Criminal Justice Theory

Criminal Justice Theory was the first comprehensive volume on the theoretical foundations of criminal justice. The authors argue that theory in criminal justice is currently underdeveloped and inconsistently applied, especially in comparison to the role of theory in the study of crime itself. In the diverse range of essays included here, the authors and contributors integrate examples from a range of criminal justice topics, building the argument that students of criminal justice must not evaluate their discipline solely on the basis of the effectiveness of specific measures in reducing the crime rate. Rather, if they hope to improve the system, they must acquire a systematic knowledge of the causes behind the structures, policies, and practices of criminal justice. This second edition has been updated to include four new articles and a wealth of material for teaching theory to students of criminal justice.

Edward R. Maguire is Professor of Justice, Law & Criminology in the School of Public Affairs at American University in Washington, DC. Professor Maguire received his Ph.D. in Criminal Justice from the University at Albany in 1997. He has held previous positions at George Mason University, the University of Nebraska, the U.S. Department of Justice, and the United Nations. From 2004–2010, he led a series of studies that examined gangs, guns, and violence in Trinidad and Tobago. From 2006–2010, he led a field study of sex trafficking in minors in the

Philippines. He is currently leading impact evaluations and other studies related to policing, gangs, firearms, violence, and youth risk in El Salvador, Uruguay, the United States, and several Caribbean nations. He has written or edited three books and more than sixty journal articles and book chapters on a variety of topics in criminology and criminal justice.

David E. Duffee is Professor Emeritus of Criminal Justice, University at Albany, and former dean of the School of Criminal Justice, from which he received his Ph.D. in 1973. His research interests are in planned change in criminal justice agencies and communities and in criminal justice theory. His first work in criminal justice theory, *Explaining Criminal Justice*, received the Outstanding Book Award from the Academy of Criminal Justice Sciences. His two most recent projects were (1) as a member of the research team of Service Outcomes Action Research (SOAR), a continuing partnership between two child welfare agencies and the University at Albany, and (2) as study director for the Assessment Protocol in the Arizona State University sites of Criminal Justice Drug Abuse Treatment Studies II.

Routledge
Taylor & Francis Group

Criminology and Justice Studies Series

Edited by **Shaun L. Gabbidon,** *Penn State Harrisburg*

Criminology and Justice Studies offers works that make both intellectual and stylistic innovations in the study of crime and criminal justice. The goal of the series is to publish works that model the best scholarship and thinking in the criminology and criminal justice field today, but in a style that connects that scholarship to a wider audience, including advanced undergraduates, graduate students, and the general public. The works in this series help fill the gap between academic monographs and encyclopedic textbooks by making innovative scholarship accessible to a large audience without the superficiality of many texts.

Books in the Series

Published:

Biosocial Criminology: New Directions in Theory and Research
edited by Anthony Walsh and Kevin M. Beaver

Community Policing in America
by Jeremy M. Wilson

Criminal Justice Theory: Explaining the Nature and Behavior of Criminal Justice
edited by David E. Duffee and Edward R. Maguire

Lifers: Seeking Redemption in Prison
by John Irwin

Race, Law and American Society: 1607 to Present
by Gloria J. Browne-Marshall

Today's White Collar Crime
by Hank J. Brightman

The New Criminal Justice: American Communities and the Changing World of Crime Control
by John Klofas, Natalie Hipple, and Edmund McGarrell

The Policing of Terrorism: Organizational and Global Perspectives
by Mathieu Deflem

Corrections
by Jeanne Stinchcomb

Community Policing
by Michael Palmiotto

A Theory of African American Offending
by James Unnever and Shaun Gabbidon

When Crime Appears: The Role of Emergence
by Jean McGloin, Christopher Sullivan, and Leslie Kennedy

Voices from Criminal Justice
edited by Heith Copes and Mark Pogrebin

Crime and the Life Course, 2/e
by Michael Benson

Wrongful Convictions and Miscarriages of Justice
edited by C. Ron Huff and Martin Killias

Human Trafficking: Interdisciplinary Perspectives
edited by Mary C. Burke

Research Methods in Crime and Justice
by Brian Withrow

Crime and Networks
edited by Carlo Morselli

Wrongful Conviction and Criminal Justice Reform
edited by Marvin Zalman and Julia Carrano

Questioning Capital Punishment: Law, Policy, and Practice
by James R. Acker

Understanding White-Collar Crime: An Opportunity Perspective, Second Edition
by Michael L. Benson and Sally S. Simpson

Criminological Perspectives on Race and Crime, Third Edition
by Shaun Gabbidon

Criminal Justice Theory

Explaining the Nature and Behavior of Criminal Justice

Second edition

Edward R. Maguire
and David E. Duffee
Editors

Routledge
Taylor & Francis Group
NEW YORK AND LONDON

Reprint 2025

First published 2015
by Routledge
711 Third Avenue, New York, NY 10017

and by Routledge
2 Park Square, Milton Park, Abingdon, Oxon, OX14 4RN

Routledge is an imprint of the Taylor & Francis Group, an informa business

Library of Congress Cataloging-in-Publication Data

Criminal justice theory : explaining the nature and behavior of criminal justice / edited by Edward R. Maguire and David E. Duffee. — 2nd Edition.
pages cm. — (Criminology and justice studies series)
Includes bibliographical references and index.
1. Criminal justice, Administration of—Philosophy. I. Maguire, Edward R., editor. II. Duffee, David, editor.
HV7419.C753 2015
364.01—dc23
2014033689

ISBN: 978-0-367-24036-3 (pbk)

ISBN: 978-1-315-88202-4 (ebk)

Typeset in MinionPro
by Apex CoVantage, LLC

Printed and bound in India

CONTENTS

LIST OF FIGURES

LIST OF TABLES

PREFACE

The seeds for the first edition of this volume were planted when Professor Bob Langworthy served as the program chair for the 1996 meeting of the Academy of Criminal Justice Sciences in Boston under President Ed Latessa. Bob Langworthy and Ed Latessa asked David Duffee if he would give the plenary address at the meeting on the topic of theory in criminal justice education. Duffee accepted and took an empirical approach to the issue, surveying all criminal justice doctoral programs with the assistance of Ed Maguire and Jeff Snipes. What they discovered was alarming to them. While the doctoral programs all had courses on criminological theory—often required—these programs basically ignored theory building and testing and types of theories about criminal justice. When asked to submit a syllabus for the most relevant theory course, many programs submitted a criminology syllabus. These syllabi usually provided little or no coverage of theories that explained criminal justice behavior, focusing primarily instead on explanations of crime. For the respondents, the word "theory" was synonymous with *criminological* theory.

The discoveries resulting from that survey were the motivation for this book. Just as crime can be studied scientifically, so, too, can criminal justice. But explicit attention to theory is a crucial ingredient in the scientific development of the field. There is no genuine science and no effective knowledge building without theory.

To the average undergraduate college student, the title of this book, *Criminal Justice Theory*, may represent a clash of themes. For most students, the first two words of the title, Criminal Justice, constitute an interesting and exciting topic. Criminal justice programs in colleges and universities are growing, often at the expense of enrollments in other disciplines. Studying "bad guys" and the system that processes them seems much more interesting to many students than studying traditional academic disciplines. But the third word in the title, Theory, often evokes the opposite reaction among students. Theories are frequently contrasted with "reality," as if theory is somehow the opposite, or the antithesis, of what happens in the real world.

The idea that these two themes—criminal justice and theory—might for some people represent such divergent perspectives is what sparked our interest in assembling the first edition of this book. Theory is a fundamental tool in the social scientist's tool kit. Theories play a central role in all social sciences, from economics and political science, to sociology and psychology. Yet, criminal justice, as a discipline, seems to have struggled with establishing a solid theoretical foundation. One reason may be that the field is so applied, so tightly intertwined with an audience of practitioners who work, or have worked, in "the real world." The field's practical orientation may have resulted in less tolerance for theory even though most practitioners tend to operate based on an implicit theory or set of assumptions that guides their decisions and working styles.

The idea of theory versus practice is really a false dichotomy since the two can inform and enrich one another. Explicit attention to theory can help us understand how the social world works. It can help us understand why some interventions work, why some fail, and why some might produce unintended, or perhaps even harmful, consequences. At the same time, careful attention to practice can stimulate theory development, expose weaknesses in flawed or incomplete theories, and help anchor theories in the reality of the social world.

Underlying all social policies and programs is some implicit theory of human behavior, whether in the form of individual or collective behavior. For instance, most research shows that hiring more police officers is not the antidote for crime that the public and most police think it is. The assumptions about police behavior and crime that underlie this popular remedy are based on inadequate theories. Criminology, a sister discipline to criminal justice, is full of examples of how well-intentioned programs meant to reduce crime sometimes not only fail to work, but occasionally may even *increase* crime. These unintended consequences are not simply the result of individual stupidity, human error, or laziness:

they occur because the underlying theories about the causes of crime on which the programs are based are faulty. As Kurt Lewin once wrote, "There is nothing so practical as a good theory."[1] We agree, and that is why we chose to develop this volume.

Criminal justice theory is defined by Duffee and Allan (2007) as

> "explanations of the variations in responses to crime.... Criminal justice theory seeks to explain and examine the variations in, and the causes of, aspects of government social control systems, which select the criminal sanction over other forms of social control and shape the nature of the criminal sanction to be employed."
>
> (p. 21)

In Chapter 2, Snipes and Maguire define criminal justice theory as "the study of the official response to behavior that may be labeled criminal." In Chapter 1, Duffee emphasizes that the idea of "responses to crime" in criminal justice theory should be conceived very broadly to encompass a wide range of social phenomena. All of these authors make it clear that criminal justice theory would include the basic decisions about whether and when to use the criminal sanction. Consequently, criminal justice theory includes the basic decision about whether to use punishment as a control and whether to consider people blameworthy for harmful acts.

This book is intended to advance the study of criminal justice by focusing on the role of theory in enhancing the discipline. It is meant for advanced undergraduate students as well as graduate students in criminal justice. The book presupposes that the student has had a basic course in research methods and is familiar with terms such as independent variable, dependent variable, and cause and effect. We have urged our authors to write using a language and tone that is appropriate for this audience. For those students who struggle with the challenging terminology and concepts used in this volume, we have included a series of discussion questions and exercises at the end of each section introduction. These can be used by instructors in the classroom as learning aids, assigned by instructors for homework, or used by individual students to study on their own at home.

We also begin each section with brief overviews that introduce key points in each chapter and connect the chapters to each other and to the different phases of the theory building and testing process. These introductions should help readers identify the various aspects of the theory development process that are represented in each part of the book. Each of these sections focuses on substantive theories about some aspect of criminal justice phenomena. Part I deals with criminal justice in general, Part II examines police, Part III examines courts, and Part IV examines corrections.

We recognize that not every important criminal justice phenomenon is represented in this collection, but we doubt that any single collection could do so. Our authors did a good job of covering micro-level and macro-level behaviors in police, courts, corrections, and system-wide contexts while simultaneously relying on different methodological approaches and different aspects of theory development. This idea of blending a substantive focus on a particular type of social behavior with solid theory and methodology is the great challenge of doing social science research well.

This volume is more than a textbook because in it we advocate a new method for thinking about scholarship in criminal justice. We urge our colleagues in colleges and universities around the world to present to their students more than simple descriptions or philosophical debates about criminal justice. We encourage them to think more and more about the *science* of criminal justice. This means thinking theoretically about a variety of issues. Why do police behave the way they do? How can we alter the behavior of prosecutors if we wish to do so? What factors explain how the innocent are convicted, or even worse, executed? Why do some agencies generate more complaints or lawsuits than others? These are the types of compelling and very real questions that criminal justice theory seeks to answer.

In thinking about the future of criminal justice theory, many questions remain unanswered. What are its central questions? In what areas does research contribute to knowledge about criminal justice? In what areas are there major research gaps? In what ways might theories of criminal justice play a role in filling these gaps and enhancing practice? Using this volume in upper-level undergraduate courses and graduate courses in the administration of criminal justice will enable instructors to expose the science of criminal justice to their students.

This volume, like others, was not born in a vacuum. Theoretical perspectives on criminal justice have played a central role for many years at the School of Criminal Justice at the University at Albany. While still a graduate student at Albany in the early 1990s, Ed Maguire had the benefit of learning these perspectives from a number of esteemed scholars, including David Bayley, David Duffee, Graeme Newman, and Rob and Alissa Worden. As a long-time faculty member as well as a former graduate student and dean at the school, Duffee was particularly influenced by some of the founding faculty of the school: Vincent O'Leary, Hans Toch, and the late Donald Newman and Leslie Wilkins. While each was quite different in his or her interests and approaches to criminal justice, all were equally devoted to the scientific study of criminal justice. We thank all of those who paved the intellectual path on which this volume rests. We owe a special thanks to the School of Criminal Justice at the University at Albany for its long-standing intellectual devotion to the ideas espoused in this volume.

We want to thank the chapter authors who contributed to this second edition of the volume. They run the gamut from an advanced Ph.D. student to highly accomplished leaders in their field of study. Some worked on short notice to prepare or revise drafts of their chapters. We thank all of them for their fine contributions. We are also grateful to Betty Fernandes for her assistance in assembling the manuscript for the second edition.

We would also like to thank the many instructors who were kind enough to share their reactions to the first edition and provide us with recommendations on how this second edition might be made more useful as a primary or supplementary text for their undergraduate and graduate courses. Based on their helpful feedback, we made number of changes, including reorganizing the book, revising and updating several chapters, and removing others. We also added five chapters (1, 3, 6, 9, and 11) to the second edition. We hope this edition will be more useful to instructors in preparing the next generation of students to think carefully about what criminal justice theory is, why it is important, and how it might be further developed. We also hope this edition will help communicate these same themes more effectively to our colleagues interested in incorporating criminal justice theory into their own work.

Finally, we also want to acknowledge our intellectual debt to Bob Langworthy, whose 1996 request set this volume in motion.

We look forward to the readers' reactions.

Edward R. Maguire
David E. Duffee

NOTE

1. Lewin, K. 1951. *Field Theory in Social Science; Selected Theoretical Papers*, ed. D. Cartwright. New York: Harper & Row.

REFERENCE

Duffee. D. and L.E. Allan. 2007. Criminal justice, criminology, and criminal justice theory. In *Criminal justice theory: Explaining the nature and behavior of criminal justice*, eds. D. Duffee and E. Maguire (pp. 1–26). New York: Routledge.

Part I

The Idea of Criminal Justice Theory

The three chapters in Part I introduce the idea of criminal justice theory. Taken together, they help readers decide what is, and what is not, criminal justice theory; they explore its breadth and its boundaries; and they explore its relevance to issues like reducing crime and disorder and enhancing justice and equity. More importantly, they help readers think about why the idea of criminal justice theory is important and worth pursuing.

In Chapter 1, Duffee asks why criminal justice theory is important, providing a personal account of his own efforts to get people to think theoretically about criminal justice. He describes an intellectual journey that is sometimes humorous and sometimes maddening. Duffee articulates the unfortunate tendency in academic criminology and criminal justice to view "theory" as synonymous with criminological theory. The problems with this approach are not simply academic. He provides clear examples to illustrate an important theme: knowing which policies and practices are most effective in reducing crime is of little use if we don't know how to get agencies to adopt and implement them. Understanding how criminal justice systems work at multiple levels—people, groups, agencies, and networks of agencies—is not only vital, it is worthy of study in its own right.

Chapter 2 furthers the discussion on criminal justice theory by defining scientific theory in more detail and distinguishing scientific theory from both non-theory and non-scientific theory. In this chapter, Snipes and Maguire observe that much of the literature that is labeled "theoretical" in criminal justice is not scientific theory because it cannot be empirically investigated. The most typical example of this is the concept of "punishment theory." Writings about punishment theory are generally philosophical tracts concerning why punishment ought to be done in certain ways and not others. As Snipes and Maguire point out, these tracts are certainly important in criminal justice policy, but they do not constitute scientific theory. Following their clarification of scientific theory, Snipes and Maguire review different approaches to scientific criminal justice theory. They articulate seven dimensions on which theory differs. They also describe the phases of scientific knowledge-building, from theory development to theory revision, and preview the types of theories and phases of knowledge-building covered in later chapters.

In Chapter 3, Hagan begins with a bold but unfortunately accurate assertion: that "criminal justice research lacks theoretical initiative." He asks why there is so little criminal justice theory. His answer focuses on the idea that criminal justice operations behave in a seemingly random way. Hagan develops a structural-contextual theory that is built on the premise that criminal justice systems are "loosely coupled." Put differently, the various components of criminal justice systems (such as police, courts, and corrections agencies) tend not to operate in a tightly coordinated fashion like the gears inside a motor. While this loose coupling provides certain benefits that are valuable in a democracy, it also results in a system that behaves in a chaotic and seemingly random fashion. Hagan outlines a provisional theory of criminal justice that focuses on the influence of the political environments in which criminal justice systems are embedded. A key aspect of the theory worth paying attention to is how changes in one part of the system are likely to influence other parts, often in unexpected and perhaps unwanted ways.

All three of the chapters in Part I probe the boundaries of criminal justice theory, in some cases arguing that those boundaries are too loose (such as when theories of crime are mistakenly identified as criminal justice theories), and in other cases arguing that they do not extend far enough. Readers should come away from Part I with their own ideas about what criminal justice theory is, what it ought to be, and where it is going.

DISCUSSION QUESTIONS

1. Two important concepts in theorizing and theory testing are "units of analysis" and "dependent variables." Units of analysis are what or who is being studied, while dependent variables are something that varies across those units that the theory

is meant to "explain." Criminal justice theories are meant to explain variation in attitudes, behaviors, or other phenomena at multiple levels, including individuals (such as police officers), working groups, agencies, neighborhoods, cities, states, and nations. Each of these levels represents a potential unit of analysis for theorizing or theory testing. Select any three units of analysis and describe some dependent variable on which those units might vary. For instance, you might select U.S. states as a unit of analysis. One way that states might vary from one another is in the rate with which people are executed.

2. In answering Question 1, you practiced selecting a unit of analysis and specific dependent variables. Now select any one of the units of analysis that you listed in your response. Propose your own theory about the factors that influence the dependent variable. What forces might make that variable fluctuate? These factors that influence variation in the dependent variable are called independent variables. This term connotes that we are interested in the effects or consequences of these variables rather than their causes. Following up on the example in Question 1, one might argue that the rate of executions in a state is a function of four factors: state laws regarding capital punishment, local legal culture, the proportion of voters who are politically conservative, and the amount of violent crime within the state. Remember that in selecting independent variables, it is important not only to identify factors that occur prior in time to the dependent variable, but also that the proposed causal connection be plausible and measurable.
3. If you answered the first two questions, you have selected a unit of analysis and one characteristic or aspect of that unit, which is the dependent variable, and one or more independent variables. You are on your way to constructing a theory! Now, does your theory meet the definition of criminal justice theory as outlined by Snipes and Maguire in Chapter 2? Why or why not? If not, can you change the theory so that it does?
4. In Chapter 1, Duffee criticizes some criminologists for their naive assumption that scientific evidence on how to reduce crime will be embraced with vigor by criminal justice agencies. Suppose a new study comes out that suggests police agencies should adopt a certain style of policing—say problem-oriented policing in "hot spots" of crime. Why might some agencies not alter their operations immediately in response to the new study?

Please take a moment and observe that in answering this question about why criminal justice agencies behave as they do, you engaged in a bit of criminal justice theorizing.

5. In Chapter 3, Hagan notes that the political environment can have a big impact on how the criminal justice system operates. How might politics influence the behavior of criminal justice agencies or those working within them?

Once again, if your answer is responsive to the question, then you engaged in another bit of criminal justice theorizing.

1

WHY IS CRIMINAL JUSTICE THEORY IMPORTANT?

David E. Duffee

This new first chapter to the second edition of *Criminal Justice Theory* is a personal rather than a scholarly statement about criminal justice theory, which is poorly understood and often ignored by scholars and students alike in both the fields of criminology and, oddly enough, criminal justice. I also intend this chapter to be an invitation both to persons interested in research and to those interested in practice to make at least part of their contribution to the field through a systematic, theory-driven understanding of criminal justice in addition to an understanding of crime.

Why do I distinguish the understanding of criminal justice from the understanding of crime? When he was trying to start the new discipline of criminology, Sutherland (1947) defined criminology as the study of crime and responses to crime. Defined in this way, criminology would seem broad enough to include the study of the causes of, the nature of, and the consequences of crime, as well as the study of the causes of, the nature of, and the consequences of criminal justice, provided that criminal justice is defined as a "response to crime." The problem with Sutherland's definition is that it has not worked, at least for promoting the study of criminal justice. In Chapter 2, Snipes and Maguire will provide more detailed, systematic definitions of criminal justice and criminal justice theory. What I wish to do here, instead, is (1) provide several examples of how the study of "crime and responses to crime" has played out for criminal justice study and (2) make a case for the importance of criminal justice theory and the research it guides.

CRIMINAL JUSTICE AS THE OFFICIAL "RESPONSE TO CRIME"

Many scholars and students jump to the conclusion that crime is more basic, primal, or fundamental than the response to crime. If crime did not occur, they argue, then there would be no responses, and, therefore, no field of criminal justice. This view assumes that crime—a harmful event—occurs prior in time to the response and therefore is more "basic" or fundamental in some sense than criminal justice. The problem with this view is apparent in the cursory examination of any common definition of crime—for example: "A reasonable definition of delinquency and crime is the commission of behaviors that violate criminal law and that place the individual at some risk of arrest if the behavior were known to the police" (Thornberry & Krohn, 2000, 50). In other words, crimes can be defined only through some criminal justice action, such as the prohibition of a behavior or the enforcement of the prohibition. In agreement with Thornberry and Krohn's definition, but written ten years earlier, Wilkins (1991, 13) concluded: "We may therefore consider 'punishability' [not crime] as the central factor. It is the use of punishment which must be studied in its own right: it is not explained away by reference to 'crime.'" If societies did not designate some events as blameworthy or punishable, those events would not be considered crimes. Indeed, there are societies that do not rely on punishment and do not conceive of some deviant behaviors as crimes. Such societies are free of criminal justice and therefore also free of crime. Societal processes that lead to criminal justice controls, as opposed to other formal or informal controls on difficult and harmful events, would therefore appear to be a basic topic for social research. Looking for the causes of criminal justice actions is a scientific undertaking that examines behavior fundamental to the human condition. Why do some societies punish while others do not? Why does a society select punishment rather than treatment or social approbation or forgiveness as the appropriate approach to some behavior but not to other harmful behaviors? Why do some societies punish more severely than others?

Whether it was intended or not, Sutherland's definition of criminology has led to an interest in the causes of crime but has retarded an interest in the causes of criminal justice. In 1968, in the first Criminal Justice Administration Proseminar at the new University at Albany

School of Criminal Justice, Donald J. Newman lamented that there were no theories of criminal justice, only of crime; consequently, there were no coherent plans for analyzing criminal justice phenomena. There were no frameworks for explanation or theory. Research was ad hoc and scattered. I am glad to say that the state of criminal justice theory has improved since Newman's observation. There are now a large number of theory building and theory testing papers about criminal justice or some aspect of it. Nevertheless, when compared to theorizing about crime, theorizing about criminal justice is still disorganized, infrequent, and, at times, disdained or dismissed as unnecessary. For example, in my pre-retirement semester, in a faculty meeting discussion of faculty recruitment needs, I tried to make a case for more interest in criminal justice theory among the faculty and was immediately rebuked sharply by one senior colleague, who said that advocating for criminal justice theory "was not collegial." Shortly before, we had concluded a discussion about the value of recruiting a noted crime theory scholar to the faculty. The same faculty member did not object to that discussion as "not collegial."

This swift negative reaction to the importance of criminal justice theory rather mystified me until I recalled an earlier, private conversation with another senior faculty member about the same issue. On the way to lunch one day, I observed that the school was getting quite thin in criminal justice expertise because of retirements. I observed that when the school had started, there had only been one or two criminologists on the faculty while all others were interested in studying criminal justice. Now, the situation had flipped. I expressed hope that we would manage to keep a balance, since the school had become known for being strong in both areas. I pointed out that we had only one person studying corrections, one studying courts, and two studying police, and two of those people were preparing to retire. My friend's response was that it did not matter. "The way I see it, police, courts, and corrections are just topics, like white collar crime, and delinquency, and homicide are topics. The school will be okay, I think, if we have a couple of those topics represented on the faculty—we don't need all of them."

After that lunchtime discussion, I realized that there was a fundamental but unacknowledged difference between the study of criminal justice as I understood it and the study of criminal justice as my friend comprehended it. To him, criminal justice "topics" were no different from any other criminological topic—they were all equal and up for grabs, depending on the interests of the persons on the faculty. There was no need to balance or structure this mix of interests in our hiring decisions—we should simply go after the "best person available."

Recalling my friend's view of criminal justice as "just other criminological topics" helped me to put in perspective the other faculty member's complaint that I was not being collegial by arguing that criminal justice theory should have a place in our curriculum. To this person, like my friend, there was simply no intellectual or scientific distinction between criminology and criminal justice. If we were going to invest in a well-known criminological theorist, there was scarcely need to also invest in criminal justice theory.

I have experienced similar reactions from several other quarters. One came from a publisher with whom Maguire and I discussed the proposal for the first edition of this book. That publisher said he already had one book on criminal justice theory and the field was not big enough for two. (We are grateful that the editor at Routledge thought differently!)

When I was a dean and spending a good deal of time recruiting doctoral students around the country, I often got into discussions with graduate students in other programs about the requirements that they faced. Inevitably, we would talk about the number and nature of comprehensive examinations for doctoral study. I often heard students say, "I am preparing to take the theory exam." "Theory of what?" I always would ask. They looked at me as if I were an idiot, or at least certainly not a dean in a well-regarded criminal justice program. "Theory of crime," they would say, perplexed by my ignorance. If I pressed further and asked if there was a similar requirement for an examination in theories of criminal justice, they would either shrug and say no or explain: "Well, not theory, but there is an exam in criminal justice administration." Either way, they would then get away from me as soon as possible.

The reactions of these graduate students were explained by the environment in which they studied. When I surveyed all doctoral programs in criminology and criminal justice in 1995 and asked them to send me the syllabus from their core course in criminal justice theory, I was inevitably sent the syllabus for a course on theories of crime (Duffee, 1995). There was no similar explicit attention to theories of criminal justice. In other words, these students were learning that one asks "Why?" only about crime. About criminal justice, one simply learns "how the system operates."

CRIMINAL JUSTICE AS APPLIED CRIMINOLOGY

Another slightly different slant on the lack of concern for criminal justice theory comes from the view of criminal justice as "applied criminology." For example, in a *New York Times* article on the proliferation of criminal justice programs in colleges and universities across the nation, Professor Lawrence Sherman stated that criminal justice is "applied criminology," a subset of criminology that focuses specifically on studying criminal justice agencies (Butterfield, 1998, B9). The article argued that criminology is an older and more expansive field that examines the causes of crime and criminal behavior. This view of criminal justice as a narrow applied slice of criminology also turned up in the contents of older introductory criminology textbooks, which often devoted most of their space to describing and explaining crime, but typically ended with a brief section about how offenders were processed. While the offender-processing sections of criminology texts have now given way to criminal justice texts and courses, there is generally little attention to theory in the criminal justice texts, while theory receives significant space in the criminology texts (see, for example, Henderson & Boostrom, 1989; Willis, 1983).

What is wrong with thinking about criminal justice as "applied criminology"? By thinking of crime and criminals as the primary, dominant concepts for study, criminal justice becomes of interest only in relationship to that primary concern with crime. This idea of "applied criminology" narrows the definition of criminal justice to the application of knowledge about crime and criminals by criminal justice actors. If we took this idea to its extreme, but logical, conclusion, all basic scientific knowledge (and therefore all theory) that is related to crime is about crime itself. It would also logically follow that criminal justice is limited to the application of the knowledge of crime reduction attempts by criminal justice officials. In other words, our interest in criminal justice behavior would be limited to its consequences for crime—was this criminal justice program/effort/initiative that applied our knowledge about crime effective in reducing crime? We would not be interested in the causes of the criminal justice effort (or lack of effort!).

A different example of this kind of thinking occurred in a review of a paper on types of criminal justice theories submitted to a criminal justice journal. The reviewer said the paper was trivial and should be rejected because no separate study of criminal justice theory is needed. "Every theory of crime is automatically a theory of criminal justice," that reviewer wrote. As the other reviewer on that paper, I puzzled for a long time about what this reviewer could possibly mean by such a statement. Apparently, he meant he had no interest in classifying, categorizing, or comparing types of criminal justice theory (an activity in which criminologists often engage). But what exactly could it mean to say any theory of crime is automatically a theory of criminal justice? That is, if one proposes that "X causes crime," how has one automatically made a proposition about causes of criminal justice as well? How efficient! If it only made sense.

I concluded that the only logical interpretation of this reviewer's comment is that the reviewer incorporated two different uses of the term "theory" in the same proposition. He used "crime theory" in a scientific sense: What causes this type of crime? How does it work? Why does it work that way? These are nonjudgmental, behavioral questions to be addressed by scientific theory. In contrast, the reviewer appeared to use the term "criminal justice theory" in a normative or ethical sense: if we know what causes this crime, then criminal justice actors *ought* to act to reduce it by using that knowledge. Therefore, any scientific theory of crime is automatically a moral "theory" or principle to guide criminal justice action. Responsible criminal justice actors would, of course, act to reduce a crime, if they only knew its causes. We do not need to search for causes of criminal justice because the answer always is: "It's crime, stupid!" This set of assumptions about the relationship between crime and criminal justice has been called the "rational theory" or "rational model" of criminal justice (Kraska, 2004). While such assumptions are not themselves rational, as we shall see later, this model of criminal justice is named as it is because it assumes or appears to assume that criminal justice is rational and operates like so:

1. Reducing crime is the goal of criminal justice.
2. The means of reducing a specific crime are known.
3. Since criminal justice actors are rational or goal directed, they will take the steps known to achieve their goals.
4. Therefore, they will adopt the steps known to reduce the crime in question.
5. Consequently, if we know what reduces crime, we can predict how criminal justice actors will behave, and we answer the question: "why do they behave in such a way" with the answer: "because their goal is the reduction of crime."

THE ASSUMPTION OF RATIONALITY

One can reduce the "rational model" of criminal justice to the process depicted in Figure 1.1.

Such a view of criminal justice is common despite the fact that it ignores much empirical work. Among the many different types of empirical studies that should make us question the assumptions about criminal justice in Figure 1.1, three types of findings stand out. First, there are many criminal justice program evaluation studies that report the program in question had limited, no, or negative effects on frequency

Figure 1.1 The criminologist's view of "rational" criminal justice

of crime. For example, after careful examination of community and residential programs in a large eastern state's department of juvenile corrections, one national expert in correctional programming reported to the department's executive director that if he wanted to make sure most of his clients returned to delinquency, he could scarcely do a better job (confidential communication from the evaluator to Duffee). Very often with such programs, the problem is one of implementation. The steps required and the allocation of resources needed to implement the program as planned by its developer so that it would actually work as intended simply are not enacted (Gendreau, Goggin & Smith, 1999). Frequently, these steps of program implementation are ignored because the experts focused on the forces that would affect crime, but failed to be concerned about the forces that would create the changes in the criminal justice agency that would enable program implementation to take place with fidelity to program plans.

Such a view also seems to ignore the process of criminal justice policy making. Criminal justice policy making is visibly political and driven by interest groups. While such groups might be acting rationally—that is, pursuing their own interests—it is simply not the case that criminal justice policies are selected and programs implemented on the basis of what works for a specific crime reduction goal. Many forces are at work in policy development, program adoption, and program implementation other than an interest in reduction of crime or, sadly, the use of the best evidence (Davies & Worden, 2009; McGarrell, 1988; Miller, Ohlin & Coates, 1977; Stucky, Heimer, & Lang, 2005).

Perhaps there is no better example of the irrationality of criminal justice policy behavior than the correctional consequences of the "nothing works" charge directed at correctional treatment programs (Martinson, 1974). After review of many correctional program evaluations, Martinson concluded that there was no correctional treatment program that would work with all offenders. The practical result of this conclusion of program failure was record increases in correctional clients and correctional resources. While the "nothing works" claim, as inaccurate as it was, led to reduction in resources for correctional treatment, it was a banner day for punishment. Investment in criminal justice was strengthened rather than weakened (Garland, 2001). The new policy (tougher punishment) was untested as a means of achieving publicly stated correctional goals, but was politically popular until quite recently, as evidence of its failure and its exorbitant cost have gradually become public knowledge. A more rational approach to correctional policy and program implementation would have been for policy makers to require systematic, regular adjustments to treatment programming based on program results (Gottfredson & Gottfredson, 1988). Instead, states jumped from one vast overgeneralization about correctional treatment (nothing works!) to another policy for which there was no information (therefore, we will punish instead!). Perhaps what is most troubling about this pattern is that evidence of such forces irrelevant to crime control or crime reduction are well known in the criminological field, but are ignored in the model of crime reduction depicted in Figure 1.1. That is, we know that what we have done in the past has not worked well in many cases, but our approach to improving criminal justice agency effectiveness is the same approach that did not work in the past. This approach to program improvement ignores frequent findings from the field of program implementation, where it is widely known that evidence of program effectiveness does not lead to a decision to adopt the program, and a decision to adopt a program does not lead to the program being implemented as designed (Fixsen et al., 2005).

A third type of finding that should lead people to doubt the accuracy and utility of the "rational model" of criminal justice are the studies showing that much important work and many resources are devoted to objectives and issues other than crime. Corrections is often engaged in meting out punishment even when such actions lead to more crime (Clear, 2007). Only a small portion of police effort is devoted to crime detection and enforcement (Bayley, 1994). Courts are rarely concerned with the impact of case processing on crime and are also interested in justice and fairness. Possibly, then, one problem with Sutherland's definition of criminology for the study of criminal justice is that it limits criminological interest to those few aspects of criminal justice that are responses to crime and ignores the rest. The result is depicted, in simplified form, in Figure 1.2.

The researchers most interested in having criminal justice agents, agencies, or systems "do something" are usually more interested in achieving a specific outcome than they are in determining how to bring that outcome about. In other words, the theories in which criminal justice is most often implicated are not theories that explain or predict

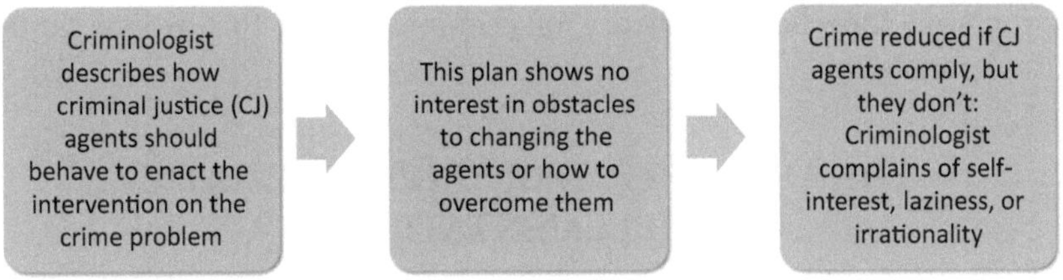

Figure 1.2 Lack of knowledge (and lack of interest) in "manipulating the independent variable"

criminal justice behavior, but theories that explain or predict a potential or real outcome of criminal justice, such as change in crime, justice, fairness, a sense of safety, and so on. In these instances, criminal justice variables are thought of and utilized as independent variables that might make the desired outcome happen. But, if we wish to "manipulate" the independent variable in such a way as to bring the desired outcome about, then we also need to think of criminal justice variables as dependent variables so that we can understand what affects criminal justice rather than think only about what criminal justice might affect. Figure 1.2 proposes that persons interested in crime as a dependent variable are often not very adept or interested in thinking about criminal justice this way.

This is the "rational model" of criminal justice at work, as Kraska (2004) pointed out. What needs to be done to create changes in criminal justice is often unknown or ignored, under the unspoken and generally faulty assumption that getting criminal justice compliance with a plan that would reduce crime should not be problematic. When this does not happen, the very same people who were (perhaps unconsciously) treating criminal justice as "rational" then turn around and blame criminal justice actors for being incompetent, lazy, self-interested, or, ironically, irrational! In other words, we see conflicting evidence about the idea that criminal justice is a rational response to crime, if a response to crime at all. Therefore, understanding the causes of crime, and consequently, what might reduce crime, does not necessarily help us understand the criminal justice system and what makes it tick.

When criminal justice programs are evaluated for their effects on crime or other desired outcomes and the outcome is not achieved, it is still very possible that the theory of crime on which the program was based was valid. Rather than a "failure of theory," the failed program could be and often is a "failure of implementation" (Rosenbaum, 1988). Program designers did not know how to manipulate the independent variable effectively—they did not know how to develop the program. They had no theory of criminal justice that would guide implementation.

THE ASSUMPTION OF UNPROBLEMATIC IMPLEMENTATION

In effectiveness or program evaluation research, the behaviors of criminal justice agents and agencies are treated as independent variables that are expected to have an effect on crime. I am not questioning the policy value or intellectual interest in criminal justice effectiveness research. However, I do wish to call attention to the incompleteness in the knowledge of criminal justice that arises from the concentration on only a few of its effects (especially crime, disorder, and fear) without equal attention to its causes. Two examples from my own experience—one from community policing within a city, and one from community prosecution nationally—will serve as examples.

First, in a relatively large city, community policing was first implemented on a trial basis in one troubled neighborhood. After a year of working with residents in that neighborhood, the police department announced that community policing reduced crime (nationally, the research findings on this relationship are very mixed). There was much excitement in this city about this discovery and much pressure to replicate this result in other neighborhoods. But despite good-faith efforts by the police department, the replication did not have the same effects in other parts of the city. In many areas, crime was unaffected by the efforts, while in a few neighborhoods, crime actually increased. Residents and the police department felt a great deal of frustration.

While many different scenarios could have produced these results, in this instance, what appeared to happen was that the department had good measures of crime, which is what the department and the residents were concerned about, but very poor measures of what the officers were actually doing on their own and with residents to implement community policing (Duffee, Fluellen & Renauer 1999). After the first neighborhood experience, no one in the department or in the neighborhood was quite sure of the elements of community policing that they wished to replicate, or whether in fact different neighborhoods would benefit from the same approach. They were not sure what they had done, what should be sustained, or how to do it again. What was it about the first neighborhood's application of community policing that made it click?

While this is just one case, the findings from Maguire's national research (1997) on structural change to implement community policing is supportive of the problems illustrated in the example. Maguire examined structural changes in police departments that had claimed to have implemented community policing, to be working on implementation, or not to be implementing community policing between the years 1987 and 1993. He could find evidence of only minimal changes in policing structures, and none of the changes were associated with community policing implementation. He concluded that the conception of community policing was so vague and nebulous that there were no core structural characteristics that could be found across police departments. He speculated therefore that program adoption was more ceremonial than real and that what changes occurred in police structure during that period were influenced by other environmental forces rather than the decision to adopt a popular program. His conclusion is virtually identical to the story in Figure 1.2: police reformers knew what police structure should look like after program adoption, but they had no knowledge of how to change police department structure or of the other forces in the environment pushing for contrary structural configurations.

The second example involves a different scene: a focus group in Washington, DC of researchers and practitioners about what aspects of community prosecution should receive attention from the National Institute of Justice (NIJ). The U.S. Department of Justice had invested significant sums in supporting community prosecution in operating agencies around the country. The participants at an NIJ focus group on community prosecution were asked to identify worthwhile areas of research on community prosecution. Earlier in the seminar, the group had heard a presentation on how different prosecutorial motives might affect the nature of the program that was produced. Some prosecutors would be attracted by political benefits, such as reelection, while other prosecutors might be attracted to improving communities. The focus group participants returned to this presentation during the discussion of what research NIJ should be interested in supporting. Should there be research on motives, such as these, or on other causes of community prosecution adoption? Or should the research focus on outcomes, such as case processing, citizen satisfaction, and increased community problem-solving capacity?

There was considerable agreement in the room that impacts should be studied and that NIJ should be interested in a range of impacts other than crime rates and convictions. But there was much less interest in studying the reasons why one office might adopt such a program while another might not, or why one prosecutor might adopt program rhetoric without changing office structure and practice, while another prosecutor made significant alterations in decision making, resource allocation, assistant prosecutor behavior, and employee evaluation. The groups did recognize significant differences from office to office in what was being called community prosecution by practitioners, but they were not convinced that it was important to develop theory to explain these differences and then engage in research to examine the validity of the theory. In other words, study of the very issues that would be important to adoption and implementation was not seen as particularly important in structuring the future federal support for local departments.

Back down on the local level, prosecutors should also be interested in causal connections of another order. How is a successful community prosecution program to be implemented in different communities within one jurisdiction? This problem is quite similar to the problem noted earlier in the city disappointed with the lack of replicability of community policing. Again, being serious about the implementation side of program evaluation requires thinking seriously about the independent variables in the intervention. Thinking seriously about how to "manipulate that independent variable" (which is usually a very complex criminal justice program) would mean that we take seriously the criminal justice variables as dependent variables! We are trying to cause them to change. This requires knowledge of how and why criminal justice behaves as it does, rather than knowledge of what criminal justice affects. It would require the building and testing of criminal justice theory.

Consequently, it would seem that even if primary political interest were in outcomes for communities (including but not limited to crime levels), knowledge of criminal justice variables as dependent rather than as independent variables is important. If we do not know how to replicate a successful intervention, it is of limited value elsewhere. We may also want to know how to avoid a damaging intervention. For example, what should we know in order to reduce the likelihood that police officers and citizens alienate each other and grow cynical about community programs (e.g., Grinc, 1998)? If we know what causes crime outcomes but do not expend equal efforts to know what causes criminal justice outcomes, we may not have deployable knowledge.

Figure 1.3 is a simple graphic depiction of the location of criminal justice theory in relation to the concentration of criminological (including "applied criminological") knowledge. The large horizontal arrows depict the "story" that most people are interested in: what steps should be taken to produce the societally desirable result? The vertical arrow represents the knowledge needed to make the changes in criminal justice, and the large horizontal arrow on the left side would be the criminal justice outcomes. Criminological and criminal justice theory are

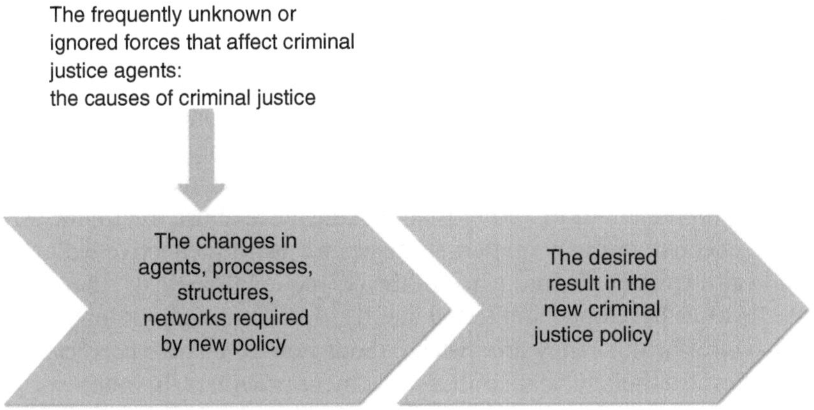

Figure 1.3 The location of criminal justice theory

often independent of each other, but they intersect in a very important way at this point.

HEALTH PROGRAM IMPLEMENTATION AS AN ANALOGY TO CRIME AND CRIMINAL JUSTICE

A strikingly similar situation is occurring in the health and behavioral health fields. Numerous research studies have found that disseminating knowledge about new treatments or practices in the health field does not lead to their implementation. As a result, seventeen years transpire, on average, from a discovery of treatment efficacy to implementation in practice. The National Institutes of Health and other research and health advocacy organizations have consequently begun a major push to focus on implementation, including the founding of the journal *Implementation Science* and an annual conference in Bethesda on implementation research. In their view, the problem is making the "pipeline" from findings to take-up shorter.

One large initiative in this movement is Criminal Justice Drug Abuse Treatment Studies 2, or CJDATS2. Because of the involvement of correctional agencies in this large study of behavioral health program implementation, I shall focus on the CJDATS example, but I could select just as readily any number of implementation studies dealing with issues as far ranging as cancer prevention to the prevention of sepsis in operating rooms. CJDATS1 was a five-year project that focused on identifying or developing effective treatment procedures for substance-abusing offenders (with a focus primarily on prison inmates). One of the most important findings in this large, multisite, national study was that there were many more treatments known to be efficacious than there was uptake of effective treatments by correctional agencies. CJDATS1 discovered that telling correctional officials about effective treatments for drug-abusing offenders did not lead to program adoption or implementation. CJDATS2, therefore, focused on the problem of implementation, rather than on substance abuse treatment. Are there effective implementation strategies for getting effective behavioral health treatments into place in the correctional context? Therefore, the theories developed and tested in CJDATS2 are not about improving behavioral health. They are instead about how to change correctional agencies and their substance abuse treatment providers. In other words, knowledge about how to improve behavioral health is not sufficient to improve behavioral health. One also has to learn how to change correctional and treatment provider management, clinicians, correctional counselors and officers, probation and parole officers, and how the correctional agencies and treatment agencies interact with each other. In this and other health-related implementations studies, the starting point included the recognition that relying on agencies' and providers' adoption of practices simply because they had been shown to be effective was not an effective implementation strategy. One would have to deal directly with behavioral change in health organizations rather than rely on practitioners to learn about and implement new treatments on their own.

This fresh examination of what it takes to change a system of health service provision is quite similar to learning what it takes to change a criminal justice system. One needs a totally different set of theories, research strategies, and research expertise than one needs to study illness or addiction. In the health and behavioral health field, therefore, new research partnerships with business, management, and public administration schools, among others, have been forged to obtain knowledge of how to change hospitals and health workers. For those interested in reducing crime, improving justice, increasing safety, and similar conditions, there needs to be similar recognition of the importance of studying criminal justice just as systematically and just as theoretically guided as is true of the study of crime.

THEORIES OF NONMANIPULABLE CRIMINAL JUSTICE VARIABLES

I would not want readers to misunderstand this discussion of the importance of criminal justice theory for bringing about planned change to conclude that criminal justice theory could or should concentrate only on manipulable causes of criminal justice behavior. Far from it. As readers proceed through the other chapters in this volume, they will readily observe that many of the forces affecting particular criminal justice characteristics cannot be or are unlikely to be changed through conscious human effort. This, of course, is also true of crime, or, I dare say, of most variables of interest. For example, in Maguire and Uchida's Chapter 4 on explaining variation in police organizations, Worden's Chapter 8 examining the bidirectional influences of courts and communities, and McGarrell and Duffee's Chapter 12 seeking to explain the level of correctional resources, it should be clear that many environmental variables with powerful effects on criminal justice organizations probably cannot be changed through conscious effort on the part of researchers or practitioners seeking to achieve a specific program goal. Does this make theories that involve such massive, distant, unalterable variables useless? Absolutely not. Theories that include such variables (and most will) set the context within which change will need to be attempted, or, perhaps, will alert researchers or managers that the changes proposed cannot be accomplished within that kind of context.

Context is a vital element in program development and program evaluation because it is critical to understanding what happened where and why (Pawson & Tilley, 1997). If we return to the previous examples of community policing and community prosecution, we should be able to see that many practitioners and researchers run into trouble when they ignore contextual forces. Therefore, any good, useable theory will include careful consideration of constraints that cannot be changed but to which the change contemplated might be adapted. For instance, if NIJ wished to advocate for and support a particular form or type of community prosecution, then it might be well served to draw upon theories of community and courts as proposed by Worden in Chapter 8 in order to identify the community (and political) context within which the desired type of community prosecution might be welcome. Funding only studies of program outcomes will not suffice.

ARE CRIMINAL JUSTICE OUTCOMES TRIVIAL?

In one of his last works, Leslie Wilkins, one of the original experts in the study of correctional decision making, expressed his frustrations with what he saw as a preoccupation with crime and a lack of serious interest in criminal justice. He pointed out that there was more variation across nations in punishment rates than in crime rates, that variation in crime did not explain why criminal justice varied as it did. He asked his colleagues about their lack of interest in understanding why punishment fluctuated: is punishment trivial? (Wilkins, 1991, 6).

A few years later, I was asked to give a colloquium for my colleagues in Albany on the Police-Community Interaction Project (PCIP), funded by NIJ (Renauer's theoretical paper, now Chapter 5 in this volume, was a product of that project, in which we compared how community policing was defined and implemented in different city contexts and in different communities). After the colloquium concluded, one of my colleagues sidled up to me in the hallway and said he enjoyed hearing about how police and neighbors interacted with each other and whether police could be community organizers. Somehow, I knew that there was a "but" coming. He then asked: "Isn't the research a bit empty, if crime isn't the outcome?" I immediately thought of Professor Wilkins' frustration and added to myself: Ah yes, dear Leslie, punishment isn't the only important issue that some folks see as trivial!

Why the empty feeling if variation in crime is not the end of the story? What other criminal justice outcomes besides the level of punishment or police–community co-production are being dismissed as not important? Figure 1.4 displays just a brief sampling of key independent and dependent variables at three different levels of analysis in criminal justice (individual agents, agencies, and linked agencies or networks). Some of the chapters in this volume and selected other research are highlighted as beginning places for persons interested in any of these relationships.

I fully understand that what will intrigue any particular scholar or researcher is largely a personal matter. Who knows why one person is

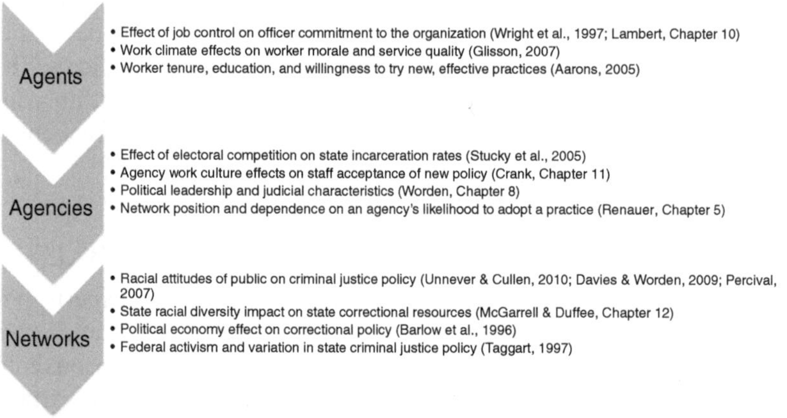

Figure 1.4 Examples of forces affecting agents, agencies, and networks

interested in crime rates and another the history of Russia or changes in the environment? So if one of my colleagues finds a theoretical story "empty" unless the last chapter is about crime, that is fine, as long as that person is speaking about his own personal preferences for scientific investigation. I do not seek to challenge that person's research preferences. Perhaps my other colleague accusing me of being "noncollegial" was actually accusing me of trying to make him interested in criminal justice issues when he was not? In any case, this is not my desire. However, I stand by the assertion that any of the outcomes listed in Figure 1.4—job commitment, service quality, morale, willingness to try new work techniques known to be efficacious, worker compliance with new requirements, incarceration rates, qualifications of judges, program adoption, level of correctional resources, correctional policy—to focus on just a smattering of criminal justice outcomes, are just as socially important as crime outcomes and can be just as intriguing as research problems. Indeed, as I have argued earlier, some of these criminal justice outcomes can be critical to the work of achieving specific crime outcomes.

EXAMPLES OF TWO CORRECTIONAL OFFICERS

Perhaps putting a human face on some correctional outcomes will suffice. I still recall vividly very different interactions with two correctional officers in neighboring eastern states. One, a captain near retirement, I met during an organizational development project in a prison system on which I was the research assistant. I shall call him Captain Johnnie. The other encounter was with a corrections officer in a maximum security prison that I visited while I was the dean of the Albany School of Criminal Justice. I shall call him Officer Mike.

Captain Johnnie had little formal education. His introduction to security happened during Prohibition, when he was a bouncer in an illegal establishment. He was one of the top-level custodial officers in a minimum security prison that was undergoing a transformation. Its superintendent was a key player in a department-wide development effort that began with intensive executive team training, but then focused on the prison where Captain Johnnie worked in an attempt to bring the development effort down to the frontline staff and the inmates on a pilot basis. Captain Johnnie was highly regarded by other officers, and therefore the superintendent wanted to involve Johnnie, if possible, to increase the chances that other officers would accept as legitimate the changes in policy and management that the super wanted to implement. I found it remarkable that such a man, with no college education, within a year of retirement, would make the effort to improve communication between officers and counselors and between staff and inmates. When I asked him about this one day, he said, "Oh, I know I am not a key person in this. Heck, I didn't finish high school and I got only a year left to serve before I retire. The key people are the young guys we just hired in the last year or two and even those who aren't working for the department yet. But if the super's program will help those people do more rewarding work and make this a better place, then I will do whatever I can to help."

Perhaps some of this attitude from this security officer certainly stemmed from his own personality. He was a warm and friendly person who liked people and wanted his work to be meaningful for people. But, much of his attitude about trying a new and innovative approach to correctional management also had to do with "the super," a man whom Eric Trist, a leader in work innovation at the Wharton School, called "the most innovative correctional manager in the country" (Trist communication with Duffee). The super had fully accepted the logic of newly espoused reintegration policy and was energetic in seeking ways to break down barriers between custody and treatment staff and between staff and inmates. He also accepted the basic premise of the development effort: that managers had to involve frontline staff in policy decisions if they wanted to reduce alienation and increase commitment.

In contrast, Officer Mike had previously been a master's student at my school. He graduated from the university during an economic downturn. Perhaps he had trouble finding a job, despite his master's degree. In any case, he was marching in formation with other officers at the changing of shifts one day when I happened to be visiting a new program for lifers in this maximum security prison. I was standing with a small group of visitors who were to be ushered into the prison as soon as the changing of the guard had been accomplished. Officer Mike happened to see me waiting and immediately exploded with venom, broke formation, leaned over, and pointed menacingly at me. "You did this to me! This is what I got at your place!" he shouted while pulling at the badge on his chest and his uniform. His rant continued as he finally marched off with the rest of his shift. The other visitors looked at me curiously. What could I possibly have done to that man? Shame on you. I wanted to disappear. And I also felt very sorry for Officer Mike, who obviously hated his job and the criminal justice degree that preceded it. And I felt sorry for the inmates in his charge.

Why was the uneducated, former bouncer Captain Johnnie motivated to improve work climate for officers and services for inmates while the educated Officer Mike hated his job and his former school? Is an inmate better off in Johnnie's care or Mike's? Is officer turnover likely to be higher in Captain Johnnie's prison or Officer Mike's prison? Where are officers more likely to behave inhumanely toward their clients or their families? What does it do to an officer's family to live every day with someone who hates going to work? Can he possibly leave all that anger at the prison gate? How much better is life with a worker like Johnnie who sees every day as an interesting and rewarding challenge? How can more officers be engaged in this way?

These are important outcomes that have occupied researchers (e.g., Lambert in this volume; Toch & Grant, 1982) and should continue to do so in the future. They are not trivial issues, and they deserve the attention of theory building and theory testing.

CONCLUSION

The subsequent chapters in this volume provide a wide range of theoretically driven endeavors in the field of criminal justice. The next chapter provides a systematic approach to defining criminal justice theory and, just as importantly, delimiting its boundaries. The authors provide examples of theory building, theory testing, and theory integration. The final chapter takes stock of the state of criminal justice theory and makes suggestions for different ways to advance theoretical thinking and research. We have sought to provide coverage of police, courts, and corrections, as well as the broader system. Of course, many important topics are unrepresented. We have also tried to provide examples of different kinds of theories and of different methods of testing theory.

We hope this volume stimulates the reader's imagination about the many intriguing, perplexing problems that criminal justice presents and helps to orient those excited by the challenge of explanation to some of the many relevant models and lenses that can be used in the attempt to understand these puzzles. I would hope that were I to set foot in a criminology or criminal justice conference in the future and query doctoral students about their upcoming comprehensive exams that at least a few of them would not shy away from me when I asked about their preparation in criminal justice theory.

REFERENCES

Barlow, D.E., M.H. Barlow, and W.W. Johnson. 1996. The political economy of criminal justice policy: A time series analysis of economic conditions, crime, and federal criminal justice legislation 1948–1987. *Justice Quarterly*, 13: 223–42.

Bayley, D.H. 1994. *Police for the future.* New York: Oxford University Press.
Butterfield, F. 1998. A newcomer breaks into the liberal arts: Criminal justice. *The New York Times* (December 5). Retrieved from http://www.nytimes.com/1998/12/05/arts/newcomer-breaks-into-liberal-arts-criminal-justice-with-little-help-movies-tv.html.
Clear, T. 2007. *Imprisoning communities: How mass incarceration makes disadvantaged neighborhoods worse.* New York: Oxford University Press.
Davies, A.L.B. and Worden, A.P. 2009. State politics and the right to counsel: A comparative analysis. *Law and Society Review*, 43(1): 187–219.
Duffee, D.E. 1995. Structuring criminal justice theory. Plenary Address, Annual Meeting of the Academy of Criminal Justice Sciences, Boston.
Duffee, D.E., Fluellen, R. and Renauer, B. 1999. Community variables in community policing. *Police Quarterly*, 2: 5–35.
Fixsen, D.L., Naoom, S.F., Blasé, K.A., Friedman, R.M. and Wallace, F. 2005. Implementation research: A synthesis of the literature. Tampa, FL: University of South Florida, Louis de la Parte Florida Mental Health Institute, The National Implementation Research Institute. Retrieved from http://nirn.fmhi.usf.edu/resources/publications/Monograph.
Garland, D. 2001. *The culture of control: Crime and social order in contemporary society.* Chicago: University of Chicago Press.
Gendreau, P., Goggin, C. and Smith, P. 1999. The forgotten issue in effective correctional treatment: Program implementation. *International Journal of Offender Therapy and Comparative Criminology*, 43(2): 180–187.
Glisson, C. (2007). Assessing and changing organizational culture and climate for effective services. *Research on Social Work Practice*, 17: 736–747.
Grinc, R. 1998. Angels in marble: Problems in stimulating community involvement in community policing. In D. Karp (Ed.), *Community justice: An emerging field* (pp. 167–202). Lanham, MD: Rowman and Littlefield.
Gottfredson, M.R. and Gottfredson, D.M. 1988. Decision making in criminal justice: Toward a rational exercise of discretion, 2nd ed. New York: Plenum.
Henderson, J.H. and Boostrom, R.L. 1989. Criminal justice theory: Anarchy reigns. *Journal of Contemporary Criminal Justice*, 5(1): 29–39.
Kraska, P.B. 2004. *Theorizing criminal justice: Eight essential orientations.* Prospect Heights, IL: Waveland.
Maguire, E.R. 1997. Structural change in large municipal police organizations during the community policing era. *Justice Quarterly*, 14(3): 547–576.
Martinson, R. 1974. What works? Questions and answers about prison reform. *Public Interest*, 35: 22–54.
McGarrell, E.F. 1988. *Juvenile correctional reform: Two decades of policy and procedural change.* Albany, NY: State University of New York Press.
Miller, A.D., Ohlin, L.E. and Coates, R.B. 1977. *A theory of social reform: Correctional change processes in two states.* Cambridge, MA: Ballinger.
Pawson, R. and Tilley, N. 1997. *Realistic evaluation.* London: Sage.

Percival, G.L. 2007. Testing the impact of racial diversity and racial attitudes on prisoner reentry policies in the U.S. states. Paper prepared for the seventh annual State Politics and Policy Conference, Austin, TX.

Rosenbaum, D.P. 1988. Community crime prevention: A review and synthesis of the literature. *Justice Quarterly*, 5: 323–395.

Stucky, T.D., Heimer, K. and Lang, J.B. 2005. Partisan politics, electoral competition and imprisonment: An analysis of states over time. *Criminology*, 43(1): 211–248.

Sutherland, E.H. 1947. *Principles of criminology*, 4th ed. Philadelphia: J.B. Lippincott.

Taggart, W.A. 1997. The nationalization of corrections policy in the American states. *Justice*

Thornberry, T. and Krohn, M. 2000. The self-report method of measuring delinquency and crime. In Measurement and analysis of crime and justice. Duffee, D.E., McDowall, D., Ostrom, B., Crutchfield, R.D., Mastrofski, S.D. and Mazerolle, L.G. (Eds.), *Criminal Justice 2000* (4): 33–84. Washington, D.C., National Institute of Justice.

Toch, H. and Grant, J.D. 1982. *Reforming human services: Change through participation*. Beverly Hills, CA: Sage.

Unnever, J.D. & Cullen, F.T., 2010. The social sources of Americans' punitiveness: A test of three competing models. *Criminology*, 48(1): 99–129.

Wilkins, L.T. 1991. *Punishment, crime, and market forces*. Brookfield, VT: Dartmouth Press.

Willis, C.L. 1983. Criminal justice theory: A case of trained incapacity? *Journal of Criminal Justice*, 11: 447–458.

Wright, K., Saylor, W., Gilman, E., & Camp, S. (1997). Job control and occupational outcomes among prison workers. *Justice Quarterly*, 14: 524–546.

2

FOUNDATIONS OF CRIMINAL JUSTICE THEORY

Jeffrey B. Snipes and Edward R. Maguire[1]

INTRODUCTION

Criminal justice has been developing as an academic field since the appearance of several influential studies and the inception of its first doctoral program in the 1960s at the University at Albany. There are now about three dozen programs in the United States and Canada. As the field continues to grow, there is a need to monitor its evolution and identify any shortcomings, inconsistencies, or other constraints that might inhibit its development. We argue that the academic study of criminal justice must overcome a major hurdle that will otherwise limit its growth and vitality: There is no common understanding or teaching of theory. Instead, academic programs consist of scattergun approaches to study, with little effort toward unity and coherence beyond very basic organizational divisions such as police, courts, and corrections.

Criminal justice differs from other social sciences in this regard. For example, sociology programs teach doctrinal theory, typically in a two-semester sequence. Criminology, as an interdisciplinary field, offers nicely bounded areas of theory with a common enterprise (to explain criminal behavior). Anthropological theory is well established and heavily integrated into graduate curricula. By contrast, scholars in criminal justice, even some who are quite prominent, still lack a coherent vision of what theory entails. Some even confuse domains, not accurately differentiating criminal justice from criminology. If insiders are disoriented, outsiders are even more at a loss: When pressed, few noncriminal justice scholars can identify what the field stands for or attempts to study. Part of this can be attributed to its newness; however, part can also be explained by our collective failure to carve out clear boundaries and to develop a clear and focused theoretical foundation. This chapter explores the foundations of criminal justice theory as a means of clarifying the way forward.

THE STATE OF CRIMINAL JUSTICE THEORY

Criminal justice theory is underdeveloped for several reasons. Chapter 1 has already isolated some of these reasons, so we will only discuss them briefly. First, criminal justice is often confused with criminology. Some view criminal justice as applied criminology, and others see it as a field of study that can be subsumed within criminology (Pelfrey, 1980, 52).[2] Criminology as a field of study is focused primarily on the study of criminal behavior. Criminal justice, on the other hand, is focused primarily on the official responses to such behavior. While theoretical criminology has been criticized for being overly fragmented, the field is largely united by a common interest in explaining crime and criminal behavior (Bernard & Snipes, 1996). As an academic field of study, criminal justice lacks any such shared orientation. Second, since criminal justice is often viewed as an applied field in which an important part of the mission is to educate criminal justice practitioners (in so-called "cop shops"), the importance of theory is sometimes downplayed.[3] Third, criminal justice is taught in departments as diverse as criminology, sociology, political science, public affairs, law, psychology, philosophy, and various other hybrid programs. Thus, the very structure of the field, including its location within universities, its reward structures, its preferred publication outlets, and its diverse disciplinary background, all interfere with its ability to develop a coherent league of its own.

Perhaps the biggest question is whether criminal justice represents enough of a unitary, cohesive, or coordinated domain to deserve its own field of study. One helpful way of thinking about the answer to that question is to trace the development of the "contemporary criminal justice paradigm" as described by Samuel Walker (1992). In the late 1950s and early 1960s, based on the pioneering work of the American Bar Foundation, scholars began to look at criminal justice in two new ways. First, based on intensive field research, they discovered the important role of discretion in the criminal justice process (e.g., Goldstein, 1960; Lafave, 1965). Second, and not independent of the first, they began to conceive of criminal justice for the first time as a "system" (Blumberg, 1967). Before this, in what Walker (1992) calls the "progressive era paradigm," criminal justice was viewed as a more legalistic, formalized process consisting of a series of independent institutions, including police, courts, and corrections. The work of these institutions was in some ways related, but essentially separate. The new "systems perspective" recognized that these institutions are interdependent upon each other in many important ways. At the simplest level, police outputs become court inputs, and court outputs become correctional inputs. This conception of criminal justice as a series of outputs and inputs became particularly popular following the report of the President's Commission on Law Enforcement and Administration of Justice in 1967 (President's Commission, 1967; also see Duffee, 1990). This systemic approach, which focuses on the importance of discretion and the interplay between the various facets of the system, is what Walker (1992) calls the "contemporary criminal justice paradigm."

However, not all scholars agree with this systemic approach. Many have argued that criminal justice is not a system, but a loosely integrated and coordinated set of institutions with separate but related duties and goals. Duffee (1990) rejects portions of the systemic approach to criminal justice for several reasons. He challenges the assumptions that criminal justice systems are uniform across localities, that criminal justice agencies within a locality are well integrated, and that there is any integrated control mechanism available at a system level. He further argues that many criminal justice analysts "gloss over" the differences between systems in order to stress their commonalities. Others argue that criminal justice does not function as a system since each component is governed by "perverse incentives" (Wilson, 1983),[4] that its components serve functions that are unrelated to criminal justice (police officers deal with traffic safety; courts attend to torts and contract disputes), or that the criminal justice process is not structured as a formal system.[5]

Therefore, the debate over the domain of criminal justice is enmeshed in a separate debate about whether the criminal justice system is actually a system. We argue that criminal justice might best be described as a loosely coupled system, with features like the separation of powers and checks and balances built in for various reasons (see Hagan, Chapter 3 in this volume). For example, police and prisons in most developed countries are based in the executive branch, and the courts in the judicial branch. Some argue that criminal justice institutions should remain separate so that they maintain an equitable distribution of power. In the United States, for example, the Fourth Amendment generally prevents the police from searching citizens' homes without prior judicial approval. In developing countries without these types of checks on police power, police may be used as agents of oppression by the ruling classes (e.g., Arthur, 1988; Clinard & Abbott, 1973; Harriott,

2000).[6] Thus, Wright (1981) argues that goal conflict, rather than hindering the effectiveness of the criminal justice system, serves a variety of beneficial roles, such as maintaining system stability and ensuring an even distribution of power among component institutions.

Furthermore, critics of the systemic perspective who focus on the differences between criminal justice institutions may not realize the importance of the informal linkages that connect actors and networks in these institutions. These informal linkages are a central theme in exchange theory, described generally by Blau (1964) and applied to criminal justice by Cole (1970). Exchange theorists argue that much of what occurs between organizations can be attributed to informal exchanges between actors from different organizations. Thus, for example, although the formal linkages between courts and police departments may be tenuous, there exists a much more powerful set of informal linkages between police officers, prosecutors, and judges. These linkages are forged on a daily basis, as the actors from each organization find themselves in repeated contact with one another (e.g., Feeley, 1991).[7] One example of such linkages is Eisenstein and Jacob's (1977) "courtroom workgroup." Although the actors brought together in the courtroom—judges, defense attorneys, prosecutors, and police officers—are from different institutions, have different goals, and are formally arranged in an adversarial relationship, they often bind together in mutually convenient, informal networks. This perspective is important because it helps us to understand the complex relationships between the component institutions of the criminal justice process.

It is precisely that these linkages across institutions exist that gives criminal justice its own domain. Aside from one's stance on the systems debate, criminal justice involves relationships between several different institutional areas, all of which participate in formal social reaction to crime. Although the study of criminal justice relies heavily on the application of theories from other academic disciplines (such as sociology, organization theory, anthropology, and political science), the domain of criminal justice is large and complex enough to justify the existence of a separate academic field. Having now explored the basic foundations of what *criminal justice* is, we now discuss *criminal justice theory*. We begin this discussion by explaining the two most common misrepresentations of criminal justice theory.

WHAT CRIMINAL JUSTICE THEORY IS NOT

Many discussions of criminal justice theory either use the term "theory" to refer to something other than scientific theory, or address substantive areas that are not within the scope of "criminal justice." It is surprising to find that scholars misuse the term "theory" so frequently. Theory has been the building block of scholarly inquiry since the birth of the scientific method. Theory is to scholars as clay is to sculptors and lumber to carpenters: It is the raw material of science. Many definitions of "theory" have been offered throughout the history of science. One of the most respected authorities of theory development in modern social sciences is Dubin (1978), who delineates four elements that must be present for a theory to be complete: (1) what; (2) how; (3) why; and (4) who, where, when (see Whetten, 1989 for a review).

What refers to the factors that explain some phenomenon of interest. In empirical research, social scientists refer to these factors as independent variables. Scientists strive to ensure that the list of explanatory factors is both comprehensive (including all relevant factors) and parsimonious (excluding trivial factors). *How* refers to the causal relationship between the independent variables and the dependent variable. For example, what form does the relationship take? Is it linear or nonlinear? Is it direct or indirect? Is it additive or multiplicative? *Why* involves the process by which the independent variables influence the phenomena, or dependent variables, being studied. For instance, these processes may be sociological, psychological, organizational, economic, or historic, to name a few possibilities. The articulation of these processes must explain why an independent variable (often denoted as X) influences a dependent variable (Y).

The *what, how*, and *why* elements are sufficient for establishing the basic structure of a theory. We can make a theory more complete by qualifying it with *who*, *where*, and *when* statements. To what extent will the basic theoretical propositions hold up with different types of people, different locations, and different time periods? In other words, to what extent is the theory generalizable?

Bacharach (1989, 498) differentiates the *elements* of a theory (such as those covered by Dubin) from the *boundaries* of a theory:

> Values are the implicit assumptions by which a theory is bounded. Theories cannot be compared on the basis of their underlying values, because these tend to be the idiosyncratic product of the theorist's creative imagination and ideological orientation or life experience. This may explain why perpetual debates such as those between Marxists and Structural Functionalists have made so little progress over the years.

Confusing the boundaries of theories with theories themselves is one of the most serious issues with past criminal justice "theories."

Let us treat Braithwaite and Pettit's (1990) republican theory as an example. The central premise of the theory is that "while there are many goods or values engaged in social and political life, a single goal for the criminal justice system can be the basis of a sophisticated policy . . . . The goal in question we describe as republican or civic freedom; in a word, 'dominion'" (Braithwaite & Pettit 1990, 765). The theory also consists of theorems, such as, "The criminal justice system should implement a presumption in favor of parsimony . . ." and, "The system should be designed, not primarily to punish offenders but, rather, out of community-based dialogue, to bring home to them the disapproval of others . . ." (Braithwaite & Pettit, 1990, 767).[8]

While republican theory may be interesting or informative, it is not scientific theory in the conventional sense of the term. Instead, it is an ideological perspective. Theorists may choose to adopt this perspective and to include the values on which it is based as the boundary assumptions of the criminal justice theories they develop. In fact, some of Braithwaite and Pettit's theorems may qualify as theories—or at least as theoretically grounded hypotheses—because they explore the effect of different policies on dominion. However, "republican theory" as a whole, much like "retribution theory," is a philosophical perspective, not a scientific theory. Both of these ideological or philosophical perspectives may play an important role in dialogue and debates within the field, but they should not be confused with traditional scientific theories, which focus on explaining why one or more social phenomena cause or influence another, including the reasons, processes, or dynamics underlying the proposed chain of effects.

A second problem with many "criminal justice theories" is that they are not really theories of criminal justice. Instead, they are theories meant to explain other social phenomena. Criminal justice, you may recall, is the study of the official response to crime. In *Theories of Criminal Justice: A Critical Reappraisal*, Ellis and Ellis (1989, ix) set out to "critically re-examine several of the most prominent approaches to the *philosophy* of criminal justice" (emphasis added). Their discussion focuses on the "three main types of *theories* of criminal justice" (1989, xxxi): deterrence, rehabilitation, and retribution. Note that in deterrence and rehabilitation, the dependent variable is crime, not the official response to crime. These theories focus on the proposed effects of different criminal justice sanctions on crime. In both theories, crime is the dependent variable, and the criminal justice response to crime is an independent variable. As Akers (1992) points out, the study of something means that the "something" is a dependent variable. Thus, in a study of criminal justice, we would expect the dependent variable to be criminal justice, not crime. If the dependent variable is crime, it is criminological theory. Retribution, as noted earlier, is not even a theory of crime because it does not seek to explain the cause or influence of one or more phenomena on another. Instead, it is a moral justification for punishment, and therefore falls more within the realm of philosophy or ideology than scientific theory.

The first step in furthering criminal justice theory is thus to clarify the terms "criminal justice" and "theory." We begin this effort by discussing some of the ambiguities that may cloud the definition of criminal justice theory. We propose a series of relatively simple "tests" for determining what constitutes criminal justice theory.

WHAT CRIMINAL JUSTICE THEORY IS

Criminal justice theory is the study of the official response to behavior that may be labeled criminal. We propose four tests for determining whether a particular statement is consistent with our definition of criminal justice theory. These include the dependent variable test, the reasonableness test, the parts-of-a-system test, and the valid theory test.

Dependent Variable Test

If criminal justice theory is meant to explain official response to a behavior that may be labeled as criminal, then crime or criminal behavior cannot be the dependent variable. If the dependent variable in a statement is crime or criminal behavior, then the statement falls within the realm of criminological theory, not criminal justice theory.

One might ask whether a study of official response to potentially criminal behavior must involve actual behavior (i.e., decisions, actions) exhibited on the part of the criminal justice system, its components, or its actors. Put differently, should non-behavioral phenomena such as attitudes, ideologies, philosophical orientations, structures, or policies be considered dependent variables worthy of study? We view it as necessary to adopt an expansive definition of "response" when setting parameters on what constitutes criminal justice theory. Responses do not necessarily have to be behavioral, and indeed, many types of non-behavioral responses are closely linked with behavioral responses. For example, a theory that explains judicial attitudes toward white-collar criminals may employ such attitudes as an intermediate variable, where the theorist ultimately wishes to explain the severity of punishment of street criminals. Even if a theorist does not link a non-behavioral response variable to an ultimate behavioral response, the theory can still be classified as constituting criminal justice theory.

Reasonableness Test

The problem with defining criminal justice as the official response to crime is that it is the official response itself that transforms behavior into "crime." If an incident occurs in which the criminal justice system responds to a certain behavior by not labeling it as a crime, this may be just as theoretically relevant as if the system had labeled it criminal. Hence, criminal justice includes our response to deviance, as long as one believes that the form of deviance being studied has a reasonable chance of being labeled criminal. By broadening the definition of criminal justice in this fashion, we incorporate into its domain studies that, for example, seek to understand why legislatures criminalize some behaviors and not others.

Parts-of-a-System Test

We have already mentioned the debate about whether criminal justice is a system. In light of this debate, it would be inappropriate to require criminal justice theory to study only system-wide responses. Theoretical statements about police, judicial, and correctional responses to potentially criminal behavior would all constitute forms of criminal justice theory. In fact, the dependent variable may be any type of response, as long as the possibility of invoking the formal criminal justice system is relevant to the theory. Thus, legislative, media, victim, and public responses to potentially criminal behavior may all be classified as legitimate dependent variables in criminal justice theory.

The Valid Theory Test

In an earlier section we laid out the basic properties of scientific theories. Since criminal justice theory is a subset of scientific theory, valid criminal justice theories should conform to more general standards for what constitutes valid scientific theory.

Table 2.1 summarizes the definition and tests of criminal justice theory. A proposed theoretical statement must pass all four tests to be consistent with our definition of criminal justice theory. Statements that do not pass all four tests may still represent valuable scholarly contributions of various types, but may not constitute valid *scientific* theories or *criminal justice* theories.[9]

Note that merely testing a theory within a criminal justice institution does not make it a criminal justice theory. For instance, deterrence theory is regularly tested in police agencies, but the dependent variable in deterrence theory is crime; therefore, these are tests of criminological theory, not criminal justice theory. The arenas in which theories are

Table 2.1 Criminal justice theory: Definition and tests

Criminal justice theory is the study of official response to behavior that may be labeled criminal.

- ☐ The *Dependent Variable Test* indicates that response to potentially criminal behavior must be the dependent variable studied; in no way can the potentially criminal behavior itself be the dependent variable.
- ☐ The *Reasonableness Test* indicates that the behavior to which the response applies must have a reasonable chance of being labeled criminal, such that the formal criminal justice system is invoked.
- ☐ The *Parts-of-a-System Test* indicates that as long as the entity responding to the behavior is integrally tied to the criminal justice system, the "official" part of the definition is met.
- ☐ The *Valid Theory Test* indicates that the theory must conform with traditionally accepted social science standards for theories, as delineated by such scholars as Dubin (1978).

developed or tested are not sufficient to classify them as criminal justice theories. Our aim is not to denigrate any scholarly work that fails these tests, but merely to suggest that it doesn't fall within the boundaries of criminal justice theory as defined in this chapter.

EXAMPLES OF CRIMINAL JUSTICE THEORY

Having discussed what criminal justice theory is and is not, we now review some work that we believe constitutes valid criminal justice theory. We are careful to avoid condensing criminal justice theory into a simplistic typology that presents an overly narrow perspective of the field. On the other hand, our aim is not to present an encyclopedic accounting of every possible type of criminal justice theory. Thus, following the principle of parsimony, we pose seven dimensions along which criminal justice theories may lie and provide examples within each dimension: (1) historical vs. ahistorical; (2) organizational perspective; (3) sociopolitical perspective; (4) objective vs. subjective; (5) type of response; (6) level of explanation; and (7) institutional arena.

There are certainly other dimensions along which theory could be measured, but we think these dimensions capture substantial variation in criminal justice theory. They are not mutually exclusive dimensions, and any given theory can be classified somewhere on the continuum (or in some cases, in one of the categories) in each dimension. Another reason for using these dimensions as a method of reviewing some criminal justice theory is that several of our suggestions for future directions in criminal justice theory involve integrating approaches within these dimensions.

Historical vs. Ahistorical

Theories may "freeze time" when explaining criminal justice phenomena, or they may attempt to explain either the source (origination) or development of criminal justice responses over time. This dimension applies to virtually any area of theoretical enterprise. To the extent that a theory relies inherently or explicitly on our understanding of a phenomenon in different historical periods (or over time), it is historical theory.

One example of a historical theory of criminal justice is Robinson and Scaglion's (1987) theory of the police. Their dependent variable is the origin of the police institution. Whereas most theories of the police might ask how the police respond to behavior that is potentially criminal, their theory asks why the institution of policing exists in the first place. Their primary independent variable is the extent to which a society is class dominated. As a society moves from kinship based to class dominated, it is more likely to develop a formal police institution to deal with forms of threatening behavior. Robinson and Scaglion support their theory with anthropological examples of societies in different historical eras, at different places along the kinship-class–dominated continuum, and with different types of police functions.

Ahistorical theories are plentiful. One such example is Klinger's (1994) notion that when a suspect exhibits a nasty demeanor toward the police, the suspect is more likely to be arrested because the officer perceives the behavior as an act of resistance. Although this notion could be expanded into a historical theory (for example, by arguing that over time, police are becoming more likely to label resistance as crime), as it stands now, it is an ahistorical theory of police behavior.

Organizational Perspective

Although criminal justice theory has adopted frameworks from many disciplines, two of the most influential have been organizational and sociopolitical perspectives. Although organizational theory is massive, three organizational approaches have arguably had the greatest impact on criminal justice theory: the rational-goal model, the functional systems model, and more recently, the institutional model.

Feeley (1973) has provided an eloquent description of the first two organizational perspectives, as adapted from Etzioni (1960). Feeley merges Etzioni's goal model with Weber's rational-legal model, forming a rational-goal model of the criminal justice system. This perspective is preoccupied with formal goals and rules, and the assumption is that it is possible to approach goals (such as organizational effectiveness) with rational organization and procedures, as characterized by Weber's vision of the formal bureaucracy. As applied to criminal justice, this model "[implies] an elaborate apparatus which processes arrests according to highly defined rules and procedures undertaken by 'experts' who perform the functions ascribed to them by highly defined formal roles, under a rigorous division of labor, and who are subject to scrutiny in a systematic and hierarchical pattern" (Feeley 1973, 410).

Theories within the rational-goal perspective might employ criminal justice effectiveness or efficiency as the dependent variable, and the rationality of procedures and decisions as the independent variable. One example of such a theory may be the effect of judicial compliance with *In re Gault* on the effectiveness of the criminal justice system (Lefstein, Stapleton, & Teitelbaum, 1969). The problem with most theories employing the rational-goal model is that they assume effectiveness (an ambiguous term in these theories) is influenced by such factors as judicial compliance, and the theorists spend their efforts simply assessing the extent to which compliance exists and inferring the extent to which the system is effective. These theories are tautological because they define effectiveness by such factors as compliance and then measure compliance to determine effectiveness. Some theories stemming from the rational-goal perspective may squeak by our proposed tests of criminal justice theory, but they are generally not well-constructed theories.

According to Feeley (1973, 413–414), whereas the rational-goal model deals with "the rational organization pursuing its single set of goals," the functional-systems perspective has to do with "rational individuals who comprise the system . . . prosecutor, defense counsel, police, defendant, clerks . . . pursuing their various individual goals." This perspective results in more complex theories than those stemming from the rational-goal model because individuals often have different, and frequently conflicting, goals from the organizations in which they work. Unlike the rational-goal model, the functional systems model pays special attention to non-goal-oriented functions, such as the activities and means by which workers carry out their jobs. This approach recognizes the reality that organizations are complex entities that often behave in ways that are inconsistent with their goals. In fact, organization theorists have spent decades trying to understand how entities that are supposed to be rational can sometimes behave so irrationally (Maguire, 2014).

Probably the best example of a theory that is consistent with the functional-systems perspective is exchange theory (Blau, 1964), which has to do with the nature and effects of the informal linkages and exchanges that occur *between* organizations. An excellent example of exchange theory applied to criminal justice is *Felony Justice* by Eisenstein and Jacob (1977). This classic study of criminal courts finds that the strongest influences on plea bargaining rates are the characteristics of the courtroom workgroup, which is composed of actors with different interests (defense attorneys, prosecutors, judges) who recognize their collective interest in cooperating with one another for the smooth functioning of the overall system. The stronger these informal linkages (the more familiar and stable the workgroup is), the more rationalized the court processes, with greater plea bargaining rates and fewer trials.

The functional systems perspective has probably had more impact on the development of criminal justice theory than any other organizational model. Its focus on the informal linkages between individuals from different organizations reminds us that what is written on a formal organizational chart is only part of the story. Understanding informal structures and patterns of interorganizational behavior is essential for understanding the criminal justice system as a whole.

Whereas the functional systems perspective explores the relationship between individuals and organizations, the institutional approach is interested primarily in how organizations interact with their social, political, and economic environments. The introduction of modern institutional theory (Meyer & Rowan 1977) into the organizational theory literature has led to a groundswell of applications to criminal justice phenomena (e.g., Burruss, Giblin, & Schafer, 2010; Crank & Langworthy, 1992; Crank, 1994; Maguire, 2014; Mastrofski & Ritti, 2000). According to institutional theory, organizations face environmental pressures to which they must succumb in order to survive. However, at its core, the organization lacks commitment to these changes and responds by adopting symbolic or ceremonial structures, policies, and practices. For instance, research has shown that police departments are heavily institutionalized organizations whose activities are often motivated by the need to appear progressive, regardless of whether the practices that generate this appearance are effective from a technical perspective. A prominent example is the development of community policing, which in some cases is a symbolic or ceremonial response to the public's demand for better (or different) policing and the department's need to secure resources necessary for its own economic survival (e.g., Burruss & Giblin, 2014; Crank, 1994). Removal of police chiefs after negative incidents (such as the Rodney King beating) may also be viewed as ceremonial or institutional responses to solving crises in policing (Crank & Langworthy, 1992). Note that several chapters in this volume discuss institutional theory and its applications to various facets of criminal justice.

Sociopolitical Perspective

Many of the sociopolitical perspectives associated with criminal justice theory stem from the conflict and consensus perspectives (Hagan, 1989). The conflict and consensus perspectives offer contrasting views on the nature of society and, more specifically, the role of government in society. According to the consensus perspective, government's role is to reconcile the interests of different groups of people. Society comes together in forming a broad consensus about what sorts of behaviors are harmful or pathological and defines them as criminal, punishing people who commit these behaviors. This perspective was influenced strongly by the work of French sociologist Emile Durkheim. It stems from a view that crime serves a functional role for society. Since it is deviant and abnormal, it brings the common public together in attempting to extinguish it.

The conflict perspective, on the other hand, views society as divided into interest groups between which there will always be conflict as these groups compete for power, prestige, and material goods. The government is unable to reconcile all their differences, so instead it represents the interests of the most powerful groups, which continually attempt to preserve their position by oppressing the less powerful. Conflict theory was strongly influenced by the work of the German philosopher Karl Marx, who believed that the very basis of society is a class struggle between the "haves" and the "have nots." From the conflict perspective, the criminal justice system functions to establish and enforce laws in such a way that (to paraphrase a popular book title) "the rich get richer and the poor get prison" (Reiman, 2007).[10]

An example of a consensus theory of criminal justice is Gottfredson and Hindelang's (1979) examination of how an offense's "seriousness"—as measured by the degree of harm to the victim—influences whether the victim reports the crime to the police. Gottfredson and Hindelang note that there is a widely held consensus that behavior that exceeds a certain threshold of seriousness falls within the proper domain of the criminal justice system. Their article was written in response to Black's (1976) *The Behavior of Law*, which was not written explicitly from a conflict perspective, but which made many assertions that were clearly compatible with conflict theory.

Conflict theory is applicable at every phase of the criminal justice process, including generating laws; reporting crimes; arresting, prosecuting, and sentencing offenders; and holding parole hearings. Myers and Talarico's (1986) study of sentencing in Georgia is an excellent example of a conflict theory that goes beyond asking the standard question: "Are minorities discriminated against in the criminal justice system?" Myers and Talarico (1986) examined the interaction between a county's racial political representation and an offender's race in influencing the offender's sentence. In counties where blacks had political control, whites were actually more likely to get prison sentences than were blacks. In counties where whites had political control, blacks were more severely sentenced than were whites.

Although conflict theory has perhaps been more commonly explored in terms of criminal justice discrimination once a behavior has been labeled criminal, the most broad-based conflict theories examine the beginning of the criminal justice process—namely, the formulation of laws. McGarrell and Castellano (1991), drawing from three theories (Chambliss & Seidman, 1982; Galliher & Cross, 1983; Scheingold, 1984), developed a three-level, integrated conflict theory of the criminal law formulation process. At the first level, highly differentiated social structures lead to more conflict, and thus an increased number of behaviors end up being defined as criminal. Intertwined with high social differentiation are cultural attitudes reinforcing myths of crime. Factors at the first level produce actual crime, victimization, fear, and concern about crime, thus generating a punitive response by the criminal justice system. Because fear of crime, along with media attention, results in increased enforcement of laws defining behavior as criminal, these responses actually bring about more crime. Triggering events are the third level of influences on legislative policy. In this "unstable and volatile public policy arena . . . [a] slight dislocation, a random event, a vocal political opportunist, or a disgruntled governmental bureaucrat, can trigger events which mobilize the political arena to consider and enact crime legislation and policy" (McGarrell & Castellano 1991, 188). Once a new law is passed, making even more behaviors illegal, the amount of crime and criminal justice is increased, and the feedback cycle continues.

Even though some scholars (such as Hagan, 1989) believe that conflict and consensus theories can only take us so far in exploring criminal justice phenomena, there is little evidence that their use by criminal justice scholars is decreasing. Because research in the conflict vein has focused very little on the exact processes by which discrimination occurs, there is still much room for theoretical development and elaboration in conflict approaches to criminal justice.

Objective vs. Subjective Perspective

Whereas the conflict and consensus perspectives relate to fundamental views of our political and social system, another dimension on which theory may be classified relates to our fundamental views of reality. Although it has been discussed by ancient philosophers, the debate over whether objective reality exists or reality is socially constructed by observers has only been influencing social science theory for the past three or four decades.[11] A highly influential work by Burrell and Morgan (1979) divides the entire field of organization theory into four paradigms, organized along two dimensions. One of these dimensions ranges from objective to subjective (the other ranges from radical change to regulation). To Burrell and Morgan (1979), and many modern organizational theorists, whether a scholar views reality as objective or subjective is a basic division in the field.

According to Burrell and Morgan, if a theorist who is examining the world without trying to change it adopts an objective approach, he or she is operating within the functionalist paradigm. A theorist who adopts a subjective stance is operating within the interpretivist paradigm. Much criminal justice theory has been driven by both of these paradigms. From a functionalist standpoint, the world is treated "as if it were a hard, external, objective reality" (1979, 3). A theorist approaching criminal justice from such a perspective would consider crime to be a social fact. In contrast, theorists working in the interpretivist paradigm view the world as composed of "the subjective experience[s] of individuals in the creation of the social world" (1979, 3). To subjectivists, facts are rarely facts; instead, they are part of a socially constructed reality. The same behavior may be viewed by some as criminal and by others as non-criminal. Some argue that behavior is observable, but can be construed in multiple ways; others argue that the very nature of subjective perception implies that any "objective" behavior is itself unobservable.

Some versions of conflict theory are consistent with the interpretivist paradigm. For instance, some formulations propose that certain types of behavior are more likely to be labeled as criminal or treated as serious under certain power conditions. For instance, Quinney (1970, 18) notes: "the probability that criminal sanctions will be applied varies according to the extent to which the behaviors of the powerless conflict with the interests of the power segments." Such specifications of conflict theory are interpretivist because they imply different realities depending upon power dynamics.

A broader approach to crime within the interpretivist paradigm is constructionism. The constructionist view suggests that different realities may exist for different people, but it is possible to manipulate commonly accepted conceptions of reality. Rafter (1990) cites Gusfield's (1963) treatment of Prohibition and Erikson's (1966) work on the Puritans' behavior toward deviance as classic examples of moral incentives to construct realities. More recently, Gusfield (1981) has shown how moral crusaders (such as Mothers Against Drunk Driving) have been able to bring certain behaviors (such as drunk driving) further into the realm of the criminal justice system by redefining it as criminal behavior instead of traffic negligence.

The objective-to-subjective continuum can be used to classify many more types of theories than those addressed earlier. For example, some influential scholarship views crime rates less as measures of actual crime and more as organizational outputs. Put differently, crime rates constructed using police data reported to the Uniform Crime Reports may reflect as much about the agencies that collect data as about crime levels (McCleary, Nienstedt, & Erven, 1982).

Type of Response

Earlier we mentioned some of the response types that fall within the domain of criminal justice theory. Here we elaborate on the response types mentioned earlier. Criminal justice theorists have studied a variety of response types, some of which may appear more obvious than others. In this section we discuss seven categories of responses: lawmaking, decisions, attitudes, ideologies, structures, styles of behavior, and routines.[12]

Development of Laws

McGarrell and Castellano's (1991) theory (described earlier in this chapter) is aimed toward explaining the formulation of laws, which in turn determine what sorts of behavior are treated as criminal in our society. Most of the theoretical literature on lawmaking is guided by consensus, conflict, or constructionist perspectives.

Decisions

Probably the most studied dependent variable in criminal justice theory pertains to the gap between the laws as formulated and actual enforcement decisions. The difference is often characterized as the law on the books versus the law in action. Only since the 1960s have scholars truly recognized the importance of discretion and begun to study it seriously (Walker, 1992). The most commonly studied forms of discretion are the decision to arrest, the decision to use force, the decision to prosecute, and the sentencing decision. Gottfredson and Gottfredson (1988) have provided what is probably the most comprehensive overview of research on discretionary decision making in the criminal justice system. Theories about the decision to report a crime also fall clearly within the scope of criminal justice theory because the citizen's report invokes the formal criminal justice process.

Attitudes

Attitudes are usually studied as intermediate variables, with the assumption that they eventually influence behavioral response. Of course, there is a longstanding debate in social psychology about the extent to which this assumption is valid (Ajzen, 1982, 1987; Schuman & Johnson, 1976). The study of attitudes is often associated with the study of culture. For example, Church (1985), in testing a theory that court participants establish legal cultures to cope with the organizational demands placed upon them, measured the extent of overlap in the views of various courtroom actors. Church stated explicitly that in doing so, he was assuming that attitudes translated into behavioral patterns. Nardulli, Flemming, and Eisenstein (1985), on the other hand, studied similar phenomena but looked at behavioral patterns instead of attitudes. Both approaches have their shortcomings: Church (1985) had to infer that behavior resulted from process (the process was established with cultural attitudes); Nardulli and his colleagues (1985) had to assume process (a model of legal culture) from behavioral patterns.

Ideologies

Whereas attitudes usually contain rather specific (or at least easily identifiable) targets, ideologies are more general philosophical orientations or outlooks. In the realm of criminal justice, examples of popular ideologies are retribution (believing criminals should get what they deserve) and rehabilitation (believing we should try to help reform criminals). Some have summarized the primary ideological dimension in criminal justice as simply liberal or progressive ("soft" on crime) versus conservative or punitive ("tough" on crime) (Walker, 1985). One example of criminal justice theory that focuses on ideologies is Duffee's (1990) *Explaining Criminal Justice*. Duffee argues that the extent to which a local criminal justice system is moralist (promoting retribution) or welfare-oriented (promoting rehabilitation) depends on the community's independence from non-local sources and the degree of cooperation within subsystems in the community. A significant body of theory and research has also focused on explaining the ideological orientations of individuals, including criminal justice officials as well as citizens.

Structures

We have already noted that structures can be viewed as another type of response, whether as direct or indirect responses to crime or the threat of crime. Examples of theories of structure in criminal justice include Langworthy's (1986) and Maguire's (2003, 2009) studies of police organizational structure, DiIulio's (1987) examination of correctional organization structure, and Eisenstein and Jacob's (1977) work on court structure. An emerging line of theory and research in criminal justice looks at the extent to which agencies adopt symbolic structures to satisfy the demands of their institutional environments (e.g., Burruss & Giblin, 2014; Crank, 1994; Burruss, Giblin, & Schafer, 2010; Maguire, 2014).

Styles of Behavior

In addition to enacting specific laws or policies or making specific decisions about how to handle people engaging in potentially criminal behavior, criminal justice actors tend to adopt overt styles of behavior on the job. Scholars have explored differences in the behavioral styles exhibited by criminal justice actors in their day-to-day work. For example, Muir (1977) has studied police officer styles in dealing with suspects and others (see Snipes & Mastrofski, 1990 for a review of other work in this area). Muir formed a well-known typology of four styles of police behavior (Avoiders, Enforcers, Reciprocators, and Professionals). The behavioral styles that officers adopt are developed from their capacity to project themselves into the circumstances of others, and from their ability to integrate the use of coercion within their moral framework. Carter (1974) has developed a similar typology for prosecutors, forming four types: Teachers, Analysts, Competitors, and Crime Fighters. The style of behavior a prosecutor develops tends to be associated with his or her commitment to due process and crime control. It is not difficult to imagine other types of criminal justice officials—including defense attorneys, judges, probation officers, and prison guards—developing their own working styles. Moreover, as James Q. Wilson (1968) demonstrated so aptly in *Varieties of Police Behavior*, styles of behavior develop not only at the individual level, but also at the organizational level (and presumably at other levels, including the shift level or the unit level). Theories that explain variations in these working styles fall well within the domain of criminal justice theory.

Routines

In addition to discrete decision making, criminal justice theorists frequently study work routines: informal methods developed by criminal justice employees to help them deal with processing cases. In this type of research, the process by which a case is handled is an outcome variable in itself, regardless of the final disposition. Prominent examples of this type of theoretical research include Waegel's (1981) study of how police detectives respond to organizational pressures in developing routines for slotting, selecting, and investigating cases, and Sudnow's (1965) analogous study of the methods developed by public defenders to classify cases. These studies typically involve examining the organizational influences on the routinization of response to potentially criminal behavior. These working routines may overlap to some extent with behavioral styles, but for the most part, they are separate. Styles involve more overt behaviors exhibited during interactions with clients, whereas work routines typically involve less overt methods used to manage difficult or unreasonable workloads.

Level of Explanation

One could classify criminal justice theories as micro or macro, but this distinction is rather arbitrary (Alexander, Giesen, Munch, & Smelser, 1987). Levels of explanation range from small units, such as individuals, to large structures, such as societies. It is safe to say that the predominant level of explanation employed in the "progressive era paradigm" described earlier in this chapter (Walker, 1992) is the individual. The dependent variable is frequently the behavior or attitudes of individual actors within the criminal justice system. The set of independent variables includes individual attributes, and may also include variables at higher levels of explanation, such as characteristics of the city or region in which they reside. Other examples of higher levels of explanation include situations, groups, or subcultures (such as police subcultures or courtroom work groups), local organizations (such as police departments), communities, local governments, state governments, criminal justice agencies, and so on.

Most theories use the same level of explanation for both independent and dependent variables. It is rare for a higher level of explanation to be explained by lower-level concepts. For example, we would not typically explain variations in state incarceration rates using the characteristics of individuals. More commonly, lower-level phenomena are explained by concepts at that level and higher levels. For example, Worden's (Chapter 6 in this volume) explanation of police use of force draws upon factors measured at the individual, situational, and organizational levels. In other words, when a police officer decides to use force against a suspect, the decision is motivated by characteristics of the individual officer and suspect (such as age, sex, temperament, etc.), characteristics of the situation (such as whether the suspect is resisting arrest), and characteristics of the police organization (such as the departmental policies on use of force). Theories like this, in which one or more of the independent variables are from a higher level of explanation than the dependent variable, are known as "contextual" theories. These theories are growing more popular, in part due to the availability of applied statistical tools for testing these complicated models (e.g., Raudenbush & Bryk, 2002).

Institutional Arena

Theories of criminal justice may focus on the criminal justice system as a whole or its components (police, courts, or corrections). In addition, these theories might focus on other social entities like legislatures, interest groups, the media, actual or potential victims, community groups, and citizens, among others. Some criminal justice theories are contained entirely within one institutional arena. Others examine responses to potentially criminal behavior that crosses arenas in some fashion. For instance, earlier in the chapter we discussed exchange theory, which explicitly concerned people's connections across organizational or institutional boundaries. This seems to be the direction in which much criminal justice theory is moving, and as we will discuss in the conclusion, it is a movement that we expect to generate considerable insights.

While some theories are targeted toward one aspect of the criminal justice system, others are so broadly construed as to apply to the system as a whole or any of its parts. A good example of such a theory is outlined in Donald Black's (1976) *The Behavior of Law*. Black treats the amount of law as a dependent variable in such a way that it can be applied to many different outcomes at different levels, including public perceptions of the seriousness of crime, victim reporting of crime, police use of arrest, prosecutorial decision to charge, judicial sentencing severity, and parole board decisions. It could also be applied to larger units of analysis like neighborhoods or communities. In each of these examples, the amount of law varies from less to more. For instance, when a victim reports a crime or a police officer makes an arrest, more law is invoked than if the victim doesn't report a crime or a police officer doesn't make an arrest. Black outlines a parsimonious theory in which five types of variables, broadly construed, explain the variation in law.[13] Black's theory is unique in that it is not limited to a narrow range of decisions or units of analysis. It operates at a level of generality that is both intriguing and uncommon.

FUTURE DIRECTIONS

Stephen Fuchs (1993) articulates a theory of scientific change in which competition (which tends to be present in most academic fields of study) leads to scientific change. However, the type of change depends on two factors: task uncertainty and mutual dependence. Task uncertainty refers to the degree of ambiguity in how scientists perceive their mission. Mutual dependence pertains to the extent to which individuals in the field are socially integrated. The field of criminal justice is characterized by high task uncertainty and low mutual dependence: high uncertainty because there is little consensus on such basic ideas as what constitutes criminal justice theory, and low dependence because instead of a core group of scholars focusing on criminal justice, research is done by scientists and practitioners working in a number of different domains, often ignorant of each other's work. According to Fuchs (1993, 946), this combination tends to result, like a perfect storm, in a fragmented scientific field:

> Such fields lack the strong and dense networks necessary to produce facts, and so they engage in informal conversation instead... There is not a great deal of confidence in the possibility to become scientific and objective, and so the self-understanding of weak fields is skeptical and critically reflexive . . . Lacking unified research fronts that could define the overall direction of the discipline, weak fields do not really believe in the continuous progress of knowledge, and so there is a strong tendency to look back to the classics instead.[14]

We believe Fuchs's description of a fragmented scientific field eloquently captures the current state of criminal justice as an academic discipline. Fuchs also proposes that high task uncertainty and high mutual dependence can result in the potential for "permanent discoveries," similar to Kuhn's (1970) notion of revolutionary change. The implication is that in order to advance to the point where dramatic paradigm shifts are possible and a more robust body of theory can develop, criminal justice would need to become more integrated as an academic field of study. A sufficient number of interested scholars would have to begin guiding the field toward this more integrated approach, forming some basic level of consensus on where the field should go. This does not mean that everybody in the field would need to proceed in lockstep, embracing the same theories and doing the same kinds of work. But it does mean that the field would need to embrace some common ideas about what criminal justice theory entails and what its goals are.

In this chapter, we have shown that scholars in criminal justice cannot even agree upon what criminal justice is and what constitutes criminal justice theory. We have tried to present an initial framework for understanding criminal justice theory, one which may be controversial, but also may generate some meaningful discussion about the future of this academic field of study. Because criminal justice theory is so fragmented, we believe some basic level of integration will be important for developing a more cohesive theoretical enterprise. Several of the dimensions along which we have classified criminal justice theory are ripe for integration.

Sociopolitical perspectives that are seemingly bipolar may actually be compatible if brought together in the right theoretical context. Conflict notions may apply under some circumstances, and consensus under others. Durkheimian theory suggests that certain conditions (such as war) can create social solidarity. Under certain political environments and idiosyncratic historical processes, then, a consensus perspective may be appropriate in explaining criminal justice phenomena. In other times and circumstances, the conflict perspective may better explain the same phenomena. An integrated theory would develop a framework for predicting when conflict and when consensus concepts would more powerfully explain our response to potentially criminal behavior. Objective and subjective perspectives may seem too disparate to bring together, yet postmodernists have begun to do just this. For example, Giddens's (1979) theory of structuration proposes that we construct phenomena subjectively, but that these phenomena then begin to take on objective properties that can in turn influence those who constructed them. Given that crime is partly subjective and partly objective, and that both behavior and our response to behavior feed off each other reciprocally, it seems that structuration might be relevant to our understanding of crime and criminal justice.

Criminal justice theories explain many different types of responses, but there are numerous linkages between these responses, and these linkages could be explored more fully in the context of integrated theory. Attitudes, behaviors, ideologies, and decisions undoubtedly affect each other. As criminal justice theory progresses, it should begin to explore the relationships between multiple response types rather than just one response type at a time.

Criminal justice theorists are already bridging levels of explanation as they develop contextual theories that feature independent variables measured at two or more levels (such as students, classrooms, and schools). On the other hand, very rarely do theories examine the interactional relationships across levels. In other words, the nature and magnitude of an effect at the individual level (such as race) may be contingent on where that individual is positioned in a higher-level context (such as at the neighborhood level). For example, police officers with discriminatory attitudes towards African Americans may be less likely to translate their attitudes into discriminatory behaviors in progressive agencies that don't tolerate such behaviors than in troubled agencies that do. Finally, we have already stressed the need to link institutional arenas when developing criminal justice theory. Of all the possible types of integration discussed earlier, this has probably been the most common in recent applications of criminal justice theory that explore boundary-spanning behaviors and interorganizational networks. Nonetheless, much remains to be done.

This chapter has documented what we view as weaknesses in the current state of criminal justice theory. However, we remain optimistic that as the field continues to grow, more scholars will embrace the need to develop a science of criminal justice that is built upon a foundation of theory. If criminal justice theory is to come into its own right, scholars who see the need for it must begin to organize, settling on parameters and basic definitions, and beginning to forge its future. The chapters in this volume provide a useful framework for thinking about the contours of criminal justice theory.

NOTES

1. We dedicate this chapter to the memory of Thomas "Nino" Castellano, whose kindness inspired us, and whose comments on an earlier draft of the manuscript helped shape our thinking on this topic.
2. See also Akers (1992, 10), arguing that confusion between these fields of study may have impaired the academic standing of criminology among sociologists.
3. Several evaluations of criminal justice education in the early to mid-1970s noted that criminal justice curricula were too oriented toward professional training. Brandstatter and Hoover (1976, 47), for example, argued that criminal justice programs "include far too many professionally oriented courses" and "place undue emphasis on curricula designed to train students to perform specific operational tasks."
4. These perverse incentives can generate interagency conflict, as is often portrayed by the media. Consider the words of the Weasel, in Wambaugh's *The Glitter Dome*, who complained, "Times are pretty goddamn bad . . . when cops started using the same lies to each other that they should save for the real Enemies in the judiciary" (Wambaugh 1981, 142).
5. Some take this perspective one step further, arguing that because the ubiquitous conflict between the components of the criminal justice system hinders the system's performance, it should be reorganized. In *Organizing the Non-System*, Skoler (1977) argues that the separate criminal justice institutions should be unified and integrated so they can function together more smoothly.
6. In some countries, such as Uganda and Zambia, the police are closely linked with the military force. Although overlap between internal and

external security functions may enhance the crime control capacity of the police in certain ways, it also tends to raise concerns about due process and human rights.

7. The importance of informal relationships among groups of actors, both within and between organizations, now occupies a central role in organizational theory. The study of these informal relationships is known as network analysis. From a network perspective, the structure of an organization can only be fully understood by observing the numerous networks of relationships both within an organization and with actors from other organizations (Nohria, 1992). Of particular interest to criminal justice is the networking that occurs between actors at the border of different organizations that work together. From the network perspective, Nohria argues, "the environment consists of a field of relationships that bind organizations together." This environment, known in organization theory as an "interorganizational field" (DiMaggio and Powell, 1983, 148; Warren, 1967), is where actors from different organizations perform "boundary-spanning" roles (Lipsky, 1980; Reiss & Bordua, 1967) which enhance the reliance of each organization upon the other. These boundary-spanning roles play a key role in many aspects of criminal justice and homeland security (Maguire and King, 2011).
8. From *Not Just Deserts: A Republican Theory of Criminal Justice* by J. Braithwaite and P. Pettit, 1990, pp. 756–757. By permission of Oxford University Press, Inc.
9. Or it may belong in that murky area of "normative theory," which is valid theory but not traditional scientific theory, and is best classified as ideology or philosophy.
10. For a review of different versions of conflict theory, and for an integrated conflict theory, see Vold, Bernard, and Snipes (1998).
11. Berger and Luckmann's (1966) *Social Construction of Reality* is often hailed as the seminal work in this area.
12. Although this is probably not a comprehensive list of potential outcomes for legitimate criminal justice theory, it probably covers at least nine-tenths of existing theory.
13. Black calls these dimensions stratification, organization, culture, morphology, and social control. His book consists of a number of hypotheses relating each dimension with the amount of law.
14. From *Social Forces*, Vol. 71: Issue 4. Copyright © by the University of North Carolina Press. Used by permission of the publisher.

REFERENCES

Ajzen, I. 1982. On behaving in accordance with one's attitudes. In *Consistency in social behavior: The Ontario Symposium*, Eds. M.P. Zanna, E.T. Higgins, and C.P. Herman, (2): 3–15. Hillsdale, NJ: Erlbaum.

Ajzen, I. 1987. Attitudes, traits, and actions: Dispositional prediction of behavior in personality and social psychology. In L. Berkowitz (Ed.), *Advances in Experimental Social Psychology* (Vol. 20). (pp. 1–56) New York: Academic Press.

Akers, R.L. 1992. Linking sociology and its specialties: The case of criminology. *Social Forces* 71(1): 1–16.

Alexander, J.C., B. Giesen, R. Munch, and N.J. Smelser. 1987. *The micro-macro link*. Berkeley: University of California Press.

Arthur, J.A. 1988. *Social change and crime in Africa*. Ann Arbor, MI: University Microfilms International.

Bacharach, S.B. 1989. Organizational theories: Some criteria for evaluation. *Academy of Management Review* 14(4): 496–515.

Berger, P. and T. Luckman, 1966. *The social construction of reality: A treatise in the sociology of knowledge*. Garden City, NY: Doubleday.

Bernard, T.J. and J.B. Snipes. 1996. Theoretical integration in criminology. In *Crime and justice: A review of research*. Ed. M. Tonry, Chicago: University of Chicago Press.

Black, D. 1976. *The behavior of law*. New York: Academic Press.

Blau, P.M. 1964. *Exchange and power in social life*. New York: John Wiley.

Blumberg, A.S. 1967. *Criminal justice*. Chicago: Quadrangle Books.

Braithwaite, J. and P. Pettit. 1990. *Not just deserts: A republican theory of criminal justice*. New York: Oxford University Press.

Brandstatter, A.F. and L.T. Hoover. 1976. Systemic criminal justice education. *Journal of Criminal Justice* 4(1):47–55.

Burrell, G. and G. Morgan. 1979. *Sociological paradigms and organizational analysis*. London: Heinemann.

Burruss, G.W. and M.J. Giblin. 2014. Modeling isomorphism on policing innovation: The role of institutional pressures in adopting community-oriented policing. *Crime and Delinquency* 60(3): 331–355.

Burruss, G.W., M.J. Giblin, and J.A. Schafer. 2010. Threatened globally, acting locally: Modeling law enforcement homeland security practices. *Justice Quarterly* 27(1): 77–101.

Carter, L.H. 1974. *The limits of order*. Lexington, MA: Lexington Books.

Chambliss, W. and R. Seidman. 1982. *Law, order, and power*, 2nd ed. Reading, MA: Addison-Wesley.

Church, T.W. 1985. Examining local legal culture. *American Bar Foundation Research Journal* 10(3): 449–518.

Clinard, M.B. and D.J. Abbott. 1973. *Crime in developing countries: A comparative perspective*. New York: John Wiley.

Cole, G. 1970. The decision to prosecute. *Law and Society Review* 4: 331–345.

Crank, J.P. 1994. Watchman and community: Myth and institutionalization in policing. *Law and Society Review* 28(2): 325–351.

Crank, J.P. and R.H. Langworthy. 1992. An institutional perspective of policing. *The Journal of Criminal Law and Criminology* 83: 338–363.

DiIulio, J.J. 1987. *Governing prisons*. New York: Macmillan.
DiMaggio, P. and W.W. Powell. 1983. The iron cage revisited: Institutionalized isomorphism and collective rationality in organizational fields. *American Sociological Review* 48: 147–160.
Dubin, R. 1978. *Theory development*. New York: Free Press.
Duffee, D.E. 1990. *Explaining criminal justice: Community theory and criminal justice reform*. Prospect Heights, IL: Waveland Press.
Eisenstein, J. and H. Jacob. 1977. *Felony justice: An organizational analysis of criminal courts*. Boston: Little, Brown.
Ellis, R.D. and C.S. Ellis. 1989. *Theories of criminal justice*. Wolfeboro, NH: Longwood.
Erikson, K.T. 1966. *Wayward puritans: A study in the sociology of deviance*. New York: John Wiley and Sons.
Etzioni, A. 1960. Two approaches to organizational analysis: A critique and a suggestion. *Administrative Science Quarterly* 5(2): 257–278.
Feeley, M.M. 1973. Two models of the criminal justice system: An organizational perspective. *Law and Society Review* 7(3): 407–425.
Feeley, M.M. 1991. *Court reform on trial: Why simple solutions fail*. New York: Basic Books.
Fuchs, S. 1993. A sociological theory of scientific change. *Social Forces* 71(4): 933–953.
Galliher, J. and J. Cross. 1983. *Morals legislation without morality: The case of Nevada*. New Brunswick, NJ: Rutgers University Press.
Giddens, A. 1979. *Central problems in social theory: Action, structure, and contradiction in social analysis*. Berkeley: University of California Press.
Goldstein, J. 1960. Police discretion not to invoke the criminal process: Low visibility decisions in the administration of justice. *Yale Law Journal* 69: 543–594.
Gottfredson, M.R. and D.M. Gottfredson. 1988. *Decision making in criminal justice: Toward the rational exercise of discretion*, 2nd ed. New York: Plenum.
Gottfredson, M.R. and M.J. Hindelang. 1979. A study of The Behavior of Law. *American Sociological Review* 44: 3–18.
Gusfield, J.R. 1963. *Symbolic crusade: Status politics and the American temperance movement*. Urbana: University of Illinois Press.
Gusfield, J.R. 1981. *The culture of public problems: Drinking-driving and the symbolic order*. Chicago: University of Chicago Press.
Hagan, J. 1989. Why is there so little criminal justice theory? Neglected macro and micro-level links between organization and power. *Journal of Research in Crime and Delinquency* 26: 116–135.
Harriott, A. 2000. *Police and crime control in Jamaica: Problems of reforming ex-colonial constabularies*. Kingston, Jamaica: University of the West Indies Press.
Klinger, D. 1994. Demeanor or crime? An inquiry into why "hostile" citizens are more likely to be arrested. *Criminology* 32: 475–493.

Kuhn, T. 1970. *The structure of scientific revolutions*, 2nd ed. Chicago: University of Chicago Press.

Lafave, W. 1965. *Arrest: The decision to take a suspect into custody*. Boston: Little, Brown.

Langworthy, R.H. 1986. *The structure of police organizations*. New York: Praeger.

Lefstein, N., V. Stapleton, and L. Teitelbaum. 1969. In search of juvenile justice. *Law and Society Review* 5: 491–563.

Lipsky, M. 1980. *Street-level bureaucracy: Dilemmas of the individual in public services*. New York: Russell Sage.

Maguire, E.R. 2003. *Context, complexity and control: Organizational structure in American police agencies*. Albany, NY: State University of New York Press.

Maguire, E.R. 2009. Police organizational structure and child sexual abuse case attrition. *Policing: An International Journal of Police Strategies and Management* 32(1): 157–179.

Maguire, E.R. 2014. Police organizations and the iron cage of rationality. In *Oxford handbook on police and policing*, eds. M. Reisig and R. Kane. New York: Oxford University Press.

Maguire, E.R. and W.R. King. 2011. Federal-local coordination in homeland security. In *Criminologists on terrorism*, eds. B. Forst, J. Greene, and J. Lynch. New York: Cambridge University Press.

Mastrofski, S.D. and R.R. Ritti. 2000. Making sense of community policing: A theoretical perspective. *Police Practice and Research: An International Journal* 1(2): 183–210.

McCleary, R., B.C. Nienstedt, and J.M. Erven. 1982. Uniform Crime Reports as organizational outcomes: Three time series experiments. *Social Problems* 29(4): 361–372.

McGarrell, E.F. and T.C. Castellano. 1991. An integrative conflict model of the criminal law formation process. *Journal of Research in Crime and Delinquency* 28(2): 174–196.

Meyer, J.W. and B. Rowan. 1977. Institutionalized organizations: Formal structure as myth and ceremony. *American Journal of Sociology* 83: 340–363.

Muir, W.K., Jr. 1977. *Police: Streetcorner politicians*. Chicago: University of Chicago Press.

Myers, M.A. and S.M. Talarico. 1986. The social contexts of racial discrimination in sentencing. *Social Problems* 33(3): 236–251.

Nardulli, P.F., R. Flemming, and J. Eisenstein. 1985. Criminal courts and bureaucratic justice: Concessions and consensus in the guilty plea process. *Journal of Criminal Law and Criminology* 76(4): 1103–1131.

Nohria, N. 1992. Introduction: Is a network perspective a useful way of studying organizations? In *Networks and organizations: Structure, form, and action* eds. N. Nohria and R.G. Eccles (pp. 1–22). Boston: Harvard Business School Press.

Pelfrey, W.V. 1980. *The evolution of criminology*. Cincinnati: Anderson.

President's Commission on Law Enforcement and Administration of Justice. 1967. *The challenge of crime in a free society*. Washington, D.C.: U.S. Government Printing Office.

Quinney, R. 1970. *The social reality of crime*. Boston: Little, Brown and Company.

Rafter, N.H. 1990. The social construction of crime and crime control. *Journal of Research in Crime and Delinquency* 27(4): 376–389.

Raudenbush, S.W. and A.S. Bryk. 2002. *Hierarchical linear models*, second edition. Thousand Oaks, CA: Sage.

Reiman, J. 2007. The rich get richer and the poor get prison (8th edition). Boston, MA: Pearson/Allyn & Bacon.

Reiss, A.J. and D.J. Bordua. 1967. Environment and organization: A perspective on the police. In *The police: Six sociological essays* ed. D. Bordua (pp. 25–55). New York: John Wiley.

Robinson, C.D. and R. Scaglion. 1987. The origin and evolution of the police function in society: Notes toward a theory. *Law and Society Review* 21(1): 109–152.

Scheingold, S.A. 1984. *The politics of law and order: Street crime and public policy*. New York: Longman.

Schuman, H. and M.P. Johnson. 1976. Attitudes and behavior. *Annual Review of Sociology* 2: 161–207.

Skoler, D.L. 1977. *Organizing the non-system*. Lexington, MA: DC Heath.

Snipes, J.B. and S.D. Mastrofski. 1990. An empirical test of Muir's typology of police officers. *American Journal of Criminal Justice* 14(2): 268–296.

Sudnow, D. 1965. Normal crimes: Sociological features of the penal code in a public defender's office. *Social Problems* 12: 255–276.

Vold, G.T., T. Bernard, and J. Snipes. 1998. *Theoretical criminology*, 4th ed. New York: Oxford University Press.

Waegel, W.B. 1981. Case routinization in investigative police work. *Social Problems* 28(3): 263–275.

Walker, S. 1985. *Sense and nonsense about crime: A policy guide*. Belmont, CA: Wadsworth.

Walker, S. 1992. Origins of the contemporary criminal justice paradigm: The American Bar Foundation Survey, 1953–1969. *Justice Quarterly* 9(1): 47–76.

Wambaugh, J. 1981. *The glitter dome*. New York: Bantam Books.

Warren, R. 1967. The inter-organisational field as a focus for investigation. *Administrative Science Quarterly* 12: 396–419.

Whetten, D.A. 1989. What constitutes a theoretical contribution? *Academy of Management Review* 14(4): 490–495.

Wilson, J.Q. 1968. *Varieties of police behavior: The management of law and order in eight communities*. Cambridge, MA: Harvard University Press.

Wilson, J.Q. 1983. *Thinking about crime*. New York: Basic Books.

Wright, K. 1981. The desirability of goal conflict within the criminal justice system. *Journal of Criminal Justice* 9: 209–218.

3

WHY IS THERE SO LITTLE CRIMINAL JUSTICE THEORY? NEGLECTED MACRO- AND MICRO-LEVEL LINKS BETWEEN ORGANIZATION AND POWER

John Hagan

Criminal justice research lacks theoretical initiative. Much criminal justice research in the 1970s and 1980s was derivative in the sense of drawing its theoretical initiative from consensus and conflict theories of society. These broadly framed theories of social relations were useful in stimulating work that was concerned with the influence of legal and extralegal variables on criminal justice outcomes. A consensus theory of social relations predicted a powerful role for legal variables, reflecting the influence of broadly shared societal values in the punishment of criminal norm violations. A conflict theory of social relations predicted a substantial role for extralegal variables, reflecting the influence of power imbalances on the punishment of crimes that posed threats to existing power relationships.

While the larger debate that organized discussions of consensus and conflict theories in the social sciences proved useful in stimulating and framing much of the early research on criminal justice operations, the results of this research did not offer much support for either theory. Where consensus theory led researchers to expect the influence of legal variables, such as offense seriousness and prior record, to be strong and persistent, the results of this research found the influence of these variables to be moderate and inconsistent. Where conflict theory led researchers to expect the influence of extralegal variables, such as class and race, to be substantial and pervasive, the results of this research found the influence of these variables to be modest and uncertain. Literature reviews vary somewhat with regard to these summary statements (e.g., see Zatz, 1984; Wilbanks, 1987), but the larger point nonetheless holds: Neither consensus nor conflict theory generated large-scale empirical support.

Meanwhile, no other theory of criminal justice has emerged to fill the void.[1] This is remarkable in that there is so much research in this field. The thesis of this chapter is that broadly framed consensus and conflict theories fail to accommodate unique aspects of criminal justice processes and outcomes and that new theoretical developments are necessary to stimulate more meaningful research. More specifically, consensus and conflict theories do not provide sufficient attention to the structural relationships that emerge from a joining of organizational and political forces in the direction of criminal justice operations. In the following sections, we review studies that illustrate regularities observed in the joint influence of organizational and political factors in criminal justice operations. However, before turning to these illustrations we outline a theoretical framework within which these studies are considered. This framework is the base for a "structural-contextual theory of criminal justice."

THE STRUCTURE AND CONTEXT OF A LOOSELY COUPLED SYSTEM

There is important variation in the degree to which criminal justice systems and subsystems are connected or coupled internally. Criminal justice operations are not unique in this respect. This is true of schools, churches, hospitals, and many other kinds of formal organizations (see Meyer & Rowan, 1977; Meyer & Scott, 1983). Nonetheless, many commentators in particular have called attention to a looseness that characterizes American criminal justice policies and operations. Gibbs (1986, 330) writes that "American penal policy is a mishmash." Eisentein and Jacob (1977) observe that even at the highest levels of decision making in this system, "the judge does not rule or govern, at most, he manages, and often he is managed by others." The same impression is conveyed by Reiss (1971, 114–120) when he speaks of the American criminal justice system as a "loosely articulated hierarchy of subsystems." Reiss suggests that this hierarchy is so loosely articulated that "the major means of control among the subsystems is internal to each," with the result that "each subsystem creates its own system of justice." It has been argued that this degree of looseness in criminal justice policies and operations is necessary to provide "individualized" treatment for suspects and offenders (see Hagan, Hewitt, & Alwin, 1979; Gibbs, 1986), but Jerome Skolnick implied something more when he titled his classic study of the police *Justice Without Trial.* In any case, our interest is in the consequences of this loose form of organization for our theoretical understanding of criminal justice operations.

A key point in our argument is that in the absence of political power that is directed toward particular crime-linked goals, American criminal justice systems and subsystems tend to be loosely coupled. This is a common condition in the U.S. federal, state, and local systems of criminal justice we know best, but this condition may not characterize many or most criminal justice systems of the world. For example, totalitarian regimes of the right and the left are often characterized by tightly coupled criminal justice systems and subsystems linked to specific crime-related goals. In the Appendix, we offer an illustrative comparison of the U.S. and West German criminal justice systems, which indicates that democratic societies also can be characterized by much more tightly coupled operations. Meanwhile, the loose coupling that is characteristic of American systems of criminal justice may be one way of accommodating diverse societal interests, while at the same time preserving autonomy, and in this sense impartiality, for the judicial branch of government. By these means, a loosely coupled criminal justice system can sometimes serve powerful legitimation needs in a democratic society.

However, our more immediate concern is with another appearance this loose coupling sometimes gives to day-to-day American criminal justice operations. This appearance is one of randomness that is conveyed, for example, in media portrayals of the justice system as chaotic, in Gibbs's description of this system as a "mishmash," and, most important for our immediate purposes, in empirical results of studies of the justice system that leave great amounts of unexplained variance in decisions about arrest, prosecution, and sentencing. For example, the single finding that is consistent throughout the large research literature on judicial sentencing is that whether legal or extralegal factors are the focus of analysis, the unexplained variance in sentencing looms large. This observation holds even in studies where the two types of variables are combined (e.g., Hogarth, 1971; Hagan & Bumiller, 1983; Myers & Talarico, 1987).

This situation is characteristic of what organizational theorists call a loosely coupled system. In connotative terms, loose coupling is meant to evoke the image of entities (e.g., court subsystems) that are responsive to one another, while still maintaining independent identities and some evidence of physical or logical separateness (Weick, 1976). Meyer and Rowan (1977) add to this conception a denotation of characteristics associated with loosely coupled formal organizations—structural elements are only loosely linked to one another and to activities, rules are often violated, decisions often go unimplemented or if implemented have uncertain consequences, and techniques are often subverted or rendered so vague as to provide little coordination. Many of these characteristics are manifest in the criminal justice system, so that, for example, as the literature on sentencing reviewed earlier suggests, many of the consequences of this loose coupling can be recognized at the level of individual sentencing decisions. At this level of analysis, Glassman (1973) suggests that entities may be considered loosely coupled to the extent that (1) they share few variables in common, (2) the variables shared in common differ substantially in their degree of influence, or (3) the variables shared in common are weak in comparison to other variables considered. The interesting and neglected questions of criminal justice research are why these loosely coupled micro-level patterns of individual decision making are characteristic of American criminal justice operations, and how and when we might look for these patterns to vary. To find answers to these kinds of questions, we need to consider neglected macro- and micro-level links that can occur between organizational and political forces, often involving shifts in political power in criminal justice operations.

First, however, we should emphasize that loosely coupled organizations have a unique capacity to absorb changes in the surrounding political environment. For example, when challenged to change, such organizations can take on new appendages, while at the same time selectively ignoring the activities of these new appendages. An example of this pattern from the first half of this century involved the introduction of probation officers into the presentencing process. In response to many of the macro-level political changes associated with the Progressive era in North American politics, probation departments and probation officers were added to juvenile and adult courts throughout the United States and Canada. A major innovation accompanying this change was that probation officers were to prepare presentencing reports that were intended to individualize dispositions through their impact on judicial sentencing decisions. However, there is little evidence that sentencing patterns in North America changed much as a result of this innovation (see Hagan et al., 1979; Rothman, 1980). The loosely coupled structure of North American systems of criminal justice absorbed this innovation with little threat to the established judicial and prosecutorial roles in sentencing.

Yet it is also the case that loosely coupled criminal justice organizations do sometimes change, with important consequences for their operations. This brings us to the first of the case studies we consider in developing a structural-contextual theory of criminal justice.

GHETTO REVOLTS AND THE ABANDONMENT OF "NORMAL" COURT OPERATIONS

When a political change or challenge comes swiftly or unexpectedly, even a loosely coupled organization will have difficulty absorbing its effects with no more than ritual or ceremonial consequences. Such a situation is described by Balbus (1973) in his study of court responses to black ghetto revolts in the mid-1960s in Los Angeles, Detroit, and Chicago. Balbus (p. 39) is explicit in noting that these events were exceptional in the sense of posing a substantial threat to "normal" court operations.

The threat derived from the need of the courts to strike a balance among three interests that Balbus identifies as constituting the core functions of courts and their authorities in the liberal state: order, formal rationality, and organizational maintenance. Normally, these functions can be served jointly with the loosely structured kinds of operations apparent, for example, in studies of sentencing referenced earlier. In these studies, a mixture of predominately legal variables exercises a modest and variable influence on sentencing decisions. However, the nature and volume of the cases involved in the American ghetto riots challenged the normal mode of court operation, with results that Balbus suggests were predictable given system needs.

These results were most apparent at the bail stage, where prior appearances of individualization that we have associated with loosely coupled court operations apparently gave way to more tightly coupled procedures necessary to achieve a massive and uniform processing of cases. Some of the micro-level processes involved must be inferred from the accounts Balbus offers, since the analysis Balbus provides is concentrated at the macro-level of the political events, with only summary use of micro-level data.

Nonetheless, some very important patterns are observed as well as suggested by this analysis. In the aftermath of uprisings in each of the cities, bail releases were far less frequent during the first few days following arrest than normal, while releases subsequent to this initial period were dramatically *more* frequent. The explanation of this sequence is that during the revolts, an interest in achieving *order* by "clearing the streets" was paramount, while subsequently, an interest in *formal rationality* and *organizational maintenance* (created by the earlier priority given to order) combined to produce a major effort aimed at "clearing the jails." Balbus notes that this pattern was particularly striking in Los Angeles and Detroit, in part because it represented a reversal of normal criminal justice operations.

> Thus we found in both cities a striking reversal of the standard model of the criminal process which posits a series of screens whose holes progressively diminish in size and from which the defendants thus find it increasingly difficult to escape; following the Los Angeles and Detroit major revolts, in contrast, the "holes" became progressively larger, and it was much easier to "escape" at the preliminary hearing and trial stages than it was at the earlier prosecution stage.

Although Balbus does not present micro-level data to make the following points, the implications of his analysis are that this shift from "normal" court operations could not have occurred without (1) a tightening of the coupling between the police, prosecutorial, and judicial subsystems, so that bail decisions became less variable; and (2) systematic changes in the "normal" sanctioning of black suspects and defendants, first resulting in unusual restrictiveness, and later in uncharacteristic leniency. The combined result should markedly increase over most prior research the variation that could be explained in bail outcomes through consideration of organizational (e.g., prosecutorial recommendations), legal (e.g., offense specific), and extralegal (e.g., race) variables.

For reasons explained earlier, we have here needed to infer results at the micro-level from the largely macro-level account provided by Balbus. This will not be necessary in case studies we consider later. However, regardless of the speculative nature of some of this discussion, the point is made that there is a need to link the study of micro- and macro-level organizational and political forces to account more fully for criminal justice operations and to understand the important kinds of variations that can occur in these operations across contexts. To better establish this point, we turn now from this case study of unexpected social and political events and their impacts on court operations to two classic studies of policing that together highlight the consequences that more crescive and purposive undertakings in law enforcement can produce, again through context-specific variation in the organization of justice system operations.

PROACTIVE POLICING AND THE COURTS

Black and Reiss (1970; Reiss, 1971) and Skolnick (1966) provide two classic analyses of policing in different parts of the United States. These studies emphasize very different aspects of police work, but taken together, they have a unique importance for our understanding of justice system operations. Early in their work, Black and Reiss (1970) drew a now well-known distinction between reactive and proactive police work, with reactive police work organizing enforcement activity around responses to citizen complaints about crime, and proactive police work organizing enforcement activity around initiatives taken by the police in seeking out crime. The two kinds of police work are quite different in organization and results, and while Reiss and Black focus their research on the nature of the more numerous reactive responses to crime, Skolnick focuses his research on the consequences of the more provocative, proactive responses to crime.

As a result, Reiss and Black reach different conclusions about modern policing than does Skolnick. Where Black and Reiss tend to see police work as having a more democratic cast that is often highly regularized and routine, Skolnick tends to see police work as more selective and biased. The key point for our purposes is that reactive policing seems to fit with the "normal" mode of North American police operations based on loosely coupled processes and outcomes, while proactive policing requires more tightly coupled practices.

Proactive policing requires a more tightly coupled organizational response because of the absence of complainants that is the distinguishing difference between these two modes of modern police work. In the absence of complainants, it is necessary for the police to develop other sources of information and assistance in developing cases. Skolnick establishes this point primarily through his observations and analysis of narcotics law enforcement. Like Reiss and Black, Skolnick sees narcotics enforcement, and the work of what he more generally calls law officers, as being much different from the work of more conventional patrol officers.

Skolnick notes that to acquire information and cooperation in narcotics work, it is necessary to adopt one or more of three kinds of tactics involving going undercover, using entrapment, or developing informants. The results of doing so are often important not only for narcotics work, but also as sources of information about other kinds of underworld activities, which make narcotics officers powerful actors in the justice system more generally. In particular, prosecutors must often rely on narcotics officers for the information they need in developing cases, and they therefore are often willing to give these officers extra consideration. The key forms this consideration takes involve charging decisions and plea and sentence bargaining, which both narcotics officers and prosecutors depend on to develop cooperation and assistance from otherwise unwilling informants and codefendants. Of course, judges, too, must ultimately be brought into these arrangements, since judges must implement and ratify the forms that plea and sentence bargains and charge reductions finally take.

Proactive police work therefore involves a tightening of the coupling among the police, prosecutorial, and judicial subsystems. Reactive police work can thrive in a more loosely coupled organizational environment, through its access to and reliance on complainants, whom it is often useful to keep decoupled from the criminal justice process. Were victim-complainants more closely coupled into a more tightly linked criminal justice system, it would be difficult if not impossible to maintain the autonomy of law from victim demands. In the "normal" course of North American criminal justice, loose coupling serves as a brake on the potential vindictiveness of citizen input (Hagan, 1982).

However, insofar as a political environment demands a more proactive response to particular kinds of crime in specific times and places, a tightening of subsystem operations will often, if not always, be necessary. Skolnick's work articulates how and why proactive policing operates as it does, but like Balbus, Skolnick's purpose is not to provide the micro-level detail necessary to establish what the consequences of this tightening of justice system operations looks like in correlational terms. We turn next to an analysis of changes over time in the politics of drug law enforcement in the federal district court in Manhattan. This analysis provides the mixture of micro- and macro-level detail that is necessary to reveal what the consequences of this kind of political change are for the processing of crime in changing contexts of enforcement.

THE CHANGING POLITICS OF DRUG LAW ENFORCEMENT

A concern with drug law enforcement has been a recurrent theme in American politics, dating at least to the turn of the century and the emergence of drug law legislation to deal with narcotic and other kinds of drugs (see, e.g., Musto, 1973). A contemporary example of the ebb and flow of the political environment that surrounds drug law enforcement is provided in Peterson and Hagan's (1984) analysis of the rise and decline in justice system activity surrounding drugs that occurred during the Nixon administration in the United States.

This study divides its attention to the prosecution and sentencing of drug offenders into three periods: from 1963 to 1969, a period of relative calm in the pursuit of drug law violations; from 1969 to 1973, a period of great political activity and public concern in relation to drug use and abuse; and 1974 to 1976, a period of consolidation in which politicians and the public were less preoccupied with drug issues. The middle period in this study is characterized as an antidrug crusade in which well-developed relational distinctions between "victims" and "villains" within the drug trade were embedded in law and enforcement efforts. The key to the political discourse of this period was a compromise between conservative and liberal impulses in which "big dealers" were identified as villains, while middle-class youth and blacks (but only insofar as the latter were not, of course, big dealers in what was then, and still largely remains, a racially stratified drug trade) were reconceived as victims. Peterson (1985) points out that this compromise, involving the assignment of a victim status, was made possible by the relative power of middle-class parents. The resulting leniency was then generalized to more ordinary drug offenders.

In any case, the intriguing consequences of this shifting political environment included an increased punitiveness in the sentencing of big dealers in the period from 1969 to 1973, combined with lenient treatment of ordinary black drug offenders and the very severe sentencing of black big dealers. But perhaps most important for our purposes is the apparent role played by plea bargaining during this period. Peterson and Hagan's analysis reveals that the plea variable became uniquely important in the sentencing of big dealers and that levels of explained variance in sentencing outcomes increased substantially during the period of this antidrug crusade. These effects are consistent with the point we have been making about the coupling of subsystem operations in periods that involve changes in the political environment and the imposition of political power. To accomplish the political goal of singling out the villainous big dealers in this antidrug crusade, it was necessary to reward cooperating players in the development of major cases, while also imposing especially severe sanctions on those who did not cooperate and/or who were the primary targets of major drug prosecutions. This combination of rewards and punishments, which is characteristic of the kind of proactive narcotics enforcement identified by Skolnick, involves a tightening of police, prosecutorial, and judicial subsystems that is ultimately reflected in the allocation of penal sanctions. The plea effects identified in this case study, the especially severe treatment of black big dealers, the lenient treatment of most others, and the overall increases in explained variance in outcomes are suggestive of the kinds of departures from "normal" court operations that can accompany important shifts in the political environment and newly proactive criminal justice operations.

THE PROSECUTION AND SENTENCING OF WHITE-COLLAR CRIME

Thus far, we have considered an area of proactive law enforcement—narcotics—that is focused disproportionately on the poor and minorities. While proactive law enforcement may most often be imposed on such defendant populations, this need not always be the case. A counterinstance involves the prosecution of white-collar crime, which during the post-Nixon era in North America briefly became an area of proactive prosecution in some jurisdictions (see Katz, 1980).

Hagan, Nagel, and Albonetti (1980) analyze sentencing decisions in one such American federal jurisdiction that pursued a proactive prosecutorial policy toward white-collar crime. They compare individual-level data from this jurisdiction with nine other federal district courts. It is crucial to note here that while narcotics and whitecollar crime may involve somewhat different offender populations, they share in common the absence of complainants who can knowledgeably inform and assist enforcement efforts. The thesis of the Hagan et al. (1980) study is that the proactive prosecution of white-collar defendants and their white-collar crimes therefore comes down to the problem of how to get the leverage required to "turn witnesses," and the key to obtaining this leverage, it is argued, is to forge a connection between negotiations and concessions and coercion in sentencing. In other words, prosecutors must overcome the tendency toward loose coupling that we have identified as the norm in most criminal justice systems, and establish instead a direct connection between plea negotiations and sentencing decisions in white-collar cases. Hagan et al. (1980) suggest that this is accomplished in two ways: by carefully managing the severity of the charges in these cases so that judges can use statutory guidelines in arriving at lenient sentences, and by getting judges to reward negotiated pleas directly.

The results of this study reveal both of these processes at work in a district that is uniquely proactive. First, the seriousness of the charges placed against white-collar offenders in this proactive district is much more influential for college-educated, white-collar offenders than in the more reactive districts; and, second, the plea variable we saw earlier that was so important during the Nixon administration crusade against drugs is now again important in the sentencing of college-educated, white-collar offenders in the proactive district, but of negligible importance elsewhere. Overall, Hagan et al. (1980) find that the explained variance in sentencing in the proactive district is much higher than in the other districts. They also find that while the proactive prosecutorial policies result in increased convictions for white-collar crime, the net result for college-educated, white-collar offenders is more lenient sentencing. Together, these findings again suggest a tightening of links between the prosecutorial and judicial subsystems that we have argued is characteristic of criminal justice operations in proactive political environments.

The crucial role of charging practices is further revealed in a subsequent Canadian study by Hagan and Parker (1985) of the proactive prosecution of a specific form of white-collar crime, securities violations, consequent to Watergate and related scandals in Canada. This study focuses on a choice between quasi-criminal securities acts and criminal code charges in the prosecution of securities violators. Like the earlier American study, this analysis also reveals a variation in charging practices that accompanies proactivity in relation to whitecollar crime, and that again results in increased convictions and reduced sentences. The overall implication is that proactive prosecution results in selective patterns of enforcement and sanctioning, involving increased levels of intersystem coordination and exchanges that can combine increased enforcement with reduced sanctions.

A PROSECUTORIAL EXPERIMENT

The last several case studies we have considered have involved political initiatives aimed at increasing the prosecution of selected crimes that characteristically are pursued most actively through a tightening of connections between prosecutorial and judicial subsystems. The last of the case studies we consider consists of a quasi-experiment in which, for different political purposes, this kind of prosecutorial activity effectively is reversed. This study involves an analysis by Rubenstein and White (1980) of a period during the mid-1970s in which plea bargaining was banned by the attorney general of Alaska.

In this instance, the political initiative bore no direct or intended relationship on the prosecution of crimes without complainants. The initiative instead was aimed at changing the public and justice system perception of the place of plea bargaining in the courts of Alaska. Rubenstein and White note that until the mid-1970s, Alaskan judges and lawyers took plea bargaining for granted. However, in December

1984, a new attorney general, Avrum Gross, was appointed to office and established the following policy:

> District Attorneys and assistant District Attorneys will refrain from engaging in plea negotiations with defendants designed to arrive at an agreement for entry of a plea of guilty in return for a particular sentence . . . While there continues to be nothing wrong with reducing a charge, reductions should not occur to obtain a plea of guilty . . . Like any general rule, there are going to be exceptions to this policy which must be approved by the Chief Prosecutor or myself.

Our interest is not in whether this was a good or bad policy initiative or in whether or not it worked, but rather in its consequences for the criminal justice process more generally, and specifically in relation to proactive areas of prosecutorial activity. Rubenstein and White point out that an explicit purpose of the ban on plea bargaining in Alaska was to "return the sentencing function to the judges." This meant that a further provision of the ban was that while prosecutors were expected to go to an open sentencing hearing and to present to the judge "factors relevant to a consideration for sentence," they were not to offer agreed-upon recommendations for a specific sentence.

Rubenstein and White argue that the overall effect of the ban on plea bargaining was to reduce dramatically, if not eliminate, the occurrence of plea negotiations in the Alaskan courts. Apart from whether this was the case or whether this experiment could be replicated in larger, more urbanized jurisdictions, however, Rubenstein and White also report several more specific findings that are important for our purposes. First, they found that after the ban, prosecutors gave far fewer recommendations for sentencing: There was a reduction of recommendations from about 50 percent of cases to fewer than 20 percent. Second, they found that sentences for several groups of offenders increased significantly: The length of prison sentences for drug felony cases increased 233 percent, while sentences in check fraud and related white-collar offenses increased 117 percent. These are, of course, the two areas of proactive prosecutorial activity that we have focused on in the preceding case studies. In each area there was clear evidence that sentence reductions were a key part of the tightened/proactive prosecutorial efforts.

Overall, the picture that emerges from the ban on plea bargaining in the Alaskan courts is one in which the tightening of connections between prosecutors and judges, involving plea bargaining and charge reductions that are ratified with sentence reductions, was substantially reduced. With regard to the specific issue of sentence recommendations and their impact, Rubenstein and White cite one Alaskan prosecutor as explaining, "We're just sulking—why bother saying anything if we can't be specific?" The implication of such a pattern is a radically decoupled system in which subsystems become highly self-contained and in which political initiatives aimed at the proactive pursuit of targeted kinds of criminal enterprise become more difficult to organize, and consequently, less likely to occur.

Between the Alaskan experiment in banning plea bargaining and the similarly atypical American and Canadian efforts at specific kinds of proactive prosecution are found the more characteristic loosely coupled systems that are most frequently encountered in North American criminal justice research.

TOWARD A STRUCTURAL-CONTEXTUAL THEORY OF CRIMINAL JUSTICE

We began this chapter with a question: Why is there so little criminal justice theory? We are now in a position to offer some speculative answers to this question that are linked to an effort to suggest new possibilities in the development of criminal justice theory. One answer may be that criminal justice researchers are bewildered by the results their studies have produced. As we have noted, these studies are characterized by unexpected evidence of randomness and inconsistency in the influence of legal and extralegal variables. Our premise is that these results should not be ignored. They form an important starting point for a theory that posits that the normal mode for North American, and perhaps most Western democratic systems of criminal justice, is a loosely coupled form of organization. Our structural-contextual theory therefore begins with the following premises.

Orienting Premises

(1) North American criminal justice systems tend to be loosely coupled, with low levels of explained variance in outcomes across subsystems.
(2) To the extent these outcomes can be explained, they are explained by different variables within different subsystems.

From these premises follow some preliminary propositions.

Preliminary Propositions

(1) The flow of crimes with complainants is more resistant to control by political forces, so political initiatives to increase

levels of law enforcement activity most often increase the prosecution of crimes without complainants.

(2) The prosecution of crimes without complainants increases the use of proactive prosecutorial techniques, including plea negotiations, charge bargaining, and sentence reductions.

(3) Increases in the use of proactive prosecutorial techniques lead to increases in levels of explained variance within and across subsystems, as the connections between these subsystems are tightened.

(4) These increased levels of explained variance are reflected in the increased influence of organizational (i.e., plea and prosecutorial recommendations), legal (i.e., offense and prior record), and extralegal (i.e., race, class, and status) variables.

These premises and propositions obviously provide no more than a provisional base for the development of a theory of criminal justice. Beyond this, however, their importance may lie as much in their implications for research methodology as for the purposes of theory construction. This is because the implication of the structural-contextual approach proposed is that we should move away in this field of research from so frequently focusing on normal or conventional criminal justice operations, while giving more attention to contexts that depart from the norm, particularly in terms of political environment.

The case studies we have considered all are atypical in that they involve contexts where the surrounding political environment has mandated departures from normal criminal justice operations. Characteristically, these departures involve the imposition of political power, sometimes targeting the prosecution of a particular form of crime and criminal, often involving morals offenses and sometimes white-collar crimes, or less frequently, targeting some feature of system operations, such as plea bargaining. We learn a great deal about system operations in these circumstances. Most significant, research of this kind suggests the means by which criminal justice operations can be tightened for the purpose of focusing attention on political goals.

In the end, of course, the purpose of criminal justice research is not simply to increase explained variance in criminal justice outcomes, but rather to increase our understanding of criminal justice operations. The thesis of this chapter is that neglected connections between the imposition of political power and organizational forms in the criminal justice system hold a key to understanding the operations of this system in typical as well as atypical situations. Attention to structure and context can increase our understanding of what too often seems to be a system in random disarray.

NOTES

Hagan, John (1989). Why is There So Little Criminal Justice Theory? Neglected Macro- and Micro-Level Links Between Organizations and Power. *Journal of Research in Crime and Delinquency*, 26(2): 116–135. Reprinted with Permission.

1. This does not discount that important explanatory efforts have been made. Feeley (1973) describes a theory of criminal justice process based on organization; Wilson (1968, chap. 8) describes a theory of police behavior based on "political culture"; Black (1976) describes a theory of the behavior of law in terms of structure, organization, and culture; Duffee (1980) describes a theory of criminal justice as a function of local community; and Packer (1968) describes two models of criminal justice based on differing philosophical orientations. Yet none of these initiatives has taken hold, for example, in the way the consensus and conflict paradigms did in the 1970s and early 1980s.

REFERENCES

Balbus, Isaac. 1973. *The dialectics of legal repression*. New York: Russell Sage.

Black, Donald. 1976. *The behavior of law*. New York: Academic Press.

Black, Donald and Albert Reiss. 1970. "Police Control of Juveniles." *American Sociological Review* 35:63–77.

Duffee, David. 1980. *Explaining criminal justice*. Cambridge, MA: Deigeschlager, Gunn & Hain.

Eisentein, James and Herbert Jacob. 1977. *Felony justice: An organizational analysis of criminal courts*. Boston: Little, Brown.

Feeley, Malcolm. 1973. "Two models of the criminal justice system: An organizational perspective." *Law & Society Review* 7:407–425.

Gibbs, Jack. 1986. "Punishment and Deterrence: Theory, Research, and Penal Policy." In *Law and the Social Sciences*, edited by Leon Lipson and Stanton Wheeler. New York: Russell Sage.

Glassman, R.B. 1973. "Persistence and loose coupling in living systems." *Behavioral Science* 18(2): 83–98.

Hagan, John. 1982. "The Corporate Advantage: The involvement of corporate and individual victims in a criminal justice system." *Social Forces* 60:993–1022.

Hagan, John and Kristen Bumiller. 1983. "Making sense of sentencing: A review and critique of sentencing research." In *Research on Sentencing: The Search for Reform*, edited by Alfred Blumstein, Jacqueline Cohen, Susan Martin, and Michael Tonry. Washington, DC: National Academy Press.

Hagan, John and Patricia Parker. 1985. "White collar crime and punishment: The class structure and legal sanctioning of securities violations. *American Sociological Review* 50:302–316.

Hagan, John, John Hewitt, and Duane Alwin. 1979. "Ceremonial justice: Crime and punishment in a loosely coupled system. *Social Forces* 58:506–527.

Hagan, John, Ilene Nagel, and Celesta Albonetti. 1980. "The differential sentencing of white-collar offenders in ten federal district courts." *American Sociological Review* 45: 802–820.

Hogarth, John. 1971. *Sentencing as a human process.* Toronto: University of Toronto Press.

Katz, Jack. 1980. "The social movement against white-collar crime." In *The Criminology Review Yearbook*, Vol. 2, edited by Egon Bittner and Sheldon Messinger. Beverly Hill, CA: Sage.

Langbien, John. 1979. "Land without plea bargaining: How the Germans do it." *Michigan Law Review* 78:204–255.

Lynch, James. 1988. "A comparison of prison use in England, Canada, West Germany, and the United States: A limited test of the punitive hypothesis." *Journal of Criminal Law & Criminology* 79:180–217.

Meyer, John and Brian Rowan. 1977. "Institutionalized Organizations: Formal structure as myth and ceremony." *American Journal of Sociology* 83:340–363.

Meyer, John and W. Richard Scott. 1983. *Organizational Environments: Ritual and Rationality.* Beverly Hills, CA: Sage.

Musto, David. 1973. *The American Disease: The origins of narcotic control.* New Haven, CT: Yale University Press.

Myers, Martha and Susette Talarico. 1987. *The social contexts of criminal sentencing.* New York: Springer-Verlag.

Packer, Herbert. 1968. *The limits of the criminal sanction.* Stanford, CA: Stanford University Press.

Peterson, Ruth. 1985. "Discriminatory decision-making at the legislative: An Analysis of the Comprehensive Drug Abuse, Prevention and Control Act of 1970." *Law and Human Behavior* 9:243–270.

Peterson, Ruth and John Hagan. 1984. "Changing conceptions of race: Towards an account of anomalous findings of sentencing research." *American Sociological Review* 49:56–71.

Reiss, Albert. 1971. *The police and the public.* New Haven, CT: Yale University Press.

Rothman, David. 1980. *Conscience and Convenience: The asylum and its alternatives in Progressive America.* Boston: Little, Brown.

Rubenstein, Michael and Teresa White. 1980. "Alaska's ban on plea bargaining." In *Plea Bargaining*, edited by William McDonald and James Crammer. Lexington, MA: Lexington Books.

Skolnick, Jerome. 1966. *Justice without trial.* New York: John Wiley.

Waller, Irvin and Janet Chan. 1975. "Prison Use: A Canadian and international comparison." *Criminal Law Quarterly* 17(1): 47–71.

Weick, Karl. 1976. "Educational organizations as loosely coupled systems." *Administrative Science Quarterly* 21:1–19.

Wilbanks, William. 1987. *The myth of a racist criminal justice system*. Monterey, CA: Brooks / Cole.
Wilson, James Q. 1968. *Varieties of police behavior: The management of law and order in eight communities*. Cambridge, MA: Harvard University Press.
Zatz, Marjorie. 1984. "Race, ethnicity and determinate sentencing: A new dimension to an old controversy." *Criminology* 22:147–172.

APPENDIX

An Illustrative Comparison of the Coupling of American and West German Criminal Justice Operations

A striking illustration of the loosely coupled form of the U.S. criminal justice system is found in contemporary efforts (e.g., Waller & Chan, 1975) to establish what might seem a simple and essential knowledge of the extensiveness of imprisonment in the United States. The most recent and sophisticated attempt to inform this issue is found in the work of James Lynch (1988), who has compared statistics on prison use in England, Canada, West Germany, and the United States. The two extremes of this comparison in terms of use of imprisonment and organizational form are clearly the United States and West Germany. The substantive as well as theoretical importance of this comparison is signaled by the fact that even when a revealing arrest-based calculation of national imprisonment rates is introduced in Lynch's analysis, Germany appears to use incarceration much less frequently than the United States, which indeed may have the highest use of imprisonment per thousand population in the world.

Equally important for our purposes, however, are the striking differences in organizational form that are revealed by the computations that Lynch must undertake to establish these fundamental comparative facts. Lynch begins with the United States, where he notes that responsibility for corrections is shared by local, state, and federal governments, without a unified statistical reporting system. This situation is complicated further when Lynch seeks to establish for what offenses imprisonment is used. The complication is that final charges in the U.S. system are so often the product of charge reductions involved in plea bargaining. The result is that the U.S. system provides no centralized or unified source of information about how many Americans are incarcerated for what crimes.

The result is that Lynch must engage in complicated estimation procedures to generate offense-based imprisonment rates. First, he must estimate how many persons are in local jails rather than the state and federal prisons that generate centralized annual reports. There are no centralized annual reports for local jails. Information on the latter comes from a *Survey of Jail Inmates* whose data are unpublished and available not from the government, but from the Institute for Political and Social Research at the University of Michigan, for a single cross-sectional sample that allows no systematic accumulation of information over time. Lynch also estimates the local jail population of the United States by using the National Prisoners Statistics (NPS) data on admissions and information from the Offender-Based Transaction System (OBTS). An indication of how tentative is our resulting knowledge of U.S. imprisonment is that the second estimated total is nearly 50 percent larger than the first, with a difference of more than a half million people, who may or may not be locked up in local U.S. jails. We simply do not know what this number is.

Furthermore, because of the extensive use of charge reduction in plea bargaining in the United States, we do not know for what crimes persons are incarcerated. Charge reduction is the changing of original or arrest charges to less serious charges for which the person is ultimately sentenced; charges are routinely changed in the U.S. system, usually downward. When offense-specific incarceration rates (persons incarcerated for specific offenses /persons arrested for specific offenses) are calculated, persons who have experienced charge reductions wind up in the numerators and denominators of different rates. Lynch gives the example of persons who are arrested for homicide and incarcerated for simple assault: Such persons enter the denominator of the incarceration rate for homicide and the numerator of the incarceration rate for simple assault. An example of the effect of charge reductions on the estimation of offense-specific incarceration rates is that the total of U.S. incarcerations for rape is reduced more than 14 percent by charge reductions; nearly 2,000 persons a year more than we would otherwise realize are incarcerated for a crime identified originally as rape.

Only through these complicated computations is Lynch able to generate imprisonment figures that tell us how many Americans are being incarcerated for what crimes, and he is able to do this only on a short-term basis rather than over time, or in other words, in a way that would tell us where we have been or where we are going in terms of our use of imprisonment. The system is so loosely coupled that it is difficult to do much more, and doing this much depends on the use of survey-based data collected by nonsystem means.

Contrast this situation with that in the Federal Republic of Germany (FRG) and its much more tightly coupled criminal justice system. Lynch (1988, 192) first notes that statistics on crime and prison admissions are collected annually and centrally for the entire republic. Jurisdictions report routinely, and there is more uniformity in definitions and collection procedures. Furthermore, prosecutors do not exercise the kind of discretion found in the United States to reduce charges and plea bargain (Langbien, 1979). Calculating an imprisonment rate is therefore far simpler for the FRG. The numerator is simply the number of admissions to prison for particular offenses, as indicated by sentences given to persons convicted for these offenses in the *Strafverfolgung, Rechtspflege* (prosecution statistics). The denominator for the rate is slightly more problematic because the FRG does not have a legal category exactly equivalent to the U.S. arrest status. Rather, the police have a more inclusive suspect status (*Tatverdachtge*) and a less inclusive charge status (*Anklage*). The latter is the charge of sentencing and is most like the portion of arrests that U.S. prosecutors actually prosecute. However, both figures can be used, and either confirms that many more U.S. than German offenders are incarcerated.

So the looseness of the U.S. criminal justice system leaves it without crucial information that can be used to evaluate how the system operates. This is a characteristic of loosely coupled systems more generally, and we indicate in the text further organizational and political consequences of this situation. We have already noted that one symptom of this situation is that it has been necessary to collect sample survey data on local jail populations to establish how many offenders are in these institutions. It is interesting to note that a broader indication of the distrust U.S. citizens and public officials have in their criminal justice record collection is provided in the increased reliance on the survey collection of victimization data in the United States. To date, the FRG has expressed no urgent need to develop such independent measures of public behavior and system response. In Germany, criminal justice system data are much more likely to be taken at face value as a meaningful reflection of serious crime and system reactions to it.

Part II

Theories of Policing

The police are in many ways the gatekeepers of the criminal justice system. Once the police make an arrest or issue a citation, they invoke the remaining elements of the criminal justice process. A fruitful body of criminal justice theory has focused on the police. These theories have been developed at many levels, from those designed to explain the behavior of individual police officers, to those meant to explain the development of policing as an institution over time and place.

Part II features three chapters on policing. In the first two chapters in this section, the unit of analysis is the police organization, and the important research question is why police organizations differ from one another. In Chapter 4, Maguire and Uchida explore this question from a bird's-eye view, showing how police organizations vary in many ways, and considering a variety of explanations for why this is true. In Chapter 5, Renauer takes a much closer look, focusing in on one element of policing that varies across agencies—the implementation of community policing—and one theory that can be used to explain that variation—institutional theory. Inherent in both chapters is the important idea that policing is not a monolith; it varies across police organizations. The important question, of course, is why. In Chapter 6, Worden takes on a crucial public policy question: what factors influence the use and abuse of force by police officers? The unit of analysis in this study is not police organizations—it is police-citizen encounters.

In Chapter 4, "Explaining Police Organizations," Ed Maguire and Craig Uchida survey the landscape of theory and research on police organizations. The chapter begins by demonstrating that police departments differ from one another in many ways: in structures, policies, processes, and outputs. For example, some arrest offenders aggressively, while others may rely on different, less formal methods for achieving compliance with the law. A large body of research has developed to explain these variations. Maguire and Uchida review this research, showing how these approaches contribute to a theoretical understanding of police organizations and the factors that influence, shape, and constrain them. Theories explaining police organizations are an important element of criminal justice theory, and scholars have been conducting tests of these theories for nearly four decades. These theories have enabled us to learn a great deal about police organizations and the factors that influence them, though, as Maguire and Uchida conclude, much remains to be learned.

In Chapter 5, "Understanding Variety in Urban Community Policing: An Institutional Theory Approach," Brian Renauer presents a theory that attempts to explain interagency variation in a specific police practice: the adoption of a particular kind of community policing. In particular, he focuses on those elements of community policing that are designed to stimulate community-building activities with the intention of enhancing sustainable neighborhoods. Renauer argues that there are important variations in the adoption of the community building components of community policing in urban police organizations, and more importantly, that these variations are both measurable and explainable.

To explain variation in the implementation of community policing, Renauer draws on institutional theory, a specific organizational theory that has been applied to many different types of organizations, and which was introduced briefly by Maguire and Uchida in Chapter 4. According to Renauer, institutional theory provides a number of insights about variation in urban community policing. First, it focuses attention on the different levels that influence police organizations: "centrist" forces, such as government agencies and national police professional organizations (such as think tanks focusing on policing issues); "local" forces, such as mayors, city councils, and the citizenry; and "internal" forces, such as police unions, organizational culture, and tradition. Second, it focuses attention on the routes through which organizational change efforts arrive at and are introduced into police organizations. Government agencies, police professional organizations, and other police departments all play a role in stimulating organizational change in policing, as do more localized forces internal and external to the agency. Running throughout these mechanisms for influencing organizational change is the central idea that organizations change to maintain the appearance of legitimacy. Renauer explores how variation in the implementation of community policing results from the intersection of these various forces at different levels, all with the goal of enhancing the perceived legitimacy of the organization. Renauer concludes by outlining several ways that researchers can collect data to test the hypotheses he has outlined.

In Chapter 6, "The 'Causes' of Police Brutality: Theory and Evidence on Police Use of Force," Rob Worden examines the individual, situational, and organizational factors that influence the use and abuse of force by officers in police-citizen encounters. To do so, Worden blends insights from psychological, sociological, and organizational theories. Moreover, he tests his assertions using sophisticated, multivariate, statistical analysis of data from a classic observational study of police behavior. Based on this analysis, Worden draws a number of interesting conclusions. For instance, all else held equal, police officers were more likely to use inappropriate force against citizens who were black or inebriated. As expected, situational and organizational factors influenced the police use of force. However, officer-level characteristics exerted little effect. Two features of Chapter 6 are particularly noteworthy. First, Worden draws on theories from multiple disciplines in thinking about the various factors that are likely to influence the behavior of police officers during encounters with citizens. Second, he carries out a detailed statistical analysis to test insights derived from those theories. In so doing, he illustrates a key aspect of social science—subjecting theories to rigorous tests of their validity.

Together, the first two chapters in Part II illustrate rather pointedly that while police organizations share many characteristics, they also differ from one another in a number of important ways. Various theories exist for explaining these variations. The final chapter in Part II examines a different unit of analysis: police-citizen encounters. These three chapters cover two very different but equally important units of analysis: organizations and encounters. However, it is important to note that many other units of analysis are worthy of theoretical and empirical investigation. For instance, theories could focus on individual police officers or groups of police officers (such as those working in certain assignments or working certain shifts). At a more macro level, some theories might explain why different nations employ fewer numbers of police officers than other nations, or why some nations adopt different styles or structures of policing. In sum, explaining different facets of policing at different levels is all within the purview of criminal justice theory. Chapters 4 through 6 present three useful examples of theorizing about the police.

DISCUSSION QUESTIONS

1 Chapters 4 and 5 make the claim that police departments differ from one another in many ways. Think about one or two ways in which they might differ, and generate a potential explanation for these differences. Consider whether Hagan's argument in Chapter 3 might be applicable here.

2. Chapters 4 and 5 both discuss a specific theory that has been applied to policing: institutional theory. In a nutshell, this theory argues that organizations are heavily influenced not only by the technical requirements of the work they perform, but also by widely held beliefs of certain individuals and groups about how they should do their work. Some institutional theorists have made the argument that if the theory is true, organizations within a certain sector (such as all police organizations) will grow to resemble one another more and more over time after repeatedly trying to conform to expectations about what they should look like. We know from the history of policing that experiments with alternative types of police uniforms (such as blazers, or those without traditional police insignias) have failed and resulted in a return to the traditional police uniform. The same has occurred when departments have attempted to eliminate in a wholesale fashion the typical rank structure of police departments.
   - What kinds of specific forces might influence a department's inability to change its uniforms, its rank structure, or other elements of traditional policing?
   - Do the forces you have just identified act only as constraints, in the sense that they only inhibit change in police organizations? Or, might these same forces also act as enablers, supporting some changes in policing while trying to thwart others?
   - Recent research has demonstrated that many police organizations have begun to adopt gang units to focus specifically on youth gang problems. However, many police organizations without a gang problem have also adopted gang units. What kinds of forces might lead a police organization in a community without a gang problem to adopt a gang unit?

3. The first two chapters in this section focused on police organizations as their units of analysis, while the third focused on police-citizen encounters. Both are premised on understanding how policing varies, whether across organizations or

encounters. Criminal justice theories can explore variation across many other units of analysis as well. For instance, they can also explore variation in policing across police officers, across geographic districts within police departments, across states, or across nations. With this in mind:

- Select a unit of analysis other than police organizations or encounters.
- Select a dependent variable; something that varies across the unit you have chosen.
- Select one or more independent variables that you believe play a role in influencing the variation in your dependent variable.

4. Chapter 6 is a good example of a long tradition of research that relies on systematic social observation of police officers on patrol to study police behavior. One of the major distinctions in this body of research is between the legal and extralegal factors that might influence police behavior. The term "legal" is meant to refer to the various laws, policies, and rules that govern police decision-making. The term "extralegal" is meant to refer to factors that police officers are not permitted to take into account in making decisions. Research has demonstrated consistently that police use a mix of legal and extralegal factors in making decisions. With this idea in mind, select one of the following decisions:
   - The decision to stop a vehicle or a person
   - The decision to search a vehicle or a person
   - The decision to issue a citation
   - The decision to make an arrest
   - The decision to use force in executing an arrest

For whatever decision you have selected, make a list of the legal and extralegal factors that a police officer might take into account in making that decision.

4

EXPLAINING POLICE ORGANIZATIONS[1]

Edward R. Maguire and Craig D. Uchida

INTRODUCTION

The introductory chapters in this volume have established the basic boundaries of criminal justice theory. This chapter examines one tradition of research and theory in criminal justice: efforts to identify the factors responsible for producing interagency variations in policing. We explore the ways that researchers and theorists explain differences in police organizations over time and place. Police organizations share much in common, but they also vary widely. Some are large, but many are quite small; some patrol aggressively, arresting offenders for minor public-order offenses, while others enforce the law with less vigor; some have tall hierarchies and formal command structures, while others are less formal, with only a handful of separate levels; some work closely with communities and spend time formulating customized solutions to local problems, while others shun community involvement and provide a more impersonal or distant style of police services. This variation in both what organizations *do* and what they *are* is not unique to police agencies. As W.R. Scott (1992, 1) notes, "While organizations may possess common, generic characteristics, they exhibit staggering variety—in size, in structure, and in operating processes." This chapter explores efforts to explain variation in American police organizations: variation in what they are and what they do; variation in form and function, in structure and process, in policy and practice.

The subject of this chapter is police organizations. The study of police agencies as organizations is a growing field, owing its theoretical roots to the sociological and social psychological study of organizations more generally.[2] This organizational focus on policing is the common thread linking each section of the chapter. Thus, we do not examine other frequently studied features of policing, including culture, discretionary behaviors (and misbehaviors), individual attributes of police officers, and many other important phenomena occurring at units of analysis that are larger (e.g., states or nations) or smaller (e.g., incidents, officers, or workgroups) than police organizations.[3]

Furthermore, the focus of this chapter is on broad organizational properties rather than particular policies, programs, activities, or structural features. Researchers have produced a wealth of valuable research on particular features of police organizations such as pursuit policies; Drug Abuse Resistance Education (DARE) programs; the use of one- and two-officer patrol cars; and the establishment of special units for various tasks, such as narcotics, child abuse, or gangs. The line between general and specific organizational properties is admittedly arbitrary. Nevertheless, the focus of the chapter is on drawing together a diverse body of scholarship on American police organizations. Research on very specific (and sometimes esoteric or idiosyncratic) organizational properties will make it much more difficult to consolidate this vast body of theory and research. Thus, while we do not discuss the prevalence of specialized bias-crime units, we do discuss specialization more generally; we do not discuss the implementation of various new technologies for processing offenders, but we do examine the adoption of innovation; we do not discuss drunk driving enforcement or use of force, but we do discuss aggressive patrol strategies and styles of policing.

Although the definition of police is seemingly straightforward, there is some ambiguity over what constitutes a police organization (Maguire et al., 1998). As Bayley (1985, 7) notes, "Police come in a bewildering variety of forms . . . moreover, many agencies that are not thought of as police nonetheless possess 'police' powers." To reduce the scope of our task, we shall focus on public police organizations in the United States whose primary purpose is to provide generalized police service, including responding to calls-for-service for a distinct residential population.[4] Even after narrowing the focus in this way, there remain considerable variations among police organizations over time and place.[5]

A substantial body of theory and research has developed to measure and explain these variations. As one way to organize the large body of scholarship on police organizations, we draw an important distinction between what they *do* and what they *are*. These categories sometimes overlap in practice, but there is some precedent in the development of organization theory for treating them separately.

WHAT POLICE ORGANIZATIONS DO

Like corporations, police organizations do many things. Most people are unaccustomed to thinking of organizations as doing things. After all, organizations are composed of people, and it is the people within them who think, plan, act, decide, debate, respond, cooperate, and all of the other activities and behaviors in which people engage. Yet, as Maguire (2003, 9–10) has argued:

> Organizations are greater than the sum of their parts. They expand and contract, rise and fall, and generally take on lives of their own. Organizations, like individuals and social groups, do not only act, but are acted upon as well. They are influenced, shaped and constrained by a complex interaction of political, social, economic, cultural, and institutional forces. Organizations exhibit patterned regularities, and they can (and indeed should) be studied apart from the people within them.
>
> (Maguire, 2003)

King (2009) takes this argument one step further, using a biological or life-course perspective to study the birth, death, and aging processes of police agencies. Thinking about organizations as separate from the people within them—as "corporate persons"—is essential to understanding what they do (Coleman, 1974).

Police organizations do many things: they make arrests, quell disturbances, respond to emergencies, solve problems, form relationships with the community, and perform other activities too numerous to summarize briefly. These activities constitute the outputs of police organizations. Systematic collection of data from large samples of police agencies has shown that there is considerable variation in the quantity and quality of these outputs over time and place. These data are used in many ways. Arrest and clearance statistics, for instance, are frequently used as measures of a police organization's productivity. The use of these kinds of performance indicators is beginning to fall out of fashion as police executives, scholars, and reformers focus on alternative measures (e.g., Maguire, 2004, 2005).

These data have also been used by researchers as indicators of a police organization's working style.[6] Some agencies, for instance, may emphasize aggressive enforcement of panhandling ordinances, while others may tend to ignore such minor offenses. While the concept of organizational style is intangible and difficult to measure, researchers have attempted to draw inferences about policing styles by examining arrest patterns for discretionary offenses such as drunkenness or disorderly conduct (Wilson, 1968b). While police organizations do many different things, data are systematically collected on only a handful of these activities. Organizational measures constructed from these data are therefore limited.

One focus of this chapter is to examine variations in police activities, processes, performance, and style over time and across agencies. We will trace efforts to explain what police organizations do, from the traditional focus on arrests and clearances, to more recent efforts to embrace problem-solving and community partnership strategies.

WHAT POLICE ORGANIZATIONS ARE

What a police organization does is external, typically taking place outside of the organization: in the community, on the streets, in residences. The features that define what a police organization *is* tend to be internal: administrative arrangements, processing routines, structures, communication patterns, and overall "corporate" personalities.[7] In short, what police organizations *do* takes place within the framework (or context) of what they *are*. The social scientific study of what police organizations are has a much shorter history than the study of what they do. This history parallels a similar split in the study of organizations more generally. While outputs and performance have always been a primary focus of organizational research, it wasn't until the late 1950s that "researchers began to conceive of organizations as more than just rationally-derived mechanisms for the production of goods and services, but as entities worthy of understanding for what they are in addition to what they produce" (Maguire, 2003, 9).

The internal features of police organizations vary considerably from one agency to the next. Researchers began to measure this variation using systematic surveys in about the late 1920s. Attempts to explain this variation came later, with theoretical explanations appearing in the 1960s and empirical studies beginning in the mid-1970s. Much of this research focuses on why we have the police organizations we have, seeking to isolate local contingencies (such as regional, historical, governmental, cultural, or demographic factors) that would lead to variations in police organizational form from one jurisdiction to another.

EXPLANATION

The first step in explaining why differences exist between police organizations (or any social entity, from people to nations) is to measure those differences. The problems in measuring the properties of police organizations are noteworthy, though there is not sufficient space in this chapter to explore these measurement issues in detail. Thus, we simply acknowledge the challenges inherent in developing valid and reliable measures of organizational attributes in policing (Maguire & Uchida, 2000).

Once researchers have measured variations across police organizations, the next natural step is to ask why such differences exist. That is the goal of explanation. Like measurement, explanation is one of the principal goals of social science research. Social scientists usually arrive at explanations for social phenomena through induction and deduction. Using the inductive method, they begin by collecting data and then analyze or search for patterns in the data. Based on their observations and analyses, they develop theories. Using the deductive method, they begin by specifying a theory, and then collect and analyze data to test the theory. In reality, these two processes tend to overlap. Frequently, social scientists begin by stating an explicit theory and collecting data to test the theory (deductive method). Upon finding only partial support for the theory in the data, they will often modify the theory accordingly (inductive method).

Police organizations, like many other units of analysis studied by social scientists, vary widely on some dimensions, and are very similar on others. When social scientists use the term "explanation," they are nearly always referring to explanations for why some trait varies across time and place. For instance, some police organizations are steeped heavily in paramilitary culture, while others appear to be more democratic and less rigid. When social scientists try to explain paramilitarism in police organizations, they mean that they are trying to explain why some organizations are more paramilitary than others. In other words, explanations in social science nearly always have the goal of explaining variation among units of analysis.[8]

If, for example, we believe police organizations in turbulent political climates are less productive (say, in terms of clearance rates) than others, then to properly test the theory, we must collect data from a sample of police organizations in different political climates. If we were to only study police organizations in hostile political climates, we could not test the theory because we would have nothing with which to compare them. In social science terms, this test would be flawed because the independent variable does not vary. A similar logical flaw, in which the dependent variable does not vary, is present in much of the current popular management literature. Many of the books in this genre study successful companies, identifying attributes that are common across each. The flaw, of course, is that these same attributes might be present in unsuccessful companies, but we cannot know for sure because they were not studied (Aupperle et al., 1986; King, 1999).[9]

Thus, the key to developing, testing, modifying, and understanding social science explanations is comparison. The comparative method has come to be associated with multinational research, but comparative research can focus on many types of organized collectivities, from police departments and schools, to nations and societies (Blau et al., 1966; Ostrom & Parks, 1973; Ragin, 1987). It is a cornerstone of sociological research on organizations (Langworthy, 1986; Scott, 1992). The comparative method is featured prominently throughout this volume.

The selection of a unit of analysis within which to conduct comparisons depends heavily on the research question. If our research question focuses on why some police organizations are more effective than others, our unit of analysis is police organizations. If, on the other hand, our interest is in how a single organization changes over time, our unit of analysis is the organization at specific points in time (like the month or year). Sometimes the unit of analysis is more complex, combining cross-sections (organizations) and times (years). For instance, if we want to determine whether changing the number of officers in municipal police departments has an effect on clearance rates, we would need to collect and analyze data from multiple organizations at multiple times. Whether we are comparing multiple organizations, the same organization at multiple times, or both simultaneously, comparison is central to understanding social science explanations.

This section examines how social scientists have sought to develop explanations for various features of police organizations. Throughout this section, the concepts we have just discussed—explaining variation, units of analysis, and comparison—will appear over and over again as central and important themes. The most common unit of analysis in our discussion is the individual police organization, and the studies we discuss usually allow for comparisons by including data from a sample of such organizations. Nearly all of these studies are focused on explaining why some police organizations are different from others, isolating the causal factors thought to be responsible for these variations. One thing that should become very clear throughout the remainder of this chapter is how measurement is inextricably linked with explanation (Maguire & Uchida, 2000).

EXPLAINING VARIATION IN POLICE ORGANIZATIONS

The scholarly study of variation in police organizations was born in the early 1960s. Following a trend in the sociology of organizations and the administrative sciences more generally, policing scholars began to devote serious attention to the role of the environment in determining the nature of a police organization. Organizational scholars of that era were profoundly influenced by a series of studies stressing the importance of the environment on organizations. Burns and Stalker (1961), Eisenstadt (1959), Emery and Trist (1965), and Lawrence and Lorsch (1967) introduced a new way of thinking about organizations and their problems. Based on their influence, scholars, managers, and others interested in organizational life could now be heard talking about the "fit" between an organization and its environment. The environment consists of everything external to an organization that is important for its functioning and survival. "Funding agencies, raw materials, clients, potential employees, the media, politicians, rumors, legislation, and employees' unions all reside in an organization's environment" (Maguire, 2003, 26).

Initial discussions of the linkage between police organizations and their environments were both subtle and implicit. For instance, Stinchcombe (1963) argued that the distribution of public and private spaces within a community has important effects on administrative practices and aggregate patterns of police behavior. Of particular importance here is his notion that different concentrations of public places within communities might account for differences between urban and rural policing. At around the same time, Wilson (1963) developed a theory linking the professionalism of police agencies to local government structure and political ethos. Though both of these early works seem to have disappeared from the landscape of modern police scholarship, they helped to plant the seeds for a growing wave of police research and theory.

Presumably influenced by these earlier works both inside and outside the study of policing, Reiss and Bordua (1967) highlighted some of the effects that the environment might have on police organizations.[10] They argued that the environmental perspective was especially important for police organizations, since "the police have as their fundamental task the creation and maintenance of, and their participation in, external relationships" (Reiss & Bordua, 1967, 25–26). Reiss and Bordua described the "internal consequences" of three broad environmental features: the nature of the legal system, the nature of illegal activity, and the structure of civic accountability. They also noted several other environmental features that might be important in shaping police organizations. It is perhaps one indicator of the halting progress in the study of police organizations since the mid-1970s that important theoretical propositions outlined by Reiss and Bordua still have not been tested empirically.[11]

These early works had the effect of focusing attention on some of the factors responsible for variation in police organizations—both what they are and what they do—across time and space. Yet, the appearance in 1968 of James Q. Wilson's *Varieties of Police Behavior* signified the first attempt to formulate a theory of police departments as organizations and to test the theory using a variety of qualitative and quantitative methods (Langworthy, 1986; Maguire, 2003). Wilson's book continues to influence police scholarship today, though sadly, empirical research has yet to test the full range of his propositions (Slovak, 1986).[12] Nevertheless, these early works set the stage for more than four decades of research on interagency variation in police organizations. With this brief historical backdrop in mind, we now discuss the evolution of this body of research, starting with what police organizations do.

EMPIRICAL RESEARCH ON WHAT POLICE ORGANIZATIONS DO

In this section, we discuss various efforts to explain some of the external features of American police organizations, including their outputs, styles, and performance. *Varieties of Police Behavior* (Wilson, 1968b) was the first and most influential attempt to explain the outputs and behaviors of police agencies (their arrest rates and styles of policing). Wilson's theory essentially posited that local contingencies such as characteristics of the population, the form of government, and political culture shape agency behaviors (and therefore outputs). Wilson's work was the first in a long line of research on the causes and correlates of police organizational outputs, which are most frequently operationalized as aggregate-level arrest rates for various offenses (Crank, 1990; Langworthy, 1985; Monkkonen, 1981; Slovak, 1986; Swanson, 1978).[13]

More recent research extends these traditional output measures to include community policing activities, attempting to generate theoretical and empirical explanations for interagency variation in these activities (Maguire et al., 1997; Zhao, 1996). Overall, this body of research seeks to determine whether the environmental, historical, and other contextual circumstances (known in organization theory as contingencies)[14] of police organizations play a role in shaping their outputs and performance. This literature includes a broad range of theoretical explanations that have not yet been tested empirically (e.g., Crank, 1994; Crank & Langworthy, 1992; Duffee, 1990). In addition, there is a large body of empirical research in this area that ranges from being nearly atheoretical to almost wholly guided by theory.

Maguire and Uchida (2000) identified twenty studies seeking to explain variation in what police organizations do. All of these studies meet several criteria: (1) the dependent variable is an organizational property; (2) there is at least one explanatory variable; (3) the study is based on quantitative data; (4) it reports the results of a statistical analysis (loosely defined) of the data; and (5) the total number of observations in the analysis is at least twenty (to allow for adequate comparison). In addition, since their focus is on what police organizations do, they do not include studies in which the dependent variable is a measure of crime. Although police organizations may have an effect on crime rates, crime is not necessarily an organizational property; in the parlance of performance measurement, it is an outcome rather than an output.[15] The remainder of this section explores some of the issues that Maguire and Uchida (2000) identified based on these twenty studies.

Wilson (1968b) was the first to use quantitative data from a sample of police agencies in an attempt to explain what police organizations do. This analysis was separate from the well-known details of his taxonomy of police styles (legalistic, watchman, and service). Wilson's theory was that local political culture constrains (but does not dictate) the style of policing within a community. Wilson argued that measuring both style and political culture would be "exceptionally difficult if not impossible" (p. 271). Nevertheless, considering it to be a worthwhile exercise, he constructed a "substitute" measure of political culture focusing on the form of government, the partisanship of elections, and the professionalism of city managers (based on their education and experience). Nodding to the presence of measurement error in his constructs, Wilson concludes: "the theory that the political culture of a community constrains law enforcement styles survives the crude and inadequate statistical tests that available data permit" (p. 276).[16]

A number of empirical studies of police organizational style have appeared since 1968. All of them measure police style using arrest rates for some mix of offense types, usually less serious offenses thought to be subject to greater discretion. Most of these studies find that organizational and environmental characteristics play a significant role in shaping police style, though there is little consensus or uniformity about what kinds of explanatory variables are important. Several other studies use arrest rates as a dependent variable but do not treat them as measures of police style. They are usually referred to more generally as indicators of organizational activity, behavior, or productivity.

Other empirical studies have focused on effectiveness or performance, which is usually measured using objective criteria such as clearance rates or subjective criteria such as citizen evaluations of local police performance (Alpert & Moore, 1993; Bayley, 1994; Parks, 1984).[17] One issue these studies address, in part, is whether bigger police departments are necessarily better, as some critics of American policing have claimed (e.g., Murphy & Plate, 1977). Subjective studies of police performance conducted by Elinor Ostrom and her colleagues suggest that bigger is not necessarily better.[18] Cordner's (1989) examination of investigative effectiveness in Maryland found that the region of the state (a proxy for urbanization) was an important predictor, but that crime, workload, and department size were generally insignificant. Davenport (1996) is the only scholar to our knowledge who has tested a model in which the environment has a direct effect on department performance, and an indirect effect on performance through organization structure. His findings are too numerous to summarize, but the most import predictor of department performance was the complexity of the environment. Probably the most consistent finding is that larger police organizations are not necessarily more effective, and in many cases, they are less effective than smaller agencies.

In recent years, responding to the need for better measures of what police organizations do, researchers began to focus their attention on measuring other facets of police behavior. Using data from a national survey of police organizations, Zhao (1996) was the first researcher to test an empirical model explaining community policing. Zhao divided community policing into external and internal components, measuring and estimating models for each one separately. Zhao's findings span the sections of this chapter, since his findings regarding externally focused change refer to those community policing activities that occur outside the police organization and in the community, while his results for internally focused change consist primarily of administrative reforms. All of these studies construct measures of community policing using various methods and then try to explain interagency variations in these measures. Probably the most consistent finding in these studies is the important role of region and department size in shaping community policing.[19] Emerging research continues to address the causes and consequences of the adoption of community policing (e.g., Wilson, 2006; Schaefer, 2010). In Chapter 5, Renauer presents a theory to explain variation across American cities in urban community policing, particularly in those activities related to community building.

EMPIRICAL STUDIES SEEKING TO EXPLAIN WHAT POLICE ORGANIZATIONS ARE

The topic of this section—explaining what the police are—has received less attention from researchers and theorists than the study of what the police do. The reason, as in organizational studies more generally, is probably that most people are far more interested in how organizations behave and what they produce than in more mundane administrative details like how they are structured. This is especially the case in policing, where the "bottom line" is typically considered to be crime, a subject of endless fascination to the populace. While reams of paper have been expended by reformers trying to convince police administrators to change the structures and internal operating processes of police organizations, scholarly progress in producing theory and research on these organizational features has been slow. In this section, we trace the development of research on internal variation in police organizations, including structure, policy, and other administrative attributes.

We find ourselves once again returning to Wilson's (1968b) *Varieties of Police Behavior*. Wilson's analysis did not explicitly consider internal organizational attributes as an object of study, but throughout the book, he makes references to the structural correlates of police style. Langworthy (1986) considered Wilson's work "the only empirically derived theory of police organization to date." Langworthy (1986, 32) summarized Wilson's implicit linkage between style and structure as follows:

> Watchman police departments were said to emphasize order maintenance, to be hierarchically flat, unspecialized, and decentralized. Legalistic departments were characterized as oriented toward vigorous law enforcement, hierarchically tall, specialized in law enforcement function, and centralized. Service-style departments were described as responsive to requests for aid or action, highly specialized across a broad range of functions, decentralized in operations, and centralized administratively.

Thus, although Wilson's work is best remembered as a theory of police style, it also contains an implicit theory of police organizational structure.

The first empirical studies in this genre didn't appear until the mid-1970s, emerging, like Wilson's work, from political science and urban studies. In 1975, T.A. Henderson published a study on the correlates of professionalism in sheriffs' agencies. The study falls within the class of theory and research that Langworthy (1986) classifies as normative, since defining and measuring police professionalism requires the researcher to make personal judgments about what it means to be professional.[20] It was the first (and perhaps only) study to treat professionalism as an organizational, rather than an individual, attribute. In 1976, Morgan and Swanson examined a number of attributes of police organizations. Rather than relying on theory as a guide for constructing their measures, the researchers used a multivariate statistical technique called exploratory factor analysis to construct both their independent and dependent variables.[21] Unlike Wilson's (1968b) classic book, which according to Google Scholar has been cited more than 2,000 times, neither study has been cited very often (20 for Henderson and 3 for Morgan and Swanson), suggesting that some of the early empirical research on the causes and correlates of police organization was rather anonymous.

During the 1970s, Elinor Ostrom (who later won the Nobel Prize in Economics) and her colleagues collected a considerable amount of data on American police organizations. They examined policing as an "industry," focusing on patterns in the production and consumption of police services. In a number of publications, Ostrom, Parks, and Whitaker (1978) described and explained how police organizations in metropolitan areas rely on one another for mutual support and to provide various specialized services. Their work defied critics who argued that American policing was a loosely connected patchwork of small and untrained police agencies, often consisting of only a handful of officers (Murphy & Plate, 1977; Skoler & Hetler, 1970). While the work of Ostrom and her colleagues made enormous contributions to the study of policing in general, the unit of analysis in nearly all of their publications was the metropolitan area and its patterns of service production and consumption, not police organizations.[22] For that reason, most of their work falls outside the scope of this chapter. Their focus on the internal consequences of police organizational size, however, was one of the earliest studies seeking to explain variations in police organizational structure (Ostrom et al., 1978).

Probably the most influential work in this area is Robert Langworthy's 1986 book, *The Structure of Police Organizations*. Langworthy argued convincingly that with the exception of James Q. Wilson's work, scholarly attention to police organizations had been restricted to normative theories and prescriptions about how they should be structured and what they should be doing. This tendency to focus on prescription rather than description and explanation, on what police should be doing rather than what they are doing and why they are doing it, left a large empirical gap in our understanding of police organizations.[23] As a first step toward filling this gap, Langworthy borrowed a series of propositions from organization theory (and once again from Wilson's work), constructing his own unique theory to explain variation in the structure of police organizations. Using data from two national surveys (including data from Ostrom and her colleagues and the Kansas City General Administrative Survey), Langworthy then tested his theory empirically. His analysis was the first comprehensive, comparative empirical study to treat the structure of police organizations as a dependent variable. He concluded that the causal forces in his study did not appear to exert a significant constraint on organization structure (p. 136):

> "It seems plain that the explanations, size, technology, population mobility, population complexity, and type of local government, although theoretically significant determinants or correlates of agency structure, explain very little of the variance in agency structure. The constraints, when they are suggested by the data, do not appear insurmountable."

These findings suggest that American police executives are, by and large, free to design police organizations as they see fit.

Research studies on the causes and correlates of police organizational structure continue to emerge. Crank and Wells (1991) found that size exerts a nonlinear effect on structure. King (1999) found that older police organizations employ fewer civilians than younger ones. Davenport (1996) found that violent crime, resource capacity, and environmental turbulence have mixed effects on measures of structure. Maguire's (2003) replication and extension of Langworthy's study found a series of mixed effects of age, size, technology, and environment on structure. Maguire divided the structure of police organizations into two domains: (1) structural complexity, and (2) structural coordination and control mechanisms. Structural complexity is the extent to which the organization divides itself into vertical or hierarchical levels (such as different levels of command), functional divisions (such as special units or teams), and spatial divisions (such as different precincts). Those organizations with many vertical, functional, and spatial divisions are more complex. Structural coordination and control mechanisms are elements that are built into the structure of the organization to help managers and administrators maintain coordination and control. Maguire considered three such mechanisms: the use of administrative staff, formal written policies, and centralization of command. Maguire found strong evidence that the context of police organizations exerts constraints on structural complexity (vertical, functional, and spatial divisions), but not on structural coordination and control (administration, formalization, and centralization). Overall, the study of police organizational structure has entered a stage of incremental development.

Other studies in this genre examined the environmental and organizational correlates of police innovation and various internal (administratively oriented) community policing reforms. Based on the literature on "innovation diffusion," Weiss (1997) examines two questions: do police organizations rely on informal communications with other agencies (peer emulation), and if so, do these contacts result in the diffusion of innovation across agencies? Diffusion of innovation is the general notion that innovative practices, whether new vaccines to cure the sick or new managerial practices in policing, tend to spread in predictable ways. Weiss found that agencies do engage in informal information sharing, and that peer emulation and cosmopolitanism both shape the adoption of innovations. King (1998) also examines the sources of innovation in police agencies, but his research is rooted more in traditional organizational theory than the diffusion literature. King found that innovation is a multidimensional concept consisting of at least five separate dimensions: radical, administrative, technical, line-technical, and programmatic.

Furthermore, he found additional evidence that at least some of these dimensions can be further reduced into multiple subdimensions. The findings are too numerous to summarize here, but overall, organizational factors played a stronger role in shaping innovativeness than environmental or "ascriptive" factors.

Several studies have examined just one category of innovativeness: the various kinds of administrative changes occurring under the banner of community policing. Zhao (1996) was the first researcher to examine the causes of "internally-focused" changes occurring under community policing. He constructed a measure of internal change and then sought to explain variation in the measure using a number of organizational and environmental predictors. His models were able to explain more of the variation in externally focused change than in internally focused change. In their evaluation of the Justice Department's COPS Office (Office of Community Oriented Policing Services), Roth and Johnson (1997) found that while federal funding may have affected external elements of community policing, agencies receiving the funding were not more likely than nonfundees to have made internal organizational changes. Finally, in a study focusing on measurement rather than explanation, Maguire and Uchida (2000) developed reliable measures of internal change which they referred to as "adaptation." Although region and department size were only included in the model as predictors for statistical reasons, once again, both were found to exert a significant effect on adaptation.

Explaining what the police are—their policies, structures, programs, and other internal elements—represents the next frontier of research on police organizations. The research in this area is relatively undeveloped, and there is an untapped pool of theories to test. For instance, promising theories that were developed in the 1960s have still not been fully tested. These include the work of Reiss and Bordua (1967) and a number of propositions about police agency structure implicit in Wilson's (1968b) theory of police behavior (Langworthy, 1986). In addition, there have been a number of more recent theoretical contributions in the areas of contingency theory (Maguire, 2003), institutional theory (Crank, 1994; Crank & Langworthy, 1992; Katz, 1997; Mastrofski & Uchida, 1993), resource dependency theory (Worrall & Zhao, 2003), and various combinations of these theories (Burruss, Giblin, & Schafer, 2010; Katz, Maguire, & Roncek, 2002; Maguire & King, 2007; Mastrofski & Ritti, 2000; Mastrofski & Willis, 2010). Next, we describe these theories and their promise for helping us to understand police organizations.

WHAT FACTORS SHAPE POLICE ORGANIZATIONS?

Many of the same variables are used to explain interagency variation in both what police organizations do and what they are. One reason for this is undoubtedly the availability of these measures in common sources such as Census Bureau publications and data or the Municipal Yearbook. Another reason is that the same theories are often used to explain a wide range of differences across police agencies, from their internal administrative structures to their community policing or homeland security practices.

Isolating the factors that shape police organizations with any degree of certainty and rigor would require a full-length book. The studies listed by Maguire and Uchida (2000) contain at least eighty-five separate independent variables, even after combining those that are similar but not exactly the same (two different measures of political culture, for instance). The following list contains the fourteen measures that had at least one statistically significant effect in at least three separate studies. They are sorted in descending order by the number of studies in which they demonstrated a significant effect:

- Organizational Size (18)
- City Governance (5)
- Region (5)
- Concentration (4)
- Crime Patterns (4)
- Organizational Age (4)
- Political Culture (4)
- Population Size (4)
- Population Heterogeneity (4)
- Poverty/Income (4)
- Urbanization or Ruralization (4)
- Span of Control or Supervisory Ratio (3)
- Time (3)
- Vertical Differentiation (3)

We are careful not to make too much of these findings. This list is simply intended to illustrate the kinds of variables that scholars have used in empirical research to explain differences in police organizations, as well as those that have been found important. These findings pertain to several different dependent variables, and neither the direction of effects nor the quality of the studies is considered. Nevertheless, this list illustrates some of the factors commonly thought and found to influence police organizations.

The most frequent and consistent finding in organizational research on police is the importance of organization size. The effects of size are not universal, as Ostrom and her colleagues have repeatedly demonstrated; the research suggests that size has an important effect on style, structure, and processes, but not necessarily on effectiveness and efficiency. Region also continues to exert significant effects on the administration of public organizations. Yet, to date, researchers have not done a very good job in isolating the theoretical reasons for these effects, though many possibilities have been suggested (Maguire et al., 1997). The structure of city governance, together with local political culture, also exerts significant effects on police organizations, suggesting that any comprehensive theory of police organizations needs to account for political effects. Note that this idea is consistent with Hagan's theoretical perspective in Chapter 3. Another particularly noteworthy finding is the presence of two variables suggesting a historical effect on police organizations: the department's age and the passage of time. Police organizations constantly change. The appearance of time and age in this list suggests that they change in ways that are sometimes predictable. Thus, any comprehensive theory of police organizations needs to account for historical effects (King, 2009). The remaining variables are all elements of the organization or its environment, and most are represented in traditional organizational theories.

FUTURE PROSPECTS

The scholarly study of police organizations has not evolved in a progressive, orderly fashion. Much of the research contains methodological and theoretical shortcomings, and for that reason it has been of limited utility for understanding police organizations and the forces that shape them. A byproduct of this limitation is that this research has been of little practical use for police executives and policy makers. More than two decades ago, Dorothy Guyot (1977) bemoaned the lack of empirical research on police organizations, citing Wilson's *Varieties of Police Behavior* as the lone exception. Nearly a decade later, Robert

Langworthy (1986, 32) echoed Guyot's complaints, arguing that Wilson's work "remains the only empirically derived theory of police organization to date." Through the mid-1980s, police organizational scholarship had not substantially evolved beyond Wilson's seminal work.

Langworthy's *The Structure of Police Organizations* was an important turning point in police organizational scholarship. It is among a handful of studies that have blended theory and research in an effort to further our understanding about the structure and function of American police organizations. Perhaps even more importantly, it inspired a new generation of police organizational scholarship (Crank & Wells, 1991; King, 1999, 2009; Maguire, 1997, 2003, 2014).

Thus, we cannot complain as forcefully as our predecessors about the status of the scholarship regarding police organizations. Since the mid-1990s, there have been a number of improvements in theory, data, and method, though certainly much remains to be done. This section has two simultaneous goals: to diagnose some of the weaknesses in this line of research, and to suggest some ways that researchers might continue to breathe into it some new life. We will consider three primary areas: theory, research, and policy.

Theory

Throughout this chapter we have made reference to theories used by scholars to explain interagency variation in police organizations. Some of these theories have received empirical support, others have not, and others remain untested. This section briefly reviews the state of theoretical explanation in the study of American police organizations.

We begin by restating contingency theory, since it is an inclusive theory of structure, process, and performance. Briefly stated, contingency theory holds that organizations will only be effective if they remain dynamic, adapting to changes in technology and environment. Technology here is used in the broadest sense, referring to the tools and strategies used by the organization to process raw materials. Thus, in addition to the material technologies that are having such a profound influence in policing (Ericson & Haggerty, 1997; Manning, 1992), it includes the social technologies used by the police to process and change people and communities (Maguire, 2003; Mastrofski & Ritti, 2000). Contingency theory focuses predominantly on the "task environment"—those elements of the environment with direct relevance for the work of the organization. In policing, the task environment would include citizens, courts, and other parts of the criminal justice system; patterns of crime and criminality; the sources available for recruiting and training officers; the physical and social attributes of the community; and numerous other external forces that shape the structure and function of police agencies.

Contingency theory is the foundation of nearly every study of police organizations. It is the implicit source of most of the explanatory variables used in models explaining organizational features: size, technology, and the various elements of the environment. It assumes that effective organizations are rational entities seeking to maximize their levels of effectiveness and efficiency. It also assumes that organizations failing to adapt to changes in technology and environment will be ineffective, fail, and be replaced by others (Langworthy, 1992).[24]

This inherent rationality is why many organizational scholars have abandoned contingency theory (Donaldson, 1995). Most of the people who study police organizations would probably not describe them as rational, dynamic, or adaptive (Maguire, 2014).

The failure of contingency theory to effectively explain the structure and function of organizations has led to the development of numerous other theories. We now discuss three alternative perspectives on the role of organizational environments: as sources of legitimacy, resources, and information.

Institutional theory has its roots in the early study of organizations by such influential theorists as Talcott Parsons and Philip Selznick. For example, Selznick described institutionalization as the process by which organizations develop an "organic character" (Perrow, 1986) and become "infused with value beyond the technical requirements of the task at hand" (Selznick, 1957, 17). Selznick was fascinated by the paradox that organizations are created for rational action, but that they never quite succeed in conquering irrationality. Institutional theory has experienced a revival since the mid-1980s, a trend that many attribute to an influential article by Meyer and Rowan in 1977. Meyer and Rowan argued that the environment is not just a source of raw materials, clients, technologies, and other technical elements essential to the function of an organization. Environments are also the source of such intangible elements as standards, norms, rumors, myths, symbols, knowledge, ceremonies, and traditions. These elements constitute the institutional environment, and though they are often less rational than elements in the technical environment, they are nonetheless essential sources of organizational legitimacy. Since organizations require legitimacy to survive and prosper, they are often more responsive to institutional concerns than they are to technical concerns. Institutional theory has begun to occupy an increasingly important role in the study of police organizations (Burruss, Giblin & Schafer, 2010; Crank, 1994; Crank & Langworthy, 1992, 1996; Maguire, 2003, 2014; Maguire and Mastrofski

2000; Mastrofski 1998; Mastrofski and Ritti 1996; Mastrofski, Ritti, and Hoffmaster, 1987). Enough has been written about institutional theory now that continuing to find ways to capture its full complexity remains an important challenge.

While institutional theory is based on the role of the environment as a source of legitimacy, credentialing, and support for the organization, resource dependency theory focuses on the environment as a source of valuable resources. The principal statement of resource dependency theory is Pfeffer and Salancik's (1978) *External Control of Organizations*. Resource dependency theory is essentially a theory of power and politics that focuses on the methods used by organizational actors to secure the flow of resources. Because organizations are frequently dependent on securing resources from the environment, they are, to a certain point, "externally controlled." Resource dependency theory has not yet been applied to policing in a comprehensive way, though several studies have described its relevance to police organizations (e.g., Katz, Maguire, & Roncek, 2002; Maguire & Mastrofski, 2000; McCarty, Ren & Zhao, 2012; Zhao, Scheider & Thurman, 2003; Worrall & Zhao, 2003).

While the first two theories focus on the environment as a locus of resources, the third sees it as a source of information. Weick (1969) and Duncan (1972) have both demonstrated how various sectors of the environment contain "pools" of information that are critical to the organization, which then processes this information in such a way as to decrease "information uncertainty." As the pace of computerization in police agencies continues to grow, the role of information may become even more relevant. Two discussions have focused on the centrality of information to police organizations. Manning (1992) outlines the link between organizations, environments, and information-processing technologies such as computer-aided dispatch (CAD) systems, centralized call collection (911) mechanisms, "expert" systems, management information systems, and other tools designed to increase the organization's capacity to intake and process information. Manning concludes by suggesting that information technologies have "an indeterminate effect on the organizational structure of policing; technology is used to produce and reproduce traditional practices, yet is slowly modifying them" (1992, 391). Ericson and Haggerty (1997) explore similar themes in *Policing the Risk Society*. They view police organizations as part of a larger network of institutions responsible for the identification, management, and communication of risks. They argue that policing (at multiple levels) is shaped by external institutions and their need for information about risks. Theories of the environment as a source of information are not very well developed at this point. In addition, they contain a host of ambiguities about the proper unit of analysis.[25] Nonetheless, given the emergence in policing of sophisticated technologies for collecting and processing information, this perspective deserves further attention.

While all of these theories offer substantial promise for understanding police organizations, we cannot ignore classical explanations. Stinchcombe (1963) made a series of early propositions in which the distribution of public and private spaces within communities serves as an important source of variation in police practice administration. His work foreshadowed the emergence of large private spaces policed by private entities, such as malls, amusement parks, and gated communities. Other classic theoretical statements appearing in the 1960s (Bordua & Reiss, 1966; Reiss & Bordua, 1967; Wilson, 1963, 1968b) have still not been adequately tested. These classics need to be dusted off and revived.

Many of the studies reviewed earlier in this chapter have not been adequately rooted in theory. In diagnosing the current state of police organizational scholarship in the United States, we find little reason for concern about the nature or volume of theories upon which to base solid empirical research. One area for improvement that should be explored is how a good theory of police organization might differ from a theory of organizations in general, or of public service organizations in particular. There is already some evidence that theories designed to explain private organizations, especially those in manufacturing rather than service industries, are inadequate to explain police organizations (Maguire, 2003). The answer may exist in either the artful blending of existing theories or the emergence of new and better ideas.

RESEARCH

Data Collection

Data collection in policing is currently in an exciting and rapid state of development. Much of this can probably be attributed to the emergence of new technologies for recording, collecting, processing, and distributing data. Police organizations are now experimenting with technology at a record pace, implementing or updating their management information systems, GAD centers, geo-mapping and other modern forms of crime analysis, mobile data terminals in patrol cars, and many other advances emerging in the past decade. One consequence of the proliferation of information-processing technologies is that police agencies now contain vast archives of data. While much of this data is not very useful for national comparative research, it is changing the face of policing in important ways.

There are currently reasons to be both optimistic and pessimistic about the state of national data collection on police organizations in the United States. On the bright side, police agencies are now more open than ever. Careful surveys conducted by researchers, government agencies, and survey firms routinely obtain response rates of 70 to 90 percent. There are numerous sources of data, and although most could be improved, they are, on average, of decent quality. We have criticized some of the data inventories used by government agencies for counting the number of police agencies and officers in the United States over the past several decades (Maguire et al., 1998). Many of the problems cited in that article have been rectified, though some remain. Consequently, current efforts to enumerate the American police are more accurate than ever. Finally, several agencies within the Justice Department now routinely include in their police agency databases a unique agency code, thus enabling researchers and policy makers to link separate databases and test interesting new hypotheses. While there is always room for improvement in the kinds of data that are collected, the methods used to collect data from police organizations tend, on average, to be fairly good.

On the other hand, the Bureau of Justice Statistics (BJS) has not maintained the continuity of its Law Enforcement Management and Administrative Statistics (LEMAS) data collection series. LEMAS serves as the principal data platform for comparative studies of American police agencies. As Matusiak, Campbell, and King (2014, 639) note: "The data have fueled a vibrant and healthy academic industry in the empirical study of, and theory testing with, police agencies." From 1987 to 2012, LEMAS was administered nine times, during which the shortest gap between successive waves was one year (1999–2000) and the longest gap was five years (2007–2012). As this chapter goes to press (in 2014), the latest wave of data available to researchers is from 2007, which limits the capacity of the research community to capture current dynamics in policing. Instability in questionnaire content and wording over time has limited the ability of researchers to carry out analyses of changes in policing (Matusiak, Campbell, & King, 2014). Unfortunately, the most recent wave (2012) eliminated many of the survey items traditionally used by researchers carrying out the kinds of research on police organizations discussed in this chapter.

Research on police organizations is challenging in many ways. For instance, in response to the 1994 Crime Act, the BJS and the National Institute of Justice (NIJ) undertook efforts to measure the use of force by police agencies throughout the nation. BJS added supplemental questions on police use of force to its national household survey. While this strategy is useful for some purposes, it undercounts at least three classes of people who may be more likely to have force used against them by the police: the homeless, the incarcerated and institutionalized, and those without telephones.[26] A second strategy, undertaken by the International Association of Chiefs of Police (IACP) with funding from BJS and NIJ, attempted to develop a national Police Use of Force Database based on confidential reporting by police departments of use-of-force incidents. This method, too, contains a number of problems. Most importantly, it relies on official records that may reflect as much about the organization's willingness to record use-of-force incidents as the actual number of incidents that take place. Other agencies, including the Police Complaint Center and the American Civil Liberties Union, collect data on excessive force and patterns of discrimination from citizens alleging to be victims of these offenses. While these may serve a useful social purpose, neither attempts to (nor claims to) carefully enumerate use-of-force incidents nationally.

Police agencies continue to face challenges with regard to "racial profiling" data: collecting detailed information on the characteristics of those who are stopped and the reasons for conducting searches (Engel, 2008; Tillyer, Engel, & Cherkauskas, 2010; Walker, 2001). This enterprise is fraught with the potential for error (and possibly subversion) and will be very difficult to implement nationally. The demand for these kinds of measures reflects a point we raised throughout the chapter—policing doesn't have one bottom line—it has many. The demand for these types of data collection efforts reflects a concern for something other than the war on terrorism, crime, and drugs. It reflects a growing concern for equity and fairness on the part of the police. Once again, data collection will play a central, if challenging, role.

Explanation

The methodologies used in the comparative study of police organizations have improved over the past four decades. Yet, many of the studies we examined are flawed in both theory and method. If we had to identify the single most serious problem in the entire line of research, our choice would undoubtedly be the failure to consistently root empirical studies in theory. Some of the studies with the worst methodological flaws contained flawless reviews of the relevant literature and theory. The indiscriminate use of statistical methods without proper attention to theory is common in much of the research. Judging from this literature alone, it appears that a crucial point in the research process that many people either ignore or find difficult is the translation of a theoretical model into an empirical one. Careful attention should be paid to these issues in training the next generation of researchers.

A Modest Vision for Future Research

Sometimes it seems that empirical research on police organizations is a lot like making minestrone soup: in the absence of a good recipe (theory), find whatever vegetables that happen to be convenient (the data), toss them into the pot (the model), cook it (execute the statistical program), and see if it tastes good (check the statistical results). Continue to make adjustments (capitalizing on statistical chance) to the soup until you like the way it tastes.

Our vision for the future of police organizational research is rather simple. Begin by explicating a reasonable theory, spend a considerable amount of time translating the theory into an empirical model, collect reasonably good data that are useful for testing the theory, spend some additional time turning those raw data points into theoretically meaningful and reliable measures, and then test a model that posits some type of causal order among the measures. Don't capitalize on statistical chance by endlessly tinkering with the model if it doesn't fit. If this is the case, return to step 1 and modify the theory. Recent advances in statistical modeling techniques and the software packages in which these techniques are implemented make it easy for most social scientists to become skilled and careful theory testers. This is our "recipe" for achieving incremental progress in the study of police organizations.

Policy

Theoretically inspired research on police organizations sometimes has direct implications for policy and practice, and other times these implications are less direct. This is okay. Many academic fields, including medicine, have a similar division between "basic" and "applied" research. A healthy balance between the two types of research is useful for keeping an academic field vibrant.

For obvious reasons, police executives and policy makers are much more interested in applied research since they are concerned with the day-to-day realities of their professional worlds. They want measures that assist them in making decisions and policy. They want explanations for why things occurred. In the academic world of theories and data, researchers want precision and statistically significant findings. They want analysis driven by theory. Coming to grips with both of these worlds is difficult, but not insurmountable. The policy implications that derive from theory and analysis need to be made explicit and digestible by researchers. Our experience suggests that police executives and policy makers want good measures and explanations, but they want them in ways that are much more understandable. They want direct answers to questions about "How does my department compare to others in terms of community policing or officer performance?" and "If there are differences, how can we overcome them?" As researchers, at least one of our jobs is to assist policy makers in answering these types of questions. Balancing all of these competing interests—using adequate theory, collecting good data, formulating accurate measures, developing sound explanations, and outlining the implications for policy—is a significant but worthwhile challenge.

CONCLUSION

This chapter is meant to serve as an introduction to research and theory on the comparative study of American police organizations. Police organizations differ, and understanding those differences is an important area of focus for both research and theory. We have tried to escort readers on a journey from the early research on why police organizations vary and the birth of scholarly theories meant to explain these variations, to the more sophisticated research that is now taking place. Along the way there have been many pitfalls: insufficient attention to conceptualization and theory, unrealistic measures, inadequate statistical methods, and an overall lack of appreciation for previous research. While looking back upon the classics in the field provides a sense of foundation, with perhaps a touch of nostalgia, there remain countless avenues for refinement and rediscovery. Chief among these are two responsibilities that may seem at first glance like strange bedfellows: doing research that (1) is based firmly in existing or new theories, and (2) contributes to the understanding or practice of policing. By tracing the evolution of research on police organizations from past to present, bumps and all, we hope this chapter provides a clear road map for what is to come. As we progress through the twenty-first century, much remains to be learned.

NOTES

1. Portions of this chapter appeared in Maguire and Uchida (2000).
2. This research also grew out of the political science tradition of exploring variations in local government policies and structures (Meyer & Baker, 1979; Wilson, 1968a, 1968b).
3. Several different levels of analysis are commonly used within organization studies. The level of analysis used in this chapter is called the "organization set," which "views the environment from the perspective or standpoint of a specific (focal) organization" (Scott, 1992, 126). This is an important detail because it limits the scope of the chapter to a particular

analytical framework. Many studies of police organizations are implicitly based on a different level of analysis. For instance, Ostrom, Parks, and Whitaker (1978) used an "areal organization field," while Bayley (1985, 1992) used the "organizational population" (Scott, 1992).

4. This definition purposely excludes agencies that are specialized by function (e.g., fish and wildlife police) or territory (park or airport police), including most federal law enforcement agencies, many county sheriffs and state highway patrol agencies, and private security firms. While using such a restrictive definition reduces the overall level of variation across the organizations under study, it defines a common set of core tasks and functions.
5. There are also numerous similarities among police organizations. As Wadman (1998) points out, all of the largest municipal police agencies have hierarchical rank structures (though some may be flatter than others); they all have divisions for patrol, investigations, and administration; and they all devote a disproportionate share of their resources to motorized patrol. Wadman overstates the similarities between police agencies, but his point is well taken. There is variation among police agencies, but it is variation "within a theme." We are grateful to Graeme Newman for this observation.
6. Although there is some overlap, the style of a police organization is conceptually different from the style of an individual officer (Talarico & Swanson, 1979; Wilson, 1968b).
7. We are careful to distinguish what an organization does from what it is by the location of the activity, behavior, or program, rather than its degree of visibility to the public. Much of what the police do externally, as Goldstein (1960) has argued, occurs in low-visibility settings. On the other hand, Marshall Meyer (1979) and other organizational theorists have shown how internal features of organizations (such as their structures) are sometimes designed to serve as visible signals to external constituents that the organization is doing the right things.
8. Most serious organizational scholars would probably agree that much of what goes on in organizations is random or unexplainable. Weick (1976) suggests that explaining the regularities across organizations is less interesting than explaining this seeming randomness. He suggests using alternative methods that enable researchers to understand the "loose coupling" or unexplained variance in organizational relationships.
9. A similar issue arises in mortality studies. Studying only the dead to learn about causes and correlates of death is a flawed strategy because we cannot know whether these same conditions are present in people who lived (Kaufman, 1976; King, Travis, & Langworthy, 1997).
10. Bordua and Reiss (1966) explore these same themes (to a lesser extent) in an earlier article.
11. For example, Reiss and Bordua (1967) discussed two environmental variables that are important to the organization: the security of the police

chief's tenure and the degree of accountability that the government executive demands from the chief. Cross-classifying these two variables, they formed a crude taxonomy of four department types that might reflect variation in political interference into police department affairs. They suggested that these and other environmental variables were important because they "structure the effective range of command and control" (p. 49) in municipal police departments.

12. Slovak (1986) laments that "there is a very real sense in which the promise offered by Wilson's original analysis has gone unfulfilled" (p. 5).
13. Aggregate-level arrest rates for various offenses are frequently used as an indicator of police style. Note that these studies focus on organizational style (or some other aggregate), not the style of an individual officer (Slovak, 1986).
14. In general, structural contingency theory suggests that no single organizational form is ideal for all circumstances (Donaldson, 1995; Lawrence & Lorsch, 1967). Successful organizations survive by adapting to the contingencies of their specific tasks and environments.
15. This is not meant to imply that police organizations have no effect on crime, because crime is the product of numerous social forces, including the police and other institutions. Therefore, it is awkward to think of the volume of crime within a community as an organizational measure that describes the police. For a review of the available research evidence in this area, see Eck and Maguire (2000).
16. Reprinted by permission of the publisher from *Varieties of Police Behavior: The Management of Law and Order in Eight Communities* by James Q. Wilson, p. 276, Cambridge MA: Harvard University Press, Copyright © 1968b, 1978 by the President and Fellows of Harvard College.
17. We have chosen not to examine studies that use measures of organizational properties (such as performance) that are aggregated based on individuals' subjective impressions or opinions. For instance, if we ask 1,000 citizens in each of ten cities to rate their local police and then compute a summary measure of citizen ratings for each agency, we would be forming an aggregate subjective measure. Such measures are not considered here, though they are clearly important.
18. Ostrom and Parks (1973), for instance, found curvilinear relationships between city size and citizen ratings of police performance in their secondary analysis of data from 102 cities. For central cities, performance ratings increased as city size approached 100,000 residents, after which ratings decreased; the same curvilinear relationship was found for suburbs, but the population threshold was only 20,000 residents. Whitaker (1983) also concludes that the size of the police organization is more important than the size of the political jurisdiction, thus lending support to reform strategies that seek to simulate the feel of small-town policing in large cities through the use of precinct stations, substations, and other

decentralization and spatial differentiation strategies. Whitaker's (1983) chapter contains the most comprehensive (though dated) review of the effect of department size on police organizations.

19. There is a shortage of theory to explain either of these consistent findings. Region may simply be a proxy for any number of political, historical, economic, or demographic differences between regions. Organizational size seems to affect nearly every aspect of what organizations do. One possible reason that larger police agencies may report engaging in more community policing activities is simply that they have more employees to assign to such functions.
20. This point is controversial. Some might argue that measuring any concept involves normative judgments. Our view is that the concept of professionalism is inherently normative because it implies a rank ordering and a value judgment: more professionalized organizations are better than those that are less professionalized.
21. Exploratory factor analysis is a method used by researchers to combine multiple variables into a single measure. Like any other tool, it can be, and is often, abused. One way that it can be used in an atheoretical manner is to combine variables that are seemingly unrelated into a single measure for statistical rather than theoretical or conceptual reasons.
22. Clark, Hall, and Hutchinson (1967) treat interorganizational relationships as "contextual" variables rather than organizational variables in their study of police performance.
23. According to Duffee (1990), this problem is rampant in all sectors of criminal justice. His advice to criminal justice scholars is particularly appropriate—we should focus on describing and explaining what criminal justice organizations do, rather than what they should be doing.
24. Conventional wisdom in policing is that police organizations do not "go out of business" (Travis & Brann, 1997). Recent work by William King and his colleagues (King, 1999; King, Travis, & Langworthy, 1997) challenges this assumption. Based on a survey of county sheriffs in Ohio, King documented the death of 104 police agencies (and the birth of an additional 15). King is now replicating this study in several other states.
25. Weick's (1969) discussion is inherently social psychological, while Manning (1992) and Ericson and Haggerty (1997) span levels from the individual to the institution.
26. We are grateful to Paula Kautt for this observation.

REFERENCES

Alpert, G., and M.H. Moore. 1993. Measuring police performance in the new paradigm of policing. In *Performance measures for the criminal justice system: Discussion papers from the BJS-Princeton project.* Washington, D.C.: Bureau of Justice Statistics.

Aupperle, K.E., W. Acar, and D.E. Booth. 1986. An empirical critique of In Search of Excellence: How excellent are the excellent companies? *Journal of Management* 12(4): 499–512.
Bayley, D.H. 1985. *Patterns of policing: A comparative international analysis.* New Brunswick, NJ: Rutgers University Press.
Bayley, D.H. 1992. Comparative organization of the police in English-speaking countries. In *Modern policing*, eds. M. Tonry and N. Morris (pp. 509–46). Chicago: University of Chicago Press.
Bayley, D.H. 1994. *Police for the future.* New York: Oxford University Press.
Blau, P.M., W.V. Heydebrand, and R.E. Stauffer. 1966. The structure of small bureaucracies. *American Sociological Review* 31: 179–91.
Blau, P.M. and R.A. Schoenherr. 1971. *The structure of organizations.* New York: Basic Books.
Bordua, D.J. and A. Reiss, Jr. 1966. Command, control and charisma: Reflections on police bureaucracy. *American Journal of Sociology* 72: 68–76.
Burns, T., and G.M. Stalker. 1961. *The management of innovation.* London: Tavistock.
Burruss, G.W., M.J. Giblin, and J.A. Schafer. 2010. Threatened globally, acting locally: Modeling law enforcement homeland security practices. *Justice Quarterly* 27(1): 77–101.
Clark, J.P., R.H. Hall, and B. Hutchinson. 1967. Interorganizational relationships and network properties as contextual variables in the study of police performance. In *Police and society*, ed. D.H. Bayley (pp. 177–93). Beverly Hills, CA: Sage.
Coleman, J.S. 1974. *Power and the structure of society.* New York: W.W. Norton.
Cordner, G.W. 1989. Police agency size and investigative effectiveness. *Journal of Criminal Justice* 17: 145–55.
Crank, J.P. 1990. The influence of environmental and organizational factors on police style in urban and rural environments. *Journal of Research in Crime and Delinquency* 27(2): 166–89.
Crank, J.P. 1994. Watchman and community: Myth and institutionalization in policing. *Law and Society Review* 28(2): 325–51.
Crank, J.P., and R.H. Langworthy. 1992. An institutional perspective of policing. *The Journal of Criminal Law and Criminology* 83: 338–63.
Crank, J.P. and R.H. Langworthy. 1996. Fragmented centralization and the organization of the police. *Policing and Society* 6: 213–29.
Crank, J.P., and L.E. Wells. 1991. The effects of size and urbanism on structure among Illinois police departments. *Justice Quarterly* 8(2): 170–85.
Davenport, D.R. 1996. Public agency performance and structure: Assessing the effects of the organizational environment. PhD diss., Lubbock, TX: Texas Tech University.
Donaldson, L. 1995. *American anti-management theories of organization: A critique of paradigm proliferation.* Cambridge: Cambridge University Press.
Duffee, D.E. 1990. *Explaining criminal justice: Community theory and criminal justice reform.* Prospect Heights, IL: Waveland Press.

Duncan, R.B. 1972. Characteristics of organizational environments and perceived environmental uncertainty. *Administrative Science Quarterly* 17: 313–27.

Eck, J., and E.R. Maguire. 2000. Have changes in policing reduced violent crime: An assessment of the evidence. *The crime drop in America* eds. A. Blumstein and J. Wallman (pp. 207–65). New York: Cambridge.

Eisenstadt, S.N. 1959. Bureaucracy, bureaucratization, and debureaucratization. *Administrative Science Quarterly* 4(3): 302–20.

Emery, F., and E.L. Trist. 1965. The causal texture of organizational environments. *Human Relations* 18: 21–32.

Engel, R.S. 2008. A critique of the "outcome test" in racial profiling research. *Justice Quarterly* 25(1): 1–36.

Ericson, R.V., and K.D. Haggerty. 1997. *Policing the risk society*. Toronto: University of Toronto Press.

Goldstein, J. 1960. Police discretion not to invoke the criminal process: Low visibility decisions in the administration of justice. *Yale Law Journal* 69: 543–94.

Guyot, D. 1977. Police departments under social science scrutiny. *Journal of Criminal Justice* 5: 68–81.

Henderson, T. 1975. The relative effects of community complexity and of sheriffs upon the professionalism of sheriff departments. *American Journal of Political Science* 19(1): 107–32.

Katz, C.M. 1997. Police and gangs: A study of a police gang unit. PhD diss., University of Nebraska at Omaha.

Katz, C.M., E.R. Maguire, and D.W. Roncek. 2002. The creation of specialized police gang units: A macro-level analysis of contingency, social threat, and resource dependency explanations. *Policing: An International Journal of Police Strategies and Management* 25(3): 472–506.

Kaufman, H. 1976. *Are government organizations immortal?* Washington D.C.: Brookings Institution.

King, W.R. 1998. Innovativeness in American municipal police organizations. PhD diss., University of Cincinnati.

King, W.R. 1999. Time, constancy, and change in American municipal police organizations. *Police Quarterly* 2(3): 338–64.

King W.R. 2009. Toward a life-course perspective of police organizations. *Journal of Research in Crime and Delinquency* 46: 213–44.

King, W.R., L.F. Travis, III, and R.H. Langworthy. 1997. Police organizational death. Paper presented at the annual meeting of the American Society of Criminology, San Diego, CA.

Langworthy R.H. 1985. Police department size and agency structure. *Journal of Criminal Justice* 13: 15–27.

Langworthy, R.H. 1986. *The structure of police organizations*. New York: Praeger.

Langworthy, R.H. 1992. Organizational structure. In *What works in policing?* eds. G.W. Cordner and D.C. Hale (pp. 87–105). Cincinnati, OH: Anderson.

Lawrence, P.R., and J.W. Lorsch. 1967. Differentiation and integration in complex organizations. *Administrative Science Quarterly* 12(1): 1–47.

Maguire, E.R. 1997. Structural change in large municipal police organizations during the community policing era. *Justice Quarterly* 14(3): 701–30.

Maguire, E.R. 2003. *Context, complexity and control: Organizational structure in American police agencies*. Albany, NY: State University of New York Press.

Maguire, E.R. 2004. Police departments as learning laboratories. *Ideas in American Policing*. Washington, DC: Police Foundation.

Maguire, E.R. 2005. Measuring the performance of law enforcement agencies. *Law Enforcement Executive Forum* 5(1): 1–31.

Maguire, E.R. 2014. Police organizations and the iron cage of rationality. In *Oxford handbook on police and policing*, eds. M. Reisig and R. Kane. New York: Oxford University Press.

Maguire, E.R. and W.R. King. 2007. The changing landscape of American police organizations. In *Policing 2020: Exploring the future of crime, communities, and policing*, ed. J.A. Schafer. Washington, DC: Federal Bureau of Investigation.

Maguire, E.R., J.B. Kuhns, C.D. Uchida, and S.M. Cox. 1997. Patterns of community policing in nonurban America. *Journal of Research in Crime and Delinquency* 34: 368–94.

Maguire, E.R., and S.D. Mastrofski. 2000. Patterns of community policing in the United States. *Police Quarterly* 3(1): 4–45.

Maguire, E.R., J.B. Snipes, C.D. Uchida, and M. Townsend. 1998. Counting cops: Estimating the number of police departments and police officers in the USA. *Policing: An International Journal of Police Strategies & Management* 21(1): 97–120.

Maguire, E.R., and C.D. Uchida. 2000. Measurement and explanation in the comparative study of American police organizations. In *Measurement and analysis of crime and justice*, eds. D. Duffee, D. McDowall, B. Ostrom, R.D. Crutchfield, S.D. Mastrofski, and L.G. Mazerolle. *Criminal Justice 2000* (4): 491–558. Washington, D.C.: National Institute of Justice.

Manning, P.K. 1992. Information technologies and the police. In *Modern policing*, eds. M. Tonry and N. Morris (pp. 51–98). Chicago: University of Chicago Press.

Mastrofski, S.D. 1998. Community policing and police organization structure. In *How to recognize good policing: Problems and issues*, ed. J.P. Brodeur (pp. 161–89). Washington, D.C.: Police Executive Research Forum; Thousand Oaks, CA: Sage.

Mastrofski, S.D and R.R. Ritti. 1996. Police training and the effects of organization on drunk driving enforcement. *Justice Quarterly* 13: 291–320.

Mastrofski, S.D., and R.R. Ritti. 2000. Making sense of community policing: A theoretical perspective. *Police Practice and Research: An International Journal* 1(2): 183–210.

Mastrofski, S.D., R.R. Ritti, and D. Hoffmaster. 1987. Organizational determinants of police discretion: The case of drinking-driving. *Journal of Criminal Justice* 15: 387–402.

Mastrofski, S.D., and C.D. Uchida. 1993. Transforming the police. *Journal of Research in Crime and Delinquency* 30(3): 330–58.

Mastrofski, S.D. and J.J. Willis. 2010. Police organization continuity and change: Into the twenty-first century. *Crime and Justice* 39(1): 55–144.

Matusiak, M.C., B.A. Campbell, and W.R. King. 2014. The legacy of LEMAS: Effects on police scholarship of a federally administered, multi-wave establishment survey. *Policing*. 37(3): 630–648.

McCarty, W., L. Ren, and J. Zhao. 2012. Panel analysis of the determinants of police strength during the 1990s. *Crime & Delinquency* 58: 397–424.

Meyer, F.A., Jr., and R. Baker, eds. 1979. *Determinants of law-enforcement policies*. Lexington, MA: Lexington Books.

Meyer, J. and B. Rowan. 1977. Institutionalized organizations: Formal structure as myth and ceremony. *American Journal of Sociology* 83: 430–63.

Meyer, M.W. 1979. Organizational structure as signaling. *Pacific Sociological Review* 22: 481–500.

Monkkonen, E.H. 1981. *Police in urban America: 1860–1920*. Cambridge: Cambridge University Press.

Morgan, D.R. and C. Swanson. 1976. Analyzing police policies: The impact of environment, politics, and crime. *Urban Affairs Quarterly* 11(4): 489–510.

Murphy, P.V., and T. Plate. 1977. *Commissioner: A view from the top of American law enforcement*. New York: Simon & Schuster.

Ostrom, E., and R.B. Parks. 1973. Suburban police departments: Too many and too small? In *The urbanization of the suburbs*, eds. L.H. Masotti and J.K. Hadden (pp. 367–402). Beverly Hills, CA: Sage.

Ostrom, E., R.B. Parks, and G.P. Whitaker. 1978. *Patterns of metropolitan policing*. Cambridge, MA: Ballinger.

Parks, R. B. 1984. Linking objective and subjective measures of performance. *Public Administration Review* 44: 118–27.

Perrow, C. 1986. *Complex organizations: A critical essay*, 3rd ed. Glenview, IL: Scott, Foresman.

Pfeffer, J., and G.R. Salancik. 1978. *The external control of organizations*. New York: Harper & Row.

Ragin, C.C. 1987. *The comparative method: Moving beyond qualitative and quantitative strategies*. Berkeley: University of California Press.

Reiss, A.J., and D.J. Bordua. 1967. Environment and organization: A perspective on the police. In *The police: Six sociological essays*, ed. D. Bordua (pp. 25–55). New York: John Wiley.

Roth, J.A., and C.C. Johnson. 1997. COPS context and community policing. Paper presented at the annual meeting of the American Society of Criminology, San Diego, CA, November.

Schaefer Morabito, M. 2010. Understanding community policing as an innovation: Patterns of adoption. *Crime and Delinquency* 56(2): 564–87.
Scott, W.R. 1992. *Organizations: Rational, natural, and open systems*, 3rd ed. Englewood Cliffs, NJ: Prentice-Hall.
Selznick, P. 1957. *Leadership in administration*. New York: Harper & Row.
Skoler D.L. and J.M. Hetler. 1970. Governmental restructuring and criminal administration: The challenge of consolidation. *The Georgetown Law Journal* 58: 719–40.
Slovak, J.S. 1986. *Styles of urban policing: Organization, environment, and police styles in selected American cities*. New York: New York University Press.
Stinchcombe, A.L. 1963. Institutions of privacy in the determination of police administrative practice. *American Journal of Sociology* 69: 150–60.
Swanson, C. 1978. The influence of organization and environment on arrest practices in major U.S. cities. *Policy Studies Journal* 7: 390–98.
Talarico, S.M., and C.R. Swanson. 1979. Styles of policing: An exploration of compatibility and conflict. In *Determinants of law-enforcement policies*, eds. F.A. Meyer, Jr. and R. Baker (pp. 35–44). Lexington, MA: Lexington Books.
Tillyer, R., R.S. Engel, and J.C. Cherkauskas. 2010. Best practices in vehicle stop data collection and analysis. *Policing: An International Journal of Police Strategies and Management* 33(1): 69–92.
Travis, J., and J.E. Brann. 1997. Introduction. In *Measuring what matters, Part Two: Developing measures of what the police do*. Research in Action. Washington, D.C.: U.S. Department of Justice, National Institute of Justice.
Wadman, R.C. 1998. Organizing for the prevention of crime. PhD diss., Idaho State University.
Walker, S. 2001. Searching for the denominator: Problems with police traffic stop data and an early warning system solution. *Justice Research and Policy*, 3: 63–95.
Weick, K.E. 1969. *The social psychology of organizing*. Reading, MA: Addison-Wesley.
Weick, K.E. 1976. Educational organizations as loosely coupled systems. *Administrative Science Quarterly* 21: 1–19.
Weiss, A. 1997. The communication of innovation in American policing. *Policing: An International Journal of Police Strategies and Management* 20(2): 292–310.
Whitaker, G.P. 1983. Police department size and the quality and cost of police services. In *The political science of criminal justice*, eds. S. Nagel, E. Fairchild, and A. Champagne (pp. 185–96). Springfield, IL: Charles C. Thomas.
Wilson. J.M. 2006. *Community policing in America*. New York: Routledge.
Wilson, J.Q. 1963. The police and their problems: A theory. *Public Policy* 12: 189–216.
Wilson, J.Q. 1968a. *City politics and public policy*. New York: John Wiley.

Wilson, J.Q. 1968b. *Varieties of police behavior: The management of law and order in eight communities*. Cambridge, MA: Harvard University Press.

Worrall, J. and J. Zhao. 2003. The role of the COPS office in community policing. *Policing: An International Journal of Police Science and Management* 26(1): 64–87.

Zhao, J. 1996. *Why police organizations change: A study of community oriented policing*. Washington, D.C.: U.S. Department of Justice, Police Executive Research Forum.

Zhao, J., M. Scheider, and Q. Thurman. 2003. A national evaluation of the effects of COPS grants on police productivity (arrests), 1995–1999. *Police Quarterly* 6: 387–409.

5

UNDERSTANDING VARIETY IN URBAN COMMUNITY POLICING

An Institutional Theory Approach[1]

Brian C. Renauer

INTRODUCTION

Numerous police agencies in the United States report involvement in community policing strategies (Maguire, Kuhns, Uchida, & Cox, 1997; Maguire & Mastrofski, 2000; Zhao, Lovrich, & Thurman, 1999; Zhao, Thurman, & Lovrich, 1995). The 1999 Law Enforcement Management and Administrative Statistics survey, based on a representative sample of 13,000 local police departments, estimates that more than 90 percent of departments serving 25,000 or more residents had some type of community policing plan in operation (Hickman & Reaves, 1999). Sixty-four percent of local police departments report having full-time community policing officers (Hickman & Reaves, 1999). No one doubts there is a proliferation of police departments that claim to do community policing. The term community policing has evolved into a household phrase recognized by many (Maguire & Mastrofski, 2000).

There continues to be speculation over the activities that characterize "ideal" community policing, the accuracy of department claims regarding their involvement in particular community policing activities, and how to assess the "dosage" or intensity of community policing efforts (Bayley, 1994; Crank & Langworthy, 1992; Maguire & Mastrofski,

2000). The effectiveness of community policing strategies at lowering crime, reducing fear, and building strong neighborhoods is still unclear—although we are exposed to numerous community policing success stories (University of Maryland, 1997; Walker, 2001). Nonetheless, community policing continues to be implemented under a variety of strategies and activities, without a universally agreed-upon definition or theory of crime prevention (Cardarelli, McDevitt, & Baum, 1998; Maguire et al., 1997; Maguire & Mastrofski, 2000; Zhao, Lovrich, & Thurman, 1999; Zhao, Thurman, & Lovrich, 1995).

This chapter proposes that there are important measurable variations in urban community policing implementation efforts. In particular, community policing as implemented in one city may take on a more "community building" style than in other cities (described in the next section). Institutional theory is employed to make sense of such variation and investigate why community policing may involve more community building efforts in some cities than in others. By attempting to explain variation in community policing—an official criminal justice response to behaviors labeled as criminal—this chapter falls squarely within the domain of criminal justice theory as described in Chapter 2 (Snipes & Maguire, this volume).

Institutional theory perspectives describe institutionalizing forces that cause structural, strategic, and policy innovations in an organizational field, such as the innovation of community policing and its adoption by police organizations. Institutional theory also explains how strategic innovations may be molded or changed to fit a particular organization's operating context or "task environment." A simple analogy for institutional theory is the children's game "telephone." Children in the game are supposed to verbally pass along to the next child an original message, yet as the message is passed from child to child, it inevitably changes. The original message of community policing can be changed and adapted to be congruent with the institutionalizing environment of any specific urban police department. This chapter develops multiple propositions regarding the institutionalizing forces and contexts of urban police departments that are likely to create a "community building" style of community policing implementation. Empirically testing these propositions will help in identifying the conditions that support or resist a certain style and intensity of policing operation. An empirical test of these propositions is not undertaken here, but a heuristic device to further theoretical elaboration and eventual empirical examination of community policing variation is developed.

POLICE COMMUNITY BUILDING

Bayley (1994) and Kelling and Coles (1996), early proponents of community policing, agree that community policing activities should contribute to the formal and informal institutions within urban neighborhoods and not negatively interfere with their functions (Duffee, Fluellen, & Renauer, 1999). Bayley (1994, 145)[2] states:

> The challenge is to find ways of using the police for crime prevention without . . . discouraging the strengthening of other social processes that are critical to the enterprise.

Kelling and Coles write:

> [Policing should] help to create conditions in neighborhoods and communities that will allow other institutions—the family, neighborhood, church, community, and government and commerce—to deal with these basic problems of society.

The comments of Bayley (1994) and Kelling and Coles (1996) suggest that the police and groups in the communities in which the police work can "jointly produce" certain public safety outcomes, such as feelings of safety or fear, levels of disorder and crime, and levels of trust and cooperation. Their research and other studies indicate that police alone cannot maintain temporary improvements in communities unless something else occurs in the neighborhood. Thus, the ultimate goal in police–community collaboration is getting "something else" to transpire that will sustain a community over the long-term. That something else is commonly referred to as "community capacity." Community capacity is "the extent to which members of a community can work together effectively, including their abilities to develop and sustain strong relationships, solve problems and make group decisions, and collaborate effectively to identify goals and get work done" (Mattessich & Monsey, 1997).[3] Another way of thinking about community capacity is the old saying about the hungry peasant: "give him a fish, and he is full today but hungry again tomorrow; teach him to fish, and he need never be hungry again." Neighbors who observe that the police reduce crime do not represent the same situation as neighbors who gain experience in controlling crime with the police. Some things that the police do to reduce or prevent crime may promote dependency of the citizenry on the police and thereby reduce the strength of civic institutions, even if they have short-term positive effects on crime. Other things the police may do to reduce or prevent crime may promote neighborhood resident experience in civic engagement that strengthens civic institutions and allows residents to solve other problems in the future. When police make this contribution to civic engagement, we can talk about police community building. "Community building" processes are community activities that build community capacity. In contrast, Lyons (1999) and DeLeon-Granados (1999) indicate police activities (under the guise of community policing) have in fact neutralized neighborhood independence; reasserted centralized policing after initial decentralized partnering; and increased community divisiveness, distrust, and ill-feeling.

The theoretical ideal that community policing should contribute to important processes that build neighborhood efficacy or community capacity has been developed elsewhere (Bennett, 1998; DeLeon-Granados, 1999; Duffee, 1996; Duffee, Fluellen, & Renauer, 1999; Duffee, Fluellen, & Roscoe, 1999; Lyons, 1999). One particular research effort, the Police-Community Interaction Project (PCIP), has identified general processes of community building and asked how the police might be involved in such community processes (Duffee, Scott, Renauer, Chermak, & McGarrell, 2002). PCIP has defined five major community building dimensions in which the police are often active. These dimensions recognize different ways in which the police can interact with community groups that improve community capacity. For the purposes of this study, only three police community building processes will be discussed.

Steps to Identify with Neighborhoods

Definition: the manner and extent to which a neighborhood is recognized as a unique place to be considered separately from other neighborhoods in the city by agencies making policies that affect the neighborhood or providing services to the neighborhood. In terms of policing, steps to identify with neighborhoods would measure the broad steps that provide for police presence in the neighborhood, for increased knowledge about the neighborhood, for accessibility of police to residents, and for police responsiveness to residents' concerns. Police steps to identify with neighborhoods would include levels and dispersion of (1) physical decentralization; (2) permanency of personnel assignment; (3) aligning patrol with place boundaries; (4) place-specific information gathering and analysis; (5) regular foot and bike patrol; and (6) a policy of police attendance at neighborhood meetings.

Steps to Encourage Resident Efforts

Definition: the types and levels of activities to encourage residents in a neighborhood to contribute their efforts to concerted or collective action to improve the neighborhood. In terms of policing, encouragement consists of five activities, including (1) disseminating information about neighborhood problems, common bonds among neighbors, and the importance of collective action; (2) taking active steps to recruit any willing individuals in the neighborhood to work on projects; (3) helping to design and structure neighborhood organizations or collective endeavors; (4) suggesting to specific groups or individuals (e.g., to persons already identified as willing and available) particular actions or tactics; and (5) providing material resources, transportation, equipment, or other supports that either enable citizen participation to proceed or increase the level of participation.

Steps for Resident Participation

Definition: the forms and degree of resident involvement and decision making about the collective interests in a neighborhood. In terms of resident interactions with the police, this measure would entail assessing (1) resident involvement with police on problem/goal identification, solution/means identification, and division of labor; (2) resident levels of decision-making input based on their ability to raise issues, discuss issues, and make final decisions over issues in interaction with the police; and (3) balance in the decision-making process—with decisions among the police, residents, and other organizations participating in the community endeavor.

VARIATION IN POLICE COMMUNITY BUILDING

There is evidence that police do engage in the aforementioned "community building" activities (Duffee, Fluellen, & Renauer, 1999; Duffee et al., 2002; Renauer, Duffee, & Scott, 2003; Scott, Duffee, & Renauer, 2003). Police often identify with neighborhoods by having a physical presence there in terms of a storefront station, permanent officers, and neighborhood planning (Giacomazzi, McGarrell, & Thurman, 1998; Skogan, 1990). Police often encourage residents in a neighborhood toward collective efforts by distributing newsletters describing neighborhood problems and passing around signup sheets so neighbors can become involved in a project (Skogan, 1990; Skogan & Hartnett, 1997). Many community policing initiatives allow participation of neighborhood residents in decision-making processes (Renauer et al., 2003; Skogan, 1995; Skogan & Hartnett, 1997). Sometimes, resident participation only comes in the form of identifying neighborhood problems, but in other neighborhoods, residents may also be involved with police in the formulation of problem solutions and the actual carrying out of crime prevention tasks (Duffee et al., 2002; Skogan, 1995).

A crucial component to researching the propositions presented in this chapter is that the aforementioned police community building processes exhibit variation across locales and measurement tools exist to examine such variation. Thus, there is a need to classify departments according to the intensity of their involvement in these three community building processes (Renauer, Duffee, & Scott, 2003). Detailed measures of police community building will be needed to classify a police department as exhibiting a high or low strength (dosage) of community building (see Scott et al., 2003). For example, a high measure of community building by police would indicate police involvement in most of the six steps to identify with neighborhoods and five steps to encourage resident efforts. Police attempts to encourage resident efforts should also be consistent over time, not a single encouragement attempt. A high measure of community building would occur if residents are involved in all areas of decision making, not just problem identification, and residents have an equal balance of participation with other organizations. A high measure of community building would entail large turnouts of resident participants at neighborhood meetings by residents who are representative of the neighborhood population and its concerns. Throughout this chapter, propositions are developed that connect descriptions of police community building to the institutional forces that are likely to produce them.

VARIATIONS IN POLICE COMMUNITY-BUILDING ACTIVITIES: AN INSTITUTIONAL THEORY APPROACH

Community policing is considered an organizational and strategic innovation, just as the professional model of policing, which advocated for motorized police forces and rapid responses to calls for service, was a predecessor innovation. Organizational and policy innovations spread or diffuse (i.e., are adopted by organizations) through society at particular rates and forms, and this is no different for the diffusion of policing innovations (DiMaggio & Powell, 1983; Walker, 1977). The ideal descriptions of community policing philosophy contained in academic books or government documents may be molded into different types of community policing implementations (Maguire & Mastrofski, 2000). One form of community policing implementation would be strong police department involvement in neighborhood community building as described earlier. Other departments may interpret community policing as the implementation of an aggressive order-maintenance style of policing, or as the use of police-controlled problem-solving strategies, or as a community relations program (Maguire & Mastrofski, 2000; Zhao, Thurman, & Lovrich, 1995). This chapter describes the contexts and institutionalizing processes that are likely to create a certain form of community policing adoption: police departments highly involved in community building. Institutional theory is introduced in this section to help us understand how such innovation diffusion could take place.

INSTITUTIONAL THEORY: LOCAL CONTROL VS. FIELD AND CENTRIST CONTROL

Institutional theory attempts to develop a greater understanding of organizational-environment relations (Kraatz & Zajac, 1996). Thus, it essentially addresses the question of how an organization's environment (which is composed of other organizations, resources, and clients) influences its operations, structure, and service delivery. There exist two "camps" or competing institutional theory perspectives: "old" institutional theory and "new" institutional theory (Kraatz & Zajac, 1996). The traditional, or "old," institutional perspective is often referred to as adaptation theory, contingency theory, or resource dependency theory (Kraatz & Zajac, 1996). Old institutional theory proposes organizational change as a direct response to technical environmental demands. In other words, rational leaders of organizations choose operational strategies that address customers' demands and competition from other organizations, or other factors in their immediate task environment (Kraatz & Zajac, 1996). Therefore, police departments should seek to implement organizational structures and operations that will accomplish goals desired by their clients, such as reducing crime and fear of crime. According to the traditional institutional theory perspective, an organization's structure and operation are highly influenced by the local or immediate context in which services are delivered.

The recognition that innovations in criminal justice are influenced by the local context and implemented in a variety of forms at the local, municipal level is not a new insight. Maguire and Mastrofski (2000) use the term refraction to describe localized filtering and adaptations of nationally promoted and funded criminal justice innovations. Thus, criminal justice organizations often shape operational strategies promoted (or demanded) by other organizations or law to fit the demands of their local context (Walker, 2001). Good examples of local adaptations of criminal justice policy can be found in the studies that evaluated the administration of federal money and grant programs by the Law Enforcement Assistance Administration (LEAA) in the 1970s. These studies revealed that conceptual uncertainty of goals and strategies, lack of coordination, and distance between coordinating agencies resulted in distortion, misinterpretation, and "willful avoidance" of the national program ideals and strategies promoted by LEAA (Duffee, 1990; Feeley & Sarat, 1980; Gray & Williams, 1980). Feeley and Sarat (1980, 33) in their review of federal funding for LEAA law enforcement initiatives have cautioned: "The success and failure of a policy is determined, in the first instance, by the conceptual, technical, and political constraints within which the policy delivery system must work."

The new institutional theory perspective differs from the traditional in two important ways: (1) the source of organizational change and stability is primarily from a broad "organizational field" rather than the local level, and (2) the mechanism that influences organizational change and stability is maintenance of organizational legitimacy rather than constant improvement of technical efficiency and service delivery to meet customer or local demands (Crank & Langworthy, 1992; DiMaggio & Powell, 1983; Maguire & Mastrofski, 2000). New institutional theory proposes that an "organizational field" composed of organizations with similar purposes and goals and spanning many locales is a primary source that stimulates organizational change (DiMaggio & Powell, 1983; Scott, 1995). It follows that police department structures and operations are often the result of copying what other police departments are doing around the nation. Police are also influenced by the ideas of police professional organizations and national powers (Police Foundation, Police Executive Research Forum [PERF], International Association of Chiefs of Police [IACP], U.S. Department of Justice programs). Thus, police departments are part of a national field of like organizations with similar concerns that collectively exert a powerful influence over the direction of policing.

According to new institutional theory, if an organizational field is highly structured and cohesive, the national organizational field will have a greater influence on organizational change and operational strategies than the local technical environment of an organization (Kraatz & Zajac, 1996). In order to understand variation in community policing implementation across this nation, we must explore how the national policing field intersects with the local context of police departments, simultaneously creating a certain community policing style.

POLICE ORGANIZATIONAL RELATIONSHIPS

This chapter utilizes a similar perspective for understanding policing described by Langworthy and Travis (1998)—police department structures and operational strategies result from a "balance of forces."

Hence, a variety of relationship networks can influence urban policing forms (Crank & Langworthy, 1992; Maguire & Mastrofski, 2000). Ideas, norms, rules, laws, and resources generated by other organizations or institutions influence urban police departments (Crank & Langworthy, 1992). Urban police departments are also influenced by their own internal policies, culture, and leadership (Greene, Bergman, & McLaughlin, 1994; Guyot, 1991; Langworthy & Travis, 1998). This study proposes that there are three important relationship networks that influence the diffusion of community policing into different forms of implementation. These three networks are as follows:

1. *Centrist Level:* This level is concerned about the relationships between local police agencies and national and state organizations that have an influence over policing operations (e.g., legislatures, judiciary bodies, administrative bodies, professional policing organizations, university research). A good example of a centrist relationship in policing would be the link between a police department and services offered by the Office of Community Oriented Policing Services (COPS) run by the U.S. Department of Justice. The COPS program has been integrally involved in promoting the spread of community policing through the provision of financial and technical resources to thousands of local police departments (Office of Community Oriented Policing Services, 2001). The Police Executive Research Forum and the Police Foundation, which hold national conferences and publish policing research and training materials, are also examples of centrist influences on policing (Maguire & Mastrofski, 2000). An equally important centrist influence would be an organization's perception of a national trend among like organizations in their "organizational field" or "policy sector" (Scott, 1995). Thus, police departments may look to see what strategies other departments are implementing or stay abreast of the operations used by "cutting edge" departments.
2. *Local Level:* The important relationships in a police department's local context are relations with local political leaders, government agencies, businesses, and organized resident groups. It is important at this network level to understand how police department operations intersect with the urban vision and policy-making approaches of the city executive and his or her regime. Cities that strongly support neighborhood decision making and even offer monetary support to resident-based

neighborhood organizations are perhaps more likely to pressure police departments to engage in a community-building style of policing. In contrast, community policing in Seattle was an outgrowth of business and chamber of commerce pressures, not resident-based organizational pressures (Lyons, 1999).

3. *Internal Police Department Level:* The importance of internal police department influences on organizational change toward community policing is illustrated by Greene, Bergman, and McLaughlin (1994). They state, "Organizational adaptation in police bureaucracies has tended to be one way: the change efforts adapt to the organization, rather than the organization adapting to the intended change" (93). Based on their experiences with Philadelphia's move toward community policing, Greene et al. (1994, 93) suggest that the police internal culture will "greatly shape the success or failure of community policing implementation efforts." To understand police operational choices, it is important to examine the relationships between the chief of police and the city executive (mayor or city manager), and also the relations of the chief with the internal police culture, especially organized police unions or fraternal police organizations.

INSTITUTIONALIZING FORCES: MIMETIC, NORMATIVE, AND COERCIVE

Scott (1995) and DiMaggio and Powell (1983) describe three mechanisms (institutionalizing processes) that support or constrain organizational activities and influence organizational change and stability. These institutionalizing processes are as follows:

1. *Mimetic Forces:* Organizations, especially those in the same field, often mimic, copy, or imitate one another (Maguire & Mastrofski, 2000). Another term for such "copycat" behavior by organizations is "isomorphism" (DiMaggio & Powell, 1983). Organizations often change operational policies to mirror organizational models they perceive as superior or prevalent in their organizational field. In order to maintain organizational legitimacy, organizations often perceive a need to do what others are doing ("jump on the bandwagon"), especially when an organizational change is widely considered the "right" thing to do. Thus, police departments may develop a community

policing program because they recognize most other police departments are doing so. Imitating other organizations' operations is usually done with haste, often disregarding whether such operations are actually proven to produce desired outcomes or whether they are technically efficient activities (Mastrofski, 1998). Isomorphic organizational changes are often just symbolic gestures to look progressive and legitimate on the surface, with perhaps little substantive change occurring in actual implementation (Crank & Langworthy, 1992; Maguire & Mastrofski, 2000; Mastrofski, 1998). Thus, police organizations may appear to be doing community policing, but only on paper, on a website, or in a survey questionnaire. Mimetic forces are part of the new institutional theory perspective.

2. *Normative Forces:* Organizational structures, policies, and behaviors can be based on norms that define the proper social purposes (goals) of organizations and strictly prescribe the legitimate activities (means) needed to fulfill social purposes (Crank & Langworthy, 1992; Meyer & Rowan, 1977). Organizations in the same field will often create standards for themselves (Maguire & Mastrofski, 2000). An organization's conformity to norms and values that define proper organizational goals and means is based on the affective ties an organization develops with other organizations, not a fear of coercion or punishment (Scott, 1995). Sometimes, diverse organizations within the same locale can develop shared meanings and a collaborative purpose, thus feeling obliged to make organizational changes in accordance with such shared beliefs.
3. *Coercive Forces* (called "regulatory institutionalizing elements" by Scott [1995]): Coercive forces involve an organization's capacity to create rules and laws, monitor others' conformity, offer incentives, and impose sanctions when needed (Scott, 1995). Organizations that are attempting to stimulate change and conformity toward new (or old) operations exert coercive forces upon other organizations in hopes they will adopt or adhere to such operations. For example, police are offered numerous monetary incentives to innovate, implement new strategies, and change organizational structures (e.g., grant monies to hire community policing officers or to engage in crime mapping). Coercive forces can be effective in producing change because rational organizational leaders make decisions that will maintain organizational stability and avoid resource punishments or adverse publicity (Scott, 1995).

POLICE INSTITUTIONALIZING ENVIRONMENT

Figure 5.1 provides an illustration of the institutionalizing environment. Urban police organizations are embedded in multiple relationships involving centrist, local, and internal level forces. Each relationship network simultaneously influences the range of operational choices a police department can engage in by exerting mimetic, normative, or coercive institutionalizing forces. Police departments are offered incentives to engage in certain strategies and are constrained by rules, laws, and potential sanctions. The operational choices of police departments are also influenced by their desires for organizational legitimacy, their shared beliefs with other organizations, and their recognition of progressive ideas. Police responses to organizational influences can range from complete compliance, refusal, mirroring actions (isomorphism), negotiation, and adaptation to deception (Scott, 1995). In the next section of the chapter, propositions are developed that characterize institutional relationships that would foster strong police community building efforts by an urban police department.

PROPOSITIONS

Since the IACP meetings in 1893, the enactment of civil service laws, and increased federal funding for criminal justice, national and state organizations have utilized a variety of institutionalizing forces to stimulate change in urban police department operations and policies (Crank & Langworthy, 1992; Walker, 1977). For example, laws and court rulings have established regulations on police practices and behaviors (e.g., search and seizure, use of deadly force). Police departments are baited with a variety of technological and monetary resources/grants in exchange for applying new strategies and techniques of law enforcement (Feeley & Sarat, 1980; Gray & Williams, 1980). Experts and think tanks describe legitimate police goals and provide the training necessary for police departments to adopt new styles and missions (Crank & Langworthy, 1992). National and state interests can extend or withdraw political support and resources to police departments. Thus, a broader organizational field, which extends beyond the local environments of police departments, can influence the direction of policing.

Institutionalizing forces from national and state sources are not exclusively directed at influencing local policing. National and state institutionalizing forces also influence city governments, community organizations, and the characteristics of urban space. National and state efforts to promote urban renewal, model cities programs, revenue sharing, interstate highway construction, improved social services, and civil rights have had enormous impacts on urban politics and neighborhood

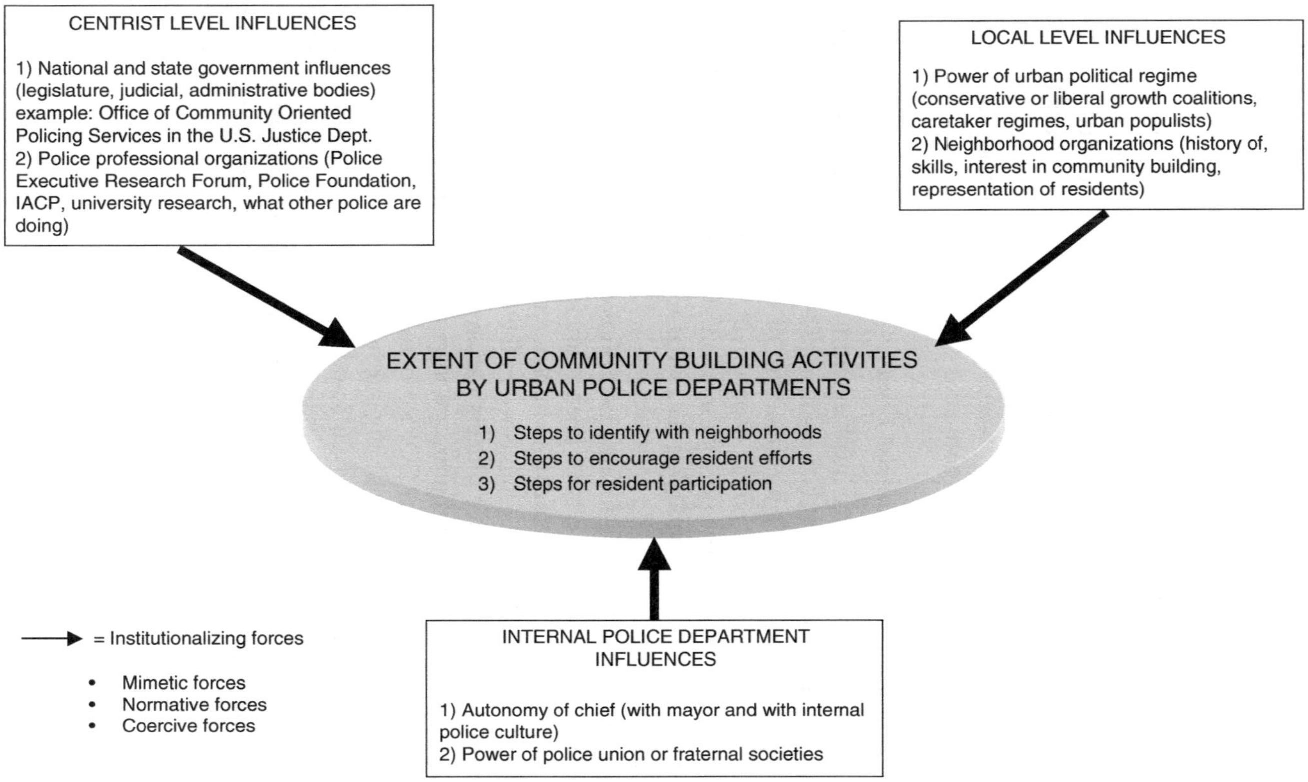

Figure 5.1 Police institutionalizing environment

environments (Judd & Swanstrom, 1998; Logan & Molotch, 1987). For example, the federal government in the 1950s and 1960s agreed that cities should become more accessible to the automobile age and thus funded massive highway construction programs, which unfortunately displaced large minority populations that were in the path of the highways (Jacobs, 1961; Judd & Swanstrom, 1998). In the late 1960s, the federal government felt that cities should tap the knowledge and expertise of citizens for improved public service delivery so it funded the Model Cities Program (Warren, Rose, & Bergunder, 1974). A variety of historic policies have shaped the physical and social environments that police operate in, and new centrist-level policies will continue to shape the police operational environment.

Centrist-Level Influences

To understand how police involvement in community building can be connected to centrist institutionalizing forces, two important linkages should be explored: (1) the structure of current financial incentives that directly connect a police department to national and state funding sources; and (2) the policy direction and influence of the broader organizational field of policing (i.e., what are "legitimate" police organizations doing?).

Since passage of the federal 1994 Violent Crime Control and Law Enforcement Act, there have been numerous financial incentives for municipal police departments to implement community policing. As of November 2001, COPS, established in the 1994 Crime Act, had funded more than 100,000 police officers nationwide. Officers funded by the COPS universal hiring program are supposed to be engaged in community policing activities. The COPS program has also supported a variety of local problem-solving policing partnerships. In order to understand the potential influence that COPS and other centrist funding agencies could have on police department involvement in community building, the following links need to be examined: (1) the level of monetary input from national/state funding agencies relative to a department's total budget; (2) the amount of expert guidance and training in community policing received as a result of the grant; (3) the clarity of community policing goals and strategies and their connection to community building activities; and (4) the intensity of oversight mechanisms regarding the use of grant monies.

There is a general consensus that community policing still lacks conceptual clarity regarding its goals and strategies (Maguire & Mastrofski, 2000; Zhao, Lovrich, & Thurman, 1999). In fact, national survey data by Zhao et al. (1999) show that departmental confusion over what community policing actually means is one of the highest-rated community policing implementation impediments reported by police chiefs. Confusion over the meaning of community policing remained a consistently expressed impediment across two waves of surveys in 1993 and 1996 (Zhao et al., 1999, 86). Can we therefore expect community policing to be the same everywhere? There is no contractual language in COPS universal hiring grants that describes how much community policing must be accomplished in a month or whether community policing must aggressively adhere to a community building style. Therefore, strong police–community building efforts are likely caused by interactions/coordination with neighborhood organizations and city organizations knowledgeable and supportive of community building processes and not as a result of federal guidance.

According to resource dependency theory ("old" institutional theory), organizations that provide the bulk of a target agency's resources are more likely to engineer an organizational change (Gray & Williams, 1980). A rational organization will first and foremost appease organizations or clients that have the most influence over organizational resources (Gray & Williams, 1980). Most urban police department budgets are overwhelmingly locally funded; thus, their organizational policies (especially intensity of implementation) are more likely to be influenced by local politics (Gifford, 1999; Scheingold, 1991). Given that police department budgets are dominated by local funding sources and there exists little national guidance on how (and to what extent) police should help build community capacity in neighborhoods, high levels of community building by urban police will be largely determined by the structure of the local political context and relationships internal to police departments.

The phenomenon of local refraction or filtering of federally supported policies to fit the local policing environment suggests the following propositions regarding variation in police community building:

Proposition A: A lack of conceptual clarity in the goals, strategies, and activities of community policing provides an opportunity for the local political economy and internal police processes to reinterpret, misinterpret, or add idiosyncratic touches to community policing operations. In addition, since municipal police department budgets are almost exclusively locally funded, their operations are more likely to be tied to the agenda of the local political context rather than the paper ideals of their centrist funding sources. (see similar propositions by Crank and Langworthy (1992) and Maguire and Mastrofski (2000). Therefore, this chapter proposes that strong police community building efforts are more likely the result of influences from local and internal police department dynamics ("old" institutional theory), rather than the influences of centrist forces ("new" institutional theory).

Such a proposition does not mean that centrist institutionalizing forces have had no influence on police involvement in community building; they have had a tremendous influence (at least on the surface). Police across this nation report the implementation of a number of community building activities (e.g., opening storefront stations, attending community meetings, increasing resident input into problem identification) (Hickman & Reaves, 1999; Maguire & Mastrofski, 2000; Zhao et al., 1999). Thus, there is some evidence of isomorphism toward a community building style of policing.[4] In the broader organizational field of policing, implementing community policing is considered a very legitimate operational choice. This chapter proposes that the national trend toward reported widespread involvement in community policing is more symbolic and the dosage of community policing implementation, especially a strong community building style, is very weak in many urban places (Crank & Langworthy, 1992; Manning, 1988).

Proposition B: Centrist forces have influenced police departments to copy other departments' operations and experiment with many community policing components, some of which are related to community building. Police departments are experimenting with storefront stations, distributing neighborhood newsletters, and attending community meetings because such activities are considered legitimate and common in the broader policing field. Centrist forces only have the power to influence the experimentation with some community building components in urban locales. High levels of police community building are related to certain types of local contexts and internal police dynamics.

LOCAL-LEVEL INFLUENCES

Police departments are also influenced by their relationships within a local interorganizational system (Crank & Langworthy, 1992). Local relationships may solicit, reinforce, and often demand a particular style of policing. The relations between police and the local mayor/city manager are the most common political linkages recognized in policing literature (Andrews, 1985; Fogelson, 1977; Fraser, 1985; Hudnut, 1985; Murphy, 1985; Walker, 1977). This section proposes that local influence on police department operations is based upon the strength of a dominant political coalition, how the dominant coalition values urban space, and the strength of resident-based neighborhood organizations.

How Should Urban Space Be Valued? Exchange vs. Use Value

A common policy and political dilemma continually challenges city administrators in America: with an expanding world economy and mobile market, how can cities remain competitive with other cities and suburbs to maintain current economic investment and ensure future growth and stability, while satisfying residents' needs and securing a healthy fiscal balance (Judd & Swanstrom, 1998; Swanstrom, 1985)? A theory of growth politics has developed to explain the varied responses by city administrations to this continual dilemma (Logan & Molotch, 1987; Swanstrom, 1985). At the core of growth politics theory is the understanding of how urban space is valued. Urban space is composed of different elements: land, natural resources, transportation systems, buildings, commerce, housing, neighborhoods, and residents. City administrators can value these urban elements in terms of their worth in an exchange relationship (exchange value) and improving profitability of urban space (Logan & Molotch, 1987; Stoecker, 1994; Swanstrom, 1985). City administrations concerned with improving the exchange value of urban space coordinate with supporters (speculators, developers, city council, zoning boards, banks) to implement political strategies and policies that support urban development approaches that "increase the chances of further commodifying urban land and infrastructure toward making profit" (Stoecker, 1994, 11). An example of an exchange value project would be supporting the construction of high-density apartment units in neighborhoods, which allow landlords to make more profit by bringing in more residents, yet increase anonymity and congestion.

Alternatively, city administrators may value urban elements in terms of their "usefulness in providing services, sustenance, and quality of life" (use value) (Stoecker, 1994, 11). City administrations concerned with use values coordinate with supporters (neighborhoods, city council, zoning boards, environmental or social activist groups) to implement urban development strategies that preserve urban land, infrastructures, and policies that contribute to the convenience of neighborhood residents' daily round (Logan & Molotch, 1987; Stoecker, 1994). A use value orientation by a city government is concerned with supporting residents and neighborhoods and ameliorating the costs of urban growth. A use value project would support the construction of low-density apartment units with playgrounds and increased public green space (e.g., parks) in neighborhoods. The advocates of exchange value policies are often in opposition to the advocates of use value policies.

Growth Politics and Institutional Theory

Although it appears this study is introducing a new theory, there are some strong similarities between theories of growth politics and institutional theory. It is arguable that theories of growth politics are really applications of institutional theory (Clingermayer & Feiock, 2001). In other words, theories of growth politics explain the sources, both individual and organizational, that influence urban change and the mechanisms by which urban space is rearranged over time. Theories of growth politics use institutional theory language. For example, growth politics focuses on the power (coercive, normative, and mimetic influences) and coalition building used by city administrations to carry out their vision for urban growth and stability. City administrators need the help of other organizations and constituents to establish ordinances, laws, standards, resources, publicity, norms, and symbols in order to develop urban space or maintain quality neighborhoods (Logan & Molotch, 1987; Stoecker, 1994; Swanstrom, 1985). Urban growth coalitions, which have the power to influence policing resources, may pressure police departments to change operations to be complementary with the urban policy agenda. The ways in which the urban growth coalition values urban space, either toward exchange or use values, will influence the range of policing strategies and operations considered locally legitimate.

TYPES OF URBAN GROWTH COALITIONS AND COMMUNITY POLICING

At a local level, the key to understanding variation in police community building is (1) to examine the dominant type of urban growth coalition and its strength; (2) examine the connection between the police department and the agenda of the urban growth coalition; and (3) examine how neighborhoods, organized or not, fit into local growth politics.

Todd Swanstrom (1985) has outlined a typology of urban growth coalitions based on their growth politics (exchange vs. use value interest) and strategies. The dominant urban growth coalitions found in American cities are labeled conservative growth coalitions, liberal growth coalitions, caretaker regimes, and urban populists (Swanstrom, 1985). Logan, Whaley, and Crowder (1997) advocate a need for increased research on the social consequences—such as disparities in police and fire protection between and within cities, gaps between rich and poor neighborhoods, and racial segregation—that can be connected to different types of urban growth coalitions. This study proposes that the policies and values of specific types of growth coalitions are more likely to support and foster strong police community building initiatives.

The remainder of this section will detail Swanstrom's (1985) four growth coalition types and their potential influence on policing operations. The section ends with a discussion of how neighborhoods fit into growth politics and policing strategy.

The Conservative Growth Coalition and Community Policing

Conservative coalitions stimulate urban growth through promotion of the following exchange value strategies: intensification of land usage, increasing rent levels, increasing tax base, tax abatement for corporations, cutting utility costs for corporations, and decreasing social service budgets. Exchange value strategies often require "risky" investment projects and policies that put all neighborhoods of the city in jeopardy or increase "collective liability" (Swanstrom, 1985). Conservative growth coalitions argue that risky investment projects and policies are necessary to remain competitive in today's mobile economy. They believe that future benefits of these investments will trickle down to all city residents, who are left out of such decision-making arenas (Logan & Molotch, 1987).

The key characteristic that separates the conservative growth coalition from the liberal growth coalition is the level of confidence placed in the belief that all increased economic activity and investment will eventually benefit every city resident and neighborhood (Logan & Molotch, 1987; Swanstrom, 1985). The conservative growth coalition will cut city and social services and lower taxes to attract or maintain corporate investment. Instead, the liberal growth coalition believes it must improve urban livability, which requires the enhancement of public services and taxes, in order to attract or maintain corporate investment. The liberal coalition recognizes urban growth often translates into costs for certain urban neighborhoods and residents (Swanstrom, 1985).

In contrast to liberal coalitions, the policy development process of conservative coalitions is typified by a small, tight-knit group of professional politicians, bureaucrats, and investors (Swanstrom, 1985). The conservative coalition attempts to ensure government actions and decisions are streamlined and efficient. Centralizing and "trimming" the decision-making processes over urban development translates into less recognition of the specific needs of urban neighborhoods and residents.

Police efforts to identify with neighborhoods, encourage resident efforts, and increase resident participation/representation (i.e., community building) appear antithetical to the values of conservative growth coalitions. A city administration concerned with governmental efficiency and tight centralization does not mix well with increased community participation and decentralized decision making. Therefore, the following proposition is made:

Proposition C: Police steps to identify with neighborhoods, encourage resident efforts, and promote resident decision making will be uncommon and poorly developed (weak dosage) in conservative growth cities. The local legitimacy of engaging in such community building processes by a police department would be suspect and perhaps threatening to a conservative regime. Ultimately, there are more incentives for police administrators to adopt the centralized decision-making values of the conservative regime.

Urban growth projects initiated by conservative coalitions generally target the central business district (CBD), CBD-adjacent land, and wealthy residential areas located within city boundaries (Swanstrom, 1985). "Community policing" in conservative growth coalition cities is likely to include zero-tolerance enforcement within the CBD and its border neighborhoods. For example, the presence of a highly transient population and panhandlers in the CBD district would be considered a threat to city commuters and local businesses, thus requiring a quick removal or sanction by police. Such a strategy may be considered a successful partnership between police and local business. Police departments in conservative growth cities are likely to utilize problem-solving activities (e.g., hot-spot analysis) that don't require extensive citizen involvement, but do produce increased arrests, crackdowns, stings, and patrol in target areas. Such tactics would be publicized and supported by growth coalition leaders in order to show the city's no-nonsense approach to crime, protecting urban investors and business commuters.

Proposition D: Policing in conservative growth cities is more likely to include strategies and/or special units for identifying high problem areas and using aggressive, traditional law enforcement tactics that increase arrests. These activities would be classified as part of the department's community policing strategy.

There are no incentives for police departments to become a strong wedge between use value–oriented neighborhoods, especially feisty ones, and a conservative political regime. Police departments in conservative coalition cities will not ignore neighborhoods, but may stress that neighborhoods are the source of crime and advocate for residents to increase their reporting of crimes. The community partnership role stressed by police in conservative coalition cities would entail being the police's "eyes and ears" on the street and reporting all disturbances. Emphasizing such a community role conceals the broader political and economic forces impacting neighborhood crime and may not help foster the type of community capacity needed for revitalizing poverty-stricken neighborhoods and addressing root causes of crime (Duffee, Fluellen, & Roscoe, 1999). Police partnership efforts are more likely to occur with homeowners, businesses associations, and chambers of commerce, who will embrace community policing as a method of increasing property values and commerce, and to keep undesirables out of the neighborhood (Crank & Langworthy, 1992; Lyons, 1999; Skogan, 1990). In the short term, community policing may be perceived as useful by conservative growth coalitions because it can provide extra policing funds and political relief (e.g., announcing a new program that will address crime).

Proposition E: Police community building activities occurring in conservative coalition cities are more likely to happen in predominately homeowner neighborhoods and business districts. The scope of community policing activities in these cities will be narrow. Activities will be primarily focused upon increasing crime reporting and target hardening. Police are not likely to be involved in noncrime issues and will not actively encourage broader resident participation and decision making.

The Liberal Growth Coalition and Community Policing

The primary difference between the conservative and liberal growth coalition is how each goes about the process of urban development (Swanstrom, 1985). Liberal growth coalitions will devote extensive time to planning growth projects and researching the potential costs of development and growth (Swanstrom, 1985). This sense of responsibility pushes liberal growth coalitions to accommodate collaborative decision making with neighborhoods on growth projects. The degree of neighborhood–government consultation will be dependent on the strength of neighborhood organizations and their pressure for involvement. Neighborhood organizations in liberal growth coalition cities may actually be funded by the city. In general, a liberal coalition city will embrace more use value concerns and attempt to sustain neighborhood livability. Development projects in liberal growth cities may include enhancing public green spaces, protecting and promoting unique neighborhood characteristics, improving public transportation and schools, and aiding less prosperous residents. The liberal growth coalition must persuade investors/partners that quality public services produce competent laborers, reduce neighborhood tensions, and increase the attractiveness of the city—not just higher taxes (Logan & Molotch, 1987; Swanstrom, 1985). Public services can be maintained by keeping risky investment strategies to a minimum (few tax or utility breaks for corporations), garnering federal and state grant monies for urban redevelopment projects, and seeking voluntary contributions to provide aid to economically disadvantaged areas (Stoecker, 1994; Swanstrom, 1985).

Since police department budgets are primarily locally funded, departments in strong liberal growth coalition cities are likely to share the dominant political concern for extensive neighborhood planning, improving neighborhood livability (especially enhancing the use value of space), and providing quality public services.

Proposition F: Community policing in liberal growth cities is more likely to be characterized by strong efforts to identify with neighborhoods, encourage resident efforts, and increase resident participation in decision making (i.e., community building). Police-community partnerships in liberal growth cities are more likely to respond to social issues outside of traditional law enforcement and involve extensive coordination efforts involving social service agencies, businesses, schools, faith-based groups, and neighborhood organizations. Thus, the scope of community policing activities is more likely to address broader social issues.

Police community building efforts in liberal coalition cities are more likely to involve numerous organizations with diverse interests and specialties. Unfortunately, such broad and complex coordination may cause intense conflict and slow implementation ("too many cooks in the kitchen"). The coordination of multiple organizations always sounds good in theory, yet unintentional consequences often occur in practice. Evidence from the Model Cities Program revealed that attempts at increasing resident collaboration are often resisted by entrenched public service agencies (Warren et al., 1974). Neighborhood organizations can easily become co-opted into the "clientelism" philosophy of public service organizations, at the expense of broad resident participation (Stoecker, 1994). Often, the representation of neighborhoods in broad coordination efforts is trivial (Hallman, 1984; Judd & Swanstrom, 1998).

Proposition G: Community policing in liberal coalition cities that lack the strong neighborhood organizations, which would fight for broad resident participation and decision-making powers, will be characterized by a "service-provider" mentality. Efforts will be made to bring to neighborhood residents a wide variety of programs and services carried out by professional service organizations, as opposed to developing grassroots programs and strategies carried out by residents. These partnerships are not likely to be characterized by creative problem-solving processes, but are efforts to use, expand, and protect existing programs.

Caretaker Regimes, Urban Populism, and Community Policing

The final types of local political coalitions, caretaker and urban populist regimes, are less likely to develop a strong presence in urban politics. Caretaker regimes are similar to the political machines that dominated urban governance from the mid-1800s to World War II, yet rarely occur today (Judd & Swanstrom, 1998; Swanstrom, 1985). Caretaker regimes tend to be antigrowth; their only concern is meeting the needs of the constituency that brought them into power (Haller, 1976; Swanstrom, 1985). In today's modern economy and complex urban environment, caretaker regimes are more likely to occur in small towns or university towns (Judd & Swanstrom, 1998). Caretaker regimes tend to provide low-quality services to their constituents, yet public services are more informal and personal in contrast to large bureaucratic institutions (Judd & Swanstrom, 1998). As long as the interests of mobile corporate wealth in a city can coexist with the interests of the caretaker regime and the service needs of voters are maintained, a caretaker regime may develop and stay in power (Swanstrom, 1985).

The traditional police department in a caretaker regime city works closely with the representatives of the political party and is integrally involved in addressing all public service needs of residents (Fogelson, 1977; Haller, 1976; Judd & Swanstrom, 1998). Thus, policing in caretaker regimes will exhibit strong neighborhood identification. Police–neighborhood identification would not entail encouragement of collective action or organizing, but would entail listening to residents' personal problems. Caretaker regimes are always accessible to hear residents' problems, which translates into votes (Grondahl, 1997). The goal of increasing resident participation in broad policy decisions or urban planning is foreign to caretaker regimes and their police departments; city services are already very personal. The biggest problems for caretaker regimes are appeasing local capital interests and maintaining a solid urban infrastructure. Caretaker regimes are often reluctant to apply for grants from state or federal agencies, which require oversight. Caretaker cities are unlikely to respond to centrist institutionalizing forces that attempt to mold the direction of policing (Grondahl, 1997).

Urban populist parties are also a rare occurrence in cities today. The recent resurgence of urban populist parties was set off by the loss of manufacturing jobs, loss of family farms, civil rights movements, and religious movements (Boyte, 1986). According to Boyte (1986, 8), "Populism is a language of inheritance. It grows from a sense of aggrieved 'peoplehood.'" Urban populist leaders are known for their rousing speeches that attempt to expose the bald political reality of society. Common populist spins exclaim how politicians and corporations are duping the American worker, or how American culture has lost its moral foothold. Urban populism thrives on the creation of belief systems through which urban problems should be viewed. Unlike conservative and liberal growth coalitions, urban populist parties are generally unable to develop strong coalitions of partner organizations and institutionalizing power in order to implement their urban agendas (Swanstrom, 1985).

Swanstrom's (1985) analysis of Mayor Dennis Kucinich's urban populist movement in Cleveland in the late 1970s illustrates how an overly boisterous urban populist party can garner the popular vote, but quickly enrages necessary political and economic allies. Without the support of banks, corporations, the legislature, and police, the populist party, which advertised the abuses of power by these same institutions, was eventually voted out of office at the next election. Voters eventually perceived more harm than good being wrought because the populist party couldn't get anything accomplished (Swanstrom, 1985).

If other urban institutions and key urban figures do not back a populist party, it is unlikely the party will be able to influence police strategies. The typical urban populist platform, which spotlights accountability of governance to citizen needs, would appear to favor many aspects of police community building, especially neighborhood decision making.

If the local police have already gravitated toward a community policing strategy, the connection to an urban populist party may generate exemplary community building activities. It is more likely, though, that the police are a target of populist rhetoric, and would therefore support antipopulist political parties.

Neighborhood Organization and Community Policing

Neighborhood organizing efforts can differ in the attention given to community building (Cortes, 1993; Hess, 1999; Stoecker, 1994). Thus, not every neighborhood organizing initiative aggressively attempts to build community, broaden resident participation, and train future resident leaders (Renauer, 2000; Stoecker, 1994). For example, Weingart, Hartmann, and Osborne's review of community antidrug efforts reports (1994, 12), "Citizens do not always aspire to create robust and long-lasting institutions." Therefore, a neighborhood's existing community capacity and interest in community building will impact the level of police community building likely to occur in that neighborhood.

Proposition H: Organized neighborhoods, led by community building activists, are more likely to resist co-optation by police and other service agencies. These neighborhoods will struggle for an increased resident influence over the types of crime prevention strategies implemented in the neighborhood. Police departments may learn how to better identify with neighborhoods, encourage resident efforts, and increase participation from these organizations. The power of neighborhood organization influence over the direction of policing strategies will improve if neighborhoods form cross-neighborhood coalitions.

INTERNAL DEPARTMENT INFLUENCES

Despite all the external institutionalizing forces that impact police departments, the internal actions and beliefs of police leaders, police subcultures, and police associations are equally critical components in shaping police behavior and organizational structure (Andrews, 1985; Bouza, 1985; Crank & Langworthy, 1992; Fraser, 1985; Greene et al., 1994; Jacobs, 1985). This section will examine two important relationships vital to the formation and implementation of policing operations. The first relationship is between the chief of police and the city executive (mayor or city manager). The second is the influence of police unions or associations on the direction and implementation of police operations.

The Police Chief and the City Executive

The independence and creative power of police chiefs exist in an unwritten, informal, political, and invisible state of nature (Andrews, 1985). Sometimes, city executives specifically inform police chiefs to take free rein over department structures, operations, and policies necessary to get the job done (Murphy, 1985).[5] The relationships between police chiefs and city executives can also be tenuous and arbitrary, and may change according to political, economic, and crime emergencies (Andrews, 1985). There are arguments for the complete independence of police chiefs from the city executive branch (Andrews, 1985) and arguments for strong cooperation between police and city executives in order to successfully accomplish all urban policies (Hudnut, 1985). In order to link the influence of a city's growth politics to policing operations, research must better understand the negotiations and shared values between police chiefs and city executives regarding the autonomy of chiefs and the role of policing within broad urban agendas.

Murphy (1985) provides a list of issues concerning the role of police chiefs and their autonomy. The following are Murphy's (1985) examples of negotiable issues: What is the role of the mayor and chief regarding media relations? Can the chief go directly to the mayor even when there is not a crisis? What are the lines of authority between the chief and the city's budget office regarding the police budget? Who decides personnel additions and changes—is the mayor allowed input? Who has ultimate control over discipline? Can there be a contract with the chief for a set number of years of employment? Does the mayor have any role in the deployment of personnel and organization of the agency? Gathering accurate information about the history of these issues within an urban setting and on the ability (or lack) of the police chief to negotiate with the city executive on these issues is integral to understanding the development of police structures, operations, and policies (Murphy, 1985).

Police chiefs with set contracts and strong autonomy over operations are less likely to feel the overriding pressure to structure police operations to be consistent with the growth agenda of the city. If there is strong police autonomy in a conservative growth city, the chances of intense police community building efforts are improved if the chief is attracted to such a style of policing. A reverse situation could happen in a liberal growth city, where an autonomous chief could maintain a more law enforcement–oriented and centralized style of policing in operation.

Proposition I: Police chiefs with set contracts and given free rein by city executives will not feel the overriding pressure to structure police operations to be consistent with the growth agenda of the city. These chiefs will follow their own vision and agenda for policing or adhere to an agenda consistent with the internal culture of the department.

Police Culture, Police Unions, and Collective Bargaining

Regardless of how a chief is connected to the city politics, if the chief is unable to garner support from top police administrators and middle managers, any community policing activities may be carried out in a haphazard or "loosely coupled" manner. Greene et al. (1994) feel the influence of the internal police culture, which is often organized in unions and associations, is the most important impediment to organizational change.

One of the major challenges to police administrators is dealing with police unions or associations and collective bargaining policies (Walker, 1977). Police unions have spread across the nation at a varied pace, and most are generally distinct from one another (Bouza, 1985). Unions negotiate for patrol officers on employment contracts and specific grievances (Bouza, 1985).

Efforts to change policing operations in Philadelphia toward community policing were strongly opposed by the police officers' bargaining unit, the Fraternal Order of Police, which resisted virtually all attempts at personnel changes (Greene, Bergman, & McLaughlin, 1994). Police union reaction to greater resident involvement and decision making has also consistently been one of repugnance (Bouza, 1985; Walker, 1977). Local movements that have advocated civilian review boards and the introduction of volunteer or civilian officers have been strongly resisted by police unions (Bouza, 1985; Perez, 1994; Walker, 1977). To engage in effective community building, police may have to work flexible hours, use different modes of patrol, attend community meetings, and be isolated from other officers. These are the same operational issues that many police unions have effectively addressed with institutionalized department policies.

Proposition J: Strong efforts by police to identify with neighborhoods, encourage resident efforts, and increase resident participation are not likely to occur when there are restrictive policies regarding officer duties and attendance at off-duty community meetings/events. Community building efforts will be hampered and short-lived if police–neighborhood collaborations are based exclusively upon overtime for officer involvement in such activities. Strong union cities are more likely to have small community policing subunits composed of volunteer or new recruit officers funded by grant monies and focused on small target areas.

CONCLUSION

Hagan (1989) argues that criminal justice theory would advance by seeking to predict where and when the couplings between policy goals and quality application would loosen or tighten. A fruitful avenue for this theory development is in the community policing area. Community policing is a sufficiently ambiguous and wide-ranging strategy, thus allowing several configurations or styles of implementation to occur. One potential style could involve strong police community building efforts that seek to identify with neighborhoods, encourage resident efforts, and develop broad resident participation and representation. This chapter proposes that the balance of institutionalizing forces (coercive, normative, mimetic) from centrist, local, and internal levels will determine the extent of police community building in urban neighborhoods (see Figure 5.1). Institutional theory is used to describe the characteristics of institutionalizing relationships that are likely to support a certain style of policing operation—police community building.

The propositions developed earlier suggest intense police community building is more likely to develop in liberal growth coalition cities, where there are organized neighborhoods concerned about community building and support from police chiefs and internal police cultures. This chapter argues that the causes of police–community building are primarily from local-level influences within a police department's immediate task environment and constituency. Local-level and internal police department influences are more powerful because they have more severe impacts on police resources and organizational flexibility, and certain local forces are more experienced with community building. Centrist-level influences ("new" institutional theory) can push police departments to experiment with police community building activities, but ultimately, the strength and direction of local and internal influences ("old" institutional theory) will impact the extent of police community building actually carried out.

By understanding the various institutionalizing relationships influencing urban community policing implementation, we can learn more about the obstacles, resistances, and achievements of community policing as a national movement and as a local project (Crank & Langworthy, 1992). If these forces do influence community policing implementation toward (or away from) strong community building, there are important policy implications.

Since no data are presented here, it can only be hypothesized what the potential policy implications of research that may support such a theory of community policing variation would be. If centrist, local, or internal police forces advocate one form of community policing over another, they should be interested in such theoretical research. In point of fact, research on the balance of forces perspective presented here would point out where constraints against a desired policing agenda would occur and where certain policies could take a firm hold, thus decreasing the chances of a decoupling phenomenon or weak implementation. For students of criminal justice, recognition of the potential refraction and adaptation of criminal justice policies at the local level is an important lesson to take into their careers. Public pronouncements, websites, and training manuals do not have the institutionalizing power to translate criminal justice policies into aggressive, quality implementations everywhere—many other factors come into play.

The research propositions presented here are integrally tied to a need for measuring the extent to which police departments engage in community building (see Duffee et al., 2002). This chapter did not arbitrarily choose to explore why policing may involve more or less community building in neighborhoods. Community building is theoretically linked to the development of community capacity and hence long-term impacts on community safety and livability. It would behoove criminal justice research to explore not only where police community building is more likely to be manifested, but also its connection to long-term public safety improvements.

NOTES

1. This chapter was made possible by the Police Community Interaction Project supported by Grant No. 97–IJ–CX–0052 awarded by the National Institute of Justice, Office of Justice Programs, U.S. Department of Justice. Points of view in this chapter are those of the author and do not necessarily represent the official position or policies of the U.S. Department of Justice.
2. From *Police for the Future* by D.H. Bayley, 1994. By permission of Oxford University Press, Inc.
3. We liken community capacity to "social capital" and "collective efficacy." All three concepts are concerned with social processes that increase the likelihood of residents engaging in social action for the common good of their community. Despite the basic similarity, all three concepts focus on

slightly different social processes, and different measurement techniques have been used to indicate each (Renauer & Scott, 2001).

4. Evidence of community policing involvement from national surveys may be tainted or lack validity because some surveys were tied to funding applications (Maguire & Mastrofski, 2000).
5. Murphy (1985) states that this is the exception rather than the rule.

REFERENCES

Andrews, A.H. 1985. Structuring the political independence of the police chief. In *Police leadership in America: Crisis and opportunity*, ed. W.A. Geller (pp. 5–19). Chicago: American Bar Foundation; New York: Praeger.

Bayley, D.H.1994. *Police for the future*, New York: Oxford University Press.

Bennett, S.F. 1998. Community organizations and crime. In *Community justice: An emerging field*, ed. D. Karp (pp. 31–46). Lanham, MD: Rowman & Littlefield.

Bouza, A.V. 1985. Police unions: Paper tigers or roaring lions? In *Police leadership in America: Crisis and opportunity*, ed. W.A. Geller (pp. 241–80). Chicago: American Bar Foundation; New York: Praeger

Boyte, H.C. 1986. Introduction. In The New Populism: The politics of empowerment, eds. H.C. Boyte and F. Riessman (pp. 1–10). Philadelphia: Temple University Press.

Cardarelli, A.P., J. McDevitt, and K. Baum. 1998. The rhetoric and reality of community policing in small and medium-sized cities and towns. *Policing: An International Journal of Police Strategies & Management* 21(3): 397–415.

Clingermayer, J.C., and R.C. Feiock. 1991. The adoption of economic development policies by large cities: A test of economic, interest groups, and institutional explanations. *Policy Studies Journal* 18(3): 539–52.

Cortes, E. 1993. Reweaving the fabric: The iron rule and the IAF strategy for dealing with poverty through power and politics. Working Paper No. 56, Center for Urban Policy Research, Rutgers University.

Crank, J.P. and R.H. Langworthy. 1992. An institutional perspective of policing. *The Journal of Criminal Law and Criminology* 83: 338–63.

DeLeon-Granados, W. 1999. *Travels through crime and place.* Boston: Northeastern University Press.

DiMaggio, P., and W.W. Powell. 1983. The iron cage revisited: Institutionalized isomorphism and collective rationality in organizational fields. *American Sociological Review* 48: 147–60.

Duffee, D.E.1990. *Explaining criminal justice: Community theory and criminal justice reform.* Prospect Heights, IL: Waveland Press.

Duffee, D.E. 1996. Working with communities. In *Community policing in a rural setting*, eds. Q. Thurman and E. McGarrell (pp. 85–96). Cincinnati: Anderson.

Duffee, D.E., R. Fluellen, and B. Renauer. 1999. Community variables in community policing. *Police Quarterly* 2: 5–35.

Duffee, D.E., R. Fluellen, and T. Roscoe. 1999. Constituency building and urban community policing. In *Measuring what matters: Proceedings from the policing research institute meetings*, ed. R.H. Langworthy (pp. 91–119). Washington, D.C.: U.S. Department of Justice, National Institute of Justice.

Duffee, D.E., J.D. Scott, B.C. Renauer, S. Chermak, and E.F. McGarrell. 2002. *Measuring community building involving the police: The final research report of the police-community interaction project*. Washington, D.C.: U.S. Department of Justice, National Institute of Justice.

Feeley, M.M., and A. Sarat. 1980. *The policy dilemma: Federal crime policy and the Law Enforcement Assistance Administration*. Minneapolis: University of Minnesota Press.

Fogelson, R.M. 1977. *Big-city police*, Cambridge, MA: Harvard University Press.

Fraser, D.M. 1985. Politics and police leadership: The view from city hall. In *Police leadership in America: Crisis and opportunity*, ed. W.A. Geller (pp. 41–7). Chicago: American Bar Foundation; New York: Praeger.

Giacomazzi, A.L, E. McGarrell, and Q. Thurman. 1998. Reducing disorder, fear, and crime in public housing: An evaluation of a drug crime elimination program in Spokane, Washington. Final Report submitted to the National Institute of Justice.

Gifford, L.S. 1999. *Justice expenditures and employment in the United States 1995*. Washington, D.C.: U.S. Department of Justice, Bureau of Justice Statistics.

Gray, V., and B. Williams. 1980. *The organizational politics of criminal justice: Policy in context*. Lexington, MA: Lexington Books.

Greene, J.R., W.T. Bergman, and E.J. McLaughlin. 1994. Implementing community policing: Cultural and structural change in police organizations. In *The challenge of community policing: Testing the promise*, ed. D.P. Rosenbaum (pp. 92–109). Newbury Park, CA: Sage.

Grondahl, P. 1997. *Mayor Erastus Corning: Albany icon, Albany enigma*. Albany, NY: Washington Park Press.

Guyot, D. 1991. *Policing as though people matter*. Philadelphia: Temple University Press.

Hagan, J. 1989. Why is there so little criminal justice theory? Neglected macro- and micro-level links between organization and power. *Journal of Research in Crime and Delinquency* 26: 116–35.

Haller, M.H. 1976. Civic reformers and the police. In *Police in urban society*, ed. H. Hahn (pp. 39–56). Beverly Hills, CA: Sage.

Hallman, H.W. 1984. *Neighborhoods: Their place in urban life*. Beverly Hills, CA: Sage.

Hess, D.R. 1999. Community organizing, building, and developing: Their relationship to comprehensive community initiatives. Paper presented on COMM-ORG: The On-Line Conference on Community Organizing and Development. Available from: http://comm-org.wisc.edu/papers99/hesscontents.htm

Hickman, M.J., and B.A. Reaves. 1999. *Local police departments 1999*. Washington, D.C.: U.S. Department of Justice, Office of Justice Programs, Bureau of Justice Statistics.

Hudnut, W.H. 1985. The police and the polis: A mayor's perspective. In *Police leadership in America: Crisis and opportunity*, ed. W.A. Geller (pp. 20–29). Chicago: American Bar Foundation; New York: Praeger.

Jacobs, J. 1961. *The death and life of great American cities*. New York: Random House.

Jacobs, J.B. 1985. Police unions: How they look from the academic side. In *Police leadership in America: Crisis and opportunity*, ed. W.A. Geller (pp. 286–90). Chicago: American Bar Foundation; New York: Praeger.

Judd, D.R., and Swanstrom, T. 1998. *City politics: Private power and public policy*, 2nd ed. Reading, MA: Addison-Wesley.

Kelling, G., and K. Coles. 1996. *Fixing broken windows: Restoring order and reducing crime in our communities*. New York: Free Press.

Kraatz, M.S., and E.J. Zajac. 1996. Exploring the limits of the new institutionalism: The causes and consequences of illegitimate organizational change. *American Sociological Review* 61: 812–36.

Langworthy, R.H. and L.F. Travis. 1998. *Policing in America: A balance of forces*, 2nd ed. Upper Saddle River, NJ: Prentice-Hall.

Logan, J.R., and H. Molotch. 1987. *Urban fortunes: The political economy of place*. Berkeley: University of California Press.

Logan, J.R., R. Whaley, and K. Crowder. 1997. The character and consequences of growth regimes: An assessment of 20 years of research. *Urban Affairs Review* 32(5): 603–30.

Lyons, W. 1999. *The politics of community policing: Rearranging the power to punish*. Ann Arbor: University of Michigan Press.

Maguire, E.R., J.B. Kuhns, C.D. Uchida, and S.M. Cox. 1997. Patterns of community policing in nonurban America. *Journal of Research in Crime and Delinquency* 34: 368–94.

Maguire, E.R., and S.D. Mastrofski. 2000. Patterns of community policing in the United States. *Police Quarterly* 3(1): 4–45.

Manning P.K. 1988. Community policing as a drama of control. In *Community policing: Rhetoric or reality*, eds. J.R. Greene and S.D. Mastrofski (pp. 27–46). New York: Praeger.

Mastrofski, S.D. 1998. Community policing and police organization structure. In *How to recognize good policing: Problems and issues*, ed. J.P. Brodeur (pp. 161–89). Washington, D.C.: Police Executive Research Forum; Thousand Oaks, CA: Sage.

Mattessich, P., and B. Monsey. 1997. *Community building: What makes it work, a review of factors influencing successful community building*. Saint Paul, MN: Amherst H. Wilder Foundation, Fieldstone Alliance.

Meyer, J.W., and B. Rowan. 1977. Institutionalized organizations: Formal structure as myth and ceremony. *American Journal of Sociology* 83: 340–63.

Murphy, P.V. 1985. The prospective chief's negotiation of authority with the mayor. In *Police leadership in America: Crisis and opportunity*, ed. W.A. Geller (pp. 30–40). Chicago: American Bar Foundation; New York: Praeger.
Office of Community Oriented Policing Services. 2001. Homepage. www.cops.usdoj.gov/ (accessed January 21, 2001).
Perez, D.W. 1994. *Common sense about police review*. Philadelphia: Temple University Press.
Renauer, B.C. 2000. Why get involved? Examining the motivational, identity, and ideological aspects of resident involvement in place-based organizations. PhD diss., State University of New York at Albany.
Renauer, B.C. and J. Scott. 2001. Exploring the dimensionality of community capacity. Paper presented at the annual meeting of the American Society of Criminology, Atlanta, GA.
Renauer, B.C., D.E. Duffee, and J. Scott. 2003. Measuring police-community co-production: Tradeoffs in two observational approaches. *Policing: An International Journal of Police Strategies and Management* 26: 9–28.
Scheingold, S.A. 1991. *The politics of street crime: Criminal process and cultural obsession*. Philadelphia, PA: Temple University Press.
Scott, W.R. 1995. *Institutions and organizations*. Thousand Oaks, CA: Sage.
Scott, J.D., D.E. Duffee, and B.C. Renauer. 2003. Measuring police-community co-production: The utility of community policing case studies. *Police Quarterly* 6(4): 410–39.
Skogan, W.G. 1990. *Disorder and decline: Crime and the spiral of decay in American neighborhoods*. Berkeley: University of California Press.
Skogan, W.G. 1995. Evaluating problem solving policing: The Chicago experience. Paper presented at the conference on Problem Solving Policing As Crime Prevention. Stockholm, Sweden (September 1996).
Skogan, W.G., and S. Hartnett. 1997. *Community policing Chicago style*. New York: Oxford University Press.
Stoecker, R. 1994. *Defending community: The struggle for alternative redevelopment in Cedar-Riverside*. Philadelphia: Temple University Press.
Swanstrom, T. 1985. *The crisis of growth politics: Cleveland, Kucinich, and the challenge of urban populism*. Philadelphia: Temple University Press.
University of Maryland. 1997. *Preventing crime: What works, what doesn't, what's promising*. Washington, D.C.: U.S. Government Printing Office.
Walker, S. 1977. *A critical history of police reform: The emergence of professionalization*. Lexington, MA: Lexington Books.
Walker, S.E. 2001. *Sense and nonsense about crime and drugs: A policy guide*. Belmont, CA: Wadsworth/Thomson Learning.
Warren, R.L., S.M. Rose, and A.F. Bergunder. 1974. *The structure of urban reform*. Cambridge, MA: Lexington.
Weingart, S.N., F.X. Hartmann, and D. Osborne. 1994. *Case studies of community anti-drug efforts*. Washington, D.C.: National Institute of Justice.

Zhao, J., N. Lovrich, and Q. Thurman. 1999. The status of community policing in American cities: Facilitators and impediments revisited. *Policing: An International Journal of Police Strategies & Management* 22(1): 74–92.
Zhao, J., Q. Thurman, and N. Lovrich. 1995. Community-oriented policing across the U.S.: Facilitators and impediments to implementation. *American Journal of Police* 14: 11–28.

6

THE "CAUSES" OF POLICE BRUTALITY: THEORY AND EVIDENCE ON POLICE USE OF FORCE[1]

Robert E. Worden

Social scientific theories and evidence concerning police behavior, and particularly research on the factors that contribute to—or "cause"—police brutality, can provide insights into the promise (and pitfalls) of governmental, administrative, managerial, and policy reforms. Indeed, every serious prescription for controlling police brutality rests at least implicitly on some theory of police behavior.[2] Fortunately, over the past twenty-five years social scientists have given considerable attention to some forms of police behavior, and scholars have made some headway in developing theories that account, at least in part, for these behaviors. The use of officers' authority to make arrests has been analyzed in a number of studies, as has the use of *deadly* force, and a substantial (but still inadequate) body of empirical evidence has accumulated. Unfortunately, very little social scientific evidence has accumulated on the use and abuse of nonlethal force, and little effort seems to have been made to consider whether the theories applied to other forms of behavior apply equally well (or at all) to the use of nonlethal force.[3]

This chapter seeks to connect theories of police behavior with new evidence on the use of force by police. First, I briefly review the theories of police behavior, along with the evidence that bears on those theories, drawing principally from empirical analyses of arrest and of deadly force. I then review the handful of studies that have examined the use of nonlethal force and evaluate the data—collected through in-person observation of police officers—on which most of these analyses are based. I then turn to the new empirical evidence on the use of force, which is also based on an analysis of observational data. I conclude by discussing whether and how further research might contribute to the development of theory and to the deliberation about reform.

THEORIES OF POLICE BEHAVIOR

Existing research on police behavior reflects the diverse training and backgrounds of those who study the police—sociologists, political scientists, psychologists, and others. Even so, much of this research can be subsumed within three explanatory rubrics: sociological, psychological, and organizational.

Sociological Theory

One prominent sociological approach to understanding the behavior of police officers is based on the premise that police behavior is influenced by the social dynamics of police-citizen encounters. For example, Donald Black's sociological theory of law holds that the "quantity of law" is influenced by the social attributes of concerned parties—victims and suspects, or plaintiffs and defendants, as well as the agents of social control themselves (see esp. Black, 1976).[4] According to this theory, police officers are least likely to take legal or other coercive action against lower-status persons—especially the poor, and racial and ethnic minorities—whose accusers are also of low status, but more likely to take such action against lower-status persons whose accusers are of higher status (Black, 1980: ch. 1). Somewhat more generally, this line of inquiry has directed analytical attention to the structural characteristics of the situations in which officers and citizens interact: the social class, race, and gender of complainants, and their dispositional preferences—i.e., whether they want offenders arrested or prefer that offenders not be arrested; the social class, race, age, gender, sobriety, and demeanor of suspects; the seriousness of the offense (if any); the nature of the relationships between complainants and suspects; the visibility of the encounters (whether they transpire in public or private locations, and whether bystanders are present); the numbers of officers at the scene; and the character of the neighborhoods in which encounters take place. From this theoretical perspective, these "situational" factors (Sherman, 1980a) are the cues on which officers form judgments about how incidents should be "handled" (Berk & Loseke, 1980). Perhaps the most comprehensive and succinct statement of this explanatory approach is Bittner's, who posited that "the role of the police is best understood as a mechanism for the distribution of non-negotiably coercive force *employed in accordance with the dictates of an intuitive grasp of situational exigencies*" (Bittner, 1970: 46).

Most empirical research that is grounded in this theory has examined the use of arrest powers (e.g., Black, 1971; Lundman, 1974; Smith & Visher, 1981; also see Sherman, 1980a: 77–85). This research has consistently shown that arrest is influenced by the demeanor of suspects—arrest is more likely if the suspect is antagonistic or disrespectful to police (but cf. Klinger, 1992)—and by the preferences of complainants (if any)—arrest is more likely if complainants wish to press charges, and less likely if complainants express a preference for informal dispositions. This research has also produced somewhat inconsistent results. For example, some analyses indicate that nonwhite suspects are more likely than white suspects are to be arrested (Lundman, 1974; Smith & Visher, 1981), while others show that the relationship between race and arrest is either null (Berk & Loseke, 1980; Worden & Pollitz, 1984; Smith & Klein, 1984; Worden, 1989) or spurious—that black suspects are more likely to be arrested because they are more likely to be disrespectful and that race has no independent effect (Black, 1971; Sykes & Clark, 1975, but cf. Black, 1980: ch. 5; Smith, Visher, & Davidson, 1984).[5] Overall, research of this genre has demonstrated that officers' arrest decisions are influenced by situational factors; but it also shows that at least half of the variation in arrest remains unexplained by this theoretical perspective.

Research on the use of deadly force has dwelt on one hypothesis that is quite compatible with this theory, namely that minorities are more likely to be shot (or shot at) by police. The empirical evidence confirms that minorities are, in fact, overrepresented among the human targets at which police shoot, relative to their numbers in city populations, but it also indicates that minorities are overrepresented among those whose actions precipitate the use of deadly force by police (e.g., Milton, Halleck, Lardner, & Abrecht, 1977; Fyfe, 1980, 1981b; Blumberg, 1981; Geller & Karales, 1981; Alpert, 1989). Insofar as this alternative explanation for the racial disparities is captured in the available data (e.g., on felony arrests), this hypothesis—that minorities are more likely to be the objects of police deadly force merely because of their race—has, then, received support in only a few analyses (Meyer, 1980; Geller & Karales, 1981: 123–125; Fyfe, 1982).

Psychological Theory

A second approach to understanding the behavior of police officers is psychological. This approach highlights variation among officers in their behavioral predispositions, variation that is obscured by the sociological approach. This perspective directs attention to the outlooks and personality characteristics that presumably produce different responses to similar situations by different officers. This perspective also underlies many propositions (or suppositions) about behavioral differences related to officers' race, gender, and educational background, inasmuch as black officers, female officers, and college-educated officers are supposed to have outlooks that differ from their white, male, less educated colleagues, and these differences in attitude are presumed to manifest themselves in officers' behavioral patterns. Hypotheses that specify a linkage between attitudes and behavior have intuitive appeal, but social psychological research has shown that people's behavior is often inconsistent with their attitudes; one review of this research concluded that "in most cases investigated, attitudes and behaviors are related to an extent that ranges from small to moderate in degree" (Schuman & Johnson, 1976: 168).

This theory (or some version thereof) is reflected in portions of the report by the Christopher Commission (Independent Commission on the Los Angeles Police Department, 1991), which identified a small group of "problem officers" who were disproportionately involved in incidents in which force was either used or allegedly misused. In its discussion of problem officers, the commission reported its findings from a survey of Los Angeles Police Department (LAPD) officers that "a significant percentage . . . agreed with the statement that 'an officer is justified in administering physical punishment to a suspect who has committed a heinous crime' (4.9 percent) or 'to a suspect with a bad or uncooperative attitude' (4.6 percent)" (p. 34). The commission could not link officers' survey responses with departmental data on uses of force or on personnel complaints, and it acknowledged that "the precise size and identity of this problem group cannot be specified (at least without significant further investigation)" (p. 38). However, the commission rejected the alternative explanation that officers' assignments (to active, high-crime areas or to specialized units) produced the skewed distribution of use of force involvement. While the commission focused on what management could and should do after the fact, once these problem officers were identified, it implicitly presumed that the outlooks or personalities of these officers are at the root of their seemingly distinctive behavioral patterns.[6]

One more specific hypothesis might be that officers who are predisposed to use force have "authoritarian" personalities (Balch, 1972, and more generally, Adorno, Frenkel-Brunswik, Levinson, & Sanford, 1950). Research on the personality characteristics of police has been concerned primarily with whether officers are psychologically homogeneous and, moreover, different as a group from the citizenry. These efforts to establish a modal (and pathological) "police personality" have proven no better than inconclusive (Balch, 1972, cf. Lefkowitz, 1975). Moreover, such analysis is misguided if one seeks to account for behavioral variation among officers. As Toch (1996) suggests, these findings do not refute the proposition that those officers who score high on indices of authoritarianism are also those who use force with unusual frequency. Unless research examines officers' authoritarianism or other personality traits as characteristics that vary among officers, then these concepts will be of no value in explaining officers' use of force.

The richest discussions of psychological hypotheses about police behavior can be found in studies that have constructed four-fold typologies of police officers (White, 1972; Muir, 1977; Broderick, 1977; Brown, 1981), with each typology based on two (or in one case, three) attitudinal dimensions. For example, William Muir (1977) classifies officers according to their outlooks on human nature and their moral attitudes toward coercive authority. Although these four studies together define sixteen categories of officers, a careful comparison of the types of officers described in these studies shows that five composite types can be isolated (Worden, forthcoming). These types do appear to differ in their propensities to use force.

One type of officer, for which I have borrowed White's (1972) label of the "tough cop," is perhaps the most likely to use force improperly. Tough cops are cynical, in the sense that they presume that people are motivated by narrow self-interest. They conceive the role of police in terms of crime control, focusing especially on "serious" crime, and they see themselves as a negative force in people's lives. They believe that the citizenry is hostile toward police, and they identify with the police culture. They believe that experience and common sense are the best guides in dealing with the realities of the street, and that "curbstone justice" is sometimes appropriate and effective.

By contrast, "problem-solvers" (also White's term) have what Muir (1977) calls a "tragic" perspective: they recognize that people's actions are influenced by complex sets of physical, economic, and social circumstances and not simple self-interest. They conceive the role of police as one of "offering assistance in solving whatever kind of problem . . . [their clientele] face" (White, 1972: 72), and thus they see themselves as a positive force. They are skeptical of traditional police methods, as they are unable to reconcile the use of coercive measures with their moral codes. This type of officer is probably the least likely to use force improperly (or at all).

The descriptions of these and the other types of officers (Worden, forthcoming) suggest that if there are officers with pronounced propensities to use force, they share several outlooks that distinguish them from other officers.[7] Officers who are the most likely to use force could be expected to (1) conceive the police role in narrow terms, limited to crime fighting and law enforcement, (2) believe that this role is more effectively carried out when officers may use force at their discretion, and (3) regard the citizenry as unappreciative at best and as hostile and abusive at worst.[8]

Much of the evidence that supports psychological hypotheses about police behavior is impressionistic, based on limited and/or unsystematic observation of officers. The few efforts to systematically test these hypotheses have produced little or no support. Brown's (1981: Ch. 9) analysis, based on officers' responses to hypothetical scenarios, indicates that—as hypothesized—there is more variation across than within categories of officers in the ways that they handle common incidents (such as family disputes and drunk driving), but it also shows that officers' behavior is affected by the organizational context in which they work; behavior is not a simple extension of attitudes, as organizational and other social forces can attenuate the impact of attitudes on behavior. Snipes and Mastrofski (1990) undertook a small-scale examination of hypotheses derived from Muir's framework by conducting in-depth interviews with and observations of nine officers in one department; they found little consistency between officers' attitudes and behaviors, and little consistency in each officer's behavior from one incident to the next. My own analyses (Worden, 1989) indicate that officers' attitudes are only weakly related to their discretionary choices—in the initiation and disposition of traffic stops, in the initiation of field interrogations, and in the disposition of disputes. The results of these studies certainly do not constitute evidence sufficient to reject psychological hypotheses, however, and none of these studies examined the use of force. But these findings suggest that the connections between officers' attitudes and behavior are probably more complex (and perhaps more tenuous) than many have supposed.

A larger body of evidence has accumulated on the relationship of officers' behavior to their background and characteristics—race, gender, length of police service, and especially education. Officers' educational backgrounds has been the subject of a number of studies, and although this research has shown that education bears no more than a weak relationship to officers' attitudes (e.g., Weiner, 1974; Miller & Fry, 1976; Hudzik, 1978; Worden, 1990) and no relationship to the use of deadly force (Sherman & Blumberg, 1981), it also indicates that college-educated officers generate fewer citizen complaints (Cohen & Chaiken, 1972; Cascio, 1977). The reason for this difference is not clear (but see Worden, 1990: 589).

Similarly, the most systematic comparison of male and female officers shows small or no differences in attitudes other than job satisfaction (Worden, 1993). Other research reveals some behavioral differences—in the frequency with which men and women initiate encounters and make arrests—but on most behavioral dimensions, the differences are nil (Bloch & Anderson, 1974; Sherman, 1975; cf. Grennan, 1987). One study of the effects of officers' race on behavior (Friedrich, 1977: 307–319) found that black officers patrol more aggressively, initiate more contacts with citizens, are more likely to make arrests, and more frequently adopt a neutral "manner" toward citizens of either race. Other research has found that black officers are more likely than white officers are to use deadly force, either on duty (Geller & Karales, 1981) or on *and* off duty (Fyfe, 1981a); but these differences in the use of deadly force can be attributed to black officers' duty assignments and to where they choose to live (also see Blumberg, 1982). Finally, analyses of officers' length of service indicate that less experienced officers are more active, in that they patrol more aggressively and initiate more contacts with citizens, and that they are more likely to make arrests, to write crime reports (Friedrich, 1977: 280–290; Worden, 1989), and to use deadly force (Blumberg, 1982; cf. Alpert, 1989).

Organizational Theory

Some approaches to understanding the behavior of police officers emphasize features of the organizations in which officers work. A theory that highlights organizational properties as influences on police behavior would seem to hold the greatest potential as a guide for police reform, since organizational factors are more readily manipulated than are the demeanors of suspects or the outlooks of officers. Unfortunately, organizational analyses of police are seldom undertaken, probably because of the expense and difficulty of collecting comparable data on multiple police agencies, and thus organizational theories of police behavior are not well supported by empirical evidence.

One theory emphasizes the influence on police officers' behavior of the formal organizational structure, especially the system of incentives and disincentives and the content and application of rules and regulations. The principal statement of this approach is Wilson's (1968), whose exploratory research formed the basis for the delineation of three organizational styles of policing—the legalistic, watchman, and service styles—and for hypotheses that these styles can be attributed to the orientations of chiefs, which influence officers' behavior through the medium of organizational structure. While Wilson acknowledges that the capacity of police administrators to shape officers' behavior is constrained by the nature of police tasks, he seems to see the glass of managerial influence as half (or partly) full rather than half (or partly) empty. Wilson's study has more to say about the use of the law than about the use of physical force; however, it suggests that improper force is more likely to be used by officers in watchman-style departments, usually in response to perceived disrespect for police authority. Some research has tested hypotheses derived from Wilson's framework (Gardiner, 1969; Wilson & Boland, 1978; Smith, 1984) with results that are generally supportive, but only Friedrich (1980), whose study I discuss later, tested hypotheses about the use of force.

Some research on the use of deadly force has shown rather convincingly that administrative controls can have salutary effects on the frequency with which officers use their firearms. Policies that set clear boundaries around the use of deadly force and that provide for effective enforcement (by, say, establishing review procedures) have reduced the number of shootings (Fyfe, 1979, 1982; Meyer, 1980; Sherman, 1983), especially the more discretionary or "elective" shootings (Fyfe, 1988: 184–187). Whether such controls are, by themselves, equally effective in controlling the use of nonlethal force is an open question in the sense that no study has produced an empirical answer. But there is good reason to be skeptical; the use of deadly force is a more visible act—or, more precisely, an act with more visible outcomes—which probably makes this form of behavior more susceptible to administrative controls.

Another theory emphasizes the limitations of formal structure in directing and controlling the behavior of patrol officers and the importance of the informal organization or peer group, i.e., the police culture. According to this perspective, the formal, more obtrusive controls on police—rewards and punishments, rules, regulations, and standard operating procedures (SOPs)—extend to the more observable and, for the most part, more mundane aspects of police work, such as the use of equipment, report writing, and officers' appearance (Manning, 1977; Brown, 1981; more generally see Prottas, 1978). At the same time, the application of unobtrusive controls on police, in the form of socialization and training, is governed by the work group. Analyses of the socialization process are quite scarce, but the available evidence indicates that new officers learn the police craft on the job (not in the academy) from more senior officers, especially their field training officers or FTOs (Van Maanen, 1974; Fielding, 1988). Rookies are quickly led to believe that their academy experience was merely a rite of passage, that the training they received there is irrelevant to the realities of policing, and that they will learn what they need to know on the street. Thus, according to this line of argument, the police culture is not only the primary reference group for officers, but also the principal mechanism of organizational control (to the extent that control is exerted at all) over the substantive exercise of police discretion.

One must be careful not to confuse what has been called the police culture with the cultures of police organizations. "The" police culture is an occupational culture, consisting of outlooks and norms that are commonly found among patrol officers in police agencies. This culture emphasizes the danger and unpredictability of the work environment, the consequent dependence of officers on each other for assistance and protection, officers' autonomy in handling situations, and the need to assert and maintain one's authority (Westley, 1970; Skolnick, 1975; Brown, 1981; Manning, 1989). The police culture does not prescribe the substance of officers' working styles so much as it serves to protect officers from administrative scrutiny and sanction and to insulate them from administrative pressures for change (Reuss-Ianni, 1983); thus it allows officers the latitude to develop and practice their own styles.[9] These cultural elements can, presumably, be found among patrol officers in all or most police agencies.

One may find variation in the *organizational* cultures of police departments, even while one finds consistency in the elements of the *occupational* culture. Wilson maintains that the administration of police departments produces differing styles both directly, by shaping the calculus on which officers' choices are based, and indirectly, by cultivating a "shared outlook or ethos that provides for [officers] a common definition of the situations they are likely to encounter and that to the outsider gives to the organization its distinctive character or 'feel'" (1968: 139). Officers in both legalistic and watchman departments might subscribe to a norm of loyalty, but according to Wilson's analysis, they would differ in their beliefs about the nature of the police role and about the proper use of police authority. Brown (1981) disputes this argument, finding officers with very different individual styles within each of the three departments he studied. These arguments can perhaps be reconciled, inasmuch as any organization that is differentiated by task and authority might well develop multiple subcultures (Reuss-Ianni, 1983; Worden & Mastrofski, 1989; Jermier, Slocum, Fry, & Gaines, 1991), and even where multiple subcultures exist among patrol officers, one may predominate. Unfortunately, the distinction between the occupational culture of police and the organizational cultures of police departments is seldom made; most previous research has attended to the former but ignored the latter.

The report of the Christopher Commission makes reference to both of these theories. The commission identified LAPD's "assertive style of law enforcement" as a reason for "aggressive confrontations with the public" (p. 97), and traced this style of policing to a "'professional' organizational culture" that has been cultivated by LAPD administration through training and the incentive structure. Officers in LAPD are rewarded for hard-nosed enforcement that is likely to (occasionally) produce arrests and (often) bring police into conflict with citizens. The commission further found that the administration of LAPD fails to discourage the improper use of force, in that (1) the complaint intake process discourages citizens from filing complaints, (2) many complaints that are filed are not substantiated as a result of inadequate resources and procedures for investigating complaints, and (3) the sanctions imposed on officers against whom complaints have been substantiated have been too light, both as a deterrent and as a message that such behavior is inappropriate. Like Wilson (1968), then, the commission concluded that the LAPD's incentive structure influences officers' behavior directly, and that there is a link between the (formal) administrative structure and the (informal) organizational culture. The implications for administrative practice are fairly straightforward: reduce the incentives for hard-nosed enforcement and increase the sanctions for the improper use of force.[10]

But the commission also acknowledged the limitations on the formal structure in controlling police conduct, reporting that "perhaps the greatest single barrier to the effective investigation and adjudication of complaints is the officers' unwritten 'code of silence', [which] consists of one simple rule: an officer does not provide adverse information against a fellow officer" (p. 168). From this conclusion one cannot easily draw practical implications, and the commission's recommendations do not address this "barrier." Since this culture originates to a significant degree in the nature of the work itself, and is not unique to LAPD or even to policing (see Gouldner, 1954), it is not likely to be altered by traditional organizational reforms (Van Maanen, 1974; Toch, 1979).

This analysis of the LAPD is instructive, to be sure, but it suffers all the limitations of a case study. Indeed, the LAPD may represent an extreme and unrepresentative case, where formal and informal organizational forces tend to reinforce one another in producing an aggressive style of policing and an elevated probability of the use of force. Most American police departments are smaller, less bureaucratic, and less insulated from the communities they serve;[11] as a result, the content of formal expectations in such departments might be less unambiguously crime-control oriented, and the potentially restraining influence of administrative controls might be greater. Any characterization of the problem of police brutality must take this variation among departments into account. So too must research on police brutality, because if large departments can be structured to simulate the relevant conditions that prevail in smaller departments, there is much to be learned by studying small and medium-sized police departments.

Internally, one might expect that in smaller police departments, which typically have fewer levels of hierarchy, administrators could more closely monitor and supervise street-level performance by taking advantage of the less distorted information that flows through the shorter formal channels of communication, and of the greater information that flows through the wider informal channels of communication (Whitaker, 1983). In principle, managers in smaller agencies could more directly, and hence effectively, communicate their priorities and expectations to street-level personnel. In addition, since they need not rely so heavily on statistical summaries of individual performance, managers can base their evaluations of officers' performance on a richer and probably more accurate base of information; consequently, patterns of (problematic) behavior are likely to be more readily detectable, and the incentive system need not emphasize quantifiable, enforcement-related activities at the expense of the more qualitative aspects of police performance. Brown's (1981) analysis, even while it led him to conclude that the police culture is more important than formal organizational structure in shaping the exercise of police discretion, also confirms the expectation that administrative controls are more palpable in smaller departments, where Brown found that officers are more reluctant to take the risk of administrative sanction that they would run by practicing an aggressive style of patrol. Furthermore, insofar as work groups are more stable in smaller departments, immediate supervisors could be expected to more frequently and effectively play an instrumental role in the development of subordinate officers' judgment and moral outlooks (see Muir, 1977).

Externally, one might expect that smaller agencies would be subject to closer oversight both by the public and by its representatives. Insofar as smaller municipalities are more homogeneous and their residents are in greater agreement about the delivery of police services, public officials have less latitude in setting policy and priorities (Wilson, 1968). Citizens in smaller municipalities also might take a more active part in local affairs (Dahl, 1967), so that municipal officials might better apprehend citizens' preferences regarding municipal services. Moreover, if in smaller municipalities public officials—including councilors, mayors, and city managers—play more active roles in policymaking and oversight (Mastrofski, 1988), then one might expect that the direction of administrative influence in their police departments would be more toward restraint and less toward aggressive enforcement, inasmuch as aggressive policing could be expected to generate political friction from which the department is not insulated.

THEORY AND RESEARCH ON THE USE OF FORCE

As Reiss (1968a) points out, "What citizens mean by police brutality covers the full range of police practices," including the use of abusive language and seemingly unjustified field interrogations, but "the nub of the police-brutality issue seems to lie in police use of physical force." Of course, some of the problems with which police deal may require the use of force, and under many of these circumstances, the line between proper and improper force is a rather fuzzy one; where force is necessary, judgments must be made about the *amount* of force that is reasonable. Whenever judgments must be made, some misjudgments are probably inevitable; such cases of *excessive* force involve the use of more force than is reasonably necessary. Other cases of improper force, however, involve the use of force where *none* is necessary; these are instances of *unnecessary* force. Reiss (1968a) focused mostly on such cases of gratuitous violence by police; he explains:

A physical assault on a citizen was judged to be "improper" or "unnecessary" only if force was used in one or more of the following ways:

> If a policeman physically assaulted a citizen and then failed to make an arrest; proper use involves an arrest.
>
> If the citizen being arrested did not, by word or deed, resist the policeman; force should be used only if it is necessary to make the arrest.
>
> If the policeman, even though there was resistance to the arrest, could easily have restrained the citizen in other ways.
>
> If a large number of policemen were present and could have assisted in subduing the citizen in the station, in lockup, and in the interrogation rooms.
>
> If an offender was handcuffed and made no attempt to flee or offer violent resistance.
>
> If the citizen resisted arrest, but the use of force continued even after the citizen was subdued.

It may be important, for both theoretical and policy purposes, to distinguish between the use of *excessive* force and the use of *unnecessary* force. Although this distinction rests on overt and thus observable behavior, it is admittedly an elusive one, inasmuch as officers not only respond to situations but also help to create them; sometimes, officers' choices early in police-citizen encounters can contribute to the emergence of circumstances that require the use of force (Binder & Scharf, 1980; Bayley, 1986; also see Klockars, 1996). Insofar as these two forms of behavior can be distinguished, we may find that they are sufficiently different phenomena—that each of them is influenced by a different set of situational, individual, and organizational factors. We may also find that interventions intended to reduce excessive force, such as (re)training officers, have little effect on the incidence of unnecessary force, and conversely, that other interventions, such as disincentives, have a greater effect on unnecessary force than on excessive force (but cf. Fyfe, 1996).

Most empirical research on the use of nonlethal force by police is based on data collected through the observation of officers on patrol. Generally, observation of police enables one to collect data on forms of behavior that cannot be reliably measured based on other sources. These are the forms of behavior that are least visible, such as field stops or the resolution of disputes, and that often result in no official record. Observation also enables one to collect data on the setting in which police action takes place; even when such information is contained in officers' reports, it is frequently incomplete or of dubious validity. Analyses of observational data make unique contributions to our understanding of police use of force, since observation by independent observers enables one to enumerate, describe, and analyze instances in which force is used, whether or not they result in citizen complaints or departmental disciplinary actions. Like survey data on victimizations, which uncover the "dark figure" of unreported crime, observational data on police behavior reveal unreported instances of police use of force (see Adams 1996).

Observational data are not without shortcomings, as they may be biased as a result of "reactivity"—that is, officers might refrain from the use of force in some instances due only to the presence of observers. But efforts to assess the bias introduced by reactivity suggest that the validity of observational data, in general, is quite high (Mastrofski & Parks, 1990); moreover, evidence shows that the relationships between some forms of police behavior and other variables (such as characteristics of the situation) are unaffected by reactivity (Worden, 1989: fn 8). As Reiss (1971b: 24) observes, "It is sociologically naive to assume that for many events the presence or participation of the observer is more controlling than other factors in the situation." More specifically, based on the results of one observational study (to be discussed later), Reiss maintains that "the use of force by the police is situationally determined by other participants in the situation and by the officer's involvement in it, to such a degree that one must conclude the observer's presence had no effect" (Reiss, 1971b: 24; also see Reiss, 1968a, 1968b). At a minimum, the bias in observational data is almost certainly no greater, and probably less, than that in archival data.

The first large-scale observational study of police was undertaken by Black and Reiss (1967) for the President's Commission on Law Enforcement and Administration of Justice. This research was conducted during the summer of 1966 in Boston, Chicago, and Washington, DC. Observers accompanied patrol officers on sampled shifts in selected high-crime precincts:

> "In the data collection, emphasis was placed upon gaining detailed descriptions of police and citizen *behavior*. . . . The social and demographic characteristics of the participants as well as a detailed description of the settings and qualities of the encounters were also obtained."
>
> (Black & Reiss, 1967: 15; emphasis in original)

Reiss (1968a, 1971a) applied a sociological approach to police brutality in analyzing these data. He describes the incidents in which officers used undue force in the following terms:

> Seventy-eight percent of all instances where force was used unduly took place in police-controlled settings, such as the patrol car, the precinct station, or public places (primarily streets). Almost all victims of force were characterized as suspects or offenders. They were young, lower-class males from any racial or ethnic group. Furthermore, most encounters were devoid of witnesses who would support the offender. In general, persons officers regarded as being in a deviant offender role or who defied what the officer defines as his authority were the most likely victims of undue force. Thirty-nine percent openly defied authority by challenging the legitimacy of the police to exercise that authority, 9 percent physically resisted arrest, and 32 percent were persons in deviant offender roles, such as drunks, homosexuals, or addicts.
>
> (Reiss, 1971a: 147–149)

Reiss also points out, however, that "many instances where the citizen behaved antagonistically toward the police officer and many encounters with deviants did not involve uncivil conduct or misuse of force by the police" (1971a: 149), and, more generally, that police-citizen encounters do not follow a rule of reciprocity in incivility—"whenever incivility occurs in an encounter, the chances are only 1 in 6 that the other party will reciprocate with incivility" (1971a: 144).

In a 1980 article, Robert Friedrich reviewed the problems with then-existing research on police use of force and outlined three approaches to explaining police use of force—"individual," "situational," and "organizational"—that correspond to the theories discussed earlier. From each approach, he pointed out, one can derive a number of specific hypotheses about the use of force; using the Black-Reiss data, Friedrich tested some of those hypotheses to produce what was at that time the most thorough and sophisticated analysis of the phenomenon.

Friedrich found, first, that physical force was used only infrequently by police, and that the use of excessive force was still less frequent. Force was used in 5.1 percent of the 1,565 encounters that involved suspected offenders (and in only one of the remaining 3,826 incidents that involved no suspects). "Excessive" force was used in 1.8 percent of the encounters with suspects, or in no more than twenty-nine incidents.[12]

Friedrich further found that situational, individual, and organizational hypotheses were, with few exceptions, unsupported by the data. Bivariate and multivariate analyses showed that characteristics of the police-citizen encounters bore the strongest relationship to the use of force, which was more likely if the suspect was antagonistic, agitated, intoxicated, or lower class; if the offense was a felony; and if other citizens or officers were present. Be that as it may, situational characteristics together had no more than modest explanatory power. The characteristics of officers—their length of service, attitudes toward the job, race, and (among white officers) attitudes toward blacks—accounted for little of the (limited) variation in the use of force. Differences across departments were of marginal significance and, moreover, did not conform to Friedrich's expectations. The incidence of the use of force overall, and of improper force particularly, was (as Friedrich hypothesized) somewhat lower in the "professional" department (Chicago) than in the "traditional" department (Boston); but the incidence of force, and especially of improper force, was (contrary to Friedrich's hypotheses) lowest in the "transitional" department (Washington, DC).[13]

Other analyses of the use of nonlethal force tend to corroborate Friedrich's findings. Analyses of other observational data have shown that force is used infrequently. Sykes and Brent (1980, 1983) analyzed sequences of interactions between officers and citizens, and they concluded that officers "regulate" or control their interactions with citizens primarily by asking questions or making accusations, and secondarily by issuing commands; they found that "coercive regulation [including threats as well as the actual use of force] is rare" (1980: 195). Bayley and Garofalo (1989), who conducted a smaller-scale observational study under the auspices of the New York State Commission on Criminal Justice and the Use of Force, found that even in encounters that qualified as "potentially violent mobilizations," police used force in only 8 percent of cases, and that the force "consisted almost exclusively of grabbing and restraining" (p. 7).

Croft (1985) analyzed reports of the use of force filed by officers in the Rochester, New York, police department from 1973 through 1979, along with a comparison sample of arrests in which no force was used. Like Friedrich's, Croft's analysis indicates that the use of force was infrequent—2,397 reported uses of force, and 123,491 arrests over the period—and that it was typically prompted by citizens' actions—threatening or attacking officers and/or other citizens or attempting to flee. Croft's analysis also suggests that many of the citizens against whom force was used were antagonistic and/or uncooperative, either verbally abusing officers or disobeying officers' commands.[14] Neither gender nor race bore the expected relationship to the use of force. Furthermore, Croft found that some officers were much more likely to use force than others were, even after controlling for officers' "hazard status," or the risk of "being exposed to police-citizen incidents having a potential for use of force" (p. 160); 119 of 430 officers selected for analysis were classified as "high force" officers, who used force in 6.1 percent or more of the arrests they made. However, "high force" officers could not, for the most part, be distinguished from "low force" officers in terms of their background characteristics; officers' use of force was related only to their age and length of service, and was unrelated to their gender, race, education, prior military service, or civil service test ranking. Neither did the two groups differ in their arrest productivity or in their numbers of citizen complaints, internally initiated complaints, or disciplinary charges. Thus, this analysis of official police records yields results that mirror those based on observational research.

ANALYSIS OF THE POLICE SERVICES STUDY DATA

Data collected for the Police Services Study (PSS) afford another opportunity to analyze police use of force based on in-person observations. The PSS was funded by the National Science Foundation and conducted by Elinor Ostrom, Roger B. Parks, and Gordon P. Whitaker. The study was designed to examine the impact of institutional arrangements on the delivery of police services. The second phase of the PSS provided for the collection of various kinds of data about twenty-four police departments in three metropolitan areas (Rochester, New York; St. Louis, Missouri; and Tampa-St. Petersburg, Florida); attention focused particularly on sixty neighborhoods served by those departments. During the summer of 1977, trained observers accompanied patrol officers on 900 patrol shifts, fifteen in each of the sixty neighborhoods. Observers recorded information about 5,688 police-citizen encounters in field notes and later coded that information on a standardized form; in many cases, narrative accounts of the encounters were also prepared. In addition, the observed officers (and samples of other officers) were surveyed. These data form the principal basis for the analyses reported later.

Compared with the Black-Reiss data and other observational data, the PSS data are broader and deeper. The Black-Reiss study focused on high-crime precincts in three major cities. The departments included in the PSS range in size from one with only 13 officers to one with over 2,000, serving municipalities whose populations range from 6,000 to almost 500,000. Within jurisdictions, neighborhoods were selected with explicit reference to racial composition and wealth to ensure that different types of neighborhoods were represented. The departments and neighborhoods provide a rough cross-section of organizational arrangements and residential service conditions for urban policing in the United States. Thus, the PSS data provide a much firmer basis for generalizing about police practices in American metropolitan areas (and not only in urban, high-crime areas).

The Use of Force

While they were observed for the PSS, officers used no more than reasonable force to restrain or move a citizen in thirty-seven encounters.[15] In twenty-three encounters, officers used force that the observer judged to be unnecessary or excessive;[16] in three of those, officers hit or swung at citizens with a weapon.[17] This analysis will focus on these two categories of behavior, i.e., the use of reasonable force, and the use of improper (i.e., unnecessary or excessive) force. It should be obvious already that the use of force was uncommon, and the use of improper force was rare as a proportion of police-citizen encounters. According to the coded data, reasonable force was used in less than 1 percent of the encounters, and improper force was used in less than one half of 1 percent; in encounters with suspects, who one would presume to be the most likely targets of police force, reasonable force was used in 2.3 percent, and improper force in 1.3 percent. Even so, incidents in which improper force was used represent a substantial proportion of the incidents in which any force (reasonable or improper) was used (Adams, 1996).

This trichotomization of officers' behavior—no force, reasonable force, improper force—for present analytic purposes should be recognized for what it is: a simplification. Officers' use of force can be conceived (if not precisely measured) along a continuum, say from minimal force to extreme (even deadly) force; these differences of degree are largely lost in this trichotomy. Moreover, this conceptualization of officers' behavior also obscures differences in the use of improper force, but the PSS data do not permit one to reliably differentiate the use of excessive force from the use of unnecessary force.[18]

Table 6.1 displays the characteristics of encounters in which reasonable force was used, encounters in which improper force was used, and for reference, all encounters and all encounters that involved suspected offenders (other than traffic violators). To illustrate, 3.7 percent of all 5,688 encounters involved a violent crime, and 16.8 percent involved a nonviolent crime; 5.8 percent of the 1,528 encounters with (nontraffic) suspects involved a violent crime, and 9.8 percent involved a nonviolent crime. These data indicate that most encounters in which force is used do not take place in seclusion: most transpired in public locations, and in three-quarters a number of bystanders were looking on.[19] All but a small fraction of the encounters in which force was used also involved one or more officers other than the observed officer, and a substantial fraction also attracted a supervisor to the scene. Force was used disproportionately in those encounters that involved violent crimes and in those that involved automobile pursuits, but most encounters in which force was used—reasonably or improperly—involved neither of these events. It might be added that none of the encounters in which force was used originated as a suspicion stop or police-initiated field interrogation; indeed, few of these encounters were initiated by officers. If the use of force is a byproduct of police aggressiveness, then it would seem not to be a *direct* outgrowth of an "aggressive" style of patrol that involves frequently stopping suspicious persons or vehicles (Wilson & Boland, 1978; Whitaker, Phillips, & Worden, 1984); it might nevertheless be a consequence of an overly assertive or confrontational posture vis-a-vis citizens in any of a number of different contexts.

Table 6.2 displays the characteristics of the citizens against whom force was used, citizens against whom improper force was used, and, for reference, all citizens who were involved in observed encounters and all citizens who were initially regarded as suspected offenders. Most citizens against whom the police used force were suspects. That the police used force against some citizens whom observers coded as sick or injured, or as the subjects of concern,[20] might seem curious, but further analysis of both the coded data and the narrative data shows

Table 6.1 Characteristics of encounters

	All Encounters	Encounters with Suspects*	Reasonable Force Used	Improper Force Used
Type of Problem				
Violent crime	3.7	5.8	21.6	21.7
Nonviolent crime	16.8	9.8	16.2	13.0
Suspicious circumstances	10.0	23.8	13.5	13.0
Interpersonal conflict	8.6	20.8	24.3	13.0
Dependent person	4.8	4.9	5.4	17.4
Morals offense	1.4	3.7	2.7	0.0
Public nuisance	9.1	20.8	10.8	13.0
Traffic	22.6	—	5.4	0.0
Medical problem	1.8	0.1	0.0	0.0
Assistance	8.8	3.9	0.0	0.0
Information	6.3	0.7	0.0	0.0
Internal operations	4.4	3.8	0.0	8.7
Other/miscellaneous	1.7	2.0	0.0	0.0
Car chase	0.9	0.5	2.7	13.0
Location				
Street, sidewalk, parking lot	57.2	55.4	59.5	34.8
Public/commercial bldg.	8.4	7.3	10.8	17.4
Private residence	29.4	30.4	24.3	39.1
Other	5.0	6.9	5.4	8.7
Bystanders				
None	52.3	48.2	24.3	17.4
1–3	29.9	26.1	2.7	8.7
4–10	13.9	18.7	37.8	30.4
More than 10	3.8	7.0	35.1	43.5
Other Officers				
None	62.3	44.5	10.8	4.3
One	23.7	32.0	29.7	17.4
2–5	13.0	21.4	46.1	34.8
More than 5	1.0	2.1	13.5	43.5
Supervisor(s) present	9.9	15.8	35.1	60.9
N	5688	1528	37	23

* Excluding those suspected only of traffic violations.

Table 6.2 Characteristics of citizens

	All Citizens	Suspects Only*	Reasonable Force Used	Improper Force Used
Role				
Suspect	33.0	100	94.9	73.1
Victim	28.3	—	0.0	3.8
Sick/injured person	1.4	—	2.6	7.7
Subject of concern	1.3	—	0.0	7.7
Person requesting service	13.8	—	2.6	0.0
Witness/person with information	18.4	—	0.0	3.8
Other	3.8	—	0.0	3.8
Race				
White	65.3	53.6	35.9	50.0
Black	32.0	43.4	64.1	50.0
Other	2.1	1.9	0.0	0.0
Mixed	0.6	1.2	0.0	0.0
Gender				
Male	59.8	75.6	84.6	72.0
Female	33.9	18.6	15.4	28.0
Mixed	6.3	5.8	0.0	0.0
Age				
Under 18	16.1	30.9	17.9	19.2
19–35	41.9	45.4	53.8	53.8
Over 35	38.7	20.2	28.2	26.9
Mixed	3.3	3.5	0.0	0.0
Sobriety				
Sober	89.7	77.8	42.1	48.0
Drinking/using	6.1	12.8	15.8	8.0
Drunk/stoned	4.2	9.4	42.1	44.0
Mental Disorder	1.3	2.1	12.8	16.7
Weapon				
None in possession	98.8	96.4	84.6	76.9
Possessed gun	0.4	1.1	5.1	3.8
Possessed knife	0.8	2.5	10.3	19.2
Tried to use	0.1	0.2	2.6	7.7
Demeanor				
Detached	1.5	4.3	10.3	3.8
Hostile, antagonistic	1.8	5.0	23.1	46.2
Other	96.6	90.7	66.7	50.0
Fought with officer	0.3	0.9	17.9	57.7
N	8666	1819	39	26

* Excluding those suspected only of traffic violations.

that about half of those were citizens who appeared to have mental disorders. About half of the citizens against whom force was used showed evidence of drinking or drug use, and most of those were drunk. Nearly half of the citizens against whom improper force was used displayed a hostile or antagonistic demeanor,[21] more than half of them fought with the officer, and one-fifth of them had a weapon. Most of the citizens were adult men, and two-thirds of the adults were young adults; half were black.[22]

Table 6.3 displays the characteristics of officers who used force, officers who used improper force, and, for reference, all surveyed officers with a rank below sergeant.[23] In general (and taking into account the small numbers of officers on which some of the percentages are based), the officers who used force (reasonably or improperly) resemble the larger sample of officers in their race, gender, length of service, and educational background; most were white, all were men, their average length of service was about six years, and most had no college degree. Somewhat greater differences can be found along attitudinal dimensions. Most of the officers who used force agreed that police "should help to quiet family disputes when they get out of hand," but most also indicated that police should *not* "handle cases involving public nuisances, such as barking dogs or burning rubbish"; a majority agreed with the statement that "police should not have to handle calls that involve social or personal problems where no crime is involved." Two-thirds of the officers who used improper force, and half of those who used force, agreed that "if police officers in tough neighborhoods had fewer restrictions on their use of force, many of the serious crime problems in those neighborhoods would be greatly reduced"; similar

Table 6.3 Characteristics of officers

	All Officers	**Reasonable Force Used**	**Improper Force Used**
Race			
White	88.4	83.8	88.9
Black	10.4	13.5	5.6
Other	1.1	2.7	5.6
Gender			
Male	93.6	100	100
Female	6.4	0.0	0.0
Mean Age	30.5	30.5	29.5
Mean Length of Service	6.1	6.2	5.7

(Continued)

Table 6.3 *(Continued)*

	All Officers	Reasonable Force Used	Improper Force Used
Education			
No college degree	68.3	56.8	72.2
Associate's degree	15.8	18.9	16.7
Bachelor's degree	15.9	24.3	11.1
Should quiet family disputes			
No	7.2	5.7	11.1
Yes	92.8	94.3	88.9
Should handle public nuisances			
No	61.6	77.1	83.5
Yes	38.4	22.9	16.7
Should not handle personal problems			
Strongly agree	8.0	13.5	11.1
Agree	24.1	29.7	44.4
Disagree	57.0	51.4	44.4
Strongly disagree	10.9	5.4	0.0
Fewer restrictions on use of force			
Strongly agree	12.4	16.2	27.8
Agree	30.2	35.1	38.9
Disagree	45.7	40.5	33.3
Strongly disagree	11.6	8.1	0.0
Only officers can judge use of force			
Strongly agree	16.8	16.2	11.1
Agree	30.1	37.8	55.6
Disagree	47.9	43.2	33.3
Strongly disagree	5.2	2.7	0.0
Most citizens respect police			
Strongly agree	6.3	2.7	0.0
Agree	69.9	62.2	55.6
Disagree	19.6	29.7	38.9
Strongly disagree	4.2	5.4	5.6
Citizens likely to abuse police			
Strongly agree	11.6	29.7	22.2
Agree	34.7	29.7	55.6
Disagree	47.5	32.4	22.2
Strongly disagree	6.2	8.1	0.0
N	1069	37	18

proportions agreed that "when a police officer is accused of using too much force, only other officers are qualified to judge such a case." Almost half of the officers who used improper force, and one-third of those who used force, disagreed with the statement that "most people in this community respect police officers"; three-quarters of the former and over half of the latter agreed that "the likelihood of a police officer being abused by citizens in this community is very high."

The Effects of Situational Characteristics

The data presented thus far are useful primarily for describing the incidents in which force was used: Table 6.1 displays for encounters in which force was used the percentages with specified characteristics; Table 6.2 displays for citizens against whom force was used the percentages with specified characteristics. Tables 6.4 and 6.5 lend themselves more to the identification of encounter-level correlates of the use of force.

Table 6.4 breaks down the use of force by the characteristics of encounters; it displays for encounters with specified characteristics the percentages in which force was used. The more illuminating set of figures is probably that for encounters with suspects, which are those in which the use of force is most likely in the first place. This analysis indicates that the use of reasonable force and the use of improper force (1) are more likely in encounters that involve violent crimes than in those that involve other kinds of problems; (2) are more likely in encounters that involve automobile pursuits than in those that do not; (3) are more likely in encounters with at least four bystanders, and still more likely in encounters that involve ten or more bystanders; and (4) are more likely in encounters in which more than one officer is involved, and much more likely in encounters in which at least five officers are involved.

Table 6.5 breaks down the use of force by the characteristics of citizens; it displays for citizens with specified characteristics the percentages against whom force was used. Once again, the more illuminating set of figures is probably that for suspects. This bivariate analysis indicates that the use of reasonable force and the use of improper force (1) are somewhat more likely if the citizen is black, male, and over eighteen; (2) are more likely if the citizen exhibits signs of drunkenness or mental disorder; (3) are more likely if the citizen has a weapon, and still more likely if the citizen attempts to use a weapon; and (4) are more likely if the citizen is hostile or antagonistic, and especially if the citizen fights with the officer(s).

Tables 6.4 and 6.5 show only bivariate associations; they do not enable one to isolate the independent effects of individual variables, nor do they form the basis for an assessment of the explanatory power of

Table 6.4 Use of force by characteristics of encounters

	All Encounters		Encounters with Suspects*	
	Reasonable Force Used	**Improper Force Used**	**Reasonable Force Used**	**Improper Force Used**
Type of Problem				
Violent crime	3.8	2.4	9.1	5.7
Nonviolent crime	0.6	0.3	4.0	1.3
Suspicious circumstances	0.5	0.9	1.4	0.6
Interpersonal conflict	1.8	0.6	2.8	0.9
Dependent person	0.7	1.5	1.3	1.3
Morals offense	1.2	0.0	1.8	0.0
Public nuisance	0.8	0.0	1.3	0.0
Traffic	0.2	0.2	—	—
Medical problem	0.0	0.0	0.0	0.0
Assistance	0.0	0.0	0.0	0.0
Information	0.0	0.0	0.0	0.0
Internal operations	0.0	0.8	0.0	1.7
Other/miscellaneous	0.0	0.0	0.0	0.0
Car chase	2.0	5.9	12.5	12.5
No car chase	0.6	0.4	2.2	0.9
Location				
Street, sidewalk, parking lot	0.7	0.2	2.4	0.5
Public/commercial bldg.	0.8	0.8	3.6	2.7
Private residence	0.5	0.5	1.7	1.3
Other	1.3	1.3	2.9	1.4
Bystanders				
None	0.3	0.1	0.8	0.4
1–3	0.1	0.1	0.3	0.3
4–10	1.8	0.9	4.9	1.1
More than 10	6.0	4.6	12.3	6.6
Other Officers				
None	0.1	0.0	0.4	0.1
One	0.8	0.3	2.0	0.4
2–5	2.3	1.1	5.2	0.9
More than 5	8.6	17.2	12.5	25.0
Supervisor(s) present	2.3	2.5	4.6	4.1

* Excluding those suspected only of traffic violations.

Table 6.5 Use of force by characteristics of citizens

	All Citizens (N = 8666)		Suspects Only* (N = 1819)	
	Reasonable Force Used	**Improper Force Used**	**Reasonable Force Used**	**Improper Force Used**
Role				
Suspect	1.3	0.7	1.9	0.9
Victim	0.0	0.0	—	—
Sick/injured person	0.8	1.7	—	—
Subject of concern	0.0	1.8	—	—
Person requesting service	0.1	0.0	—	—
Witness/person with information	0.0	0.1	—	—
Other	0.0	0.0	—	—
Race				
White	0.2	0.2	1.2	0.7
Black	0.9	0.5	2.9	1.1
Other	0.0	0.0	0.0	0.0
Mixed	0.0	0.0	0.0	0.0
Gender				
Male	0.6	0.3	2.2	1.0
Female	0.2	0.2	1.5	0.6
Mixed	0.0	0.0	0.0	0.0
Age				
Under 18	0.5	0.4	1.3	0.2
19–35	0.6	0.4	2.3	1.1
Over 35	0.3	0.2	2.5	1.6
Mixed	0.0	0.0	0.0	0.0
Sobriety				
Sober	0.2	0.2	1.1	0.4
Drinking/using	1.2	0.4	2.7	0.4
Drunk/stoned	4.4	3.0	7.8	4.8
Mental Disorder				
No evidence of disorder	0.4	0.2	1.8	0.7
Evidence of disorder	4.5	3.6	10.8	2.7
Weapon				
None in possession	0.4	0.2	1.7	0.7
Possessed gun	5.6	2.8	10.0	5.0

(*Continued*)

Table 6.5 (*Continued*)

	All Citizens (N = 8666)		Suspects Only* (N = 1819)	
	Reasonable Force Used	Improper Force Used	Reasonable Force Used	Improper Force Used
Possessed knife	5.7	7.1	8.9	6.7
Tried to use	20.0	40.0	25.0	25.0
Demeanor				
Detached	3.0	0.8	5.1	1.3
Hostile, antagonistic	5.7	7.6	9.9	11.0
Other	0.3	0.2	1.3	0.3
Fought with officer	28.0	60.0	41.2	47.1

* Excluding those suspected only of traffic violations.

these sets of variables. For example, the citizen's race and demeanor are both related to the use of force. Some previous research has found that the citizen's race and demeanor are both related to arrest, but that when one statistically controls for the effect of demeanor, race has no effect. A multivariate analysis, using suspects as the units of analysis, permits one to impose statistical controls and thus to estimate the independent effects of these variables, summarized in the form of regression coefficients, and it also provides an estimate of the extent to which these variables together account for the use of force.

The results of a multinomial logit analysis are shown in Table 6.6.[24] This analysis produces two sets of coefficients: one set reflects the estimated effects of the variables on the use of reasonable force, and the other reflects the estimated effects of the variables on the use of improper force. The statistical significance of each coefficient indicates the confidence that one can have in rejecting the null hypothesis that the variable has no effect. Otherwise, however, the coefficients have no intuitive interpretation. Thus, the table also presents for each variable (X) the estimated probability that force will be used, i.e., Pr(Y), given that X has the value shown in brackets, and given that all of the other variables have their modal values. The last column shows the estimated change in the probability given that X changes from its modal value to the value in brackets.

Several variables have statistically significant effects both on the use of reasonable force and on the use of improper force. Either reasonable or improper force is more likely in incidents that involve violent crimes, and against suspects who are male, black, drunk, antagonistic, or who

Table 6.6 The effects of situational factors on the use of force

	Reasonable force			Improper force		
Variable (mode)	**Coefficient**	**Pr(Y|x = [])**	**Change**	**Coefficient**	**Pr(Y|x = [])**	**Change**
Violent crime (0)	1.555*	.01777[1]	.01394	2.436*	.00076[1]	.00009
Nonviolent crime (0)	1.108**	.01150[1]	.00767	−1.582	.00001[1]	.00005
Car chase (0)	1.271	.01341[1]	.00958	4.640*	.00692[1]	.00685
Street, sidewalk, parking lot (1)	0.335	.00274[0]	−.00109	0.928	.00003[0]	−.00004
Public/commercial bldg. (0)	0.397	.00568[1]	.00185	2.144	.00006[1]	.00051
Police station/car (0)	−14.191	.00000[1]	−.00383	−11.096	.00000[1]	−.00007
Number of bystanders (0)	0.034*	.00396[1]	.00013	0.004	.00007[1]	.00000
		.00453[5]	.00070		.00007[5]	.00000
		.00636[15]	.00253		.00007[15]	.00000
Number of other officers (0)	0.141	.00440[1]	.00057	0.293**	.00009[1]	.00002
		.00771[5]	.00388		.00029[5]	.00022
		.01547[10]	.01164		.00126[10]	.00119
Supervisor(s) present (0)	−0.785	.00175[1]	−.00208	0.821	.00015[1]	.00009
Citizen black (0)	1.265*	.01342[1]	.00959	2.133*	.00057[1]	.00050
Citizen male (1)	1.549*	.00082[0]	−.00301	3.440*	.00000[0]	−.00007
Citizen 19–35 (1)	0.711	.00188[0]	−.00195	1.034	.00002[0]	−.00004
Citizen over 35 (0)	0.692	.00761[1]	.00378	1.381	.00027[1]	.00020
Citizen drunk/stoned (0)	1.453*	.01615[1]	.01232	1.992*	.00049[1]	.00042
Citizen mentally disordered (0)	1.479**	.01658[1]	.01275	−0.226	.00005[1]	−.00001
Citizen possessed weapon (0)	0.990	.01023[1]	.00640	1.600	.00033[1]	.00027

(Continued)

Table 6.6 (*Continued*)

	Reasonable force			Improper force		
Variable (mode)	**Coefficient**	**Pr(Y|x = [])**	**Change**	**Coefficient**	**Pr(Y|x = [])**	**Change**
Citizen used weapon (0)	–4.295*	.00052[1]	–.00378	–5.238	.00000[1]	–.00007
Citizen hostile, antagonistic (0)	1.280*	.01361[1]	.00978	2.795*	.00110[1]	.00103
Citizen fought with officer (0)	5.501*	.45310[1]	.44927	7.595*	.06531[1]	.06524

* p<.05, two-tailed test

** p<.10, two-tailed test

physically resist the police. Physical resistance has by far the greatest effect on the use of force. But even when the effects of physical resistance are statistically controlled, the suspect's demeanor has significant effects on the use of force. And even when the effects of physical resistance and of demeanor are statistically controlled, the suspect's race has significant effects on the use of force. That officers are more likely to use even reasonable force against blacks might suggest that officers are, on average, more likely to adopt a penal or coercive approach to black suspects than they are to white suspects.[25] For example,

> Shortly after midnight we received a call of disturbance and [the observed officer] proceeded to the scene without delay. We were the first to arrive and noticed two older women and a man standing on the south side of the street and a large group of younger women standing on a porch on the north side of the street. There was no disturbance upon arrival. [The observed officer] pulled up by the smaller group of people and asked them if they had called the police. They said that they had not. The [officer] apparently assumed (correctly) that the man in the group was the source of trouble, for he told the man that someone had called the police about a disturbance and that it would be necessary for them to go inside. The man (black, 30) said that there was no problem and stood his ground. At this point another [officer] and a friend of the man walked up to our car. [The observed officer] said that whether there was a problem or not they would have to get off the street. One of the women (the mans [sic] mother) told him to go inside but the man began muttering about how no one was going to tell him what to do. It was then that I realized that he was very drunk. [The observed officer] said that if the man didn't get off the street and the police got another call to come out he would be arrested. The man didn't like this at all and began raving about how there was no problem and about how the police were just trying to hassle him. The friend pleaded with the man to come inside but the man would not move and continued his muttering. [The observed officer] got out of the car and placed himself very near the man. He began saying something about not going anywhere and [the officer] told the man that he was under arrest. [The second officer] helped handcuff the man who was being very uncooperative. His friend told him that he was ignorant and asked the [officer] if he could go to the station with them. [The officer] said yes. They placed the man in the back seat of our car and we drove to the station, all the while being accussed [sic] of harassment

> and racism. The man threatened to kill us and [the officer] said he would have his chance when we got to the station. When we arrived [the officer] took him out of the car but the man started pulling away. [The second officer] grabbed him by the hair and [the observed officer] said that he had originally planned to let the man go when they got to the station but since the man was being such an ass he was going to book him.

In this case, the officer's actions early in the encounter—ordering the man to get off the street and then confronting and challenging him—were, arguably, precipitous and ill advised, making it all the more likely that force would later need to be used.

Several additional variables have statistically significant effects on the use of reasonable force, but *not* on the use of improper force.[26] The likelihood that reasonable force will be used rises with the number of bystanders. The use of reasonable force is also more likely if the encounter involves a nonviolent crime and if there is some evidence that the citizen has a mental disorder. Curiously, the use of reasonable force is *less* likely if the citizen uses a weapon.

The effect of bystanders, and perhaps even of mental disorder, may reflect some officers' judgment that such encounters are best handled with dispatch. For example,

> We were on routine patrol when flagged down by an [officer] waving a flashlight. He was out of breath from chasing a "mental", a black woman about 22 years old. We noticed an ambulence [sic] in the parking lot of an apartment complex, and [the observed officer] decided to check it out. The first officer explained that the young woman had been drinking heavily and had put her head through a plate glass window, sustaining minor (but bloody) injuries. Her mother had called both the police and the ambulence because the woman had a history of drinking and mental disorder and might abuse her two children. When the police arrived, the woman ran away, covering about two blocks before the police and her mother caught her. When we arrived, the woman was having a heated discussion with her mother about whether or not she should go to the hospital. A third [officer] arrived. Two National Ambulence attendants were also trying to persuade the woman to go along. She became more and more distraught, and began yelling and cursing the attendants and officers. Lights began appearing in apartment windows, and several people began filtering out toward the confrontation. The woman kept screaming, "Momma, you done me wrong." Suddenly, [the observed officer]

> and the first [officer] grabbed the woman by the arms and began dragging her, kicking and screaming, to the ambulence. She was rather large, and put up a good struggle. The third [officer] and an attendant each had to grab a leg. They threw her on a stretcher. [The observed officer] sat on her legs while the other two officers held her arms and the attendants tied her hands and feet to the stretcher. She cursed and spit at the officers. [The observed officer] bounced on her legs and grinned. (She was wearing a bathrobe and underwear, and the bathrobe lost its effectiveness in the struggle. [The observed officer] mocked the woman, saying that her spit was 100 proof. The mildest epithet used was "Get your white ass offa me, motherfucker." An attendant put a pillow over her face to keep her from spitting.). . . . In reflecting on the case as we patrolled, the [observed officer] mentioned that he had stopped even though there were two officers on the scene because both were young and sometimes indecisive. He said that the officers let the situation drag on too long, that people were beginning to come out of their apartments, and that he had to act.

This officer apparently believed that the encounter was better resolved before a large crowd formed, and the dynamics of the encounter were thereby altered (as Muir [1977: Ch. 7] illustrates in his discussion of "the crowd scene").

Two variables have statistically significant effects on the use of improper force, but not on the use of reasonable force. Improper force is more likely if the encounter involves a car chase, even controlling for physical resistance by the suspect. One reason may be that pursuits are emotionally and physiologically intense experiences that are *sometimes*—i.e., in some cases and/or for some officers—"catalytic" (see Toch, 1996); one would do well to remember that most pursuits do not conclude with the use of excessive or unnecessary force. Another reason may be that a suspect's flight is another form of disrespect for police authority, as is a hostile or antagonistic demeanor, which sometimes prompts officers to unduly assert their authority. Either explanation could account for the following:

> At about 18:05, we were sitting in the car in a parking lot on the corner of B and LK talking to a patrol supervisor, when a Lilliput [a pseudonym for another municipality] police car went by chasing a motorcycle. Both the patrol car and the supervisor took off after the bike, which had turned onto LK Avenue. We chased him down LK to S, where he turned right and onto LT and back into Lilliput. By the time a Lilliput car and our car stopped him, two

> other Lilliput cars and another Metro [also a pseudonym] car had arrived. Two Lilliput officers and a Lilliput detective jumped out of their cars, tackled the suspect, roughed him up a bit, and handcuffed him. . . . The suspect was frisked and loaded into the back of a Lilliput patrol car.

The likelihood of improper force also rises with the number of officers at the scene. This finding too is open to at least two interpretations (Friedrich, 1977: 93). One is that an officer is more likely to use force when other officers are there to provide physical and social psychological reinforcements. Another is that incidents in which force is used are also those to which other officers come or are summoned; according to this interpretation, the presence of other officers is an effect rather than a cause. Unfortunately, the analysis does not permit one to eliminate either interpretation.

In some respects, these results parallel Friedrich's, who found that "police use of force depends primarily on two factors: how the offender behaves and whether or not other citizens and police are present" (1980: 95). In particular, Friedrich's results show that the use of force is affected by the citizen's demeanor and sobriety. This analysis of the PSS data corroborates these findings: drunkenness, a hostile demeanor, and especially physical resistance all make the use of force more likely. But Friedrich's analysis indicated that the use of force is unaffected by other characteristics of citizens, such as race and gender. The results of this analysis indicate that the use of force *is* affected by race as well as by gender.[27]

The explanatory power of situational factors can be assessed in terms of the success of the model in "predicting" the use-of-force outcomes of these encounters; the proportion of cases that are correctly classified can be compared with the proportion that one could correctly classify based on knowledge only of the frequencies of the outcomes. Given that the use of force is so uncommon, however, predictions based only on the frequencies would be quite accurate. Indeed, one could correctly classify over 97 percent of the cases if one predicted that force was *never* used; if one randomly classified cases to reproduce the frequencies, one could correctly classify 94.6 percent. So overall, the model would seem to have little room for improvement in predictive success—no more than a 5.7 percent improvement over random classification. In fact, the model's predictions correctly classify 97.7 percent of the cases, a 3.3 percent improvement over chance. A fairer assessment of the model, perhaps, is its success in classifying cases in which force was used; random classification would result, on average, in 2 percent correct (one of forty-nine cases), while the model yields 24.5 percent correct. Furthermore, this analysis also suggests that, together, these situational factors better predict the use of improper force than they do the use of reasonable force. Five of thirty-five cases (14 percent) are correctly classified as those in which reasonable force was used, while seven of fourteen cases (50 percent) are correctly classified as those in which improper force was used.

The Effects of Officers' Characteristics

Table 6.7 breaks down the use of force by the characteristics of officers; it displays for officers with specified characteristics the percentages who used force. (Table 6.3 displays for officers who used force the percentages with specified characteristics.) This bivariate analysis indicates that black officers and officers with college degrees are somewhat more likely to use force, but also that black officers and officers with bachelor's degrees are somewhat less likely to use improper force. The analysis also indicates that the two forms of force bear modest relationships to officers' attitudes. Officers who conceive their role in narrow terms, by excluding public nuisances and personal problems, are somewhat more likely to use force. Officers who believe that force is effective and officers who believe that the use of force should be regulated by police themselves are somewhat more likely to use force. Finally, officers whose views of citizens are negative—who believe that citizens do not respect

Table 6.7 Use of force by characteristics of officers

	Reasonable Force Used	Improper Force Used	N
Race			
White	3.3	1.7	948
Black	4.5	0.9	112
Other	8.3	8.3	12
Gender			
Male	3.7	1.8	1003
Female	0.0	0.0	69
Length of Service			
Less than 1 year	0.0	0.0	20
1 to 3 years	3.7	2.1	326
4 to 8 years	3.8	1.7	476
More than 8 years	2.8	1.2	250

(Continued)

Table 6.7 *(Continued)*

	Reasonable Force Used	Improper Force Used	N
Education			
No college degree	2.9	1.8	733
Associate's degree	4.1	1.8	169
Bachelor's degree	5.3	1.2	171
Should quiet family disputes			
No	2.6	2.6	76
Yes	3.4	1.6	974
Should handle public nuisances			
No	4.2	2.4	638
Yes	2.0	0.8	397
Should not handle personal problems			
Strongly agree	5.9	2.4	85
Agree	4.3	3.1	257
Disagree	3.1	1.3	608
Strongly disagree	1.7	0.0	116
Fewer restrictions on use of force			
Strongly agree	4.5	3.8	133
Agree	4.0	2.2	323
Disagree	3.1	1.2	489
Strongly disagree	2.4	0.0	124
Only officers judge use of force			
Strongly agree	3.3	1.1	180
Agree	4.3	3.1	322
Disagree	3.1	1.2	512
Strongly disagree	1.8	0.0	56
Most citizens respect police			
Strongly agree	1.5	0.0	67
Agree	3.1	1.3	747
Disagree	5.3	3.3	209
Strongly disagree	4.4	2.2	45
Citizens likely to abuse police			
Strongly agree	8.9	3.2	124
Agree	3.0	2.7	371
Disagree	2.4	0.8	508
Strongly disagree	4.5	0.0	66

and are likely to abuse police—are somewhat more likely to use force. However, judging from the percentage differences alone, these relationships are as weak as they are consistent with expectations.

Multivariate analyses using officers as the units of analysis form a better basis for assessing the impacts of officers' characteristics on their use of force. For such an analysis, one may measure officers' use of force as counts—the numbers of occasions on which each officer was observed to use reasonable force and improper force, respectively—or as dichotomies—whether or not each officer was observed using reasonable force and improper force, respectively. As it turns out, the results are very much the same, regardless of the measure and the statistical technique used.[28] Since OLS coefficients are more intuitively interpretable than logit or Poisson regression coefficients, Table 6.8 displays the results of two OLS regression analyses: one on the use of reasonable force and the other on the use of improper force.

Only three variables (other than the amount of time for which officers were observed) have significant effects on one or both forms of force. First, officers' attitudes toward citizens—i.e., citizens' respect for police and the perceived likelihood that officers would be abused by citizens—have significant effects both on officers' use of reasonable force and on their use of improper force;[29] officers with more negative attitudes toward citizens are more likely to use force, reasonably or

Table 6.8 The effects of officers' characteristics on their use of force—OLS Estimates

	Reasonable Force	Improper Force
Constant	.199	.138
Race (black = 1)	.003	–.015
Gender (female = 1)	–.079	–.044
Associate's degree	.058	.003
Bachelor's degree	.078**	–.011
Length of service	.003	–.001
Role orientation	.007	–.010
Attitude toward force	.000	.010***
Attitude toward citizens	–.045*	–.017*
Time observed (in 100s of mins)	.061**	.001
R^2	.037	.031
N = 463		

* p<.05, two-tailed test
** p<.10, two-tailed test
*** p<.10, one-tailed test

unreasonably. Second, the effect of officers' attitudes toward the use of force on their use of improper force is of marginal statistical significance (at the .10 level with a one-tailed test); officers with more positive attitudes toward the use of force tend to use force improperly with greater frequency.[30] Third, the effect of officers' education on their use of reasonable force is statistically significant (at the .07 level in the OLS regression and at the .05 level in the Poisson regression); in particular, officers with bachelor's degrees are more likely to use reasonable force.

Overall, then, officers' characteristics contribute very little to an explanation of the use of reasonable or improper force in these data. In OLS analyses, these variables explain hardly any of the variation—less than 3 to 4 percent—in officers' use of force. (In logit analyses, this set of variables has practically no predictive power; all of the officers were classified as having not used force.) Furthermore, one might suspect that even these modest relationships are partially or entirely spurious, inasmuch as officers who are assigned to the more active, violent, and socially disorganized police districts, in which the use of force is more frequently necessary, might as a result have more negative attitudes toward citizens; those officers might also be those with less seniority, and thus younger, less experienced, and more highly educated. When officers' characteristics are included with situational factors in an analysis using suspects as the units of analysis, only one of these three variables—officers' attitudes toward citizens—has a statistically significant effect, and only on the use of reasonable force. Psychological hypotheses about officers' use of force find some, but not much, support in these analyses of the PSS data.

The Effects of Organizational Characteristics

As one might expect, given the infrequency with which force was used in the observed encounters, the incidence of force varies very little across the twenty-four departments. In eleven departments there were no observed uses of force; in each of five other departments there was only one observed case of reasonable force; and in each of another five departments observers recorded two or three uses of force. In each of the remaining three departments, observers recorded ten, sixteen, and nineteen incidents in which force was used, respectively. These raw numbers are potentially misleading, however, as these three departments were not only the largest departments, but also those in which the largest numbers of shifts were observed. Taking into account the varying amount of observation across departments as well as the frequency with which officers in the respective departments encounter suspected offenders, one finds, for example, that the incidence of improper force in three smaller departments equals or exceeds that in the largest departments. But even when the use of force is standardized across departments for the duration of observation, these estimates of the use of force as an *organizational* property rest on a narrow foundation of data collection; in the smaller departments, observation extended over only fifteen to thirty shifts, or 120 to about 250 hours.

Rather than use the departments as the units of analysis, one can include the theoretically relevant characteristics of the departments with situational factors in the same model, using suspects as the units of analysis. This approach has the advantage of controlling for the frequency with which officers in different departments confront the kinds of situations in which force is more likely. Three characteristics of the departments, which are featured in organizational theory, can be measured with PSS data.

First, the bureaucratization of the departments can be measured in terms of their size (the number of full-time employees), their levels of hierarchy or vertical differentiation (the number of separate ranks), their degree of specialization (the number of separate units, such as traffic, juvenile, etc.), and the extent to which the departments are civilianized. These characteristics can be analyzed as individual variables, or they can be combined to form a single index of bureaucratization.[31] In either case, bureaucratization is conceived as a continuum, rather than as a dichotomy (or as a synonym for organization).

Second, the priority that the chiefs of the departments place on law enforcement and crime fighting can be gleaned from in-depth interviews with the chiefs and with other high-ranking police administrators. Respondents' answers to one or more of three questions in these interviews provide some clues to their priorities:

(1) Would you characterize the department's emphasis as being one of primarily providing service to residents, as primarily trying to suppress crime, or as something in between?
(2) Are there any specific departmental policies regarding patrol style or emphasis?
(3) What kinds of reports do you [does the chief] get on day-to-day operations of your patrol officers? (Probes: What things get brought to the chief's attention immediately? What kinds of indicators does the chief think are important regarding patrol?)

On the basis of these interview data, three departments appear to have a decidedly "legalistic" or "professional" orientation (Wilson, 1968), in the sense that their chiefs place primary emphasis on fighting crime. One chief, for example, told the PSS interviewer that

> the department's first priority was the suppression and prevention of crime, and its second priority was responding to calls for service. The respondent felt that the department receives many trivial or "bullshit" calls for service. . . . The department does what it can to respond to all calls, but such calls as these take low priority.

Furthermore, administrators in that department monitored patrol officers' performance through time sheets, filled out by each officer,

> indicating how much time he spent on a variety of activities and various production measures: hours on patrol, hours traffic control, hours accident investigation, hours special duty, hours court, hours office duty, hours writing reports, hours approved overtime, sick leave, number of field interrogation reports filed, number of miscellaneous investigations conducted, number of complaints investigated, number of accidents investigated, number of non-traffic arrests, number of traffic arrests, number of accident arrests, number of warrant arrests, number of juvenile arrests, number of warnings issued.

This chief's express priority on crime fighting was reinforced by the department's information system.

Predictably, perhaps, not all chiefs' answers revealed an unambiguous and well-ordered set of priorities. Of course, some chiefs may have been reluctant to tell interviewers that, in effect, "service" was secondary to suppressing crime; they may have shared the orientation, but not the candor, of other chiefs whose departments have been coded as legalistic. But it is equally or more likely that ambiguous answers reflected truly ambiguous priorities. For better or worse, police administrators typically are not compelled to establish clear priorities among the multiple and sometimes competing goals and functions of the police; the LAPD may be exceptional in the clarity of its priorities. Be that as it may, priorities can be communicated, even unwittingly, in the form of activity report categories, the criteria for evaluation, the reasons for sanctions, orders, memoranda, and the like. The PSS interviews with police administrators do not suffice to measure priorities established in these ways, but the measure based on these data certainly represents an improvement over those available for previous research (e.g., Friedrich, 1980).[32]

Third, survey data on patrol officers in each department can be aggregated to measure some features of the informal cultures of the departments. Besides the observed officers, all or a sample of the other officers in each department were included in the survey.[33] Their responses to seven questionnaire items, described earlier for the analysis of officers, reveal wide variation in the collective attitudes of the departments. For example, the proportions of respondents who agreed that police should not have to handle social or personal problems ranged from 6.3 percent in one department to 62.5 percent in another. The proportion of respondents who agreed that fewer restrictions on the use of force would reduce the serious crime problems in tough neighborhoods ranged from 14.3 percent in one department to 69.2 percent in another.

When these variables—bureaucratization, the priority placed on crime fighting, and the collective attitudes of patrol officers—are added to situational factors in analyses of the use of force, the estimated effect of one organizational characteristic achieves statistical significance: the likelihood that reasonable force will be used increases with the bureaucratization of the department (see Table 6.9).[34] The effect of bureaucratization on the use of improper force does not achieve a customary level of statistical significance (although it too has a positive sign), and the estimated effects of the other organizational variables are negligible. The inclusion of organizational factors modestly improves the explanatory power of the model: 28.6 percent of the cases in which force was used are classified correctly, compared with 24.5 percent correctly classified based only on the situational factors.

It would seem, then, that compared with officers in more bureaucratized departments, officers in less bureaucratized departments either are less likely to use force when it would be justified, seeking instead to handle problems in other ways, or are less likely to take actions early in an encounter that make it more probable that force will be necessary later in an encounter. These results may thus offer some support for the proposition that in smaller, less bureaucratic departments, administrators can more effectively monitor the performance of officers, and perhaps that supervision can more frequently extend to the development of subordinates' judgment. These are long inferential leaps, to be sure, but they are consistent with the quantitative results.

These conclusions find some additional support in the interviews with administrators. The chief of one department pointed out that his "is a small enough department to allow [him] to read each crime report every day or two." When asked about the reports that are used to get a feel for day-to-day operations, another chief, whose department was relatively small (with twenty-seven full-time patrol officers),

> pointed out that he does have the daily activity sheets that comes [sic] in to rely on. But his further comments indicate that he relies

Table 6.9 The effects of organizational factors on the use of force

	Reasonable Force			Improper Force		
Variable (mode)	**Coefficient**	**$Pr(Y \mid x=[])$**	**Change**	**Coefficient**	**$Pr(Y \mid x=[])$**	**Change**
Violent crime (0)	1.503*	.01541[1]	.01194	2.579*	.00033[1]	.00030
Nonviolent crime (0)	1.127**	.01063[1]	.00716	−1.816	>.00001[1]	−.00003
Car chase (0)	1.662	.01791[1]	.01444	5.567*	.00643[1]	.00640
Street, sidewalk, parking lot (1)	0.339	.00248[0]	−.00099	1.586	.00001[0]	−.00002
Public/commercial bldg. (0)	0.391	.00365[1]	.00018	2.863**	.00009[1]	.00006
Police station/car (0)	−15.956	.00000[1]	−.00347	−12.562	.00000[1]	−.00003
Number of bystanders (0)	0.030*	.00358[1]	.00011	0.010	.00003[1]	.00000
		.00403[5]	.00056		.00003[5]	.00000
		.00543[15]	.00196		>.00003[15]	.00000
Number of other officers (0)	0.065	.00370[1]	.00023	0.231	.00003[1]	.00000
		.00480[5]	.00133		.00008[5]	.00005
		.00663[10]	.00316		.00025[10]	.00022
Supervisor(s) present (0)	−0.454	.00221[1]	−.00126	1.485	.00011[1]	.00008
Citizen black (0)	1.043*	.00978[1]	.00631	2.370*	.00027[1]	.00024
Citizen male (1)	1.577*	.00072[0]	−.00275	4.275*	.00000[0]	−.00003
Citizen 19–35 (1)	0.733	.00167[0]	−.00180	0.543	.00001[0]	−.00002
Citizen over 35 (0)	0.555	.00291[1]	−.00056	0.732	.00003[1]	.00000
Citizen drunk/stoned (0)	1.514*	.01558[1]	.01211	2.134*	.00021[1]	.00018
Citizen mentally disordered (0)	1.243***	.01193[1]	.00846	−0.268	.00002[1]	−.00001
Citizen possessed weapon (0)	1.272**	.01227[1]	.00880	1.859**	.00016[1]	.00013
Citizen used weapon (0)	−19.302	.00000[1]	−.00347	−20.517	.00000[1]	−.00003

Citizen hostile, antagonistic (0)	1.257*	.01208[1]	.00861	3.303*	.00068[1]	.00065
Citizen fought with officer(0)	20.521	.95369[1]	.95022	22.425	.04631[1]	.04628
Legalistic department (0)	−16.435	.00000[1]	−.00347	−14.635	.00000[1]	−.00003
Bureaucratization (a)	0.166*	.00208[b]	−.00139	0.220***	.00001[b]	−.00002
		.00503[c]	.00156		.00004[c]	.00001

* p<.05, two-tailed test
** p<.10, two-tailed test
*** p<.10, one-tailed test
a = 1.13 (see footnote 34)
b = −1.97 (see footnote 34)
c = 3.38 (see footnote 34)

> at least as heavily on other means of keeping tabs on day-to-day operations. Just listening to the radio, he said, is a good way to tell how things are going. And he pointed out that he can tell by the tone of voice of the officers, the way they are answering calls, whether there is anything wrong, and he said that listening to the men talking around the department is also a good way to keep track of daily operations. He emphasized that not anyone can do this; one has to know the individual officer's personality to be able to tell if the person is quieter than usual.

Needless to say, the chiefs of larger departments are scarcely in a position to take advantage of these sources of information. Larger, more bureaucratic agencies tend to rely on quantitative measures of performance, both of individuals and of the agency as a whole, and the less quantifiable aspects of police performance may thus receive too little attention. Indeed, the chief of one larger department (with 381 full-time patrol officers)

> "mentioned that a big problem in law enforcement was an overwhelming concern for statistical measures of performance, such as arrest rates, clearance rates, crime rates. [The chief] indicated that many of the statistics are misleading, but that nearly all professional departments use them, people come to expect their use, and it is difficult to come up with other more meaningful comparative measures of police performance."

Quantitative indicators of performance are useful primarily for measuring officers' productivity in enforcement; they reveal little about officers' performance of other police tasks, or even about some aspects of their enforcement activities, such as the judiciousness with which they use force. Police administrators are not blind to this problem. But as the Christopher Commission's analysis suggests, a higher incidence of the use of force may be one consequence of relying too heavily on such performance measures. A decentralized administrative structure, which would permit mid-level managers to monitor officers' performance through a more complete range of information channels, might enable the subunits of a large department to capture some of the managerial advantages of smaller departments (see Brown, 1981: Ch. 10; Whitaker, 1983). An explicit and vigorous commitment to addressing the problems of the community as the community defines them might also be steps in the right direction, insofar as it underscores both the multiplicity of the functions that police perform and the legitimacy of citizen preferences in shaping police policy.

CONCLUSIONS

Analyses both of the Black-Reiss data and the PSS data, as well as of other data, show that physical force is infrequently used by the police, and that improper force is still less frequently used. Is police brutality, then, "rare"? The incidence of the use of improper force is rare in the sense that aircraft fatalities are rare: it is infrequent relative to the large volume of interactions between police and citizens, just as deaths in aircraft accidents are infrequent relative to the large number of passenger-miles flown. That these events are rare does not, of course, mean that no effort need be devoted to making them still rarer. Both types of events are almost certainly inevitable to some degree, so long as neither officers nor pilots are recruited from the ranks of philosopher-kings. But as we extend our understanding of how best to structure and regulate human behavior, we may expect that the frequency of either event can be further reduced.

Analyses of the Black-Reiss data and the PSS data also show that to some extent, the use and abuse of force by police is influenced by characteristics of the situations in which officers and citizens interact. Of course, it would be very surprising indeed to find that the use of force is distributed randomly across police-citizen encounters; that officers are more likely to use force, say, against suspects who offer physical resistance is hardly startling. That officers are more likely to use force—and especially improper force—against suspects who are inebriated or antagonistic (other things being equal) is—if not unexpected—cause for concern. That officers are more likely to use improper force against black suspects (other things being equal) is cause for grave concern. Unfortunately, although these results form the basis for causal inferences, they are open to different interpretations. For example, one might interpret the effect of race simply as the behavioral manifestation of hostile police attitudes toward African Americans. A somewhat different interpretation was offered by one chief of police (in a private communication with the author), who thought that some of his officers were especially fearful of black suspects; the unstated implication, I take it, is that those officers might either use force preemptively (and unnecessarily) or act unwittingly in such a way that provokes resistance to which they must respond with force. These different interpretations, moreover, would seem to have different implications for the form and likely efficacy of managerial interventions. In general, a sociological approach to *explaining* police use of force may not suffice for *understanding* the use of force.[35] Further research on the dynamics of police-citizen encounters in which force is used, with a view toward how those dynamics may be affected by—and the ways in which officers interpret—specific situational factors, could improve our understanding of these results (Worden, 1989; Mastrofski & Parks, 1990).

Neither this analysis nor previous analyses demonstrate that officers' characteristics or attitudes have a substantively (rather than merely statistically) significant effect on the use of force. Such results are consistent with the negative results of recruit screening (Grant & Grant, 1996). Even so, this analysis does offer some—albeit weak—support for psychological hypotheses, and perhaps the most prudent conclusion at this juncture is that, if officers' propensities to use force are affected by their backgrounds and beliefs, then those effects are probably contingent on other factors—such as the characteristics of the situations in which officers interact with citizens and the characteristics of the organizations in which officers work—and the effects may be interactive rather than additive—that is, officers' propensities to use force may be affected by a constellation of outlooks rather than by each outlook independent of others. For example, the officers who are most likely to use and abuse force might be those who define the police role exclusively in terms of crime fighting *and* who are inclined to bend or break rules that regulate their authority in order to bring about outcomes that they consider desirable *and* whose formal and informal training has provided them with few alternatives to the use of force; such officers might be more likely to use force *if* they work in more bureaucratic agencies that emphasize hard-nosed enforcement and that measure and reward performance accordingly. Put more succinctly, officers' attitudes and personality characteristics may bear a systematic but complex relationship to their use of force.

Research on these questions should be designed to capture these complexities. Previous observational studies have not been so designed. For both the Black-Reiss and PSS studies, the units of sample selection (within precincts and neighborhoods, respectively) were shifts. Active or busy shifts were oversampled in order to maximize the number of police-citizen encounters that observers could record. For the Black-Reiss study, 589 officers were observed for one or more shifts; the average period of observation per officer was two-and-one-half shifts (Friedrich, 1977). For the PSS, 522 officers were observed; more than half of the officers were observed for only one shift, only 60 officers were observed for as much as twenty-four hours (or about three shifts), and only 24 for as much as thirty-two hours.[36] But if the use of force is infrequent, and if the distribution of the incidence of force across officers is skewed, then officers should serve as the units for sample selection. Officers who use force most frequently could be oversampled;

the sampling frame could be stratified according to the numbers of sustained or unsustained citizen complaints, arrests for resisting arrest, use of force reports, or other departmental indicators (including the reports of other officers—see Bayley & Garofalo, 1989). The balance of the sample would be composed of other officers with similar assignments, and officers would be weighted for analysis. If observation were extended to include debriefing officers about individual encounters to obtain data on the decision rules by which they choose courses of action (Mastrofski & Parks, 1990; Worden & Brandl, 1990), and if these observations were complemented by a well-conceived survey instrument, then one might conduct a relatively powerful test of psychological hypotheses.

Finally, this analysis provides modest support for an organizational explanation of police brutality. It suggests that elements of formal organizational structure affect the incidence with which force is used. It does not, however, suggest that this effect is a simple product of restrictive policies, in terms of which discussions of administrative controls are too frequently cast. The theory on which this analysis is based, and the structural variables that were conceptualized and measured, point toward more fundamental—and less easily altered—features of the organization. Future research should continue to explore the ways in which organizational forces affect the incidence with which officers use force, but it should cast a broad theoretical net, one that reaches beyond policy and procedure with respect to the use of force and complaints about the use of force. Evidence on these propositions will accumulate slowly because comparable data on the use of force in multiple departments will be difficult to find or very expensive to collect (see Adams, 1996). But evidence will not accumulate at all unless research is guided by theory.

NOTES

Worden, Robert E. (1995). "The 'Causes' of Police Brutality: Theory and Evidence on Police Use of Force." In William A. Geller and Hans Toch, eds., *And Justice for All: Understanding and Controlling Police Abuse of Force*. Washington, DC: Police Executive Research Forum. Reprinted with permission.

1. Alissa Pollitz Worden, Gordon P. Whitaker, Hans Toch, and Dennis Blass all read an earlier draft of this paper, and I am grateful to them for their thoughtful comments.
2. However, the converse—that every theory has implications for reform—is not true.
3. See, for example, Sherman (1980b), whose discussion of violence by police focuses almost exclusively on the use of deadly force.

4. Black holds that the quantity of law can be conceived as a continuous variable, but quantitative research on police has, with few exceptions, conceived and measured it as a dichotomy.
5. I return to the issue of race later, when I review studies of the use of non-lethal force. Also see Locke (1996).
6. See Toch (1996) for a more thorough assessment, both of the commission's analysis of problem officers and of violence-prone officers more generally.
7. The other types are "professionals," "clean-beat crime-fighters," and "avoiders" (see Worden, forthcoming):

   "Professionals . . . are . . . willing to use coercive means to achieve desirable ends, but they use it with a keen sense of when, and in what proportion, it is necessary. . . . they believe that . . . the application of the law should be tempered by a sensitive appreciation of its consequences, justifying the enforcement of the law in terms of helping people. . . . these officers are neither overly aggressive on the street nor resentful of legal restrictions on their authority."

   "Clean-beat crime-fighters . . . stress the law enforcement function of the police. . . . they justify uniform (non-selective) enforcement in terms of its deterrent effect." They are very energetic and aggressive on the street, although they lack the street sense of the tough cop.

   "Avoiders . . . [are] unable to cope with the characteristic exigencies of police work. . . . They prefer to do as little police work as possible, only that amount of work necessary to meet the minimum expectations of supervisors; otherwise, they adopt what has elsewhere been called a 'lay-low-and-don't-make-waves' approach to policing."
8. Also see Lester (1996).
9. Brown (1981) makes the argument that one of the core themes of the police culture is individualism, and Fielding (1988) maintains that some officers ostensibly go along with the dominant value system but "once confident of their place, and ability to use the necessary justifying rhetoric in relation to their own complex of values, officers begin to move in and through the culture to secure their own ends" (p. 185). However, many other (less convincing) accounts of the police culture tend to highlight the forces that have homogenizing effects, both on officers' outlooks and on their behavioral patterns; little attention is given to the differing interpretations of and conformity with the norms of the culture. For example, Hunt (1985) describes the effects of peers on individual officers' conceptions of proper force and their justifications for the use of force, and while she also observes that some "violence-prone" officers repeatedly "exceed working notions of normal force" and are "not effectively held in check by routine means of peer control" (p. 336), her analysis does not allow for officers who use less than "normal" force.
10. Such a shift in expectations and incentives could perhaps be affected with the adoption of community policing, which the commission

recommended. That such a model of policing—and of police administration—would reduce the incidence of improper force is itself a largely untested (albeit plausible) hypothesis. For a theoretically rich and illuminating study that offers some support for this proposition, as well as a sobering account of the likely obstacles to implementing this model, see Guyot (1991); also see Goldstein (1987).

11. About half of all state and local police agencies employ fewer than ten full-time sworn officers (Reaves 1993: 9).
12. Reiss's (1968a) analysis of the same data reports that force was used improperly in thirty-seven cases. Friedrich's analysis rests on the characterizations of the coders, who "examined pertinent passages of the observation reports to determine if physical force had been used and if it was justified in terms of self-defense or the need to make an arrest," while Reiss "had an expert panel decide whether or not force on the order of an aggravated assault was used" (1980: fn. 12; also see Reiss, 1968a).
13. These expectations were based largely on Wilson's (1968) analysis of police styles and the organizational contexts with which they are associated. In the light of more recent research, especially Brown's (1981), it should be clear that these expectations are faulty. For many years, the LAPD was regarded as the epitome of police professionalism; elements of that professionalism, we now realize, may make the use of force *more* likely.
14. Her analysis also shows that when citizens in these incidents verbally abused or disobeyed officers, officers typically responded by issuing a command, whereupon citizens attacked the officers.
15. According to a PSS memorandum (coding update number 3, dated 29 May 1977), this category encompasses "instances where the officer is attempting to make a citizen come with him, or is attempting to separate citizens who are fighting, or similar acts. The sense here is that the officer is restraining or moving the citizen without the intent to beat the citizen."
16. The aforementioned PSS coding memo specifies that this code should be used "for instances where the officer is 'kicking ass'."
17. A gun was *drawn* by one or more officers in each of fifty-three encounters, and in one of those, the gun was fired (albeit at a rattlesnake); another type of weapon was drawn in thirty-three encounters.
18. The coded data provide little information about the temporal sequences of events. For example, the data indicate whether the citizen fought with the officer and whether the officer(s) used improper force, but they do not indicate whether the force preceded the citizen's resistance or continued after the resistance ceased—a case of unnecessary force—or the force was more than that required to subdue the citizen—a case of excessive force.
19. The location shown in Table 6.1 is the location at which the encounter began (or at which the observed officer entered). The coded data provide for up to three changes in the location of the encounter, e.g., from inside

a house to the front porch, to the squad car, and to the police station. However, these data do not enable one to determine the point (and thus the location) at which the officer(s) used force. The location changed at least once in twenty-six of the thirty-seven encounters in which reasonable force was used, in fifteen to the squad car, and in eleven to the police station or jail; both logic and the narrative data suggest that these changes accompanied arrests. The location changed at least once in thirteen of the twenty-three encounters in which improper force was used, in four to the squad car, and in seven to the police station or jail. In at least two of these, the impropriety consisted of "throwing" suspects into police cars, and in one other it involved excessive force in searching an arrestee at a jail. Otherwise, it appears that improper force was not observed in these locations.

20. "Subjects of concern" might include, for example, juveniles or drunks—people who could not be expected to care for themselves.
21. Each citizen's demeanor was coded at three points in time: at the beginning of the encounter, during the encounter, and at the end of the encounter. This analysis conservatively uses the citizen's demeanor at the beginning of the encounter, lest we confuse antagonistic behavior that prompts the use of force with antagonistic behavior prompted by the use of force.
22. A small number of the "citizens" coded by observers were actually groups of citizens; if the group was not homogeneous with respect to race, gender, or age, it was coded as "mixed."
23. In some encounters, the officer who was designated as the "primary" or observed officer, and for whom survey data could be connected to coded observations, was not among those who used force. Thus, the figures in Table 6.3 for officers who used force are based on only the primary officers who were observed to use force, and exclude other officers who used force in the observers' presence.
24. Since I have conceived the use of force as a nominal variable with three categories, I have estimated the parameters of a multinomial logit model, which is the "standard method" (Aldrich & Nelson, 1984: 37–40) for analyzing a polytomous, unordered dependent variable. As an alternative, one could operationalize the use of force—reasonable and/or improper force—as a dichotomy and apply other multivariate techniques, including the widely used Ordinary Least Squares (OLS) regression; this is the analytic approach that Friedrich (1980) used. In the PSS data, when regression equations for reasonable force and improper force, respectively, are estimated using OLS, some but not all of the findings are congruent with the multinomial logit results. Binomial logit results are largely—but not entirely—consistent with the multinomial logit results. Since OLS regression is not appropriate for dichotomous dependent variables (Hanushek & Jackson, 1977: Ch. 7; Aldrich & Nelson, 1984: Ch. 1; and, more generally, King, 1989), there is good reason to prefer the logit

results. Also see Brehm and Gates (1992) for a discussion of alternative techniques and applications to the Black-Reiss data.

25. Black (1980: Ch. 5) comes to a similar conclusion based on his analysis of dispute resolution by police using the Black-Reiss data.
26. This is not the same as saying that for each of these variables the two coefficients are significantly different from one another; to the contrary, in each case the confidence intervals for the two coefficients overlap.
27. The OLS results indicate that race has a statistically significant effect on the use of reasonable force, but not on the use of improper force. Perhaps the discrepancy between the results of the logit analysis and those of Friedrich's analysis are methodological artifacts.
28. The two measures of officers' use of force differ very little from one another, inasmuch as no officer was observed to use excessive force more than once, and only seven officers were observed to use reasonable force more than once (five used it twice and two used it on three occasions). Moreover, the estimation of model coefficients hinges neither on the measure nor on the statistical technique that is used. When the use of force is measured as an event count, both OLS regression and Poisson regression (see Inn & Wheeler, 1977; and more generally, King, 1989) yield comparable results; when the use of force is measured as a dichotomy, binomial logit yields results that are congruent with the OLS and Poisson regressions.
29. This variable is an index formed by summing officers' responses to the two questionnaire items. Neither of the items by itself achieves statistical significance in separate OLS analyses, although both are significant (one at .07 and the other at .03) in the Poisson regression.
30. This, too, is an index formed by summing officers' responses to the questionnaire items about the use of force in "tough neighborhoods" and about who (if anyone) besides police are qualified to judge allegations of improper force. In a separate analysis, the former item achieves this same marginal level of statistical significance, and the effect of the latter is insignificant.
31. This index is the sum of the standardized variables. Smith's (1984) analysis of the PSS data is based on an index of bureaucratization that was formed in a similar fashion, but using a somewhat different set of variables.
32. It is also nearer the mark of police "professionalism" than are indicators of officers' educational achievement (cf. Smith, 1984).
33. Because the survey was intended to collect information relevant to the sixty study neighborhoods, selection procedures generally identified would-be respondents who had responsibilities in those areas—for patrol, supervision, or administration. In the six largest departments, samples of officers and supervisors assigned to those areas were selected in addition to command staff; in the smaller departments, all officers, supervisors, and command staff were selected. In two departments, samples

of all officers were selected, regardless of their assignments to study neighborhoods or to other areas. Overall, of the 1,435 officers selected, 2 refused to be interviewed, 8 could not be contacted, and 8 others were not interviewed for unidentified reasons. Aggregated responses in each department are based only on respondents with a rank below sergeant, i.e., those whose primary responsibility is patrol, and who are most likely to use force or have occasion to use force.

34. The results presented in Table 6.9 are based on a model that omits measures of the collective attitudes of patrol officers, none of whose effects achieve statistical significance; results are available from the author.

    The values of bureaucratization on which predicted probabilities are calculated are not modal values, but rather scale values that correspond to hypothetical departments that are more or less bureaucratized: 1.13 is the scale score for a department with 6 ranks, 10 separate divisions, and 200 employees, 25 percent of whom are civilians; –1.97 is the score for a (less bureaucratic) department with 4 ranks, 6 divisions, and 70 employees, 20 percent of whom are civilians; 3.38 is the score for a (more bureaucratic) department with 7 ranks, 12 divisions, and 800 employees, 25 percent of whom are civilians.

35. Black (1976: 7) points out that his theory of the behavior of law "predicts and explains . . . without regard to the individual as such. . . . It neither assumes nor implies that he is, for instance, rational, goal directed, pleasure seeking, or pain avoiding. . . . It has nothing to do with how an individual experiences reality."

36. In fairness to the PSS, it should be noted that it was not designed for the purpose of analyzing police brutality.

REFERENCES

Adams, K. (1996) Measuring the prevalence of police abuse of force. In W. A. Geller & H. Toch (eds.), *Understanding and controlling police abuse of force* (pp. 52–93). New Haven, CT: Yale University Press.

Adorno, T.W., Else Frenkel-Brunswik, Daniel J. Levinson, and R. Nevitt Sanford (1950) *The authoritarian personality* (New York: Harper and Row).

Aldrich, John H., and Forrest D. Nelson (1984) Linear probability, logit, and probit models, *Quantitative Applications in the Social Sciences* (45). Beverly Hills: Sage.

Alpert, Geoffrey P. (1989) "Police use of deadly force: The Miami Experience," in Roger G. Dunham and Geoffrey P. Alpert (eds.), *Critical issues in policing: Contemporary Readings* (Prospect Heights, IL: Waveland).

Balch, Robert W. (1972) "The police personality: Fact or fiction?" *Journal of Criminal Law, Criminology, and Police Science* 63: 106–119.

Bayley, David H. (1986) "The tactical choices of police patrol officers," *Journal of Criminal Justice* 14: 329–348.

Bayley, David H. and James Garofalo (1989) "The management of violence by police patrol officers," *Criminology* 27: 1–27.

Berk, Sarah Fenstermaker, and Donileen R. Loseke (1980–81) "'Handling' family violence: Situational determinants of police arrest in domestic disturbances," *Law & Society Review* 15: 317–346.

Binder, Arnold, and Peter Scharf (1980) "The violent police-citizen encounter," *Annals of the American Academy of Political and Social Science* 452: 111–121.

Bittner, Egon (1970) *The functions of the police in modern society*. Washington: U.S. Government Printing Office.

Black, Donald (1971) "The social organization of arrest," *Stanford Law Review* 23: 1087–1111.

Black, Donald (1976) *The behavior of law* (New York: Academic Press).

Black, Donald (1980) *The manners and customs of the police* (New York: Academic Press).

Black, Donald and Albert J. Reiss, Jr. (1967) "Patterns of behavior and citizen transactions," in President's Commission on Law Enforcement and Administration of Justice, *Studies in crime and law enforcement in major metropolitan areas*, field studies III, vol. II, sec. I (Washington: U.S. Government Printing Office).

Bloch, Peter B., and Deborah Anderson (1974) *Policewomen on Patrol: Final Report* (Washington: Police Foundation).

Blumberg, Mark (1981) "Race and police shootings: An analysis in two cities," in James J. Fyfe (ed.), *Contemporary issues in law enforcement* (Beverly Hills: Sage).

Blumberg, Mark (1982) "The use of firearms by police: The impact of individuals, communities, and race," unpublished Ph.D. dissertation, State University of New York at Albany.

Brehm, John, and Scott Gates (1992) "Policing police brutality: Evaluation of principal-agent models of noncooperative behavior," paper presented at the Annual Meeting of the Midwest Political Science Association, April, Chicago.

Broderick, John J. (1977) *Police in a time of change* (Morristown, NJ: General Learning Press).

Brown, Michael K. (1981) *Working the street: Police discretion and the dilemmas of reform*. (New York: Russell Sage Foundation).

Cascio, Wayne F. (1977) "Formal education and police officer performance," *Journal of Police Science and Administration* 5: 89–96.

Cohen, Bernard, and Jan M. Chaiken (1972) *Police background characteristics and performance* (New York: Rand).

Croft, Elizabeth Benz (1985) "Police use of force: An empirical analysis," unpublished Ph.D. dissertation, State University of New York at Albany.

Dahl, Robert A. (1967) "The city in the future of democracy," *American Political Science Review* 61: 953–970.

Fielding, Nigel G. (1988) *Joining forces: Police training, socialization, and occupational competence* (London: Routledge).
Friedrich, Robert J. (1977) "The impact of organizational, individual, and situational factors on police behavior," unpublished Ph.D. dissertation, University of Michigan.
Friedrich, Robert J. (1980) "Police use of force: Individuals, situations, and organizations," *Annals of the American Academy of Political and Social Science* 452: 82–97.
Fyfe, James J. (1979) "Administrative interventions on police shooting discretion," *Journal of Criminal Justice* 7: 309–323.
Fyfe, James J. (1980) "Geographic correlates of police shooting: A microanalysis," *Journal of Research in Crime and Delinquency* 17: 101–113.
Fyfe, James J. (1981a) "Who shoots? A look at officer race and police shooting," *Journal of Police Science and Administration* 9: 367–382.
Fyfe, James J. (1981b) "Race and extreme police-citizen violence," in R.L. McNeely and Carl E. Pope (eds.), *Race, crime, and criminal justice* (Beverly Hills: Sage).
Fyfe, James J. (1982) "Blind Justice: Police Shootings in Memphis," *Journal of Criminal Law and Criminology* 73: 707–722.
Fyfe, James J. (1988) "Police use of deadly force: Research and Reform," *Justice Quarterly* 5: 165–205.
Fyfe, James, J. (1996). Training to reduce police-civilian violence. In W.A. Geller & H. Toch (eds.), *Understanding and controlling police abuse of force* (pp. 165–179). New Haven, CT: Yale University Press.
Gardiner, John A. (1969) *Traffic and the Police* (Cambridge, MA: Harvard University Press).
Geller, William A., and Kevin J. Karales (1981) "Shootings of and by Chicago Police: Uncommon Crises. Part I: Shootings by Chicago Police," *Journal of Criminal Law and Criminology* 72: 1813–1866.
Goldstein, Herman (1987) "Toward community-oriented policing: Potential, basic requirements, and threshold questions," *Crime and Delinquency* 33: 6–30.
Gouldner, Alvin W. (1954) *Patterns of industrial bureaucracy* (Glencoe, IL: Free Press).
Grennan, Sean A. (1987) "Findings on the role of officer gender in violent encounters with citizens," *Journal of Police Science and Administration* 15: 78–85.
Guyot, Dorothy (1991) *Policing as though people matter* (Philadelphia: Temple University Press).
Hanushek, Eric A., and John E. Jackson (1977) *Statistical methods for social scientists* (New York: Academic Press).
Hudzik, John K. (1978) "College education for police: Problems in measuring component and extraneous variables," *Journal of Criminal Justice* 6: 69–81.

Hunt, Jennifer (1985) "Police accounts of normal force," *Urban Life* 13: 315–341.

Independent Commission on the Los Angeles Police Department (1991) *Report of the Independent Commission on the Los Angeles Police Department* (Los Angeles: Author).

Inn, Andres, and Alan C. Wheeler (1977) "Individual differences, situational constraints, and police shooting incidents," *Journal of Applied Social Psychology* 7: 19–26.

Jermier, John M., John W. Slocum, Jr., Louis W. Fry, and Jeannie Gaines (1991) "Organizational subcultures in a soft bureaucracy: Resistance behind the myth and facade of an official culture," *Organization Science* 2: 170–194.

King, Gary (1989) *Unifying political methodology: The likelihood theory of statistical inference* (Cambridge: Cambridge University Press).

Klinger, David A. (1992) "Deference or deviance? A note on why 'hostile' suspects are arrested," paper presented at the Annual Meeting of the American Society of Criminology, November 4–7, New Orleans.

Klockars, C.B. (1996). A theory of excessive force and its control. In W.A. Geller & H. Toch (eds.), *Understanding and controlling police abuse of force* (pp. 1–22). New Haven, CT: Yale University Press.

Lefkowitz, Joel (1975) "Psychological attributes of policemen: A review of research and opinion," *Journal of Social Issues* 31: 3–26.

Lester, David (1996) "Officer opinion about police abuse of force." In W.A. Geller & H. Toch (eds.), *Understanding and controlling police abuse of force* (pp. 180–190). New Haven, CT: Yale University Press.

Lundman, Richard J. (1974) "Routine police arrest practices: A commonweal perspective," *Social Problems* 22: 127–141.

Manning, Peter K. (1977) *Police work: The social organization of policing* (Cambridge, MA: MIT Press).

Manning, Peter K. (1989) "The police occupational culture in Anglo-American societies," in William G. Bailey (ed.), *Encyclopedia of Police Science* (Dallas: Garland).

Mastrofski, Stephen (1988) "Varieties of police governance in metropolitan America," *Politics and Policy* 8: 12–31.

Mastrofski, Stephen and Roger B. Parks (1990) "Improving observational studies of police," *Criminology* 28: 475–496.

Meyer, Marshall W. (1980) "Police shootings of minorities: The case of Los Angeles," *Annals of the American Academy of Political and Social Science* 452: 98–110.

Miller, Jon, and Lincoln Fry (1976) "Reexamining assumptions about education and professionalism in law enforcement," *Journal of Police Science and Administration* 4: 187–198.

Milton, Catherine H., Jeanne W. Halleck, James Lardner, and Gary L. Abrecht (1977) *Police use of deadly force* (Washington: Police Foundation).

Muir, William Ker, Jr. (1977) *Police: Streetcorner Politicians* (Chicago: University of Chicago Press).

Prottas, Jeffrey Manditch (1978) "The power of the street-level bureaucrat in public service bureaucracies," *Urban Affairs Quarterly* 13: 285–312.

Reaves, Brian A. (1993) "Census of state and local law enforcement agencies, 1992," Bureau of Justice Statistics Bulletin (Washington: Bureau of Justice Statistics).

Reiss, Albert J., Jr. (1968a) "Police Brutality—Answers to key questions," *Trans-action* 5(8):10–19.

Reiss, Albert J., Jr. (1968b) "Stuff and nonsense about social surveys and observation," in Howard S. Becker, et al. (eds.), *Institutions and the Person* (Chicago: Aldine).

Reiss, Albert J., Jr. (1971a) *The police and the public* (New Haven: Yale University Press).

Reiss, Albert J., Jr. (1971b) "Systematic observation of natural social phenomena," in Herbert L. Costner (ed.), *Sociological Methodology 1971* (San Francisco: Jossey-Bass).

Reuss-Ianni, Elizabeth (1983) *Two cultures of policing* (New Brunswick, NJ: Transaction).

Schuman, Howard, and Michael P. Johnson (1976) "Attitudes and Behavior," *Annual Review of Sociology* 2: 161–207.

Sherman, Lawrence W. (1975) "An evaluation of policewomen on patrol in a suburban police department," *Journal of Police Science and Administration* 3: 434–438.

Sherman, Lawrence W. (1980a) "Causes of police behavior: The current state of quantitative research," *Journal of Research in Crime and Delinquency* 17: 69–100.

Sherman, Lawrence W. (1980b) "Perspectives on police and violence," *Annals of the American Academy of Political and Social Science* 452: 1–12.

Sherman, Lawrence W. (1983) "Reducing police gun use: Critical events, administrative policy, and organizational change," in Maurice Punch (ed.), *Control in the police organization* (Cambridge, MA: MIT Press).

Sherman, Lawrence W. and Mark Blumberg (1981) "Higher education and police use of deadly force," *Journal of Criminal Justice* 9: 317–331.

Skolnick, Jerome H. (1975) *Justice without trial: Law Enforcement in Democratic Society* (2nd ed.; New York: John Wiley).

Smith, Douglas A. (1984) "The organizational context of legal control," *Criminology* 22: 19–38.

Smith, Douglas A. and Jody R. Klein (1984) "Police control of interpersonal disputes," *Social Problems* 31: 468–481.

Smith, Douglas A., and Christy A. Visher (1981) "Street-level justice: Situational determinants of police arrest decisions," *Social Problems* 29: 167–177.

Smith, Douglas A., Christy A. Visher, and Laura A. Davidson (1984) "Equity and discretionary justice: The influence of race on police arrest decisions," *Journal of Criminal Law and Criminology* 75: 234–249.

Snipes, Jeffrey B., and Stephen D. Mastrofski (1990) "An empirical test of Muir's typology of police officers," *American Journal of Criminal Justice* 14: 268–296.
Sykes, Richard E. (1983) *Policing: A social behaviorist perspective* (New Brunswick, NJ: Rutgers University Press).
Sykes, Richard E., and John P. Clark (1975) "A theory of deference exchange in police-civilian encounters," *American Journal of Sociology* 81: 584–600.
Sykes, Richard E., and Edward E. Brent (1980) "The regulation of interaction by police: A systems view of taking charge," *Criminology* 18: 182–197.
Toch, Hans (1979) *Peacekeeping: Police, prisons, and violence* (Lexington, MA: Lexington Books).
Toch, Hans. (1996). The violence-prone police officer. In W.A. Geller & H. Toch (eds.), *Understanding and controlling police abuse of force* (pp. 94–112). New Haven, CT: Yale University Press.
Van Maanen, John (1974) "Working the street: A developmental view of police behavior," in Herbert Jacob (ed.), *The potential for reform of criminal justice* (Beverly Hills: Sage).
Weiner, Norman L. (1974) "The effect of education on police attitudes," *Journal of Criminal Justice* 2: 317–328.
Westley, William A. (1970) *Violence and the police: A sociological study of law, custom, and morality* (Cambridge, MA: MIT Press).
Whitaker, Gordon P. (1983) "Police department size and the quality and cost of police services," in Stuart Nagel, Erika Fairchild, and Anthony Champagne (eds.), *The political science of criminal justice* (Springfield, IL: Charles C. Thomas).
Whitaker, Gordon P., Charles David Phillips, and Alissa P. Worden (1984) "Aggressive patrol: A search for side-effects," *Law & Policy* 6: 339–360.
White, Susan O. (1972) "A perspective on police professionalization," *Law & Society Review* 7: 61–85.
Wilson, James Q. (1968) *Varieties of police behavior: The management of law and order in eight communities* (Cambridge, MA: Harvard University Press).
Wilson, James Q., and Barbara Boland (1978) "The effect of the police on crime," *Law & Society Review* 12: 367–390.
Worden, Alissa Pollitz (1993) "The attitudes of women and men in policing: Testing conventional and contemporary wisdom," *Criminology* 31: 203–241.
Worden, Robert E. (1989) "Situational and attitudinal explanations of police behavior: A theoretical reappraisal and empirical assessment," *Law & Society Review* 23: 667–711.
Worden, Robert E. (1990) "A badge and a baccalaureate: Policies, hypotheses, and further evidence," *Justice Quarterly* 7: 565–592.
Worden, Robert E. (1995) "Police officers' belief systems: A framework for analysis," *American Journal of Police* 14(1): 49–81.

Worden, Robert E., and Steven G. Brandl (1990) "Protocol analysis of police decision making: Toward a theory of police behavior," *American Journal of Criminal Justice* 14: 297–318.

Worden, Robert E., and Stephen D. Mastrofski (1989) "Varieties of police subcultures: A preliminary analysis," paper presented at the Annual Meeting of the Law & Society Association, June 8–11, Madison, WI.

Worden, Robert E., and Alissa A. Pollitz (1984) "Police arrests in domestic disturbances: A further look," *Law & Society Review* 18: 105–119.

Part III

Theories of the Courts

The three chapters in this section address explanations of "court" behaviors. These chapters share a broad concern for what happens in the middle portion of the criminal justice system, where suspects are charged, defendants are adjudicated, and those who plead or are found guilty are sentenced. Courts are complex social systems in which a number of actors (defendants, defense attorneys, prosecutors, judges, and others) come together and a wide variety of discretionary decisions are made, often behind closed doors. This section features theories meant to explain these phenomena at multiple levels, from the case or individual level to the courtroom or jurisdictional level.

Chapters 7 and 8 provide critical reviews of existing theory on courts. Much like Maguire and Uchida's review of the application of organization theory to police agencies in Chapter 4, these two chapters examine a broad class of theories that seek to explain court-related phenomena. In both chapters, the authors pose a framework for comparing and evaluating theories. These frameworks for comparing explanations provide a helpful means for determining what kinds of research are needed to test existing (but insufficiently tested) theory, as well as what kinds of theoretical explanations should be developed to guide future research. The behaviors on which these two chapters focus are related, since they both address why certain court outcomes occur. But these two chapters cover quite different theoretical territory.

In Chapter 7, Paula Kautt and Cassia Spohn develop a framework for assessing judicial sentencing decisions. In Chapter 8, Alissa Pollitz Worden assesses the nature of theories that use community variables to explain court outcomes and court variables to explain community outcomes. The distinction between these two chapters might be characterized as the difference between microtheories about individuals in Chapter 7, and macrotheories about complex social systems in Chapter 8. It is worth remembering, however, that the meaning of the terms micro and macro is not fixed, as Snipes and Maguire point out in Chapter 2.

The exact use of these terms varies by discipline, but in general, they are used to acknowledge the importance of distinguishing between smaller social units like encounters, cases, or individuals, and larger social units like agencies, communities, states, or nations. A simple way of illustrating the idea of these micro and macro social levels is the idea of a "hung jury." A hung jury is, by definition, an indecisive group that is unable to make a collective decision. But that group is composed of individuals who have made firm decisions as individuals, but in conflicting directions. Consequently, while it would be appropriate to call the jury as a whole indecisive, it would be inappropriate to describe the individuals in the jury that way. Different social levels behave differently.

Similarly, it is not difficult to envision a community that is, on average, racially fair but that nevertheless contains some prejudiced individuals who make racially biased decisions. We can also conceive of a racially biased community that contains some individuals whose attitudes and decisions are not racially biased. Certainly, society may want to eliminate or at least control injustice and bias at both levels. However, fixes at one level (such as controls on individual discretion) may not be relevant to problems at the higher level (such as criminal penalties that punish sale of one form of cocaine more severely than another form). Consequently, it is critical that we recognize the need for theories at multiple levels and encourage theoretically guided research at each appropriate level.[1]

In Chapter 7, Kautt and Spohn devise a framework for organizing different theories about individual judicial sentencing decisions. Their framework has two dimensions: a vertical dimension that identifies the level of the social phenomena that are expected to affect the decision (from attributes of the case at the low end to attributes of the jurisdiction at the high end) and a horizontal dimension that organizes the nature of the explanatory variables at any one level (such as physical attributes, internal commitments, perceptions, and experience of individual decision makers).

Kautt and Spohn argue that this means of organizing theories of decision making could be applied to any criminal justice decision. In other words, while Kautt and Spohn focus on explanations of judicial sentencing in this chapter, they assert that the framework proposed should also work for assessing theories of police arrest decisions, prosecutorial charging decisions, prison guard disciplinary write-ups, and so on. If they are correct, then this framework would also be useful in examining whether the same kinds of variables affect other discretionary decisions by different actors or whether different kinds of explanations are more relevant for different parts of the criminal justice system. Chapter 6 provided a good example of an important discretionary decision to which this framework might apply: the decision by police officers to use force.

Kautt and Spohn cover five of the seven themes that Snipes and Maguire used to consider criminal justice theories in Chapter 2, including organizational, sociopolitical, objective/subjective, type of response, and level of explanation themes. Kautt and Spohn are deeply concerned with *how* to theorize. They suggest that understanding decision making can be advanced if we are very systematic in thinking about the placement of a theory in the universe of possible explanations of a phenomenon. They illustrate their framework by reviewing various theories of judicial sentencing decisions, beginning with those that examine attributes such as age, race, and gender of the judge, moving on to perceptual theories that explain judicial decisions as outcomes of the judge's internal assessment processes. Finally, they examine some integrated theories that draw on different domains of explanatory variables at the same time.

In Chapter 8, Alissa Worden examines theories that try to link communities and courts. She begins by asking what we should consider "court theory." She briefly appraises the conceptual domains that are necessary to the court–community connection and how variations in these domains would affect the nature of those theoretical connections. She then asks how theorists should try to link the communities and courts. She proposes that current theories about this linkage can be divided into three broad categories: theories that examine how a constituency is represented in a public organization, theories that pose conflict among constituents, and theories that rely on organizational or working group "communities" to explain court processes and outcomes. She then asks what might be compatible or conflictual among these different approaches, with an aim, ultimately, of developing each more completely by combining or integrating them.

Worden's critical review of theory utilizes five of Snipes and Maguire's "theoretical themes," including the level of explanation embedded in a theory, the sociopolitical perspective or assumptions about society underlying a theory, the types of criminal justice responses that the theory sets out to explain, the organizational perspectives employed in typifying the criminal justice phenomenon, and the institutional arena to which the theory applies.

Worden clearly indicates that dividing the "system" up neatly into different institutional areas may be easier said than done (or too simplistic to carry us very far). From one point of view, the court is a local phenomenon influenced by a local "community." But as we add the institutional perspective about organizations and get involved in the symbolic politics of courts, theorists rapidly leave the "local" for broader concerns of culture and political structure. It would appear that a very difficult and intriguing part of court theory is how the local and the national or societal come together—a question that was also at the heart of Renauer's theory of police community building in Chapter 5.

On a more abstract level, Worden's concerns about the linkages between communities and courts share some overlap with several other chapters in this volume, including Hagan's structural-contextual theory in Chapter 3, Maguire and Uchida's review of the connections between police organizations and their environments in Chapter 4, and McGarrell and Duffee's investigation of state environments and correctional structures in Chapter 12. This pattern suggests that a great deal of criminal justice theory, whether focused on specific institutions or not, involves connecting broader social, political, and cultural systems to the government control system called criminal justice. That these attempts are constantly wrestling with the local and nonlocal and how they mix is not surprising or unique to criminal justice. Perhaps the main theme of Warren's classic book *Community in America* (1978) is precisely this: the variation in community that we seek to understand is often a product of the confluence of national forces that affect all communities and the local characteristics or filters through which those national forces become distinct in particular localities.

Unlike Chapters 7 and 8, which provide overarching reviews of existing theory, Chapter 9 provides a test of theory using qualitative research methods. In Chapter 9, Megan Kennedy notes that prosecutors are among the most powerful officials in the criminal justice system, and thus understanding their decision-making processes is a matter of key importance for criminal justice theory. Prosecutors serve a key gatekeeping role in the criminal justice system, deciding which defendants will be charged with a crime. Kennedy focuses specifically on the prosecutor's decision to charge defendants in sexual assault cases. She points out that existing research relies heavily on quantitative research methods, and as a result, tends to overlook certain nuances in the prosecutor's decision-making process. Instead, she relies on qualitative data based on interviews in three prosecutors' offices in two states. This is the first of two chapters in this volume (together with Chapter 11, which focuses on probation and parole) that presents the results of qualitative research.

Note that in qualitative research, the "data" are not the numerical quantities that play such an important role in quantitative research. Instead, the data used here are the more than 400 single-spaced pages of transcripts from the interviews Kennedy carried out with prosecutors. She relies on a series of inductive and deductive methods in analyzing this rich textual data source. Recall that inductive methods involve the researcher discovering patterns in the data and developing theory as a result of those patterns. Deductive research involves approaching the job of data analysis with a theory already in mind and allowing the data to validate or invalidate that theory. These two very different pathways to the development and testing of theory tend to work well together, allowing researchers to draw a variety of insights from their data.

Kennedy finds that the most important factor in the prosecutor's decision to move forward with a sexual assault case is whether the victim is "on board" with pursuing charges against the suspect. Another important factor includes the perceived strength or weakness of the case, though even in weak cases, prosecutors still often defer to the victim. Kennedy's findings about the prominent role of the victim are inconsistent with theories suggesting that prosecutors' charging decisions are influenced heavily by their need to avoid uncertainty with regard to case outcomes. Put simply, prosecutors in Kennedy's study appear to care less about their batting average and more about whether the victim is a willing participant in the prosecution.

Taken together, the chapters in this section provide three different vantage points for thinking about courts, how they function, and why they function in the way they do. One theme will become very clear after reading these chapters. Rational theories that view courts from purely legalistic or mechanical perspectives are insufficient to explain how these complex social systems behave. Efforts to implement court reform often fail because they are based on inaccurate and overly simplistic assumptions about how these social systems operate. The theories discussed in this section provide a useful perspective on the many factors that influence how courts operate.

DISCUSSION QUESTIONS

1. Take the challenge issued by Kautt and Spohn in Chapter 7. See if you can take their schema for individual decision making

and apply it to a different institutional sector or to different decision making within the court sector. Can their model for systematically varying the level and domain of explanation help with understanding police decisions to use force, issue a citation, or make an arrest? What about the prosecutor's decision to charge or the judge's decision to release a defendant on bail? How about prison disciplinary charges or discretionary prison releases? What about some less studied decisions, such as a victim's decision to call the police or a legislator's decision to treat a specific type of harm as a crime rather than a tort?

2. Examine Worden's proposed examination of court impact on community in Chapter 8. Is this criminal justice theory under the four tests proposed by Snipes and Maguire in Chapter 2?
3. Review the dependent variables proposed by both Kautt and Spohn in Chapter 7 and Worden in Chapter 8. Are any of these consistent with a desire to explain justice (or injustice) or outcomes other than crime?
4. In Chapter 9, Kennedy uses qualitative research methods to test theories about prosecutors' charging decisions in sexual assault cases. Earlier in Chapter 6, Worden used quantitative research methods to test theories about police officers' decisions to use force against citizens. Based on your reading of these two chapters, list the strengths and weaknesses of qualitative and quantitative research methods for understanding the decisions made by criminal justice officials. Under what conditions would it be better to use each approach? Why?

NOTE

1. Social scientists have a term—the "ecological fallacy"—to describe the inferential error that occurs when people draw inferences about individuals based on data from aggregates.

7

ASSESSING BLAMEWORTHINESS AND ASSIGNING PUNISHMENT

Theoretical Perspectives on Judicial Decision Making

Paula M. Kautt and Cassia C. Spohn

> Dynamic theories of the judicial process . . . picture the judge as a policy oriented decision-maker who derives . . . premises both from within and without the courtroom and whose functions far exceed the mechanical task of applying settled rules of law to clear fact situations . . . the judge operates in an institutional framework which places certain restraints on the pure expression of personal preferences, but which also allows significant latitude for such expression.
>
> (Grossman, 1967, 334–335)

INTRODUCTION

More than other components of the criminal justice system, the criminal courts possess a certain mystique. There, defense and prosecution join in battle over the facts of a criminal case and the guilt or innocence of a defendant in order to achieve the ideal of "justice." The judge, physically and symbolically removed from the combatants, is the impartial primary arbiter of these adversarial proceedings: he or she weighs the evidence, interprets the rules of engagement, and metes out decisions from the lofty bench. Yet, when a decision of guilt is finally reached, how do judges, these supposed paragons of impartiality, decide the sentence to be imposed upon the convicted offender? Intuitively, the answer seems simple: the more serious the infraction, the harsher the punishment. In other words, the law and the interests of justice alone dictate sanction. All other factors are simply irrelevant. Such an idealized explanatory framework has been with us since ancient times. Its simplicity and symmetry have an intuitive appeal that evokes the ideals of equity and fairness while its longevity and tradition attractively cloak it in the fabric of historical "truth." Academically, this simple, commonsense explanation of criminal sentencing outcomes is also known as the legal metaphor (Eisenstein, Flemming, & Nardulli, 1988).

However, despite its rich heritage, it seems clear that the legal metaphor's concept of courtroom actors who objectively apply the rule of law to each case is misleading. As indicated by the introductory quotation, factors deemed legally irrelevant do affect punishment. Consider, for example, the offender's income. Clearly, how much money someone makes is irrelevant as to whether or not he or she is factually guilty of a criminal offense or deserves punishment. Yet, one need only think of the expensive legal defenses mounted in recent high-profile criminal cases to quickly recognize that this seemingly extraneous factor does indeed play a role in determining criminal sanction (or lack thereof). With brief additional reflection, one can readily conceive of a host of other factors that can influence judicial sentencing decisions. Personal biases, political influence, court resources, or past experiences might all play a role. As a result, common sense tells us that the legal metaphor does not accurately portray or comprehensively explain the realities of judicial decision making and criminal sentencing.

Existing empirical research bolsters this commonsense conclusion, indicating that a myriad of factors—many of which are completely independent of the case at hand—influence court decision makers (Jacob, 1997; Ulmer, 1997) and the sentences they mete out (Gibson, 1977; Blumstein et al., 1983). For example, defendants who go to trial are more likely to be incarcerated and receive longer sentences than their nonjury counterparts (Uhlman & Walker, 1980; Spohn, 1992). Likewise, defendant gender (Steffensmeier et al., 1993; Daly & Tonry, 1997), age (Steffensmeier et al., 1995), race (Steffensmeier et al., 1998; Spohn & DeLone, 2000; Kautt & Spohn, 2002), and socioeconomic status (Smith, 1991) all have been shown to affect case outcomes. There also is evidence that judges are more likely to impose the death penalty in jurisdictions where they are elected rather than appointed (Bright &

Keenan, 1995) and that city political environments have a direct impact on judicial sentencing philosophy and behavior (Levin, 1972). Such findings clearly indicate that factors from a wide variety of sources affect sentencing outcomes. As a result, perspectives that are more comprehensive and sophisticated than the legal metaphor are necessary to explain the punishments assigned to criminal defendants. Meeting this challenge is one purpose of court and sentencing theory.

While it has often been said that empirical investigations of the criminal justice system are atheoretical (see Snipes and Maguire in this volume as well as Hagan [1989b]), the notable exception to this is the arena of criminal courts—specifically, judicial decision making. There, substantive theories have rapidly developed over the past several decades. Collectively, these frameworks provide a global perspective for understanding the criminal courts, their function, and their outcomes. Yet, not all court theories are created equal. In fact, the theoretically relevant factors vary widely in the existing court perspectives. For example, some focus exclusively on a single level of influential factors—such as only case, organizational, or jurisdictional attributes—while others simultaneously account for multiple influential levels. Likewise, single-level theories (e.g., case) may address only one group of factors from that level—such as defendant characteristics—while others incorporate multiple factor categories from that same level (defendant characteristics in conjunction with offense and processing factors). Such variability clearly demonstrates how the explanations of the courts and their outcomes can differ radically by the vertical and horizontal dimensions they encompass.

While the existing theories exhibit numerous variations in the elements believed to have predictive and explanatory importance, such differences can be translated into an organizing framework for discussing and categorizing existing sentencing theories. The aforementioned vertical and horizontal dimensions are the key to this approach. The vertical element or hierarchy broadly refers to the level of the theory. This dictates both the level and unit of analysis for empirical investigation. Much more specific than micro, meso, or macro levels, hierarchy represents the level of the theory both in terms of which and how many levels are accounted for by a given perspective (see Figure 7.1 for a graphic representation). Conversely, different groups of influential factors that occur at the same level of analysis comprise the horizontal elements or spheres (see Figure 7.2). At the individual level, for example, and as illustrated by Figure 7.3, physical judicial characteristics (gender,

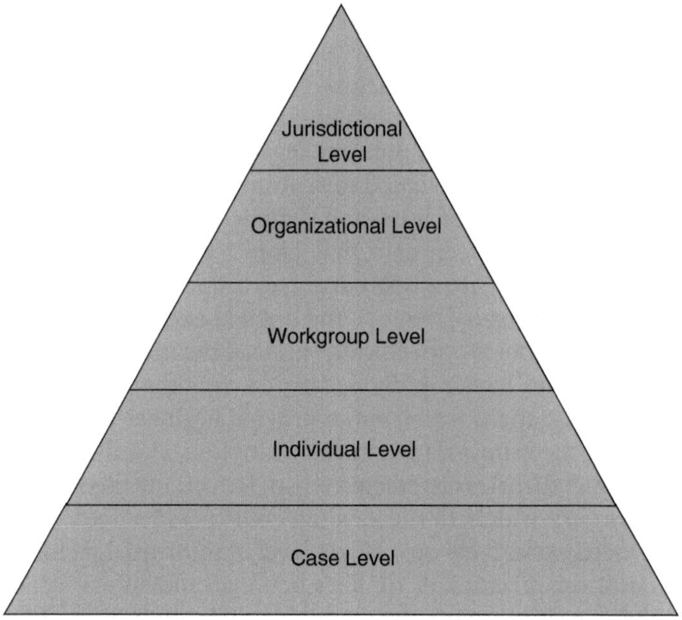

Figure 7.1 Vertical hierarchies

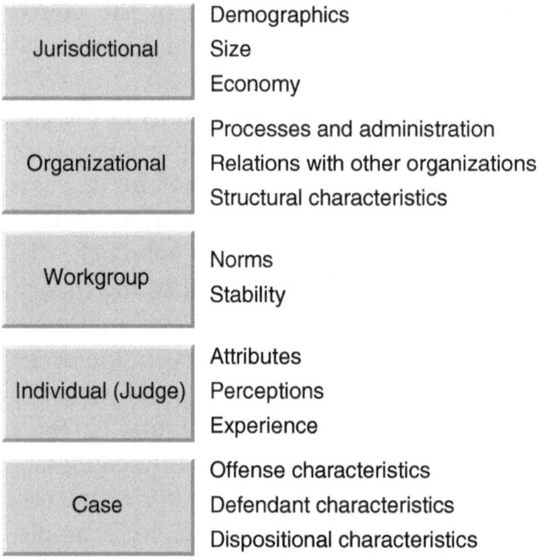

Figure 7.2 Horizontal spheres

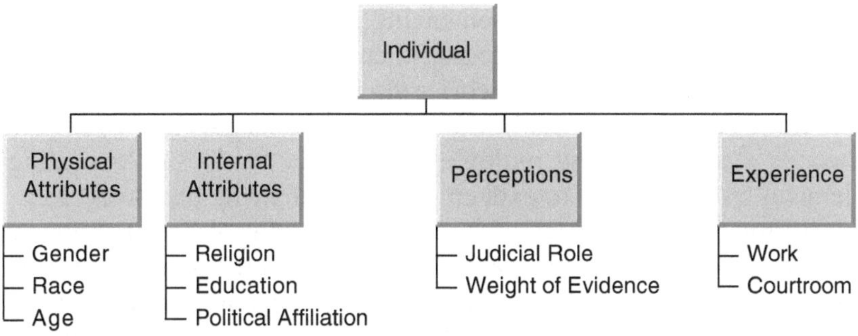

Figure 7.3 Horizontal spheres: The individual level

race, age) comprise one sphere of influence, while nonphysical judicial characteristics (experience or education) comprise another.

Using hierarchy and spheres together, one can categorize court theories by the breadth and width of factors they incorporate. Practically speaking, theories can be labeled horizontally integrated, vertically integrated, both, or neither. A horizontally integrated theory would capture multiple spheres of influence occurring at the same hierarchical level. Conversely, a vertically integrated theory would incorporate theoretical influences from two or more hierarchical levels. Beyond this categorization, theories can be differentiated further by which specific hierarchies or spheres they address. However, it is important to note that not all theories simultaneously incorporate vertical and horizontal dimensions or even all spheres from within the same level; in fact, most do not. Many theories are neither horizontally nor vertically integrated—although there has been movement toward this ideal since the late 1990s (Ulmer, 1997; Ulmer & Kramer, 1998; Henham, 2001).

Although our initial model identifies several potential hierarchies and spheres, our current examination of judge-based theories of sentencing outcomes will cover only three major groupings representing a gradual theoretical evolution from simple or unidimensional theories to complex and integrated ones. These are judicial attributes, judicial perceptions, and integrated theories. The judicial attributes section describes theories positing that two individual-level spheres—physical (gender, race, age) and nonphysical (education, experience, and values) judicial characteristics—affect sentencing outcomes. This section also discusses the emergence of horizontally integrated individual-level theories. The judicial perceptions section addresses theories concerning how judicial views of particular external factors (such as the defendant, case, workgroup, environment—which may be located on different hierarchical levels) affect the sentencing decision reached. Such theories represent a preliminary step that attempts to incorporate multilevel factors into individual-level theories via individual perception of factors from other levels. Finally, the integrated theory section addresses theories that encompass multiple hierarchical levels—incorporating elements from several—to explain judicial sentencing decisions. Thus, addressing Snipes and Maguire's seven dimensions of criminal justice theories (Chapter 2 of this volume), the frameworks reviewed in this chapter include the organizational, sociopolitical, and objective versus the subjective, type of response, and level of explanation perspectives.

Obviously, our listing of examined hierarchies and spheres is not comprehensive—nor was it intended to be. Rather, they are chosen in a deliberate effort to reflect the evolution and range of judicial theory—from the flat one- or two-dimensional traditional frameworks to the modern multifaceted picture of judicial decision making. Moreover, they are illustrative of the utility of our proposed framework in discussing the existing judicial decision-making theories. We believe that this classification system can serve as a tool for categorizing existing research and theories. We also believe that it will facilitate the development of new models and theories by providing a precise framework for considering, organizing, and incorporating any theoretically relevant factors. Such theoretical innovations will produce more accurate depictions of reality as well as predictions of and explanations for sentencing outcomes. What follows is a discussion of each of the aforementioned theory groups.

JUDICIAL ATTRIBUTES AND JUDICIAL DECISION MAKING

Social scientists and legal scholars, who acknowledge that the legal metaphor is an inadequate explanation for sentencing decisions, have developed other theoretical perspectives for explaining how judges determine the appropriate sentence for any given offense and offender. Some scholars maintain that sentencing decisions are affected by the personal characteristics of the judge. As Myers (1988, 649) states, "The social background of judges is presumed to affect early and professional socialization experiences, which in turn are hypothesized to affect attitudes, role orientations, and ultimately, behavior." According to this perspective, judges' background characteristics, attitudes, and values influence—either directly or indirectly—the sentences they impose. This and other such theories are classic examples of the sociopolitical and the objective versus subjective perspectives as articulated by Snipes and Maguire earlier in this volume.

Early studies of judicial decision making suggested that the influence of the judge's personal characteristics was predicated on one of three theoretical concepts: conversion, consensus, or rationality (Grossman, 1967). The most basic concept, conversion, refers to the direct translation of social background characteristics into judicial decisions (Goldman, 1969). Sentencing theories based on conversion assume that individual thought and decision making are the products of one's social identity, which is shaped by physical attributes such as race, gender, and age. As a result, the sentences imposed by black judges will differ from those imposed by white judges, and the sentencing decisions of male judges and younger judges will differ from those of female judges and older judges.

THE EFFECT OF THE GENDER, RACE/ETHNICITY, AND AGE OF THE JUDGE

Several theories have been put forth about the effect of specific physical attributes on judges' sentencing decisions. Many theorists, for example, contend that female judges will dispense a different type of justice than will male judges as a result of differences in their outlooks, orientations, and experiences. In support of the argument that women judges "speak in a different voice," some point to the work of Carol Gilligan (1982), who claimed that women's moral reasoning differs from that of men: whereas men emphasize legal rules and reasoning based on an ethic of justice, women, who are more concerned about preserving relationships and more sensitive to the needs of others, reason using an ethic of care. Others, who counter that "the language of law is explicitly the language of justice rather than care" (Berns, 1999, 197), claim that the differences women bring to the bench stem more from their experiences as women than from differences in moral reasoning. They maintain, for example, that women are substantially more likely than are men to be victimized by rape, sexual harassment, domestic violence, and other forms of predatory violence, and that their experiences as crime victims or their fear of crime shape their attitudes toward and their response to crime and criminals.

Although researchers generally agree that the attitudes and experiences of women and men on the bench are different, they disagree about the ways in which these differences will influence the sentencing patterns of female and male judges. Some researchers contend that because females are socialized to be nurturing, sympathetic, and understanding, female judges will be more lenient than male judges (Gruhl, Spohn, & Welch, 1981). Others suggest that the fact that women are more likely to be victims of sexualized violence and are more fearful of crime in general might incline them to impose harsher sentences than men, particularly for violent crimes, crimes against women, and crimes involving dangerous repeat offenders (Steffensmeier & Herbert, 1999). A third school of thought holds that because the presence of women in positions of authority—such as judges—is relatively rare, females in those positions will tend to view themselves as tokens. As a result, female judges will be uniformly harsher than male judges because of a psychological need to prove that they are not "soft on crime" and that they are "worthy" of judges' robes, despite so many years of formal exclusion from the profession (Kanter, 1977). Still others argue that the life experiences of female judges—and particularly black or Hispanic female judges—will make them more sensitive to the existence of racism or sexism; as a result, they might make more equitable sentencing decisions than white male judges (Gruhl, Spohn, & Welch, 1981).

Researchers who contend that the race of the judge will affect sentencing decisions advance similar arguments. Because the life histories and experiences of blacks differ dramatically from those of whites, the beliefs and attitudes they bring to the bench also will differ. Justice A. Leon Higginbotham Jr., an African American who retired from the U.S. Court of Appeals for the Third Circuit in 1993, wrote: "Someone who has been a victim of racial injustice has greater sensitivity of the court's making sure that racism is not perpetrated, even inadvertently" (Washington, 1994, 11–12). Welch and her colleagues make an analogous argument. Noting that blacks tend to view themselves as liberal rather than conservative, they speculate that black judges might be "more sympathetic to criminal defendants than white judges are, since liberal views are associated with support for the underdog and the poor, which defendants disproportionately are" (Welch, Combs, & Gruhl, 1988, 127). Others similarly suggest that increasing the number of black judges would reduce racism in the criminal justice system and produce more equitable treatment of black and white defendants.

Regarding the age of the judge, researchers generally expect older judges to be more traditional and more conservative and hence to impose more punitive sentences than younger judges. Myers (1988, 654), however, speculates that older judges might be "selectively punitive"—that is, older judges might "impose harsher sanctions on certain offenders with whom, because of their age, they are least able to sympathize." Myers states that while drug offenders are the most likely candidates for harsher treatment by older judges, these judges also might impose more punitive sentences on "members of disadvantaged and potentially troublesome groups (e.g., black, young, single, unemployed)" (p. 654).

Although several studies concluded that older judges sentenced defendants more harshly than younger judges (Cook, 1973; Kritzer, 1978; Myers, 1988; Steffensmeier & Herbert, 1999), the results of research examining the effect of the gender and race of the judge on sentencing decisions are inconsistent. While some research finds that female judges impose harsher sentences than do male judges in certain contexts (Spohn, 1990b; Steffensmeier & Herbert, 1999), most studies conclude that there are more similarities than differences between the sentences handed down by male and female judges (Gruhl et al., 1981; Myers, 1988; Spohn, 1990b; Laster & Douglas, 1995). Moreover, the studies that do find a "judge gender effect" conclude that the relationship between the gender of the judge and sentence outcomes is neither simple nor straightforward. Rather, several studies find that contextual factors—such as defendant or case characteristics (Spohn, 1990a; Steffensmeier & Herbert, 1999)—interact with judge gender to affect both the incarceration and sentence length decisions. Recent research also argues that these varied gender effects are not the product of women's socialization patterns, but instead reflect other factors such as the judge's professional background (Laster & Douglas, 1995) or the judicial selection process (Songer & Crews-Meyer, 2000). These results suggest a bridge between judges' physical and nonphysical attributes in the decision-making process.

The findings regarding the effect of the judge's race/ethnicity on sentencing decisions also are contradictory. Most researchers find few overall differences in the sentences imposed by black and white judges. Engle (1971) concluded that there were only minor differences in the sentences imposed by black and white judges on the bench in Philadelphia. Uhlman (1979) found that while the sentencing patterns of individual black judges varied considerably, their overall sentencing patterns did not differ from those of white judges, and Spohn (1990b) concluded that there were "remarkable similarities" in the sentencing decisions of black and white judges. One study (Spohn, 1990a) found that black female judges imposed longer sentences on offenders convicted of sexual assault, while another (Spears, 1999) found that black male judges sentenced offenders to prison at a lower rate but imposed longer sentences on those who were incarcerated. Depending upon the time period, the jurisdiction, and the types of offenses included in the analysis, black judges sentence no differently, more harshly, or more leniently than do white judges.

The evidence regarding the degree to which black and Hispanic judges impose more racially equitable sentences also is mixed. Two studies found that black judges imposed similar sentences on black and white offenders, while white judges gave more lenient sentences to white offenders than to black offenders (Spears, 1999; Welch, Combs, & Gruhl, 1988). Another found a similar pattern of results for Hispanic judges and Anglo judges (Holmes et al., 1993). All three studies concluded that white judges discriminate in favor of white offenders. A fourth study, on the other hand, found no race-of-judge differences in the sentences imposed on black and white offenders convicted of violent felonies (Spohn, 1990b).

In sum, existing research finds that the gender and race of the judge generally have little or no direct effect on sentencing decisions; when effects are present, they are often inconsistent and indirect. Such findings clearly indicate that judicial decision making is not merely a conversion of physical attributes into sentencing outcomes. This is not surprising, since theoretical frameworks grounded in the physical attributes of the decision maker often ignore individual perception, learning, and experience. In other words, these perspectives are limited to a single sphere of individual-level factors when the evidence suggests that multiple individual-level spheres come into play during the sentencing process. Such linkage between the individual-level spheres is consistent with the maximalist perspective (Steffensmeier & Herbert, 1999), where on-the-job decisions and behaviors are the product of beliefs, attitudes, and norms developed and located within the individual. Thus, judicial decisions are not a direct product of physical characteristics, but rather are derived from psychological and socialization differences—only some of which may stem from physical attributes such as gender, race, or age.

THE EFFECT OF THE JUDGE'S PERSONALITY ATTRIBUTES AND PROFESSIONAL EXPERIENCE

Theories of judicial decision making also highlight the role played by the judge's personality attributes and prejudicial professional experience. Some researchers focus on judicial self-esteem; they contend that judges with weak self-images seek personal validation through their sentencing decisions. According to Gibson (1981), judges can accomplish this validation either through decision conformity (they demonstrate that they "belong" on the bench because they conduct themselves in the accepted and expected manner) or nonconformity (they flout convention in order to prove to themselves and others that they are both confident and independent). Other scholars maintain that sentencing outcomes will vary by the religious beliefs of the judge: judges with more fundamentalist religious beliefs are expected to impose more punitive sentences (Nagel, 1962; Myers, 1988). Additional judicial characteristics predicted to affect sentencing decisions include the judge's background (Ball, 1980; Myers, 1988), political affiliation (Rowland et al., 1984), and professional experience (Frazier & Bock, 1982; Myers, 1988).

Research exploring the effect of these background characteristics generally reveals that they either do not affect sentence outcomes at all (Spohn, 1990a; Spears, 1999) or have only weak effects (Steffensmeier & Herbert, 1999). They also demonstrate that such characteristics do not always affect sentencing decisions as expected. Three studies (Gibson, 1978; Myers, 1988; Steffensmeier & Herbert, 1999), for example, found that judges with prior prosecutorial experience imposed harsher sentences, while one (Welch et al., 1988) found that former prosecutors imposed more lenient sentences. Similarly, two studies found that judges who had been on the bench longer imposed more severe sentences (Gibson, 1978; Welch et al., 1988), while two others found that longer tenure on the bench led to more lenient sentences (Spohn, 1990a; Steffensmeier & Herbert, 1999). Two studies concluded that judges who were members of fundamentalist churches meted out more severe punishment than those who were not (Gibson, 1978; Myers, 1988). The fact that most of these effects were relatively weak, coupled with the fact that some of them were in the opposite direction of what was predicted, indicates that these background characteristics do not consistently affect the sentences that judges impose. These results also suggest that any judicial variation in sentencing decisions is more the product of other factors—such as case differences—rather than individual attributes.

This position is further bolstered by research exploring the influence of judicial characteristics while simultaneously controlling for case-level attributes. Such findings indicate that judicial characteristics have little direct effect on sentencing outcomes, but do condition the weight attached to particular case-level factors. These results demonstrate the importance of considering individual judicial characteristics in conjunction with factors from other levels—such as case attributes—as conditioners of sentencing outcomes (Frazier & Bock, 1982; Myers, 1988). Such findings clearly indicate that individual-level theories alone—even multispherical ones—are inadequate to explain the complexities of judicial decisions and sentencing outcomes.

Returning to the three historical bases for explaining the impact of judicial characteristics on sentencing decisions, the aforementioned concepts of consensus and rationality suggest an approach for bridging these multilevel factors. Consensus-based theories posit that personal characteristics become relevant only when the judge perceives the case as being ambiguous. Conversely, rationality-based perspectives argue that the judge uses his or her own personal preferences and attributes to choose between the variety of sentencing alternatives that each case presents (Grossman, 1967). In both instances, judicial perceptions of characteristics from other levels—most notably case characteristics—dictate the influence of personal characteristics on the sentencing outcome. Similarly, in the psychometric model (Schubert, 1961), case attributes are stimuli that elicit responses (sentencing decisions) representing individual judicial attitudes toward and perceptions of the case (Goldman, 1969). Likewise, role orientation links individual attributes to case characteristics at the individual level. There, judicial beliefs about the relevance and rank importance of case criteria dictate the sentencing decision (Gibson, 1977, 1978, 1981). Such concepts linking individual judicial attributes to case characteristics gave rise to a new breed of theories explaining sentencing outcomes. These perspectives, however, are only pseudo-integrated because, while they address factors that stem from multiple levels, these factors are accounted for only as perceived by the sentencing judge. As a result, they remain exclusively at the individual level.

JUDICIAL PERCEPTIONS AND JUDICIAL DECISION MAKING

The theoretical perspectives discussed thus far suggest that judges' back ground characteristics, attitudes, and role orientations have inconsistent and contradictory effects on their sentencing decisions. A second category of theories focuses on the ways in which judges' perceptions of and reactions to external factors such as the crime, the defendant, other members of the courtroom workgroup, and the environment affect their sentencing decisions. According to these theories, judges' sentencing decisions reflect both their beliefs about the factors that ought to be taken into consideration in determining the appropriate punishment and their perceptions of these factors. If, for example, judges generally believe that more serious crimes and more blameworthy or dangerous offenders deserve harsher punishment, the sentences they impose will depend upon their perceptions of the types of crimes that are most serious and the types of offenders who are most blameworthy and dangerous. As John Hogarth (1971, 279) wrote over thirty years ago, sentencing "is a cognitive process in which information concerning the offender, the offense, and the surrounding circumstances is read, organized in relation to other information and integrated into an overall assessment of the case."

The theories discussed next attempt to explain "how the values and beliefs of individuals and groups are transformed into the policies and practices of controlling organizations" (Bridges & Steen, 1998, 568). They attempt to account for how judges develop "an overall assessment of the case." Each of these judge-based theories seeks not simply to identify the relevant predictors of sentencing decisions, but also to describe the mechanisms by which characteristics of the crime, the defendant, the organization, and the environment influence the sentences that judges impose. All of the theories assume, explicitly or implicitly, that sentencing is discretionary, that the information available to the judge at sentencing is incomplete, and that judges therefore simplify or routinize the decision-making process by categorizing or classifying crimes, defendants, and cases. As shown next, each of the theories also purports to explain why certain categories of offenders—racial minorities, males, young adults, the unemployed—may be singled out for harsher treatment.

CAUSAL ATTRIBUTION THEORY

A number of scholars argue that judges' sentencing decisions reflect their beliefs about an offender's potential for rehabilitation, which rest, in turn, on their perception of the causes of criminal behavior (cf., Bridges & Steen, 1998; Carroll & Payne, 1976; Hawkins, 1981). According to this perspective, decision makers attribute causality either to the individual's personal characteristics (i.e., internal characteristics, such as antisocial personality, lack of remorse, refusal to admit guilt or cooperate with officials) or to factors within the environment/ external characteristics (e.g., delinquent peers, a dysfunctional family, drug or alcohol use, poverty). Individuals whose crimes are attributed to internal factors are viewed as more responsible, and, thus, as more blameworthy, than those whose crimes are viewed as stemming from external forces; more importantly, these attributions affect the sentences that judges impose. As Hawkins (1981, 280) states, "Perceptual differences such as this may in turn lead to conclusions regarding the . . . offender's rehabilitation potential, the threat posed to society, and the type of criminal sanction imposed."

Bridges and Steen (1998, 555), who contend that most studies of racial bias in the courts fail to identify the mechanisms by which race affects court outcomes, suggest that causal attribution theory can be used to explain "the race-punishment relationship." Building on theories of social cognition, which hold that racial and ethnic stereotypes affect officials' perceptions of minority offenders, Bridges and Steen propose that the harsher treatment of racial minorities may be due to the fact that criminal justice officials perceive their crimes as caused by internal forces and crimes committed by whites as caused by external forces. They further argue that these "differential attributions about the causes of crime by minorities and whites may contribute directly to differential assessments of offender dangerousness and risk" and, thus, to "racial differences in perceived risk and recommended punishment" (Bridges & Steen, 1998, 557).

Bridges and Steen used juvenile probation officers' narrative reports and sentence recommendations to test these propositions. They found that reports on black youth were more likely to mention negative personality characteristics (internal attributions), while those on white youth were more likely to mention negative environmental factors (external attributions). They also discovered that these causal attributions shaped probation officers' assessments of the risk of reoffending and sentence recommendations. Because the crimes of black youth were more often attributed to negative personality traits or attitudes, black youth were judged to have a higher risk of recidivism than white youth; as a result, probation officers recommended harsher sentences for black youth than for white youth. Thus, Bridges and Steen (1998, 567) note, "Attributions about youths and their crimes are a mechanism by which race influences judgments of dangerousness and sentencing recommendations." Causal attribution theory represents a direct challenge to the legal metaphor. It suggests that sentences result, not from a static process in which "the law" is applied objectively to individual cases, but from a causal sequence that involves subjective perceptions, assessments, and decisions. In fact, subsequent research (Steen et al., 2005) has expanded this framework to incorporate judicial "stereotypes" about crime and offense type—effectively demonstrating that even "the law" and how judges perceive it can change with the characteristics of the defendant before the court.

THE THEORY OF BOUNDED RATIONALITY/ UNCERTAINTY AVOIDANCE

A second theory focusing on the linkages between judges' perceptions of offenders and their crimes and judges' sentencing decisions is the theory of bounded rationality/uncertainty avoidance, which incorporates both organizational theory and causal attribution theory. Albonetti (1991, 248) suggests that "[t]he salience of these two theoretical perspectives to judicial sentencing decisions lies in each perspective's sensitivity to discretionary use of information in decision making." Structural organizational theorists (Simon, 1957; Thompson, 1967), for example, contend that decision makers rarely have the information needed to make fully rational decisions; because they cannot identify all of the possible alternatives or the costs and benefits of each known alternative, they cannot always select the alternative that will provide the greatest benefit at the lowest cost. Instead, they use a decision-making process characterized by "bounded rationality" to search for a solution that will avoid, or at least reduce, the uncertainty of obtaining a desirable outcome.

Applied to the sentencing process, the theory of bounded rationality/uncertainty avoidance suggests that judges' sentencing decisions hinge on their assessments of the likelihood of recidivism. Because judges typically do not have the information they need to make accurate predictions regarding the odds of reoffending, they develop perceptual sentencing standards (i.e., "patterned responses") based on case and offender characteristics that they believe will increase or decrease the risk of recidivism. Judges, in other words, attempt to reduce the uncertainty of their predictions by using stereotypes of crime seriousness, offender blameworthiness, and offender dangerousness to classify or categorize offenders and their crimes. Offenders who commit crimes perceived to be more serious are treated more harshly, as are offenders who are deemed more blameworthy and dangerous. According to Albonetti (1991, 250), these perceptions "are themselves the product of an attribution process influenced by causal judgment." Thus, stereotypes linking race, gender, and social class to the risk of recidivism result in harsher sentences for racial minorities, men, and the poor. More to the point, "Discrimination and disparity in sentencing decisions . . . may be the product of judicial attempts to achieve a 'bounded rationality' in sentencing by relying on stereotypical images of which defendant is most likely to recidivate" (Albonetti, 1991, 250).

Albonetti's (1991) analysis of the sentences imposed on offenders convicted of felonies in a federal district court in 1974 revealed substantial support for her theoretical perspective. She found that sentence severity was affected by the offender's prior record, race, use of a weapon, and bail status; offenders with a prior record of felony convictions received more punitive sentences, as did black offenders, offenders who used a weapon during the commission of the crime, and offenders who were required to post bail as a condition of release. Moreover, being required to post bail had a more aggravating effect on sentence severity for black offenders than for white offenders. These findings, which generally are consistent with the results of other research on sentence outcomes (for reviews, see Blumstein, Martin, & Tonry, 1983; Zatz, 1987; Spohn, 2000), support Albonetti's assertion that judges attempt to reduce uncertainty by imposing harsher sentences on defendants perceived to pose a greater risk of reoffending. They also support assertions regarding the salience of racial stereotypes in judicial decision making.

THE FOCAL CONCERNS THEORY OF SENTENCING

The focal concerns theory of sentencing incorporates and builds on the uncertainty avoidance perspective. As developed by Steffensmeier and his colleagues (Steffensmeier, Ulmer, & Kramer, 1998; Steffensmeier & Demuth, 2001), this theoretical perspective suggests that judges' sentencing decisions are guided by three "focal concerns": their assessment of the blameworthiness of the offender; their desire to protect the community by incapacitating dangerous offenders or deterring potential offenders; and their concerns about the practical consequences, or social costs, of sentencing decisions.

The first focal concern—offender blameworthiness—reflects judges' assessments of the seriousness of the crime, the offender's prior criminal record, and the offender's motivation and role in the offense. Thus, offenders convicted of more serious crimes or who have more serious criminal histories will be viewed as more blameworthy; consequently, they will be sentenced more harshly. Offenders who suffered prior victimization at the hands of others or who played a minor role in the offense, on the other hand, will be seen as less culpable and will, therefore, be sentenced more leniently. The second focal concern—protecting the community—rests on judges' perceptions of dangerousness and predictions of the likelihood of recidivism. Like judges' assessments of offender blameworthiness, these perceptions are predicated on the nature of the offense and the offender's criminal history. Thus, judges seek to protect the community by imposing harsher sentences on repeat violent offenders or offenders whose risk of reoffending is high. The third focal concern—the practical consequences or social costs of sentencing decisions—reflects judges' perceptions regarding such things as the offender's "ability to do time," the costs of incarcerating offenders with medical conditions or mental health problems, and the "social costs" of imprisoning offenders responsible for the care of dependent children. It also includes judges' concerns about maintaining relationships with other members of the courtroom workgroup and protecting the reputation of the court.

Like Albonetti's theory of bounded rationality, the focal concerns theory assumes that judges typically do not have the information they need to accurately determine an offender's culpability, dangerousness, or likelihood of recidivism. As a result, they develop a "perceptual shorthand" based on stereotypes and attributions that are themselves linked to offender characteristics such as race, gender, and age. As Steffensmeier, Ulmer, and Kramer (1998, 787) note:

> Younger offenders and male defendants appear to be seen as more of a threat to the community or not as reformable, and so also are black offenders, particularly those who also are young and male. Likewise, concerns such as "ability to do time" and the costs of incarceration appear linked to race-, gender-, and age-based perceptions and stereotypes.

Recent studies of sentencing decisions—and particularly studies exploring the effect of race and ethnicity on sentence outcomes—have produced compelling evidence in support of the focal concerns perspective (Steffensmeier, Ulmer, & Kramer, 1998; Spohn & Holleran, 2000; Steffensmeier & Demuth, 2001; Schlesinger, 2005; see also Wheeler et al., 1988). These studies reveal that African Americans and Hispanics are sentenced more harshly than whites (Spohn & DeLone, 2000; Spohn & Holleran, 2000) or that Hispanics are sentenced more harshly than either whites or blacks (Steffensmeier & Demuth, 2000; Steffensmeier & Demuth, 2001; Schlesinger, 2005). They also reveal that men receive more punitive sentences than do women (Spohn & Beichner, 2000; Steffensmeier, Kramer, & Striefel, 1993), that young adults are sentenced more harshly than are teenagers or older adults (Steffensmeier, Kramer, & Ulmer, 1995), and that the unemployed receive harsher sentences than do those who are employed (Chiricos & Bales, 1991; Nobiling, Spohn, & DeLone, 1998).

These studies also reveal that judges' perceptions of deviance and dangerousness are shaped by a combination of offender characteristics. One study (Steffensmeier, Ulmer, & Kramer, 1998), for example, used statewide data on sentencing outcomes in Pennsylvania to explore the interrelationships among race, gender, age, and sentence severity. Consistent with the focal concerns perspective, this study revealed that each of the three offender characteristics had a significant direct effect on both the likelihood of incarceration and the length of the sentence: blacks were sentenced more harshly than whites, younger offenders were sentenced more harshly than older offenders, and males more harshly than females. More importantly, the three factors interacted to produce substantially harsher sentences for one category of offenders—young, black males—than for any other age-race-gender combination. According to the authors, their results illustrate the "high cost of being black, young, and male" (Steffensmeier, Ulmer, & Kramer, 1998, 789). Spohn and Holleran's (2000) analysis of sentencing outcomes in Chicago,

Kansas City, and Miami revealed that offenders with constellations of characteristics other than "young black male" also pay a punishment penalty. They found that young black and Hispanic males faced greater odds of incarceration than did middle-aged white males, and unemployed black and Hispanic males were substantially more likely to be sentenced to prison than were employed white males.

Each of the theoretical perspectives discussed earlier—causal attribution, bounded rationality/uncertainty avoidance, and focal concerns—posits that judges' sentencing decisions are shaped by their perceptions of the seriousness of the crime and the offender's blameworthiness, dangerousness, and potential for rehabilitation. The fact that the information judges have is typically incomplete and the predictions they are required to make are uncertain helps explain why offender characteristics—including the legally irrelevant characteristics of race, gender, and social class—influence sentencing decisions. Because they lack all the information needed to fashion sentences perfectly fitting both crimes and offenders, judges may resort to stereotypes of deviance and dangerousness that rest on considerations of race, ethnicity, gender, age, and unemployment. Thus, men may be perceived as more dangerous than women, younger offenders may be regarded as more crime prone than older offenders, gang members may be viewed as more threatening than nongang members, the unemployed may be seen as more likely to recidivate than the employed, and those who abuse drugs or alcohol may be viewed as less amenable to rehabilitation that those who abstain from using drugs or alcohol. Similarly, racial minorities—particularly those who are also male, young, members of gangs, and unemployed—may be seen as more dangerous and threatening than whites. Judges use these perceptions to simplify and routinize the decision-making process and to reduce the uncertainty inherent in sentencing. As a result, men may be sentenced more harshly than women, African Americans and Hispanics may be sentenced more harshly than whites, the unemployed may be sentenced more harshly than the employed, and gang members may receive more punitive sentences than nongang members.

INTEGRATED THEORIES

In contrast to the perceptual theories discussed earlier, in which judges' *perceptions* of multilevel factors are incorporated into individual-level theories, integrated theories posit that *actual* factors from the different hierarchical levels influence sentencing decisions. Under such perspectives, varied combinations of individual-, case-, workgroup-, organizational-, and environmental-level factors mutually influence judicial decisions and determine sentencing outcomes. These frameworks improve upon the aforementioned perceptual theories in that they account for more than only the individually perceived impact. While, as the saying goes, "perception is reality," the reality represented by individual perception is often conditioned by the attributes of the individual perceiver. Because perception is filtered through the lens of individual experience and biases, it does not necessarily reflect conditions as they actually occur and exist. Thus, two judges within the same jurisdiction, for example, might have very different views of the ways in which local characteristics such as demographics or court resources affect their caseload—both of which might misrepresent reality. Along similar lines, the fact that female defendants are perceived to pose a lower risk of recidivism than are male defendants, or black defendants are seen as more threatening than are white defendants, does not mean that these perceptions are true. As a result, theories and research based solely on judicial perception of these factors may misrepresent or distort their true influence. Thus, multilevel theoretical alternatives intuitively are logical improvements of perceptual frameworks that exemplify Snipes and Maguire's "level of explanation" dimension.

In one respect, such hierarchical frameworks can be visualized as a multilevel funnel into which various hierarchical factors enter and from which the final sentencing decision is extruded. Yet, a more tangible and concrete analogy of the causal mechanisms of these perspectives is the vintage arcade game "Plinko" (Cheatwood, 2000). There, a ball or token is slid from the top of a steeply angled, nearly vertical board with multiple horizontal rows of pegs. The token passes through each row before reaching the bottom. As it falls, the token strikes pegs at every level—with each collision affecting its downward trajectory. At the bottom of the board, there is a series of labeled cells—any one of which can be the token's final resting place. The object of the game is for the falling token to come to rest in one specific cell (generally that with the highest point value or best prize assigned to it). The Plinko board is comparable to the sentencing decision process under multilevel sentencing theories. Here, the cells along the bottom of the board are the possible sentencing decisions. Each horizontal row of pegs represents a different hierarchical level, while the individual pegs themselves depict the varied horizontal spheres. Finally, the token is the individual case, and its final resting place is the sentencing decision—both of which are affected by various factors (pegs) from different hierarchical levels and spheres. The widely accepted object of the criminal sentencing process is, of course, to reach the most "just" sentence for the given offense.

While Plinko boards never represent such simple models, the most basic multilevel perspectives are bilevel theories where two levels of factors are paired to form explanations for sentencing outcomes. There are several examples of these simplified frameworks. For instance, substantive rationality bridges the gap between judicial perception theories and integrated theories because it includes components of both perspectives (Ulmer & Kramer, 1996). First, like the perceptual theories, it takes into account judicial perceptions of offender dangerousness, rehabilitation potential, and the practical consequences of sentencing in its explanation of judicial decisions. Yet, at the same time, actual variation between local courts is accounted for and expected to influence sentencing outcomes. Thus, this perspective focuses on how both judicial perception and local context—two distinct hierarchical levels—affect judicial decision making. Ulmer and Kramer's findings indicate support for their theoretical linkage between these levels—showing county variation in the effects of plea agreements, trial penalties, and defendant characteristics over sentencing outcomes.

Another series of bilevel perspectives pair individual- and organizational-level factors. Such frameworks attempt to explain how system factors and individual attributes shape judicial decisions and sentencing outcomes. For example, political system variation has been thought to affect judicial decisions through its impact on the judicial selection process. Such differences can lead to differential patterns of judicial socialization and recruitment that, in turn, influence the judges' views as well as their decision-making processes. Many studies support this proposition. One early study examined the sentencing behavior of Pittsburgh and Minneapolis judges—finding that differences in sentencing decisions are the indirect product of the cities' political systems (Levin, 1972). Similarly, organizational coupling (Jacob, 1997) merges organizational and interpersonal perspectives, describing the organizational impact on the work and activities of trial judges—specifically focusing on how intraorganizational relationships and individual perceptions mutually affect judicial decisions. In other words, this perspective captures how organizational factors affect the degree to which judges will "collaborate with one another or stand in one another's way" (Jacob, 1997, 4). Here, judicial sponsoring organizations exert from loose to tight control, or "coupling," over their members, which affects the predictability of court interactions and outcomes. The degree of "coupling" has direct implications for the efficiency and effectiveness of the sentencing process, as well as the equity of the sentences imposed by individual judges within that particular organization. For example, in organizations with tight coupling, strict authority over judicial case assignment, the caseload volume given to individual judges, and even scheduling of vacations is maintained—resulting in predictable outcomes and consequences. At the same time, tight control can impact judicial perceptions of their organization and, as a result, affect performance and decision making.

Thus, assignments or directives perceived to be undesirable can produce tension and resentment between judges and their organization, which can stifle innovation and slow the process of change. Conversely, loose coupling—while to a large degree alleviating such tension—reduces the predictability of court decisions and therefore increases the chances for disparate decisions. Thus, as Jacob notes, "Both tight and loose coupling provide benefits and costs to organizations" (1997, 8) as well as to individual defendants.

However, as suggested earlier, bilevel theories oversimplify the judicial decision-making process in a way that more complex multilevel theories do not. One approach that addresses the bilevel limitation—structural-contextual theory (Hagan, 1989a, 1989b, 1995)—posits that three levels of characteristics (case, organizational, and jurisdictional) interact to determine individual sentencing decisions. In the context of the courts specifically, this theory argues that sentences vary dramatically for common crimes because, for such cases, criminal justice organizations are loosely controlled and judicial discretion is relatively unconstrained; as a result, sentences are based on a variety of individual-level factors. However, in extreme cases, such as acts of domestic terrorism, a proactive political jurisdiction (such as one exhibiting strong media pressure) is argued to tighten the organizational constraints on sentencing outcomes through the invocation of proactive techniques (such as mandatory sentencing statutes), which make the sentencing decision more predictable. Thus, this perspective proposes an interactive relationship between factors from different hierarchical levels, suggesting that the predictive value of one level of influences (case level) varies by factors emanating from two other hierarchical levels (organizational and jurisdictional). In other words, legal factors better explain sentence outcomes when the jurisdictional political environment tightens organizational control over sentencing outcomes and when the offense is very severe (Smith & Damphousse, 1998). Unfortunately, there is mixed support for this perspective—with some studies supporting it (Spohn & Cederblom, 1991; Smith & Damphousse, 1998) and others refuting it (Smith & Damphousse, 1996).

Using a somewhat different approach, the court community framework (Eisenstein & Jacob, 1991) also includes explanatory factors from multiple hierarchical levels, but focuses primarily on how the courtroom workgroup interactions affect sentencing decisions. Here, while the judge is seen as the formal leader, he or she must still negotiate with the other workgroup members—especially the prosecutor and the defense attorney. Although many strategies are available for reaching a mutually acceptable sentencing outcome, workgroups mainly rely on negotiations in reaching a final sentence. However, the possibility of negotiations depends heavily upon workgroup factors such as familiarity, level of interaction, member stability, and going rates. In addition, factors from other hierarchical levels enter the explanatory equation in terms of how they affect the negotiation process. For example, case factors come into play in terms of the strength of the evidence, while sponsoring organizations (organizational level) affect workgroup negotiations through case assignment practices and through their relationships with the other sponsoring organizations. Likewise, environmental factors influence the negotiation process—and therefore the sentencing decision—through caseload, legislative standards, appellate decisions, and political environment, and media influences wield power over the workgroup.

Along these same lines, rationalized justice suggests an interaction between factors from multiple hierarchical levels that affects sentencing outcomes (Heydebrand & Seron, 1990). Specifically, it posits that environmental, structural, workgroup, and individual forces all influence judicial sentencing decisions. The relevant jurisdictional forces include the range and variability of the cases and the resources available to handle these cases, as well as the overall demographic and economic stability of the jurisdiction. Pertinent organizational aspects include court management techniques, the administrative orientation, and the degree of judicial autonomy permitted, as well as the levels of bureaucratization, formalization, and centralization. The workgroup characteristics include the degrees of coalition formation, co-optation, and exchange, as well as negotiation strategies. Finally, individual-level influences mainly stem from the roles and role orientations of the individual workgroup players. According to this perspective, variation in each of these factors across the four hierarchies impacts the ultimate sentencing decision. Thus, judicial activities and decisions vary by organizational, workgroup, environmental, and individual characteristics (Heydebrand & Seron, 1990). In much the same vein, other perspectives such as organizational context and tenor of justice incorporate variations in sentencing processing across these hierarchical levels, holding that individual sentencing decisions are influenced by the political, social, and organizational context of the court in which they occur (Nardulli et al., 1988; Dixon, 1995).

Currently, the most complex multilevel framework is the processual order or social worlds perspective (Ulmer, 1997; Ulmer & Kramer,

1998). Here, individual, case, workgroup, organizational, and environmental influences each affect sentencing decisions. As opposed to the other multilevel perspectives, however, this framework discourages static depictions of the courts and their decisions by focusing on the activities and interaction strategies of participants. It argues that, as varied court actors—most notably judges—confront sentencing decision situations, they continually engage in various interaction strategies with other court players to reach solutions that further their individual and collective interests. Such strategies or processes become a part of the court environment as social orders. These social orders, in turn, are created, maintained, and changed over time by these same interaction processes. Thus, this perspective views several hierarchical levels as inherently linked because they mutually compose and influence one another through the existing conditions, negotiation activities, and practical consequences—suggesting a nonrecursive relationship between all of these factors (Ulmer & Kramer, 1998). For example, individual and workgroup interaction processes and outcomes maintain, develop, and change the local institutional organization. Such organizations, in turn, affect both the individual role and workgroup interactions. Similarly, the boundaries of court communities are not established by formal organizational structures, but by lines of communication, participation, and influence in case processing. As a result, the relative importance of each component varies with location, time, and institution (Ulmer, 1997). Simply, "case processing and sentencing practices develop through the ongoing interaction of courtroom workgroup members, which is in turn contextualized by local court interorganizational relationships and state policies" (Ulmer & Kramer, 1998, 252). In other words, court actors interpret and use the formal criteria subjectively in a manner that both helps them deal with uncertainty and furthers their political and organizational interests (which are shaped by local context).

While each of the aforementioned theorists provides empirical analyses that support their own theoretical perspectives, until recently, there has been limited research assessing multilevel theories. Prior to this, the most common approach had been the separate case-level analysis of sentencing data as categorized by factors of another hierarchical level—such as environment or organization. While such research confirms sentencing variation by organizational factors (Kirsch, 1995) and workgroup characteristics (Flemming et al., 1992), the bulk of these studies focuses on cross-jurisdictional differences—finding significant variation in the effect of case-level factors by environment (Myers & Talarico, 1986a, 1986b; Dixon, 1995; Crawford et al., 1998; Nobiling,

Spohn, & DeLone, 1998). Another strategy for investigating multilevel theories, which has become increasingly popular, is the use of multilevel modeling techniques to analyze data from multiple hierarchical levels. Superior to single-level analytical alternatives, such strategies can differentiate between and identify the specific multilevel factors responsible for outcome differences (Kreft & De Leeuw, 1998; Heck & Thomas, 2000).

In recent years, this latter approach has been widely used to test a variety of macrolevel perspectives. Using case-level data for Pennsylvania sentencing outcomes in conjunction with county-level census data, the first such study (Britt, 2000), similar to research using the simpler partitioning approach, found that jurisdictional characteristics impact sentencing decisions even when case characteristics are controlled. However, unlike previous studies, this multilevel analysis further indicates that county attributes condition the influence of most case-level factors—suggesting an interactive effect between the two levels. Yet, at the same time, it also demonstrates minimal direct effect for environmental factors such as urbanization, racial composition, economic conditions, and crime level on sentencing outcomes.

Other multilevel sentencing research yields similar findings. For example, one analysis of federal drug sentences finds that the district in which a case is sentenced significantly affects the influence of case-level factors—such that the effect that both legal and extralegal factors wield over the final outcome varies significantly from one district to another. However, those higher-level factors explain only 10 percent of the sentence variation in drug offenses (Kautt, 2002). Similarly, research on sentences under the Pennsylvania system demonstrates that while higher-level factors such as court caseload, organizational culture, and demographic makeup significantly influence sentences, they account for only a small amount of the variance (Ulmer & Johnson, 2004). Conversely, other research using sentencing data from multiple U.S. jurisdictions also indicates that county factors wield minimal effects over case-level outcomes (Weidner, Frase, & Schultz, 2005). The implications of such results for multilevel theories are unclear. Supporting the propositions of many perspectives, these findings show that contextual variation in sentencing decisions exists. At the same time, they refute elements of these same theories by showing contextual factors are of limited explanatory power when case-level factors are controlled.

Despite the previous findings, however, it is important to keep in mind that the utility of these studies in testing the aforementioned multilevel perspectives is limited. To date, and despite additional calls for it (Kautt & Spohn, 2002), no studies of judicial sentencing decisions that rely upon this multilevel strategy have incorporated the sentencing judge as a level of analysis. As Britt (2000, 729) himself notes, "By ignoring the individual decision maker, this research assumes that judges will reach decisions in a uniform manner" and goes on to point out that his study also "assumes that judges within the same court jurisdiction will respond in the same way to broader contextual issues." As a result, existing research has yet to fully test the assumptions and propositions of the aforementioned multilevel theories attempting to explain judicial decision making.

CONCLUSION

This chapter has elaborated on various theoretical frameworks that describe the process by which judges reach sentencing decisions—tracing the gradual evolution of such explanations from simple unidimensional perspectives to complex multispherical and multilevel theories. Specifically, we focused on single and multispherical individual-level theories as well as those that integrate multiple hierarchical levels. Our examination of the relevant literature revealed only limited support for the unidimensional perspectives and suggests that multilevel and multispherical frameworks most accurately capture the realities of judicial decision making.

Beyond this, we used the characteristics of these theories and their evolution to illustrate and propose an organizational framework for categorizing existing theories of judicial decision making (see Table 7.1). However, this framework's utility is not limited solely to classifying explanations of sentencing outcomes. Rather, it has a wide range of applicability—from categorization of other court-specific theoretical explanations (such as prosecutorial charging decisions or probation officer assessments of offense seriousness and prior record) to that of

Table 7.1 Classifications of discussed theories

Unidimensional	Horizontally Integrated	Vertically Integrated	Both Horizontally and Vertically Integrated
Individual Physical Attributes Individual Internal Attributes Conversion	Maximalist Perspective Consensus Rationality Causal Attribution Bounded Rationality Focal Concerns	Substantive Rationality Organizational Coupling Structural-Contextual Court Community Rationalized Justice	Processual Order / Social Worlds

more broadly based explanations of criminal justice behaviors such as decisions made by police officers (arrest or use-of-force decisions) or correctional personnel (revocation decisions by probation or parole officers). Simply, the organization framework proposed here can be used to classify any type of theory and serve as a valuable tool for researchers who are new to either using or creating criminal justice theory.

With this structured perspective, we sought to provide an easy framework within which both novice researchers and theorists alike can methodically consider the various spheres and hierarchies they wish to include in their intended research. This formal assessment would, in turn, help them to determine the best theoretical perspective to use or the most appropriate form that any new theory they create should take. With thoughtful consideration of the multilevel and multispherical characteristics we identify, both the researcher and the theory framer alike will easily be able to formally examine the pertinent aspects of the area he or she intends to research, as well as make concrete choices concerning the theoretical perspectives to be used or created.

We hope such an organizational guide will spark innovative and comprehensive explanations for criminal justice outcomes and processes that incorporate all theoretically relevant influences, regardless of sphere or hierarchy. We feel that such a movement would signal the end of "atheoretical criminal justice," as well as result in more comprehensive explanations of the criminal justice process.

REFERENCES

Albonetti, C.A. 1991. An integration of theories to explain judicial discretion. *Social Problems* 38: 247–66.

Ball, H. 1980. *Courts and politics: The federal judicial system*. Englewood Cliffs, NJ: Prentice-Hall.

Berns, S. 1999. *To speak as a judge: Difference, voice, and power*. Aldershot, UK: Ashgate.

Blumstein, A., S.E. Martin, and M.H. Tonry. 1983. *Research on sentencing: The search for reform*, vol. 1. Washington, D.C.: National Academy Press.

Bridges, G.S., and S. Steen. 1998. Racial disparities in official assessments of juvenile offenders: Attributional stereotypes as mediating mechanisms. *American Sociological Review* 63: 554–70.

Bright, S.B. and P.J. Keenan. 1995. Judges and the politics of death: Deciding between the bill of rights and the next election in capital cases. *Boston University Law Review* 75: 759–835.

Britt, C. 2000. Social context and racial disparities in punishment decisions. *Justice Quarterly* 17(4): 707–32.

Carroll, J.S. and J.W. Payne. 1976. The psychology of the parole decision process: A joint application of attribution theory and information processing psychology. In *Cognition and human behavior*, eds. J.S. Carroll and J.W. Payne (pp. 13–32). Hillsdale, NJ: Erlbaum.

Cheatwood, D. 2000. Getting rid of cause: Improving the impact of theory on policy. Paper presented at the Academy of Criminal Justice Sciences, New Orleans, LA.

Chiricos. T.G. and W.D. Bales. 1991. Unemployment and punishment: An empirical assessment. *Criminology* 29(4): 701–24.

Cook, B.B. 1973. Sentencing behavior of federal judges: Draft cases—1972. *University of Cincinnati Law Review* 42: 597.

Crawford, C., T. Chiricos, and G. Kleck. 1998. Race, racial threat, and sentencing of habitual offenders. *Criminology* 36(3): 481–512.

Daly, K. and M. Tonry. 1997. Gender, race and sentencing. In *Crime and justice: A review of research*, ed. M. Tonry (pp. 201–52). Chicago: University of Chicago Press.

Dixon, J. 1995. The organizational context of criminal court sentencing. *American Journal of Sociology* 100: 1157–98.

Eisenstein, J. and H. Jacob. 1991. *Felony justice: An organizational analysis of criminal courts*. Lanham, MD: University Press of America.

Eisenstein, J., R.B. Flemming, and P.F. Nardulli. 1988. *The contours of justice: Communities and their courts*. Boston: Little, Brown.

Engle, C.D. 1971. Criminal justice in the city: A study of sentence severity and variation in the Philadelphia court system. PhD diss., Temple University.

Flemming, R, P. Nardulli, and J. Eisenstein. 1992. *The craft of justice: Politics and work in criminal court communities*. Philadelphia, PA: University of Pennsylvania Press.

Frazier, C. and E.W. Bock. 1982. Effects of court officials on sentence severity: Do judges make a difference? *Criminology* 20: 257–72.

Gibson, J. 1977. Discriminant functions, role orientations and judicial behavior: Theoretical and methodological linkages. *The Journal of Politics* 39: 984–1007.

Gibson, J. 1978. Judges' role orientations, attitudes, and decisions: An interactive model. *American Political Science Review* 72: 911–24.

Gibson, J. 1981. Personality and elite political behavior: The influence of self-esteem on judicial decision-making. *The Journal of Politics* 43: 104–25.

Gilligan, C. 1982. *In a different voice: Psychological theory and women's development*. Cambridge, MA: Harvard University Press.

Goldman, S. 1969. Backgrounds, attitudes, and the voting behavior of judges: A comment on Joel Grossman's social backgrounds and judicial decisions. *The Journal of Politics* 31: 214–22.

Grossman, J.B. 1967. Social backgrounds and judicial decisions: Notes for a theory. *The Journal of Politics* 29: 334–51.

Gruhl, J., C. Spohn, and S. Welch. 1981. Women as policymakers: The case of trial judges. *American Journal of Political Science* 25: 308–22.

Hagan, J. 1989a. *Structural criminology.* New Brunswick, NJ: Rutgers University Press.

Hagan, J. 1989b. Why is there so little criminal justice theory? Neglected macro- and micro-level links between organization and power. *Journal of Research in Crime and Delinquency* 26: 116–35.

Hagan, J. 1995. *Crime and disrepute.* Thousand Oaks, CA: Pine Forge Press.

Hawkins, D. 1981. Causal attribution and punishment for crime. *Deviant Behavior* 2(3): 207–30.

Heck, R.H. and S.L. Thomas. 2000. *Introduction to multilevel modeling techniques.* Mahwah, NJ: Erlbaum.

Henham, R. 2001. Theory and contextual analysis in sentencing. *International Journal of the Sociology of Law* 29(3): 253–76.

Heydebrand, W. and C. Seron. 1990. *Rationalizing justice: The political economy of federal district courts.* Albany, NY: State University of New York Press.

Hogarth, J. 1971. *Sentencing as a human process.* Toronto: University of Toronto Press.

Holmes, M.D., H.M. Hosch, H.C. Daudistel, D.A. Perez, and J.B. Graves. 1993. Judges' ethnicity and minority sentencing: Evidence concerning Hispanics. *Social Science Quarterly* 74: 496–506.

Jacob, H. 1997. The governance of trial judges. *Law and Society Review* 31(1): 3–30.

Kanter, R.M. 1977. *Men and women of the corporation.* New York: Basic Books.

Kautt, P.M. 2002. Location, location, location: Interdistrict and intercircuit variation in sentencing outcomes for federal drug-trafficking offenses. *Justice Quarterly* 19(4): 633–71.

Kautt, P. and Spohn, C. 2002. Cracking down on black drug offenders? Testing for interactions between offender race, drug type, and sentencing strategy in federal drug sentences. *Justice Quarterly* 19(1): 1–35.

Kirsch, C.P. 1995. Federal criminal justice: The decision process from complaint to trial. PhD diss. Graduate School of Public Service, New York University.

Kreft, I. and J. De Leeuw. 1998. *Introducing multilevel modeling.* Thousand Oaks, CA: Sage.

Kritzer, H.M. 1978. Political correlates of the behavior of federal district judges: A "best case" analysis. *Journal of Politics* 40: 25–58.

Laster, K. and R. Douglas. 1995. Feminized justice: The impact of women decision makers in the lower courts of Australia. *Justice Quarterly* 12 177–205.

Levin, M.A. 1972. Urban politics and policy outcomes: The criminal court. In *Criminal justice: Law and politics*, ed. G.F. Cole (pp. 330–52). Belmont, CA: Wadsworth.

Myers, M.A. 1988. Social background and sentencing behavior of judges. *Criminology* 26(4): 649–75.

Myers, M.A. and S.M. Talarico. 1986a. The social contexts of racial discrimination in sentencing. *Social Problems* 33(3): 236–51.

Myers, M.A. and S.M. Talarico. 1986b. Urban justice, rural injustice? Urbanization and its effect on sentencing. *Criminology* 24: 367–91.

Nagel, S. 1962. Ethnic affiliations and judicial propensities. *The Journal of Politics* 24: 92–110.

Nardulli, P.F., J. Eisenstein, and R.B. Flemming. 1988. *The tenor of justice: Criminal courts and the guilty plea process.* Urbana, IL: University of Illinois Press.

Nobiling, T., C. Spohn, and M. DeLone. 1998. A tale of two counties: Unemployment and sentence severity. *Justice Quarterly* 15: 459–85.

Rowland, C.K., R.A. Carp, and R.A. Stidham. 1984. Judges' policy choices and the value basis of judicial appointments: A comparison of support for criminal defendants among Nixon, Johnson, and Kennedy appointees to the federal district courts. *Journal of Politics*, 46: 886–902.

Schlesinger, T. 2005. Racial and ethnic disparity in pretrial criminal processing. *Justice Quarterly* 22(2): 170–92.

Schubert, G. 1961. A psychometric model of the supreme court. *American Behavioral Scientist* 5: 14–18.

Simon, H.A. 1957. *Administrative behavior: A study of decision making processes in administrative organizations.* New York: Macmillan.

Smith, B.L. and K.R. Damphousse. 1996. Punishing political offenders: The effect of political motive on federal sentencing decisions. *Criminology* 34: 289–322.

Smith, B.L. and K.R. Damphousse. 1998. Terrorism, politics, and punishment: A test of structural-contextual theory and the "liberation hypothesis." *Criminology* 36:67–92.

Smith, C.E. 1991. *Courts and the poor.* Chicago: Nelson-Hall.

Songer, D.R. and K.A. Crews-Meyer. 2000. Does judge gender matter? Decision making in state supreme courts. *Social Science Quarterly* 81: 750–62.

Spears, J.W. 1999. Diversity in the courtroom: A comparison of the sentencing decisions of black and white judges and male and female judges in Cook County Circuit Court. PhD. diss., University of Nebraska at Omaha.

Spohn, C. 1990a. Decision making in sexual assault cases: Do black and female judges make a difference? *Women and Criminal Justice* 2: 83–105.

Spohn, C. 1990b. The sentencing decisions of black and white judges: Expected and unexpected similarities. *Law and Society Review* 24(5): 1197–1216.

Spohn, C. 1992. An analysis of the "jury trial penalty" and its effect on black and white offenders. *The Justice Professional* 7: 93–112.

Spohn, Cassia. 2000. Thirty years of sentencing reform: The quest for a racially neutral sentencing process. In *Criminal Justice 2000, Volume 3* (pp. 427–501). Washington, DC: National Institute of Justice.

Spohn, C. and D. Beichner. 2000. Is preferential treatment of female offenders a thing of the past? A multi-site study of gender, race, and imprisonment. *Criminal Justice Policy Review* 11: 149–84.

Spohn, C. and J. Cederblom. 1991. Race and disparities in sentencing: A test of the liberation hypothesis. *Justice Quarterly* 8(3): 305–27.
Spohn, C. and M. DeLone. 2000. When does race matter? An analysis of the conditions under which race affects sentence severity. *Sociology of Crime, Law and Deviance* 2: 3–37.
Spohn, C. and D. Holleran. 2000. The imprisonment penalty paid by young, unemployed black and Hispanic male offenders. *Criminology* 38: 281–306.
Steen, S., R.L. Engen, and R.R. Gainey. 2005. Images of danger and culpability: Racial stereotyping, case processing, and criminal sentencing. *Criminology* 43(2): 435–67.
Steffensmeier, D. and S. Demuth. 2000. Ethnicity and sentencing outcomes in U.S. federal courts: Who is punished more harshly? *American Sociological Review* 65: 705–29.
Steffensmeier, D. and S. Demuth. 2001. Ethnicity and judges' sentencing decisions: Hispanic-black-white comparisons. *Criminology* 39: 145–78.
Steffensmeier, D. and C. Herbert. 1999. Women and men policymakers: Does the judge's gender affect the sentencing of criminal defendants? *Social Forces* 77: 1163–96.
Steffensmeier, D., J. Kramer, and C. Striefel. 1993. Gender and imprisonment decisions. *Criminology* 31: 411–46.
Steffensmeier, D., J. Kramer, and J. Ulmer. 1995. Age differences in sentencing. *Justice Quarterly* 12: 583–601.
Steffensmeier, D., J. Ulmer and J. Kramer. 1998. The interaction of race, gender, and age in criminal sentencing: The punishment cost of being young, black, and male. *Criminology* 36: 763–98.
Thompson, J.D. 1967. *Organizations in action*. New York: McGraw-Hill.
Uhlman, T.M. 1979. *Racial justice: Black judges and black defendants in an urban trial court*. Lexington, MA: Lexington Books.
Uhlman, T.M. and N.D. Walker. 1980. He takes some of my time; I take some of his: An analysis of judicial sentencing patterns in jury cases. *Law and Society Review* 14: 323–39.
Ulmer, J.T. 1997. *Social worlds of sentencing: Court communities under sentencing guidelines*. Albany, NY: State University of New York Press.
Ulmer, J.T. and J.H. Kramer. 1996. Court communities under sentencing guidelines: Dilemmas of formal rationality and sentencing disparity. *Criminology* 34(3): 383–408.
Ulmer, J.T. and J.H. Kramer. 1998. The use and transformation of formal decision making criteria: Sentencing guidelines, organizational contexts and case processing strategies. *Social Problems* 45: 248–67.
Ulmer, J.T. and B. Johnson. 2004. Sentencing in context: A multilevel analysis. *Criminology* 42(1): 137–77.
Washington, L. 1994. *Black judges on justice: Perspectives from the bench*. New York: The New Press.

Weidner, R.R., R.S. Frase, and J. Schultz. 2005. The impact of contextual factors on the decision to imprison in large urban jurisdictions. *Crime and Delinquency* 51(3): 400–24.

Welch, S., M. Combs, and J. Gruhl. 1988. Do black judges make a difference? *American Journal of Political Science* 32: 126–36.

Wheeler, S., K. Mann, and A. Sarat. 1988. *Sitting in judgment: The sentencing of white-collar offenders*. New Haven, CT: Yale University Press.

Zatz, M.S. 1987. The changing forms of racial/ethnic bias in sentencing. *Journal of Research in Crime and Delinquency* 24: 69–92.

8

COURTS AND COMMUNITIES

Toward a Theoretical Synthesis

Alissa Pollitz Worden

INTRODUCTION

The political and historical origins of American criminal courts cast them as distinctly local, community-based institutions. As Americans sorted out the details of postcolonial government, they drew upon a common-law heritage of local judicial administration, as well as their own distrust of centralized legal authority, and established criminal courts that were more directly accountable to local citizens than to state authorities. Two centuries later, this decentralization of criminal adjudication is still manifested in criminal codes as well as court structures. Criminal statutes define what constitutes crime and punishment in general terms, which are subject to the interpretation of local court actors. In most states, judges and prosecutors are elected by local constituencies. Most defendants are represented by counsel appointed by local judges, or by public defenders authorized and paid by county governments. Linkages to central authorities are limited: few criminal convictions are appealed, and professional associations exercise little control over judges and lawyers. The U.S. Supreme Court regularly reaffirms the role of community values in setting local legal practices (Friedman, 1984; Finckenauer, 1988).

This tradition of fragmentation and local autonomy is accompanied by institutionalized rules, practices, and structures that reflect unresolved conflicts among social values (Wright, 1981, 217; Goodpaster, 1987). Courts are expected to apply the law fairly, consistently, rationally, and publicly, but verdicts emerge from the secret, idiosyncratic, and unrecorded deliberations of lay jurors. Verdicts are in theory the result of adversarial challenges of evidence and testimony, but research tells us that defense lawyers and prosecutors face moral and practical incentives to quickly "settle the facts," avoid trials, and instead negotiate the terms of guilty pleas. Judges are supposed to be independent and impartial, yet in most jurisdictions they keep their jobs by winning elections. Court actors must reach equilibrium among these competing values. There is little reason to predict that courts in differing social, political, and economic environments will arrive at the same balances.

In short, the delegation of adjudication and sentencing functions to local courts, the geographic and political isolation of courts from each other, combined with the highly discretionary nature of court actors' work, and the need to reconcile competing values are conditions that favor the evolution of distinctive local legal cultures. While the broad outlines of the criminal process are sketched by state lawmakers, the substantive details are filled in at the local level by court actors themselves, in the form of norms, practices, and customs that prescribe how these actors do their jobs and what constitutes justice.

This chapter takes as a premise that courthouse culture—court actors' unwritten rules and understandings about local justice—has important political dimensions, and that understanding the relationships among communities and their courts merits social scientists' attention. As two observers of trial courts have noted, "Few government decisions affect citizens more than those made in the criminal process, for courts decide who shall be labeled a criminal and who shall be deprived of liberty or even life. Such decisions shape the context and dynamics of public order" (Eisenstein & Jacob, 1977, 4).

The purpose of this essay is to assess the state of theory about the relationships between communities and their criminal courts. This entails cataloging the relevant conceptual domains across which courts and communities vary, and taking stock of social scientists' attempts to theorize about the relationships among these concepts, as a prelude to deciding which lines of thinking are worth pursuing, what linkages have been overlooked but merit exploration, and what obstacles and challenges might stand in the way of theory development.[1]

This is not an easy task, for several reasons. Early attempts to theorize about trial courts were largely derivative; political scientists and sociologists borrowed theories about individual, social, organizational, and political behavior from other contexts and attempted to fit them, with uneven success, onto courts. Second, court research has emerged from several disciplines, but so far has inspired little integration of theoretical questions or propositions across disciplinary lines. Third, scholars began studying courts' community contexts almost as an afterthought, when they happened upon the topic while trying to explain important and troubling discoveries: first, the pervasiveness of guilty pleas and bargaining in urban courts (Newman, 1956; Sudnow, 1965; President's Commission on Law Enforcement and Administration of Justice, 1967; Blumberg, 1967); and second, evidence of disparities and discrimination in sentencing (Hagan, 1974).

Hence we have come to study the relationships between courts and communities in a roundabout way. In order to sort out the most promising directions for theory development, we must begin with some simple tasks: first, to clarify the meaning of theory as it is applied in this essay; second, to identify key elements and concepts; third, to review theoretical linkages that social scientists have suggested or developed, and critique their efforts to empirically test those theoretical propositions; and then, finally, turn our attention to emerging and unexplored theoretical perspectives among these linkages in order to identify promising directions for future research.

THE ROLE OF THEORY IN CRIMINAL COURT SCHOLARSHIP

A complete inventory of scholarship on criminal courts and communities would far exceed the scope of this essay, for a good deal of what has been written about the courts falls outside the definition of social science theory adopted here. A full catalog of court scholarship would include normative, doctrinal, and historical works as well as scientific studies, but the boundaries around scientific theory are drawn here around testable propositions about causes of individual, organizational, and community behavior in response to crime (Snipes & Maguire, Chapter 2 this volume). This approach sets aside some familiar types of intellectualizing about courts, which are worth noting.

For instance, during the 1960s and 1970s, a lively philosophical argument over the coercive evils and convenient virtues of plea bargaining occupied many journal pages (Vetri, 1964; Brunk, 1979; Church, 1979), only occasionally punctuated by empirical tests of authors' assumptions (Feeley, 1973; Friedman, 1979; Mather, 1979, 3). Perhaps because legal scholars started writing about courts before social scientists did, treatments of case law and legal reasoning are sometimes described as theoretical studies—but they are typically philosophical and value-based analyses rather than theoretical studies of variation in social or political behavior (e.g., Schulhofer, 1984; Lynch, 1999). Trials make good stories, so most students of the courts are familiar with historical and autobiographical accounts of casework, often involving particularly spectacular, influential, or publicized cases, but these accounts are not generalizable to routine court behavior (Lewis, 1964; Dershowitz, 1983; Wishman, 1986).

These sorts of work can illustrate theory, and may inspire theorizing, particularly insofar as they prompt reflection on important aspects of decision processes or sincere concerns about unjust outcomes. Unfortunately, they can also obscure or distract from social scientific thinking about courts. Theory-based work tends to set aside the spectacular trial, the landmark case, the famous attorney, in favor of modeling the routine processes that ordinary actors apply to typical cases. This is hard work, so why do it?

First, theoretical thinking is explanatory rather than descriptive, so it leads to clearer statements of interesting and important questions, and sometimes improved predictions about the likely success of policy changes. Relatedly, theoretical thinking permits us to formalize conventional wisdom and test it. What "everyone knows" often turns out to be incorrect, or correct only at the extremes. For instance, marked disparities in the incarceration rates of whites and minorities may be reasonable cause for alarm, but without an understanding of the causes for the disparity, one cannot argue persuasively about the need to address social prejudice, economic inequalities, discriminatory police and court practices, or sentencing statutes.

Second, theory obliges us to discipline our thinking about core concepts and about cause and effect relationships. Few research tasks prompt more careful reflection than the practical problems of specifying units of analysis, figuring out what aspects of those units should be measured, and diagramming the possible causal connections among variables.

Third, theoretical work is (or ought to be) iterative and cumulative, channeling the opportunities and activities of researchers toward common questions. Over time, the result of this kind of work is greater confidence in social science answers to these questions—and in the study of criminal justice, answers are socially and politically, as well as intellectually, important.

For the purposes of studying courts and communities, theory directs us toward some intriguing questions: Whose "behavior" should we examine, and of what does it consist? What formal and informal structures in courts are related to that behavior, and how? How should we conceptualize communities (an important first step in figuring out what aspects of communities we should model and measure)? How have theorists modeled the relationships among these variables, and how might we add to that work?

DEFINING CONCEPTUAL DOMAINS: COMMUNITY AND COURT CHARACTERISTICS

Figure 8.1 presents six conceptual domains, which can be broadly (but not exclusively) grouped as court characteristics, elite characteristics, and community characteristics. The diagram directs our attention first to characteristics of courts themselves: courthouse cultures composed of case processing norms and practices, court organizations' structure, and court actors' priorities and attitudes. Key courthouse actors—judges, prosecutors, and criminal defense lawyers—are specialized members of a community's political elite. They share this status with other individuals who occupy positions of political power, control over resources, responsibility for local criminal justice policy, and accountability to constituents. This group might include both elected officials (mayors, county commissioners), as well as directors of criminal justice organizations (police executives, local jail administrators) and local bar associations. These political elites are part of a broader social and political landscape. That landscape is defined by characteristics of community residents (social, political, and economic), as well as the missions and priorities of community organizations and agencies, both public and private, who claim a stake or interest in the work of the courts (and, usually, in the work of the criminal justice system more generally).

The following sections briefly describe these conceptual domains, with particular attention to four sets of questions. First, what variables are included in each domain, and how should they be differentiated for purposes of theorizing about linkages among them? Second, how (and how much) do these concepts vary, and do they vary in ways that are likely to be relevant to our understanding of court–community relationships? Third, how are these concepts meaningful as variables in models of court behavior (do they help us build hypotheses? have they distracted us from less obvious but important constructs?) and, fourth, are they measurable using social science research strategies? Cataloging these constructs is a first step toward mapping their theoretical relationships; and as the following discussion will suggest, the relationships among these variables are not necessarily simple.

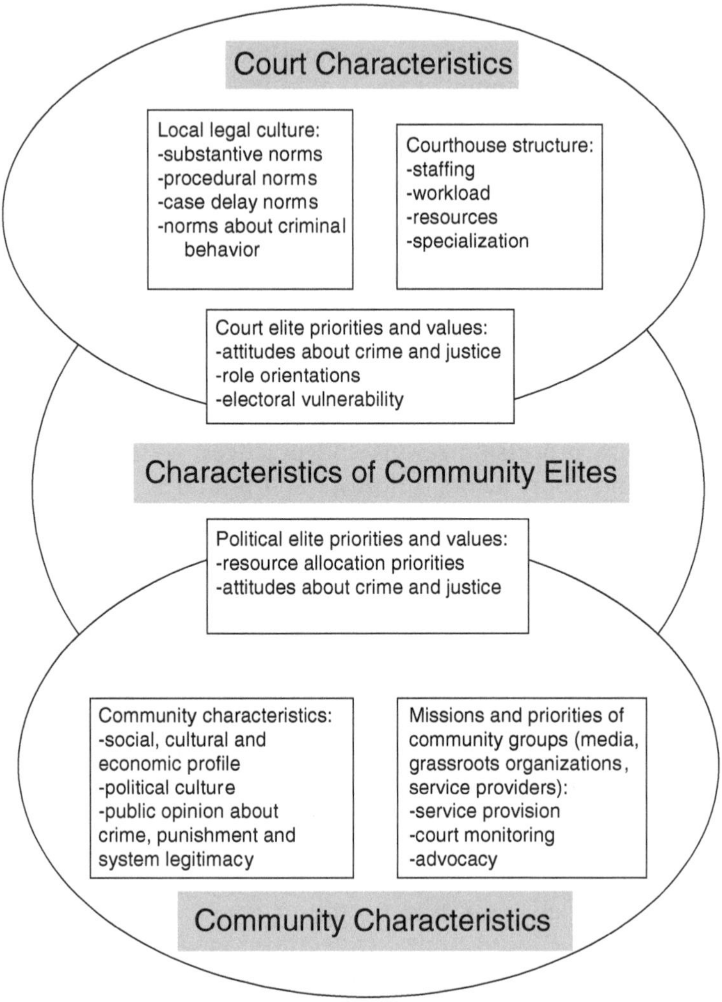

Figure 8.1 Conceptual domains in court-community research

Courthouse Culture

Courthouse culture, or local legal culture, is made up of the norms, customs, practices, and policies that characterize a court's decision processes (Church, 1985). The term serves as shorthand for court actors' shared beliefs and understandings about how their court works, although the content of those beliefs, and the level of agreement on them, varies across several important dimensions. The concept was initially developed to account for the displacement of jury trials by plea bargaining, as social scientists concluded that the very low trial rate in most courts resulted from the widespread belief among court actors that trials were an inefficient and inappropriate means of disposing of most criminal accusations (Eisenstein & Jacob, 1977; Heumann, 1978). As court observers developed the concept of legal culture, they recognized its value in accounting for variation in plea bargaining norms (as well as rates), its applicability to domains of decision making besides guilty pleas and trials, and its potential value in explaining why courts in otherwise similar communities could generate very different patterns of verdicts and sentences.

Eisenstein and Jacob's (1977) landmark study of Chicago, Baltimore, and Detroit criminal courts explored legal culture as the product of court actors' converging objectives and interests in avoiding time-consuming and unpredictable trials. They hypothesized that structural and organizational features of courts (such as stable workgroups and large volumes of cases) accounted for the development of norms about sentencing in the form of "going rates" for particular types of offenses or offenders. Later researchers extended and refined this concept, and have measured sentencing norms directly, as collective attitudinal constructs of court actors (Church, 1985; Worden, 1987; Luskin & Luskin, 1987).

Norms encompass procedural as well as substantive dimensions. For example, court actors might agree that the appropriate (or inevitable) outcome of most cases is a guilty plea and a highly predictable sentence and gear their preparation, time commitment, and conversations with victims and defendants accordingly (Heumann, 1978); elsewhere, court actors might agree that a plea is inevitable, but routinely plan to negotiate over sentences (McIntyre, 1987); and in still other (but probably rare) courts, lawyers may approach each other as adversaries and may subscribe to traditional advocacy positions (Emmelman, 1996). Court cultures, therefore, might be categorized in terms of consensus, negotiation, and adversariness.

Norms about procedural and substantive justice entail more than expectations about whether defendants should (or will) plead guilty and on what terms, however. They also include expectations about pretrial decisions. Court actors' discretion to withhold formal accusations and sanctions may be more powerful in shaping community standards of crime and justice, and may be more immune to community oversight, than their discretion in setting punishments (Myers & Hagan, 1979; Horney & Spohn, 1991). Court actors' norms about how to handle many misdemeanor or low-level felony charges can include unwritten rules about the quality of evidence necessary to sustain charges, about the role of the victim in prosecution, and about the use of legal controls other than sentencing, such as pretrial detention and orders of protection. Examples of de facto decriminalization would include the hands-off practices of some courts in drunk driving cases and domestic violence incidents. When court actors agree that certain types of cases do not merit prosecution, or merit it only under unusual conditions, that agreement may have important consequences: it may discourage police from making arrests, and may send signals to complainants and defendants that some offenses are beneath the court's notice.

Local legal culture, adequately conceptualized and measured, is arguably the key construct in any community-level model of court behavior. Researchers have hypothesized, with some empirical support, that courthouse cultures evolve as the products of court structure and elite values, and they have also hypothesized that culture accounts for observable differences in patterns of adjudication and sentencing (Feeley, 1973; Nardulli, 1978; Alschuler, 1979; Ryan, 1980; Jacob, 1983; Glick & Pruet, 1985; Scheingold & Gresset, 1987; Vance & Stupak, 1997; Ulmer, 1998). If these hypotheses are correct, then legal culture constitutes the community's unwritten legal code: it defines for a community what protections or burdens are imposed on victims, what costs and risks are faced by defendants, what offenses shall and shall not be sanctioned by the court, and what punishments are faced by convicted offenders.

Court Structure and Organization

Courts are really networks of organizations—the local judiciary and its staff, the prosecutor's office, and the members of the criminal defense bar—who are bound to each other through their formal shared responsibility for adjudicating criminal charges. A comprehensive inventory of the dimensions of court and court organizations' structure is beyond the scope of this discussion; here we simply illustrate three constructs that might influence the character of local legal culture: court caseload, staffing and workload distribution, and indigent defense systems.

Caseload has been conceptualized in two ways: as volume of work processed in a court, and as relative workload or case pressure experienced by court actors. The first measure is, of course, associated with jurisdictional size and urbanization. Early researchers typically conducted their studies in urban, high-volume courts, and often concluded that sheer volume of cases desensitized court workers to individual differences among defendants, fostering routinization and plea bargaining norms (Sudnow, 1965; Skolnick, 1967). However, few attempted to test this hypothesis by directly comparing low-volume and high-volume jurisdictions (but see, e.g., Jacoby, 1977; Austin, 1981; Myers & Reid,

1995), and case studies of moderately sized cities uncovered evidence of routinization as well (Cole, 1970; Eisenstein et al., 1988). Another seemingly obvious hypothesis, that heavy case pressure compelled actors to short-circuit adversarial processes, also failed to find much empirical support in comparative studies (Heumann, 1975; Church, 1985; Worden, 1995) or in historical research (Feeley, 1978; Friedman, 1979).

By the early 1970s, theorists looked more closely at what happened inside courts, recognizing more complex dynamics at the individual and organizational level. One of the most influential among them, Malcolm Feeley, argued that understanding (and reforming) the legal process was "clearly . . . more than a problem of overcoming workload so that good men can do good work" (1973, 422). The structure and interorganizational relationships among court actors, he suggested, has more to do with courthouse norms than case volume; after all, court actors are largely autonomous and have considerable discretion in regulating and organizing their work. Eisenstein and Jacob (1977) hypothesized that organizational conditions that favor the formation of stable workgroups tend to produce high rates of guilty pleas and consensus on sentencing norms for common types of offenses. Although many assume that these conditions are obtained primarily in urban courts, contemporary researchers have noted that the economies of scale in urban courts may allow for specialized structures and work assignments that promote more adversarial and individualized adjudication. Examples would include specialized court parts, community courts, and dedicated units in public defender and prosecutors' offices (Weimer, 1980; McIntyre, 1987; Chaiken & Chaiken, 1991).

Finally, court scholars have hypothesized that the organization of criminal defense work shapes the character of courthouse culture. Early studies that simply asserted or assumed the inferiority of publicly paid counsel (e.g., Blumberg, 1967; Casper, 1972; Lizotte, 1978) were soon supplanted by research that models both public and private lawyers' incentives, role definitions, organizational settings, and performance (Mather, 1979; Stover & Eckart, 1975; Houlden & Balkin, 1985; Nardulli, 1986; McIntyre, 1987), although few such studies utilized comparative data on two important variables, resources and caseload (but see Worden, 1995; Priehs, 1999).

These examples illustrate the challenges of making sense of empirical findings on court structure and culture. First, some community and structural variables covary (e.g., urbanization, caseload, and use of public defender agencies), which complicates the development of causal models about court behavior. Second, most studies are of highly urbanized courts, and few studies are truly comparative. Third, interesting variables are hard to measure, or to measure reliably at the community and courthouse level, so we tend to measure what we can see and overlook less visible (but more theoretically important) variables.

Furthermore, court researchers have reasonably focused on formal and structural constructs, giving less attention to more subtle characteristics of court cultures such as openness to innovation and nontraditional structuring of work. While researchers are quick to evaluate the impact of innovations and reforms, such as community prosecution, alternative sentencing, priority prosecution programs (e.g., Chaiken & Chaiken, 1991), and specialized courts, they have devoted less effort to the more challenging task of testing theories about why some courts innovate and others do not.

Finally, the remarkable diversity of court structures frustrates efforts to theorize parsimoniously about them; with so many variants to observe and describe, it is easier to simply continue the work of documenting local idiosyncrasies. However, a more constructive solution might be to inventory structural variables in order to cull the list for those that hold most promise in explaining court behavior.

Priorities and Attitudes of Courthouse Elites

Because the legal system grants so much discretion to courthouse actors, particularly judges and prosecutors, it is commonsensical to predict that their attitudes, beliefs, and experiences affect their decisions. Early research based on interviews and observations in trial courts provided evidence that court actors indeed hold diverse views about crime, justice, and their roles and functions (Becker, 1966; Mather, 1979; Carter, 1974; Bohne, 1978). However, a full accounting of how attitudes and priorities vary and what difference that might make for courts and communities has yet to be conducted.

Such an accounting might begin with a simple categorization of beliefs. Like other people, court actors hold beliefs about the absolute and relative seriousness of offenses, about the virtues and limitations of procedural safeguards, about punishments and punishment rationales, and about their own roles in the court. Unlike other people, however, court actors have daily opportunities to act upon their beliefs. Although judges and prosecutors remain a socially homogeneous group, their views about crime and justice are diverse (Church, 1985; Scheingold & Gressett, 1987; Worden, 1990, 1995). Defense lawyers vary in their commitment to due-process norms, in their beliefs about the integrity of the legal process, and in their feelings of loyalty to clients (Flemming, 1986).

Court actors' beliefs about their own roles and functions, independent of their substantive beliefs and values, may shape their use of discretion. Judges who define their job in terms of enforcing community norms may transmit community values more directly into decisions than do judges who rely on their own experience and expertise as trustees of community justice (Gibson, 1980). Judges may play an active role in their courts, or they may become referees rather than decision makers, ensuring that prosecutors and defense lawyers play by the rules, but routinely ratifying the results of their contests over verdicts and sentencing (Alpert, Atkins, & Ziller, 1979). Role orientation encompasses perspectives on policy as well as case-by-case practice. Some judges may be innovators, willing to experiment with new strategies (such as victim assistance programs, alternative sentencing plans, or specialized courts), while others may limit their job description to traditional particularized adjudication.

Likewise, prosecutors' and defense lawyers' role orientations vary. Like judges, prosecutors are political actors and must come to terms with their constituents' expectations. Furthermore, some prosecutors adopt an adversarial and combative approach to casework, while others place a premium on finding common ground with their opponents (Nardulli, Flemming, & Eisenstein, 1984). Defense lawyers may see their jobs in terms of winning cases, meeting clients' needs, developing good working relationships with others in the courthouse, or defending abstract conceptions of constitutional rights. Few, if any, lawyers could successfully pursue all these objectives simultaneously.

These attitudinal variables are relevant to understanding courts and communities if we suspect that court actors behave like the elected (or appointed) politicians that they are. Unfortunately, beyond courthouse folklore about hanging judges, relentless prosecutors, and valiant defense lawyers, researchers interested in court actors' political links to their communities have had few opportunities to develop and test hypotheses about constituency preferences and court behavior. First, studies seldom construct replicable measures of actors' beliefs, or even directly measure beliefs, instead relying on proxy measures (such as race, sex, or career background; e.g., Myers, 1988; Spohn, 1990a, 1990b). Second, researchers have targeted judges to the neglect of prosecutors or defense lawyers, overlooking the fact that case outcomes are more often the products of attorneys' bilateral negotiations than judges' unilateral judgments. Finally, the findings of most theoretically based studies suggest that the attitude–behavior link may hold only under some conditions: when actors define their role in terms of community responsiveness (Gibson, 1978, 1980), when information about public preferences is clearly communicated (Kuklinski & Stanga, 1979), or when they feel unconstrained by the expectations of other system actors (Spohn & Cederblom, 1991; Worden, 1995).

Priorities and Values of Community Elites

Community elites are defined as individuals and organizations who possess political power within their communities. This includes criminal justice agents outside the courts (law enforcement agencies, probation departments, jail authorities), local government authorities (mayors, local funding authorities, some criminal justice task forces), and groups with direct access to and influence on the courts (local bar associations). Elite priorities, political motivations, and resources may shape court behavior in several ways.

First, the policies and practices of criminal justice agencies, particularly police departments, generate the raw material of court work. Proactive departments staffed with well-trained officers produce caseloads of differing size and evidentiary quality than understaffed and less professionalized departments. The organizational culture of probation departments can filter the types of information and recommendations that judges receive about defendants (Vance & Stupak, 1997).

Second, because courthouse budgets are often highly dependent on city and county funds, funding authorities' capacity and willingness to support key functions affect the structure and capacity of the system. Examples include indigent defense, prosecutors' offices, and courthouse infrastructure, as well as support for treatment programs, victim assistance programs, and jail capacity.

Third, local politicians and political groups exercise influence on who sits on the bench and practices at the bar. Judges' and prosecutors' elections often end in lopsided victories, but important and contested endorsement and nomination decisions are made behind closed doors by local political party chiefs, and often are influenced by the formal or informal endorsements of local bar associations. The crime and justice priorities of local mayors or council members may have more impact on court outputs when those elites hold the political strings of nominations (e.g., Levin, 1972).

These variables—agency priorities, policies and practices, resource allocation, and political power—vary at the community level, and anecdotal evidence suggests that these variables are linked to court behavior. However, community elites, and community groups more generally, have typically been relegated to a position of secondary interest in studies of communities and courts. Researchers acknowledge the role of these groups as part of courts' political environments (e.g., Eisenstein &

Jacob, 1977; Eisenstein, Flemming, & Nardulli, 1988), although seldom at a theoretical and generalizable level. This may be due in part to the difficulty of measuring the behavior of such groups at the community level and the tendency to assume that these factors are unique to communities.

Community Organizations' Missions and Objectives

Community organizations are defined for our purposes as groups whose self-defined mission includes service provision, advocacy, oversight, or mobilization around crime and justice issues. These organizations have been the least studied elements in research on courts and communities; like political elites, they are sometimes credited with particular changes or outcomes in particular jurisdictions, but seldom researched systematically by court scholars.

A catalog of such groups would include neighborhood associations, reform-oriented political action groups, organizations that provide services to offenders and to victims, political entrepreneurs who import and attempt to implement innovations into local legal systems, and local media. These organizations vary across many dimensions: some are grassroots organizations (shelters for domestic abuse victims), while others are local branches of larger state or national groups (Mothers Against Drunk Driving—MADD). Some are founded to change or reform court practices (courtwatch organizations), while others operate side by side with court actors (offender counseling programs). Some are long-standing features of the local political landscape (newspapers), while others may be mobilized by a controversial case or highly publicized crime (task forces). Some identify with public safety and victim protection, while others work to improve defendants' rights. Some projects are housed in established community institutions (e.g., church-based groups); others may have independent staff, office space, funding, and infrastructure (alternative sentencing programs).

The objectives of these groups may include providing auxiliary or alternative services for courts, lobbying for more or different crime control activities, or challenging the legitimacy of court practices. While theories of community mobilization and change would probably help us conceptualize and theorize about the relationships of these groups to courts and communities, that task has yet to be undertaken. There are glimmerings of interest in these questions, however. For example, researchers who analyze restorative justice initiatives recognize the role of reform advocates in getting such programs underway and the remarkable diversity of such programs in different community settings (Bazemore, 1997; Rose & Clear, 1998). Studies of specialized drug courts and domestic violence courts take into account the key roles of service providers as both promoters of and contributors to these innovations (Shepard & Pence, 1999).

Community Environment

Researchers often sum up community environments in very simple and general terms: rural, urban, middle-class, crime-ridden, Democratic, conservative, Midwestern, black or white. These words are meant to signal what is (and what is not) relevant for understanding courts' relationships with their social, economic, and political environments. For the purpose of sketching backdrops for community case studies, this level of generality is sufficient. But theorizing about sociopolitical environments and institutional behavior calls for more careful discrimination among social and economic constructs, political culture, and public opinion on crime and justice topics.

COMMUNITIES' SOCIOECONOMIC CHARACTERISTICS

Economic and social conditions, particularly urbanization, crime, and poverty, define the demands placed on, and to some extent the resources available to, court organizations. All else being equal, communities with higher crime rates place greater demands on the criminal justice system and require more resources for functions such as indigent defense. Unemployment rates (and their implications for labor markets) might be either a cause or a consequence of high incarceration rates in communities. Community size may influence the level of bureaucratization and routinization in case processing. Furthermore, researchers have scrutinized court behavior in distinctively rural (Hagan, 1977; Austin, 1981; Eisenstein, 1982), predominantly black (Myers & Talarico, 1986a, 1986b), and midsized (Eisenstein, Flemming, & Nardulli, 1988) communities.

Political Culture

The essence of political culture, as originally described by Elazar (1972, 1988), consists of the public's views about the relationship between government and the governed. Elazar theorized that political culture develops from the shared values and experiences of a region's residents; for example, Southern political culture has been described as traditionalistic, marked by deference to local political and economic elites, and acceptance of social (and racial) stratification, a consequence of a highly skewed race and class system. The political culture of areas populated by working-class immigrants has been characterized as individualistic, implying an opportunistic, self-interested, and pragmatic view of government, giving rise to patronage and machine politics, as well as career politicians. New England and Midwestern political cultures have been described as moralistic, molded by the attitudes of affluent Northern European settlers whose local political structures reflected a communitarian, reform-minded, "good government" perspective.[2]

The links between political culture and court behavior are largely unexplored, but merit continued development. That political culture may account for court behavior is suggested (although by no means conclusively demonstrated) by intriguing bits of evidence. For example, traditionalistic communities in the South produce unusually high incarceration rates (especially for African American defendants). Communities that would be classified as moralistic were the first to experiment with comprehensive community-based reforms in the area of domestic violence and victim assistance (Minnesota, Massachusetts). Levin (1972) observed that party-dominated machine politics in Pennsylvania tended to select judges with particularistic, individualistic orientations toward defendants, compared with those in Minnesota, where the selection system tended to tap lawyers from private practices with strong public safety orientations.

Public Opinion about Crime and Justice

Public opinion is multidimensional, and understanding its relationships with court behavior requires that we distinguish at the community level among the objects of opinions, the level of salience, and levels of consensus or heterogeneity.

People's normative opinions about crime can be sorted into at least three dimensions of variation. First, beyond consensus on serious (and relatively rare) crimes of violence and property, people hold different views about what behaviors should and should not be punished as crimes (Glick & Pruet, 1985) and about what justifications might excuse criminal acts (Robinson & Darley, 1995). Examples might include driving while intoxicated, many instances of domestic violence, firearms possession, sexual assaults, possession of controlled substances, and some incidents of child abuse, as well as the legitimacy of the insanity defense and the meaning of self-defense.

Second, people vary even more in their views about appropriate punishments for specific crimes, and more generally in their willingness to see harsh punishments imposed on offenders (Blumstein & Cohen, 1980; Durham, 1988; Bohm et al., 1990). A third set of normative beliefs involves the perceived legitimacy of the legal system. Researchers have assessed attitudes about procedural justice, as well as opinions about the legitimacy of local criminal justice institutions (Merry, 1985; Tyler, 1988; Olson & Huth, 1998). Finally, in addition to normative beliefs, individuals hold different empirical beliefs about crime itself—its prevalence and their own risk of victimization.

Attitudes and beliefs about criminal justice have been examined primarily at the individual level, and from this research, we have gleaned a few important observations. First, differences in attitudes about the relative gravity of many common misdemeanors (and minor felonies) are correlated with social background and individual characteristics such as race, sex, and age (Miller, Rossi, & Simpson, 1986). Second, views about punishment may be related to deep-seated cultural values, including religious views (Grasmick et al., 1992). Third, views about appropriate punishments may be quite different from (and often harsher than) actual sentencing practice (Durham, Elrod, & Kincade, 1996; Blumstein & Cohen, 1980). Fourth, views about system legitimacy may be related to personal experiences with the criminal justice system (Casper, 1978). Fifth, fear of crime is not closely related to objective risk of victimization across social groups (Glick & Pruet, 1985).

These observations offer some guidance in conceptualizing public opinion at the community level. First, because belief dimensions are not correlated in altogether predictable ways, we should be cautious of overgeneralizing about community attitudes and pay close attention to which dimensions are theoretically and empirically related to court decisions. For example, rural residents may be more punitive than urban counterparts, but also more libertarian in their ideas about what behaviors the criminal justice system should monitor.

Second, an assessment of the relationships between public opinion and court behavior requires attention to the salience of opinion, as well as levels of consensus. One might predict weak associations between opinion and system behavior if opinions, regardless of their content, are casually formed. Most data collection strategies offer no opportunity to measure salience, and may therefore lead to overprediction of the impact of public opinion.

Finally, we should hypothesize not just about whether opinion influences court behavior and under what conditions, but also about whose opinions are influential and how these opinions are transmitted to court decision makers (a topic to which we shall turn in the next sections). Public opinion varies when measured at the community level, but not all variation is meaningful. For example, two communities whose residents favor tougher driving while intoxicated (DWI) sentencing by majorities of 70 and 95 percent, respectively, may be indistinguishable in terms of their impact on local criminal justice practice, although smaller differences located at a different place on the scale—say, 45 and 60 percent—might prove much more politically interesting. While it is tempting to express public opinion data in terms of interval-level variables, more careful thinking suggests it might be better conceived for some purposes in categorical or ordinal terms. Furthermore, because attitudes on some crime issues are not distributed in the same way across social groups, and some social groups may have more influence on court behavior than others, community-level soundings of opinion may mask heterogeneity across subpopulations and lead us to underestimate criminal justice agents' responsiveness to constituencies.

SUMMARY

In summary, explorations into community attributes have generated a menu of intriguing variables, but little conceptual clarity or empirical certainty about what is, or theoretically might be expected to be, related to court behavior. Social and economic profiles have sometimes served as shorthand for community values and beliefs, but many conceptual questions remain unsettled, including questions about how best to measure community-level attributes and what dimensions to measure. Some of the most interesting questions about public opinion may be about criminal acts that are at the edge of unlawful behavior, yet more research has examined public opinion on high-end criminal justice practices (such as capital punishment), where consensus levels are high.

How might communities' political, social, and economic characteristics be associated with court behavior? Crime, and crime's economic correlates of poverty, unemployment, and social disorganization, generates caseloads for the courts through police arrest practices, as well as through the availability of public resources for supporting the courts' work. Political culture may shape the ways in which court elites reach office; attitudes about crime and justice may influence courthouse decision makers who are attuned to public opinion. Controversies among subgroups, or perceived injustices, may materialize in the form of community organizations that lobby for reforms, victim protections, or defendant rights. In short, aggregate characteristics of communities' residents influence court behavior, if at all, through indirect paths.

Theoretical Linkages among Court and Community Variables

These broadly defined conceptual domains—dimensions of court structure, local legal culture, the values and priorities of courthouse elites, community elites, and community-based organizations, and social and political environment—are all seemingly relevant to understanding the relationships among courts and communities, but how does theory direct us toward mapping those relationships? Do community characteristics define the way courts do their work? Does court behavior affect communities above and beyond individual case outcomes? Or do causal arrows run in both directions?

As it turns out, these three simple questions are illustrated (but by no means exhausted) by three theoretical perspectives that have been adapted to studying courts. Political scientists have adapted theories of constituency representation to account for sentencing patterns, hypothesizing that community values and political elites constrain or guide judges' decisions. Drawing on conflict theory, sociologists have attempted to explain disparate sentencing patterns as consequences of self-interested elite behavior, resulting in court behavior that perpetuates race and class inequalities in communities. Scholars who are trained in organizational theory model local legal culture as the product of local court structure, workgroup relationships, and organizational constraints and incentives shaped indirectly by political environments.

These theoretical perspectives have dominated thinking about how courts work and how they relate to their communities—so much so, in fact, that a casual consumer of court literature might be forgiven for concluding that these perspectives have transcended their status as theories and instead become postulates about court behavior. In fact, however, the discrepancies among these theoretical perspectives have seldom been scrutinized, much less reconciled. These linkages are mapped in Figures 8.2, 8.3, and 8.4, which are discussed briefly next.

Representational Theory

Political scientists have borrowed theories of constituency representation to model the relationships between public opinion and judicial behavior (see Figure 8.2). Implicitly casting judges as local policy makers, and courts' aggregate decisions (usually sentencing decisions) as policy, researchers speculated that as elected officials, judges would serve as a conduit for the public opinions about crime and justice. These initial efforts turned out to be overly simplistic, but they have led to theoretical refinements about the conditions under which judges might incorporate public opinion into decisions.

Specifically, researchers hypothesized that judges would transmit public opinion if they subscribed to delegate role orientations (defining their job at least partly in terms of public responsiveness) (Cook, 1977; Gibson, 1981), if they believed themselves to be electorally vulnerable (Gibson, 1980), or if they shared constituency views (Gibson, 1978;

Flango, Wenner, & Wenner, 1978; Glick & Pruet, 1985), or if, as is seldom the case, they were provided with data about their constituents' opinion, particularly on controversial matters (Kuklinski & Stanga, 1979).

There is little reason to believe that the electorate is very interested in court electoral politics, and some reason to believe that court actors know this (Sheldon & Lovrich, 1982), so court actors' sense of vulnerability may prove to be a weak link between community opinion and court behavior. However, this representational theoretical perspective

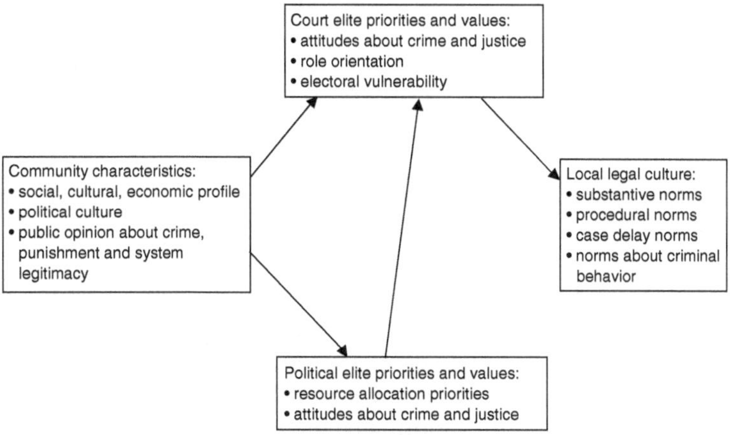

Figure 8.2 Representational theory

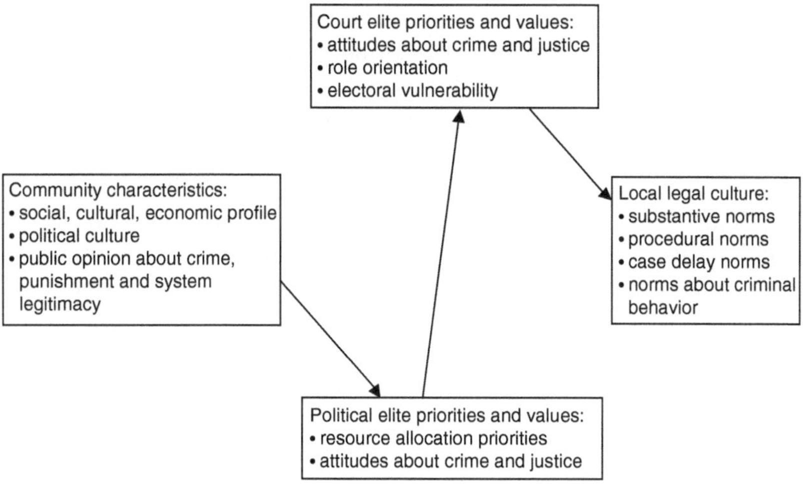

Figure 8.3 Conflict theory

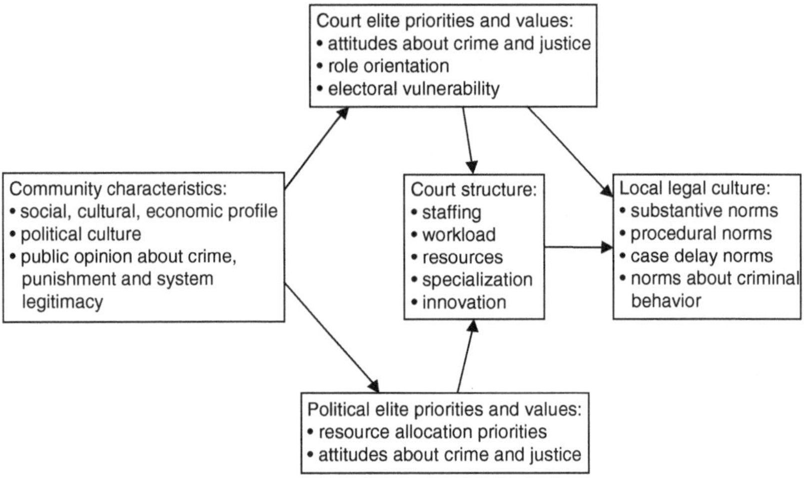

Figure 8.4 Local legal culture and workgroup theory

suggests a second and less direct linkage between public opinion and court behavior: political culture (rather than specific opinions about crime) may define informal elements of judicial and prosecutorial selection processes, as suggested by Levin's comparative study of party machine careerists and bar-nominated amateurs (Levin, 1972; see also Scheingold & Gressett, 1987).

Most of the empirical research developed from this theoretical perspective falls short of providing convincing tests of a representational model of court behavior, for several reasons. First, as discussed earlier, public opinion is a complex set of dimensions, which are difficult to measure. Second, researchers have applied this theory almost exclusively to judges as political decision makers. Yet prosecutors may be more influential in settling case outcomes than judges, and are also more likely to feel politically vulnerable and electorally accountable (Worden, 1990). Third, most studies measure court "policy" in terms of felony case sentencing; but court actors exercise more discretion in less serious, more common, and more normatively marginal offenses (Spohn & Cederblom, 1991).

Moreover, multijurisdictional studies have yielded contradictory findings about the correlations among community attributes and court behavior: political culture appears to be associated with sentencing outcomes in some studies (e.g., Gibson, 1978; Broach, Jackson, & Ascolillo, 1978) but not others (Bowers, 1997). Studies of community demographic characteristics (Britt, 2000; Myers & Talarico, 1986a, 1986b vs.

Crawford, 2000) and crime rates (Glick & Pruet, 1985; Worden, 1990 vs. Britt, 2000) produce the same sorts of inconsistencies.

If statistics could talk, perhaps these studies' findings would tell us that we should take a more careful look at representational theory, remembering that it is a theory about elite responsiveness to perceived political conditions, and the original question posed by the theory is about how court actors see their responsibilities to their courts, their constituents, and their careers. These questions are interesting, not just because the answers might account for some variation in aggregate outputs, but even more, because the theory, if correct, tells us something important about the roles and functions of these public officials.

Conflict Theory: Courthouse Elites and the Underclass

Since the 1960s, conflict theorists have invoked the notion of elite oppression of an underclass in attempting to account for some patterns of court outcomes, particularly racial and economic disparities (Chambliss & Seidman, 1982; see Figure 8.3). Cast as a community-level theory, conflict theory predicts that community elites, including court actors, will use their political power to maintain social and economic stratification, and to reduce threats to their privileged status.

Interpreted as a very general perspective about the creation and behavior of coercive criminal justice institutions and punitive sanctions, this theory might shed some light on cross-cultural comparisons of legal systems (Lynch & Groves, 1981; Shelden, 2001). However, cast as a theory about American courts, communities, and elites, it has not yet been developed sufficiently to permit a rigorous empirical test of its assumptions and hypotheses.

Instead, many self-described tests of conflict theory are assessments of statistical associations at the individual level between defendants' race or social class and case outcome, usually measured in terms of relative sentencing severity. Absent from these studies are measures of elite intent or motivation. As more critical reviewers point out, even when such correlations are found, they might be attributable to unmeasured variables such as court actors' racial prejudice, judgments about the amenability of unemployed defendants to community rather than institutional corrections, or inadvertent structural biases (such as the quality of defense counsel available to the poor) (Hagan, 1974; Lizotte, 1978). Key elements of conflict theory, such as the incentive and ability to manage underclass populations for economic or other benefits and the co-optation of working and middle-class citizens into elite strategies, have seldom been discussed. Scholars have not reached agreement on who, exactly, is part of the underclass for purposes of this theory: the poor, the unemployed, the working class, members of racial minorities, immigrants?

This theoretical perspective might offer more insight into court behavior if core assumptions of the theory were substantiated and if it were more carefully adapted to the question of how communities influence courts. This is neither an original nor a recent observation. Chiricos and Waldo (1975), finding no significant relationships among offenders' socioeconomic status and length of prison terms, judiciously concluded that their own empirical model was missing too many links to provide a valid test of conflict theory. Similar research designs continue to produce contradictory findings (e.g., Pruitt & Wilson, 1983; Katz & Spohn, 1995).

Further, it is not enough to presume that court actors are aligned and behave in concert with social and economic elites at the local level, or that elite priorities are homogeneous; these are variables, not constants. Care should be taken to discern what attributes of communities might prompt more punitive decisions (social heterogeneity? pervasive poverty? economic distress and unemployment? racial tensions?) and whether these characteristics tend to be stable over time or are instead episodic. Chiricos and Bales argue against settling for generalizations about community conditions and argue for the importance of attending to local actors' motivations, observing that "[t]he relevance of such macro-analyses [of crime and punishment] are compromised by the fact that both labor markets and punishment policies are highly localized and are imperfectly approximated by national or state level measures" (1991, 720).

Hypotheses derived from conflict theory are most plausible (and hence worth the effort of empirical testing) under some simple conditions: first, when they explain changes in the use of criminal court powers over time; second, when the use of court sanctions and power is plausibly related to elite objectives; and third, when they take into account the conditions under which coercive power is likely (or unlikely) to be successfully deployed for strategic purposes.

These conditions are aptly illustrated by Myers's (1993) longitudinal study of the use of incarceration and chain gangs in the early twentieth century. Myers hypothesized that fluctuating needs for cheap local labor motivated court elites to strategically deploy misdemeanor-sentencing options in rural Georgia counties. She mapped elites' economic needs in an unstable cotton economy in terms of fluctuating demands for publicly controlled road-building labor (chain gangs) and privately available farm labor. She further observed that courts practiced highly discretionary sentencing practices with both black and white misdemeanants, and she conducted her study in a state characterized by a traditionalistic political culture, in which decisions of local political and economic leaders were seldom questioned by poor whites or blacks. Her key hypothesis, that court elites manipulated sentences (and hence both the free, and the indentured, labor markets) to respond to the needs of economic elites, is a complex but elegant expression of conflict theory.

As this illustration suggests, conflict theory's applicability to courts and communities is more complex than most sentencing severity studies contemplate. Focusing on elites' motivations might suggest dependent variables such as courthouse norms about what merits prosecution (and what does not)—for example, under what conditions is prostitution problematic for community elites (and under what conditions is it tolerable)? Whose victimizations merit prosecutors' time and resources—and whose do not (Myers & Hagan, 1979; Paternoster, 1983)? Conceiving of elite motivations as a variable (or set of variables) directs our attention toward community organizations and interests, and toward controversies among groups and interests, as well as toward the linkages among those interests and courthouse elites.

A final comment on conflict theory is in order. One might maintain that conflict theory is less useful as a theory about communities and courts and more useful as an historical theory about how courts came to be what they are—formal, adversarial, often unforgiving, and punitive, where decisions about largely poor, minority, and unemployed defendants (and victims) are made by privileged lawyers and career politicians (Snipes & Maguire, this volume). This perspective would imply that variability across communities is less interesting or important than apparent commonalities across courts (Lynch & Groves, 1981). This is perhaps a defensible position, at least for heuristic purposes. But respect for the intellectual integrity of the theory itself leads us to remember that good theories must be falsifiable, and the tremendous variability in community characteristics (and the lack of strong centralizing or standardizing influences in local courts) may provide that opportunity.

Local Legal Culture and Workgroup Theory

A theoretical perspective on court behavior based on workgroup relationships and courthouse culture directs our attention toward structure, court actors' incentives, common perspectives on court processes, and patterns of decisions. In principle, this theoretical perspective almost stands on its own, independent of community attributes; in fact, the most extensive treatments of workgroup theories fail to develop systematic hypotheses about the effects of community characteristics on workgroup cultures. While we have evidence that courthouse cultures, measured as norms about court work, vary across jurisdictions (Church, 1985; Worden, 1987), social scientists rarely have measured cultural and community variables in enough sites to permit systematic hypothesis testing anyway. All the same, given theoretical reasons to draw linkages among community environments, elite priorities, and court structure, and given that social scientists have as yet only incompletely mapped the dimensions of community culture, it makes sense to continue to explore the relationships among community variables and courthouse norms.

This exploration should begin with some simple but important questions. First, which aspects of legal culture are plausibly shaped by community variables? Once again, it may turn out that sentencing norms may be less important than norms about charging practices, pretrial decisions (bail setting, expectations for victim participation and cooperation), and nonincarcerative controls and sanctions (orders of protection, treatment programs).

Second, can we model and assess at the community level linkages between variables such as court structure and organization and informal norms about procedure? For instance, can we determine whether better-funded public defender offices contribute to more advocacy-oriented, adversarial defense practices? Do courts with specialized caseloads (such as drug courts, community courts, domestic violence courts) generate new norms about the use of victim assistance programs, rehabilitation options, or offender accountability?

Finally, an impressive line of case studies has led many experts to believe that most of the time courts successfully resist, deflect, or simply ignore externally imposed attempts to change how they do business (Feeley, 1991). Reformers have tried with only limited success to modify court structure (Church & Heumann, 1989; Taxman & Elis, 1999), substantive and procedural law (Ross & Foley, 1987; Horney & Spohn, 1991), sentencing codes (Ulmer & Kramer, 1996), and sometimes several of these at once (Heumann & Loftin, 1979; McCoy, 1984). Even when they adopt new ideas, courts adapt them to their own routines, in short order producing a variety of local variants on the original plans (Torres & Deschenes, 1997; Harris & Jesilow, 2000). Leaving aside the optimism of reform advocates, what do evaluations of these reforms tell us about the power of larger political forces over local courts? Put another way, do these studies reinforce the notion of local legal culture as a durable feature of communities' courts and prompt us to search more carefully for its distinctive community roots?

Table 8.1 Dimensions of theoretical perspectives (adapted from Snipes and Maguire [this volume])

	Representation theory	Local legal culture	Conflict theory
Level of explanation	Community Individual (judges, prosecutors)	Community Courthouse Workgroup	Society Community Era/historical period
Socio-political perspective	Consensus	Contingent on authors' assumptions about courthouse elites	Conflict
Type(s) of responses	Substantive norms Attitudes Role orientations	Substantive norms Routines Role orientations	Substantive norms Patterns of decisions

EXPLORING NEW LINKAGES

The foregoing discussion suggests that social scientists' sketches of the linkages among courts and communities still need development, testing, and synthesis. We might get some guidance on this challenging undertaking if we briefly review, compare, and contrast these perspectives along some of the dimensions of criminal justice theory proposed by Snipes and Maguire (this volume). Snipes and Maguire propose that theory can be sorted along seven dimensions; Table 8.1 indicates how each of the three perspectives discussed here might be classified on three selected dimensions. First, and most importantly, although these perspectives may be operationalized to apply to different units of analysis or levels of explanation, they have in common the community. Representational theory ties decision makers to their own perceptions of community values (although as we have seen, they may perceive those values quite differently, and not always accurately); local legal cultures are bounded by the structures, resources, and leadership of communities; conflict theory, at its origins a theory about society generally, nonetheless is most appropriately understood in the context of criminal courts as a theory about how to manage groups in community populations.

Community Mobilization, Symbolic Politics, and Community Impacts

To array these perspectives along a sociopolitical dimension may prove overly simplistic, but attempting to do so reminds us that understanding local legal culture requires that we make assumptions (or get some data) about the motivations of courthouse elites. In principle, this theoretical perspective is compatible with either consensus or conflict theory, but research has not yet told us whether we should expect court actors to organize their working norms around notions of public values or notions of elites, nor much about the conditions under which we might expect either.

Finally, these perspectives draw our attention to the "what" question: what kinds of behavior does each theory attempt to explain? Representational theory helps us map judges' (and potentially prosecutors') attitudes, beliefs, and role orientations, both as products of community values and as predictors of cumulative decisions—norms about what is or is not criminally culpable, and what shall or shall not be done about it. These substantive norms define legal culture, and that theoretical perspective invites us to measure differences and similarities in those norms across work settings, examining individuals' orientations toward work and the routines that workgroups develop to account for norms. Conflict theory is likewise about norms of justice, measured as patterns of decisions as well as substantive standards about crime and punishment.

This brief review oversimplifies the potential and the complexities of these perspectives, to be sure. However, it provides some evidence of commonalities that might serve the needs of greater theoretical integration as well as parsimony. All three perspectives have been built on the assumption that communities vary in ways that influence how justice is carried out. These perspectives diverge, however, in their assumptions about the motivations of actors.

Figure 8.5 depicts what might happen if these theories were superimposed upon each other, and also suggests theoretical linkages that have seldom captured the attention of social scientists. Of course, any attempt at synthesizing these very complex perspectives is vulnerable to a skeptic's charge of oversimplification, especially when that attempt follows a lengthy discussion of previous studies' failures to capture the complexity of core concepts and to fully specify causal links. Perhaps one should be particularly suspicious of diagrams that approximate symmetry. Figure 8.5 is therefore offered for heuristic purposes only, as a point of departure for continued theorizing about courts and communities. In this speculative spirit, the following observations might be made.

First, this model adds a conceptual domain; community impacts. One might argue that these linkages are out of place in a chapter on court behavior, but there are good reasons to include them in this discussion of theory. Some theoretical perspectives (such as conflict

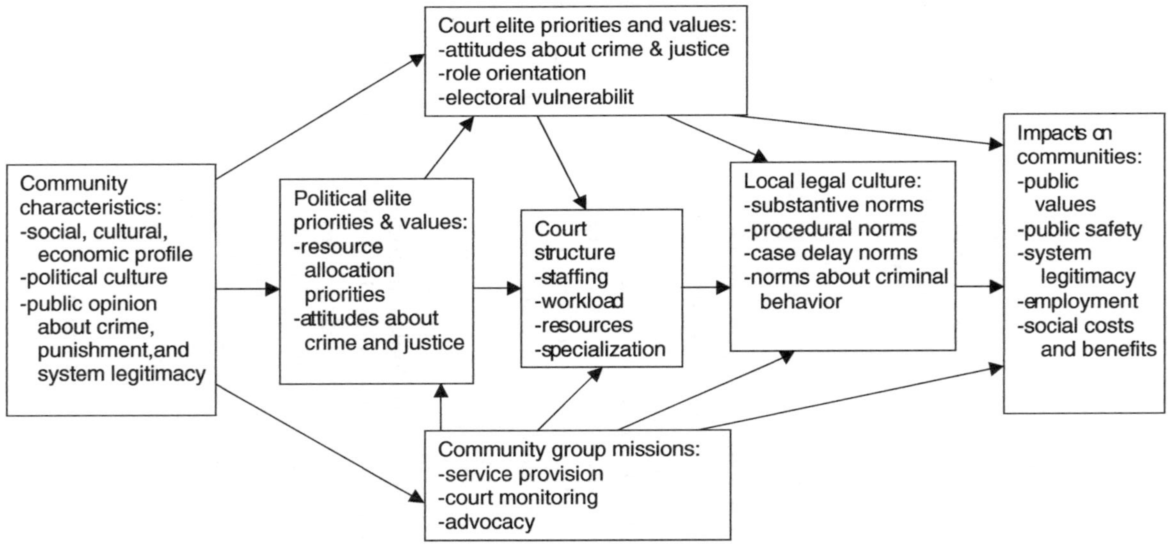

Figure 8.5 Reassessment of theoretical linkages between courts and communities

theory) were initially applied to criminal courts precisely because scholars detected social impacts of court behavior at odds with abstract legal norms; moreover, the relationships between courts and communities is probably reciprocal (Figure 8.5 could be redrawn to illustrate this by sketching feedback loops from courthouse culture to community characteristics). Neglecting one set of arrows could lead to misspecification and misestimation of other important linkages.

Second, this diagram suggests that court actors, other political elites and criminal justice agencies, and groups in communities (including the media) mediate the effects of community characteristics on court behavior, suggesting that we may have overestimated the direct significance of public opinion, political culture, and social and economic profiles as causes of court practices and outcomes. These variables may shape court decisions and outputs, but they are filtered through the priorities of actors who have more direct interests in the criminal courts and criminal justice.

Third, court structure, organization, workload, and resources may influence local legal norms, but these sets of variables may be relatively independent of community attributes. As noted previously, empirical research has yielded little evidence that even crime rates and caseloads have direct consequences for courthouse norms about plea bargaining and about case delay (Church, 1985; Flemming, Nardulli, & Eisenstein, 1987), and these variables have been found to influence plea bargaining practices only indirectly through prosecutors' perceptions of the seriousness of local crime problems (Worden, 1990).

Finally, three intriguing paths emerge from this picture, linkages that have been largely overlooked in court–community studies. The first is the role of community groups in transmitting and mediating community values and in influencing court structure. The second are the direct links between community elites' and community organizations' politically motivated behavior, and community views about crime and justice—links that bypass the routinized norms of courthouse culture. The third type of linkage includes the relationships between courthouse norms and communities' expectations about crime and justice, as well as their social and economic health.

Community Mobilization

The role of community groups is changing court structure and culture. The activities of community organizations are plausibly related to court behavior in at least three ways. Some may contribute resources, expertise, or leadership to courthouse innovations, particularly when they sponsor the adoption of new or experimental programs. For example, grassroots domestic violence organizations may provide victim advocacy services to courts. Law school internship programs may supply legal research or other forms of assistance to public defenders. Other organizations may define their mission in terms of challenging court practices or holding court actors accountable.

A second path of organization influence is political influence. Groups may mobilize to influence elections or to endorse candidates or support (or oppose) nominations for court offices. Scheingold and Gressett (1987) document the impacts of this sort of activity in a Midwestern community experiencing a rise in public concern about crime; other case studies have reported similar dynamics (Olson & Batjer, 1999).

Third, groups may influence courthouse norms directly, through participation in courtrooms. Victim advocacy programs provide an example: advocates play an active role in encouraging and assisting crime victims to file impact statements and to make appearances (Erez & Tontodonato, 1990). Mediation program staff may take up stations in the courtroom itself to invite and encourage complainants and defendants to participate.

Case studies of community groups often acknowledge activity of these actors, but seldom cast their behavior in theoretical terms. However, community organizations may become more salient to studies of courts if notions of community prosecution, community courts, and problem-solving special courts continue to proliferate. We should be cautious in jumping to optimistic conclusions about the success of these wholesome-sounding undertakings, however. Treating communities and their self-appointed representative groups as sources of information, problem definitions, and resources is an unfamiliar role for court actors. Partnerships between community groups and court workers have not always proven mutually beneficial or durable. Courts notoriously resist innovations not of their own design. Perhaps the most important questions to pursue on this topic, therefore, are the following: first, under what political or resource conditions are courts most likely to adopt community-sponsored innovations, and of what sort? Second, under what conditions are innovations most likely to be fully implemented and incorporated into routine practices? Third, what organizational and political factors account for organizations' failures to influence how courts work?

Symbolic Politics

Local legal culture has served as a key variable in this chapter, in large part because courthouse norms are thought to define the boundaries of court actors' routine, ordinary decisions and thereby to define justice as communities experience it. However, not all cases are ordinary, and not all court behavior is routine; and it is the extraordinary events or behaviors that are most likely to register with the public. An assessment of the impacts of courts on communities would be incomplete without mention of the potentially powerful role of symbolic acts and statements, especially those made by court actors themselves and those made by visible community organizations and agents (including the media). Such statements may be isolated and anomalous; they may be sparked by an unusual incident or case; they may involve inaccurate generalizations about court behavior; and they may bear little or no relationship to the ordinary, normal behavior of court actors. However, they may be more likely to register on public consciousness and influence public perceptions about criminal justice than actual routine practices.

Examples would include accounts of a judge's highly visible (but ultimately ineffective) campaign against drunk driving (Ross & Voas, 1990), and a Detroit prosecutor's well-publicized (but unsuccessful) attempt to ban plea bargaining by his staff (Heumann & Loftin, 1979). Community activists who publicize a new restorative justice program, who successfully lobby for use of victim impact statements at sentencing, or who rally against a prosecutor's attempt to seek the death penalty may have little effect on how cases are handled, but may create strong impressions about how the courts operate among the public. A mayor's campaign promises to crack down on prostitution and drug dealing may leave voters with an image of a tough, intolerant criminal justice system, even as prostitutes and drug dealers continue to ply their trades. A prosecutor's careless racist remark may undermine his office's legitimacy, regardless of his staff's behavior. A newspaper's coverage of a sensational trial may be all the education some people ever get on how the legal system works.

It is difficult to place such behavior in the context of a general theory of criminal justice behavior; after all, these sorts of behaviors seem to be idiosyncratic and episodic, and they seldom register in the places social scientists go to gather data. They may not even be legal, or within the legitimate bounds of court actors' authority (Maschke, 1995). But social scientists must be very cautious if they choose to disregard evidence of purposive political behavior, particularly when that behavior intentionally (or unintentionally) influences public beliefs about the courts' priorities, punitiveness, or fairness. Exponents of theories about symbolic political behavior have long suggested that social scientists overestimate people's awareness of real political and governmental behavior, and underestimate their appetite for public, eye-catching acts of political elites (Edelman, 1964).

Courts' Behavior and Impacts on Community Well-Being

The political behavior of political elites and community groups, although difficult to fit into existing theoretical models of community values, is at least observable (if not easily measurable) and its consequences are often predictable. The impacts of local legal culture on court communities are seldom scrutinized, perhaps because they seem self-evident. If a community's legal culture is very punitive, offenders in that town are punished more; if the culture tolerates long court delays, defendants must bide their time. But the question of how legal culture impacts communities is both more complex and more interesting than this. Courthouse practices may influence economic and social conditions, public safety, public opinion, and beliefs about crime, and it is only recently that social scientists have begun to argue for more careful attention to these linkages, as illustrated by the following examples.

Conventional applications of conflict theory, for example, predict not only high incarceration rates (at least under some circumstances), but also incarceration rates that disproportionately punish poor, unemployed, and minority defendants. More recently, critics have observed that where such trends exist, they raise equity concerns for defendants, but also for these defendants' communities, whose populations are temporarily depleted and suffer permanent economic handicaps as a result of incarceration practices (Rose & Clear, 1998).

Feminist theorists have argued that the courts' treatment of women as victims of acquaintance assaults can be interpreted as patriarchal protection of men's social autonomy. There is ample historical evidence of this argument in American legal codes (Friedman, 1985; Estrich, 1987; Horney & Spohn, 1991). Statutory and common law that defines assaults on women have been subject to dramatic reforms since the mid-1970s, violence against women has become a federal priority, and these forms of victimization are treated seriously by mainstream media. Yet research tells us that there remains great variability in how courts respond to incidents of domestic violence and sexual assault, so the questions for contemporary theorists and empiricists are these: first, why are such offenses still treated casually in some courts, but taken quite seriously in others? Second, do courts that remain indifferent to these victims inadvertently legitimize this behavior in the eyes of community residents? Third, are victims (and potential victims) at risk, and is their autonomy compromised, where courts treat this behavior as a private matter rather than a public norm violation?

Court norms that prescribe what is (and is not) treated as an offense meriting conviction constitute de facto criminal codes; courts vary in how they handle incidents such as drunk driving and drug possession. These behaviors are quite common, so there is reason to believe that many people have formed first- or second-hand beliefs about the legal system's responses to them. Therefore, courthouse norms may tacitly legitimize (or tolerate) these behaviors in the eyes of many, creating an environment that calls for little accountability from or shaming of offenders. Young people may be socialized to believe drug use or impaired driving is not risky behavior.

In short, if we understand local legal cultures as informal and unwritten codes of justice, we should begin to recognize that they may influence community norms about what is, and is not, criminal behavior, fair treatment, and reasonable protection. Community residents are unlikely to think about their courts this formally, of course; laypeople typically do not know exactly what the law stipulates, nor how matters are handled in other communities. They may simply come to know and accept their own courts' definitions of crimes and their going rates of punishment, and their labeling of what constitutes crime and what counts as victimization. At the margins, beliefs about what is and is not legally acceptable may shape behavior. These effects will not materialize around crimes that are universally condemned, to be sure, but rather, around those that occupy the borderlines between socially tolerated and socially condemned behavior.

COURTS AND COMMUNITIES: NOTES TOWARD THEORY DEVELOPMENT

The argument in this chapter can be summed up as follows: because American communities exhibit wide variation in social, economic, and political characteristics, because their criminal courts are historically defined by links of local rather than state accountability, and because court structure and functions grant actors great discretion but also the imperative to balance competing and sometimes conflicting values about crime and justice, courts develop distinctive norms, practices, and policies. The ways in which these practices are shaped by community environments, elites, and organizations, and their impacts on community values and well-being, have been studied from three distinct theoretical perspectives. Although none of these theories has been fully developed in the community context, these theories are not incompatible. But neither do they exhaust the range of plausible and potentially fruitful theoretical perspectives.

Further development and testing of theories about these concepts would benefit from lessons learned through previous research, particularly lessons about theory specification and research design. Ultimately, we may come to understand courts' connections with their communities if we broaden our thinking about how we define communities and how we define court behavior.

Specifying Theoretical Linkages

Early attempts to model court–community relationships have sometimes settled for oversimplified, inadequately adapted versions of theories that were originally developed to explain something quite different—such as congressional voting behavior, economic disparities—with predictably anemic results. The fault lies not with the theories, though. After all, judges and prosecutors are politicians, and incarceration and unemployment have something in common. The problem is with the adaptation of theory to local settings, and to the special case of court behavior. Sociolegal and institutional theories will tell us the most about courts (as about anything else) if they are crafted with court actors in mind. Studying court behavior is, after all, about studying human decision making (Hogarth, 1971). One could argue that court decisions are more peculiarly human than those made by many politicians: court actors share authority for the fates of individuals whom they meet face to face, and are obliged to evaluate acts carried out under emotional states of anger, jealousy, greed, and fear. Case by case, they must challenge each other's interpretations of events and of law, and they chalk up their wins and losses to their own professional skills (McIntyre, 1987).

Often, however, empirical court research has tended to leave these actors as sketchy shadows, and to leave readers making broad inferences about their motivations and behavior based on associations between community variables and aggregate court outcomes. On the other hand, court research has benefited from some valuable examples of careful theoretical thinking; examples include longitudinal and historical studies that capture and attempt to account for changes in practices at the local level. This sort of research suggests that modeling the nature of linkages, not just their direction, is critical to understanding variations in court behavior. For example, in simple terms, conflict theory may suggest that defendants' race or socioeconomic status is associated with case outcome; a more sophisticated version would suggest that under particular economic, cultural, or political conditions, court actors are motivated to incarcerate unemployed or minority defendants at higher rates. Relationships between community attributes and court behavior may be conditional, indirect, spurious, or simply collinear; the one thing that empirical research tells us with certainty is that they are seldom direct, linear, and additive.

Finally, our understanding of courts and communities would be enriched by further specification of relationships among local political groups (elites, community organizations, and the sponsoring organizations within courts themselves), structure, and behavior. Conceiving of communities as pluralistic environments may lead us to more systematic measurement of the dimensions of community variation, and hence to more accurate models of political and social influences on court behavior.

Research Design Challenges

Many of the lessons one might glean from critiquing court–community research apply to most social science research. Research design problems can compromise faithful application of theory and hypotheses to data; when this happens, it is often the theory that is sacrificed. Limited resources and the labor-intensive nature of data collection have led researchers to rely heavily on databases maintained by courts or state criminal justice agencies. Predictably, however, these databases do not always serve the purpose of testing community-level hypotheses. They are often limited to felonies, are most likely found in highly urbanized jurisdictions, and seldom include critical process and outcome variables. Moreover, they tempt the researcher to analyze data at the individual case level, not the community level.

The most basic, but overlooked, lessons one might derive from community–court studies are these: first, we should begin theorizing and data collection at the community or courthouse level of analysis and measure variables at that level. Second, we should "measure what matters" theoretically, avoiding proxy measures that may be inadequate. Third, we should match research designs to the dynamics of theories. Cross-sectional designs are appropriate for comparing communities, but not for explaining change over time, such as adaptations to legal or structural innovations or responses to political activity by community groups.

Further, we should match the precision of methodology to the precision of theory. Criminal court research has benefited tremendously from a tradition of exploratory and qualitative case studies, and a student setting out to understand what we know about how courts work and their connections to communities would probably be well advised to immerse herself in these studies, and even better advised to carefully compare the findings of scholars across sites.

Rethinking Communities and Courts

It is difficult to liberate recommendations for future theoretical work from critiques of existing efforts. Social scientists tend to rely on what they have done (well or badly) as the point of departure for thinking about what they should do next. This sort of intellectual incrementalism is probably functional, but it can also be limiting, and court research may suffer from some of these limitations. Theorists might do well to set aside conventional ideas about how we define communities and court behavior, reconsider their political and social dynamics, and redirect empirical research efforts toward refining familiar theories and developing overlooked relationships.

While researchers have explored many aspects of communities, they have seldom questioned what a community is for the purposes of court research. Communities have been generally and seemingly consensually defined as the political, geographically based jurisdiction of a court, bounded by city, county, or circuit lines. Communities are the populations from which cases are drawn and processed. (Even more specifically, they are the places where crimes take place, since one is tried in the jurisdiction of an alleged offense, not in one's hometown.) For some purposes, this definition works: those boundaries constitute judges' and prosecutors' electoral constituencies, for example. We know that communities are not homogeneous (and are certainly less so than when the tradition of community-based courts was institutionalized in this nation); however, we can in principle measure and assess heterogeneity if we believe it affects court behavior.

But that may not be sufficient. If we suspect that community politics and grassroots organizations are elements in understanding court behavior, we may need to reconceptualize communities in pluralistic terms. This is true whether we are interested in local "politics as usual"—understanding decisions about the impact of other criminal justice agencies, public resource allocations, and elections—and also if we are interested in studying grassroots political mobilization around justice issues at the local level or innovation efforts in court organizations. Community case studies present considerable evidence that court actors think of communities in these terms—as institutions, political forces, dominant social and political groups—rather than as aggregates of citizen characteristics.

We should also revisit long-standing conceptualizations of court behavior. This chapter has argued against relying on variation in final outcomes (such as sentencing) and in favor of closer examination of courthouse norms about what is to be treated as crime, how it is to be processed, and what sorts of outcomes are imposed. Not all courts have consensual norms on these matters; in fact, in some courts, it is "normal" for court actors to be adversarial and in perpetual disagreement over cases. Further work on developing typologies of courthouse norms would allow testing of hypotheses about why these procedural and substantive norms of justice are different across communities.[3]

Lastly, rethinking what is important about communities and court behavior might prompt us to rethink how these concepts might be related and to decide whether it is time to set aside some long-standing hypotheses in order to pursue and prioritize other lines of theory. These judgments can be based on normative or empirical criteria; for example, we might prioritize studying the impacts of incarceration rates on communities because that is an urgent social problem, or we might focus on the relationships between court actors' attitudes and priorities and legal culture because research tells us that those linkages really exist. Either strategy is likely to contribute to our understanding of court behavior if it is guided by the primary objective of mapping the theoretical relationships that link courts to their communities.

NOTES

1. This chapter focuses almost exclusively on trial courts because they are uniquely and purposefully local institutions in ways that federal and appellate courts are not. However, readers should note that federal courts have been the subject of studies of community context as well (Cook, 1977; Kritzer, 1979; Albonetti, 1998).
2. A highly mobile and increasingly diverse population places the permanence of these categories, and their geographical associations, in some doubt, as periodic recalibrations of this concept demonstrate. However, the concept remains valuable for studying state and local government structure and policy.
3. It is worth noting here that almost all studies of court behavior are studies of reactive behavior: responses to the steady supply of criminal charges. There are other dimensions of court actors' behavior that have gone virtually unexamined or that have been described but not developed theoretically. Judicial leadership (Wice, 1995; Jacobs, 1978), prosecutorial innovation, and public defense management are just a few examples of topics that may be shaped by community politics.

REFERENCES

Albonetti, C.A. 1998. Direct and indirect effects of case complexity, guilty pleas, and offender characteristics on sentencing for offenders convicted of a white-collar offense prior to sentencing guidelines. *Journal of Quantitative Criminology* 14(4): 353–78.

Alpert, L., B. Atkins, and R. Ziller. 1979. Becoming a judge: The transition from advocate to arbiter. *Judicature* 62: 325.

Alschuler, A. 1979. Plea bargaining and its history. *Law and Society Review* 13: 211–45.

Austin, T. 1981. The influence of court location on type of criminal sentences: The rural-urban factors. *Journal of Criminal Justice* 9: 305–16.

Bazemore, G. 1997. The "community" in community justice: Issues, themes, and questions for the new neighborhood sanctioning models. *Justice System Journal* 19(2): 193–228.

Becker, T. 1966. Surveys and judiciaries: Or who's afraid of the purple curtain? *Law and Society Review* 1: 133.

Blumberg, A.S. 1967. *Criminal justice*. Chicago: Quadrangle Books.

Blumstein, A. and J. Cohen. 1980. Sentencing of convicted offenders: An analysis of the public's view. *Law & Society Review* 14(2): 223–61.

Bohm, R., T. Flanagan, and P. Harris. 1990. Current death penalty opinion in New York State. *Albany Law Review* 54: 819–43.

Bohne, B. 1978. The public defender as policy maker. *Judicature* 62: 176.

Bowers, D. 1997. Political culture and felony sentencing: An examination of trial courts in 300 counties. *Criminal Justice Policy Review* 8(4): 343–64.

Britt, C. 2000. Social context and racial disparities in punishment decisions. *Justice Quarterly* 17(4): 707–32.

Broach, G., P. Jackson, and V. Ascolillo. 1978. State political culture and sentence severity in federal district courts. *Criminology* 16(3): 373–82.

Brunk, C. 1979. The problem of voluntariness and coercion in the negotiated plea. *Law and Society Review* 13: 527.

Carter, L.H. 1974. *The limits of order*. Lexington, MA: Lexington Books.

Casper, J.D. 1972. *American criminal justice: The defendant's perspective*. Englewood Cliffs, NJ: Prentice-Hall.

Casper, J.D. 1978. Having their day in court: Defendant evaluations of the fairness of their treatment. *Law and Society Review* 12(1): 237–51.

Chaiken, M. and J. Chaiken. 1991. *Priority prosecution of high-rate dangerous offenders*. Washington, D.C.: National Institute of Justice.

Chambliss, W. and R. Seidman. 1982. *Law, order, and power*, 2nd ed. Reading, MA: Addison-Wesley.

Chiricos, T.G. and W.D. Bales. 1991. Unemployment and punishment: An empirical assessment. *Criminology* 29(4): 720.

Chiricos, T.G. and G. Waldo. 1975. Socioeconomic status and criminal sentencing: An empirical assessment of a conflict proposition. *American Sociological Review* 40: 753–72.

Church, T. 1979. In defense of "bargain justice." *Law and Society Review* 13: 509.

Church, T. and M. Heumann. 1989. The underexamined assumptions of the invisible hand: Monetary incentives as policy instruments. *Journal of Policy Analysis and Management* 8(4): 641–57.

Church, T.W. 1985. Examining local legal culture. *American Bar Foundation Research Journal* 1985: 449–518.

Cole, G. 1970. The decision to prosecute. *Law and Society Review* 4: 331–45.
Cook, B. 1977. Public opinion and federal judicial policy. *American Journal of Political Science* 21: 567–600.
Crawford, C. 2000. Gender, race, and habitual offender sentencing in Florida. *Criminology* 38(1): 263–80.
Dershowitz, A. 1983. *The best defense*. New York: Vintage Books.
Durham, A., III. 1988. Crime seriousness and punitive severity: An assessment of social attitudes. *Justice Quarterly* 5(1): 131–53.
Durham, A., H. Elrod, and P. Kincade. 1996. Public support for the death penalty: Beyond Gallup. *Justice Quarterly* 13(4): 705–36.
Edelman, M. 1964. *The symbolic uses of politics*. Urbana: University of Illinois Press.
Eisenstein, J. 1982. Research on rural criminal justice: A summary. In *Criminal justice in rural America*, ed. S. Cronk. Washington, D.C.: National Institute of Justice.
Eisenstein, J, R.B. Flemming, and P.F. Nardulli. 1988. *The contours of justice: Communities and their courts*. Boston: Little, Brown.
Eisenstein, J. and H. Jacob. 1977. *Felony justice: An organizational analysis of criminal courts*. Boston: Little, Brown.
Elazar, D. 1972. *American federalism: A view from the states*, 2nd ed. New York: Crowell.
Elazar, D. 1988. *The American mosaic*. Boulder, CO: Westview.
Emmelman, D. 1996. Trial by plea bargain: Case settlement as a product of recursive decision-making. *Law and Society Review* 30(2): 335–60.
Erez, E. and P. Tontodonato. 1990. The effect of victim participation in sentencing on sentence outcome. *Criminology* 28(3): 451–73.
Estrich, S. 1987. *Real rape*. Cambridge, MA: Harvard University Press.
Feeley, M.M. 1973. Two models of the criminal justice system: An organizational perspective. *Law and Society Review* 7(3): 407–25.
Feeley, M.M. 1978.The effects of heavy caseloads. In *American court systems: Readings in judicial process and behavior*, eds. S. Goldman and A. Sara (pp. 125–33). San Francisco: W.H. Freeman.
Feeley, M.M. 1991. *Court reform on trial: Why simple solutions fail*. New York: Basic Books.
Finckenauer, J. 1988. Public support for the death penalty: Retribution as just deserts or retribution as revenge? *Justice Quarterly* 5(1): 81–100.
Flango, V., L. Wenner, and M. Wenner. 1978. The concept of judicial role: A methodological note. *American Journal of Political Science* 19: 277.
Flemming, R. 1986. Client games: Defense attorney perspectives on their relations with criminal clients. *American Bar Foundation Research Journal* 1986: 253–77.
Flemming, R., P. Nardulli, and J. Eisenstein. 1987. The timing of justice in felony trial courts. *Law and Policy* 9(2): 179–206.

Friedman, L. 1979. Plea bargaining in historical perspective. *Law and Society Review* 13: 247.

Friedman, L. 1984. *American law: An introduction*. New York: W.W. Norton.

Friedman, L. 1985. *A history of American law*. New York: Simon & Schuster.

Gibson, J. 1978. Judges' role orientations, attitudes, and decisions: An interactive model. *American Political Science Review* 72: 911–24.

Gibson, J. 1980. Environmental constraints on the behavior of judges: A representational model of judicial decision making. *Law and Society Review* 14: 343.

Gibson, J. 1981. Personality and elite political behavior: The influence of self-esteem on judicial decision-making. *The Journal of Politics* 43: 104–25.

Glick, H. and G. Pruet, Jr. 1985. Crime, public opinion, and trial courts: An analysis of sentencing policy. *Justice Quarterly* 2(3): 319–43.

Goodpaster, G. 1987. On the theory of the American adversary criminal trial. *Journal of Criminal Law and Criminology* 78(1): 118–53.

Grasmick, H., E. Davenport, M. Chamlin, and R. Bursik, Jr. 1992. Protestant fundamentalism and the retributive doctrine of punishment. *Criminology* 30(1): 21–45.

Hagan, J. 1974. Extra-legal attributes and criminal sentencing: An assessment of a sociological viewpoint. *Law and Society Review* 3: 357–83.

Hagan, J. 1977. Criminal justice in rural and urban communities: A study of the bureaucratization of justice. *Social Forces* 55: 597.

Harris, J. and P. Jesilow. 2000. It's not the old ballgame: Three strikes and the courtroom workgroup. *Justice Quarterly* 17(1): 185–203.

Heumann, M. 1975. A note on plea bargaining and case pressure. *Law and Society Review* 9: 515–28.

Heumann, M. 1978. *Plea bargaining: The experiences of prosecutors, judges, and defense attorneys*. Chicago: University of Chicago Press.

Heumann, M. and C. Loftin. 1979. Mandatory sentencing and the abolition of plea bargaining: The Michigan Felony Firearm Statute. *Law and Society Review* 13: 393.

Hogarth, J. 1971. *Sentencing as a human process*. Toronto: University of Toronto Press.

Horney, J. and C. Spohn. 1991. Rape law reform and instrumental change in six jurisdictions. *Law and Society Review* 25(1): 117–53.

Houlden, P. and S. Balkin. 1985. Quality and cost comparisons of private bar indigent defense systems: Contract vs. ordered assigned counsel. *Journal of Criminal Law and Criminology* 76(1): 176–200.

Jacob, H. 1983. Courts as organizations. In *Empirical theories about courts*, eds. K. Boyum and L. Mather. New York: Longman.

Jacobs, D. 1978. Inequality and the legal order: An ecological test of the conflict model. *Social Problems* 25(5): 515–25.

Jacoby, J. 1977. *The prosecutor's charging decision: A policy perspective*. Washington, D.C.: National Institute of Law Enforcement and Criminal Justice.

Katz, C. and C. Spohn. 1995. The effect of race and gender on bail outcomes: A test of an interactive model. *American Journal of Criminal Justice* 19(2): 161–84.
Kritzer, H.M. 1979. Federal judges and their political environments: The influence of public opinion. *American Journal of Political Science* 23: 194.
Kuklinski, J. and J. Stanga. 1979. Political participation and government responsiveness: The behavior of California superior courts. *American Political Science Review* 73: 1090.
Levin, M.A. 1972. Urban politics and policy outcomes: The criminal court. In *Criminal justice: Law and politics*, ed. G.F. Cole (pp. 330–52). Belmont, CA: Wadsworth.
Lewis, A. 1964. *Gideon's trumpet*. New York: Vintage Books.
Lizotte, A. 1978. Extra-legal factors in Chicago's criminal courts: Testing the conflict model of criminal justice. *Social Problems* 25: 564.
Luskin, M. and R. Luskin. 1987. Case processing times in three courts. *Law and Policy* 9(2): 207–32.
Lynch, D. 1999. Perceived judicial hostility to criminal trials. *Criminal Justice and Behavior* 26(2): 217–34.
Lynch, M. and W. Groves. 1981. *A primer in radical criminology*. Albany, NY: Harrow & Heston.
Maschke, K. 1995. Prosecutors as crime creators: The case of prenatal drug use. *Criminal Justice Review* 20(1): 21–33.
Mather, L. 1979. *Plea bargaining or trial? The process of criminal case disposition*. Lexington, MA: Lexington Books.
McCoy, C. 1984. Determinate sentencing, plea bargaining bans, and hydraulic discretion in California. *Justice System Journal* 9(3): 256–75.
McIntyre, L. 1987. *The public defender: The practice of law in the shadows of repute*. Chicago: University of Chicago Press.
Merry, S. 1985. Concepts of law and justice among working-class Americans: Ideology as culture. *Legal Studies Forum* 9(2): 59–69.
Miller, J., P. Rossi, and J. Simpson. 1986. Perceptions of justice: Race and gender differences in judgments of appropriate prison sentences. *Law and Society Review* 20: 313.
Myers, M.A. 1988. Social background and sentencing behavior of judges. *Criminology* 26(4): 649–75.
Myers, M.A. 1993. Inequality and the punishment of minor offenders in the early 20th century. *Law and Society Review* 27(2): 313–43.
Myers, M.A. and J. Hagan. 1979. Private and public trouble: Prosecutors and the allocation of court resources. *Social Problems* 26(4): 439–51.
Myers, M.A. and S. Reid. 1995. The importance of county context in the measurement of sentence disparity: The search for routinization. *Journal of Criminal Justice* 23(3): 223–41.
Myers, M.A. and S.M. Talarico. 1986a. The social contexts of racial discrimination in sentencing. *Social Problems* 33(3): 236–51.

Myers, M.A. and S.M. Talarico. 1986b. Urban justice, rural injustice? Urbanization and its effect on sentencing. *Criminology* 24: 367–91.

Nardulli, P.F. 1978. *The courtroom elite: An organizational perspective on criminal justice*. Cambridge, MA: Ballinger.

Nardulli, P.F. 1986. "Insider" justice: Defense attorneys and the handling of criminal cases. *Journal of Criminal Law and Criminology* 77(2): 379–417.

Nardulli, P.F., R. Flemming, and J. Eisenstein. 1984. Unraveling the complexities of decision making in face-to-face groups: A contextual analysis of plea bargained sentences. *American Political Science Review* 78: 912.

Newman, D. 1956. Pleading guilty for considerations: A study of bargain justice. *Journal of Criminal Law, Criminology, and Police Science* 46: 780.

Olson, S. and C. Batjer. 1999. Competing narratives in a judicial retention election: Feminism versus judicial independence. *Law and Society Review* 33(1): 123–60.

Olson, S. and D. Huth. 1998. Explaining public attitudes toward local courts. *Justice System Journal* 20(1): 41.

Paternoster, R. 1983. Race of victim and location of crime: The decision to seek the death penalty in South Carolina. *Journal of Criminal Law and Criminology* 74(3): 754–85.

President's Commission on Law Enforcement and Administration of Justice. 1967. *Task force reports: The courts*. Washington, D.C.: U.S. Government Printing Office.

Priehs, R. 1999. Appointed counsel for indigent appellants: Does compensation influence effort? *Justice System Journal* 21(1): 57–79.

Pruitt, C. and J. Wilson. 1983. A longitudinal study of the effect of race on sentencing. *Law and Society Review* 17: 613.

Robinson, P. and J. Darley. 1995. *Justice, liability, and blame*. Boulder, CO: Westview Press.

Rose, D. and T. Clear. 1998. Incarceration, social capital, and crime: Implications for social disorganization theory. *Criminology* 36(3): 441–80.

Ross, H. and J. Foley. 1987. Judicial disobedience of the mandate to imprison drunk drivers. *Law and Society Review* 21: 315.

Ross, H. and R. Voas. 1990. The new Philadelphia story: The effects of severe punishment for drunk driving. *Law and Policy* 12(1): 51–77.

Ryan, J.A. 1980. Adjudication and sentencing in a misdemeanor court: The outcome is the punishment. *Law and Society Review* 15(1): 79–108.

Scheingold, S.A. and L. Gressett. 1987. Policy, politics, and the criminal courts. *American Bar Foundation Research Journal* 1987: 461–505.

Schulhofer, S. 1984. Is plea bargaining inevitable? *Harvard Law Review* 97(5): 1037–1107.

Shelden, R. 2001. *Controlling the dangerous classes*. Boston: Allyn & Bacon.

Sheldon, C. and N. Lovrich, Jr. 1982. Judicial accountability vs. responsibility: Balancing the views of voters and judges. *Judicature* 65: 470.

Shepard, M. and E. Pence. 1999. *Coordinating community responses to domestic violence*. Thousand Oaks, CA: Sage.
Skolnick, J. 1967. Social control in the adversary system. *Journal of Conflict Resolution* 11: 52–70.
Spohn, C. 1990a. Decision making in sexual assault cases: Do black and female judges make a difference? *Women and Criminal Justice* 2: 83–105.
Spohn, C. 1990b. The sentencing decisions of black and white judges: Expected and unexpected similarities. *Law and Society Review* 24(5): 1197–1216.
Spohn, C. and J. Cederblom. 1991. Race and disparities in sentencing: A test of the liberation hypothesis. *Justice Quarterly* 8(3): 305–27.
Stover, R. and D. Eckart. 1975. A systematic comparison of public defenders and private attorneys. *American Journal of Criminal Law* 3: 265.
Sudnow, D. 1965. Normal crimes: Sociological features of the penal code in a public defender's office. *Social Problems* 12: 255–76.
Taxman, F. and L. Elis. 1999. Expediting court dispositions: Quick results, uncertain outcomes. *Journal of Research in Crime and Delinquency* 36(1): 30–55.
Torres, S. and E. Deschenes. 1997. Changing the system and making it work: The process of implementing drug courts in Los Angeles County. *Justice System Journal* 19(3): 267–90.
Tyler, T. 1988. What is procedural justice? Criteria used by citizens to assess the fairness of legal procedures. *Law and Society Review* 22(1): 103–35.
Ulmer, J.T. 1998. The use and transformation of formal decision-making criteria: Sentencing guidelines, organizational contexts and case processing strategies. *Social Problems* 45: 248–67.
Ulmer, J.T. and J.H. Kramer. 1996. Court communities under sentencing guidelines: Dilemmas of formal rationality and sentencing disparity. *Criminology* 34(3): 383–408.
Vance, N. and R. Stupak. 1997. Organizational culture and the placement of pretrial agencies in the criminal justice system. *Justice System Journal* 19(1): 51–76.
Vetri, D. 1964. Guilty plea bargaining: Compromise by prosecutors to secure guilt pleas. *University of Pennsylvania Law Review* 112: 865.
Weimer, D. 1980. Vertical prosecution and career criminal bureaus: How many and who? *Journal of Criminal Justice* 8: 369–78.
Wice, P. 1995. Court reform and judicial leadership: A theoretical discussion. *Justice System Journal* 17(3): 309.
Wishman, S. 1986. *Anatomy of a jury*. New York: Times Books.
Worden, A.P. 1987. The structure of local legal culture: Explorations of interorganizational models of courthouse norms. PhD diss., University of North Carolina at Chapel Hill.
Worden, A.P. 1990. Policymaking by prosecutors: The uses of discretion in regulating plea bargaining. *Judicature* 73(6): 335–40.

Worden, A.P. 1995. The judge's role in plea bargaining: An analysis of judges' agreement with prosecutors' sentencing recommendations. *Justice Quarterly* 12(2): 257–78.

Wright, K. 1981. The desirability of goal conflict within the criminal justice system. *Journal of Criminal Justice* 9: 209–18.

9

A QUALITATIVE STUDY OF PROSECUTORS' DECISION MAKING IN SEXUAL ASSAULT CASES

Megan Kennedy

INTRODUCTION

Criminal justice theory includes theories that explain the behavior of court actors and the functioning of the courts. Court actors include defense attorneys, judges, and prosecutors. More than any other actor in the criminal courts, the prosecutor wields the greatest power and authority. Although the judge may sit above all in the courtroom, it is the prosecutor who decides whether a case is brought before the judge. As a result, many scholars and commentators have called prosecutors the most powerful actors in the criminal justice system, stating that prosecutors hold the keys to the courthouse and are the gatekeepers of the criminal justice system (Frohmann, 1991; Kerstetter, 1990).

As gatekeepers, prosecutors decide which defendants will be charged with a crime and which will not, thus determining whether cases will "go forward." The question of whether a sexual assault case will go forward, or be prosecuted, is often fraught with numerous issues and considerations as a result of the nature of the crime. Nevertheless, in deciding whether the case will proceed through the system, a first decision must be made: will the defendant be charged with a crime? Regardless of the nature of the crime, this decision is always discretionary. This means that regardless of the nature of the case, neither judge nor victim can force the powerful prosecutor to bring a charge.

Since prosecutors hold so much power, understanding how and why they make decisions to charge individuals with crime is clearly of great importance. Most researchers who have chosen to study charging decisions have utilized quantitative methodologies. Although some of the researchers supplement their research with interviews, typically, these studies compile data through court documents, prosecutors' files, police reports, criminal histories, and other accessible court data. These studies provide a valuable piece of the many facets of decision making by prosecutors. Conducting in-depth interviews with prosecutors, however, may allow researchers to piece together a more complete picture.

Qualitative research, talking to prosecutors and probing their thought processes, may reveal more information about the reasons prosecutors make various decisions. This is important because quantitative methodology may not allow the researcher to directly investigate and test certain criminal justice theories. If the methodology does not allow for a full picture of the prosecutors' decision making, then it follows that the theories will not be able to fully and accurately explain the factors that influence prosecutors' decisions. The study that is discussed in this chapter will explore the value of qualitative research when studying prosecutors' decision making in sexual assault cases and reveal the importance of qualitative methods as a means of informing criminal justice theory.

THEORETICAL PERSPECTIVES ON PROSECUTORS' DECISION MAKING

Researchers have utilized several theoretical perspectives of prosecutorial decision making. Although considered separate theories, these theories are closely intertwined within one theoretical perspective: the uncertainty avoidance thesis (Albonetti, 1986; Albonetti, 1987). The uncertainty avoidance thesis includes within its framework elements of organizational theory (Littrell, 1979; Albonetti, 1986, Stanko, 1981, Albonetti, 1987, Frohmann, 1991), rationality theory (Albonetti, 1986, Albonetti, 1987), and focal concerns theory (Spohn and Holleran, 2001; Beichner and Spohn, 2005). These theories suggest that strength of the evidence and case seriousness are powerful predictors of whether a case will be charged. When applied to sexual assault cases, these theories form the basis for researchers' conclusions about prosecutors' motives in charging cases. Simply stated, researchers have shown that prosecutors use a routinized approach to charging decisions in an effort to avoid charging cases that will result in an acquittal so that the organizational goal of achieving convictions is attained.

Uncertainty Avoidance Thesis

The uncertainty avoidance thesis suggests that prosecutors are motivated to maximize their conviction rates, insofar as they believe conviction rates are used as measures of good performance (Albonetti, 1986). Hence, this theory implies that prosecutors will only move forward on those cases that are most likely to result in a conviction. The theory claims that prosecutors make decisions with an eye towards avoiding uncertainty. The uncertainty they are attempting to avoid is a case that results in an acquittal. As a result, weak cases are not prosecuted, and strong cases are pursued.

The theory was developed by Celesta Albonetti in 1986. In separate studies, Albonetti examined both the decision to go forward on a case following police charges and the decision to continue prosecution following indictment (Albonetti, 1986; Albonetti, 1987). In both studies, she examined felony cases in the U.S. Attorney's Office in Washington, DC. This varies from other research, in that most research examines cases prosecuted by city or county prosecutors' offices.

Albonetti examined cases that were presented for screening at the prosecutor's office. In one study, case screening was completed in the office's "Intake Section." The prosecutors assigned to this unit were responsible for judging the merit of police charges. In addition, she examined the decision to continue prosecution by analyzing cases following indictment to determine the factors that affected the decision to continue prosecution.

Albonetti's goal in both studies was to expand upon previous research. Studies had shown that prosecutors' offices had organizational goals of achieving convictions and efficiency (Jacoby, 1979; Littrell, 1979). In addition, studies prior to Albonetti's revealed that strength of the evidence (Miller, 1969; Neubauer, 1974) and seriousness of the offense (Miller, 1969; Neubauer, 1974) were powerful predictors of case charging. Albonetti sought to determine the net effect of case characteristics on the prosecutor's initial decision in the case. Albonetti hypothesized that types of evidence, number of witnesses, and the relationship between victim and defendant would influence the decision to prosecute.

She found that physical evidence, severity of the offense, and corroborative evidence were among the factors that influenced the decision to charge or continue prosecution. Since these were all factors that would lead to a greater likelihood of conviction, the results allowed her to infer that the guiding force in making the decision to prosecute were factors related to convictability. Supporting her conclusion was the fact that prosecutors revealed during interviews that the criteria used by the screening prosecutor was whether the case would likely result in a jury trial conviction.

Based on the results of her study, Albonetti (1986) concluded that "the exercise of prosecutorial discretion . . . is substantially and statistically influenced by a prosecuting attorney's attempts to avoid uncertainty in obtaining a jury trial conviction" (Albonetti, 1986: 638). She explained the significance of her study was the link between prosecutors' desire for promotion within the office and uncertainty avoidance.

According to Albonetti (1986), prosecutors seek convictions not to do justice, but instead to advance in one's job. This organizational goal of attaining convictions to secure promotions is a key explanation for prosecutorial discretionary decision making in criminal cases. Because the goal of the prosecutor's office is to get convictions and "win" cases, the individual prosecutor believes that professional success is determined by his or her ability to meet this organizational goal. She boldly states "[t]here is little ambiguity within the prosecutor's office regarding the criteria of successful movement within the profession and the hierarchically arranged office" (Albonetti, 1987: 295). Furthermore, "prosecutorial success, which is defined in terms of achieving a favorable ratio of convictions to acquittals, is crucial to a prosecutor's prestige, upward mobility within the office, and entrance into the political arena"[1] (Alboneti, 1987: 295). It is these clear notions of the organizational goals, combined with the results of her studies which show a greater likelihood for prosecution of a strong case, that leads Albonetti to the conclusion that uncertainty avoidance explains prosecutors' decision making.

Albonetti's and others' early research indicated that seriousness of the crime and strength of the evidence exert an effect on a prosecutor's decision to go forward, consistent with uncertainty avoidance theory and the accepted organizational goals of efficiency and promotion (Albonetti, 1986; Albonetti, 1987; Blumberg, 1967; Eisenstein and Jacob, 1977; Miller, 1969). The organization's goals directly affect the reward structure and priorities of prosecutors' offices and the goals of prosecutors. According to Albonetti (1986, 1987) and Stanko (1981), the primary organizational goal is achieving convictions. This in turn becomes the primary goal of the prosecutor. Previous researchers have also found that prosecutors' offices share the goal of efficient case processing (Littrell, 1979). This goal is often the result of limited resources and therefore results in using such resources primarily toward prosecuting cases that are more likely to result in a conviction. In order to act efficiently and meet the goal, prosecutors must reduce uncertainty.

Uncertainty is reduced by prosecuting only those cases that the prosecutor has the greatest chance of "winning." Uncertainty is also removed by employing an approach that determines how to handle a case by considering past outcomes. This potential for avoiding uncertainty is described in the theory of bounded rationality. Bounded rationality posits that prosecutors use routinized approaches to cases. This routinized approach includes assessing cases by looking for elements that have been linked to conviction in the past (Albonetti, 1986). In sexual assault cases, this results in the use of quick assessments and stereotypes to make charging decisions (Frohmann, 1991; Beichner and Spohn, 2005). As prosecutors are able to examine cases to determine whether to prosecute based on past outcomes, the prosecutor is also examining the factors in these cases guided by a set of "focal concerns."

Focal Concerns Theory

Research has shown that court actors, including both prosecutors and judges, are guided by a set of focal concerns. In studies of judges' sentencing decisions, researchers typically classify focal concerns into three categories: judgments of blameworthiness, concern about public safety, and practical constraints on sentencing options (Steffensmeier, Ulmer, and Kramer, 1998). Judges typically do not have all the information necessary to fully examine the likelihood the offender will reoffend or to determine if the offender is a danger to the community. As a result, judges will engage in shorthand assessments of defendants based on stereotypes and characteristics that are thought to be common in dangerous individuals.

Like judges, prosecutors' decisions are limited based on the potential consequences of their decisions. The potential consequences, however, are different. According to proponents of focal concerns theory, "prosecutors' charging decisions are guided by a set of focal concerns that revolve around reducing uncertainty and securing convictions" (Spohn, Beichner, and Davis-Frenzel, 2001: 232). In order to ensure that the focal concern of achieving a conviction is met, this theory posits that prosecutors examining sexual assault cases "incorporate beliefs about real rapes and legitimate victims" in their decision making (Spohn and Holleran, 2001: 233). Therefore, prosecutors' decisions to charge are guided by the enduring ideas found in rape myths. These myths include the notion that persons of a certain age, occupation, education, engaging in certain behavior, or having a certain reputation cannot be real victims (Estrich, 1987). For example, a person with a substance abuse problem, a prostitute, or a person who is walking alone through a dangerous neighborhood does not conform to the idea of "real victims." As a result, stereotypes are formed about real rape and real victims (Estrich, 1987), become the foundation for the focal concerns of victim credibility and convictability, and are applied to charging decisions (Estrich, 1987; Spohn and Holleran, 2001).

Although the many rape law reforms[2] were aimed at tearing down some of these stereotypes, the research has shown legally irrelevant victim characteristics remain significant predictors of case charging (Spears and Spohn, 1997; Spohn and Horney, 1992). From this, many researchers have concluded that prosecutors prioritize blameworthiness as a focal concern, and hence focus on victim credibility in sexual assault cases (Beichner and Spohn, 2005). Based on previous research, and in particular uncertainty avoidance theory, one would expect that prosecutors would examine sexual assault cases and other types of cases with the same concerns. Therefore, this would mean that strength of the evidence and offense seriousness are the most powerful predictors in case processing. Instead of only strength of the evidence and offense seriousness, however, it appears that many other factors contribute to prosecutors' uncertainty, including the victim's credibility as a focal concern. The results of studies of sexual assault cases are inconclusive as to prosecutors' motivations and the factors that ultimately guide their decisions.

Legally Relevant Case Characteristics in Sexual Assault Cases: Seriousness of the Offense and Evidence

Theories that examine prosecutorial decision making conclude that prosecutors' decisions are made with an eye toward avoiding uncertainty. As a result, legally relevant case characteristics, if this theory applies to sexual assault cases, should have an effect on case processing. Such characteristics include strength of the evidence and offense seriousness.

Many studies examine case characteristics in an effort to determine the effect of various elements of a case on the decision to charge. Case characteristics are generally divided into two categories. These include case seriousness and evidence factors. These characteristics are meant to measure the relative strength or weakness of a case. Case seriousness may include simply the charge filed against the offender (Spears and Spohn, 1997). Evidence factors have included injury to the victim (Spears and Spohn, 1997; Kingsnorth et al., 1999; Beichner and Spohn, 2005), weapon use (Beichner and Spohn, 2005), presence of physical evidence, (Spears and Spohn, 1997; Kingsnorth et al., 1999; Beichner and

Spohn, 2005), incriminating statements by the defendant (Kingsnorth et al., 1999), availability of a witness to corroborate (Spears and Spohn, 1997; Kingsnorth et al., 1999), and prompt reporting of the incident by the victim to law enforcement (Kingsnorth et al., 1999; Beichner and Spohn, 2005).

Previous research examining case characteristics as predictors of charging decisions in sexual assault cases has produced inconsistent results. In a 1997 study, Spears and Spohn utilized data from arrests in Detroit during the year 1989. They measured seriousness of the offense as the actual charge of the offense. Second, they measured strength of evidence with four factors: physical evidence, whether a weapon was used, whether there was a witness, and whether the victim suffered injury.

Spears and Spohn (1997) hypothesized "that prosecutors would be more likely to file charges if there was a witness to the assault, collateral injury to the victim, physical resistance by the victim, or if the suspect used a gun or knife" (p. 512). This hypothesis was based on their assessment of previous research indicating prosecutors will attempt to avoid uncertainty by only filing charges in cases where the evidence is strong. Contrary to their hypothesis, however, they learned that charging decisions were not affected by the strength of the evidence.

The findings contradict Albonetti's assertions "that strength of the evidence is one of the major predictors of convictability, and thus of prosecutor's decision making" (Spears and Spohn, 1997: 518). As a result, they conclude the difference must be attributable to differences in motivation between sexual assault cases and other cases. One potential source of difference is the existence of a victim in a sexual assault case. The victim, therefore, becomes the focus on predicting convictability. Therefore, "prosecutors attempt to avoid uncertainty by screening out cases unlikely to result in a conviction because of questions about the victim's character, the victim's behavior, and the victim's credibility" (Spears and Spohn, 1997: 519). The study's findings, as is the case with some of the findings related to victim characteristics, are inconsistent with other empirical research.

A study done in 1999 by Kingsnorth et al. (1999) is illustrative of the inconsistent findings in this body of research. They examined use of a weapon, injury to the victim, incriminating remarks by the suspect, time of reporting, whether the victim resisted the attack, and whether there were witnesses available to conflict, support, or contradict the victim's account. This is the only study to have included "victim's cooperation during prosecution" as a variable in their regression analysis. It is possible that other researchers did not have access to this information;

however, it would seem that the victim's willingness to participate is an important factor.

The results of the analysis indicate the model is "dominated by legally relevant variables" (Kingsnorth et al., 1999).

> Several legally relevant variables, closely related to the prosecutor's ability to secure a conviction, attain significance in the model: These include incriminating remarks by the defendant or accomplice, cooperation by the victim, degree of injury to the victim (for which a photographic record exists), and the availability of witnesses to corroborate the victim's account.
>
> (Kingsnorth et al., 1999: 287)

This is in stark contrast to the study by Spears and Spohn (1997) that found that evidence factors had no effect.

In another study that examined case characteristics, Beichner and Spohn (2005) examined charging differences between two jurisdictions. They hypothesized that the effect of case characteristics and evidence factors on decision making would differ between the jurisdictions because one jurisdiction included a specialized unit and the other did not. As a result, they expected the jurisdiction with the specialized unit to be less concerned with legally irrelevant characteristics. The case characteristics and evidence factors used in their analysis included injury to the victim, whether the suspect used a gun or knife, presence of physical evidence, and whether there was a witness to the assault.

Their results indicate charging decisions in the two jurisdictions "are nearly identical" (Beichner and Spohn, 2005). In Kansas City, they found physical evidence increased the likelihood of prosecution. In Miami, they found case seriousness and other factors such as injury, weapon use, and prompt reporting were the most influential predictors at increasing likelihood of charging. Based on these results, they conclude prosecutors are more likely to charge a suspect when the evidence is strong and the offense is serious (Beichner and Spohn, 2005). In keeping with the overall focus on the theory of uncertainty avoidance, the authors conclude their study shows "prosecutors select cases with a high probability of conviction and reject charges in cases in which conviction is unlikely" (Beichner and Spohn, 2005: 487). This study, therefore, supports the findings by Albonetti (1986, 1987) and previous researchers (Miller, 1969; Neubauer, 1974). They also concluded that victim credibility was a focal concern because prosecutors were less likely to file charges if there were questions of character or risk-taking behavior.

Frohmann's Framework: Applying Uncertainty Avoidance to Sexual Assault Cases

Although most studies rely primarily on quantitative data and analysis, Frohmann (1991) used a strictly qualitative approach to examining the charging decisions of prosecutors in sexual assault cases. Not only did Frohmann interview prosecutors, she also observed case filing interviews between prosecutors and victims. This is a vastly different approach from most of the other studies that examine sexual assault case processing. Her approach allowed for a deeper understanding of the reasons prosecutors may choose not to charge a defendant with a sex crime.

In her study, Frohmann concluded "that prosecutors are actively looking for 'holes' or problems that will make the victim's account of 'what happened' unbelievable or not convincing beyond a reasonable doubt, hence unconvictable" (Frohmann, 1991: 214). She argues this is the result of the office's organizational policy. First, the promotion policy provides that prosecutors will be judged based on their ability to get convictions at trial. Second, a record of acquittals is considered evidence of poor performance. Third, prosecutors are looked upon favorably if they can help to reduce the caseload for the office and the court system. Based on this organizational context, Frohmann (1991) concludes that a great number of sexual assault cases never get beyond charging, with prosecutors choosing only those cases that are "solid" or "convictable." These findings are clearly in agreement with Albonetti's, with a potential variation. While Albonetti suggests prosecutors go forward on only those cases with strong evidence and serious charges, Frohmann suggests prosecutors in sexual assault cases take a rather proactive approach in seeking out potential "holes" in the victim's story.

In her interviews and observations, Frohmann was able to ascertain how prosecutors justify their decisions to reject sexual assault cases. The central feature in these cases "is the discrediting of victims' allegations of sexual assault" (Frohmann, 1991: 215). The two primary mechanisms used to "discredit victim's complaints" are "discrepant accounts and ulterior motives" (Frohmann, 1991: 215). Based on her analysis, Frohmann developed a framework for studying decision making in these types of cases. Her framework that focuses on these mechanisms of case rejection has been utilized, at least in part, by most of the studies that followed (see Spohn, Beichner, and Davis-Frenzel, 2001; Spohn and Holleran, 2001).

"Discrepant accounts" include inconsistencies in the victim's account. During the initial investigative process following the assault, the victim is likely to give a report of the events to several individuals. If these reports vary, the prosecutor will find that there are "inconsistencies" in the victim's story. Inconsistencies are one means that prosecutors will use to explain their rejection of a case.

"Discrepant accounts" also include the prosecutor applying their "repertoire of knowledge" to these crimes. Over time, prosecutors will develop a series of "typifications of rape-relevant behavior" as "another resource for discrediting a victim's account of 'what happened'" (Frohmann, 1991: 217). These typifications include rape scenarios, post-incident interaction, rape reporting, and the victim's demeanor.

According to Frohmann (1991), prosecutors believe they know how these crimes typically occur, how true victims react to such crimes, and how true victims report these crimes. Therefore, if the incident, behavior, and reporting do not meet these "typifications," the account is likely to be discredited. If the victim's behavior is atypical, the prosecutor will anticipate problems convincing a judge or jury of the allegation. Atypical behavior includes behavior inconsistent with accepted beliefs about genuine rape. The prosecutor's concern becomes victim credibility as it relates to the "downstream" concern of a conviction.

The second mechanism prosecutors typically used in rejecting cases was finding "ulterior motives." "Ulterior motives," according to Frohmann (1991), means the prosecutor believed the woman consented to the sex act and then decided to deny the act was consensual afterwards. Prosecutors usually attribute case rejection to ulterior motives based on their knowledge of the victim's personal history and the location in which the incident allegedly occurred. For example, Frohmann (1991) suggests that "knowledge of a victim's criminal activity enables prosecutors to 'find' ulterior motives for her allegation" (Frohmann, 1991: 223). The criminal history may reveal a history of drug use or prostitution, and the location of the event may reveal her presence in a location known for prostitution. Thus, prosecutors may conclude that the victim's ulterior motive is avoiding an arrest for prostitution, so she fabricates a rape allegation.

Frohmann's (1991) study reveals grave injustices in the prosecution of sexual assault cases. For example, she found that cases were rejected even when the prosecutor believed a sexual assault happened but there was a low chance of convictability. Her study suggests the organizational concern of conviction rates and the avoidance of uncertainty are clearly applicable to sexual assault cases. Unfortunately, a qualitative study of prosecutors' decision making in sexual assault cases has not been done for more than two decades. Instead, the studies that have attempted to replicate Frohmann's work have been primarily quantitative.

Replications and Extensions of Frohmann's Framework

Frohmann's work studying the behavior of prosecutors in charging sexual assault cases has been used as the framework for subsequent studies of charging decisions in sexual assault cases by researchers (Spohn and Holleran, 2001; Spears and Spohn, 1997; Beichner and Spohn, 2005).

In an attempt to test, replicate, and extend Frohmann's work, Spohn and Holleran (2001) examined cases complete with the incident report, arrest affidavit, and closeout memorandum that indicated reasons for rejection. Although this study relied primarily on quantitative data analysis, the data were supplemented with interviews. In their analysis, they examined case rejections under the theory of focal concerns and uncertainty avoidance.

Spohn and Holleran (2001) suggest that instead of focusing on case seriousness and culpability, "prosecutors' charging decisions are guided by a set of focal concerns that revolve around reducing uncertainty and securing convictions and that incorporate beliefs about real rapes and legitimate victims" (Spohn and Holleran, 2001: 206). As a result, rape myths have survived decades of rape law reform and are a consideration in the mind of prosecutors when they examine a case. This way of thinking, they argue, is the result of an attempt to predict how the victim will be viewed by the judge and jury.[3] Because the goal is to avoid uncertainty and "these predictions are inherently uncertain, prosecutors develop a perceptual shorthand that incorporates stereotypes of real crimes and credible victims" (Spohn and Holleran, 2001: 208).

To conduct their analysis, Spohn and Holleran (2001) "examine and categorize prosecutorial justifications for charge rejection" (Spohn and Holleran, 2001: 211). As Frohmann (1991) did, Spohn and Holleran. (2001) "create a typology of reasons for case rejection and . . . highlight the victim, suspect, and case characteristics associated with each type of case" (Spohn and Holleran, 2001: 207). They "also examine the degree to which characteristics affect prosecutors' charging decisions" (Spohn and Holleran, 2001: 207).

Spohn and Holleran examined case outcomes, including cases that were rejected by the prosecutor. The sample included a total of 140 cases. Fifty-eight of the cases were rejected by the prosecutor. However, in half of those cases, the case was not prosecuted due to lack of victim cooperation. Therefore, it is important to note that it may have been impossible for the prosecutor to continue the case due to a lack of evidence. The authors examined prosecutors' reasons for those cases that were rejected.[4]

They categorized the cases into three categories: first, cases rejected due to discrepant accounts; second, cases rejected due to ulterior motives; and third, cases where the victim failed to appear, recanted, would not cooperate, or asked that the case be dropped. Although this third category was essentially out of the hands of the prosecutor, it was still coded as a rejection by the prosecutor.

The findings in the first category, discrepant accounts, show that prosecutors use inconsistent statements by the victim as a reason for case rejection. Similar to Frohmann's (1991) findings regarding the application of the prosecutor's "repertoire of knowledge," Spohn et al. (2001) assert that prosecutors will reject cases if the victim's behavior, reaction to the event, or delay in reporting do not match the prosecutor's idea of victim credibility. Quite simply, prosecutors are looking for what they believe is behavior of a "genuine" rape victim. If they fail to find it, the case is likely to be rejected because it is unlikely to result in a conviction.

The authors also find that prosecutors reject cases based on their judgment about victims' ulterior motives. As in Frohmann's (1991) work, the authors conclude that prosecutors will find reasons the victim has filed the complaint. Common reasons include the need to deny that an encounter was consensual; the prosecutors' knowledge of the area where the crime occurred, leading the prosecutor to believe the victim was actually there as a prostitute or to purchase drugs; and the victim's criminal record. It is important to note, however, that in this category the researchers include two cases where the prosecutors could not go forward with the case, yet the dismissal or failure to prosecute is attributed to a rejection by the prosecutor.

The existing research appears to show that prosecutors avoid uncertainty because it is important to achieve convictions if one wishes to advance as a prosecutor. As a result, the prosecutor wants to take only those cases that are likely to result in a conviction. In most cases, the key factors that influence this decision appear to be seriousness of the offense and strength of the evidence. In sexual assault cases, however, uncertainty comes in the form of risky behavior, questionable character, and concerns regarding the victim's credibility. Therefore, in order to explain the low rate of prosecution of sexual assault cases, it is important to understand prosecutors' motivations in general, and their customs for judging the risks of prosecuting sexual assault cases in particular.

Limitations in the Existing Research

The research to date on prosecutors' charging decisions in sexual assault cases suffers from several limitations. First, the studies that form the empirical research in this area rely on data collected in the 1980s and 1990s. This research also relies upon general theories of prosecution developed in the 1950s through 1980s. The timing of data collection and analysis is important in this area of research because laws have changed a great deal in many states, education and training have increased, and a greater understanding of the issues surrounding sexual assault crimes exist throughout society. Second, most of these studies' capacity for hypothesis testing is limited to variables that are included in quantified data sets based on archived case files, and hence they cannot examine the role of unmeasured variables. As a result, they are of limited validity in capturing prosecutors' decision processes.

For instance, they fail to take into account the large measure of influence that victims have in these cases, since victims' actions are seldom reliably recorded in data archives. The studies fail to recognize an important factor; that cases cannot, except in rare circumstances where a witness exists, go forward without a victim's cooperation.

Although the lack of victim cooperation is a potentially significant contributor to the failure to prosecute cases, it is largely ignored in the literature and is seldom included in statistical analyses. One example of this issue is illustrative. Spohn and Holleran (2001) argue that prosecutors are the gatekeepers to the courthouse and that their findings "suggest that prosecutors' concerns about convictability lead them to file charges when the evidence is strong, the suspect is culpable, and the victim is blameless" (p. 676). However, they also offer an alternative explanation in a footnote regarding the possible connection between a lack of willingness to participate and case factors. The footnote offers a clear description of the potential contributing factor. It reads:

> As suggested by one of the anonymous reviewers, the decision to prosecute or not may also be reflected by the victim's willingness to cooperate; this in turn, may be affected by the extralegal behavior and character factors. Although we could not obtain this information in either jurisdiction, in Kansas City we were able to determine the prosecutor's reasons for rejecting the charge. (Because we were not allowed to examine the prosecutor's files in Philadelphia, we could not obtain this information there.) In 41 cases, the victim either could not be located or asked that the charges be dropped; the prosecutor filed charges in only 6 of those cases. Moreover, risk-taking behavior by the victim (but not evidence regarding moral character) was associated with the victim's willingness to prosecute: that is, victims whose behavior at the time of the incident was questionable were significantly more likely to disappear or to ask that the case be dropped.
>
> (Spohn and Holleran, 2001: 676, fn 27)

Although it may be that the victims who could not be found were involved in cases that would not be prosecuted, it is nevertheless important to consider these dismissed cases. Perhaps, a qualitative study would shed light on the reasons these cases were not prosecuted because it would mean prosecutors would be asked about the cases that did not "go forward." In this particular study, the researchers were able to gather information regarding standards for case processing, but the prosecutors did not participate in interviews regarding the cases that were studied. A qualitative study would allow the prosecutor to explain what actions they might have taken had the victims been found.

Finally, because much of this research is based on correlational analysis that examines the link between case outcome and case characteristics, authors must draw inferences about the logic and motivations of prosecutors' charging decisions. The analysis of prosecutors' charging decisions has primarily entailed examining case files and police reports, absent any recent inquiry into prosecutors' judgments about how cases should be handled. As a result, prosecutors' motivations cannot be directly measured, but are instead inferred through empirical associations. This same set of variables has repeatedly been used to study prosecutors' decisions in sexual assault cases. These variables include victim characteristics, case characteristics, and the nature of the relationship between offender and victim. It is these variables that researchers suggest are the causal influences driving prosecutors not to prosecute weak cases so as to achieve convictions and protect conviction rates.

These research questions would benefit from current qualitative research that provides more complete information on both the nature of the information that prosecutors may use in making decisions, and the rationales with which they use that information. In other words, qualitative research may make a valuable contribution in this area of study, especially if based on recently compiled data. Furthermore, a mixed-methods study that employs both methods would also greatly inform this area of research.

Many factors contribute to the limitations in the current research concerning case processing of sexual assault cases. Most notably, a lack of studies that rely on recently collected qualitative data and a lack of examination of the potential significance of the victim's willingness to cooperate with prosecution of the case.

CURRENT STUDY

Methods and Data

The data for this study were collected from three research sites in two different states. The research sites were state district attorney's offices.

Data were collected using semi-structured interviews. These interviews utilized vignettes that mirrored information likely to be in the possession of the prosecutor when he or she made a decision about whether and how to proceed with a case. This included a police report, criminal record of the victim and suspect, and information regarding a meeting with the victim.

The interviews loosely followed an interview instrument that was designed to aid in the discussion.[5] The interviews, therefore, were semi-structured and followed the subject in the directions they chose to go. Some areas were specifically addressed, however, so as to probe the specific research questions. For example, prosecutors were asked about the case review process, promotion process and decision making, and the strengths and weaknesses in sexual assault cases. The vignettes provided a very useful tool to discuss and expand upon the issues prosecutors see in sexual assault cases. A total of 23 prosecutors participated in the study. Interviews were conducted between December 2011 and April 2013. All of the interviews were audio recorded. I transcribed all of the interviews verbatim. This resulted in more than 400 pages of single-spaced text. The interviews in each office continued until either I interviewed the entire sexual assault unit or reached saturation.

This study addresses the limitations in previous research. Since the current study involves recent primary data collection, the findings may provide a more reliable picture of the decisions made in the contemporary context of reformed sexual assault laws. The study, however, is still able to test the findings of previous studies because it uses vignettes that include the relevant variables previous researchers have found may be contributing to prosecutors' case-processing decisions. Finally, by conducting interviews with prosecutors, this study seeks to allow prosecutors the opportunity to explain their decision-making process.

Research Sites

The research sites included three district attorney's offices in two different states. All three offices are prosecutors' offices responsible for a specific county within the state. Two of the offices are much larger, employing between sixty and eighty prosecutors. The third office employs only twelve prosecutors. In addition, the county with the smaller number of prosecutors has a significantly smaller total population. The two offices in the same state both have populations over 600,000 and less than 800,000. The third office is responsible for a population of only 159,000. Similarly, however, all offices are located in primarily urban areas. Finally, in all three offices, the district attorney is an elected official.

Data Analysis Methods

This study relied on qualitative analytical methods, including both inductive and deductive approaches. These methods are of tremendous benefit because they allow the researcher to focus on specific questions and to test the validity and reliability of existing research and theories.

The inductive approach allows for exploration of data with no set hypotheses. Often, the inductive approach is exploratory and not aimed at testing hypotheses. The inductive approach may be based in grounded theory research and allows for what is known as open coding of the data (Glaser and Strauss, 1967). In this study, using a grounded theory approach, I was able to engage in inductive and open coding, allowing the analysis to follow the path the data set out. In other words, the inductive approach allows the research to follow the data wherever they may go. In this study, the inductive method and open coding allowed me to remain open to all of the prosecutors' potential motivations related to decision making.

The deductive approach is a method of qualitative research that generally is aimed at testing hypotheses. The data analysis method relies upon "the investigator's prior theoretical understanding of the phenomenon under study" (Ryan and Bernard, 2003: 88). In this study, this part of the analysis is necessary to examine the "already agreed on professional definitions found in literature reviews" (Ryan and Bernard, 2003: 88). In essence, the researcher is able to ask the same questions as researchers who used a quantitative analytical approach. For example, using this approach, I was able to test whether the prosecutors' decisions were affected by the same variables that other researchers have found to influence charging decisions.

A second aspect of qualitative research utilized in this study is thematic analysis. Thematic analysis allows the researcher to discover themes in the data. In this study, the data are the interview transcripts. The researcher reads the text with an eye toward determining whether the text is related to an important theme. Once themes are identified, the researcher also identifies subthemes. This process requires narrowing the themes to those the researcher believes are most important so that there are a manageable number of themes to analyze. Finally, the researcher will link themes into theoretical models (Ryan and Bernard, 2003).

As a strategy of looking for themes, I utilized a line-by-line coding of the text of each interview. Coding is a method of organizing data and is part of the analytical method because it begins the process of discovering themes (Lofland and Lofland, 1995; Ryan and Bernard, 2003).

Line-by-line coding means reading each line of an interview transcript while looking for themes to emerge and then placing the text into categories, themes, or subthemes. Since this research involved both questions previously posed by other researchers and an open approach to the emergence of new themes, coding required both looking for the themes that emerged to answer specific questions and being open to themes not coming from any set research question. Once themes were discovered, I reevaluated the codes and reexamined the transcripts to ensure data were appropriately and completely coded (Lofland and Lofland, 1995). These techniques are also known as open, initial, and focused coding (Lofland and Lofland, 1995). Placing text in thematic categories through coding themes allowed me to examine the emerging concepts that provided the important findings for this study.

As a result, this study provides recent evidence of prosecutors' decision making in sexual assault cases through qualitative data and analysis. The interviews, combined with open-ended questions and the use of hypothetical scenarios, allowed me to probe the prosecutors' decision-making process. The study relies primarily on the interviews to form a discussion regarding case-processing decisions and is supplemented by illustrations from the vignettes. The findings that come from the analysis of these discussions illustrate the importance of qualitative methods when studying the decision making of prosecutors.

Findings

Decision Making in Sexual Assault Cases

Findings in this study about decision making in sexual assault cases are based primarily on discussions with prosecutors. These discussions involved the use of interview questions as well as vignettes. The hypothetical scenarios allowed me to discuss case characteristics with prosecutors and to examine whether elements such as strength of the evidence and case characteristics had an effect on case processing. In addition, the scenarios allowed me to consider whether prosecutors used stereotypes and shorthand assessments in their consideration of each scenario.

Each hypothetical scenario contained elements that would clearly be considered weaknesses and that are meant to match the weaknesses identified by previous researchers (a summary of the vignettes can be found in Table 9.1).[6] These include risky behavior on the part of the victim such as prostitution, drug and alcohol use, and going to a male's dorm room. Case characteristics also included both weak elements, such as reporting delay, and strong elements, such as physical injuries. The vignettes provided all of the information previous researchers would typically find as they gather quantitative data, as well as many variables that would be known to police and prosecutors in any particular case but would seldom be recorded in archived case files.

The difference in this study is the ability to probe prosecutors' decision making instead of to draw inferences based on whether cases with certain variables were charged or not. This methodology led to a set of rich data and different, more complex findings. Importantly, all of the prosecutors said the vignettes were realistic and included elements they could see coming up in real cases.

Table 9.1 Vignettes administered to prosecutors

Vignette	Summary
#1	Girl alleges she was held down by a classmate and forced to have intercourse with a different classmate when she was 14 years old. The incident took place at a party. Victim was drinking alcohol. One month after the incident the victim willingly engaged in intercourse with the perpetrator. The victim reported the incident to the police one year later.
#2	A twenty-year-old female college student alleged she was raped by a male college student she met at a college party. She agreed to go back to the male's dorm room, but says she told him she would not have sex with him. The two engaged in mutual kissing and touching but she alleges she told him to stop when he began intercourse. She reported the incident to the police about one month later. The perpetrator made a statement to the police admitting to intercourse, but claiming it was consensual.
#3	The victim met a man on Craigslist. She agreed to meet him to perform oral sex in exchange for both cocaine and money. She met the man and began performing oral sex when the man took out a knife, threatening her if she did not get in the back seat. She complied. He then engaged in forcible intercourse. As he did so he beat her. The victim was bloodied and bruised as she exited the car. She was seen by two teenagers, and her screams were heard by neighbors. An ambulance was called to the scene. The victim was taken to the hospital where she submitted to a rape kit, photographs, and medical treatment. The DNA was a match to the defendant. The defendant has a criminal record that includes sexual assault.
#4	The victim reports to the police that she was sexually assaulted by her pastor ten years earlier. She alleges she was approximately fourteen when she began spending a lot of time with her church pastor who was in his twenties at the time. During their time together they kissed, he touched her breasts, and penetrated her vagina with his finger. The victim explained that she was coming forward now because she knew the defendant still worked with youth and had three young children.

Several themes emerged in these discussions to reveal the factors that influence processing sexual assault cases. This chapter discusses the effect of victim behavior and victim characteristics on the decision to prosecute a sexual assault case. To summarize the findings: First, prosecutors agree that the single greatest factor in choosing whether to prosecute a case was whether or not the victim was "on board" with prosecution. Most prosecutors explained that the victim was in charge such that if he or she did not wish to participate, the case would not be prosecuted. This is an element that has not been studied previously and may benefit from qualitative research. Second, prosecutors said that victim characteristics and case characteristics could make a case weaker or stronger, but were not necessarily determinative in their decisions about going forward. Therefore, the characteristics that quantitative research suggests spell the end of a case may be correlated with a victim who does not wish to proceed or make a case weaker. Qualitative research allows us to further explain why this is so.

Victim Is in Charge

The single greatest factor in case assessment and charging is the sexual assault victim. A common theme among the prosecutors interviewed was that the victim is in charge. There was some disagreement, however, among the prosecutors about how much influence the victim has in case processing, with most prosecutors following the victim's lead. Several, however, felt that the victim should be consulted, but that all decisions were strictly in the province of the prosecutor.

Common themes in each of the counties include the importance of meeting with a victim before charging a case. In addition, prosecutors indicated the first question asked in deciding whether to accept a case for indictment is whether the victim is "on board." These two facts underscore the role of the victim in case processing. As explained by one prosecutor:

> I start with a real simple bias and I certainly believe that if somebody is coming in and they are reporting a sexual assault and . . . we investigate and *they* want to go forward, I start with a premise that they should get their chance and their day in court, so that's kind of where I begin. . . .

When this prosecutor was asked why she would go forward with each hypothetical scenario in spite of believing a case was unlikely to result in a conviction, she explained:

> Because if you have a victim who is saying, none of these cases make me say somebody is lying, in each of these cases if the

underlying premise is that, now I read all these cases, and let's say that for me the underlying belief is these people are all telling the truth. Now granted some of their stories may be better than others in terms of whether they are winnable or not, that's using a determination of winnable in a courtroom and there are lots of other ways, as we started this conversation, in which, winnable to me isn't the same thing as winnable to a victim and winnable for me personally is even more complicated than that, so if somebody is putting forward what we believe to be a crime, they are willing to go forward, they are willing to testify in court, and we think that in good faith we can stand up and represent to the court that they've been raped, then we're gonna go forward.

Q: So winnable does not mean conviction?

A: Noooo. It never equals a conviction and ya know I think that's where it all gets all screwed up. I think it is, there is a sense of doing justice all the time. Justice sometimes is just giving somebody the chance to come in and be heard, . . . and having their day in court, that's justice.

This part of the interview exemplifies a common theme throughout the interviews: that the victim is at the center of the case and the most important aspect of the case. This is made clear by the previous statement that seeks to provide justice for the victim, regardless of whether the case is "winnable" in terms of achieving a conviction. In asking a prosecutor directly how much input the victim has, the prosecutor highlighted the importance of the victim's input.

Q: So when you meet with the victims how much does their input play in role in your decision making throughout the case?

A: A lot. An enormous amount.

Q: Why is that?

A: Because they're what the case is about, it's about their lives. So it's important that their needs are respected, but also realistically, who they are, how they feel about things, their ability to participate is gonna have a huge impact on the end result.

I pressed the prosecutor by asking how they handled explaining to a victim the many weaknesses of a particular case when discussing whether the victim wanted to go forward and whether they explained this to the victim. One prosecutor explained:

A: [T]hat's the meeting that you have and you sit down with somebody and it's a lousy case and you say, you know, "I want

> you to think about this, here are the strengths and here are the weaknesses of the case and at the end of the day I just want to make sure that if it's a not guilty that you're going to be okay with that, and that for you success isn't only going to be measured in whether or not we get a guilty cause I can't tell you that we're gonna get a guilty but if at the end of the day you're gonna know I had the chance to say what happened, that he had to listen to me as I said what happened, and that that is empowering, and that feels like something you can tolerate, if after going through all of that you hear a jury say not guilty, then let's go."

The idea that the victim is in charge was prominent in a significant majority of the interviews. It is important to consider, then, the possibility that the relationship suggested by the quantitative studies is only part of the picture. Quantitative studies draw conclusions based on inferences. One such inference is drawn from the correlation between the number of cases dismissed and negative victim characteristics that exist within those cases. Perhaps the cases that do not go forward are those cases that do indeed have many weaknesses *and* as a result of knowing those weaknesses, the victim does not wish to participate. Regardless, the prosecutors in this study in most cases were not making quick assessments of the cases, but were waiting to meet with the victim prior to forming an opinion about the case.

Victims Are Assessed as Individuals and Not as Stereotypes
The use of stereotypes and quick assessments largely affects how a case will be handled, as opposed to whether a case will actually be prosecuted. However, even the use of stereotypes and quick assessments were based only on an initial reading of the hypothetical scenario, with the prosecutors in almost all instances explaining they could not make a final determination of how the case would proceed without first meeting the victim. For example, many of the prosecutors read the vignette and reported that the "case sucks," offering reasons why. However, when asked to determine whether the case might result in a conviction, expecting the prosecutor to respond in the negative, the prosecutors largely said they couldn't possibly answer that without meeting the victim.

The responses in the three different counties studied varied slightly. First, in one county there was no evidence of the use of stereotypes and quick, routine assessments. Cases were charged and indicted so long as the victim was "on board" with prosecution. Second, in another county, although the prosecutor might offer a better plea bargain to the defendant or strongly advise the victim that the case might not be successful, the case would still be prosecuted. Third, in the final county, the prosecutors might strongly consider the use of resources for that case, choose not to indict, or offer a good plea bargain to the defendant, but in all cases, the prosecutors indicated the case would go forward. In addition, the prosecutors said they would need to meet the victim before making a final assessment.

Many prosecutors indicated to me that they would need to actually meet the victim to get a sense of their credibility and willingness to participate in the case. When I asked several of the prosecutors whether the case was weak or strong and whether it would be indicted, they responded saying things such as "I don't know, . . . I think it would come down to having to meet [the victim]." And when asked what would they most want to know, often the response was "I'd want to meet the person. I'd, I guess that's the first and foremost." For example:

Q: So you could read something on paper, like read a police report, and then meet with someone and have a totally different . . .
A: All the time it happens.
Q: Really?
A: *All the time*. Much more so where I read something, think it's stupid, meet someone and I'm like oh my God, I totally feel completely different. I've had that happen to me a zillion times, where I read on paper and am thinking "okay, I'm getting rid of this, this is going nowhere," and I meet someone and my opinion is completely different. So that's so important, without a doubt, cause when you do this for a long time you read this stuff over and over, truth is sometimes stranger than fiction you know, and you kind of forget it and you think, "Oh my God this is so dumb," and then you meet the person and you're like "holy shit, she's credible. . . ."

The preceding interview illustrates one of the advantages of the qualitative approach to studying prosecutors' decision making: data contained in police reports and court documents only paint part of the picture, and much can be ascertained by digging deeper and asking questions. As the prosecutor needed to meet the victim to determine whether the case should go forward, so, too, should the researcher meet with the prosecutor to determine how and why he makes charging decisions.

One scenario that involved the potential for a quick assessment of the case included a teenage girl who had consensual sex with the perpetrator one month after he allegedly raped her. All of the subjects believed this fact would be a weakness in the case and would be difficult for a jury to understand. Most, however, believed that the victim's behavior made sense. Some even offered their view on it. Indicating:

> A: [T]he fact that she has sex with him *after*, but her reasoning makes sense to me, I think that a lot of girls you know sort of feel that way, you know a lot of girls don't report right away, especially teens and stuff because, exactly that, they're so like, number one they blame themselves and they almost want to act like it was okay so they don't feel that they were raped.

Although prosecutors largely indicated they would prosecute the cases in spite of their weaknesses, the handling of the cases might vary depending on strengths and weaknesses. For example, in one county, prosecutors might try to "shut down" a horribly weak case, but ultimately leave it up to the victim. Shutting down a case was a phrase used by several prosecutors to explain how they would have a frank discussion with the victim about the likelihood of conviction, with this often resulting in the victim choosing not to participate in the process. Again, in a quantitative study, this might result in an inference that weak cases are not prosecuted, when it is the victim who decided not to participate, thus necessitating dismissal of the case.

Strengths and weaknesses do have an effect on the amount of time a prosecutor will devote to a case. Several prosecutors offered that their office had limited resources, there are few prosecutors, and consequently they might devote greater attention to a stronger case than a weak one, but not because it might impact their conviction rate. In addition, a weak case is more likely to result in a generous plea bargain for the defendant. This means the defendant might be offered a plea to a misdemeanor charge on a case that could potentially be indicted. However, some cases are assigned to prosecutors for indictment and therefore supervisors have decided the case must go forward. Therefore, the prosecutors cannot avoid prosecuting cases they believe are weak.

Ultimately, quick assessments of the hypothetical scenarios often included an assessment of issues that would arise for the jury. Instead of relying on stereotypes, most prosecutors use their experience to develop ways they would address the weaknesses to a jury. Much of the discussion included how there are great differences between how the prosecutor views the facts of the case and how the jury will view the facts of the case.

The idea that shorthand assessments and stereotypes are used is negated by the prosecutors' insistence that they would need to actually meet the victim before forming an opinion about the strength or weakness of the case. The importance of this meeting is to discuss the process, introduce the prosecutor, and get a sense of their credibility and willingness to participate in the case. The importance of this meeting was repeatedly mentioned by most of the prosecutors. Unlike protecting one's conviction rate, meeting with the victim and assessing their willingness to participate is a key element in processing sexual assault cases.

Victim Characteristics and the Use of Management Strategies: Educate and Convince the Jury

Many of the prosecutors found weaknesses in the cases to be problems that needed to be dealt with, as opposed to issues that might be the determinative factor in a charging decision. Such weaknesses could result in attempting to resolve the case with a plea bargain prior to indictment, having a frank discussion with the victim about the obstacles in the case such that the victim would be in agreement with either a plea bargain or dropping the case, or formulating strategies to educate and convince the jury.

One way to deal with the weakness was to face the weakness directly. For example, many prosecutors approached negative moral character and risk-taking behavior as a common issue, something they could work with, an issue that simply needed to be addressed. This is illustrated in my discussion with prosecutors regarding a hypothetical scenario where the victim meets a man on Craigslist, exchanges oral sex for cocaine, and is subsequently beaten and forced to engage in intercourse. This particular scenario sparked several prosecutors spontaneously launching into a mock closing argument. One prosecutor arguing:

> Listen like she just got up there . . . you don't have to like her, you don't have to like the decisions she made, you don't have to want to go out to dinner with her or anything like that, but she got up and she owned all of that in front of you.

Another prosecutor arguing:

> You have a girl that takes the stand and says that she would perform oral sex for cocaine, and that she agreed to do that on this occasion, and that she did it all the time. I mean, if she's gonna make up a rape she'd say she was on her way to church and this guy pulled her aside and raped her, but you didn't hear that from her, you heard, I mean, she coulda spun that any number of ways, but she told you all the dirty, nasty details, including the rape, I think that credits her testimony.

The use of vignettes allowed the prosecutors to explain how they would handle typical sexual assault cases. By discussing the vignettes, prosecutors were able to explain what affect various characteristics of the cases had on their decision making. Without actually speaking to the prosecutors, I could not have learned their methods for dealing with weaknesses in cases such as educating the jury. This information is incredibly valuable as we attempt to understand how prosecutors make decisions and exercise their discretion.

DISCUSSION

This study sought to explore the continued utility and accuracy of the uncertainty avoidance thesis. It also sought to engage in grounded theory so as to allow for the opportunity for the data to lead the way. As a result, I was able to uncover the theme that the victim has great influence in sexual assault cases in a manner that is different from what was commonly thought based on previous research. Instead of the victims' negative characteristics or character determining whether the case will go forward, it is often the victim and her willingness to participate that have the greatest influence. Qualitative research has revealed that in weaker cases, prosecutors defer to victims who prefer or choose not to participate in prosecution. That is quite a different dynamic than the conventional wisdom that prosecutors dismiss cases in order to avoid uncertain outcomes, and conserve their efforts for more certain convictions.

Uncertainty avoidance is an important thesis because the idea that prosecutors process criminal cases with an eye toward avoiding uncertainty theory so as to avoid an acquittal has been consistently applied to the research examining prosecutors' decisions. However, in this study there was no support found for the theory that prosecutors make case-processing decisions based on concerns for upward mobility within the office. In fact, prosecutors discussed the importance of the victim's willingness to participate with the prosecution as one of the most important factors in deciding whether a case would be prosecuted.

Although prosecutors seem to give the victim a lot of power in the counties studied, there were some exceptions. For example, regardless of the victims' stance, prosecutors largely said that the vignette including a defendant with a criminal record for sexual assault and horrific injuries to the victim would be aggressively pursued due to concerns for public safety. The organizational goal, however, would be neither efficiency nor achieving convictions, but protection of a vulnerable population: prostitutes. Therefore, this example reveals the focal concern of public safety that exists in decisions related to sexual assault cases. Most of the prosecutors indicated they would do everything possible to convince the victim to participate in the prosecution of the case. In the other cases, however, the prosecutors were much more ambivalent about convincing the victim to participate.

An additional focal concern in these cases is the victim. It is not, however, consistent with findings in other cases. This study revealed that prosecutors are concerned with achieving a positive result for the victim. This positive result could be a dismissal, plea bargain, conviction, or other disposition that results in closure for the victim, satisfaction with the process, or a feeling of empowerment. This is in contrast to findings from other studies, which suggest that victim credibility is a focal concern because it might impact convictability.

The idea that prosecutors routinize their processing of these cases through the application of rape myths finds little support in this study. As a result, this study does not support the theory of bounded rationality that prosecutors will examine a case through the lens of considering what has been successful in the past. Instead, this study revealed that prosecutors do not consider victim characteristics as stereotypes. To the contrary, prosecutors explained that case assessments could only be complete if they had met the victim.

This study reveals the fact that the uncertainty avoidance thesis, bounded rationality, and the focal concern of victim credibility are not applicable in the counties studied. Perhaps attitudes and values in prosecutors' offices have changed since Albonetti's study. It is also possible that the findings from Albonetti's (1986) study do not apply to state prosecutor's offices. The two original studies by Albonetti in 1986 and 1987 were both conducted using data from a U.S. attorney's office. In this study, the prosecutors worked in state offices. Certainly it is possible that a high batting average in terms of convictions is necessary for upward mobility in the federal system. Nevertheless, there was no evidence of uncertainty avoidance to protect one's conviction rate in any of the three counties included in this study.

As explained by the prosecutors, sexual assault cases generally require the participation of the victim. In many cases, the victim is traumatized and hesitant about participating in the process. It is clear from the discussions with prosecutors that their ideas about the typical sexual assault case do not conform to the notions in rape myths. In addition, prosecutors specifically stated they do not measure success in terms of achieving a conviction. Given greater knowledge and understanding, prosecutors may now have a different measure of success in a sexual assault case other than a conviction.

Specifically applying the uncertainty thesis to sexual assault cases, Frohmann (1991) suggests prosecutors discredit victims' allegations to justify their decision not to prosecute. In her research, she found the office actually "encourages prosecutors to accept only 'strong' or 'winnable' cases for prosecution by using conviction rates as a measure of prosecutorial success" (Frohman, 1991). In the three counties studied, there was no evidence of an office policy to only accept strong or "winnable" cases. To the contrary, prosecutors typically stated that the victim was in charge and the case would be prosecuted so long as the victim was "on board."

This study also revealed a different approach by prosecutors to the weaknesses that often appear in sexual assault cases. As a result, the quick assessments and stereotypes seen in Frohmann's (1991) study were not present here. Instead of seeing problems with the victim's character or risk-taking behavior as the death knell of the case, prosecutors saw these issues as problems and developed strategies to overcome the issues. These responses vary completely from the responses reported by previous researchers.

This study failed to replicate the findings by Albonetti (1986), Frohmann (1991), and the many researchers who have conducted studies of sexual assault case processing. Decades have passed since these studies were completed, and many of the more recent studies rely on data that are decades old. Recent studies will likely shed more light on how sexual assault cases are currently prosecuted. Nevertheless, it reveals that prosecutors, at least in these three counties, have a vastly different view of the difficulties in a sexual assault case and a willingness to face these issues head on.

This study is not, however, without its limitations. All research has both strengths and weaknesses. Where the quantitative approach draws inferences through the use of data that come from court records and prosecutors' files, the qualitative approach makes conclusions based on the words of prosecutors for whom there is always a possible bias in their responses. Qualitative research bears the burden of relying on subjects to tell the truth and be open in their responses. In this study, the location of the offices is confidential and the identities of the subjects remain anonymous. As a result, anonymity and confidentiality are possible means of decreasing bias that were utilized in this study.

In addition, this particular study took place in three different offices in two different states. There were differences in legal standards between the two states that affected some aspects of case processing. There is also variability between states regarding how the district attorney obtains his or her post. Some district attorneys are elected and others are appointed. This is an important point because it is possible that the handling of sexual assault cases varies between offices, and therefore research studies, in part based on statutory differences or political concerns. As a result, it may be difficult to make generalizations about the behavior of *all* prosecutors. Nevertheless, the value of using qualitative methods to study prosecutors is clear, since much can be uncovered through interviews that cannot be ascertained through case files.

CONCLUSION

This chapter has described the theoretical frameworks that describe the important components of decision making by prosecutors in sexual assault cases. Furthermore, this chapter has outlined an argument for the qualitative study of prosecutorial decision making. Unlike existing studies, this study relied on recent interviews with prosecutors, probing why a certain type of case would or would not be prosecuted, instead of drawing inferences based on a possible relationship between variables commonly found in sexual assault cases and the result of the case.

In the qualitative study that was discussed, the findings indicate this study failed to replicate the findings by previous researchers that prosecutors make charging decisions or decisions regarding whether a case will proceed through the system based on concerns for uncertainty avoidance. Instead, decisions in sexual assault cases appear to be victim focused. The fact that most of the prosecutors focused on the victim's willingness to participate in spite of weaknesses in the case means further research is needed to explore the interaction between the victim's stance and the prosecution of the case. For example, how do prosecutors determine the victim's willingness to participate, and do prosecutors ever force victims to testify? In addition, if the prosecutor needs to assess the victim's willingness, at what point does this happen and how? A deeper exploration of the victim and prosecutor relationship is needed. Important considerations include the method of study to answer these questions. Is it possible to deeply probe prosecutors' decision making without the use of qualitative research?

This study has revealed that weaknesses in a sexual assault case are often seen as issues that need to be explained to a jury, as opposed to issues that will result in a failure to prosecute the case. In addition, this study showed that prosecutors do not apply the ideas in rape myths to the processing of their cases, instead assessing victims and their respective cases individually. Research in this area should examine whether there are other potential factors that influence case processing in sexual assault cases and whether qualitative research will better inform these questions.

More research is needed to examine sexual assault case processing. Sexual assault cases have a very high attrition rate from arrest to sentencing. Yet sexual assault crimes are devastating to victims and communities. The nature and impact of the cases make it clear that further research is needed to uncover the factors that influence case attrition.

NOTES

1. Littrell (1979), however, learned that "prosecutors often view their positions as temporary opportunities to gain experience, before moving on to private practice, politics, government services, or some combination of all three" (p. 41). The idea that one's employment is temporary and geared toward a goal outside of the prosecutors' office contradicts the notion that prosecutors are focused on achieving convictions so as to ensure promotions. It is possible that the difference in locale may explain the different motivations. Littrell's study took place in a county in New Jersey, whereas Albonetti's research relied on data collected from federal court and U.S. attorneys.
2. Rape law reforms have been developed and expanded over the last three decades. Reforms have included rape shield laws, removing requirements for corroboration of sexual assault, elimination of the spousal exemption, and inclusion of both genders as possible named victims.
3. In his research, Littrell (1979) also found that prosecutors think of "imaginary jurors to consider whether a case is weak or strong."
4. If the cases that were not prosecuted due to either lack of evidence or lack of victim cooperation are not included in the analysis, however, the analysis only then included twenty-four cases.
5. The interview instrument is available from the author.
6. The complete vignettes are available from the author.

REFERENCES

Albonetti, C.A. (1986). Criminality, prosecutorial screening, and uncertainty: Toward a theory of discretionary decision making in felony case processings. *Criminology* 24(4): 623–644.

Albonetti, C.A. (1987). Prosecutorial discretion: the effects of uncertainty. *Law and Society Review* 21(2): 291–313.

Beichner, D. & Spohn, C. (2005). Prosecutorial charging decisions in sexual assault cases: Examining the impact of a specialized prosecution unit. *Criminal Justice Policy Review* 16: 461–498.

Blumberg, A. (1967). The practice of law as a confidence game: Organizational cooptation of a profession. *Law and Society Review* 1: 15.

Eisenstein, J. & Jacob, H. (1977). *Felony Justice*. Boston, MA: Little, Brown.

Estrich, S. (1987). *Real Rape*. Cambridge, MA: Harvard University Press.

Frohmann, L. (1991). Discrediting victims' allegations of sexual assault: Prosecutorial accounts of case rejections. *Social Problems* 38(2): 213–226.
Glaser, B.G. & Strauss, A.L. (1967). *The Discovery of Grounded Theory: Strategies for qualitative research.* Chicago: Aldine.
Jacoby, J. (1979). The charging policies of prosecutors. In McDonald, W. (Ed.), *The Prosecutor* (75–97). Beverly Hills, CA: Sage.
Kerstetter, W.A. (1990). Gateway to justice: Police and prosecutorial response to sexual assaults against women. *Journal of Criminal Law and Criminology* 81: 267–313.
Kingsnorth, R., MacIntosh, R. & Wentworth, J. (1999). Sexual assault: The role of prior relationship and victim characteristics in case processing. *Justice Quarterly* 16, (2): 275–302.
Littrell, W.B. (1979). *Bureaucratic Justice: Police, Prosecutors, and Plea Bargaining.* Beverly Hills, CA: Sage, Publications, Inc.
Lofland, J. & Lofland, L.H. (1995). *Analyzing Social Settings* (3rd Ed.). Belmont, CA: Wadsworth.
Miller, F. (1969). *Prosecution: The Decision to Charge a Suspect with a Crime.* Boston, MA: Little, Brown.
Neubauer, D. (1974). After the arrest: The charging decision in Prairie City. *Law and Society Review* 8: 475–517.
Ryan, G.W. & Bernard, H.R. (2003). Techniques to identify themes. *Field Methods* 15(1): 85–109.
Spears, J. W. & Spohn, C. (1997). The effect of evidence factors and victim characteristics on prosecutors' charging decisions in sexual assault cases. *Justice Quarterly* 14(3): 501–524.
Spohn, C. & Horney, J. (1992). Rape Law Reform: A Grassroots Revolution and Its Impact. New York: Plenum.
Spohn, C., Beichner, D. & Davis-Frenzel, E. (2001). Prosecutorial justifications for sexual assault case rejection: Guarding the "Gateway to Justice." *Social Problems* 48(2): 206–235.
Spohn, C. and Holleran, D. (2001) Prosecuting sexual assault: A comparison of charging decisions in sexual assault cases involving strangers, acquaintances, and intimate partners. *Justice Quarterly* 18(3), 651–688.
Stanko, E.A. (1981). The impact of victim assessment on prosecutors' screening decisions: The case of the New York County District Attorney's Office. *Law and Society Review* 16(2): 225–239.
Steffensmeier, D., Ulmer, J. & Kramer, J. (1998). The interactions of race, gender, and age in criminal sentencing: The punishment cost of being young, black, and male. *Criminology* 13: 649–679.

Part IV

Theories of Corrections

Part IV focuses on theories of corrections. The correctional sector is the portion of the criminal justice process that deals with people who have already been convicted of a crime or who are under supervision while awaiting trial. As with criminal courts, the correctional sector is a complex social system that is composed of many parts. One basic distinction in the correctional sector is between correctional institutions, such as prisons and jails, and community corrections, which encompasses probation, parole, and other community-based programs. The three chapters in this section each address a different aspect of the correctional sector.

Correctional facilities are personnel-intensive organizations. Employees constitute a massive share of correctional budgets and are responsible for delivering the services offered by these organizations. Although employees are the lifeblood of correctional facilities, little is known about how the conditions of their work shape their attitudes and outlooks. In Chapter 10, Eric Lambert examines the impact of the work environment on correctional staff job satisfaction, organizational commitment, and "turnover intent" (intention to leave the job). To do so, he draws on a rich body of theory and research on employee views and outlooks from studies of organizations both inside and outside of criminal justice.

Higher levels of job satisfaction and organizational commitment are thought to be associated with improved performance on the job and a number of other beneficial outcomes for employees and their employers. Conversely, lower levels of job satisfaction and commitment are thought to be associated with reduced job performance and other negative outcomes like chronic absenteeism and, as Lambert emphasizes, employee turnover. Training and acculturating correctional employees is expensive and time consuming. Thus, when competent employees choose to leave the job due to weak satisfaction and commitment, it is costly and disruptive to the organization.

Lambert develops a theoretical model that specifies the antecedents (causes) and consequences (effects) of job satisfaction and organizational commitment. He then tests the model using data from the Prison Social Climate Survey administered by the U.S. Federal Bureau of Prisons. Many of his findings are worthy of attention from correctional administrators, but three in particular stand out:

- Lower job satisfaction is associated with lower organizational commitment.
- Lower job satisfaction is associated with greater turnover intent.
- Lower organizational commitment is associated with greater turnover intent.

Lambert's findings reinforce the idea that theory-based research can inform policy and practice.

In Chapter 11, John Crank examines the role of organizational and occupational culture in parole and probation. In particular, he focuses on how local parole and probation organizations are influenced by broader changes in parole and probation. Unlike Lambert's quantitative analysis of survey data in Chapter 10, Crank relies on a qualitative approach through direct observation of parole and probation officers undergoing training by the Nevada Department of Probation and Parole, as well as follow-up interviews. In particular, Crank focuses on the role of linguistic devices called "tropes" for communicating meaningful themes about the organizational and occupational culture to training participants. These tropes often take the form of instructors sharing stories about their experiences in the field. As Crank notes, these stories "provide a vocabulary of precedents that construct an appropriate cultural, or intersubjective, way of seeing the world."

Crank organizes his findings into three domains of "cultural meaning," including an emphasis on parole and probation officers as crime fighters, the morality of personal responsibility on the job, and the challenges and hazards of dealing with bureaucracies. While training is ostensibly about delivering specific or technical content to participants, Crank notes that it is also about transmitting cultural meaning. For instance, a key aspect of the bureaucratic tropes he observed was how to take shortcuts around bureaucratic impediments to getting work done. Crank emphasizes both the complexity and the importance of culture in parole and probation organizations. Reform efforts that are not based on a firm understanding of organizational and occupational culture are unlikely to succeed.

In Chapter 12, McGarrell and Duffee examine the causes of correctional spending at the state level. They compare a mainstream theory to account for correctional spending (states with more crime spend more on corrections) with alternative explanations from different theoretical traditions. One is conflict theory, which has already been discussed in several earlier chapters. The second is a "genealogical" theory, which is associated with French philosopher Michel Foucault and his followers. The third is institutional theory, which has also played a prominent role in several earlier chapters. Their evidence suggests that the mainstream explanation for variations in correctional spending across states, while perhaps the most intuitive, is insufficient.

Note that the three chapters in Part IV use very different research methods. Chapter 10 relies on statistical analysis of data from surveys of prison employees. Chapter 11 relies on the analysis of qualitative data from direct observations and interviews with parole and probation training participants. Chapter 12 relies on statistical analysis of data on corrections at the state level. Although the research methods differ considerably, all three chapters rely heavily on existing theory to guide their selection of an appropriate methodology and their interpretation of findings. They then conclude their studies with proposals for theory revision and new investigation.

The reader should note that in Chapters 10 and 12, the authors combine approaches and theoretical connections from prior work. In Chapter 10, the study looks at both the causes and effects of job satisfaction, rather than just one or the other. In Chapter 12, the study combines a concern for the institutionalized environment of public organizations and a concern for social conflict (both of which are, more abstractly, two different aspects of the correctional environment). Consequently, both studies have some concern for conceptual combinations and theoretical integration that helps us assess how theories come together to produce more complicated explanations of more complicated phenomena. For example, Chapter 12 by McGarrell and Duffee can be viewed as an attempt to combine (and contrast) the rational-goal and institutional organizational perspectives from Chapter 2 with the conflict/consensus views of the sociopolitical perspective also discussed in Chapter 2.

All three chapters in this section concern corrections in important ways. Equally interesting and valuable, however, is that the correctional theories featured in these chapters can also be characterized in non-correctional terms. Chapter 10 contributes to a general literature on job satisfaction, commitment, and turnover intent. It demonstrates, for example, that the same forces that are most powerful in predicting these outcomes in private firms are also most important in explaining correctional employee attitudes, despite the obvious differences between these two sectors. Chapter 11 is about the content of training in parole and probation, but it is likely that the author's conclusions may apply equally to other sectors outside of criminal justice. Chapter 12 focuses on correctional expenditures at the state level, but it is not difficult to imagine similar analyses of spending on health care, education, or other policy domains.

Chapter 12 raises some compelling issues about criminal justice theory. The question raised by the authors is what characteristics of the state or of the correctional system make corrections more politically powerful or more "valued" by its public. Why do some state correctional systems fare better than others in the allocation of resources? The reader should recognize the deep connections between the concerns of this chapter on correctional systems and the concerns raised in Chapters 1 through 3 about entire criminal justice systems. Does examining the amount of funding allocated to state correctional systems constitute only a study of corrections? Or does it also constitute a more general study of the punitiveness of societies? If some states pay more for corrections than other states, or pay more for corrections than for other social concerns, are they being more punitive than are their peers? Is this a study of corrections or a study of choices among social policies? Put differently, Chapter 12 may not just be a study of corrections theory, but a study of criminal justice system theory, or the study of public support (in the form of tax dollars) for the criminal sanction.

These types of substantive issues would be less visible if not for the prominent role of theory that guides the research in Chapters 10 through 12. The theories underlying each study make it easier to see potential theoretical connections with other substantive domains outside of corrections and even outside of criminal justice. This is one of the great benefits of theorizing: it enhances our ability to think in the abstract and to see connections that might otherwise be less obvious. Thus, these studies become good examples, not only of theory testing, but also of the general knowledge-building process. They illustrate, for example, how a study of prison workers can contribute to general knowledge about human resources in organizations, and how a study of parole and probation training can reveal insights about the powerful role of culture in organizations.

As with earlier chapters, the two quantitative chapters in this section (Chapter 10 by Lambert, and Chapter 12 by McGarrell and Duffee) can be broadly distinguished by the level of analysis. Lambert is interested in explaining what makes correctional employees satisfied with their work, committed to their organizations, and willing to stay, or the reverse—dissatisfied, uncommitted, and intending to leave. As defined by Kautt and Spohn, Lambert's three dependent variables are micro or individual-level variables on the vertical dimension and "attitudinal" variables on the horizontal dimension. Unlike Kautt and Spohn's chapter, however, Lambert's work is not examining a criminal justice decision maker's outcomes for a case, a suspect, or an offender. Instead, he is trying to determine what aspects of the worker or the worker's environment affect the worker's internal reactions to the work. This kind of study is important for any number of reasons. One of the most obvious is that satisfied and committed workers may be more likely to implement organizational goals, such as treating prisoners in ways consistent with policy. Also important is that, if satisfied and committed workers are less likely to leave the organization, then corrections could save significant recruitment and training costs by doing things that promote employee satisfaction and commitment.

In contrast to Lambert's focus on the individual worker, McGarrell and Duffee are studying state-level correctional systems. They are not looking at individual decisions and attitudes. They are examining large structural features of bureaucracies (such as size and complexity) and structural features of society, such as class, wealth, racial composition, and political traditions. This kind of study is also important for quite different reasons. For policy makers, this is one of a growing number of studies that suggest that level of crime is only a minor influence in determining the level of punishment meted out by society. It would also suggest that a large number of social inequities are built into social control systems, even if individual decision makers are fair and unbiased. (Note that Part III was also concerned with the differences in justice outcomes at different units of analysis.)

In terms of the knowledge-building process, the three chapters in this section represent the later phases of the theory building–observing–reformulating–expanding cycle. These studies appear to confirm some expectations and disconfirm others. They also "stumble" (in the sense of did not expect) onto findings that suggest new theoretical developments are needed. In addition, they suggest more research avenues. Although the three chapters in this section examine very different questions using different research methodologies, together they illustrate the rich complexity of the correctional sector and the criminal justice theories used to understand it.

DISCUSSION QUESTIONS

1. In Chapter 10, Lambert examines job satisfaction and other attributes of prison employees. Consider the job satisfaction of other criminal justice system participants. Would you propose that police officers, prosecutors, public defenders, probation officers, or other officials are likely to be influenced by different job and organizational characteristics from those that appear to influence the federal correctional workers studied by Lambert? Where would you look to determine if Lambert's theory had been applied elsewhere in criminal justice?
2. Compare the McGarrell and Duffee study in Chapter 12 of this volume to the study of incarceration rates by McGarrell (1993). In that study, McGarrell examines whether social conflict variables are equally strong in explaining incarceration rates at different points in time. Does such a study of several points in time provide stronger evidence than the study in this chapter about the influence of sociopolitical processes on punishment rates? Compare either of the aforementioned studies to McGarrell and Duffee (1995). In that study, the investigators examine pre-release centers per state and per inmate. Why are there differences in the state-level variables that influence the adoption of pre-release centers and the state-level variables that influence dollars devoted to corrections? What do these differences say about the importance of the exact nature of the dependent variable?
3. At their root, the theories discussed by Lambert in Chapter 10 and McGarrell and Duffee in Chapter 12 hypothesize processes that unfold over time. Do the tests of these theories in Chapter 10 or Chapter 12 account for these *change* processes adequately? Put differently, are the data sufficient to make clear judgments about processes that unfold over time? If not, where and how would you gather data that did so? What are the problems with gathering such data?
4. In Chapter 11, Crank describes a qualitative study of parole and probation training through the use of direct observation and interviews. What are the strengths and weaknesses associated with this type of research? (Note: Be sure to consult

Crank's discussion of "going native" in thinking about your answer to this question.) What types of criminal justice research are more or less suitable for qualitative research? How does Crank's approach differ from the approach used by Kennedy in Chapter 9? Both are qualitative studies, but they differ in important ways.

10

A TEST OF A TURNOVER INTENT MODEL

The Issue of Correctional Staff Satisfaction and Commitment[1]

Eric G. Lambert

INTRODUCTION

Earlier chapters in this book focused on the development and discussion of theories. While theory development is critical to understand, guide, and reshape the criminal justice system, a theory is only as good as the empirical evidence that supports it. From a theory, testable hypotheses can be developed. The empirical evidence generated from hypothesis testing can support a theory or cause it to be discarded or revised. Without hypothesis testing, significant policy changes could be made based on political rhetoric or intuition rather than a sound scientific foundation. This testing of theories through the testing of hypotheses is part of the scientific process. It is through the scientific process that we develop a better, more accurate, and systematic understanding of the world, including the agencies in the criminal justice system.

In this book, many theories deal with aggregate groups, such as components of the criminal justice system and agencies—macrotheories. Criminal justice theories are not limited to aggregate groups, such as nations, states, agencies, or departments; they can also focus at the individual level, on police officers, judges, probation officers, or correctional workers. Behaviors, perceptions, values, and attitudes of individuals are also examined by criminal justice theories—micro or individual-level theories. In this chapter, the impact of the work environment on correctional staff job satisfaction, organizational commitment, and turnover intent is explored. In other words, an individual-level theory is tested.

The driving force of an organization is its workers. This is especially true for correctional facilities, where staff are a valuable and expensive resource, often accounting for over 75 percent of the annual budget of a correctional facility (Camp and Lambert 2006). Correctional facilities are labor-intensive organizations, where staff are responsible for a myriad of tasks and duties to ensure a safe, humane, and effective institution is operated. Rather than solely aiming on finding the right person for the job, correctional organizations need to focus on improving the work environment, as the work environment has real and lasting effects on staff.

While it is true that correctional staff have significant effects on the operation of correctional organizations, it is also true that correctional organizations have meaningful and real effects on their staff, which can be either positive or negative. In our society, work is viewed as a central, sometimes even the defining, factor in a person's life. What takes place at work can have rippling to enormous consequences in a worker's life, even outside of the work environment. Job satisfaction and organizational commitment are the two most important areas by which correctional organizations influence the behaviors, intentions, and attitudes of their staff, such as turnover intent and turnover. Turnover is a significant problem in the field of corrections. By improving the job satisfaction and organizational commitment of staff, both turnover intent and turnover can be significantly reduced.

JOB SATISFACTION

The concept of job satisfaction is a frequently studied concept across a wide and diverse assortment of research fields. Hopkins (1983) defined overall job satisfaction as "the fulfillment or gratification of certain needs that are associated with one's work" (p. 7). Spector (1996) contended job satisfaction is simply "the extent to which people like their jobs" (p. 214). There is general agreement in the literature that job satisfaction is an affective (i.e., emotional) response by an employee concerning his or her particular job in an organization (Cranny, Smith, and Stone 1992).

ORGANIZATIONAL COMMITMENT

Organizational commitment is a newer concept than job satisfaction, coming into prominence in the late 1970s and early 1980s. Over the years, various definitions of organizational commitment have been proposed. Early definitions equated organizational commitment with loyalty to the employing organization (Jauch, Glueck, and Osborn 1978). Early definitions of organizational commitment also described it as the level of investments (e.g., pensions) an employee had with the employing organization (Becker 1960). The greater the level of investments, the more committed the employee should be to the employing organization. More recent definitions of organizational commitment have expanded the affective (i.e., psychological) bond to include loyalty to the organization, identification with the organization (i.e., pride in the organization) and its goals (i.e., internalization of the goals of the organization), and willingness to put forth substantial effort on behalf of the organization and its goals (Mowday, Porter, and Steers 1982).

While there are numerous, differing conceptualizations of organizational commitment, two fundamental points are clear. First, organizational commitment is a bond to the whole organization, and not to the job or position, or belief in the importance of work itself. Second, Mowday et al. (1982) argued that the various definitions can be categorized on a behavioral–attitudinal continuum. At one end of the continuum is the dimension of organizational commitment that is concerned with behavioral indicators or outcomes. This dimension is typically referred to as calculative or continuance commitment, because an employee "calculates" in some manner the costs and benefits of working for a given organization (e.g., monetary, social, physical, psychological, lost opportunities, etc.). These calculations determine the level of commitment to the organization. The synonymous term continuance commitment derives its name from the premise that workers highly committed to an organization will want to continue employment with that organization because of the benefits of continued employment as compared to the costs of leaving. In general, definitions at the behavioral end of commitment argue that employees commit to varying degrees based upon the costs and benefits of organizational membership. At the other end of the continuum are definitions that focus on affective or attitudinal commitment. Affective commitment is primarily concerned with the mental and cognitive bonds an employee feels toward the employing organization. These bonds include loyalty, wanting to belong, attachment, belief in the value system and goals of the organization, and so forth (Mowday et al. 1982).

There is an ongoing debate about which dimensions of organizational commitment, attitudinal or behavioral, are theoretically accurate, especially for the purposes of measuring commitment and its effects (Meyer, Stanley, Jackson, McInnis, Maltin, and Sheppard 2012).

Measures for the behavioral dimension of organizational commitment are criticized as being underdeveloped and failing to measure organizational commitment completely (Meyer and Allen 1984). Interestingly, empirical research has found that high calculative commitment is often associated with negative consequences (Lambert, Kelley, and Hogan 2013). Less criticism is leveled at attitudinal commitment measures, which are the most frequently utilized in research outside of the field of criminal justice (Meyer et al. 2012); therefore, an affective definition of organizational commitment is used in this study. Specifically, organizational commitment is defined as "the strength of an individual's identification with and involvement in a particular organization" (Mowday et al. 1982, 27). Past empirical research has found that high affective commitment is often associated with positive consequences (Lambert et al. 2013; Lambert and Hogan 2009).

THE IMPORTANCE OF CORRECTIONAL STAFF JOB SATISFACTION AND ORGANIZATIONAL COMMITMENT

Job satisfaction and organizational commitment have powerful and far-reaching consequences for both employers and employees. High levels of job satisfaction and organizational commitment have been linked to improved job performance, creativeness, innovation, receptivity to change, support for treatment of offenders, and heightened organizational citizenship behavior (i.e., going above and beyond what is expected at work; Culliver, Sigler, and McNeely 1991; Kerce, Magnusson, and Rudolph 1994; Lambert, Hogan, and Griffin 2008; Wycoff and Skogan 1994). Lower levels of job satisfaction and organizational commitment have been associated with high rates of absenteeism, turnover intent, and turnover (Camp 1994; Lambert, Edwards, Camp, and Saylor 2005; Lambert and Hogan 2009; Stohr, Self and Lovrich, 1992). Research supports the contention that job satisfaction and organizational commitment are important work attitudes. While all the negative outcomes of low job satisfaction and organizational commitment are detrimental, turnover intent/turnover is the outcome that tends to be the most observable, costly, and disruptive to correctional organizations (Lambert and Hogan 2009).

Turnover

There are two general categories of employee turnover: voluntary and involuntary. Voluntary turnover occurs when the employee ends his or her employment with an organization. Involuntary turnover, however, is the ending of employment that is not desired or initiated by the employee (Lambert and Hogan 2009). In most cases, involuntary turnover is initiated by the employing organization (Mueller, Boyer, Price, and Iverson 1994), but not always (e.g., death; McElroy, Morrow, and Fenton 1995).

Of the two types, voluntary turnover is usually more avoidable, costly, and disruptive to an organization (Lambert and Hogan 2009; Mowday et al. 1982). Involuntary turnover, on the other hand, is usually less controllable, and, in many cases, it is not in the best interest of the organization or the employee that employment continue, such as the firing of a poorly performing staff member (Lambert and Paoline 2010; Stohr et al. 1992).

The Extent and Impact of Turnover in the Field of Corrections

Turnover is seen as a significant problem in the field of corrections. Annual turnover rates in corrections average about 20 percent and as high as 40 percent for a few correctional agencies (Matz, Wells, Minor, and Angel 2013). Moreover, Locke (1976) contends that it is usually the most competent workers who quit, as it is relatively easy for them to obtain work elsewhere. Wright (1993) found that correctional workers who voluntarily left their jobs had, on average, higher performance ratings than the staff who remained.

Voluntary turnover of correctional staff has detrimental, and even devastating, effects for most correctional organizations. Recruitment, testing, selection, and training of new correctional staff are expensive, estimated to be approximately $15,000 to $20,000 per staff member (Matz et al. 2013). Even small reductions in turnover will save correctional organizations substantial expenditures in recruiting and training alone (Lambert and Hogan 2009). For example, Crews and Bonham (2007) pointed out that one correctional agency had to spend an extra $21 million to offset the effects of staff who had quit. Furthermore, correctional staff turnover disrupts the social networks and contacts that staff members develop over time with inmates and other staff. Correctional administrators rely on staff to obtain information, directly and indirectly, on what is happening in the institution in order to avoid potential problems. It takes time for new staff to learn these subtle but very necessary skills (Lambert and Paoline 2010; Stohr et al. 1992). Moreover, should turnover be allowed to reach a critical negative mass, turnover rates may cause future staff turnover. A chronic, looping turnover pattern may emerge. Minor, Wells, Angel, and Matz (2011) pointed out that "it is not hard to envision how high staff turnover might help beget even higher turnover, as well institutional deportment of problems and recidivism among offenders" (p. 59). The costs to the employee and his or her family before, during, and after the separation process are also high (Lambert and Hogan 2009). Voluntary correctional staff turnover has many negative and costly effects for the correctional staff who have left, the staff who remain, and the correctional organization itself. While job satisfaction and organizational commitment are critical keys to understanding voluntary correctional staff turnover, they primarily influence voluntary turnover indirectly through turnover intent.

The Issue of Turnover Intent

Intentions help shape many types of behavior (Lambert and Paoline 2010). In fact, Fishbein and Ajzen (1975) argue that "the best single predictor of an individual's behavior will be a measure of his intention to perform that behavior" (p. 369). Intentions "represent a vital link—transitional link—between thought and actual behavior" (Steel and Ovalle 1984, 674). Moreover, withdrawal intentions should have a stronger impact on employee turnover than many other types of behavior (Matz et al. 2013). Leaving employment with an organization is not a decision that is typically made on the spur of the moment. For most individuals, substantial thought goes into the decision to quit before a formal resignation is tendered. The intent to leave a job within a given time period is referred to as turnover intent. Understanding the causes of turnover intent is very important, because there is still time to make changes to keep a staff member before he or she quits.

Turnover intent is also important to understand from an employee's standpoint (Lambert and Hogan 2009). Many adults accept employment with the intention of remaining with an organization. Voluntary termination of employment with a particular correctional organization is a negative and painful experience for most correctional staff, particularly in terms of economic impact; therefore, if the antecedents of turnover intent are better understood, it may be possible to avoid the actual act of turnover. This would benefit the correctional staff member planning to leave, the staff who remain, and the correctional organization. It is postulated that job satisfaction and organizational commitment help shape turnover intent, and turnover intent, in turn, directly influences actual voluntary turnover behavior.

ANTECEDENTS AND CONSEQUENCES OF JOB SATISFACTION AND ORGANIZATIONAL COMMITMENT

The consequences of job satisfaction and organizational commitment in terms of turnover intent are only part of the equation. Exploring, confirming, and understanding the key antecedents (i.e., variables that come before another variable), both direct and indirect, of job satisfaction and organizational commitment are equally important. Identifying the factors that influence job satisfaction and organizational commitment provides correctional administrators with meaningful information to make intelligent decisions regarding interventions aimed at increasing organizational commitment and job satisfaction, with the ultimate goal being a decrease in negative withdrawal intentions, such as turnover intent; therefore, one needs to look at both the potential causes and effects, or as Guion (1992) points out, "Looking independently at antecedents and consequences is a bit like looking at an art museum brochure's detail of a painting: It's intellectually stimulating and informative, but you miss the grandeur of the artist's complete vision" (p. 257).

Identifying the salient antecedents of job satisfaction and organizational commitment among correctional staff is especially important. Correctional work is often hard and dangerous. Working in a prison holds little prestige in society, unlike many other criminal justice professions, such as being a judge. Such a job in itself may help foster negative attitudes. There is no reason for correctional organizations to contribute to or even enhance the development of negative attitudes by staff; however, without knowing the salient antecedents of job satisfaction and organizational commitment, correctional organizations may be unintentionally contributing to unduly negative attitudes and behaviors of staff. There is a critical need, therefore, to identify those factors that positively or negatively influence job satisfaction and organizational commitment among correctional staff.

There are two general viewpoints on the factors that influence workers' attitudes, intentions, and behaviors (Cullen, Latessa, Kopache, Lombardo, and Burton 1993). The first is referred to as the Individual Importation Model. This approach sees workers' reactions mainly as the result of personal characteristics, such as age, tenure, race, gender, personality, or past experiences. These are characteristics that people bring with them into the organization. The second approach, the Work Environment or Organizational Reaction Model, views employees' attitudes and behaviors as predominately shaped by the organizational work environment (e.g., degree of participation, routinization, promotional opportunity, pay, discipline, role ambiguity, type and quality of supervision, etc.).

While both viewpoints have found empirical support, it is generally argued that work environment factors have a far greater impact on job satisfaction and organizational commitment (Lambert and Paoline 2008). Thus, the work environment ultimately affects employee withdrawal intentions through job satisfaction and organizational commitment. Nevertheless, in the field of corrections, personal characteristics are still given undue focus, while work environment factors fail to receive the attention they warrant.

Rather than limiting this study to either exclusively personal or work environment measures, both are included to determine whether and how they impact job satisfaction and organizational commitment and, in turn, the consequences of job satisfaction and organizational commitment on turnover intent among correctional staff. Before a causal model is proposed, it is necessary to first define and discuss briefly what is meant by the concepts of personal characteristics and work environment.

Personal Characteristics

Personal characteristics are the characteristics that individuals bring with them when they join a particular organization. These characteristics concern an individual's background (e.g., education, place and type of upbringing, etc.), demographic identity (e.g., age, sex, race, ethnicity, etc.), current situation (e.g., married, number of children, tenure, etc.), and other areas (e.g., religion, distance living from work, total family income, etc.; Cammann, Fichman, Jenkins, and Klesh 1983). Personal attributes are argued to affect how an individual views his or her world. Nonetheless, personal variables tend to be more descriptive than explanatory (Lambert et al. 2008). Because personal characteristics are frequently used in research on correctional staff, several personal characteristics have been included in this study as control variables.

Work Environment

The work a person carries out in the course of a job does not take place in a vacuum. It takes place in a setting known as the work environment, which is composed of much more than just physical elements. It encompasses all the factors that comprise the overall work conditions and situations for a particular staff member, including both the tangible and intangible. There are numerous dimensions of the work environment, such as centralization (i.e., staff participation in decision making), financial rewards, integration (i.e., creating group cohesion among the workers and departments in an organization), legitimacy (i.e., fairness in terms of workload, rewards, and punishment), mobility, promotion, supervision, job autonomy, relations with coworkers, job variety, and job stress (Lambert and Paoline 2008). Several different areas of the work environment were measured in this study and are discussed in the methods section.

THE PROPOSED COMPREHENSIVE MODEL FOR CORRECTIONAL STAFF TURNOVER

As previously stated, both the antecedents and consequences of job satisfaction and organizational commitment are important, and both deserve comprehensive analysis. This means that a causal or comprehensive model needs to be developed. Comprehensive approaches to complex human processes, such as turnover, provide structure and discipline for researchers. Lee and Mowday (1987) wrote:

> Without such direction, research on employees leaving organizations would be totally ad hoc. Each researcher would probably focus on a subset of variables he or she found interesting, with little regard for a larger network of variables that could influence the relationships under study. The likelihood that knowledge would accrue from such ad hoc research is minimal. Comprehensive models impose a degree of discipline on researchers and help ensure that evidence from various studies can accumulate in some meaningful fashion. As that process occurs, scholars can refine the theoretical models, which will in turn increase understanding of the process through which employees leave organizations. (p. 738)

In addition, comprehensive models provide a framework for correctional administrators to understand the process of correctional staff voluntary turnover more thoroughly. Many correctional managers feel that they know why staff quit, even though their knowledge is rarely based upon a systematic and complete examination of the problem (Lambert and Hogan 2009). Investigating causal processes rather than individual relationships is, therefore, important.

Causal models allow for researchers to test for both direct and indirect effects among the variables in the model. Direct effects are the effects of one variable on another that are not moderated by any other variable. Indirect effects represent the impact that a variable has on another variable that is mediated by one or more other variables. Knowing both direct and indirect effects is critical when examining causal processes of complex phenomena.

> Considering each type of effect leads to a more complete understanding of the relationship between variables than if these distinctions are not made. In the typical regression analysis the regression coefficient is an estimate of the direct effect of a variable. If we ignore the indirect effects that a variable may have

> through other variables, we may be grossly off in the assessment of its overall effect.
>
> (Bollen 1989, 37–38)

A variable that may not have a significant direct effect may still have a significant indirect effect on the outcome variable of interest. Without taking into account the indirect effects, a variable that is, in fact, very important in the causal process could conceivably be rejected as insignificant.

Five core areas have been postulated to influence the causal process of voluntary turnover among correctional staff: turnover intent, job satisfaction, organizational commitment, work environment forces, and personal characteristics of the staff member. The proposed causal model of correctional staff voluntary turnover is presented in Figure 10.1. Testing the proposed causal model can empirically demonstrate that past multivariable correctional research has missed the total effect (i.e., direct and indirect) of salient variables on correctional staff turnover intent, and underestimated the importance of job satisfaction and organizational commitment as mediating variables.

Organizational commitment was postulated to impact negative turnover intent. Correctional staff who have low commitment will be less inclined to remain with the organization. Conversely, those with higher commitment have stronger bonds with the organization, and these bonds will generally ensure that they will want to remain members of the organization. People who are highly attached or bonded to

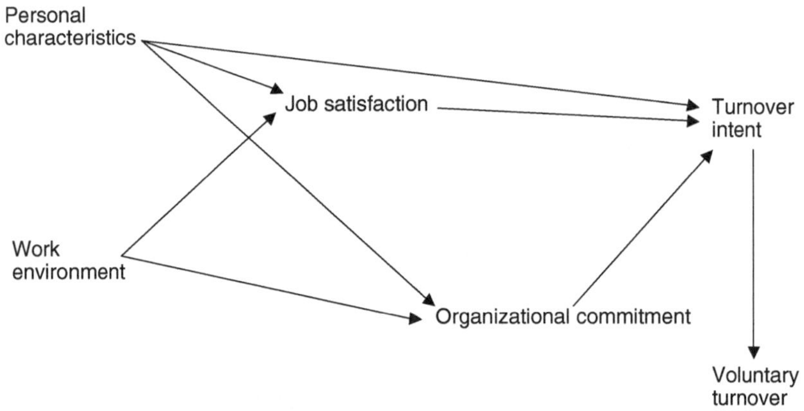

Figure 10.1 Causal model for correctional staff turnover

something are generally not likely to sever that attachment (Lambert and Hogan 2009).

Job satisfaction was also predicted to have an inverse effect on turnover intent among correctional staff. Work is a very important part of people's lives. According to Locke (1976), the reaction to something that is satisfying is to embrace it, while the response to something that is dissatisfying is to withdraw from it. If the person is highly dissatisfied with his or her job, he or she is likely to want to leave the thing that is causing him or her so much pain and discomfort, and will be more likely to voice intentions to want to leave (Lambert and Hogan 2009). Oppositely, those workers who are happy with their overall jobs have far less reason to leave. People do not readily abandon positive experiences that meet their vital needs. Humans seek stimuli that provide them with the pleasure of positive effects while meeting their other needs. While job satisfaction was predicted to have a direct inverse effect on turnover intent, it was also predicted to have an indirect effect on turnover intent through organizational commitment.

Job satisfaction is generally viewed as preceding organizational commitment. Job satisfaction occurs relatively quickly, while organizational commitment takes time to develop (Mowday et al. 1982). A person dissatisfied with his or her job has little reason to develop or remain committed to the organization that is causing the dissatisfaction in the first place. Alternatively, those workers satisfied with their jobs are more likely to see the organization in a positive light and, as such, will be more likely to bond with the organization (Lambert 2004). Job satisfaction was, therefore, predicted to impact correctional staff organizational commitment in a direct positive direction.

Work environment factors were predicted to influence organizational commitment and job satisfaction, with some of the total effects on organizational commitment being through job satisfaction. Positive work environment factors lead to a more enjoyable working experience for staff, which, in turn, is more likely to result in higher levels of job satisfaction and organizational commitment. Conversely, negative work environment factors tend to result in unpleasant and straining experiences, which often leads to lower satisfaction from the job and commitment to the correctional organization (Lambert and Paoline 2008). The specific areas of the work environment measured will dictate the type of predicted relationships (i.e., negative or positive) and, as such, these types of relationships are discussed in the upcoming section on measures. Finally, work environment factors were hypothesized to be more important than personal characteristics in shaping the level of job satisfaction and organizational commitment of correctional staff.

METHOD

Data Source

The data used in this study were obtained from the Prison Social Climate Survey collected by the Federal Bureau of Prisons. The Prison Social Climate Survey was developed by William Saylor (1983), deputy chief of the Office of Research and Evaluation in the Federal Bureau of Prisons. The survey provides a wealth of information, including demographic characteristics and staff perceptions of the workplace (Camp 1994). Each year, the Prison Social Climate Survey has been administered to a representative segment of staff at each federal correctional facility. The staff are selected through a random stratified proportional probability sample design. The sample of staff selected is based upon a set of stratifying characteristics consisting of supervisory status, race, ethnicity, gender, and job category and is representative of an institution's workforce (Camp 1994). This data set is, therefore, not limited to correctional officers, but includes food service, inmate records, unit management, education, custody, medical, maintenance, and industry staff. Staff were assured that their responses would be confidential (Camp 1994). With the Prison Social Climate Survey, it is possible to study staff across an entire agency. Most correctional staff studies have collected data limited to only one or a few prisons. Rarely have staff from an entire correctional agency been studied.

The Prison Social Climate Survey generally has a response rate above 80 percent. For the selected survey, the response rate was 88 percent. Out of 1,966 possible respondents, 1,704 were selected for use in this study because they have data on all the measures used in this study (i.e., listwise deletion was used; listwise deletion is a statistical technique where a case is dropped from analysis if a person did not answer the question).

MEASURES

Personal Characteristics

The personal characteristics of race, age, tenure, gender, and educational level were used more as control than explanatory variables. Race was measured using a dichotomous variable, with whites coded as 0 and nonwhites coded as 1. Age was measured in years. Gender is a dichotomous variable with males coded as 0 and females coded as 1. Tenure was measured by the number of months the respondent has worked for the Federal Bureau of Prisons. Finally, education was measured by asking the respondents their highest level of educational attainment. The education measure had five response categories of some high school but no degree, high school degree, some college but no degree or technical training, bachelor's degree, and graduate work or higher. The frequency percentages for the five educational categories, respectively, were as follows: .5, 20, 46, 18, and 16 percent.

Organizational Power

Organizational power refers to the ability to get things done in an organization (Kanter 1977). Centralization is one component of organizational power (Heffron 1989); another is controlling and disseminating information (Lambert and Paoline 2008). Measures of organizational power, therefore, tap into both the areas of centralization and instrumental communication. Organizational power was measured by a summated index of nine items (see Appendix A) and had a Cronbach's alpha of .90. Cronbach's alpha (Cronbach 1951) is a measure of internal reliability that provides an estimate of how the questions used to form an index are related to one another. It is important to remember that an alpha value is not an all-or-nothing proposition, but rather a matter of degrees of acceptability. Cronbach's alpha ranges from zero (no relationship between the items in terms that they are measuring the same concept) to one (complete relationship between the items in terms of measuring the concept). Cronbach's alpha values of .60 and higher are seen as acceptable, and the closer the value is to 1.0, the better (Gronlund 1981). Cronbach's alpha values lower than .60 are viewed as unacceptable.

The measure for organizational power was predicted to have a positive impact on both job satisfaction and organizational commitment. The less power an employee perceives he or she has, the more likely that employee will be dissatisfied with his or her job and with the organization as a whole. Most adults like to have a degree of input in what they do and how they accomplish their job (Lambert, Paoline, and Hogan 2006). The greater degree of power that a person perceives that he or she has, the more that individual tends to be satisfied with the job, because the work reflects, at least in part, his or her own decisions (Lambert and Paoline 2008). Similarly, the more power a staff member has, the more likely they will bond with the organization. Workers generally identify with and extend effort toward those organizations that give them a greater degree of control (Lambert et al. 2006).

Promotional Opportunity

Perceived promotional opportunity is another salient dimension of work environment (Price and Mueller 1986). The index for promotional opportunity was designed to measure a respondent's perception of promotional opportunity and practices, and was measured by a summated index of three items (see Appendix A) and had a Cronbach's alpha of .61.

The promotional opportunity index was predicted to have direct, positive effects on both organizational commitment and job satisfaction among federal correctional staff. Staff who perceive themselves as having fair opportunities to move up in the organization are more likely to be committed to the organization (Lambert and Paoline 2008). Lincoln and Kalleberg (1990) wrote, "More than earnings, we think, opportunity for promotion is a key weapon in the corporatist arsenal for winning the compliance and commitment of employees: workers who perceive that they have a career with the company are more likely to be committed to its goals and fortunes over a long period of time" (p. 105). On the other hand, correctional workers are unlikely to attach to an organization that they blame for a system that denies them promotional opportunities.

Moreover, a positive perception of promotional opportunity will influence staff members' affective views of their jobs. Most workers have career aspirations and ambitions that they expect to be met by the organization over time (Lambert et al. 2006; Lincoln and Kalleberg 1990). A perception of little chance for promotion leads many staff to view their job as a dead-end one, and, as such, they are less likely to be satisfied with the job.

Organizational Fairness

The concept of organizational fairness represents a staff member's perception of fairness in terms of official organizational recognition. This measure is rooted in the organizational justice theory. This theory is concerned with employees' perceptions of procedural justice (i.e., the perceived fairness of the methods in which important reward and punishment decisions concerning workers are made at the organizational level) and distributive justice (i.e., the fairness in terms of outcomes) (Lind and Tyler 1988). According to Mueller et al. (1994), organizational justice measures are concerned with the "degree to which rewards and punishments are related to performance inputs into the organization. It often is simply referred to as fairness" (p. 186). In this study, organizational fairness is measured by a summated index of four items (see Appendix A) and has a Cronbach's alpha of .82.

The index for organizational fairness was hypothesized to have direct, positive effects on organizational commitment and job satisfaction among correctional staff. Staff who perceive the organizational recognition system as being fair are more likely to be committed to the organization (Lambert et al. 2008). Human beings desire recognition for hard work. They also want fair outcomes. Organizational fairness demonstrates the administration's respect for staff and produces a bridge of trust that ultimately strengthens the staff members' commitment to the organization (Lind and Tyler 1988). Correctional workers are unlikely to attach to an organization that they blame for a system that denies them a chance to be properly and fairly recognized for their work. Similarly, perceptions of lack of recognition and unjust outcomes can lead to resentment on the part of staff (Lambert et al. 2008). This resentment will ultimately affect their job satisfaction. When a staff member feels betrayed by an unfair organizational process or outcome, that staff member is unlikely to feel that his or her job is satisfying. Positive perceptions of organizational fairness were predicted to have a positive influence on correctional staff job satisfaction and organizational commitment.

Supervision

A measure concerning supervision was included, as the relationship with supervisors is a significant feature of a staff member's work environment (Brough and Williams 2007; Matz et al. 2013). This supervision measure was designed to tap a respondent's view of the openness in discussing issues and expectations with his or her supervisor(s) concerning work-related matters. Supervision was measured as a single item (see Appendix A).

Considerate supervisors are important in the development of positive attitudes among employees. Supervisors are normally seen by workers as providing guidance and support (Lambert 2004). Supervisors are intended to give direction and feedback that is necessary for staff to complete their tasks within organizational specifications (Brough and Williams 2007). For most staff, supervisors represent the organization. If supervisors are perceived as failing in their functions, particularly in terms of support and consideration, staff are less likely to be satisfied with their work and committed to the organization (Lambert and Paoline 2008). On the other hand, staff who perceive positive supervisory consideration are more likely to report positive feelings toward their job and the organization; therefore, the measure of supervision was predicted to have a positive effect on job satisfaction and organizational commitment among federal correctional staff.

Job Stress

In this study, job stress was defined as feelings of job-related hardness, tension, anxiety, worry, emotional exhaustion, and distress, and was measured by a summated index using six items (see Appendix A) and had a Cronbach's alpha of .85.

While work is a significant source of stress (Davis and Newstrom 1985), the literature is unclear on the relationship between job stress and job satisfaction. While some scholars argue that job stress negatively impacts job satisfaction, other scholars contend that job dissatisfaction is a cause of job stress (Lambert 2004; Sager 1994). In this study, job satisfaction was hypothesized to have a negative effect on stress. Staff who enjoy their jobs will be less likely to feel stressed. Staff who dislike their jobs will report higher levels of job stress because they dread going to a job they dislike.

Furthermore, job stress was hypothesized to have a negative relationship with organizational commitment among correctional staff. Staff members who are highly stressed will generally hold the organization responsible for permitting the stressful situation, particularly if it persists over a significant period of time. On the other hand, workers who perceive little work stress are more likely to be committed to the employing organization because they see the organization to be responsible, at least in part, for creating a peaceful work environment (Lambert 2004).

Finally, perceived job stress was predicted to have a direct effect on turnover intent. Prolonged and intense stress has been found to have serious physical and mental consequences (Ivancevich and Matteson 1980). These consequences may influence a person to intend to leave the organization permanently (Lambert and Paoline 2010).

Job Satisfaction

A global, rather than faceted, measure of job satisfaction was used in this study. Global job satisfaction is concerned with the broader domain of an individual's satisfaction with his or her overall job, rather than with specific facets, such as pay, coworkers, benefits, type of work done, and so forth (Lambert 2004). Global measures are more appropriate for measuring overall job satisfaction and have fewer methodological concerns than measures that sum the facets to arrive at an overall measure of job satisfaction (Camp 1994). Five items were used to construct the global job satisfaction scale (see Appendix A). The job satisfaction index had a Cronbach's alpha of .84. Job satisfaction was predicted to have a positive association with organizational commitment.

Organizational Commitment

In line with the definition provided, an attitudinal measure of organizational commitment was used in this study. Unlike many organizations studied in the organizational sciences, there are two levels of commitment that must be accounted for when studying correctional staff: commitment to a particular correctional institution and commitment to the overall correctional agency (Camp 1994). The Prison Social Climate Survey measures both institution and agency commitment. The eight items for institution and agency commitment were combined to form an overall measure of organizational commitment (see Appendix A). The organizational commitment index had a Cronbach alpha of .88.

Turnover Intent

Turnover intent was measured by a single item (see Appendix A), as is frequently the case (Lambert and Paoline 2010; Matz et al. 2013). The premise that turnover intent will directly impact voluntary turnover among correctional staff cannot be tested in this study. The Prison Social Climate Survey is an anonymous questionnaire, and hence, cannot be linked to actual individuals to determine whether they continued with or left employment with the Federal Bureau of Prisons in a given time frame. The next best method is to study turnover intent because it almost always and immediately precedes voluntary turnover.

Data Analysis Technique

The proposed causal model was tested using path analysis. Path analysis is a powerful research method that allows for the examination of complex events in which there are more than one dependent variable and multiple independent variables (Bollen 1989; Lambert and Hogan 2009). A dependent variable is the outcome of interest and is so called because it is said to be dependent on other variables for its cause. Independent variables represent those forces that cause change in dependent variables. For example, a college student's grades are affected, in part, by the amount of time he or she spends studying. In this example, the number of hours spent studying is the independent variable, and course grade is the dependent variable because it depends on the amount of time studying (Bollen 1989).

A major strength of path analysis is its ability to decompose total effects into direct and indirect effects. Direct effects are the effects between one variable and another that are not moderated by any other variable. Indirect effects represent the impact that a variable has on another variable that is mediated by one or more other variables. For example, the work environment measures were proposed to affect correctional staff turnover intent indirectly through job satisfaction and organizational commitment.

There are three main areas of path analysis: path diagram, equations to correlations to estimate the effects of the independent variables on the dependent variable or variables, and decomposition of total effects. Path diagrams are a pictorial or graphical representation of the specified causal effects between variables for a given model (Bollen 1989). The graphical picture presented in Figure 10.1 is a basic path diagram.

The equation part of path analysis refers to estimating the direct effects between the independent variables and the dependent variable. The equations represent the relationships graphically presented in the path diagram; therefore, path analysis is essentially a series of mathematical equations for each dependent variable in the path model (Bollen 1989). In this study, four equations need to be estimated, one for each dependent variable. The four dependent variables in this study are job satisfaction, job stress, organizational commitment, and turnover intent.

While several estimation techniques could be used to estimate the direct effects for the four dependent variables of job satisfaction, job stress, organizational commitment, and turnover intent, the estimation technique of Ordinary Least Squares (OLS) regression was selected. OLS regression estimates the effects of an independent variable on a dependent variable while controlling for the effects of the other independent variables in the model. For example, OLS regression would estimate the effect of supervision on job stress, while controlling for the variables of personal characteristics, organizational power, promotional opportunity, and organizational fairness. In addition, OLS regression is frequently used in criminal justice research.

RESULTS AND DISCUSSION

Table 10.1 reports the descriptive statistics for the variables. The average age of the respondents was 35.7 years of age. About 26 percent were female correctional staff. Seventy-five percent of the respondents were white. Most respondents (i.e., 46 percent) had some college but no baccalaureate degree. The average tenure with the Federal Bureau of Prisons was 79.1 months (i.e., slightly less than seven years). The average values for the organizational power, promotional opportunity, organizational fairness, and supervision measures were 3.40, 2.98, 3.33, and 3.92, respectively. The average values for job stress, job satisfaction, and organizational commitment were 2.28, 3.83, and 3.80, respectively.

About 18 percent agreed in some manner (i.e., somewhat agree, agree, or strongly agree) that they desired to leave employment with the Federal Bureau of Prisons. Finally, each of the variables had a significant amount of variation as indicated by their standard deviation, which measures the amount of variation from the mean value.

Job Satisfaction

An OLS regression equation was computed with job satisfaction as the dependent variable. The coefficient of determination (i.e., R-squared) for the job satisfaction equation is .31 and is statistically significant ($F = 83.55$, $df = 9$, $p < .001$). R-squared can be interpreted as the amount of variance explained in the dependent variable by the independent variables (i.e., the percentage of error reduced by using the independent variables to predict the dependent variable rather than using the mean of the dependent variable) (Draper and Smith 1966); therefore, the model accounts for about 31 percent of the variance in job satisfaction. Variance refers to the amount of difference observed among the respondents on how they responded to the job satisfaction questions. For example, some staff may indicate that they are very satisfied with their jobs, other staff may respond that they are only somewhat satisfied with their jobs, and still other staff may indicate that they are dissatisfied with their jobs. The different responses are the variance observed in the job satisfaction index. The selected independent variables, therefore, explain about 31 percent of the different responses provided by respondents to the job satisfaction questions.

All the independent variables had a statistically significant impact on job satisfaction at a level of $p \leq .05$, except for the gender, race, and organizational fairness measures. Basically, $p < .05$ represents the chances of making a type I error. A type I error occurs when it is concluded that a variable has a real effect on another variable, when in fact there is no such relationship. For example, the chance of wrongly concluding that organizational power has a real impact on job satisfaction based upon the findings is 5 times out of 100. In other words, 95 times out of 100, the conclusion would be right. If there is no real relationship, the findings are probably due to random chance.

There was no difference between male and female federal correctional staff in terms of job satisfaction once the effects of the other independent variables were controlled. In addition, the results indicated that, among federal correctional staff, there was no significant difference in job satisfaction between whites and nonwhites.

The measure of organizational fairness had no significant impact on job satisfaction after controlling for the other independent variables in

Table 10.1 Descriptive statistics

Variable	Alpha	Mean[a]	Std. Dev.[b]	Median[c]	Min.	Max.
Age		35.71	7.01	35.00	22	69
Gender		0.26	0.44	0.00	0	1
Race		0.25	0.43	0.00	0	1
Tenure		79.10	65.51	60.00	0	399
Education		3.29	0.98	3.00	1	5
Organizational power	0.90	3.40	1.42	3.56	0	6
Promotional opportunity	0.61	2.98	1.37	3.00	0	6
Organizational fairness	0.82	3.33	1.58	3.50	0	6
Supervision		3.92	1.90	5.00	0	6
Job stress	0.85	2.28	1.23	2.33	0	6
Job satisfaction	0.84	3.83	1.38	4.00	0	6
Organizational commitment	0.88	3.80	1.22	4.00	0	6
Turnover intent		1.72	1.88	1.00	0	6

Note: Age was measured in continuous years. Gender was coded as men = 0 and women = 1. Race was coded as whites = 0 and nonwhites = 1. Tenure was measured in months. Education was coded as follows: 1 = less than high school, 2 = high school diploma, 3 = some college but no degree (including technical schooling), 4 = bachelor's degree, 5 = graduate work (including earning a degree). The specific questions for the remaining variables are presented in the appendix.

[a] The arithmetic mean is reported. To compute the arithmetic mean, the values are summed together and divided by the total number of cases.

[b] Std. Dev. stands for standard deviation and is a measure of dispersion that represents how much the values are, on average, away from the mean; therefore, the smaller the standard deviation, the tighter the cases are around the mean value, and the larger the value, the more spread out the cases are from the mean value.

[c] The median represents the point in which half of the cases fall below and half of the cases lie above. The mean and median values are similar to one another, indicating the variables are near normal distribution.

the equation. This is probably because organizational fairness has more to do with how an individual perceives the employing organization than it does with how an individual perceives his or her job. Finally, age, tenure, education, supervision consideration, promotional opportunity, and organizational power all have positive effects on job satisfaction among federal correctional staff. A positive relationship means that an increase in the independent variable is associated with an increase in the dependent variable (e.g., when perceptions of supervision consideration increase, the more satisfaction from the job is reported). Conversely, a decrease in the independent variable results in a decrease in the dependent variable (e.g., lower perceptions of organizational power are associated with a reduction in job satisfaction).

Organizational power has the largest effect on job satisfaction, followed by promotional opportunity and then supervision. The personal variables have the least impact on job satisfaction. In order to determine the amount of variance accounted for in job satisfaction, the personal variables (i.e., age, tenure, gender, race, and education) and the work environment variables (i.e., supervision, organizational fairness, promotional opportunity, and organizational power) are entered as blocks independent of one another. Blocks independent of one another means that each set of independent variables was used alone without the variables in the other sets. R-squared for the personal variables was .06. R-squared for the work environment variables was .27, and R-squared for all the independent variables was .31; therefore, as predicted, the work environment factors accounted for a far greater proportion of job satisfaction of federal correctional staff than personal characteristics.

Job Stress

Because it was theorized that job satisfaction affects job stress rather than the opposite, job stress was regressed on job satisfaction. Job satisfaction had a significant impact on job stress among federal correctional staff ($p = .001$). In other words, less than 1 time out 1,000 would job satisfaction be observed to have an impact on job stress due to random chance. It appears that there is a real negative relationship between job satisfaction and job stress. The negative relationship means that as job satisfaction increases, the level of job stress reported decreases.

Organizational Commitment

An OLS regression equation was estimated with organizational commitment as the dependent variable. R-squared for the organizational commitment equation was .53 and was statistically significant ($F = 170.50$, $df = 11$, $p = .001$); therefore, the model accounted for about 53 percent of the variance in organizational commitment. All the independent variables had a statistically significant impact on organizational commitment at a level of $p \leq .05$, except for the gender, age, and education measures. As with job satisfaction, there appeared to be no statistical difference between male and female federal correctional staff in terms of organizational commitment. In addition, the results indicated that among federal correctional staff there was no significant relationship between age and organizational commitment. Interestingly, age did have a statistically significant impact on job satisfaction. Age appears to be a significant antecedent of job satisfaction but not organizational commitment. As with age, it was interesting to note that education level had a statistically significant effect on job satisfaction. Education also appears to be a significant antecedent of job satisfaction, but not organizational commitment, among federal correctional staff.

The measures for tenure, supervision, promotional opportunity, organizational power, organizational fairness, and job satisfaction all had statistically significant positive effects on organizational commitment among federal correctional staff. This means increases in any of these variables were associated with greater satisfaction from the job.

As previously indicated, the measure of organizational fairness had no significant impact on job satisfaction among federal correctional staff after controlling for the other independent variables in the equation. It did, however, have a positive impact on organizational commitment; therefore, organizational fairness appears to have a greater impact on how an individual perceives the employing organization than it does with how an individual perceives his or her job.

Job stress, as predicted, had a significant negative effect on organizational commitment. In addition, nonwhite federal correctional staff members had statistically less organizational commitment than white staff. As previously mentioned, there was no significant difference between whites and nonwhites in terms of job satisfaction. While both have similar levels of job satisfaction, whites were more likely to have higher organizational commitment compared to their nonwhite counterparts.

Looking at the magnitude of effects, promotional opportunity and organizational power had the largest effects on organizational commitment. Job satisfaction had the third largest direct effect on organizational commitment. This was an unexpected finding. Job satisfaction was expected to have the largest direct impact on organizational commitment among federal correctional staff. The reason that job satisfaction did not have the largest magnitude of effect on organizational commitment in this study could be due to how the variables were measured or that among federal correctional staff, job satisfaction does not have the largest impact on organizational commitment, or a combination of both.

The personal variables, the work environment variables and job stress, and job satisfaction were entered as blocks independent of one another to determine the amount of variance explained of organizational commitment among federal correctional staff. R-squared for the personal variables as a block was only .01; for the work environment variables and job stress, .49; with only job satisfaction, .26; and for all the independent variables, .53. The work environment, job stress, and job satisfaction, therefore, accounted for a far greater proportion of the variance of organizational commitment for federal correctional staff than did personal characteristics.

Turnover Intent

An OLS regression equation with turnover intent as the dependent variable was estimated. R-squared for the turnover intent model was .40 and was statistically significant (F = 137.37, df = 8, p = .001); therefore, the model accounted for about 40 percent of the variance in turnover intent. All the independent variables had a statistically significant impact on organizational commitment at $p \leq .05$. Age and tenure both had a negative impact on turnover intent among federal correctional staff, which is consistent with Becker's (1960) side-bet theory. As employees get older and their tenure increases in an organization, the more sunken costs they have in the organization and, as such, are less likely to intend to leave. Conversely, education had a positive effect on turnover intent among federal correctional workers. Educated correctional workers could simply have greater ease in finding alternative employment.

Gender had a negative effect on turnover intent. Specifically, female federal correctional staff were less likely to express turnover intent than were male staff. The finding for gender could be contextual and might vary between correctional agencies. Based upon the author's personal experience, female staff in the federal prison system operate in a friendlier environment than do their female counterparts in many state and local correctional agencies. In addition, federal female correctional staff may remain in employment in the field of corrections as a career choice, whereas men may be more likely to accept a job in a correctional setting as temporary employment until something better comes along.

Race had a positive impact on federal correctional staff turnover intent. Specifically, nonwhite staff members were more likely than white staff to express turnover intent. Nonwhites could perceive the working environment as more hostile than white workers.

Job stress, as predicted, had a positive effect on turnover intent among federal correctional staff. It is likely that stress wears on a person until he or she psychologically desires to quit.

Looking at the magnitude of effects, organizational commitment, as predicted, had the largest effect on turnover intent among federal correctional staff, followed closely by job satisfaction. Job stress had the third largest direct effect on turnover intent, and had only a third to a half of the impact on turnover intent as compared to job satisfaction and organizational commitment. The personal variables had the least impact on turnover intent. Personal characteristics only had one-fourth the impact on turnover intent as compared to organizational commitment, and a third of the effect as compared to job satisfaction.

In order to determine the impact of each group of variables on turnover intent, the personal variables—job stress, job satisfaction, and organizational commitment—were entered as blocks independent of one another. R-squared for just the personal variables was .04; R-squared for job stress, job satisfaction, and organizational commitment was .37; while R-squared for job satisfaction and organizational commitment was .36. Finally, R-squared for all the independent variables was .40; therefore, job satisfaction and organizational commitment account for a far greater proportion of turnover intent variance among federal correctional staff than do personal characteristics and job stress.

Direct, Indirect, and Total Effects

Until this point, all the effects discussed have been direct effects. Besides direct effects, path analysis allows for the calculation of indirect and total effects. As previously discussed, indirect effects are the effects between two variables that are mediated by at least one intervening variable (Bollen 1989). Indirect effects are calculated by multiplying the direct standardized coefficients of the direct causal paths leading to the dependent variable of interest. Total effects of an independent variable on a particular dependent variable are calculated by adding the direct and indirect effects together (Bollen 1989; Lambert and Hogan 2009). Table 10.2 reports the direct, indirect, and total effects for turnover intent.

Age, tenure, education, gender, and race had both direct and indirect effects on turnover intent. The indirect effects were through job satisfaction and organizational commitment. Supervision, organizational fairness, promotional opportunity, and organizational power only had indirect effects on turnover intent. The indirect effects were mediated by both job satisfaction and organizational commitment. Of the work environment measures, organizational power had the largest total impact on turnover intent among federal correctional staff, followed by promotional opportunity. Supervision and organizational fairness had the smallest total effects. Moreover, the four work environment variables all had larger indirect effects on turnover intent than did the five personal characteristics. In fact, the indirect effects of the work environment variables on turnover intent were either about the same or larger than the direct effects of the personal characteristics. Finally, the total effects of the five personal characteristics on turnover intent were similar to each other in terms of size.

In the correctional staff literature, it is common to test only for the direct effects of work environment measures on turnover intent or turnover. In other words, turnover intent is regressed on all the variables in

Table 10.2 Direct, indirect, and total effects on turnover intent

Variable	Direct Effects	Indirect Effects	Total Effects
Age	−0.06	−0.04	−0.09
Education	0.06	−0.04	−0.10
Gender	−0.09	0.00	−0.08
Race	0.06	0.03	0.09
Tenure	−0.06	−0.04	−0.10
Supervision	0.00	−0.07	−0.07
Promotional opportunity	0.00	−0.16	−0.16
Organizational fairness	0.00	−0.05	−0.05
Organizational power	0.00	−0.20	−0.20
Job stress	0.12	0.05	0.17
Job satisfaction	−0.24	−0.13	−0.37
Organizational commitment	−0.38		−0.38

Note: Direct effects are the effects of one variable on another that are not moder- ated by any other variable. In other words, direct effects are the direct paths between two variables. Indirect effects represent the impact that a variable has on another variable that is mediated by one or more other variables.

the path model. Age, tenure, race, education, job stress, job satisfaction, and organizational commitment all had statistically significant effects on turnover intent, while supervision, organizational fairness, and organizational power all had statistically insignificant effects on turnover intent among federal correctional staff, and promotional opportunity only reached statistical significance at a $p < .05$ level.

If only the direct effects had been examined, one would dismiss work environment factors as not having an impact on turnover intent, let alone actual turnover, since turnover intent mediates many of the effects on actual turnover. Nevertheless, as evidenced by the total effects reported in Table 10.2, such a conclusion would be in error. While work environment factors had significant total effects on turnover intent, these effects were mainly indirect, mediated primarily through job satisfaction and organizational commitment. By dismissing work environment factors as not having a significant effect, a researcher would be missing the complex process that actually occurs during the formation of turnover intent by the employee. As predicted, the effects of the work environment on turnover intent are indirect and are mediated by job satisfaction and organizational commitment.

Organizational commitment, as positioned in the path model, has only a direct effect on turnover intent, and, as such, the total effects of organizational commitment are equal to the direct effects. Job stress had both direct and indirect effects on turnover intent. The indirect effects of job stress are mediated by organizational commitment. Job satisfaction also had both direct and indirect effects on turnover intent, and the indirect effects were mediated by job stress and organizational commitment. Organizational commitment had the largest total effect on turnover intent, followed very closely by job satisfaction. While all the total effects for organizational commitment were direct, over a third of the total effects for job satisfaction were indirect. The total effects of job stress on turnover intent were largely direct and positive. Finally, the total effects of job stress on turnover intent were less than half the size as the total effects for job satisfaction and organizational commitment among federal correctional staff. As predicted, job satisfaction and organizational commitment had the greatest impact on turnover intent of federal correctional staff.

CONCLUSION

The results support the process presented in Figure 10.1 and the core hypotheses made in this study. The work environment is very important in shaping job satisfaction of federal correctional staff. Furthermore, work environment and job satisfaction are key antecedents for shaping organizational commitment. Both job satisfaction and organizational commitment are important antecedents in shaping turnover intent, and account for a much larger variance of turnover intent than do personal characteristics. In addition, the work environment has significant effects on turnover intent, and these effects are mainly indirect. By failing to take into account indirect effects, one risks dismissing factors that are, in fact, critical in the complex process of turnover intent.

In the introduction, it was stated that in the field of corrections, there is significant focus on the selection process, while job satisfaction and organizational commitment fail to receive the attention they warrant. The results of this study suggest that this view is in error. If correctional administrators are truly interested in reducing turnover intent of their staff, they need to invest resources in improving staff job satisfaction and organizational commitment, which can be accomplished by improving the work environment. Key areas of the work environment identified in this study are organizational power, promotional opportunity, supervision, and organizational fairness. Of these, organizational power appears to be the most important; therefore, correctional administrators should attempt to improve the flow of important information (i.e., communication) and allow for greater staff participation in decision making, particularly in the area of job autonomy. Similar recommendations for better essential communication and for allowing greater staff participation, regardless of the type of organization, are abundant in the literature.

Implementation of such broad recommendations may be easier said than done, particularly in the bureaucratic setting of most correctional agencies. Nevertheless, serious consideration should be given to improving job satisfaction and organizational commitment of correctional staff through changes in the work environment. Other than reducing turnover intent and other negative work outcomes, higher levels of staff job satisfaction and organizational commitment are also predicted to have positive outcomes in other areas, such as improved home life for staff, improved staff–inmate interactions, and improved work performance. The knowledge of and ability to understand the antecedents of correctional staff work attitudes and behaviors are critical for all parties involved.

Aside from specific implications for correctional institutions, this chapter also illustrates that there are multiple layers of criminal justice theories. Some theories focus on the aggregate level, while others attempt to explain variations found at the individual level. In addition, theories are not constrained by inputs and outputs found across the study of criminal justice. Criminal justice theories can examine what the editors of this book call "throughputs." Throughputs lie between the inputs and outputs, and are elements such as values, beliefs, perceptions, and attitudes. Throughputs are appropriate and salient areas for criminal justice theories to address.

NOTE

1. The author thanks the anonymous reviewers for their comments and suggestions. The author also thanks Janet Lambert for her help in editing and proofreading this chapter. The author is indebted to William Saylor and Scott Camp of the Office of Research and Evaluation of the Federal Bureau of Prisons for the information they provided on the Prison Social Climate Survey, and he is grateful to the Federal Bureau of Prisons for granting permission to use the findings from my dissertation in this chapter. Finally, the author thanks Drs. David Duffee, Robert Hardt, David McDowall, Hans Toch, and Robert Worden for providing valuable comments while serving as members of my dissertation committee.

REFERENCES

Becker, H. (1960). Notes on the concept of commitment. *American Journal of Sociology, 66*, 32–42.

Bollen, K. (1989). *Structural equations with latent variables.* New York: John Wiley.

Brough, P. and Williams, J. (2007). Managing occupational stress in a high-risk industry. *Criminal Justice and Behavior, 34*, 555–567.

Cammann, C., Fichman, M., Jenkins, G., and Klesh, J. (1983). Assessing the attitudes and perceptions of organizational members. In S. Seashore, E. Lawler, P. Mirvis, and C. Cammann (Eds.), *Assessing organizational change: A guide to methods, measures, and practices* (pp. 71–138). New York: John Wiley.

Camp, S. (1994). Assessing the effects of organizational commitment and job satisfaction on turnover: An event history approach. *The Prison Journal, 74*, 279–305.

Camp, S. and Lambert, E. (2006). The influence of organizational incentives on absenteeism: Sick leave use among correctional workers. *Criminal Justice Policy Review, 17*, 144–172.

Cranny, C., Smith, P., and Stone, E. (1992). *Job satisfaction: How people feel about their jobs and how it affects their performance.* New York: Lexington Books.

Crews, R. and Bonham, G. (2007). Strategies for employee retention in corrections. *Corrections Compendium, 32*, 7–14.

Cronbach, L. (1951). Coefficient alpha and the internal structure of tests. *Psychometrika, 16*, 297–334.

Cullen, F., Latessa, E., Kopache, R., Lombardo, L., and Burton, V. (1993). Prison wardens' job satisfaction. *The Prison Journal, 73*, 141–161.

Culliver, C., Sigler, R., and McNeely, B. (1991) Examining prosocial organizational behavior among correctional officers. *International Journal of Comparative and Applied Criminal Justice, 15*, 277–284.

Davis, K. and Newstrom, J. (1985). *Human behavior at work.* New York: McGraw-Hill.

Draper, N., and Smith, H. 1966. *Applied regression analysis.* New York: John Wiley.

Fishbein, M. and Ajzen, I. (1975). *Belief, attitudes, intention, and behavior.* Reading, MA: Addison-Wesley.

Gronlund, N. (1981). *Measurement and evaluation in teaching.* New York: Macmillan.

Guion, R. (1992). Agenda for research and action. In C. Cranny, P. Smith, and E. Stone (Eds.), *Job satisfaction: How people feel about their jobs and how it affects their performance* (pp. 257–281). New York: Lexington Books.

Heffron, F. (1989). *Organizational theory and public organizations: The political connection.* Englewood Cliffs, NJ: Prentice Hall.

Hopkins, A. (1983). *Work and job satisfaction in the public sectors.* Totowa, NJ: Rowman and Allonheld.

Ivancevich, J. and Matteson, M. (1980). *Stress and work: A managerial perspective.* Glenview, IL: Scott Foresman and Company.

Jauch, L., Glueck, W., and Osborn, R. (1978). Organizational loyalty, professional commitment and academic research productivity. *Academy of Management Journal, 21*, 84–92.

Kanter, R. (1977). *Men and women of the corporation*. New York: Basic Books.
Kerce, E., Magnusson, P. and Rudolph, A. (1994). *The attitudes of Navy corrections staff members: What they think about confinees and their jobs*. San Diego: Navy Personnel Research and Development Center.
Lambert, E. (2004). The impact of job characteristics on correctional staff. *Prison Journal, 84*, 208–227.
Lambert, E., Edwards, C., Camp, S., and Saylor, W. (2005). Here today, gone tomorrow, back again the next day: Absenteeism and its antecedents among federal correctional staff. *Journal of Criminal Justice, 33*, 165–175.
Lambert, E. and Hogan, N. (2009). The importance of job satisfaction and organizational commitment in shaping turnover intent: A test of a causal model. *Criminal Justice Review*, 34, 96–118.
Lambert, E., Hogan, N., and Griffin, M. (2008). Being the good soldier: Organizational citizenship behavior and commitment among correctional staff. *Criminal Justice and Behavior*, 35, 56–68.
Lambert, E., Kelley, T., and Hogan, N. (2013). Hanging on too long: The relationship between different forms of organizational commitment and emotional exhaustion burnout among correctional staff. *American Journal of Criminal Justice, 38*, 51–66.
Lambert, E. and Paoline, E. (2008). The influence of demographic characteristics, job characteristics, and organizational structure on correctional staff job stress, job satisfaction, and organizational commitment. *Criminal Justice Review, 33*, 541–564.
Lambert, E. and Paoline, E. (2010). Take this job and shove it: Turnover intent among jail staff. *Journal of Criminal Justice, 38*, 139–148.
Lambert, E., Paoline, E., and Hogan, N. (2006). The impact of centralization and formalization on correctional staff job satisfaction and organizational commitment. *Criminal Justice Studies: A Critical Journal of Crime, Law, and Society, 19*, 23–44.
Lee, T. and Mowday, R. (1987). Voluntarily leaving an organization: An empirical investigation of Steers and Mowday's model of turnover. *Academy of Management Journal, 30(4)*, 721–743.
Lincoln, J. and Kalleberg, A. (1990). *Culture, control and commitment: A study of work organization and work attitudes in the United States and Japan*. Cambridge: Cambridge University Press.
Lind, E. and Tyler, T. (1988). *The social psychology of procedural justice*. New York: Plenum.
Locke, E. (1976). The nature and causes of job satisfaction. In M. Dunnell (Ed.), *Handbook of industrial and organizational psychology* (pp. 1297–1349). Chicago: Rand-McNally.
Matz, A., Wells, J., Minor, K., and Angel, E. (2013). Predictors of turnover intention among staff in juvenile correctional facilities: The relevance of job satisfaction and organizational commitment. *Youth Violence and Juvenile Justice, 11*, 115–131.

McElroy, J., Morrow, P., and Fenton, J. (1995). Absenteeism and performance as predictors of voluntary turnover. *Journal of Managerial Issues, 12*, 91–98.

Meyer, J. and Allen, N. (1984). Testing the side-bet theory of organizational commitment: Some methodological considerations. *Journal of Applied Psychology, 69*, 372–378.

Meyer, J., Stanley, D., Jackson, T., McInnis, K., Maltin, E., and Sheppard, L. (2012). Affective, normative, and continuance commitment levels across cultures: A meta-analysis. *Journal of Vocational Behavior, 80*, 225–245.

Minor, K., Wells, J., Angel, E., and Matz, A. (2011). Predictors of early job turnover among juvenile correctional facility staff. *Criminal Justice Review, 36*, 58–75.

Mowday, R., Porter, L., and Steers, R. (1982). *Employee-organization linkages: The psychology of commitment, absenteeism and turnover.* New York: Academic Press.

Mueller, C., Boyer, E., Price, J., and Iverson, R. (1994). Employee attachment and noncoercive conditions of work. *Work and Occupations, 21*, 179–212.

Price, J. and Mueller, C. (1986). *Professional turnover: The case of nurses.* New York: Spectrum.

Sager, J. (1994). A structural model depicting salespeople's job stress. *Journal of Academy of Marketing Science, 22*, 74–84.

Saylor, W. (1983). *Surveying prison environments.* Washington, DC: Federal Bureau of Prisons.

Spector, P. (1996). *Industrial and organizational psychology: Research and practice.* New York: John Wiley.

Steel, R. and Ovalle, N. (1984). A review and meta-analysis of research on the relationship between behavioral intentions and employee turnover. *Journal of Applied Psychology, 69*, 673–686.

Stohr, M., Self, R., and Lovrich, N. (1992). Staff turnover in new generation jails: An investigation of its causes and preventions. *Journal of Criminal Justice, 20*, 455–478.

Wright, T. (1993). Correctional employee turnover: A longitudinal study. *Journal of Criminal Justice, 21*, 131–142.

Wycoff, M. and Skogan, W. (1994). The effect of a community policing management style on officers' attitudes. *Crime and Delinquency, 40*, 371–383.

APPENDIX

ITEMS USED TO CREATE INDEXES USED IN CHAPTER 10

The following items are measured with the response categories of strongly disagree, disagree, somewhat disagree, undecided, somewhat agree, agree, and strongly agree. To form a summated index for those concepts with multiple items, the items were summed together and the resulting value was divided by the number of items.

ORGANIZATIONAL POWER

1. I have authority I need to accomplish my work objectives.
2. My supervisor engages me in the planning process, such as developing work methods and procedures for my job.
3. I have a great deal of say over what has to be done on my job.
4. My supervisor asks my opinion when a work-related problem arises.
5. The information I get through formal communication channels helps me perform my job effectively.
6. I am told promptly when there is a change in policy, rules, or regulations that affects me.
7. My supervisor gives me adequate information on how well I am performing.
8. I often receive feedback from my supervisor for good performance.
9. Information I receive about my performance usually comes too late for it to be any use to me (reverse coded).

PROMOTIONAL OPPORTUNITY

1. Under the present system, promotions are seldom related to employee performance (reverse coded).
2. There are job advancement opportunities in the BOP [Bureau of Prisons] for me.
3. There are job advancement opportunities in this facility for me.

ORGANIZATIONAL FAIRNESS

1. The standards used to evaluate my performance have been fair and objective.
2. My last annual performance rating presented a fair and accurate picture of my actual job performance.
3. My own hard work will lead to recognition as a good performer.
4. I will get a cash award or unscheduled pay increase if I perform especially well.

SUPERVISION

My supervisor demonstrates sensitivity to such personal needs as shift and leave requests by fairly balancing them with the needs of the facility.

JOB SATISFACTION

1. I would be more satisfied with some other job at this facility than I am with my present job (reverse coded).

2. My BOP [Bureau of Prisons] job is usually worthwhile.
3. My BOP job is usually interesting to me.
4. My BOP job suits me very well
5. If I have a chance, I will change to some other job at the same rate of pay at this facility (reverse coded).

ORGANIZATIONAL COMMITMENT

Agency level

1. The BOP is better than any of the other correctional agencies (e.g., state).
2. I have a good opinion of the BOP most of the time.
3. Most of the time the BOP [Bureau of Prisons] is run very well.
5. If I remain in corrections, I would prefer to remain with the BOP.

Institutional level

1. This facility is the best in the whole BOP.
2. I would rather be stationed at this facility than any other I know about.
3. I would like to continue to work at this facility.

TURNOVER INTENT

I am currently looking for or considering another job outside the BOP [Bureau of Prisons].

The following items are measured with the response categories of never, very rarely, rarely, now and then, often, very often, and all the time.

JOB STRESS

During the past six months, how often have you experienced . . .

1. A feeling that you have become harsh toward people since you took this job.
2. A feeling of worry that this job is hardening you emotionally.
3. A feeling of being emotionally drained at the end of the workday.
4. A feeling that you treat some inmates as if they were impersonal objects.
5. A feeling that working with people all day is really a strain for you.
6. A feeling of being fatigued when you get up in the morning and have to face another day on the job.

11

THE CONSTRUCTION OF MEANING DURING TRAINING FOR PROBATION AND PAROLE

John P. Crank

The present research is an assessment of three broad changes in the institutional environment of parole and probation and how a particular local organizational culture is responding to those changes. I argue that changes in the institutional environment of parole and probation are articulated in classes and topics selected for Peace Officer State Training (POST). These changes in turn are mediated through instructors who use linguistic devices called tropes—stories, ironies, and metaphors—to provide the cultural context for comprehending institutional changes. An assessment of tropes provides a schematic of the way in which local agency culture responds to institutional changes in terms of preexisting cultural meanings.

According to conventional wisdom on organizational reform in criminal justice, local agency culture will blunt efforts to institute meaningful change. Efforts for change have had only a limited impact on the day-to-day activities of criminal justice practitioners, as has been cited widely (Fogelson 1977; Guyot 1986; Kerner Commission 1967).[1] Among courtroom actors, the resistance of courtroom work groups to change has been described in terms of the influence of local legal culture (Church 1982). Among the police, occupational resistance to change has been characterized in terms of organizational culture and described in terms of police insularity, the blue curtain, and the code of secrecy (Manning 1970; Pollock-Byrne 1988; Stoddard 1968; Westley

1956). In the field of corrections, the guard subculture, sometimes with the support of charismatic administrators, has been associated with widespread resistance to the expansion of prisoner rehabilitation programs (Jacobs 1977) and with the use of violence to maintain social control (Marquart and Crouch 1984, 1990).

This literature has frequently described resistance to organizational change in terms of individual or group self-interest—the idea that the agent of resistance to change lies in purposeful individual or group behavior. From this perspective, advocates seeking reform through organizational change have failed because changes are perceived to be inconsistent with the self-interest of members of the particular organizational culture or subculture. For example, a factor in the failure of team policing reforms in the 1970s has been described as the resistance of mid-management personnel who feared losing their jobs in the wake of command decentralization (Skolnick and Bayley 1986; Walker 1992). Similarly, resistance to change from local legal cultures has been attributed to courtroom actors' vested interest in maintaining established relations (Walker 1985).

While acknowledging the powerful influence of self-interest as a source of resistance to change (DiMaggio and Powell 1991), I argue here that change efforts may encounter local customs regarding how action should be organized—in particular, organizational cultures (Jepperson 1991). Organization members' response to change may not be resistance for reasons of self-interest, but assimilation of that which is new into customary ways of doing and thinking about things (Meyer and Rowan 1977). In other words, how an organizational culture responds to change will depend on the meanings and values carried by its members. This point suggests that the study of the impact of change on organizational culture requires three steps: first, the identification of the changes bearing on the organization; second, an assessment of the values and meanings embedded in a particular organizational culture; and third, an analysis of how those changes are perceived in terms of prevailing patterns of cultural meaning. In this paper I perform these three steps in order to understand how a particular parole and probation organization is affected by contemporary changes in parole and probation.

POST TRAINING AND THE DIFFUSION OF INSTITUTIONAL KNOWLEDGE

Three broad areas of change affect the field of parole and probation today: the shift toward crime control and surveillance, accountability to the rule of law, and the rationalization of the work environment (Feeley and Simon 1992; Fogel 1984; Simon 1993). I argue here that these are institutional-level changes; consequently, a brief review of the institutional theory of organizations is appropriate.

Institutional influences on the behavior and activity of criminal justice organizations are being increasingly recognized (Crank and Langworthy 1992; Hagan 1989). This literature has described the relationship between institutions and organizations in terms of institutional diffusion processes, where normative and cognitive elements are transmitted across an institutional sector to particular organizations (Scott 1994). Such processes are particularly influential in highly institutionalized environments, where organizational structures and behaviors are focused outward in order to acquire legitimacy from the institutional environment (Schur 1980), rather than inward to satisfy technical criteria of efficiency or effectiveness (Meyer and Rowan 1977). This is particularly evident in public-sector organizations whose outputs are ambiguous and whose efficiency or effectiveness cannot be assessed directly (Meyer and Scott 1983). Organizations, desiring to maintain legitimacy and thus to sustain or augment their resources, seek to conform to the expectations of powerful institutional actors (Meyer and Scott 1983), and thus are highly sensitive to institutional pressures (DiMaggio and Powell 1983).

Formal training programs are one way in which institutional knowledge is transmitted among modern organizations—in particular, institutions (Scott and Meyer 1994). As forces for the transmission of institutional knowledge, training programs have been studied in the private sector (Levitt and March 1988; Monahan, Meyer, and Scott 1994). Research in the public sector has focused on criminal justice organizations and has looked primarily at informal and apprenticeship aspects of training (Van Maanen 1979; Van Maanen and Schein 1979). This literature has recognized latent functions of POST for particular organizational cultures, for example, how stress training at POST academies teaches officers that they have only fellow officers to rely on (Van Maanen 1979). The role of POST training as a transmitter of institutional knowledge has not been recognized in this literature; in the current paper, I respond to this shortcoming.

Over the past sixty years, POST training has evolved as a carrier of formal training across the institutional environment of criminal justice. As an institutional form, POST legitimates individuals as "sworn" officers: it prepares recruits who will occupy positions in corrections, parole and probation, and policing for duties associated with the status of professional peace officer with the license to carry a weapon.

POST training emerged relatively recently as an institutional form for the transmission of training and education. In the1920s and 1930s, August Vollmer and two of his protégés, William Wiltberger and O.W. Wilson, emerged as advocates of educational reform in California and in Wichita, Kansas; all three made use of facilities available at institutions of higher education for providing peace officer training (Morn 1984). In 1959, California founded a commission on POST training to establish minimum standards for hiring and training peace officers. By 1969, there were forty-five police academies in California—seventeen of these were housed in colleges, and fourteen others were affiliated with colleges.

POST in Nevada

POST in Nevada, the research setting of this paper, emerged in the spirit of peace officer reform that marked the national agenda in the late 1960s. The Nevada Peace Officer and Standards Training Division was created in 1967, and was placed within the Nevada Department of Public Safety. The reform purpose of the POST commission, as described by the enabling legislation, was to provide for and encourage training and education of peace officers, to improve law enforcement, and to develop methods for preventing and reducing crime and for detecting and apprehending criminals. POST training was expanded to the Nevada Department of Probation and Parole in 1991 in both Category I (basic) and Category II (agency-specific).

Areas of Institutional Change

POST, a means for transmitting knowledge across the institutional environment of parole and probation, also transmits changes that occur within that environment. That is, changes in values, practices, and beliefs will be reflected in the selection and content of topics and classes provided by the POST curriculum (Meyer and Rowan 1977). In the current era, these changes can be organized into three categories, discussed later: those that emphasize the role of surveillance and crime fighting, those that involve officers' accountability to the rule of law, and those that emphasize the rationalization of administrative process.[2]

The first area of institutional change is the reconstruction of the work of parole and probation officers around ideas of law enforcement and surveillance. With the decline of the rehabilitative ideal in the 1980s, probation has shifted its emphasis from traditional ideas of offender counseling to a public-safety enterprise oriented around ideas of surveillance and enforcement (Fogel 1984; Rothman 1980). This shift occurred simultaneously with the federal government's divestment of funding for community-based rehabilitation for offenders during the Reagan era (Duffee 1990). At the same time, a deinstitutionalization process has increased the population of probationers and parolees. Legislators have responded by trying to make parole and probation look "tough" (Gordon 1991). The continuing intensification of peace officers' law enforcement role has been noted in current research on community corrections (Feeley and Simon 1992; Petersilia 1989).

Many elements of the curriculum and topics of POST training reveal the emphasis of parole and probation on enforcement and surveillance. Peace officer skills, an area that includes topics such as range safety, firearms handling, and handcuffing, is the single largest block, accounting for 66 of the 240 hours of instruction. Topics such as survival skills, aimed at preparing recruits mentally for work in a hazardous environment, promote a perception of parole and probation as dangerous work dealing with lawbreakers. To illustrate the extent to which parole and probation focus on crime control, the instructors of defensive tactics, two parole and probation officers, also teach defensive tactics to the city-county police department.

The second area of institutional change is peace officers' accountability to the rule of law. Though parole and probation historically have been perceived as correctional functions, accountability concerns are increasingly comparable to those confronted by police rather than those addressed by correctional agents, whose authority is limited by the confines of a correctional institution. The traditional tasks of reintegrating offenders are being delegated to community organizations, while officers focus on control (Harris, Clear, and Baird 1989). Consequently, issues of accountability increasingly parallel those of municipal police officers.

Accountability is a topic of sustained interest in POST training, as indicated by the large numbers of classes on aspects of that subject. In this context, accountability aims to upgrade individual officers. Many of the POST courses, which focus on procedures regarding arrest and detention, paperwork preparation and timeliness, and community relations, instruct recruits in the nature and limits of their authority. Other courses related to accountability include Professional Ethics, Legal Liability, Undercover Activity, and Search and Seizure. The class titled Strategies of Case Supervision, for example, includes the topic of legal and illegal officer behavior in a practicum. The Bill of Rights is disseminated to students and discussed. In short, accountability to the rule of law is a topic of continual discussion in POST classes.

The third area of change is the rationalization of the administrative process in parole and probation work (Feeley and Simon 1992).

This rationalization also has been noted in criminal justice institutions, including police (Crank and Langworthy 1992) and the courts (Hydebrand and Seron 1990). Feeley and Simon (1992), discussing the "new penology," distinguish this process from the rightward shift in penal thinking that characterized the 1980s. The new penology, they suggest, is marked by the development of bureaucratic strategies that focus on the management of risk groups and dangerous populations (Cohen 1985). Community-based sanctions become risk-management strategies whose purpose is to maintain control and surveillance over offenders (Feeley and Simon 1992: 461, 450). System goals have shifted from the reintegration of offenders to the efficient control of internal system processes—for example, the use of urine testing to determine whether offenders are using drugs.

Preparation for rationalizing the work process is presented in diverse ways. One area of rationalization is the elaboration of record-keeping systems (Van Maanen and Bentlind 1994). Classes on topics such as urinalysis process, substance abuse, and police communications prepare recruits for record keeping through discussions of internal management systems and strategies. Competency in administrative process is also emphasized, and classes such as report writing and dictation prepare recruits for their roles as participants in a large bureaucracy. In all classes, students are exposed to the quantity of paperwork for which they will be responsible. The ability to correctly fill out and answer forms is a corollary to every aspect of the work they are learning to do as sworn officers in the department of parole and probation.

OCCUPATIONAL CULTURE, COMMON SENSE, AND TROPIC KNOWLEDGE

Information transmitted by POST across the institutional environment of parole and probation is not accepted unconditionally, but is subjected to evaluation by local organizational cultures. In this process of evaluation, institutional information is weighed against standards of "common sense."

Common sense is the lifeblood of occupational culture. Occupational cultures embody "accepted practices, rules, and principles of conduct that are situationally applied" (Manning 1989: 360). These practices and rules are recipes for behavior, and are codified loosely into organizing themes that participants perceive as common sense. The use of commonsense judgments in assessing justice has been noted at all stages of the criminal justice process (Walker 1985).

Commonsense worldviews are systems of taken-for-granted knowledge steeped in organizational culture (Manning 1989). Among criminal justice organizations, the commonsense worldview of the police has received considerable attention from researchers (Crank, Payne, and Jackson 1993; Ericson 1982). This worldview is described by what members take for granted, as well as by generalized rationales and beliefs (Manning 1970). Policing is perceived by its members as a craft, in which "learning comes exclusively through experience intuitively processed by individual officers" (Bayley and Bittner 1989: 87). Police behavior becomes the visible embodiment of commonsense knowledge (McNulty 1994). Thus, common sense is more than a simple set of unspoken propositions about the occupational environment; it provides a tool kit of cultural repertoires, including verbal and nonverbal behavioral skills (Swidler 1986).

The presence of commonsense knowledge is indicated by the use of linguistic devices called tropes (Shearing and Ericson 1991). A trope is essentially something described in terms of something else. In occupational cultures, this something else is often a story, an irony, a metaphor, or some combination of these constituted from everyday experience. The accumulation of tropes makes each organizational culture unique, depending on its work circumstances and its members' collective experiences.

Tropes are processes of "analogous reasoning" or "cultural repertoires" that "allow action to be both orderly and improvisational" (Shearing and Ericson 1991: 482). They provide culturally acceptable ways for organizing knowledge under commonsense ideas. The craft of policing, for example, can be characterized as an extensive repertoire of tropes that enable officers to move easily from one ambiguous situation to the next, practicing their craft according to commonly held ideas, embodied in a story-based vocabulary, of what policing is (McNulty 1994).

Four types of tropes are frequently cited (Eco 1984). Metaphor, defined as a "way of seeing something as if it were something else" (Manning 1979: 661), has been called the master trope in that other types of tropes are special types of metaphors. Stories are metaphors in that they explain something in terms of personal, concrete experience, although the stories themselves may be constructed of strings of tropes. The other tropes are special cases of metaphors. Synecdoche refers to seeing a part for the whole. Burke (1969) defined synecdoche as representation—that is, the presentation of one thing to represent another.[3,4] Metonymy takes a whole and reduces it to its constituent parts (Turner 1974).[5] Ironies convey meaning through their opposites.[6]

Tropes are often carried by stories about what peace officers do. Story telling among peace officers to depict their work is recognized widely (Harris 1973; Van Maanen 1979). That these stories might be the object of research, however, has been noted only recently (McNulty 1994; Shearing and Ericson 1991). Stories are not merely glosses that arise from peace officers' inability to articulate why they do what they do; rather, they represent a "narration that is the quintessential form of customary knowledge" (Shearing and Ericson 1991: 488–89). Put another way, stories provide a vocabulary of precedents that construct an appropriate cultural, or intersubjective, way of seeing the world (Mills 1940). A member of an organizational culture learns not how to act, but "rather the sensibility out of which she or he ought to act" (Shearing and Ericson 1991: 493). McNulty (1994) describes an interactive training scenario in which police recruits are taught the "problematic quality of the truth" (Ericson 1982: 62).

Because stories use the intersubjective world of occupational activity as their referent, culture is transmitted as knowledge about the natural order of things (McNulty 1994). Thus, recruits, when taught the lore of police work, simultaneously receive a vocabulary of police culture whenever tropes are used to convey information. When training occurs in a classroom provided for POST academies, the use of stories imparts a lexicon of organizational culture masquerading as commonsense knowledge.

POST instructors, by virtue of their occupational position, span the boundaries between the institutional environment and the local organizational culture. As members of the organizational culture, they participate in its commonsense language. Their natural language for organizing action is metaphoric and story based (McNulty 1994). These individuals are also responsible for providing rational instruction as it is embodied in the content of the curriculum and the topics selected for POST training.[7] Thus, they are ideological boundary spanners: as instructors, they are expected to provide the rational discourse of institutional change, while as members of the local organization, they participate in a culturally created commonsense worldview communicated by tropes.

Boundaries between areas of institutional change and local organizational culture emerge when instructors are asked a question or when they feel compelled to explain something during a class. Explanations based on the instructors' lore will be drawn from their commonsense worldview, and consequently will be expressed as a trope. These explanations thus convey organizational or cultural perspective presented as commonsense knowledge (Shearing and Ericson 1991). In this way, instructors convey cultural tools that enable trainees to organize the knowledge presented in POST training (Kappeler, Sluder, and Alpert 1994).[8] Because these tools are conveyed in regard to particular topics, trainees learn, to use Shearing and Ericson's (1991) phrase, "the sensibility out of which" to think about whatever material is being taught. When topics involve changes in the institutional environment of parole and probation, recruits are taught how to think about those changes.

This tool kit—the stories and tropes used by instructors to convey local culture—is the object of the present analysis. Because tropes emerge frequently in discussions involving institutional change, an assessment of tropes helps us to consider how local organizational culture responds to those changes.

RESEARCH DESIGN

In the summer of 1992 I conducted research as a nonparticipant observer of a POST training session offered by the Nevada Department of Probation and Parole.[9] The session lasted six weeks, from June 15 to July 27. The academy employed thirty-five POST-certified instructors during this period; all but three were members of the Department of Probation and Parole.[10] All instructors were sworn peace officers and were employed by the Department of Probation and Parole.

The integration of training into organizational structure, process, and culture was indicated by the organization of the regional Department of Probation and Parole. This department consisted of five units. Three units supervised offenders; one provided court services. The fifth, the POST training unit, was housed in the same building complex as the three supervisory units. The unit manager and both supervisors of operations carried offender caseloads, as did the district trainer, the rangemaster, and the program coordinator. These individuals also were instructors in the POST academy. The other instructors also typically carried caseloads. Consequently, the instructors' values and beliefs complemented the occupational perspectives of the members of the organization, among both administrators and line officers.

During the session, I gathered data primarily from classroom observation and conducted follow-up interviews with training staff members and students. POST instructors were informed of my presence before class. I took the role of a nonparticipant observer to minimize the impact of my presence on the conduct of the class. With the passage of time, however, I was increasingly accepted as a member of the group, and occasionally was invited to participate in class activities. In this way, my nonparticipant status was breached on several occasions. This breaching probably aided in the collection of valid data: at the outset, I suspected that information was filtered in that students and instructors, distrustful of academic outsiders, were guarding their conversations and discussions. With the relaxing of the nonparticipant barrier, however, I sensed that instructors, particularly those who appeared before the class on multiple occasions, were more "open," that is, likely to lecture, speak, or reveal their sentiments as they would if I were not present.

The shift from nonparticipant to quasi-participant status raised the possibility of another threat to validity: that of "going native," whereby loyalties to the studied group bias the observer's value-neutrality. I became more sympathetic toward members of this group during the research process. The extent to which this affected my findings is an incalculable source of potential bias.[11]

This research focused on the extent to which the tropes used by instructors could be organized into cultural themes (Spradley 1980). Tropes were said to reveal such themes; in contrast, the thematic content of "war stories" could be organized systematically to form a pattern of meaning. Analytically, when different stories and tropes appeared to convey a recurring idea, I considered this to be a cultural theme rather than a simple war story. This process is inherently interpretive (Spradley 1979). Focus on thematic replication is a conservative approach to identifying the cultural character of an organization in that it might overlook the contribution of a particular story as an element of cultural meaning.

Cultural themes in turn were organized into domains. Domains represent broad areas of meaning to the organizational culture and are derived directly from the pattern of meanings that emerge from the various themes. The domains that emerged in the POST training session were crime fighting, the morality of personal responsibility, and bureaucracy. Particular themes within and across domains provided the cultural sensibility from which recruits were taught to consider areas of institutional change.

These domains were pertinent to contemporary changes in parole and probation. Representing the most inclusive meaning of the themes presented by instructors, they provided the local cultural interpretation of the three broad changes in parole and probation discussed previously. Consequently, an analysis of the tropes making up the three domains helped to clarify that local organizational culture was responding to contemporary changes in the institutional environment of parole and probation.

FINDINGS

Findings are presented here by domain. Tropes in each domain are presented next as vignettes and are organized into themes of cultural meaning.

Crime Fighting

The first domain, crime fighting, was marked by tropes that emphasized the role of the parole and probation agent as a crime fighter. Instructors' crime-fighting stories dominated the tropic landscape. The tropes were organized into two themes.

The first theme cast probationers or parolees as lawbreakers or, in the metaphorical parlance of probation and parole officers, "the bad guys," and emphasized the need to control their behavior and surveil their activities. Tropes with this theme underscored the importance of labeling probationers or parolees as offenders and as persons probably engaged in continuous wrongdoing. The following synecdoche, in which the appropriate term *parolee* or *probationer* was replaced by the figurative term *offender*, was stated several times in academy classes:

> "Keep in mind: we do not service clients. We supervise offenders."

This dictum carried the weight of administrative authority:

> The district administrator is very adamant about that.
> They are offenders, not clients.

The following trope, from a class on home visits, emphasized the idea that offenders were engaged in continuous wrongdoing:

> A fella just got out of jail, and I gave him one of my cards. The next day Metro called, and asked me about my cards. They had found a card at the scene of a burglary. I asked them to read it to me, and they did, and it was this guy. We went to his place, and the police checked for the stolen items. When he came home we arrested him. He was out only one day.

The labeling process was reinforced with interrogative interviewing strategies. The following example and associated trope refer to "wedging the alibi with a minor admission" to uncover wrongdoing during interviews.

> Most offenders will not admit all at one time. They will admit by hints and pieces at a time. Any time you can get the offender to admit a little bit of it, you've opened the door.

An instructor told a long story of an individual who would not admit to a crime. The agent, however, by gaining admission of small units, one at a time, was able to obtain evidence that this individual had committed the crime. In the same class, this was another principle of interviewing:

> They forget to cover up their closest associations. You can get a lot of information from loved ones.

This statement was followed by a story about an offender who had thoroughly alibied his offense but had failed to provide the alibi to his sister. These tropes characterized an ordinary component of probation and parole activity—interviewing the probationer or parolee in terms of strategies that, when followed correctly, would uncover law-breaking. The tropes revealed the extent to which interviewing has shifted from rehabilitative counseling to interrogation aimed at uncovering wrongdoing (Cohen 1985).

The second theme concerns tropes that describe the potential danger of routine activities. These were the most common of the crime-fighting tropes. In a class on lethal force, the following advice emphasized the potential for danger in a home visit:

> If someone says "I can kill you six ways before you hit the ground," well, maybe they can. Get an extra one or three people before you go in. Most of the time they are bluffing, but don't take any chances.

This theme was echoed in a class on operations. Students were provided with a vocabulary list of terms used by the agency. Two of these terms were tropes that, according to the instructor, provided direction for home visits. The first was "JDLR," defined as "Just don't look right. Refer to GTHO, p. 5." The definition of GTHO was "Get the hell out." These two tropes were ironies by which a keen observer transformed apparently safe circumstances into perilous ones.

The following story, from a class on the return of violators, emphasized the dangerousness of offenders and the need to search carefully, however repugnant the process might be. The instructor was discussing body searches and was referring to the area around the groin:

> This is the place where people hide all kinds of stuff. There was a case in California where a guy was up for parole. He went before the board, and they turned him down. He bent over and pulled a stabbing tool out of his anal cavity. He jumped over the desk and stabbed a parole board member that he didn't like in the shoulder a couple of times.

Tropes can be chillingly persuasive. The following tropes were taken from a class on officer survival. The class opened with a two-minute film in which an officer was talking against the backdrop of a city street (a visual metaphor of the street as a place where the work takes place). This example illustrates the metaphorical richness of tropes that can imbue even a brief statement with meaning. In this instance, tropes (in bold type in the following quote) emphasized the crime-control aspect of the work:

> I'm not going to let any **son-of-a-bitch** (depraved animal: metaphor for violator) get me **out there** (the street: metaphor for work). No **animal** (animal: metaphor for client) **out there** (the street: metaphor for work) is going to **beat me** (physical confrontation: metaphor for doing one's job). You'll have to **cut my head off** (cutting one's head off: metaphor for keeping from doing one's job) to **stop me** (stop me: metaphor of physical resistance obstructing someone's work).

The instructor presented this statement as an example of a healthy attitude that would enable a recruit to survive in a hostile environment. It was followed by a heuristic trope, a film story of unpredictability and danger during a routine activity. The film was taken by a videocam mounted on an officer's car. The officer was engaged in a routine traffic stop of a car when he was suddenly and violently assaulted by the occupants. The footage showed the officer being beaten and murdered at the side of a dark road. In the last few minutes of the film, the officer was shown lying dead on the pavement behind the patrol car, enveloped in the somber Texas night. This story served as a powerful irony; it transformed a traffic stop into an activity with peril, in which the greatest peril was to take things as they appeared to be.

The theme of unpredictability as a basis for story telling has been noted by other scholars (Harris 1973; Van Maanen 1979). The following story, from a class on probable cause, uses the irony of difficulty in gaining entry to convey unpredictability:

> A door can *hurt* you. I've got a big foot (points at his foot). We were over at a fellow's place, and we could see him on the bed. I kicked the door, and that door it kicked back. I kicked that door nine times. When it finally broke open, there was a great big piece of the door around the deadlock still stuck to the wall. When I pulled it out, there was a deadbolt that long (gestures about nine inches) in concrete reinforced wall. It was specially reinforced.

The Morality of Personal Responsibility

Many tropes identified a precept of personal responsibility for both offenders and officers: responsibility for one's own actions morally imbued probation and parole work at all levels. Whether such responsibility involved the behavior of a probation and parole officer in the courtroom or when making house calls, or whether it involved an offender's ability to maintain personal cleanliness or conform to terms of probation or parole, these tropes emphasized the morality of responsibility for one's own behavior.

Among officers, personal responsibility involved personal demeanor, emotions, and case preparation. In a class on courtroom procedure, accountability for probation and parole officers was linked to their demeanor and case preparation, as indicated by the following tropes:

> Don't read a paper. I was in reviewing a case, leafing through the pages, and the judge stopped, pointed at me, pointed to the bailiff, and the bailiff made a big circle around the courtroom, a big show, and came up to me and said "Please don't rustle your paper." If a judge asks you a question, and you don't know the answer, he'll ask "Who knows?" He'll call for a new date for the hearing, and instruct you to bring in everyone who has that information.

In these examples, responsibility was an immediate, concrete issue of demeanor and preparation. Responsibility, however, also involved the control of emotions. The following story, stated in a class on lethal force, provided local cultural perspective on personal emotions:

> A PR24 (baton) is a deadly weapon. A few years ago an LASD officer saw a fellow he knew standing on a corner, a guy he knew was a burglar. He told him to leave. He drove around the block, and when he came back the guy was still there. He executed a power takeout with a PR24 and hit the guy across the skull, and literally knocked his brains out the side of his head. So be careful. You may be tempted to strike someone, but you'll end up in the trick bag.

The message here was to avoid being overcome by anger; this was viewed as a loss of emotional integrity.

The extent to which moral responsibility was perceived as an issue of personal integrity was underscored in a class titled "Hazardous Attitudes." Such attitudes were detrimental to the use of common sense. The five hazardous attitudes—anti-authority, impulsiveness, macho, apathy, and invulnerability—were presented ironically as exemplars of the absence of common sense.

After the instructor's opening presentation, the class divided into five groups, each charged with acting out one of the hazardous attitudes. These skits were heuristic dramas on the ironies. Thus, recruits were taught to think tropically by constructing and enacting tragic dramas that demonstrated how a hazardous attitude could conflict with the application of common sense to daily work. Inevitably, each drama ended in mock tragedy, affirming the trainees' understandings of local cultural values. The instructor's concluding trope, "Don't drive faster than your guardian angel can fly," conveyed the sentiment that agents should not let their emotions get the best of them.

Among offenders, personal responsibility was presented thematically in terms of "taking responsibility for [the offender's] life." The director of the training unit emphasized this theme in cited discussions with offenders. She stated the following trope many times:

> I had an offender accuse me of building a case against him. "Are you building the case?" No sir. I told him he was building his own case. Am I writing it down? You betcha!

This theme was echoed in the following statement that made use of a correctional metaphor: doing time for someone else.

You've got to avoid doing time for them. They'll have a million excuses. They have to be responsible for themselves.

The morality of offenders' responsibility justified retribution.

An instructor in a class on probable cause defined the probable cause standard for probation and parole: a crime has been committed, or is about to be committed, or a condition of probation or parole has been violated. The instructor then stated:

> Suppose you have a guy that is usually clean, starts dressing dirtier, makes payments late, but doesn't show drugs in his urine. Is this basis for a search? Yes. Behavioral change. This is probable cause.

In this hypothetical story, behavioral changes indicating untidiness in demeanor, even in the absence of legal or technical violations, become grounds for reinvoking the intervention of the criminal justice system.

Bureaucracy

Many classes dealt with issues salient to participants in bureaucracies, and tropes frequently were bureaucratic in reference. These tropes were organized into two themes. First, they provided guidance for organizing action in terms of local values on topics made complex by a proliferation of legal or organizational structure. Second, they allowed recruits to consider ways to offset some of the more dehumanizing aspects of the crescive rationality of the organizational and legal bureaucracy.

The following metaphorical trope I obtained in a class on case supervision that presents the offender as a construction of the record-keeping system:

> Until Central receives the Initial Risk and Needs Assessment form, the person does not *live*. They do not *die* until Central gets the Termination Data form. The computer says this person lives and dies, and no logic prevails.

In regard to the first theme, several tropes acted as cultural guideposts for action to simplify bureaucratic complexity in order to act more directly and sometimes more retributively against offenders. Drug use is one such topic for which these tropes come into play. This offense classification is highly rationalized by the state legal code. Drugs are categorized by type in five schedules; each contains several different drugs. For example, Schedule 2 includes amphetamines, methaqualone, morphine, thebaine, and hydrocodone. Moreover, three quantities differentiate the charges of trafficking; each charge carries different recommended sentences and fines. Each offense in turn is compounded by previous offenses. From this mass of legal complexity emerged cultural bases for organizing retributive action for drug violators:

> I had a woman, I work over at Gersham Park, that just wouldn't quit (using drugs). I just couldn't get her to quit. So we went in, took her kid away. Stopped her welfare, told her she couldn't get her kid back until she cleaned up her act. She was in a program in three days.

Another way to organize retribution was provided in a class on filing new charges. This example also reveals how local organizational culture was presented as commonsense knowledge. Here a trainee was told to use common sense and then was provided with a cultural recipe to organize commonsense action:

> Basically, the rule of thumb is that if you have a lot of stuff on them, go ahead. Just use common sense. We had a bad guy that was causing a lot of trouble. He was picked up, searched, and a small piece of a roach was found. They found him guilty of a gross misdemeanor, and he pled it way down to introducing a controlled substance into interstate commerce. That's the lowest of the low. They'll use that when they really want to get someone.

The following story reveals how organizational culture was masked as organizational process by adding new charges for drug violators:

> Instructor: We rarely do these (file new charges). I did three over the past year, and that's a lot. For example, you might have a pregnant mother using drugs. Trainee: Is that a case where we don't do this? Instructor: No, that's the kind of case where we usually make an arrest.

These tropes revealed how violators, particularly individuals who use drugs, were legally chastised. In these stories, tropic language simplified organizational complexity with rule-of-thumb guides for delivering sanctions to drug-using offenders.

This simplification of procedure occurred around important local values—for example, assisting one's partner. I witnessed this in a class on radio communications. Communications have become highly rationalized, and agents are expected to learn a complex array of procedures to communicate by radio. Recruits were introduced to the five types of radios used in the district, details of radio panels, basic radio functions, and the 400 code; officers were advised to memorize this code. Heuristic dramas introduced officers to the complexities of the communications system and emphasized Code 444—assisting another officer.

Dramas were scripted from known events involving officers in the department. The first drama was about a traffic accident that changed to a Code 444 when an officer received gunfire and an armed suspect was chased on foot. The second concerned an aborted holdup that changed into a siege situation when the offender escaped to the roof of a building and shot a medical officer. Both of these skits were about officers in trouble. Through the administrative and technical complexity of police communications emerged one fundamental cultural precept: always respond to officers' calls for assistance.

The second theme was that of balancing bureaucratic excess against offenders' particular needs. The first trope reveals sympathy for individuals whose circumstances make it difficult to deal with conditions of probation or parole:

> We have a bad situation in our country. A lot of times it is impossible to find work for an unemployed mother. There's no way minimum wage can provide the support [she can get] from unemployment and ADC. However, a condition of parole is employment. You may have to talk to your supervisor. A low-skill offender with three children, her children will literally starve if she has to take a minimum-wage job. They can't afford child care. You can

> write it up so that they have to work, but you can write it up so that they can take care of their children at home.

The theme of balancing bureaucracy against offenders' needs was revealed particularly by the "success story" tropes, which described how offenders had overcome particular problems in dealing with the bureaucratic apparatus of the criminal justice system. The following story was told in a class on offender services:

> There is essentially no public transportation in the city. When classes are over, people may be dumped at the terminal and be stuck. There is no bus service when classes are over at 9:15. Also, transportation is a significant problem for many of them. One woman started catching buses at 3 to be at class at 7. One kid took a skateboard every morning to get from Henderson to the Bonanza office. He always managed to get there on time.

Another story was told in a class on case supervision:

> The judge ordered a high school completion (a needs form) for a woman with an IQ of 70. What I did was put my woman into Rancho High School classes. She wrote a book report she was exceptionally proud of. I sent a report to the judge telling him what she had accomplished. The judge liked it.

These tropes suggest that probationers or parolees who have displayed the ability to overcome personal hardships become "success stories," a valued commodity in the story-telling language of the organizational culture.

DISCUSSION

Domains are a cognitive map of the organization of common sense in the local culture. Because common sense is produced in POST training, these domains become a cultural interface with the institutional environment and, by implication, with areas of institutional change. Here I discuss domains in the light of contemporary changes in the institutional environment of parole and probations.

The first domain, crime fighting, revealed local accommodation to surveillance and crime-control trends in contemporary probation and parole (Duffee 1990; Gordon 1991; Simon 1993). Themes of tropes in the crime-fighting domain—labeling the probationer or parolee as an offender, and the danger and unpredictability of routine activities—suggested that the role of crime fighter was integrated fully into the organizational culture. The commonsense worldview, with its emphasis on crime fighting, danger, and unpredictability, is similar to the worldview of occupational activity frequently attributed to police officers (Manning 1970; McNulty 1994).

Tropes favorable to crime control appear to be matched by a corresponding devaluation of rehabilitative concerns. Probationers and parolees were labeled offenders rather than clients, a label from which there was no escape as long as an offender remained under the department's administrative authority, yet if formal terms of probation or parole and informal norms of personal responsibility were honored, offenders were not subjected to further status degradation. The awkward accommodation between the supportive nature of rehabilitation and the adversarial nature of surveillance was revealed in an incident related by the director of the training unit. A prisoner said, "You don't trust us, do you?" She responded, "You're right, I don't trust you, but I care."

The second domain, the morality of personal responsibility, is particularly relevant to officers' accountability to the rule of law. Accountability issues are more complex for probation and parole officers than for other sworn officers in criminal justice. Probation and parole officers have broader search and arrest authority than do police officers. Although probation and parole officers are subject to the same due-process constraints as police officers regarding revocation of probation or parole, the due-process standard for the former is more lenient. Evidence seized in violation of the Fourth Amendment, for example, cannot be entered into evidence for any new crime, but it can be used as a basis for revocation of probation or parole. Searches of a probationer's residence do not require probable cause. Also, violation of contractual terms of probation or parole is a basis for the rearrest of offenders for existing charges, but it has no legal bearing on new charges. These examples reveal that issues of accountability vary according to the legal situation encountered by the officer.

Throughout the six-week period, not a single trope disdained due-process concerns. Tropes suggested that these issues were interpreted in terms of preexisting cultural meanings—specifically, the morality of individual responsibility. These criteria were behavioral: how an individual dresses, courtroom demeanor, and the following of technical procedures for arrest. Thus, contrary to the often-cited resistance of policing cultures to accountability, probation and parole instructors provided tropes favoring such accountability. The officer's personal integrity and, by application, the integrity of the organization were of utmost importance.

The third domain, bureaucracy, revealed how the local organizational culture accommodated the contemporary process of rationalizing the administrative environment of parole and probation (Feeley and Simon 1992). Rationalization was revealed in the elaboration of record-keeping systems. The increasing emphasis on surveillance facilitates the rationalization and centralization of the record-keeping and information-collecting systems used by criminal justice agencies; officers were taught detailed procedures when dealing with interstate compacts, for returning violators, and in court services. As one student noted, "P and P stands for paperwork and more paperwork."

Tropes emerged to facilitate problem solving in bureaucratically complex areas. I noted simplifying strategies in the sanctioning of offenders in areas that were organizationally or legally complex, and also in limited efforts to counter the bureaucratic rigor of particularly stringent probation contracts or parole conditions. In institutional terms, tropes instructed how officers could "loosely couple" their behavior to areas of administrative or legal complexity by using local cultural recipes for action.

CONCLUSIONS

> One must pick one's root metaphors carefully.
>
> (Turner 1974: 25)

A POST training class, viewed through the lens of culture, is a practical theory of action grounded in the experiential world, steeped in rational knowledge, and based on powerful metaphorical imagery. Its metaphors are consequential. The previous quote by Turner (1974), with its suggestion that foundational metaphors may have far-reaching implications, is accepted here as an invitation to illuminate some of those implications.

First, the "crime fighting" metaphor has sweeping implications for the organization and activity of parole and probation. That crime fighting is accomplished by individual officers with superior skills was made evident in tropes that labeled probationers or parolees as offenders, and in the use of investigative skills to uncover possible wrongdoing. This metaphorical imagery is similar to Manning's (1979) description of the master detective as the organizing principle for much of police work, in which the ability to ferret out and control offenders' crime stems from the skill of the individual peace officer. Tropes also scripted surveillance and enforcement with stories of the danger and unpredictability of enforcement activity. In a national climate of intense crime control activity and in the face of cultural expectations of controlling crime among offenders, temptations to circumvent due process may become strong, particularly in view of the already relaxed due process protections for probation and parole officers. Organizational pressures to make arrests have strongly influenced the corruption of undercover police officers (Manning and Redlinger 1978). Probation and parole officers, facing increased pressures to convert to a crime-control mode, may find it difficult to avoid similar problems with due process, particularly in view of their expanded enforcement authority.

Second, personal responsibility infuses cultural morality; this finding supports Simon's (1993) important work on the history of parole. Simon (1993: 105) conceptualizes parole officers' perceptions of their work in terms of controlling "poor discipline." Parole provides an ideological corrective; it seeks to ensure that offenders are returned to a condition of social normality (also see Garland 1985). I observed this ideological corrective in the current research in the use of streamlined disciplinary tactics to sanction drug offenders. The diverse accounts of organizational shortcuts for penalizing drug violators suggest that normalization of offenders is pursued with a moral vengeance. On the other hand, offenders who display moral responsibility in the face of administrative adversity become "success stories." These stories consequently may serve as a moral counterweight to the legal degradation of offenders who violate precepts of morality, and thus, in an ironic logic, may justify retribution for offenders who violate the local culture's moral sensibility.

Third, bureaucratic tropes provide organizational shortcuts for dealing with areas swathed in technicality to facilitate control of offenders. Put another way, the bureaucratization of probation and parole appears to be accompanied by the development of informal processes to facilitate the organization of officers' day-to-day routines. This was particularly evident in the development of shortcuts for dealing with problem cases in areas dense with legal complexity. If, as Feeley and Simon (1992) suggest, the process of system rationalization continues to accelerate for probation and parole, one might anticipate the increasing decoupling of probation and parole officers' work from the administrative processes of the organization, and the increasing isolation of line-level probation and parole officers from the administrative process.

In the aggregate, findings suggest that rather than resisting change, as suggested by common wisdom, the local organizational culture absorbed changes in terms of existing areas of meaning, such as offenders' and agents' morality. In doing so, however, the culture itself changed: it adapted to increased legal complexity, for example, by developing rules of thumb for dealing with particular types of offenders. The organizational culture apparently responded to the content of POST training by incorporating areas of change into a continual redefinition of itself. Organizational culture thus is passed on to each new cohort in ever-changing form, providing the flexibility to adapt and survive, regardless of changes imposed externally on the organization.

The literature on reform presented at the outset of this paper created an image of organizational reform frustrated by the self-interest of organizational members. Findings in the current research provide a different image, in which the relationship between institutional change and local culture is more complex than suggested by ideas of self-interest, and in which efforts for change may be accepted, rejected, or modified depending on the nature of the change and the values and beliefs of the local organizational culture.

These findings have a number of implications for efforts at organizational reform. First, local organizational culture should not be dismissed as an inevitable source of resistance to change; the relationship of culture to change is much more complex than suggested by the literature. Second, because institutional changes are subjected to an interpretive process at the level of the local organizational culture, the outcome of change efforts will never be fully predictable. Third, though I have argued here that change efforts must account for the values and beliefs of local organizational culture, one should not assume that the self-interest of particular organizational actors might not also come into play. Researchers on change and resistance in organizational environments should recognize that both individual self-interest and value-laden organizational culture will influence desired organizational reforms.

Fourth is the finding that stories are integral to the language of motive. Stories are not simply illustrative fillers that ground a technical lecture empirically; they imbue an account with cultural meaning and value. By the tropes an instructor uses, he or she adds organizational "spin," or cultural interpretation and value, to an area of instruction. This point has a powerful policy implication: a class is a transmitter of organizational culture. POST leaders at the agency level should not only monitor the technical quality of classes, as they do currently through an assessment of testing materials, instructor evaluations, and evaluations of performance. They also should be sensitive to the tropic devices used by instructors to convey information. The transmission of information through tropes will affect recruits' loyalties and the meanings they acquire about their work as powerfully as the technical knowledge will affect their skills and abilities. POST leaders who fail to recognize the power of tropes for instilling cultural knowledge may find that all of their efforts to instill change or knowledge in a particular area are circumvented by offsetting cultural precepts and values.

Using the training unit of a parole and probation department as an empirical referent, I have undertaken to construct theoretical links between institutional and cultural ideas of organizational processes. In this chapter, I do little more than hint at the potential fruitfulness of such efforts.

Beyond the writings of a few police theorists (Ericson 1982; Manning 1970, 1979, 1989; McNulty 1994; Shearing and Ericson 1991; Van Maanen 1979), the intuitional and interpretive nature of cultural knowledge in criminal justice is untapped. Only recently have researchers begun to recognize the power of institutional perspectives (Crank 1994; Hagan 1989). Currently, there is a great need for insights into patterns of internal (cultural) and external (institutional) influence that empirical investigations can provide through these perspectives, and into non-rational bases of organizational knowledge in criminal justice organizations.

Both cultural and institutional perspectives rely heavily on case-study methods of observing and presenting information. The usual call to develop quantifiable measures for future research will not be issued here. I believe that additional and more elaborate case-study research can contribute most to these perspectives. We need to assess the wellsprings of organizational meaning and to learn how meanings are modulated through cultural and institutional contexts.

I have examined here only one source of organizational change. Actors have sought to change the administration and behavior of criminal justice organizations in many ways: through the efforts of the chief executive, college education, civilian review boards, media supervision, and policy-oriented research. The central thesis of this chapter, however—that organizational culture will influence how particular changes are perceived, and ultimately will determine the success or failure of those changes—should apply to those sources of change as well.

NOTES

Crank, John P. (1996). The Construction of Meaning during Training for Probation and Parole. *Justice Quarterly*, 13(2): 265–290. Reprinted with permission from Sage.

1. The reformer's frustration is expressed in Dr. Kenneth Clark's comments to the Kerner Commission (Kerner 1967: 27). In comparing the Kerner Commission's findings and recommendations on the urban riots of 1963–1967 with commission reports on the 1919 riot in Chicago and the Harlem riots of 1935 and 1943, Dr. Clark stated, "I must again in candor say to you members of the commission that it is a kind of Alice in Wonderland, with the same moving picture shown over and over again, the same analysis, the same recommendations, and the same inaction."
2. Nevada POST training also offers a POST III training course. Category HI includes peace officers whose legal authority and primary duties are limited to the care and custody of juveniles in a correctional or detention facility. It is not provided for parole and probation officers who belong to the Nevada Department of Public Safety.

3. Berger and Luckmann (1967: 57) describe this idea in terms of highly institutionalized belief systems that consist of "taken-for-granted routines." Also see Scott (1991).
4. For example, a parolee or probationer may be referred to as a "bad guy"; thus, the meaning of the probationer's status is shifted from the relatively neutral term *client* to the negatively sanctioned term *criminal.*
5. Metonymy occurs when an instructor, in attempting to respond to a "how to" question, tells what he or she did on a particular occasion (Shearing and Ericson 1991). Manning (1979: 662) also noted that metonymy is the representation of a concept in terms of its characteristics—for example, describing an organization in terms of its size, its body of rules, or the degree and type of structural differentiation.
6. Umberto Eco (1984: 87) characterizes four types of tropes as follows. The metaphor, the "most luminous" of tropes, is the master trope, of which all other tropes are types. Eco says it is impossible to define a metaphor because any definition of a metaphor is itself a metaphor and hence a tautology. A synecdoche is a substitution of two terms for each other according to a relation between them—for example, a part for the whole, or vice versa. Metonymy is a substitution for a relation of contiguity (a definition Eco admits is "fuzzy"); irony is substitution by the opposite of something; by this definition, a story is always a metaphor but may contain the other types of tropes as well.
7. As an institutional form, POST training is highly rationalized. Training protocols offer a standardized means for providing training to new recruits (Scott and Meyer 1994). These include a well-defined and explicit curriculum, testing and evaluation procedures, and a formal credentialing standard. Curriculum content is also rationalized; it is objective, orderly, and systematic.
8. Kappeler, Sluder, and Alpert (1994: 101) found a parallel phenomenon with regard to police training. Training instructors, they observed, used stories to reinforce the existing worldview rather than to provide recruits with education and new ways of thinking about their work.
9. Instruction for this training section was organized around the following categories: orientation (for example, agency history, OSHA safety rules, professional ethics, peace officer stress), administration (cultural awareness, sexual harassment, community resources, offender programs), pre-sentence investigation (pre-sentence investigation, special problems with street and prison gangs), case supervision (search and seizure, warrant process, home visit training and practicum, interstate compact), peace officer skills (basic firearms, return of violator process, arrest procedures, officer survival skills), and the violation process (report writing, capstan, communications, and report writing).
10. Those three instructors were from the county prosecutor's office (on courtroom demeanor), the Las Vegas Fire District (on explosives), and the county health district (on AIDS).

11. I would recommend the use of multiple observers to cross-check findings in future research of this type, where the codification of data is a subjective process and organizational pressures for loyalty are strong.

REFERENCES

Bayley, D. and E. Bittner. 1989. "Learning the Skills of Policing." Pp. 87–110 in *Critical Issues in Policing*, edited by T. Barker and D. Carter. Prospect Heights, IL: Waveland Press.

Berger, P. and T. Luckmann. 1967. *The Social Construction of Reality*. New York: Doubleday.

Burke, K. 1969. *A Grammar of Motives*. Berkeley: University of California Press.

Church, T. 1982. *Examining Local Legal Culture: Practitioner Attitudes in Four Criminal Courts*. Washington, DC: National Institute of Justice.

Cohen, S. 1985. *Visions of Social Control: Crime, Punishment and Classification*. Oxford: Polity Press.

Crank, J.P. 1994. "Watchman and Community: A Study of Myth and Institutionalization in Policing." *Law and Society Review* 28:325–51.

Crank, J.P. and R. Langworthy. 1992. "An Institutional Perspective of Policing." *Journal of Criminal Law and Criminology* 83:338–63.

Crank, J.P., B. Payne, and S. Jackson. 1993. "The Relationship between Police Belief Systems and Attitudes toward Police Practices." *Criminal Justice and Behavior* 20:199–221.

DiMaggio, P.J. and W.W. Powell. 1983. "Institutional Isomorphism and Collective Rationality: The Iron Cage Revisited." *American Journal of Sociology* 48:147–60.

DiMaggio, P.J. and W.W. Powell. 1991. "Introduction." Pp. 1–40 in *The New Institutionalism in Organizational Analysis*, edited by W. Powell and P. DiMaggio. Chicago: University of Chicago Press.

Duffee, D. 1990. *Explaining Criminal Justice: Community Theory and Criminal Justice Reform*. Prospect Heights, IL: Waveland Press.

Eco, U. 1984. *Semiotics and the Philosophy of Language*. Bloomington: Indiana University Press.

Ericson, R. 1982. *Reproducing Order: A Study of Police Patrol Work*. Toronto: University of Toronto Press.

Feeley, M.M. and J. Simon. 1992. "The New Penology: Notes on the Emerging Strategy of Corrections and Its Implications." *Criminology* 30:449–74.

Fogel, D. 1984. "The Emergence of Probation as a Profession in the Service of Public Safety: The Next Ten Years." Pp. 65–99 in *Probation and Justice: Reconsideration of Mission*, edited by P. McAnany, D. Thompson, and D. Fogel. Cambridge, MA: Oelgeschlager, Gunn and Hain.

Fogelson, D. 1977. *Big-City Police*. Cambridge, MA: Harvard University Press.

Garland, D. 1985. *Punishment and Welfare*. Brookfield, VT: Gower.

Gordon, D.I. 1991. *The Justice Juggernaut: Fighting Street Crime, Controlling Citizens*. London: Rutgers University Press.

Guyot, D. 1986. “Bending Granite: Attempts to Change the Rank Structure of American Police Departments.” Pp. 43–68 in *Police Administrative Issues*, edited by M. Pogrebin and R. Regoli. Millwood, NY: Associated University Press.

Hagan, J. 1989. “Why Is There So Little Criminal Justice Theory? Neglected Macro- and Micro-Level Links between Organization and Power.” *Journal of Research in Crime and Delinquency* 26:116–35.

Harris, P., T. Clear, and S.C. Baird. 1989. “Have Community Supervision Officers Changed Their Attitudes toward Their Work?” *Justice Quarterly* 6:233–46.

Harris, R.N. 1973. *The Police Academy: An Inside View*. New York: Wiley.

Hydebrand, W. and C. Seron. 1990. *Rationalizing Justice: The Political Economy of Federal District Courts*. New York: SUNY Press.

Jacobs, J. 1977. *Stateville: The Prison in Mass Society*. Chicago: University of Chicago Press.

Jepperson, R.L. 1991. “Institutions, Institutional Effects, and Institutionalism.” Pp. 143–64 in *The New Institutionalism in Organizational Analysis*, edited by W. Powell and P. DiMaggio. Chicago: University of Chicago Press.

Kappeler, V.E., R.D. Sluder, and G.P. Alpert. 1994. *Forces of Deviance: Understanding the Dark Side of Policing*. Prospect Heights, IL: Waveland Press.

Kerner, O. and the National Advisory Commission on Civil Disorders. 1967. *Report of the National Advisory Commission on Civil Disorder*. Washington, DC: U.S. Government Printing Office.

Levitt, B. and J.G. March. 1988. “Organizational Learning.” *Annual Review of Sociology* 14:319–40.

Manning, P. 1970. *Police Work*. Cambridge, MA: MIT Press.

Manning, P. 1979. “Metaphors of the Field: Varieties of Organizational Discourse.” *Administrative Science Quarterly* 24:660–71.

Manning, P. 1989. “Occupational Culture.” Pp. 360–64 in *The Encyclopedia of Police Science*, edited by W. Bayley. New York: Garfield.

Manning, P. and L.J. Redlinger. 1978. “The Invitational Edges of Corruption: Some Consequences of Narcotic Law Enforcement.” Pp. 147–66 in *Policing: A View from the Street*, edited by P.K. Manning and J. Van Maanen. Santa Monica: Goodyear.

Marquart, J. and B. Crouch. 1984. “Coopting the Kept: Using Inmates for Social Control in a Southern Prison.” *Justice Quarterly* 1:491–509.

Marquart, J. and B. Crouch. 1990. “Resolving the Paradox of Reform: Litigation, Prisoner Violence, and Perceptions of Punishment.” *Justice Quarterly* 7:103–23.

McNulty, E.W. 1994. “Common-Sense Making among Police Officers: The Social Construction of Working Knowledge.” *Symbolic Interaction* 17:281–94.

Meyer, J. and B. Rowan. 1977. “Institutionalized Organizations: Formal Structure as Myth and Ceremony.” *American Journal of Sociology* 83:430–63.

Meyer, J. and W.R. Scott. 1983. "Centralization and the Legitimacy Problems of Local Government." Pp. 199–216 in *Organizational Environments: Ritual and Rationality*, edited by J. Meyer and R. Scott. Thousand Oaks, CA: Sage.

Mills, C.W. 1940. "Situated Actions and Vocabularies of Motive." *American Sociological Review* 5:904–13.

Monahan, S.C., J.W. Meyer, and W.R. Scott. 1994. "Employee Training: The Expansion of Organizational Citizenship." Pp. 255–71 in *Institutional Environments and Organizations*, edited by W.R. Scott and J.W. Meyer. Thousand Oaks, CA: Sage.

Morn, F. 1984. "The Academy of Criminal Justice Sciences and the Criminal Justice Education Movement: Some History." Unpublished manuscript.

Petersilia, J. 1989. "The Influence of Research on Policing." Pp. 230–48 in *Critical Issues in Policing*, edited by R. Dunham and G. Alpert. Prospect Heights, IL: Waveland Press.

Pollock-Byrne, J. 1988. "Ethics and Criminal Justice." *Justice Quarterly* 5:475–85.

Rothman, D. 1980. *Conscience and Convenience*. Boston: Little, Brown.

Schur, E.M. 1980. The *Politics of Deviance: Stigma Contests and the Use of Power*. Englewood Cliffs, NJ: Prentice-Hall.

Scott, W.R. 1991. "Unpacking Institutional Arguments." Pp. 164–82 in *The New Institutionalism in Organizational Analysis*, edited by W. Powell and P.J. DiMaggio. Chicago: University of Chicago Press.

Scott, W.R. 1994. "Institutions and Organizations: Toward a Theoretical Synthesis." Pp. 55–80 in *Institutional Environments and Organizations*, edited by W.R. Scott and J.W. Meyer. Thousand Oaks, CA: Sage.

Scott, W.R. and J.W. Meyer. 1994. "The Rise of Training Programs in Firms and Agencies." Pp. 228–54 in *Institutional Environments and Organizations*, edited by W.R. Scott and J.W. Meyer. Thousand Oaks, CA: Sage.

Shearing, C.D. and R.V. Ericson. 1991. "Culture as Figurative Action." *British Journal of Sociology* 42:481–506.

Simon, J. 1993. *Poor Discipline: Parole and the Social Control of the Underclass, 1890–1990*. Chicago: University of Chicago Press.

Skolnick, J. and D. Bayley. 1986. *The New Blue Line: Police Innovation in Six American Cities*. New York: Free Press.

Spradley, J.P. 1979. *The Ethnographic Interview*. New York: Holt, Rinehart and Winston.

Spradley, J.P. 1980. *Participant Observation*. New York: Holt, Rinehart and Winston.

Stoddard, E.R. 1968. "The Informal Code of Police Deviancy: A Group Approach to Blue-Collar Crime." *Journal of Criminal Law, Criminology, and Police Science* 59:201–13.

Swidler, A. 1986. "Culture in Action: Symbols and Strategies." *American Sociological Review* 51:273–86.

Turner, V. 1974. *Dramas, Fields, and Metaphors: Symbolic Action in Human Society*. Ithaca: Cornell University Press.

Van Maanen, J. 1979. "Observations on the Making of Policemen." Pp. 292–308 in *Policing: A View from the Street*, edited by P. Manning and J. Van Maanen. Santa Monica: Goodyear.

Van Maanen, J. and B.T. Bentlind. 1994. "Cops and Auditors." *The Legalistic Organization*, edited by S. Sinkin. Thousand Oaks, CA: Sage.

Van Maanen, J. and E. Schein. 1979. "Toward a Theory of Organizational Socialization." Pp. 209–64 in *Research in Organizational Behavior*, edited by B.M. Shaw. Greenwich, CT: JAI.

Walker, S. 1985. *Sense and Nonsense about Crime*. Belmont, CA: Wadsworth.

Walker, S. 1992. *The Police in America*. 2nd ed. New York: McGraw-Hill.

Westley, W.A. 1956. "Secrecy and the Police." *Social Forces* 34:254–57.

12

EXAMINING CORRECTIONAL RESOURCES

A Cross-Sectional Study of the States

Edmund F. McGarrell and David E. Duffee

INTRODUCTION

This chapter examines the causes of correctional spending. We will compare the dominant, mainstream political account of why spending on corrections varies with two less popular explanations for state spending on punishment. The dominant view, the one that is usually taken for granted in political speeches, media accounts, and neighborly conversations, is that more crime produces more punishment, which costs more money. In other words, the popular account is that more spending is an inevitable reaction to the behavior of criminals. This view has also been called the "functionalist explanation" (Barlow, Barlow, and Johnson 1996), the "consensus" explanation (Bernard and Engel 2001), or the "rational model" (Kraska 2006).

To this account, we will compare two other accounts of correctional spending. In developing these other accounts, we will draw on three different theoretical traditions. One of these is the sociology of social control most notably associated with the late Allen Liska and his colleagues, who describe their approach as drawing on the "conflict perspective" (Liska 1992a; Liska and Chamlin 1984).

Within this general conflict approach to social control, there are both "structural accounts" and "elite" accounts (Liska 1992a) for the nature and level of social control. In the former, social structure and culture create pressures that permeate society for control of some groups of people, over and above the contribution of those groups to crime, and independent of the decisions of particular people. In the latter elite theories, particular groups such as economic elites or administrative elites seek control over other groups, such as the poor or minorities (e.g., Davies and Worden 2009; Unnever and Cullen 2010; Weitzer and Tuch 2004). One form of elite theory proposes that a "managerial elite," such as correctional professionals, argue for social policies that are in their interest (Inverarity 1992; Lipsky 1980).

The second tradition that we will rely upon for our theory is the "genealogical" theory associated with Foucault (1979) and his followers, such as David Garland (2001) and Jonathan Simon (1993). These scholars seek to explain the evolution of current social discourses and practice, such as beliefs about and practices of crime control, from a combination of past practices and changes in social structure and culture. We will provide a detailed example of Garland's and Simon's arguments later.

The third and final literature on which we draw is "neoinstitutionalism" (Kraatz and Zajac 1996). There are several branches of institutional theory concerned with culture, politics, and organizations (March and Olsen 1984; Meyer and Rowan 1977). The branch of most concern to us here is the institutional theory of organizations. As described by Renauer in Chapter 5, organizational institutionalism looks at the interplay among political, social, and cultural forces in society and public organizations, which administer major social institutions, such as education and corrections. In Chapter 5, Renauer asked what elements in the local and national environments of police departments would pressure departments toward more or less engagement of neighborhoods in social control. In this chapter, we ask almost the opposite question: what elements in the "correctional sector" or correctional environment would push for greater or lesser investment in state control (particularly incarceration)? We will go into greater depth about the institutionalized environment of corrections later.

Correctional genealogy is primarily, but not only, a European development. The sociology of social control and institutional theory are primarily, but by no means exclusively, developments in the United States. There is so much overlap among these theoretical approaches that it is hard at times to tell them apart, and we shall feel free to blend them. Indeed, Garland (2001) says that his most recent study is both a genealogical history and a sociology of social control. While Garland does not explicitly mention institutional theory, much of his argument, as we shall see later, comports well with that tradition as well. Despite this intellectual overlap in research questions and theoretical approaches, these three theoretical traditions are currently more separate than integrated. To some extent, this chapter is concerned with theory integration, as discussed by Snipes and Maguire in Chapter 2.

One difference in method between this chapter and typical genealogical study is that the latter is, as the name implies, historical and longitudinal. It tries to identify the confluence of forces over time that produces current practice. While that approach is highly valuable, for reasons that Snipes and Maguire describe in Chapter 2 (see the discussion of the historical dimension), it can be, as both Garland (2001) and Simon (1993) admit, difficult to test. There are, after all, only so many histories to come by, so quantitative examination is limited and expensive, although by no means impossible. What the reader will see us doing here is converting the longitudinal, genealogical argument into a cross-sectional argument in which these phenomena vary over place instead of time. That is, if Garland is right about some of the forces that have affected British and U.S. policy over time, is it possible to look for differences in those forces across different states?

PUNISHMENT EXPENDITURES

Before we get more specific about building a theory from these diverse traditions, a word about our research question is appropriate. As prison populations expanded at unprecedented rates since 1974, costs of building and maintaining correctional facilities also exploded. From 1975 to 1985, costs of operating correctional facilities in the United States increased by 240 percent. Indeed, the increase in the costs of corrections was 50 percent greater than the increase in total state and local governmental expenditures for the period from 1971 to 1985 (McDonald 1989). In per capita terms, corrections spending by state and local governments increased 218 percent from 1960 to 1985, the fastest growing policy area in that period (Yondorf and Warnock 1989; see also Taggart and Winn 1991). State aid to local governments for corrections was the fastest growing category of state aid to local governments from 1970 to 1987, increasing 400 percent in that period, easily outstripping aid for education, for example.

This chapter focuses on correctional expenditures in the mid-1980s toward the end of the period described earlier. We chose mid-1980 data because that period provided some good institutional data that were not readily available at other periods (Taggart and Winn [1991] examined similar data for similar reasons). We are trying to demonstrate the value of a theoretic approach, and therefore are not too immediately concerned about the currency of the data. However, it is relevant to indicate that public spending on corrections increased steadily through the 1990s for reasons that, according to Garland (2001), are the same as the ones we will examine for the 1980s. We recognize that there is now, in 2014, some trending away from high incarceration and a reemergence of an interest in treatment, but we would expect the same institutional theory to be useful in explaining the location and timing of such swings (see the conclusion for specific research ideas).

The trend data sketched earlier certainly indicate the importance of asking why punishment cost varies over time. This question becomes even more intriguing when we realize that crime was stable or dropping for much of that time period, at least suggesting the need for factors other than crime to explain the increase (Barlow et al. 1996; Garland 2001). However, does it make equal sense to ask why correctional expenditures vary from place to place? Using juvenile corrections data from 1979, the National Council on Crime and Delinquency (NCCD) answered in the affirmative (Krisberg, Litsky, and Schwartz 1984). The NCCD study noted large differences from state to state in admissions to detention, length of stay, youth confinement in adult facilities, confinement conditions, and expenditures. The council could not explain away the differences on the basis of crime or arrest data. Looking at Western European countries in the 1980s, Leslie Wilkins (1991) noted that incarceration rates differed more than crime rates. While he did not look directly at expenditures, the correlation between use of imprisonment and correctional expenses would be very high. Using 1984 data, Taggart and Winn (1991) found large per-capita expenditure differences across the forty-eight contiguous states in the United States. One motivation for explaining these differences across place would be the potential for finding some causal factors that are controllable and can then be the focus of interventions to control increasing costs over time (Garland 2001; Taggart and Winn 1991; Wilkins 1991). But what are these causes and can they be manipulated?

In this chapter, we consider the role of technical, political, and cultural factors in determining the level of resources available for corrections in the fifty states. We are interested in how variation in the task and institutional environments of corrections systems affects levels of correctional resources. Are variations in the state-level structures for mobilizing and distributing correctional resources differentially effective in securing funds for the accomplishment of correctional objectives? Do these characteristics of the correctional bureaucracies affect the level of correctional resources beyond the effect of technical demands for resources? Do social structure and demographic character of states make correctional claims for resources more compelling in some states than others? For example, Stucky, Heimer and Lang (2005) find that the level of political competition affects the volatility and direction of correctional policy.

THE CHARACTERISTICS OF INSTITUTIONALIZED ENVIRONMENTS

Our application of institutional theory to the study of corrections follows what Scott (1987) has referred to as the institutionalized environments approach. This approach observes that some societal sectors, or functional areas, are more governed by symbols of form and means than by assessments of outcome. Some environments are more richly endowed with deeply held and often taken-for-granted beliefs about the organization and practice of certain social endeavors (Meyer and Rowan 1977). For example, particular divisions of labor, employee qualifications, and programs may be imposed on organizations if they are to be granted legitimacy (Feeley 1989; Garland 2001; Warren et al. 1974). These forces, according to institutional theory, are embedded in organizational environments and are adopted by organizations in good-faith demonstrations of adherence to modern practice, without much attempt (or capacity) to link such elements to desired outcomes (such as recidivism rates or improved reading ability). Organizational survival depends on conformity more than on performance (Crank and Langworthy 1992; Katz 2001; although Sweeney et al. 2000 provides some evidence that attempts to conform are not always based on accurate assessments of institutional pressures). Institutional theory assumes that other societal sectors, particularly the profit sector, may be more heavily controlled by tangible outcomes, such as return on investment and market share, so that organizational behaviors are better predicted by competitive advantage and resource dependencies than by conformity to public myths about appropriate organizational conduct. While these technical and economic forces may also be important in the public sector, institutional theory alerts us to the importance of political and cultural influences as well (Garland 2001).

The institutional perspective, therefore, suggests that various characteristics of institutionalized environments may have economic as well as structural consequences for organizations, particularly, as in the case of corrections, when measures of technical proficiency are ambiguous and politically controversial (Meyer, Scott, and Deal 1983; see the discussion in Chapter 1 of the effects of the "nothing works" claim about correctional treatment). In terms of the present study of allocation of resources to corrections, this suggests that conformance to widely held beliefs about good organizational practices might be an important factor in securing funding. Actual allocation of funds for corrections will be influenced by a number of elements of the task and institutional environment of the correctional sector (McGarrell and Duffee 1995).

Certainly, the dominant political message that more deviance produces more government control expenditure has some level of credence. Treating crime as the engine for a technically rational demand for punishment has some merit: more criminals may mean more inmates and more resources for punishing. The warden has more mouths to feed. But these are marginal differences and may be offset by economies of scale (the marginal increase for punishing two inmates is not twice the cost of punishing one). Moreover the technical–rational story propounded by our official policy makers sounds circular and suspicious. More crime leads to more punishment. But less crime also leads to more punishment (usually under the argument that punishment works). In addition, there are no inevitable connections between levels and seriousness of crime and levels of punishment, even under the notion that retribution must take place. Commensurate punishment, and its costs, are set through some political and social process and vary from place to place (see Wilkins [1991] for an elaboration of these arguments).

THE CORRECTIONAL SECTOR

Our theoretical approach to variation in punishment expenditures follows Scott and Meyer, who use the term societal sector to refer to "all organizations within a society supplying a given type of product or service together with their associated organizational sets: suppliers, financiers, regulators, and the like" (1983, 129). But, in addition to the organizations in a sector, a sector would include the values and beliefs about their practices, a phenomenon that Warren called an "institutionalized thought structure." Garland's (2001) and Warren's term (Warren, Rose, and Bergunder 1974) is field rather than sector; however, we think these terms are synonymous.

The correctional sector is composed of focal organizations, such as state correctional departments, in interaction with their task and institutional environments. The task environment consists of those forces affecting economic/technical processes of organization. In subsequent sections, we refer to these forces as the rational–technical base of correctional structures and outcomes. In terms of this study, key elements of the task environment include factors such as the crime-related demand for correctional resources and the resource munificence of the state (i.e., state wealth). States with higher levels of crime should produce more clients for the corrections system, and wealthier states should be able to provide higher levels of resources for all state functions, including corrections.

The institutional environment comprises the cultural and political forces affecting the organization. It consists of values, norms, and rationalized beliefs about both the efficacy of the correctional function and the organizational structure of "good" correctional practice. In terms of norms and values, we are primarily concerned with variation among the states in the relative use of incarceration as a response to crime. We refer to this as the value base of the corrections function.

In addition, previous work on institutionalized environments suggests two related sets of characteristics that might describe the level and nature of the institutional environment in the correctional sector. One set of variables has to do with the relative strength of the formally organized forces in a society and hence their varying capacity to exert control on societal activity. In particular, we are interested in the role of the professions and similar organized interests of a given sector. The importance of these forces was suggested in a recent study that found that police organizations and prosecutors' offices were influenced by distinct environmental forces in the implementation of community policing and community prosecution (Giblin 2014). Indeed, there was little relationship at the local level between the implementation of community policing and community prosecution.

The other set has to do with the formal structural arrangements of these institutionalizing forces, such as whether they are unified or fragmented, centralized or decentralized (Carroll, Goodstein, and Gyenes 1988; Scott and Meyer 1983). In subsequent sections, we devote attention to dominant trends in the institutional environment of corrections as a way of deriving hypotheses as to how these characteristics, referred to as the organizing capacity of the correctional sector, might affect levels of resources for corrections.

THE SYSTEMATIZATION OF CORRECTIONS

In 1932, the Wickersham Commission decried the feudalism of corrections in the states and, in 1939, President Roosevelt's First National Parole Conference proclaimed it an outrageously corrupt system, bereft of either bureaucratic or professional standards (National Parole Conference 1939). Administrative reforms in corrections followed shortly, but did not really take off until after World War II, when the systems concepts promoted by operations researchers were applied to management (e.g., Beer 1966). About twenty-five states reorganized their correctional bureaucracies from 1950 to 1980, with the most potent reforms being the creation of centralized departments of correction and the state takeover or regulation of local correctional services (Council of State Governments 1977).

The most commonly spoken rationale for the structural changes in correctional services was provision of better services. Proponents of unification, state takeover, and state regulation promised improved coordination among units, better quality and enhanced continuity of services to offenders, and heightened administrative accountability (National Advisory Commission on Criminal Justice Standards and Goals 1973; Nelson, Cushman, and Harlow 1980; President's Commission on Law Enforcement and Administration of Justice 1967; Skoler 1976). The formal rationale was one of increased technical proficiency in the conduct of correctional tasks.

While increased technical proficiency is a possible result of such reorganizations, improved outcomes by public institutions, including corrections, are quite difficult to demonstrate (Nokes 1960; Salancik 1981; Mastrofski 1998). We can view the major swing to the right in correctional policy since the 1970s as an example of the public collapse of an institutionalized myth (Meyer and Rowan 1977). In the corrections case, the rehabilitation myth emerged in the 1930s as the new social science–based professions gained power (Dession 1938). Since the mid-1970s, we have witnessed the substitution of a new set of beliefs about good correctional practice—retribution, deterrence, incapacitation, and the management of risk (Feeley and Simon 1992; Garland 2001; Simon 1993). The technical proficiency of the new beliefs is just as difficult to demonstrate as was the technical proficiency of rehabilitation. However, demonstrations of technical accomplishment will be infrequently demanded and studiously avoided, so long as the forms used satisfy public notions of what works. These beliefs will have considerable impact on the administration of corrections. (It is important to note that public views of "what works" are not always defined in terms of efficacy of the practice for its intended outcome. The public, and political, views of what works might lean toward what some group deems appropriate, such as opposition to college programs for inmates because they are seen as undeserving.)

Thus, while centralization and unification may or may not have affected technical proficiency, institutional theory suggests that to the extent that such structures are associated with institutionalized beliefs regarding sound or enlightened practice, centralized and unified departments may fare better in the struggle for resources. Similarly, to the extent that centralization and unification lead to more organized and powerful correctional bureaucracies, such structures may be associated with higher levels of resources (Taggart and Winn 1991; see Taggart 1997 on the influence of federal entities on "nationalizing" correctional policy).

The main argument that we have pulled from our disparate theoretical sources is generally as follows. There has been a major shift in the economy and in social structure in the United States, although this shift has been differentially felt in the states. It has had particularly marked effects in economically developed states that have urban concentrations of poverty and ethnic and racial difference. Where these changes have occurred, the threat to the political elite will be higher and the middle class who have escaped the urban setting will be more mean-spirited. In such places, a "culture of penal welfarism" has given way to a "culture of control" (Garland 2001).

However, in these states, structures associated with the older penology, which sought to overcome the social disadvantage of correctional clients, are still very active and help to shape current policy and practice (Garland 2001; Feeley and Simon 1992). These more developed bureaucracies and correctional work forces developed and deployed tools of prediction and classification in the allocation of correctional treatment resources. Those resources have now been retracted or diminished, but the agents are still responsible for offender outcomes. They have taken to applying their people technologies to "managing risk" (Feeley and Simon 1992) rather than changing offender behavior. This trend might now be slowing if not reversing. For example, the fifth largest probation agency in the country defines its mission as changing behavior to ensure public safety (Maricopa County Adult Probation Department 2010).

The coupling of the new value system that values punishment highly and the professional capacity to marshal resources for people control has led to boomerang effects in the social control process. For example, Simon (1993) argues that the California parole system was the best endowed for provision of treatment and reintegration services, but that the supervision practices that were designed for reintegration are now used for rapid revocation. In the more professionalized systems, the new punitive policies are more successful because the more advanced social control agents are best able to make the case for the technical inevitability of greater social control responding to greater crime.

In summary, the new economy and demographic changes do cause more crime and more opportunities for punishment. But it is changes in political culture, the politics of threat, which make punishment more severe (such as more use of incarceration). It is the professional and highly organized correctional work force that can connect criminogenic forces (such as unemployment and drug use) with punishment (such as by revocation) and can best make the political demand for punishment appear most legitimate (Feeley 1989; Simon 1993).

Our principal interest is in the last part of this three-legged stool: the nature of the "organizing capacity" of the correctional sector itself. Are some correctional structures and some correctional work forces better able to secure funding than others, controlling for the crime effects and controlling for the relative threat in the political environment?

CHARACTERISTICS AFFECTING ORGANIZING CAPACITY OF THE CORRECTIONAL SECTOR

On the basis of these trends in corrections, and following the lead of Scott and Meyer (1983), we have selected five sector variables for initial study. An institutional explanation of societal functions, such as fiscal support for corrections, would propose that these characteristics can have an impact on such functions independent of (but not instead of) economic/technical explanations, such as the number of persons to be processed (McGarrell and Duffee 1995).

Professionalization

One possible measure of the degree of institutionalization in a sector is the extent to which professional bodies are organized and exert influence over how societal functions should be achieved. We would expect states with greater professionalization to spend relatively more on corrections, because the professions should increase the legitimacy of a societal function with which they are associated and impose hiring qualifications and practices that are more expensive.

Unionization

The institutional literature relies more heavily on professionalization than unionization as an institutionalizing force. Since there are many quasi-professions in corrections, and since the state dominates practice more than in other sectors (and perhaps thereby reducing professional influence), we thought unionization was another institutionalizing force to be examined. Correctional officer unions, in particular, have become increasingly concerned with the conditions of work and with the ratio of workers to offenders. While professionalism and unionism can often conflict, we think both forces should work together for the increase of resources for corrections (Lipsky 1980).

In addition to these two characteristics of the correctional staff, states vary considerably in the structures of their corrections bureaucracies. While some overall trends have been cited in the introduction, there are still remarkable differences in the ways in which corrections is structured from state to state. Among the variables that we thought could be important were fragmentation/unification, federalization/concentration, and size.

Fragmented Structure

States vary in the number of separate agencies that have correctional responsibilities. We expect greater fragmentation to increase the level of correctional spending, on the presumption that multiple voices speaking for corrections will increase legitimacy as well as increase the administrative costs associated with provision of correctional services. There is a competing hypothesis, however, that fragmentation would reduce costs by introducing competition among agencies and introduce greater concern for efficiency in the evaluation of correctional-sector activities. In this second hypothesis, a single, unified correctional bureaucracy that combined community and institutional punishments would speak louder than separate agencies about correctional needs.

Federalization

States vary on the degree to which correctional functions are concentrated at the state level or shared with local authorities (federalized). The movement toward state takeover of probation may be seen as a trend toward concentration, while the diffusion of community corrections acts (Musheno et al. 1989) may be seen as a countertrend toward federalization. We expect that federalization should increase the level of resources for corrections, again by increasing the number of organizational constituents favoring correctional expenditure. However, again, there is a counterhypothesis about this structural characteristic. Garland (2001, 202–203) appears to conclude that the state-concentrated structure is significantly different from the federalized structure. In his view, the federalized, deconcentrated forms of social control may be an emergent countertrend to state-centered social control. Lyons (1999) may be making the same argument about policing. In his study of Seattle community policing, Lyons claims that reciprocal relationships between neighborhood and police department are decentered forms of social control. His analysis of the Seattle Police Department (SPD) claims that the SPD successfully co-opted neighborhood forces, making them adjuncts to state control, and diminishing reciprocity, or federalization. Garland's and Lyons's arguments would say that federalization spreads not just the responsibility for corrections, but also the form of control (from state centered to a combination of state and community controls). If they are correct, then federalization may reduce correctional cost.

Size of Bureaucracy

The final structural variable is the size of the state corrections bureaucracy, measured as the number of employees in state correctional agencies. Size is perhaps the most frequently examined structural variable in organizational analysis. We would expect size to generate internal complexity in organizations, which in turn may lead to fragmentation of the bureaucracy itself. Second, we would expect larger correctional work forces, independent of their unionization or professionalization, to be more potent political advocates of correctional expenditure.

ADDITIONAL CHARACTERISTICS OF TASK AND INSTITUTIONAL ENVIRONMENTS

The sector characteristics described earlier comprise key aspects of the institutional environment of the correctional sector. Structural factors appear important because, to the extent these factors conform to institutionalized beliefs about good practice, they may lead to greater legitimacy and resources for the organizations that display them. In addition, sector characteristics such as professionalization, unionization, and size may indicate the greater organizing capacity of correctional interests and lead to greater effectiveness in obtaining resources. Clearly, however, these are not the only characteristics influencing levels of correctional resources. Correctional spending is also likely to be affected by other aspects of the institutional environment, such as dominant norms and values, and by elements of the task environment, such as the number of persons to be supervised. Consequently, additional variables of the institutional and task environments should be included in the explanation of correctional resources. The other variables in this analysis are discussed in the following sections.

Size

Size was previously described as a bureaucratic trait of the correctional sector that is predicted to relate to increased spending due to specialization and increased political advocacy. Size, however, is also a measure of the "technical" or economic demand for correctional resources within the state. States with larger correctional systems will likely have to spend more on corrections (see Brown and Warner [1992] for a similar argument about the size of police departments). Thus, a positive relationship between size and correctional resources will be consistent with an interpretation attributing effects to both the institutional and task environment. Size is likely to be affected by the following two variables.

Crime Rate

Crime rate refers to the index crime rate of the state for 1985. On its face, crime rate would appear to be a relatively unambiguous element of the task environment. States with higher crime rates should have greater demand for correctional resources. As a measure of demand for services, it should operate through conviction or incarceration rates. While the violent crime rate might arguably be a better gauge of demand for incarcerative punishments, Arvanites and Asher (1995) report that either violent crime or general crime rates perform about the same across the states. Clearly, not all states reserve prison space for the violent. Indeed, this is less the purpose of prison use in the new punishment culture (Garland 2001). The effects of this punishment culture are just recently causing considerable concern (New York Times Editorial Board 2014; Clifford 2014). Crime rate may not be only a measure of "technical demand for punishment." It may also act as a symbolic force, independent of the conversion of crimes into punishments—as when political leaders demand that the criminal justice system, including corrections, must be better endowed to deal with the crime problem (Barlow, Barlow, and Johnson 1996; Garland 2001, 8–20; Scheingold 1984).

Level of Development

Population size, along with levels of industrialization and urbanization, should have a direct effect on the size of the correctional system through the larger population base. The Level of Development is an index of state development based on state population, industrialization, and urbanization. More populous, industrialized, and urbanized states are rated higher on the Level of Development index.

Racial Heterogeneity

States with greater racial and ethnic heterogeneity and economic inequality are hypothesized to be more punitive than are states with more homogeneous populations (Barlow, Barlow, and Johnson 1996; Brown and Warner 1992; Garland 2001; Liska 1992b; Liska and Chamlin 1984; McGarrell and Castellano 1991). A number of different indicators were considered, including an index of income inequality, poverty level, percent black, and a composite indicator of heterogeneity based on these three dimensions. Percent black emerged as having the strongest and most consistent relationships in the analysis that follows. Percent black is predicted to affect correctional resources through incarceration rate based on the hypothesis that racial heterogeneity leads to more punitive responses to offenders. This is a principal proposition of the conflict sociology on social control, where it would be recognized as the "threat hypothesis." It is a primary proposition of correctional genealogists, who argue that new economic structures produce marginalized groups who are both at high risk for crime and for social control. In Wilkins's terms, blame allocation and punishment protect the economic and political system by explaining system consequences as individual characteristics of the morally undeserving (1991) (see Garland 2001 for an identical but apparently independent argument; see also Davies and Worden 2009; Unnever and Cullen 2010; Weitzer and Tuch 2004).

Incarceration Rate

States vary widely on their relative use of incarceration. The sources of this variation have been a matter of debate, with disagreement as to the extent to which the incarceration rate is a product of crescive forces, such as age structure and crime rate, or whether it is the product of policy decisions (Barlow, Barlow, and Johnson 1996; Garland 2001; Sherman and Hawkins 1981). To the extent that incarceration rate affects the size of the correctional system and correctional resources beyond the effect of the crime rate, it seems to be indicative of institutionalized norms and values supportive of punishment. Controlling for crime rate, incarceration rate becomes a central measure of punitive values in both the genealogical and social control studies.[1]

Traditionalistic Political Culture

An additional potential source of variation on institutional beliefs toward punishment is the political culture of the state. In particular, states tending toward traditionalistic political culture, characterized as elite dominated with minimal levels of popular participation and little concern for public welfare (Elazar 1972; Johnson 1976), are likely to have higher rates of incarceration once crime rate has been controlled. Further, because political culture relates to public spending, we would expect traditionalistic culture to affect correctional resources. For example, because of the lack of commitment to social welfare and education in traditionalistic political cultures, corrections may fare well as a proportion of state spending.

The impact of traditionalistic political culture, as measured by Elazar, would appear on its face to be consistent with higher investments in punishment relative to other social sectors; however, Garland (2001) and Feeley and Simon (1992) would argue that this is no longer true. The genealogical analysis concludes that the traditionalistic (particularly Southern) style of punishment has become outmoded (Feeley 1989). The new punitive culture appears in highly urban, diverse states, where the postindustrial service economy has done the most to marginalize the poor. Moreover, the Southern traditions did not produce the professional correctional institutions that have recently been turned on their head to increase rather than reduce return to prison. Consequently, these theoreticians would argue that the predictive value of traditionalistic political culture has been superseded.

Wealth

A final characteristic of the states that may influence resources for corrections is the general level of wealth in the state. Public organizations are expensive. The wealth in the state (measured as per-capita income) permits, but does not guarantee, greater investments in corrections and in other correctional services (Taggart and Winn 1991).

RESOURCES FOR CORRECTIONS

The level of resources for corrections can be measured in a number of ways. In this study, we have explored the use of two different measures, which capture different aspects of investment in punishment.

Correctional Spending Per Total State Spending

Correctional spending per total state spending refers to the percent of the state budget that is devoted to correctional spending. It is thus a measure of how corrections fares vis-à-vis other categories of state expenditures. We see this as a measure of strategic position of corrections, because the greater its share of state financial support, presumably the relatively more value accorded to corrections compared to education, welfare, transportation, mental health, and so on.

For Garland (2001), this is probably the most theoretically relevant dependent measure. It would arguably stand for the overall punitiveness or control orientation of the state, relative to other ways in which state resources could be used. Garland makes the point that welfare spending has gone down at precisely the same juncture for the same reasons: the disadvantaged are now portrayed as making choices to commit crimes and to be poor.

Correctional Spending Per Citizen

Correctional spending per citizen stands for correctional spending per capita. It is thus an indicator of total correctional spending normed by the population base of the state. We expect some positive relationship between the share of state dollars devoted to corrections and corrections dollars per capita. However, correctional spending per citizen should be less dependent on the demands, size, and structure of other societal sectors. For example, one state could support corrections at higher levels than another state, without the relative fiscal position of the various societal sectors being affected. If professionalization in corrections is related to professionalization of other sectors, then correctional dollars per citizen should rise in professionalized states, even if the correctional professions do not achieve a greater share of state dollars than professions in other sectors. This is the measure that Taggert and Winn used in their analysis of the impact of environmental and internal factors on correctional spending (1991). It is a measure of punishment dollars per citizen-client rather than punishment dollars per all state expenses. This measure is consistent with Wilkins' (1984) position that the real correctional client is the taxpayer.

The appendix to this chapter includes the correlation matrix for the two spending measures. The correlation coefficients indicate the extent to which the variables are related to one another. As anticipated, correctional spending per total state spending and correctional spending per citizen are strongly related. States that spend relatively high amounts per capita on corrections also devote a greater share of the overall state budget to corrections.[2]

HYPOTHESIZED RELATIONSHIPS AND FINDINGS

We shall now describe the specific hypotheses and findings for two models; the first using total state spending as the dependent variable and the second using spending per capita.

Correctional Spending Per Total State Spending

The first outcome measure of interest is correctional spending per total state spending, the proportion of total state expenditures devoted to corrections. As noted earlier, correctional spending per total state spending is a measure of the correctional share of the state budget and thus indicates how the correctional system fares in relation to other state functions.

Figure 12.1 presents our hypothesized theoretical model. States with a greater demand for correctional resources in terms of both size of the system and values supportive of incarceration and those with greater organizing capacity should be able to command a greater proportion of the state budget. Thus, correctional spending per total state spending is viewed as having a rational–technical base, a value base, and an organizing capacity base. These predicted relationships are represented by the arrows indicating direct effects on correctional spending per total state spending.

The rational–technical base of correctional spending per total state spending is represented by the path from size of bureaucracy to correctional spending per total state spending. States with larger correctional systems are likely to need greater relative correctional resources. The rational–technical component of size of the system is driven by the population base of the state and the crime rate. That is, larger states are going to have larger correctional systems because of their greater population base. Consequently, the Level of Development, based on population, real gross state product, industrialization, and urbanization, is predicted to have a direct effect on size of bureaucracy.

Correctional spending per total state spending will also be influenced by the values and attitudes toward the use of imprisonment in a state. In this analysis, punitive values are measured indirectly by the incarceration rate of the state (incarceration rate). Incarceration rate is predicted to have both a direct and indirect effect on correctional spending per total state spending. The direct effect indicates that states committed to the use of incarceration are likely to commit a greater relative share of state resources to corrections. In addition, incarceration rate is predicted to have an indirect effect through its relationship to size of bureaucracy.

Incarceration rate, in turn, is seen as driven by crime rate, percent black in the state, the Level of Development, and political culture. States with a higher crime rate are likely to have a greater demand for punishment. This can be seen as the rational–technical base of the incarceration rate, at least to the extent that American culture ascribes to incarceration as an efficacious response to crime (Currie 1985; Scheingold 1984). However, incarceration rate is also determined by racial

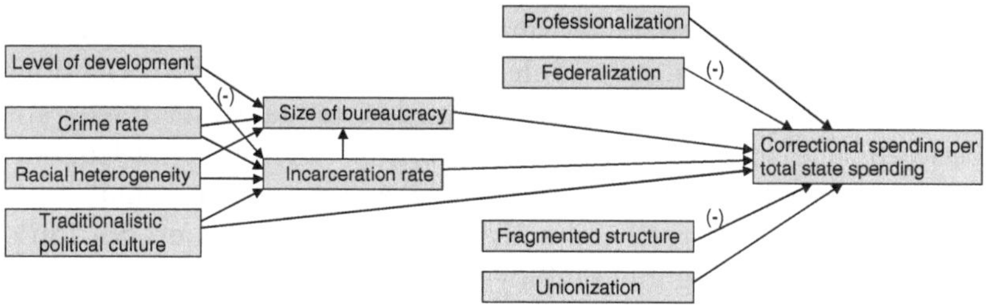

Figure 12.1 Theoretical model of correctional spending per total state spending

and economic heterogeneity. As noted earlier, we considered a number of indicators of heterogeneity. The percent of the state's population that is black consistently had the strongest zero-order relationships to incarceration rate and the spending measures and the highest standardized regression coefficients in the multivariate analysis. Therefore, we included percent black as the sole indicator of heterogeneity.

Contradictory predictions can be made for the effect of the Level of Development on incarceration rate. Industrialization and urbanization are consistent predictors of the crime rate. Thus, the Level of Development may have a spurious positive effect on incarceration rate due to its relationship to crime rate (r = .4101; see the appendix). However, Joubert et al.'s (1981) study found that having controlled for crime rate, more urbanized and industrialized states actually had lower incarceration rates. They suggested that this might reflect the inability of these states to process a larger number of offenders, or alternatively, the greater availability of alternatives in such states. Consequently, we predicted a negative effect of Level of Development on incarceration rate. Finally, we hypothesized that political culture would relate to correctional spending per total state spending indirectly through incarceration rate, as well as having a direct effect. Traditionalistic political culture is reflective of states with a tradition of elite dominance and minimal popular participation, innovation, and concern for public welfare. It is hypothesized that in such a context, correctional spending should be prioritized over other forms of state expenditure and that such a political culture will tend to favor greater relative use of incarceration.

The third set of factors predicted to influence correctional spending per total state spending relates to characteristics of the correctional sector reflecting the system's capacity to organize and capture state resources. States with a more professional work force should be able to gain a larger share of state resources. Similarly, although often considered at odds with professionalism, we predict that states in which the correctional officer work force is unionized will spend proportionately more on corrections.

Additional sector characteristics relate to two aspects of correctional system structure. First, states differ on the extent to which correctional policy and programming are concentrated at the state level or federated between state and local levels. Federalization is an index of federated structure based on whether a state makes intergovernmental transfer payments for correctional activities and the relative proportion of correctional spending and employment at the local versus state level. Competing hypotheses can be drawn on the effects of federated structure. First, federalization may be related to correctional spending per total state spending because the federated structure means more levels of government are lobbying for correctional expenditures. On the other hand, a system where policy and resources are concentrated at the state level may be more powerful and more influential over state resources.

Structure refers to the number of organizations responsible for correctional activities in the state. In some states, correctional activities (juvenile and adult institutions, probation, parole, etc.) are consolidated in a single organization. In other states, there are autonomous organizations for two or more of these functions. Fragmented structure is predicted to relate to correctional spending per total state spending because in such a context there are more organizations available to lobby for correctional resources. Again, however, a competing hypothesis can be advanced. The trend in corrections has been to unify correctional activities. To the extent unified structures conform to rational myths about good practice, unified sectors may be rewarded with greater resources.

A final sector characteristic is system size. Larger correctional agencies should be more effective at acquiring state resources than smaller agencies. This, of course, is also seen as reflecting the influence of rational-technical demand for a large correctional system. Further, to the extent that size of bureaucracy is the product of percent black and incarceration rate, independent of Level of Development and crime rate, size of bureaucracy also reflects values supporting incarceration. Thus, a relationship between size of bureaucracy and correctional spending per total state spending is consistent with the three hypothesized sources of correctional spending: rational-technical demand, values, and organizing capacity of sector. Of course, this is consistent with institutional theory that posits all three characteristics driving correctional resources.

The models depicted in Figures 12.1 and 12.2 were analyzed using Ordinary Least Squares (OLS). This is a technique that allows us to examine the influence of a set of variables on a dependent variable where the effects of the other variables in the model are taken into account. In addition, indirect effects for the full models were examined using maximum likelihood estimates computed with LISREL VII. The LISREL program allows us to consider both direct and indirect effects of the variables. However, because the key theoretical relationships of the present analysis are based on the hypothesized direct effects on the spending measures and for ease of presentation, Tables 12.1 and 12.2 present the results of the OLS equations.

The results presented in Table 12.1 indicate that the model seemed to provide a reasonable fit to the theoretical expectations. Four variables—size of bureaucracy, incarceration rate, professionalization, and federalization—have significant effects on correctional spending per total state spending. Thus, states with larger correctional systems, higher incarceration rates, a more professionalized correctional work force, and resources concentrated at the state level tend to devote proportionately more state expenditures to corrections. Three variables—unionization, fragmented structure, and traditionalistic political culture[3]—were not significantly related to correctional spending per total state spending in the multivariate analysis.

Three additional variables—the Level of Development, crime rate, and racial heterogeneity—had indirect effects through their relationships to size of bureaucracy and incarceration rate.[4] Larger, industrial, and urbanized states have larger correctional systems. Beyond the effects of these characteristics, states with a higher index crime rate and a higher proportion of black population tend to have larger correctional systems. Similarly, states with higher crime rates and those with larger black populations tend to incarcerate at higher rates. The Level of Development had a negative effect on incarceration rate indicating that once the effects of crime rate are controlled, larger, industrial, and urban states actually incarcerate at a lower rate.[5]

These findings lend support to institutional theory's emphasis on the effects of functional requisites, values, and organizing capacity of the sector. The effect of size of bureaucracy on correctional spending per total state spending is consistent with explanations pointing to the greater rational-technical demands for correctional resources in larger, industrial, urban states with higher crime rates. The finding that percent black contributes to size of bureaucracy once the effects of Level of Development and crime rate are controlled, however, also suggests the role of values. States characterized by racial heterogeneity appear to be committed to larger correctional systems beyond that expected by these other state characteristics.

The role of values also appears when we consider the role of incarceration rate on correctional spending per total state spending.[6] Here again, racial heterogeneity appears to be a prime factor in states' use of incarceration, even after controlling for the effects of crime rate.

Thus, this model is consistent with an explanation that finds the proportion of state funds devoted to corrections to be largely determined by the size of the correctional system and the incarceration rate. These characteristics, in turn, reflect the effect of broader characteristics of the state, including population, urbanization, industrialization, crime rate, and percent black. These traits create sector variation in rational-technical demands for resources and in values supportive of the greater relative use of incarceration as a response to crime. Beyond these factors, two characteristics of the correctional system, professionalism

Table 12.1 Standardized coefficients and t values of model of correctional spending per total state spending

	Incarceration Rate		Size of Bureaucracy		Correctional Spending per Total State Spending	
	Standardized Coefficient	t value	Standardized Coefficient	t value	Standardized Coefficient	t value
Level of development	–0.262	–2.12*	0.666	9.26**		
Crime rate	0.507	4.36**	0.186	2.32*		
Racial heterogeneity	0.680	3.88**	0.422	5.32**		
Traditionalistic political culture	–0.140	–0.82	–0.111	–1.30	0.126	0.98
Incarceration rate					0.383	3.39**
Size of bureaucracy					0.454	3.48**
Professionalization					0.270	2.59*
Federalization					–0.238	2.02*
Fragmented structure					–0.201	–0.19
Unionization					–0.035	–0.28
Adjusted R-square	0.458		0.820		0.562	

* t value significant < .05
** t value significant < .001

and state-level concentrated structure, seemingly indicative of greater sector capacity to secure resources, affect state spending on corrections.

Correctional Spending Per Citizen

As Figure 12.2 indicates, the hypothesized model for correctional spending per citizen is quite similar to that for correctional spending per total state spending. Size of bureaucracy and incarceration rate are predicted to have positive effects on correctional spending per citizen. However, the influence of incarceration rate may be weaker on correctional spending per citizen than on correctional spending per total state spending. A state in which values supportive of punishment are predominant may also tend to spend less on other forms of government programs such as education and social welfare. In such a setting, correctional spending per total state spending may be higher even though spending per citizen may be relatively low. Similarly, traditionalistic political culture was hypothesized, though not found, to relate positively to proportionate spending on corrections. Traditionalistic political culture may not, however, have a strong effect on per-capita spending because traditionalistic political culture is also characteristic of political values opposing governmental spending. Thus, incarceration rate and traditionalistic culture may lead to greater proportionate spending on corrections (correctional spending per total state spending) but not to elevated levels of spending per citizen (correctional spending per citizen).

The characteristics of correctional system structure—professionalization, federalization, unionization, and fragmented structure—are all hypothesized to influence correctional spending per citizen in a similar fashion to correctional spending per total state spending. The one additional variable included in the present equation is wealth. While wealth was not expected to influence proportionate spending on corrections, it should be positively related to overall levels of spending.

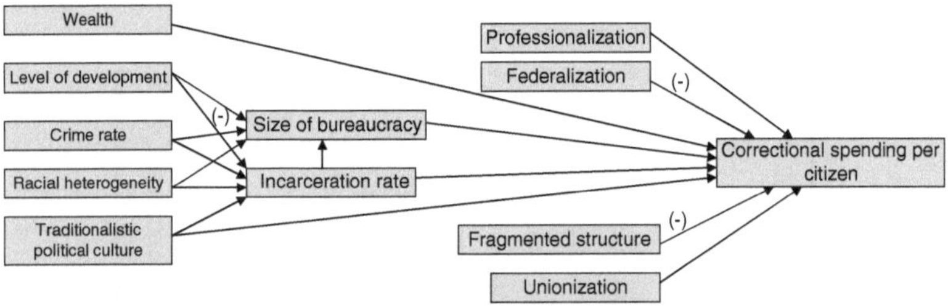

Figure 12.2 Theoretical model of correctional spending per citizen

Table 12.2 presents the results of the OLS analysis. It appears that the model is reasonably consistent with the theoretical expectations. Four variables have significant effects on correctional spending per citizen, and the model produces an R^2 of .572. States with high incarceration rates and large correctional bureaucracies tend to devote more resources per citizen to corrections. In addition, states with a more professional work force and in which resources are concentrated at the state level have higher levels of per-capita spending.

The findings on federated structure require some mention. Recall that competing hypotheses were discussed in relation to the effects of this sector characteristic. On the one hand, federalization was seen as creating more levels of government and more agencies likely to lobby for increased correctional resources. On the other hand, as noted at the outset, the trend in corrections has been to consolidate correctional programs at the state level. The finding that concentration is related to higher per-capita correctional spending may indicate that such a structure conforms to institutionalized beliefs about desired practice. In addition, state bureaucracies where correctional resources are concentrated may be more effective advocates for public expenditures than numerous but fragmented voices, or federated structures might be more efficient than large, unified bureaucracies.

Thus, the model is once again consistent with a theoretical explanation that treats technical demand, values, and organizing capacity as three important sets of forces influencing correctional resources.

Table 12.2 Standardized coefficients and t values of model of correctional spending per citizen

Correctional Spending per Citizen		
	Standardized Coefficient	**t Value**
Size of bureaucracy	0.311	2.10*
Incarceration rate	0.520	4.46***
Professionalization	0.228	2.13*
Federalization	−0.330	−2.87***
Unionization	0.151	1.16
Fragmented structure	−0.180	−1.65
Traditionalistic political culture	−0.121	−0.82
Wealth	0.086	0.60
Adjusted R-square	0.572	

* t value significant < .05
** t value significant < .01
*** t value significant < .001

CONCLUSION

These findings suggest to us the usefulness of institutional theory as a basis for understanding correctional systems. We can see at the moment more implications for research than for practice, although there are some implications for practice that could be exciting.

Future Research

Institutional theory and research are only gradually making their way into the study of criminal justice. Several researchers (notably Hagan, Chapter 3 in this volume; Hagan, Hewitt, and Alwin 1979) have borrowed the concept of "loose coupling." In Hagan's work, loose coupling has referred to the slippage in the processing of offenders from one criminal justice agency to another, while in most institutional theory, loose coupling has referred to disjointedness between the public consumables of organizations, such as rhetoric and formal structure, and frontline client processing (Meyer and Rowan 1977; Weick 1976). This more typical application of a key institutional concept has only recently been applied in criminal justice, particularly by Crank and colleagues, Katz, and Giblin (Crank and Langworthy 1992; McCorkle and Crank 1996; Katz 2001; Giblin 2006, 2014). In Chapter 11 of this volume, Crank provides an illustration of how loose coupling in corrections might occur despite management attempts to change frontline officer behavior.

Certainly the institutional approach to public organizations is far richer and more varied than the idea of loose coupling. It is surprising, given the nature of criminal justice institutions and the success of institutional study in other sectors, that more of the theoretical concerns and more of the methods associated with the new institutionalism have not been more visible in criminal justice. This does appear to be changing. Crank (Chapter 11) has been looking at symbolic communication in community corrections. Feeley (1989) has approached federal courts intervening in state corrections, both as an authoritative institutional voice and as an actor borrowing and applying punitive images promoted by other institutional actors, such as national professional groups and the Federal Bureau of Prisons. McGarrell and Duffee (1995) examined the forces leading to reintegration programming adoption. In policing, Hunt and Magenau (1993) have sought to study the power of the police executive from an institutional perspective, and Renauer (Chapter 5) has sought to tie several strands of institutional theory together to explain the nature of community policing. Katz (2001) found that institutional theory helped explain patterns of diffusion of gang units, and

Giblin (2006) similarly was able to account for the diffusion of crime analysis units in police agencies. Recently, Giblin (2014) extended this approach through a comparison of the diffusion of community policing and community prosecution (see also Maguire 1997).

Perhaps one of the reasons that the institutional perspective has not penetrated the study of criminal justice as deeply as education is that many of the traditional institutional research concerns have, in the field of criminal justice, been approached by the social control researchers on the one hand and the genealogists on the other. Both of these scholarly traditions lay claim to much of the same territory as the institutionalists: the interplay of social structure, political systems, and political culture or conventional belief systems and the connection of all three of these to the formal institutions of social control. We hope to have shown that these traditions can be productively combined, although we certainly have done little here but indicate that the boundaries between these intellectual pursuits are quite porous and easily traversed.

We would be remiss not to mention another, perhaps more substantial, barrier to the study of criminal justice as we have practiced it here. As Hagan (1989) and Sullivan (1994) have noted, research in criminal justice administration more frequently focuses on the behavior of individual decision makers facing case-by-case choices. The dominant research questions since the mid-1960s have been preoccupied with the legality or extralegality of agent decisions and whether agent discretion may be controlled (Walker 1993). While this microfocus is decidedly foreign to the sociology or the genealogy of social control, these traditions have not articulated effectively with criminal justice science. Perhaps the dominance of the individual-to-individual research in criminal justice is traceable to the influence of Black's theory of law (1976), which argued that the explanations of the variations in law would be the same at the individual and societal levels. Early research testing of Black's theory (including his own) zeroed in on decisions by victims, police officers, judges, and other individuals (Black 1970; Gottfredson and Hindelang 1979a, 1979b; and see Kautt and Spohn, Chapter 7 in this volume). This microapproach was compatible and spurred on by the American Bar Foundation survey and the President's Commission on Law Enforcement and Administration of Justice (Ohlin and Remington 1993; Walker 1993).

We are sympathetic with Hagan's desire to explain the behavior of criminal justice systems themselves, rather than concentrating so heavily on the actors in the system. As starting points, we would suggest attention to the following research issues. Clearly, the relationships examined in the present study need to be considered longitudinally.

Undoubtedly, some of these relationships are dynamic. For example, while size was shown to relate to spending on corrections, such spending may be hypothesized to lead to future expansion of the system. Similarly, while we emphasized the role of the incarceration rate in driving correctional spending per total state spending and correctional spending per citizen, such spending on corrections could also have feedback effects on the willingness of lawmakers and judicial officials to legislate and impose incarcerative sanctions (see Clifford 2014 for a judicial protest). Have the changes in crime rates experienced since the crime decline started in the 1990s affected levels of funding and the relationships between these factors? Have the stark contrasts between American values of equality and freedom and the American politics of social control begun to cast doubts on the latter (see New York Times Editorial Board 2014 for a recent complaint regarding drug enforcement)? Garland identified some possible emergent countertrends (2001, 196–204). How have these trends been influenced by the Great Recession in 2007 and its significant effect on state budgets?

The utility of the approach taken in this study could also be examined by a comparative approach such as that undertaken, in limited fashion, by Sherman and Hawkins (1981), Garland (2001), and Wilkins (1991). This type of research could examine not only cultural variation in attitudes toward punishment and incarceration, but also comparison of different institutional processes in countries with different governmental forms. Hagan's (1989) brief comparison of the tightly coupled criminal justice system in the Federal Republic of Germany with the loosely coupled system in the United States suggests the possibility of such comparative analyses.

This research also suggests the need for more research on the role of race at the macrolevel—such as the political processes through which race influences the incarceration rate. In a survey of New York State legislators, McGarrell and Flanagan (1987) found race to be a consistent predictor of criminal justice ideology. Further, such ideological stances tend to divide along geographical lines, with legislators from urban centers much more likely to endorse liberal and radical crime control positions than their suburban and rural counterparts (see also Castellano and McGarrell 1991; Weitzer and Tuch 2004). These findings suggest the potential of investigations of political conflict over crime control policy structured by factors such as overall racial heterogeneity, concentration of minorities in urban centers, and racial and party politics (for example, see Stucky, Heimer and Lang 2005 for a study of race, welfare, and party politics). Along similar lines, there is a need for research on the impact of concentrations of other racial/ethnic groups on criminal justice policy and the structure of corrections, as well as on potential outlier states such as Hawaii with its large nonwhite population yet relatively lower incarceration rate.

Most of the extant research on the connection between race and social control is associated with the conflict theorists and their "threat hypothesis" (Brown and Warner 1992; Liska and Chamlin 1984). As Liska (1992b) indicates, much data showing impacts of racial composition on social control activities, net of crime, are consistent with the threat hypothesis of the conflict theorists. As powerful groups are threatened by changes in size or behavior of less powerful groups, greater social control efforts are exerted. However, as Liska concluded, there are major challenges in converting the threat hypothesis into a real theory. He identified conceptual problems, such as defining threat and defining the powerful, independent of the social control they supposedly exert. He also identified theoretical problems, such as organizing research around different forms of social control rather than around different theoretical propositions and problems in connecting presumed structural threats with specific control processes (1992b).

Liska's general critique of social control research applies to our findings as well. While diversity—in particular, percent black in the general population—appears to exert a powerful influence on the punitiveness of state budgeting, it is necessary to ask for more direct evidence that diversity produces threat, or perceived threat, and that the threat leads directly or indirectly to policy decisions, such as choosing between health, education, and punishment investments of public dollars. There are several avenues for doing this. One is building and executing a design in which the political processes can be shown to mediate the population composition effects on the social control outcomes. This was admirably done by Brown and Warner, for example, at the city level for police arrests (1992). It has not, to our knowledge, been equally successfully pulled off at the state or national levels of comparison. At these levels, we have compelling case studies of single or a few systems, such as Garland (2001) and Simon (1993), which are suggestive of the processes and structures that should be connected but cannot control alternative explanations, and broad cross-jurisdiction comparisons, such as this one, that can control multiple variables but infer the process connections. Stucky and colleagues (2005) have made a strong case for designs that integrate broad cross-jurisdiction comparisons and detailed process-focused studies selected from the broader sample in order to examine the cause-effect details that are inferred in the large studies.

While there is much work to be done, we think it is promising that the kinds of forces highlighted in the genealogical case studies also appear influential in this comparative analysis, at least as we have measured those forces. Of particular promise is the possible interplay of administrative or organizational forces, such as the image and structure of the correctional system, and structural and demographic forces, such as the economic development, class, and race composition. Taggart and Winn's (1991) finding that "correctional strength" affected per-capita correctional spending would appear similar to our findings of the influence of professionalism, concentration, and size.

Garland (2001), Simon (1993), and Feeley and Simon (1992) propose that professional, concentrated, and large correctional bureaucracies, while devised for decidedly different ends, have become the machinery, or the processual connection, that has enabled structural and cultural changes in society and in the political system to drive the type and level of social control. Barlow et al. (1996) argue that the more progressive, modern forms of criminal justice are more effective in implementing threat politics, ironically, because they appear more politically palatable as professional and progressive. In the policing area, both Lyons (1999) and DeLeon-Granados (1999) make a similar argument about the rhetoric or political discourse of community policing. The state, in the form of a well-trained, progressive, and professional police department, has successfully translated community-policing messages into support for traditional law enforcement practices. What began as a community building enterprise has been transformed into more traditional sanctioning of marginal groups.

These proposed political functions of the "correctional sector," as we have called it, or the "field," as Garland has called it, are intriguing and should be pursued. More qualitative case studies that couple economic and structural change with bureaucratic, institutional reaction are certainly needed. It would also be fruitful to connect these theories to the studies in political extremism. Both Scheingold (1984) at the national level and Wilkins (1991) at the international level propose that certain political systems are more given to simplified and extreme social control answers to social problems. They propose that the voices of danger play better in centralized political systems with heavy reliance on mass media campaigns for elections. At the state level, do these happen to be the same states that have professional and concentrated correctional institutions? How does the prior investment in corrections connect to the dynamics of the state political system and the state political economy?

Another interesting set of questions surround the interrelationship among social control forms. Correctional spending as a percent of the state budget provided an initial comparison of correctional expenditure relative to other forms of governmental spending. It is not surprising that we found states supportive of incarceration to spend relatively more on corrections. An additional question of interest is what happens to public spending in states where incarceration is less valued? Do we find increased expenditures on alternative forms of social control such as mental health, social welfare, and education? Or, alternatively, are some states more "control-oriented" with higher levels of expenditures on all of these sources of social control? Examining these issues in the contemporary period of tight public budgets could be a promising avenue for addressing these research questions.

Finally, the role of political and cultural forces in the structure of corrections also suggests the need for studying the mobilization and implementation of reform. It is common in corrections to call for adoption in one jurisdiction of an innovation that has apparently worked in another. Such political grafts, however, are often disappointing (see the discussion of implementation in Chapter 1). They do not take, and policy makers often blame political differences for their failures. It would be useful to study the extent to which policy successes and failures (e.g., Minnesota vs. California sentencing guidelines) succeeded or failed because the political mobilizations fit, or did not fit, the political environment. The importance of the political environment may account for the variation in adoption and implementation of Project Safe Neighborhoods (PSN) in U.S. Attorney's Offices and police departments. In the case of PSN, despite significant resources and apparent political support at the federal government level, there was significant variation in implementation across the ninety-four federal districts (McGarrell et al. 2010; McGarrell 2010).

Policy Implications

We began this chapter with doubts about the contention that political and cultural variations in the use of incarceration necessarily mean that policy choices are feasible. This study does not allay that doubt. This research indicates that some political and cultural variables are as important as crime rate in predicting correctional expenditures. It is difficult to say that such expenditures will be reduced if they are dependent on the punitiveness of a culture.

However, correctional resources also appear dependent on the extent that the correctional work force is professionalized and whether correctional activity is concentrated at the state level or shared by state and local government. Like cultural beliefs, professional power may also be fairly intractable (DiMaggio and Powell 1983). But professional groups are a more concentrated target than diffuse beliefs about how to punish criminals. Policy makers might have more success negotiating with professionals about the nature of punishment and sentencing than they would seeking to alter the level of punitiveness in society (see also Giblin 2014).

Federated correctional structure seems an even more promising variable for manipulation. Planned changes in the distribution of correctional responsibility might be made. Pushing more correctional activity to the local level rather than concentrating corrections in state bureaucracies would seem to reduce expenditures. This finding is consistent with Garland's (2001) and Lyons's (1999) final speculations that restorative justice, community building, and other reciprocal forms of social control may produce less exclusionary and marginalizing results. Along the lines, local-level partnerships created between researchers, criminal justice professionals, social services, and community groups may prove to be sources of innovation (McGarrell 2010).

More important than attempts to alter any of these variables directly would be the utilization of such information about the states in two types of policy intervention. First, policy makers within a state should be tailoring policy changes to fit their own contexts. We are certain that politicians are well aware of the need for coalition building. However, some evidence (Flanagan, Brennan, and Cohen 1991) suggests that political decision makers could use far more precise information about the nature and strength of forces aligned for and against particular crime control policy choices than they now have available.

Second, the variation among the states should be useful by national organizations that can operate across the states. One of these, of course, is the federal government. Our findings would seem to support Sherman and Hawkins's (1981) contention that no single national policy is likely to be productive across all jurisdictions. Other national organizations with investment in policy change include the National Association for the Advancement of Colored People (NAACP), the American Civil Liberties Union (ACLU), Mothers Against Drunk Driving (MADD), and other victim's rights groups, and foundations such as the Burden and Edna McConnell Clark foundations. Policy makers in these groups routinely attempt to concentrate their resources where they might have the most impact. Data on the institutionalized context of corrections in each state could conceivably be used to indicate the vulnerability of a state to change and the nature of the targets in each state that a policy or program must enlist, accommodate, or defeat. Efforts such as the Pew Charitable Trust's Public Safety Performance Project (2014) and the Council of State Governments Justice Center's (2014) smart supervision and reentry initiatives may offer informative insight into planned change efforts in varied correctional policy environments.

NOTES

1. The use of incarceration rate as an indicator of punitive cultural values within a state receives support from the correlation between incarceration rate and number of death row inmates (normed by state population). For 1985, the correlation was .59 ($p < 0.01$).
2. In a longer, earlier version of this chapter, we also included an analysis of costs per inmate, which have been removed from this version because of limitations on length. However, it is interesting to note that there is no correlation (not shown) between correctional spending per inmate and either correctional spending per total state spending or correctional spending per citizen. Thus, overall spending for corrections relative to all other state expenses or relative to population may be good measures of state punitiveness, but are not useful measures of resources devoted to each offender.
3. One possible explanation for traditionalistic political culture not being related to correctional spending per total state spending in the multivariate analysis may be because of traditionalistic political culture's high zero-order correlation with racial heterogeneity ($r = -.76$). This may be indicative of conservative, traditionalistic political values and traditions predominating in racially heterogeneous states.
4. As noted, the theoretical models presented in Figures 12.1 and 12.2 were also analyzed using maximum likelihood estimates as a way to examine indirect effects. In the LISREL analysis, Level of Development ($B = -.217$, $t = 2.01$), crime rate ($B = .252$, $t = 3.45$), and racial heterogeneity ($B =.417$, $t = 4.13$) had significant indirect effects on correctional spending per total state spending. For the analysis of correctional spending per citizen, crime rate and racial heterogeneity had significant indirect effects ($B = -.312$, $t = -3.28$; $B = -.451$, $t = -3.15$, respectively), but Level of Development did not.
5. The multivariate analysis being employed examines the impact of one variable while controlling or holding constant the effects of the other variables. For example, Level of Development appears to have a negative effect on incarceration rate once one holds the effects of crime rate constant.
6. It would appear important to extend this analysis through longitudinal research to consider possible two-way effects. For example, while we emphasize the influence of incarceration rate on correctional resources, a plausible rival hypothesis is that resources influence future incarceration rates.

REFERENCES

Arvanites, T.M. and M.A. Asher. 1995. The direct and indirect effects of socio-economic variables on state imprisonment rates. *Criminal Justice Policy Review* 7: 27–55.

Barlow, D.E., M.H. Barlow, and W.W. Johnson. 1996. The political economy of criminal justice policy: A time series analysis of economic conditions, crime, and federal criminal justice legislation 1948–1987. *Justice Quarterly* 13: 223–42.

Beer, S. 1966. *Decision and control*. New York: Wiley.

Bernard, T.J. and R.S. Engel. 2001. Conceptualizing criminal justice theory. *Justice Quarterly* 18: 1–30.

Black, D. 1970. The production of crime rates. *American Sociological Review* 35: 733–46.

Brown, M.C. and B.D. Warner. 1992. Immigrants, urban politics, and policing in 1900. *American Sociological Review* 57: 293–305.

Carroll, G.R., J. Goodstein, and A. Gyenes. 1988. Organizations and the state: Effects of the institutional environment on agricultural cooperatives in Hungary. *Administrative Science Quarterly* 33: 233–56.

Castellano, T.C. and E.F. McGarrell. 1991. The politics of law and order: Case study evidence for a conflict model of the criminal law formation process. *Journal of Research in Crime and Delinquency* 28: 304–29.

Clifford, S. 2014. Citing fairness, U.S. judge acts to undo a sentence he was forced to impose. *New York Times*, July 29, A16–17.

Council of State Governments. 1977. *Reorganization of state corrections agencies: A decade of experience*. Lexington, KY: Council of State Governments.

Council of State Governments Justice Center. 2014. Justice Center. http://csg-justicecenter.org/ (accessed July 28, 2014).

Crank, J.P. and R.H. Langworthy. 1992. An institutional perspective of policing. *The Journal of Criminal Law and Criminology* 83: 338–63.

Currie, E. 1985. Confronting crime: An American challenge. NY: Pantheon Books.

Davies, A.L.B. and A.P. Worden. 2009. State politics and the right to counsel: A comparative analysis. *Law and Society Review* 43(1): 187–219.

DeLeon-Granados, W. 1999. *Travels through crime and place*. Boston: Northeastern University Press.

Dession, G. 1938. Psychiatry and the conditioning of criminal justice. *Yale Law Journal* 47(3): 319–40.

DiMaggio, P. and W.W. Powell. 1983. The iron cage revisited: Institutionalized isomorphism and collective rationality in organizational fields. *American Sociological Review* 48: 147–60.

Elazar, D. 1972. *American federalism: A view from the states*, 2nd ed. New York: Crowell.

Feeley, M.M. 1989. The significance of prison conditions cases: Budgets and regions. *Law and Society Review* 23: 273–82.

Feeley, M. and J. Simon. 1992. The new penology: Notes on the emerging strategy in corrections and its implications. *Criminology* 30: 449–74.

Flanagan, T.J., P. Brennan, and D. Cohen. 1991. Attitudes of New York legislators toward crime and criminal justice: A report of the state legislator survey: 1991. Working Paper. Albany, NY: State University of New York at Albany, School of Criminal Justice.

Foucault, M. 1979. *Discipline and punish: The birth of the prison.* New York: Vintage Books.

Garland, D. 2001.*The culture of control: Crime and social order in contemporary society.* Chicago: University of Chicago Press.

Giblin, M.J. 2006. Structural elaboration and institutional isomorphism: The case of crime analysis units. *Policing: An International Journal of Police Strategies & Management* 29(4): 643–664.

Giblin, M.J. 2014. Understanding influence across justice agencies: The spread of "community reforms" from law enforcement to prosecutor organizations. Final report to the National Institute of Justice. Washington, DC: National Institute of Justice.

Gottfredson, M.R. and M.J. Hindelang. 1979a. A study of The Behavior of Law. *American Sociological Review* 44: 3–18.

Gottfredson, M.R. and M.J. Hindelang. 1979b. Theory and research in the sociology of law. *American Sociological Review* 44: 27–37.

Hagan, J. 1989. Why is there so little criminal justice theory? Neglected macro- and micro-level links between organization and power. *Journal of Research in Crime and Delinquency* 26: 116–35.

Hagan, J., J.D. Hewitt, and D.F. Alwin. 1979. Ceremonial justice: Crime and punishment in a loosely coupled system. *Social Forces* 58: 506–27.

Hunt, R.G. and J.M. Magenau. 1993. *Power and the police chief: An institutional and organizational analysis.* Newbury Park, CA: Sage.

Inverarity, J. 1992. Extralegal influences on imprisonment: Explaining the direct effects of socioeconomic variables. In *Social threat and social control,* ed. A.E. Liska, 113–28. Albany, NY: State University New York Press.

Johnson, C.A. 1976. Political culture in American states: Elazar's formulation examined. *American Journal of Political Science* 20: 491–509.

Joubert, P.E., J.S. Picou, and W.A. McIntosh. 1981. U.S. social structure, crime, and imprisonment. *Criminology* 19: 344–59.

Katz, C.M. 2001. Establishment of a police gang unit: An examination of organization and environmental factors. *Criminology* 39(1): 37–73.

Kraatz, M.S. and E.J. Zajac. 1996. Exploring the limits of the new institutionalism: The causes and consequences of illegitimate organizational change. *American Sociological Review* 61: 812–36.

Kraska, P.B. 2006. Criminal justice theory: Toward legitimacy and an infrastructure. *Justice Quarterly* 23(2): 167–85.

Krisberg, B., P. Litsky, and I. Schwartz. 1984. Youth in confinement: Justice by geography. *Journal of Research in Crime and Delinquency* 21(2): 153–81.

Lipsky, M. 1980. *Street-level bureaucracy: Dilemmas of the individual in public services*. New York: Russell Sage.
Liska, A.E., ed. 1992a. *Social threat and social control*. Albany, NY: State University of New York Press.
Liska, A.E., ed. 1992b. Conclusion: Developing theoretical issues. In *Social threat and social control*, ed. A.E. Liska, 165–90. Albany, NY: State University of New York Press.
Liska, A.E. and M. Chamlin. 1984. Social structure and crime control among macrosocial units. *American Journal of Sociology* 90: 383–95.
Lyons, W. 1999. *The politics of community policing: Rearranging the power to punish*. Ann Arbor: University of Michigan Press.
Maguire, E.R. 1997. Structural change in large municipal police organizations during the community policing era. *Justice Quarterly* 14(3): 701–30.
March, J.G. and J.P. Olsen. 1984. The new institutionalism: Organizational factors in political life. *American Political Science Review* 78: 734–49.
Maricopa County Adult Probation Department. 2010. Annual report: A force for positive change. Phoenix, Maricopa County Adult Probation Department.
Mastrofski, S.D. 1998. Community policing and police organization structure. In *How to recognize good policing: Problems and issues*, ed. J. P. Brodeur (pp. 161–89). Thousand Oaks, CA: Sage.
McCorkle, R. and J.P. Crank. 1996. Meet the new boss: Institutional change and loose coupling in parole and probation. *American Journal of Criminal Justice* 21: 1–25.
McDonald, D.C. 1989. The cost of corrections: In search of the bottom line. *Research in Corrections* 2(1): 1–25.
McGarrell, E.F. 2010. Accumulating lessons from Project Safe Neighborhoods. In *The New Criminal Justice*, eds. J.M. Klofas, N.K. Hipple, and E.F. McGarrell (pp. 135–46). New York: Routledge.
McGarrell, E.F. and T.C. Castellano. 1991. An integrative conflict model of the criminal law formation process. *Journal of Research in Crime and Delinquency* 28: 174–96.
McGarrell, E.F., N. Corsaro, N.K. Hipple, and T. Bynum. 2010. Project Safe Neighborhoods and violent crime trends in U.S. cities: Assessing violent crime impact. *Journal of Quantitative Criminology* 26(2): 165–90.
McGarrell, E.F. and D.E. Duffee. 1995. The adoption of pre-release centers in the states. *Criminal Justice Review* 20(1): 1–20.
McGarrell, E.F. and T. Flanagan. 1987. Attitudes of New York legislators toward crime and criminal justice: A report of the state legislator survey: 1991. Working Paper. Albany, NY: State University of New York at Albany, School of Criminal Justice.
Meyer, J.W. and B. Rowan. 1977. Institutionalized organizations: Formal structure as myth and ceremony. *American Journal of Sociology* 83: 340–63.
Meyer, J.W., W.R. Scott, and T.E. Deal. 1983. Institutional and technical sources of organizational structure: Explaining the structure of educational

organizations. In *Organizational environments: Ritual and rationality*, eds. J.W. Meyer and W.R. Scott (pp. 45–67). Beverly Hills, CA: Sage.

Musheno, M.C., D.J. Palumbo, S. Maynard-Moody, and J. Levine. 1989. Community corrections as an organizational innovation: What works and why. *Journal of Research in Crime and Delinquency* 26: 136–67.

National Advisory Commission on Criminal Justice Standards and Goals. 1973. *Corrections*. Washington, D.C.: U.S. Government Printing Office.

National Parole Conference, First. 1939. Proceedings. Washington, D.C.: U.S. Government Printing Office.

Nelson, E.K., R. Cushman, and N. Harlow. 1980. *The unification of community corrections*. Washington, D.C.: U.S. Government Printing Office.

New York Times Editorial Board. 2014. The injustice of marijuana arrests. *New York Times*, July 29: A18.

Nokes, P. 1960. Purpose and efficiency in humane social institutions. *Human Relations* 13: 141–55.

Ohlin, L.E. and F.J. Remington, eds. 1993. *Discretion in criminal justice: The tension between individualization and uniformity*. Albany, NY: State University of New York Press.

Pew Charitable Trust's Public Safety Performance Project. 2014. www.pewtrusts.org/en/projects/public-safety-performance-project/about (accessed July 28, 2014).

President's Commission on Law Enforcement and Administration of Justice. 1967. *Challenge of crime in a free society*. Washington, D.C.: U.S. Government Printing Office.

Salancik, G.R. 1981. The effectiveness of ineffective social service systems. In *Organization and the human services*, ed. H.D. Stein (pp. 142–50). Philadelphia, PA: Temple University Press.

Scheingold, S.A. 1984. *The politics of law and order: Street crime and public policy*. New York: Longman.

Scott, W.R. 1987. *Institutions and organizations*. Thousand Oaks, CA: Sage.

Scott, W.R. and J.W. Meyer. 1983. The organization of societal sectors. In *Organizational environments: Ritual and rationality*, eds. J. Meyer and W.R. Scott (pp. 129–54). Beverly Hills, CA: Sage.

Sherman, M. and G. Hawkins. 1981. *Imprisonment in America: Choosing the future*. Chicago: University of Chicago Press.

Simon, J. 1993. *Poor discipline: Parole and the social control of the underclass, 1890–1990*. Chicago: University of Chicago Press.

Skoler, D.L. 1976. Correctional unification: Rhetoric, reality and potential. *Federal Probation* 40: 14–20.

Stucky, T.D., K. Heimer, and J.B. Lang. 2005. Partisan politics, electoral competition and imprisonment: An analysis of states over time. *Criminology* 43(1): 211–48.

Sullivan, R. 1994. The tragedy of academic criminal justice. *Journal of Criminal Justice* 22(6): 549–58.

Sweeney, J., C. Rivera, D.E. Duffee, and T. Roscoe. 2000. Environmental effects on probation supervision strategy. *Corrections Management Quarterly* 4(4): 34–44.

Taggart, W.A. 1997. The nationalization of corrections policy in the American states. *Justice Quarterly* 14(3): 429–44.

Taggart, W.A. and R.G. Winn. 1991. Determinants of corrections expenditures in the American states: An exploratory analysis. *Criminal Justice Policy Review* 5: 157–82.

Unnever, J.D. and F.T. Cullen. 2010. The social sources of Americans' punitiveness: A test of three competing models. *Criminology* 48(1): 99–129.

Walker, S. 1993. *Taming the system*. New York: Oxford University Press.

Warren, R.L., S.M. Rose, and A.F. Bergunder. 1974. *The structure of urban reform: Community decision organizations in stability and change*. Lexington, MA: D.C. Heath.

Weick, K.E. 1976. Educational organizations as loosely coupled systems. *Administrative Science Quarterly* 21: 1–19.

Weitzer, R. and S.A. Tuch. 2004. Reforming the police: Racial differences in public support for change. *Criminology* 42(2): 391–416.

Wilkins, L.T. 1984. *Consumerist criminology*. Totowa, NJ: Barnes and Noble Books.

Wilkins, L.T. 1991. *Punishment, crime, and market forces*. Brookfield, VT: Dartmouth Press.

Yondorf, B. and K.M. Warnock. 1989. *State legislatures and corrections policies: An overview*. Denver, CO: National Conference of State Legislatures.

APPENDIX

Descriptive Statistics and Correlation Matrix in Chapter 12

Table A.1 Variable Descriptive Statistics

	Mean	Standardized Deviation	N
Level of Development — Factor Score Based On:			
Population	4762.3	5068.9	50
Real Gross State Product	70909.8	83281.3	50
Industrialization	16463.9	19044.8	50
Urbanization (percent)	63.3	22.3	50
Wealth	13159.8	2058.9	50
Crime Rate	4750.9	1292.3	50
Racial Heterogeneity (percent Black)	9.1	9.2	50
Traditionalistic Political Culture	0.205	0.3	48
Professionalization	2.3	1.0	50
Federalization — Factor Score Based On:			
Correctional Expenditures at State/Local Level (percent)	0.74	0.13	50
Correctional Employment at State/Local Level (percent)	0.71	0.14	50
Correctional Intergovernmental Transfer Payments (0 = no; 1 = yes)	0.52	0.50	50
Unionization (0 = no; 1 = yes)	0.54	0.50	50
Fragmented Structure (range 1-4)	2.0	0.78	50
Size of Bureaucracy	2797.7	3305.9	50
Incarceration Rate	203.2	99.24	50
Correctional Spending Per Total State Spending	0.02	0.01	50
Correctional Spending Per Citizen	35.7	12.35	49

Part V

Conclusion

13

DIRECTIONS FOR THEORY AND THEORIZING IN CRIMINAL JUSTICE

David E. Duffee, Alissa Pollitz Worden, and Edward R. Maguire

Throughout this volume, our guiding principle has been to bring a scientific approach to the study of criminal justice phenomena in multiple sectors (police, courts, corrections, etc.) and at multiple levels (situations, individuals, groups, neighborhoods, etc.). Put differently, the work featured in this volume pays explicit attention to the development and testing of scientific theory as a means of improving our understanding of criminal justice. This concluding chapter gives us the opportunity to highlight key themes that we view as important for thinking about criminal justice in a more rigorous and theoretically informed way.

THE IMPORTANCE OF CRIMINAL JUSTICE THEORY

Criminal justice is one of the most pervasive and expensive forms of government social control. Federal, state, and local governments rely increasingly on criminal justice as fiscal commitments to mental health systems and public welfare have been reduced. Criminal justice is also the primary example of coercive political power. Political decisions about what values to protect, what behaviors to criminalize, how to punish criminal behavior, and how much punishment to administer are fundamental political decisions that define the nature of society. Understanding criminal justice behavior is, therefore, just as basic and just as important as other fields of study in the social sciences, including the study of crime and criminal behavior.

A scientific approach to criminal justice must be guided explicitly by theory. Theory is one of the essential ingredients in scientific investigation, along with high-quality data and the most appropriate research methodologies. Without theory, there is no real science. In the absence of theory, scientific research is a fishing expedition. The results from such research end up being subjected to pure speculation about the substantive meaning of the findings. Such speculation is inevitably colored by the analyst's personal, cultural, and political values, traditions, and interests, no matter how well intended or carefully crafted such speculations might be (Bernard and Ritti 1990).

It surely is not helpful, then, that theory is so often inappropriately mystified by scientists and denigrated by nonscientists. Theory is often contrasted with real-world pragmatism and objective facts in a misleading way. Even in our supposedly rational, scientific era, it is relatively common to hear some students and even faculty contrast what is "supposed to happen in theory" with "what actually happens in the real world." While theory and facts are not the same, this is not to say theory is not concerned with facts. Scientific theories help us understand why we should expect to observe one pattern of facts occurring rather than another. When students or faculty talk about "what should happen in theory," they most likely mean what ought to happen according to some moral or political theory, not what is likely to happen according to some *scientific* theory.

We agree with Kurt Lewin's notion that "there is nothing so practical as a good theory." Scientific theory—good theory—is a very practical activity. Scientific theory is informed by prior research and made up of logical (sensible, plausible, and noncontradictory) propositions or explicitly stated expectations about how, why, and under what conditions something happens that is worth knowing about. It is tested, and if found lacking, it is either rejected or modified. The subjective part of theorizing is in the decision about what is worth knowing. What facts do we attend to? The scientific part lies in establishing and maintaining an approach to answering the what, how, why, when, and where without letting the human interests that initiated the study interfere with the facts. Yet theory does not hold all facts equal. Theory focuses our attention toward some facts and away from others. It helps us sort out from the infinite array of factors that could influence the phenomena we are interested in studying, those that are most worth testing against logical standards and empirical evidence. If we agree that we need to understand the causes of criminal justice behavior scientifically, then a theory is the most important tool in the shed—but no more than a tool. If it works, we proceed. If it does not, we toss it out and find another theory to guide the work.

CHALLENGES OF CRIMINAL JUSTICE THEORY DEVELOPMENT

In some scientific fields like chemistry and physics, theory is relatively well developed. As a consequence, the work of many contemporary scientists is mostly in testing, refining, replicating, and comparing theories. This is often called the work of "normal science" (Kuhn 1970). This is less the case in the social sciences. Indeed, there are arguments that social science is not science but art (DiCristina 1995), or perhaps politics. Certainly the strength of arguments about the applicability of science to social facts varies from one social sector to another. For example, the theories and methods on which Eric Lambert drew for his study of employees in the Federal Bureau of Prisons in Chapter 10 are far more developed, refined, and tested than the application of institutional theory to corrections by McGarrell and Duffee in Chapter 12. Scientists examining the issues explored by Lambert—job satisfaction, job commitment, and turnover intent—can draw on a significant body of theory and empirical research, as well as useful advances in measurement methods in conducting their own studies. In contrast, researchers seeking to conduct scientific research on the level of punitiveness in society and its implications for correctional policy choices would have less of a scholarly foundation on which to build. They would need to articulate theory, developing concepts and measures, and test the theory with much less guidance from those who came before them. This is the nature of scientific discovery in the social sciences because some topics are studied much more heavily than others.

As we have argued in this volume, criminal justice as a social science is "pretheoretical" or perhaps "prototheoretical" in the sense that it remains in its infancy compared with other academic fields of study like anthropology, economics, political science, or sociology. This is not intended to denigrate the academic study of criminal justice. It is simply a young field that is at an early stage in its evolution.

As we seek to develop the science of criminal justice, there are a variety of challenges to be met. A number of these have been documented throughout this volume. For instance, Chapters 1 and 2 argue that criminology and criminal justice are often intertwined to the detriment of criminal justice science. Certainly crime and justice are connected and studies of each will inform the other. But as Duffee notes in Chapter 1, criminal justice is often treated as an *independent* variable that influences crime, but it is much less frequently treated as a *dependent* variable that we are seeking to understand. Put differently, social scientists seem much more interested in the effects of criminal justice on crime than on the factors that influence criminal justice. This is not to say that the effects of criminal justice are unimportant or uninteresting. But even if our long-term concern were reducing crime, it would be useful to understand the factors that influence the adoption or implementation of criminal justice policies, programs, and activities. Even those whose primary interest is understanding and/or reducing crime could benefit from knowledge about how to get effective solutions implemented. There is a pressing need to study criminal justice phenomena as dependent variables.

In Chapter 2, Snipes and Maguire mention another common problem with criminal justice theory: the conflation of normative or speculative theories about how the world *should* work with scientific theories that seek to describe accurately how it *does* work. By its very nature, the field of criminal justice is of interest to philosophers and moralists who ask questions like what is the rationale for punishment? What kinds of punishments are appropriate, fair, and civilized? These statements of moral positions are sometimes described loosely as "theories" of criminal justice. There is nothing wrong with such work, but it is not scientific theory.

One of the major challenges faced by criminal justice scholars is overcoming the antiscientific, or "everybody knows," approach to criminal justice. In a world filled with media portrayals of criminal justice on the evening news, in fictional and nonfictional television shows and books, and in major Hollywood films, people may assume they know a lot more than they really do about the complexities of criminal justice.

The application of scientific theory in criminal justice may also lag behind because its development is potentially threatening to important political interests, including the elites of the criminal justice system itself (Castellano and Gould 2007). To think of the contrast between the support for science in criminal justice and the support for science in other fields, consider the likelihood that a politician would claim that he knew how to get to the moon without scientific knowledge. It is quite unlikely. It is perhaps even more unlikely that such a person would actually ride in the vehicle that he designed without scientific know-how. But the same politicians reject the need for scientific knowledge about criminal justice every day. Such people usually begin with statements like "everyone knows" how to improve the work of the police or prisons, how to get criminal justice programs implemented, or how to reduce miscarriages of justice. In criminology, parallel claims usually come in the form of politicians claiming that their get-tough crime policies are responsible for the notable drop in crime. The belief that criminal justice policies can be made in the absence of science is one of the most challenging issues in the development of criminal justice science.

Another challenge to criminal justice theory is its reliance on other social science disciplines to help establish its own foundations. Many of the concepts and theories used to understand criminal justice phenomena were originally derived from political science, sociology, psychology, economics, management science, and other fields of study. There is nothing wrong with borrowing from other fields of study. In fact, it can often provide intriguing and interesting ideas and can help speed up the development of a new science. For instance, consider the many applications of organization theory to criminal justice agencies that have been discussed throughout this volume.

However, the interdisciplinary and multidisciplinary foundations of criminal justice as an academic field also pose a number of potential challenges. The traditional disciplinary-based academic employment structure sometimes inhibits orderly progress in theory development. Social scientists from different backgrounds tend to publish in different journals, use different methodologies and jargon, and attend different academic conferences, even when they are all working independently on the same theoretical questions. While this could be a potential strength, it could also be a liability if they don't understand or know about each other's work, if they talk past one another, and if they fail to build on each other's work. A good example of this dynamic comes from the field of organizational studies. Australian sociologist Lex Donaldson (1995) has argued that organizational studies is enmeshed in a series of "paradigm wars" that inhibit the growth of the discipline and render it irrelevant to those who seek real answers about how organizations work. Donaldson blames the American academic establishment for failing to provide incentives for cooperating and integrating across perspectives.

Second, researchers who are trained in criminal justice rather than one of the major source disciplines may not be educated in or fully informed about all the traditions, conventions, and findings in the fields from which they borrow concepts and theories. As a result, key elements of a theory may remain unstated or unexamined, or underlying assumptions may not be fully appreciated. For example, a doctoral student of one of the authors once sought to devise a theory of criminal justice agency cooperation with citizens using a theory from social welfare organization that had been developed to explain tokenism. As used in this example, tokenism means involving citizens in organizational decision-making processes as a symbolic gesture, with no intention of actually incorporating their input (Arnstein 1969). This student had not been sufficiently versed in the social welfare research tradition that saw interorganizational cooperation as a means of reducing and controlling citizen input rather than increasing it. This research study was eventually reframed successfully, but it got off to a rocky start by borrowing from an unfamiliar research tradition. Borrowing concepts and theoretical insights from fields in which one does not have sufficient expertise involves weighing the risks of misuse or misunderstanding against the potential benefits of achieving new insights. For example, one of us (Maguire) once had to take an econometrics class just to be able to summarize the evidence on the effects of police on crime because most of the research on that topic had been published in economics journals using econometric methods he didn't understand at the time.

Other related problems involve the confusing web of definitions for the same term across disciplines and the use of different terms to mean the same thing. It can take a very experienced researcher, and often, a well-functioning team of researchers, to recognize and appreciate such distinctions.

One of the best examples of these kinds of problems is associated with the term "community," which features prominently in a number of recent reform movements such as community policing and community corrections. To the first author of this chapter (Duffee), thirty years ago, the term community simply meant the "public" who might have opinions about corrections or seek to support it at some level (O'Leary and Duffee 1971; Duffee 1974). When Duffee arrived at Pennsylvania State University to teach in a Division of Community Development, his colleagues, who were community development experts, dismissed this work as ignorant about the meaning of community (and rightly so from their point of view). To them, Duffee had been using the term community imprecisely to refer to something like "the polity" or the "public," but certainly not the distinct, geographically defined communities that were consistent with how they conceptualized the term.

Today, we can see the same confusion in relation to community policing, community prosecution, community courts, and more generally, community justice. What criminal justice policy makers mean by this term is highly varied and generally not very programmatic in its implications. Instead, it is often used as a largely symbolic term by which agencies and programs secure approval and legitimacy rather than anything more substantively meaningful. Indeed, one of the most intriguing (and damning) accounts of the adoption of community policing in a U.S. city focused on the rhetorical use of the term community. Lyons (1999) couches the politics of community policing as a struggle between central government and neighborhoods for the power to define what community will mean and what kinds of social control those meanings will entail. There is also a great deal of variation in the use of the term community as a scientific construct. Community can be defined as cultures, interest groups, enclaves, polities, cities, neighborhoods, and other social entities. This variation is both frustrating and potentially useful. To make sense of it, criminal justice scientists must either have considerable knowledge of other disciplines or must team up with experts from those disciplines.

THE STATE OF CRIMINAL JUSTICE THEORY

What do the preceding chapters say about the state of criminal justice theory? Let us begin with a brief review.

In Chapter 1, "Why Is Criminal Justice Theory Important?," Duffee proposes that criminal justice theory is underdeveloped. He does not argue that it is missing altogether, but he does argue that explicit attention to criminal justice theory lags behind theory development in other fields. Duffee proposes that the academic study of criminal justice would be strengthened if scholars recognized explicitly the need to rely on scientific theory in explaining criminal justice.

In Chapter 2, "Foundations of Criminal Justice Theory," Snipes and Maguire begin by discussing the shortcomings of criminal justice theory, tracing the brief history of its foundations, and settling on a loose conception of its domain. Their broad definition states that criminal justice theory is the study of the official response to behavior that may be labeled criminal. They criticize current theory by arguing that much of what is labeled criminal justice theory is either not adequate theory or does not really belong to criminal justice. Most notably, they carve out a distinction between ideologies, criminological theory, and criminal justice theory. They then propose four tests that can be used to determine whether a theory falls within the domain of criminal justice theory. The essential nature of these tests is (1) that the dependent variable must be related to the official response to potentially criminal behavior; (2) that the deviance could reasonably have been labeled criminal, if it was not; (3) that the response is related in some way to official criminal justice policies, structures, or practices; and (4) that the theory conforms to basic standards for constructing social science theories. Students may find it useful to apply these four tests to the theories presented in this volume.

In Chapter 3, "Why Is There So Little Criminal Justice Theory? Neglected Macro- and Micro-Level Links between Organization and

Power," Hagan notes (like Duffee in Chapter 1 and Snipes and Maguire in Chapter 2) that criminal justice research is not sufficiently based in scientific theory. The basic question he asks is why there is so little criminal justice theory. In answering this question, he discusses the apparent randomness in criminal justice operations. He then articulates a structural-contextual theory that incorporates his observation that criminal justice systems are "loosely coupled," by which he means the components of criminal justice systems (police, courts, corrections, etc.) do not operate in a tightly coordinated manner. This loose coupling property has some utility in a democracy that values checks and balances between different branches and agencies of government. However, it also generates a sense of weak coordination or disjointedness between the various components of the criminal justice system. Hagan develops a theory of criminal justice that emphasizes the role of political environments in shaping criminal justice system behavior.

In Chapter 4, "Explaining Police Organizations," Maguire and Uchida survey the landscape of theory and research on police organizations. The chapter begins by demonstrating that police departments are different from one another in many ways: in structures, policies, processes, and outputs. For example, some arrest offenders aggressively, while others may rely on different, less formal methods for achieving compliance with the law. A large body of research has developed to explain these variations. Maguire and Uchida review this research, showing how these approaches contribute to a theoretical understanding of variations in police organization. Among the values of such a theoretical review is their discovery, which might otherwise remain hidden, that most theories of police organizations are of the "contingency" variety of organizational theory. While this is not necessarily problematic, it should alert theoreticians interested in policing that a huge variety of other kinds of organizational theory has not been adequately tapped, applied, or developed.

In Chapter 5, "Understanding Variety in Urban Community Policing," Renauer provides an example of scholarship that seeks to build a new theory to explain emergent phenomena in a police organization. His starting point is the large and contradictory variety in the structures and activities that urban police departments adopt under the banner of "community policing." Recognizing that police organizations are important legal, political, and cultural institutions, Renauer draws on the institutional theory of public organizations, which was developed initially to explain the behavior of public utilities (Selznick 1966) and public education (Meyer and Rowan 1977; Weick 1976). He proposes that some of the forces affecting choices of community policing rhetoric, organizational location, and programs are local and some are nonlocal. The nature of community policing could be predicted by knowing the power and trajectory of the relevant forces in the department itself, in the city, and in the city's and the department's transactions with nonlocal powers such as the U.S. Department of Justice.

In Chapter 6, "The 'Causes' of Police Brutality: Theory and Evidence on Police Use of Force," Worden examines the individual, situational, and organizational factors that influence police officers' decisions to use force against citizens. Worden draws on theories from psychology, sociology, and organizational theory in specifying and testing a series of statistical models in which the dependent variable is police use of force. Worden generates a number of interesting conclusions, including the notion that, all else held equal, police officers are more likely to use inappropriate force against citizens who are black or inebriated. Situational and organizational factors also influenced the police use of force, but officer-level characteristics exerted little effect. Worden's use of theories from multiple disciplines is helpful for thinking about how to combine propositions into a cohesive theoretical model. His empirical test of that model is useful for reinforcing the importance of subjecting theories to rigorous empirical testing.

In Chapter 7, "Assessing Blameworthiness and Assigning Punishment: Theoretical Perspectives on Judicial Decision Making," Paula Kautt and Cassia Spohn provide a framework for summarizing, assessing, and integrating theories about individual decision making in criminal justice. They illustrate the promise of this framework with theory and research about judicial sentencing decisions. Explicit attention to the horizontal or domain characteristics (such as demographic variables vs. belief and attitude variables at the individual level) and the vertical or social-level characteristics of independent variables (such as individual vs. organizational forces) allows researchers to determine what kinds of explanations for decisions have been explored and which have been ignored. Doing so permits them to design new theory and new research in a systematic way. It also provides for clues about possible combinations or integration across sectors and levels that could make our explanations of decision makers more complete. For example, are judges with one set of values and beliefs more or less likely than others to act on those personal beliefs, and are those tendencies affected by the community or organization in which the judge is situated?

In Chapter 8, "Courts and Communities: Toward a Theoretical Synthesis," Worden illustrates a different approach to the review and comparison of theories, as well as the use of a different unit of analysis. While Kautt and Spohn developed a framework for explaining decision outcomes by individual judges, Worden is concerned with the larger (or higher) social levels in the Kautt and Spohn vertical chain: courts and communities. Worden's review illustrates the importance of getting concepts properly defined. Some researchers conceive of the prosecutor, defense attorney, and judge meeting in the court as itself a community. Since Warren (1978) long ago argued that communities are largely and increasingly networks of organizations, this view of courts-as-community is not trivial or accidental, even if it is not what others might mean by community. Frameworks for systematically reviewing theory assist in identifying potential conceptual conflicts and assist in turning them into creative opportunities. In addition, Worden seeks to devise a framework that will work in two directions: enabling us to see the potential effects of courts on communities, and vice versa, the potential effects of communities on courts. It would be useful to ask whether investigations in both directions still meet Snipes and Maguire's "official response test." While community impacts on courts presumably affect official response to crime and therefore meet this test, do court impacts on community also meet this test? Can we think of community differences in criminal justice as connected to the official response to crime? We will return to this issue later, as we talk about units of analysis as one means of developing criminal justice theory.

In Chapter 9, "A Qualitative Study of Prosecutors' Charging Decisions in Sexual Assault Cases," Megan Kennedy notes the importance of understanding prosecutors' decision-making processes. Kennedy focuses specifically on the prosecutor's decision to charge defendants in sexual assault cases. She points out that most research on this topic relies on quantitative methods. She argues that qualitative research methods are better for capturing nuance. Kennedy finds that the most important factor in the prosecutor's decision to move forward with a sexual assault case is whether the victim is "on board" with pursuing charges against the suspect. Another important factor is the perceived strength or weakness of the case. Kennedy's findings about the role of the victim are inconsistent with theories suggesting that prosecutors' charging decisions are influenced heavily by their concern with regard to case outcomes. Prosecutors in Kennedy's study appear to be less concerned about conviction rates and more concerned about whether the victim is going to be a willing participant in the prosecution.

In Chapter 10, "A Test of a Turnover Intent Model: The Issue of Correctional Staff Satisfaction and Commitment," Lambert provides a rigorous empirical test of a theory that specifies the causes and effects of job satisfaction among corrections workers. Working in an area of management and human resources research that is rich in theory development, measurement, and research, Lambert borrows available theory to examine whether it is valid in corrections. The patterns that have been substantiated in private industry also appear to apply in work such as corrections. Worker job satisfaction is more affected by management practice than by worker characteristics. Similar in unit of analysis to the Kautt and Spohn work, Lambert examines individual worker attitudes and decisions. As Worden suggests in Chapter 8, these individual-level attitudes are, in this case like many others, strongly influenced by levels of explanation above the individual level (in this case, characteristics of the correctional organization).

In Chapter 11, "The Construction of Meaning During Training for Probation and Parole," Crank examines the role of organizational and occupational culture in probation and parole. Crank reports on the findings from a qualitative study of parole and probation officers undergoing training by the Nevada Department of Probation and Parole. He gathers data through direct observation of the training sessions and follow-up interviews with some participants. Crank focuses on the role of linguistic devices called "tropes" for communicating meaningful themes about the organizational and occupational culture to training participants. These tropes often take the form of instructors sharing stories about their experiences in the field. As Crank notes, these stories "provide a vocabulary of precedents that construct an appropriate cultural, or intersubjective, way of seeing the world." While on the surface, training is seemingly about delivering specific or technical content to participants, Crank notes that it is also about transmitting cultural meaning. Crank emphasizes both the complexity and the importance of culture in parole and probation organizations. Reform efforts that are not based on a firm understanding of organizational and occupational culture are unlikely to succeed.

In Chapter 12, "Examining Correctional Resources," McGarrell and Duffee seek to explain variations in financial support for corrections. Like Renauer, they draw on institutional theory. While institutional theory has often been more concerned with legitimacy of public organizations than with fiscal resources, the authors reason that greater legitimacy should result in a greater share of tax dollars and greater level of tax dollars per citizen. While the test of institutional theory conducted here is generally supportive of institutional theory, the test is a weak one in the sense that the authors have to assume, rather than directly measure, the underlying processes that would lead to the results that they achieve. The findings also suggest that some facets of the institutional environment are more powerful than are others. In this instance, racial or cultural heterogeneity appears more powerful than professions, unions, or bureaucracy in determining the relative strength of corrections as a public-sector investment.

Together, these chapters illustrate the richness and complexity of criminal justice as an academic field of study. They draw on a rich variety of theory, most of it imported from other disciplines to enhance our understanding of criminal justice phenomena. They also draw on or describe a variety of methods, including both qualitative and quantitative research. They examine many different units of analysis, including situations (like police-citizen encounters in Chapter 6), individuals (like prosecutors in Chapter 9 and corrections employees in Chapter 10), organizations (like police agencies in Chapters 4 and 5), and jurisdictions (like communities in Chapter 8 and states in Chapter 12). Across these units of analysis, the many outcomes or dependent variables examined in these chapters reflect the potential enormity of criminal justice theory. Together, these chapters provide sufficient variety to inspire intellectual discourse and debate about the nature, scope, and boundaries of criminal justice theory.

THE DIMENSIONS OF THEORY

In Chapter 2, Snipes and Maguire proposed several theoretical themes that might be useful in thinking about and developing criminal justice theory. Given the variety of material introduced in later chapters, we now revisit these themes briefly in the order in which they appeared in Chapter 2.

Historical vs. Ahistorical Perspective

Theories vary in their attention to history, or the extent to which they explicitly incorporate change over time. One can think of such changes both with individuals (such as changing attitudes while at work, as in Chapter 10) and with larger constructs such as polities (such as changing the value placed on punishment as the composition of society changes, as in Chapter 12). Renauer's theory of community policing (Chapter 5) probably implies development over time within a city, as a police department reacts incrementally to a mix of local and nonlocal forces. Some of the theories that Kautt and Spohn review (Chapter 7) imply changes in judicial decisions as judges age, gain experience, change their attitudes, and so on. In general, however, one should note that while some of the theories discussed in this volume are more historical or developmental than others, most of the chapters do not account explicitly for historical or developmental processes.

Clearly, stronger science will emerge when historical data are available to permit tests of theories that incorporate temporal dynamics.

Locating high-quality data that capture the same dynamics over time is very difficult. Recall Maguire and Uchida's comments (Chapter 4) about instability in the data available from the Bureau of Justice Statistics on American police organizations. Maguire and his colleagues have demonstrated in several studies that the quality and stability of longitudinal data in policing, while seemingly banal, has a direct impact on our ability to test theories of change (Maguire 2002; Maguire et al. 2003).

For instance, Maguire and Schulte-Murray (2001) found that many of the nations submitting data to the United Nations on the number of police employees used erratic definitions of what constitutes a "police officer" over time. Maguire and Schulte-Murray's graphs of the number of police officers in several nations showed large peaks and valleys from year to year, when in fact police employment changed only gradually. Testing historical theories of police employment using such data would paint a wholly inaccurate picture. The quality and stability of longitudinal data are issues facing research on many types of criminal justice phenomena, not just policing.

If one is concerned with changes in individuals, it might be easier to design a study to track individuals over time. Longitudinal studies of delinquents and offenders are commonplace in criminology. Similar studies of criminal justice officials are not as common.

Organizational Perspective

Snipes and Maguire suggest that three main organizational perspectives are most relevant (or at least most prevalent) in relation to criminal justice theory: the rational-goal perspective, the functional systems perspective, and the institutional perspective. It is likely that many other versions of organizational theory will eventually creep into the mix of explanations for criminal justice behavior. Of the three perspectives discussed in Chapter 2, arguably this volume has provided greater coverage of and more examples of the latter two than the first. Does this mean rational-goal perspectives are less common? We doubt it. In fact, the opposite is likely to be the case. The ubiquity of rational-goal perspectives is one of our main complaints. The rational-goal perspective often focuses on effectiveness and assumes that reduction in crime is the principal criterion of effectiveness. There are severe limits to the logic of such theories, as discussed by both Snipes and Maguire in Chapter 2 and Castellano and Gould (2007), including some reasonable questions about their status as scientific theories. Nevertheless, they have probably generated the most research in criminal justice. Functional systems perspectives and institutional perspectives need much more attention before we can begin to take full advantage of their potential explanatory power.

Sociopolitical Perspective

Snipes and Maguire pose the fundamental differences in sociopolitical perspective as the difference between consensus and conflict approaches to criminal justice. Hagan (1989b) and more recently Bernard and Engel (2001) have suggested that this dichotomy in political perspective is overly simplistic and limited in its explanatory value. We suspect these authors are correct. Thinking of criminal justice as resting on only a conflict among groups or consensus among groups seems less than accurate about most complex societies. While the chapters in this volume do not focus only, or often, on the sociopolitical dimension, they do appear to suggest that consensus and conflict may be operating at different levels in the same place and time. For example, there may be more political consensus about how individual criminal justice officials should behave in a system than there is consensus across groups or political interests about basic criminal justice policies.

Objective vs. Subjective Perspective

Recall from Chapter 2 that objective theories view social artifacts (such as crime rates) as reflecting reality, while subjective theories treat such artifacts as socially constructed. For subjectivists, reality is in the eye of the beholder. Sullivan (1994) argued that the subjective perspective was limiting the growth of criminal justice theory because it relied more heavily on distinguishing different individual beliefs and attitudes than on examining objective differences among larger units of analysis such as organizations and criminal justice systems. While this volume finds many roadblocks in the path of theory development, it does not portray overreliance on individual subjective experience as one of them. Indeed, most of the works reviewed and presented here would seem to fall on the objective side of the objective/subjective dimension (with the possible exception of Lambert's study in Chapter 10 and some of the individual attitudinal studies reviewed by Kautt and Spohn in Chapter 7). Both the objective and subjective perspectives might be meaningfully integrated to expand our understanding of criminal justice phenomena. We will provide two hypothetical examples to show how this might be done, one from the world of policing, and the other from corrections.

First, when police chiefs think about their departments' performance, they often rely on a series of "objective" indicators such as crime rates, use of force incidents, and citizen complaints. These indicators all have their place within a comprehensive performance evaluation scheme. However, police agencies are much less likely to rely on multiple sources of subjective data about their performance. They sometimes survey citizens, though they often do not ask the right questions. They rarely survey arrestees, crime victims, or officers about the department's performance. Combining official data and subjective survey data from multiple populations is one way of collecting multidimensional data on police performance (Maguire 2003).

Second, students of organizational theory and public administration often wrestle with the term bureaucratization. The term is intellectually empty because it combines multiple dimensions of organizations in a fuzzy or unclear way (Langworthy 1986; Maguire 2003). At the same time, it has mass appeal because we can all recall with some degree of misery the problems and hassles we have experienced in dealing with government agencies, whether local, state, or federal. Therefore, though we have intellectual concerns about the validity of the concept, it still makes for a good example to illustrate the difference between objective and subjective approaches. Bureaucratization has been measured in many ways over the years, but some of the most popular "objective" measures are the number of written rules and policies within the organization, the number of people who must sign off on a particular decision, the number of standard operating procedures, or the number of separate forms that must be filled out to accomplish a particular set of tasks. At the same time, we might also think of bureaucratization as having a strongly subjective component. Even if an organization has mountains of red tape, if the worker and the client do not view it as bureaucratic, is it? If objective and subjective measures of bureaucratization are not closely aligned, then theories of bureaucratization should also account for the subjective experiences of those who must deal with the organization, namely its workers and its clients.

Type of Response or Nature of the Dependent Variable

The nature of the dependent variable is another way of distinguishing between criminal justice theories. It is closely tied with the unit of analysis. Frequently, for instance, when the unit of analysis is the individual, the dependent variable is some measure of attitudes or behaviors that varies across individuals. When the unit of analysis is the organization, the dependent variable is some feature that varies across organizations.

Sometimes the dependent variable will be a traditional criminal justice response that involves overt behavior on the part of criminal justice personnel: examples include the use of force, arrest, citation, charging, sentencing, or releasing. Sometimes it may just be an attitude or a value. Is the police officer cynical? Does the correctional officer have high job satisfaction? Other times the dependent variable will not be an individual attitude or behavior, but rather a context within which these attitudes and behaviors operate. Examples include policies, operating standards, organizational cultures, and organizational structures. For instance, Robert Langworthy (1986) examined the effect of various political and social factors on the organizational structures of police organizations. This dependent variable passes the reasonableness test outlined by Snipes and Maguire in Chapter 2 because police organizations presumably structure themselves to deal with crime, as well as other issues.

Another way of thinking about the dependent variable is to identify the unit of analysis. All theories strive to make inferences about some entity—that entity is the unit of analysis. Alternatively, it is the level at which the dependent variable is measured. In Chapter 10, for instance, Lambert describes a theory of correctional officer job satisfaction. The unit of analysis in this case is correctional officers, or more generally, individuals. In Chapter 12, McGarrell and Duffee outline a theory of correctional spending which they then test at the state level; therefore, states are the unit of analysis.

Units of analysis can sometimes get complex when units are nested within other units. For instance, suppose we develop a theory to explain police officers' behavior in urban neighborhoods. We then test the theory using data collected by observing officers in multiple neighborhoods. If the theory seeks to explain variation in the behavior of individual officers, then the unit of analysis is individuals. If the theory seeks to explain patterns of police behavior in different neighborhoods, then the unit of analysis is neighborhoods. An example of this nesting occurs in Chapter 7, in which Kautt and Spohn seek to explain judicial decision making. Typically, we are not interested in comparing individual judges, but in the decisions they make in criminal cases. Thus, the criminal case is the unit of analysis, and to test the theory properly, one would need to observe or collect data from multiple criminal cases across multiple judges in multiple courts. Such phenomena call for multilevel or contextual theories that account for more than one level of explanation.

Level of Explanation or Nature of the Independent Variable

Closely tied with the unit of analysis is the level of explanation, or the level at which the independent variables are measured. In many theories, the unit of analysis and the level of explanation are the same. For instance, if we develop a theory in which we attribute the punitive behavior of judges to their political attitudes, both the independent variable (attitudes) and the dependent variable (behavior) are measured at the individual level. Sometimes, however, the independent variables are measured at multiple levels. For an example, we need to look no further than Chapter 7, in which Kautt and Spohn attempt to explain variation in judicial decision making. They claim that a "vertically integrated theory" is one that incorporates "influences from two or more hierarchical levels." Among the explanatory or independent variables they discuss are case characteristics, individual characteristics of the defendant and the judge (and other court actors), and the characteristics of the community in which the court is located.

We might picture level of explanation as an inverted pyramid (while Kautt and Spohn use a pyramid in Figure 7.1, the idea also makes sense upside down). The level at which the independent variables are measured can always be equal to or larger than the level at which the dependent variable is measured. If the dependent variable is the outcome in a criminal trial, then characteristics of the case can be used as independent variables because they are measured at the same (case) level. Furthermore, since cases are nested within courts and districts (both of which are a higher level than an individual case), perhaps characteristics of these levels could also help explain differences in the outcomes of trials. In this instance, we would be relying on multiple levels of explanation.

While discussions of units of analysis and levels of explanation can quickly get tangled up with the jargon of research methods and statistics, once again, the topic is actually quite simple. Picture a patrol officer who has stopped a drunk driver. Suppose the driver is belligerent and refuses to get out of the car as instructed by the officer. Think for a moment about all the potential forces acting on that individual officer when deciding what course of action to pursue. Certainly the officer's own experiences, attitudes, and values will come into play. It is not difficult to imagine two officers handling the situation very differently if one has a quicker temper than the other, for example. The individual characteristics of the suspect might play a role. For instance, the officer might handle a strapping 240-pound young man differently from how he or she might handle a well-dressed older woman. The officer will also respond to cues present in the situation. Is it dark outside? Are the windows of the car tinted? Is the area populated and busy, or is it a lonely stretch of road? Finally, the officer will also presumably be influenced by organizational factors. What does department policy dictate? How has the department interpreted recent procedural law? What would the officer's supervisor expect? In short, the officer would be influenced by a variety of individual, situational, and organizational factors like those outlined by Worden in Chapter 6. Each of these factors represents a level of explanation. A theory that accounts for police behavior in drunk driving situations using all of these factors would be relying on multiple levels of explanation.

Institutional Arena

Finally, the easiest way to distinguish among different theoretical approaches to criminal justice is probably to identify the sector in which the theory is focused. Sometimes, the theorist focuses only on one part of the criminal justice system like the police or the courts; other times, the focus is on the system as a whole. The chapters in this volume were divided up by sector, with Part I containing three chapters that address the criminal justice system as a whole and criminal justice theory generally, and Parts II through IV addressing the police, courts, and corrections, respectively.

Both Alan Liska, in his sociology of social control (1992), and Bernard and Engel (2001), in their proposal for a framework of criminal justice theory, make the case for theories that span institutional arenas. Bernard and Engel argue that if we truly have a theory of "criminal justice," then we should be making theoretical statements that would hold across police, court, and correctional officials or agencies. Similarly, but even more expansive, Liska argues that a sociology of social control should be able to deal with theories of control across control sectors, such as crime, mental health, and poverty.

In most instances, the chapters in this book do not get that far. It would seem to us that cross-institutional theories of criminal justice are indeed important, if quite deficient, as Howard and Freilich (2007) point out. But we would also suggest that requiring a theory to span sectors in order to make the grade is overly demanding and perhaps too narrow of a criterion. While it would be interesting to determine if various criminal justice officials respond in the same way to similar stimuli, it is certainly premature to cast off or denigrate studies within one sector as too narrow to be useful. Indeed, careful theoretical reviews will be needed that examine systems, organizations, and individuals for similarities and differences. We would not want to ignore what is unique to policing in the pursuit of what police have in common with correctional officers or to lose what is unique about criminal justice in pursuit of what all formal control systems have in common.

NEXT STEPS IN CRIMINAL JUSTICE THEORY: FRAMEWORKS AND ILLUSTRATIONS

Given the breadth, complexity, and relatively recent emergence of criminal justice as a research field (Cullen 1995), if we are to sort out and prioritize promising areas for study, we first need a means of organizing the work. The most useful framework would be one that facilitates thinking about causal theory, not merely prediction; one that does not confine our attention to topics and questions that already have been examined; and, similarly, one that permits us to assess readily both what has been done and what remains to be explored. There are many ways to categorize criminal justice research (Chapter 2 in this volume; Bernard and Engel 2001), but we suggest that one of the most promising ways to organize our assessments of previous research, and our recommendations for future study, is around units of analysis—the entities whose behavior we wish to explain (Snipes and Maguire's fifth theme in Chapter 2).

A simple taxonomy of units of analysis would include individuals, organizations, communities, and polities. For each of these, we might construct a schema with the following dimensions: types of behavior worth studying, areas of potentially applicable theory, and extant theoretical and empirical work. By mapping these elements of criminal justice scholarship, we may be better able to answer three interesting questions: What has theory taught us about criminal justice behavior? What has our research on behavior taught us about popular theories? Should we be asking different questions, or asking questions differently, about criminal justice behavior? Development of this schema is beyond the scope of this chapter, but the following sections offer illustrations and some observations based on this strategy.

Individuals

As Walker (1993) and others have documented, probably the most commonly studied aspect of criminal justice behavior is the discretionary decision making of practitioners. This emphasis on police officers, prosecutors, judges, and correctional officers may stem from the politics that accompanied the emergence of criminal justice as a field of study in the 1960s and 1970s. When policy makers identified challenges to improving the criminal justice process, few questioned the structure or implied objectives of the existing systems and processes; instead, they equated dysfunction with departures from legal norms of equal treatment and due process, and therefore often directed their research toward individuals' failure to perform as expected or to treat citizens fairly. In particular, they directed their attention toward discretionary decisions such as arrest, charging, and sentencing, and they sought explanations for disparities in these decisions in the behaviors of individual actors.

The simplest theories about individuals account for variation in behavior with individual-level constructs, such as social background, attitudes and beliefs, and experience. Theories linking these attributes have been developed fairly extensively for some kinds of actors (such as police and correctional officers), but much less so for others (prosecutors). For instance, scholars have hypothesized that variability in police officers' job performance (arrest, use of physical force) is influenced by age, sex, race, and family class status. Others have used these same independent variables to predict not only discretionary decisions, but also actors' role orientations, beliefs about their work and about constituencies, and commitment to occupations (Carter 1984; Gibson 1981; Muir 1977). Researchers have also predicted attitudes about work, and working styles, from preprofessional as well as on-the-job experiences (such as education, other work experiences, and training; e.g., Lambert, Chapter 10).

Much of this work stems from importation theories—theories that stipulate that work behavior is shaped by the characteristics of the individual, at least as much as the character of the work or the workplace (see Lambert, Chapter 10; Worden 1993). As commonsensical as this sounds, however, importation theory has found limited support in criminal justice research. There are at least two reasons for this. First, the causal theories have not always been carefully specified, and as a result, empirical tests only loosely mirror hypotheses. For example, gender and race often serve as proxies for very general (and often underspecified) constellations of experiences and attitudes; but null findings cannot tell us whether the theory is incorrect, or if the sampled subjects simply did not fit gender or race stereotypes.

Second, individual-level theories overlook the effects of some powerful social and organizational processes, processes that may lead individuals to change their attitudes, or to set them aside in the workplace. For example, criminal justice workers self-select into their occupations, so variance on some attitude and experience variables is limited in samples of practitioners. Furthermore, many criminal justice jobs have entrance barriers and strong socializing and training regimens that tend to standardize views about the work, and certainly are intended to standardize behavior (e.g., Heumann 1978).

Measuring key constructs in these kinds of theories—theories about organizational structure, culture, and socialization processes—is more challenging than examining individuals, but potentially more promising. Moreover, these theories introduce a larger range of interesting and important behavioral variables and questions. What do police departments or prisons do well (or poorly) to help workers adapt to their work? Is the blue-collar culture of police departments really just the aggregate result of traditional recruitment among the working class, or is it instead sustained (or undermined) by leadership, training, or departmental philosophy?

Organizations

Criminal justice organizations are agencies that process people and information. Like many other organizations, they provide services, respond to needs and complaints, and spend tax money. They are nearly unique in their prerogative to use physical force and coercion to ensure compliance from citizens (in the form of arrest, contempt citations, subpoenas, probation revocation, or solitary confinement in prison, to name a few examples).

Formally, organizational behavior is bounded by responsibilities (e.g., the obligation to respond to 911 calls), constraints (such as the prohibition on unjustified detention), and accountability (the need to answer to political powers that authorize their work, as well as professional standards). Organizations also are characterized by variables such as culture and style of leadership. Although the basic functions of the various types of criminal justice organizations are well established (and are often reflected in their formal structure), other aspects of their activities vary considerably: some police departments innovate, while others do not; some prisons offer more rehabilitative programming than others; some prosecutors create specialized units. The challenge for social scientists is to catalog the behaviors worthy of study and identify theories that might help us understand variation in those behaviors.

Most commonly, researchers (and the public) are interested in the relationships among the ways work is organized (including the allocation of resources, people, and expertise) and the way work is performed (including quality, fairness, consistency, and efficiency). As an example, in this volume, Maguire and Uchida offer an exhaustive inventory of police department organizational behaviors, including activities, processes, performance, style, administrative arrangements, processing routines, structures, communication patterns, and corporate personalities or subcultures (see also Maguire and Uchida 2000). Researchers and policy makers have asked similar questions about other sectors: do public defenders provide better representation than do appointed counsel? Do vertical prosecution bureaus achieve higher conviction rates than does the horizontal division of labor? Do drug courts result in fewer jail sentences than traditional criminal courts? A second set of questions involves organizational changes: how, how much, and under what conditions can (and will) policy makers rearrange organizations to induce different behavior? Interestingly, systematic studies that assess organizational capacity to innovate are rare in criminal justice (see Worden, Chapter 8).

Some of the most successful recent efforts to account for organizational behavior stem from institutional theory, which stipulates that organizational adaptations to environments serve not only practical, functional reasons (such as garnering sufficient resources or managing caseloads), but also the less obvious but critically important need to retain legitimacy by reflecting basic cultural values and beliefs. While criminal justice organizations have something of a monopoly on their business and are therefore unlikely to be put out of business by competitors (although private alternatives are proliferating), their roles as enforcers and arbiters of social norms generate constant potential challenges to their authority and legitimacy. Furthermore, since criminal justice agency leaders would be politically unwise to argue, as some of this volume's authors do, that criminal justice behavior may not affect the rate or amount of crime, they must sometimes justify their existence or activities in other ways.

It is important to recognize that the institutionalization of practices, beliefs, and norms that are not demonstrably connected to performance takes places in two settings, or for two kinds of constituencies. First, practices become institutionalized because they suit local actors' expectations; they may be defended as inevitable or necessary when in fact they are simply familiar, comfortable, and predictable. For example, Church's early research (1985) on case delay in urban courts revealed that pretrial lapses (which vary greatly across jurisdictions) were unrelated to caseload, resources, or personnel; instead, each jurisdiction's court workers firmly believed that their particular turnaround time was the result of case pressure, rules, or resource limits (and were, therefore, altogether defensible).

Second, practices become institutionalized for the consumption of external constituents. Renauer (Chapter 5, this volume) observes that adoption of community policing may be less the consequence of commitment to a different model of crime control and community responsiveness than the result of national peer pressure from other departments and professional organizations, or community pressure for more accountability. Not surprisingly, the prospects for a fully operational community policing system appear to be related to motivation for innovation.

Institutional theory not only helps us understand how organizations negotiate their environments; it may also help us figure out why and how they can successfully disregard important elements of those environments. For example, a small collection of excellent case studies documents the ways in which court organizations subvert externally (often legislatively) imposed procedural rules and sanctioning mandates (Feeley 1983; Heumann and Loftin 1979; Horney and Spohn 1991). Leaving aside the simple political fact that legislatures have little power to bring judges and prosecutors into compliance, these actors have no incentive to set aside norms and standards that they have spent years practicing and justifying.

In short, our theorizing about criminal justice organizations has focused largely on two kinds of questions: First, how do internal organizational arrangements affect performance? Second, how do organizational relationships with political environments affect organizational behavior? What we have learned from the limited empirical research on these questions suggests that future studies would be well served to look beyond formal organizational goals and legal constraints and focus instead on less readily measurable but powerful influences on behavior such as organizational culture and political legitimacy.

Communities

Communities historically have been the basis for criminal justice in American society. Therefore, communities, defined as legally and geographically bounded jurisdictions, are units that shape the work of local criminal justice systems and react to those systems' behavior. But as noted previously in this chapter, the notion of communities encompasses a broader array of social groupings than cities and counties: we would also want to include neighborhoods, political wards, and, perhaps, organized grassroots interest groups that cross community boundaries. These social entities practice a diverse range of activities, which have been more commonly the subject of speculation, and, sometimes theorizing, than of empirical scrutiny. Examples include political behavior such as electioneering, coalition formation, and voting; behavior more specifically directed at the performance of criminal justice agencies such as partnering and coproduction; and behavior that legitimates (or calls into question) system practices or decisions, such as protesting, mobilization, or participation (as in civilian review boards). Many would also include as behavior collective opinion formation (for example, fear of crime, beliefs about system integrity).

Community attributes often appear as independent variables explaining other things, such as organizational behavior (whether police departments adopt community policing models) and individual behavior (whether judges sentence harshly or leniently in response to perceived community preferences). These sorts of studies typically model communities as static features of the criminal justice environment to which agents and agencies react. Future researchers may expand this perspective on communities by exploring the nonrecursive relationships among criminal justice agencies and communities (e.g., Renauer's Chapter 5; Sung 2001).

Because the most important (if least remarked) feature of many communities is their lack of communal action, researchers would benefit from learning more about what sorts of communities act collectively and under what conditions. On this question, very different theoretical propositions might arise: one might hypothesize that economic marginality (neither hopeless poverty, nor comfortable affluence) motivates citizens to work together; a more pluralistic perspective would compare the activity levels of residential, commercial, and other interests (as well as their competition); still another proposition is that charismatic leadership generates some kinds of community action. Once researchers make headway on the important challenge of defining communities (perhaps by devising a more helpful lexicon to sort out the many meanings of this phrase), they would be better prepared to address other important questions about communities: for example, what attributes of communities might account for social equilibrium (rather than conflict) over enforcement priorities? What conditions incubate rather than stifle social protests over crime and criminal justice, regardless of levels of community participation? What factors in communities repress or inhibit coproduction or cooperation with authorities (Scott 2002)?

Polities

Polities are political units of analysis: states, provinces, nations, and, at the international level, policy-making bodies, including states and provinces, as well as nations and even international collectives with self-governing treaties (such as the United Nations). They are composed of citizens or members and their governing bodies. One might distinguish them from communities, certainly in a Western context, insofar as they claim explicit authority to make (not merely interpret or implement) law, including laws about what is and is not crime, and how society will deploy its power against those accused of violating law, and in protection of those who are victimized.

American history and law regard crime and justice as peculiarly local phenomena, as Worden demonstrates (Chapter 8, this volume), so why should higher-order polities be of interest to researchers who study American criminal justice? First, most criminal justice policy is formally made at this level, including substantive and procedural law, many significant organizational and administrative decisions in the area of corrections, and resource allocations. Second, states' and nations' political cultures—their expectations of their government, including their criminal justice systems—vary significantly. In particular, where crime is defined broadly, to include whatever popular culture or powerful elites find unacceptable, inappropriate, or threatening, criminal justice will be a highly visible function in society.

Therefore, the criminal justice behavior exhibited by polities will include the rules they promulgate, as well as the structures and institutions they create to enforce them; one might also include public and elite expectations for (and reactions to) the system itself. While theorizing at this level may seem rather abstract, a few familiar examples quickly make the task appear not only practical but pressing: Why do some states adopt the death penalty and others do not? Why are some acts defined as crimes in some nations, but not others? Why do Americans value due process so highly? Taking these questions one step further, one might ask whether some features of criminal justice systems (such as a strong rights orientation, punitiveness, or repressive criminal codes) are related to social features, including prevalence of crime, poverty, and education?

Answers to these questions can perhaps be found in theories designed to account, more generally, for societies' distributions of benefits and punishments. Some versions of conflict theory attribute legal definitions of crime, and enforcement priorities, to the interests of entrenched elites, who use the criminal justice system (like other social systems) to manage their investments. Consensus theory suggests that these political decisions are more likely to reflect the collective will of citizens, for whom criminal justice is particularly salient to their notions of collective security and safety, as well as their normative views. Frequently, these theories are presented as oppositional (e.g., Hagan 1989a; Lynch and Groves 1981), although a skillful (and agnostic) theoretical synthesis of them is not only conceivable but also tantalizing. Comparative and historical theoretical treatments (Beckett 1997; Garland 2001) suggest that the moral panic around crime issues that has dominated since the mid-1980s is the product of the shared exploitation of crime and victimization by the media and politicians; the unwitting consumers of this preoccupation with crime have been mainstream voters (Scheingold 1984, 1991).

These sorts of theories are powerful, but risky from a scientific perspective: they are easily expropriated for ideological purposes, and ideological debates typically leave little room for science. All too often, the standard of plausibility is substituted for the standard of probability, and we stop short of subjecting these theories to the tedious work of hypothesis development, measurement, and testing. This is understandable, since these units of analysis are big and unwieldy and change only gradually, over spans of time that exceed the average researcher's professional career. It is almost as if such theories are too grand to be put to practical use. Moreover, social scientists have an uneasy and wary relationship with historical studies, which might provide the kinds of data that would yield some tests of these theories (but see Garland 2001; Myers 1993). Yet studies of polities such as American states reveal considerable variation in criminal justice behavior, and some promise in accounting for that variation with political and social variables (Horney and Spohn 1991; McGarrell and Duffee in this volume; McGarrell and Duffee 1995; Taggart and Winn 1991; Talarico and Swanson 1979).

SUMMARY

We offer a simple strategy for taking stock of criminal justice theory: inventory what we know and what questions we have asked around the entities—the units of analysis—that behave in the context of criminal justice. This strategy puts the focus on behavior—actions, activities, decisions, responses—that can be attributed to identifiable social units. But is this strategy helpful, and if so, how?

First, organizing our understanding around social units' behavior directs us to look first at attributes of those units for theoretical causes: this is efficient and commonsensical. It also paves the way for discovering that the most proximate theoretical causes are not always the most powerful ones, however; an important discovery. For example, individuals' behavior may be more deeply influenced by their organizations, and organizations by their political environments, than by their own internal characteristics. It is always good to explore the simplest explanations first; but if and when they fail, then it is wise to move to more complex levels of explanation.

Second, the focus on social units clarifies the importance of two basic scientific tasks that too often get hasty and inadequate attention from researchers: theorizing and measurement. If one is to theorize that a particular force causes an agent's behavior, one must assume or demonstrate the plausibility of that causal relationship. This simple requirement is overlooked surprisingly often. An example occurs in the sentencing literature, where researchers have sometimes modeled case outcomes (such as conviction) as a function of defendant attributes, even when those attributes were not typically known or knowable by the decision makers at the time of conviction (such as drug dependence or parental status). One is unlikely to make such a mistake if one simply remembers that human beings (judges and prosecutors) can only base decisions (including good, bad, biased, or fair ones) on information that they actually have. Similarly, theorizing about social units' behavior raises the stakes for careful conceptualization and measurement of those units' attributes and behavior. Hypothesizing that female police officers make fewer arrests than men is much less interesting than finding out whether women (and men) with traditional gender roles do their jobs differently—but sex and gender role are quite different variables, calling for different measures.

Finally, studying more complex social units, such as communities and polities, presents more challenges but possibly more payoffs than the field's traditional prioritization on individual and organizational studies. Such research might raise our awareness of variables that masquerade as constants in studies of other units of analysis. A simple example, entailing a widely regarded theory, is Lipsky's analysis of street-level bureaucrats. Astute readers note that Lipsky (1980) accounts for what many might see as a set of pathologies (and seemingly universal ones) among those who work directly with social agency clients, including criminal justice clients. His accounting for these problematic but pervasive behaviors is compelling, in part, because it seems to apply, at least partly, to nearly every bureaucrat: police, probation officers, teachers, and social workers. More astute readers recognize, however, that Lipsky is doing more than describing a seemingly invariable state of affairs because he attributes those conditions, ultimately, to American society's unwillingness to take on full responsibility for the complexity and costs of responding to the social problems those bureaucrats face each day. Social indifference (or ignorance) of these kinds of problems is, of course, a construct that varies across states and other sorts of polities.

Lingering Questions

We are, of course, not suggesting that reviewing and formulating theory around the device of the unit of analysis is the only, or even the best, way to proceed. A number of other rubrics should also be explored. There is a great deal of such work to be done, in part because criminal justice theory has not often been taken seriously enough for long enough to generate systematic comparisons of theoretical schemas. We do not really know what they hold in common and what is different. It is time for that work to begin. While that task is far too vast for this volume, we hope that this collection will spur on such work.

As we close, we want to take another brief look at other lingering and troublesome questions. While we can provide only tentative and suggestive answers here to some of these, we anticipate that the development of criminal justice theory will enable better and more exacting answers in the future.

Is it possible to find or develop a criminal justice theory that would span different units of analysis? Is it even desirable to look? Howard and Freilich (2007) caution against grand theories. It may be very premature or even misleading and dangerous to search for a theory that "explains all criminal justice responses at all times." This, of course, is precisely what Black thought he had done with *The Behavior of Law* (1976). He proposed that the same variables that would explain individual-level behavior would explain behavior by communities or polities. Most of the evidence suggests that this was a false hope. Indeed, there often appear to be very different explanations for individual-level phenomena and those occurring at higher levels. We suspect that Howard and Freilich (2007) may be correct and that grand theories of criminal justice are unlikely and perhaps misleading.

Is it useful to think of schools of criminal justice theory, as is often the case with criminological theory? Our view is that this might occur (actually, it is probably an inevitable by-product of theory development). As criminal justice scholars become more explicitly concerned with the nature of the theories that they espouse and test, they will seek means of comparing and contrasting different kinds of criminal justice theories. If kept under control, we think this kind of development is a positive sign; it suggests some vibrancy in theoretical thinking. But the identification of schools of criminal justice theory would also suggest some hazards. Schools of thought are often reified and taught; they are valued as truths rather than as tools for research. We would be wary of intellectual (and emotional) commitments to specific theories, as schools of thought might imply. We are convinced that "conflict" and "consensus" "theories" are usually too global, too grand, or too simplistic to be of much help in describing most criminal justice reality—although both Scheingold (1984) and Wilkins (1991) have made some strides trying to think of when and where there is more or less consensus or conflict, or more or less extremism in reaction to crime. Other kinds of schools of thought about criminal justice that have been bandied about, such as radical, liberal, and conservative, seem to describe the political rather than scientific intent of some researchers. In any case, we suspect that criminal justice theory is a long way from being codified into schools of thought. It probably will occur several times over, as it has in other sciences. But criminal justice theory is relatively underdeveloped to allow much categorization of types of theory.

Can criminal justice theory develop separately from the broader study of social control? We suspect that it will and should, within limits.

First, academic programs of criminology and criminal justice continue to develop rapidly, and the fastest growth in these programs now is at the doctoral level. The field of crime and criminal justice is maturing as a scientific field. It will not continue to mature unless criminal justice theory is taken seriously. And it seems unlikely to us that the field will continue to be serious about crime theory but permit other fields such as political science and sociology to focus on criminal justice theory. Certainly, criminal justice is one form of state social control, and sociologists and political scientists will continue to be interested in criminal justice phenomena. But we also think that criminal justice is sufficiently distinct from other forms of social control and other forms of political power that it can and will benefit from criminal justice specialists developing theory uniquely suited to explaining criminal justice behavior.

Finally, how is criminal justice theory related to criminological theory? Our honest answer at the moment is that we do not know but are eager to find out. One of the authors once mentioned to another colleague that the most basic theoretical problem in criminal justice is explaining what will be called a crime. His colleague responded by saying that it was also the most fundamental criminological problem. We are not sure whether these two scholars are agreeing with each other or talking past each other, but we think it could be very productive to explore systematically the relationship between explaining crime and explaining criminal justice. Leslie Wilkins (1991) wrote that crime and the reaction to crime could not be separated because they depend on each other. A crime is not a fact, but a decision to respond to a fact in a certain way. To call something a crime means that it should be punished, or presupposes the criminal justice system (of some sort). Crime does not come before punishment; the availability of punishment leads to labeling acts as crimes and some people as criminal. This observation would lead some people to say that criminal justice "causes" crime. The observation is either trivial or profound, but it is not going to help us very much with the practical task of sorting through the theoretical and empirical connections between crime and criminal justice.

Yes, there must be some concept of "crime" in order for some harmful acts to be labeled as such, and such labeling may have its own effects on a variety of behaviors by a variety of people. And it may be very interesting to promote more studies that examine how, when, and why the idea of crime and the apparatus of criminal justice emerge in sociopolitical systems (see Robinson and Scaglion 1987; Schwartz and Miller 1965). Such studies are an important subset of theoretical and research problems in which one is trying to explain why criminal justice rather than some other social control is selected by a society in response to a problem.

Most of the connections between criminological and criminal justice theory will be more mundane and more frequent than these queries about the origins of crime and punishment. Most will start with a base in which responding to a wide range of social acts as crime is commonplace and a criminal justice system is institutionalized. The questions will not concern which is first or more primordial. Instead, we will be concerned with whether specific forms of criminal justice have specific effects on types of crime, and similarly, whether specific kinds of crime have specific effects on criminal justice. For practical and political reasons, one of the more common connections between criminal justice theory and criminological theory will probably stem from current interests in promoting crime suppression or prevention programs, including those that involve criminal justice policies, agencies, and actions. This raises an important question: governments, which fund most criminal justice research, tend to be much more interested in criminal justice effectiveness in reducing crime (e.g., in some form of criminological theory) than in criminal justice theory (Castellano and Gould 2007). But to the extent that such policy or program effects can be found, they might spur interest in replication. If we can control crime in one place, can we replicate the program in another place? While the question has often been asked, we have rarely been seriously interested in the answer, which would require the development of criminal justice theory. If we can reproduce a program, that means we can, or expect that we can, manipulate the variables that cause some forms of criminal justice behavior. Can we?

REFERENCES

Arnstein, S.R. 1969. A ladder of citizen participation. *Journal of American Institute of Planners* 35: 216–24.

Beckett, K. 1997. *Making crime pay: Law and order in contemporary American politics*. New York: Oxford University Press.

Bernard, T.J. and R.S. Engel. 2001. Conceptualizing criminal justice theory. *Justice Quarterly* 18: 1–30.

Bernard, T.J. and R.R. Ritti. 1990. The role of theory in scientific research. In *Measurement issues in criminology*, ed. K.L. Kempf (pp. 1–20). New York: Springer Verlag.

Black, D. 1976. *The behavior of law*. New York: Academic Press.

Carter, L.H. 1984. *The limits of order*. Lexington, MA: Lexington Books.

Castellano, T.C. and J.B. Gould. 2007. Neglect of justice in criminal justice theory: Causes, consequences, and alternatives. In *Criminal justice theory:*

Explaining the nature and behavior of criminal justice, eds. D.E. Duffee and E.R. Maguire. New York: Routledge.

Church, T.W. 1985. Examining local legal culture. *American Bar Foundation Research Journal* 1985: 449–518.

Cullen, F. 1995. Assessing the penal harm movement. *Journal of Research of Crime and Delinquency* 32: 338–58.

DiCristina, B. 1995. *Method in criminology: A philosophical primer*. New York: Harrow & Heston.

Donaldson, L. 1995. American anti-management theories of organization: A critique of paradigm proliferation. Cambridge: Cambridge University Press.

Duffee, D.E. 1974. *Correctional policy and prison organization*. Beverly Hills, CA: Sage.

Feeley, M.M. 1983. *Court reform on trial: Why simple solutions fail*. New York: Basic Books.

Garland, D. 2001.*The culture of control: Crime and social order in contemporary society*. Chicago: University of Chicago Press.

Gibson, J. 1981. Personality and elite political behavior: The influence of self-esteem on judicial decision-making. *The Journal of Politics* 43: 104–25.

Hagan, J. 1989a. *Structural criminology*. New Brunswick, NJ: Rutgers University Press.

Hagan, J. 1989b. Why is there so little criminal justice theory? Neglected macro- and micro-level links between organization and power. *Journal of Research in Crime and Delinquency* 26: 116–35.

Heumann, M. 1978. *Plea bargaining: The experiences of prosecutors, judges, and defense attorneys*. Chicago: University of Chicago Press.

Heumann, M and C. Loftin. 1979. Mandatory sentencing and the abolition of plea bargaining: The Michigan Felony Firearm Statute. *Law and Society Review* 13: 393.

Horney, J. and C. Spohn. 1991. Rape law reform and instrumental change in six jurisdictions. *Law and Society Review* 25(1): 117–53.

Howard, G.J. and J.D. Freilich. 2007. Durkheim's comparative method and criminal justice theory. In *Criminal justice theory: Explaining the nature and behavior of criminal justice*, eds. D.E. Duffee and E.R. Maguire. New York: Routledge.

Kuhn, T. 1970. *The structure of scientific revolutions*, 2nd ed. Chicago: University of Chicago Press.

Langworthy, R.H. 1986. *The structure of police organizations*. New York: Praeger.

Lipsky, M. 1980. *Street-level bureaucracy: Dilemmas of the individual in public services*. New York: Russell Sage.

Liska, A.E., ed. 1992. *Social threat and social control*. Albany, NY: State University of New York Press.

Lynch, M. and W. Groves. 1981. *A primer in radical criminology*. Albany, NY: Harrow & Heston.

Lyons, W. 1999. *The politics of community policing: Rearranging the power to punish.* Ann Arbor: University of Michigan Press.

Maguire, E.R. 2002. Multiwave establishment surveys of police organizations. *Justice Research and Policy*, 4 (Fall Issue): 39–60.

Maguire, E.R. 2003. *Context, complexity and control: Organizational structure in American police agencies.* Albany, NY: State University of New York Press.

Maguire, E.R. and R. Schulte-Murray. 2001. Issues and patterns in the comparative international study of police strength. *International Journal of Comparative Sociology*. 17: 75–100.

Maguire, E.R., Y. Shin, J. Zhao, and K.D. Hassell. 2003. Structural change in large police agencies during the 1990s. *Policing: An International Journal of Police Strategies and Management* 26(2): 251–75.

Maguire, E.R. and C.D. Uchida. 2000. Measurement and explanation in the comparative study of American police organizations. In *Measurement and analysis of crime and justice*, eds. D. Duffee, D. McDowall, B. Ostrom, R.D. Crutchfield, S.D. Mastrofski, and L.G. Mazerolle. *Criminal Justice 2000* (4): 491–558. Washington, D.C.: National Institute of Justice.

McGarrell, E.F. and D.E. Duffee. 1995. The adoption of pre-release centers in the states. *Criminal Justice Review* 20(1): 1–20.

Meyer, J.W. and B. Rowan. 1977. Institutionalized organizations: Formal structure as myth and ceremony. *American Journal of Sociology* 83: 340–63.

Muir, W.K., Jr. 1977. *Police: Streetcorner politicians.* Chicago: University of Chicago Press.

Myers, M.A. 1993. Inequality and the punishment of minor offenders in the early 20th century. *Law and Society Review* 27(2): 313–43.

O'Leary, V. and D. Duffee. 1971. Correctional policy: A classification of goals designed for change. *Crime and Delinquency* 17: 373–86.

Robinson, C.D. and R. Scaglion. 1987. The origin and evolution of the police function in society: Notes toward a theory. *Law and Society Review* 21(1): 109–52.

Scheingold, S.A. 1984. *The politics of law and order: Street crime and public policy.* New York: Longman.

Scheingold, S.A. 1991. *The politics of street crime: Criminal process and cultural obsession.* Philadelphia, PA: Temple University Press.

Schwartz, R. and J. Miller. 1965. Legal evolution and societal complexity. *American Journal of Sociology* 70: 159–69.

Scott, J.D. 2002. Assessing the relationship between police-community coproduction and neighborhood-level social capital. *Journal of Contemporary Criminal Justice* 18(2): 147–66.

Selznick, P. 1966. *T.V.A. and the grassroots.* New York: Harper & Row.

Sullivan, R. 1994. The tragedy of academic criminal justice. *Journal of Criminal Justice* 22(6): 549–58.

Sung, H. 2001. *The fragmentation of policing in American cities: Toward an ecological theory of police-citizen relations*. Westport, CT: Praeger.

Taggart, W.A. and R.G. Winn. 1991. Determinants of corrections expenditures in the American states: An exploratory analysis. *Criminal Justice Policy Review* 5: 157–82.

Talarico, S.M., and C.R. Swanson. 1979. Styles of policing: An exploration of compatibility and conflict. In *Determinants of law-enforcement policies*, ed. F.A. Meyer, Jr. and R. Baker, 35–44. Lexington, MA: Lexington Books.

Walker, S. 1993. *Taming the system*. New York: Oxford University Press.

Warren, R.L. 1978. *Community in America*, 3rd ed. Chicago: Rand McNally.

Weick, K.E. 1976. Educational organizations as loosely coupled systems. *Administrative Science Quarterly* 21: 1–19.

Wilkins, L.T. 1991. *Punishment, crime, and market forces*. Brookfield, VT: Dartmouth Press.

ABOUT THE CONTRIBUTORS

John P. Crank earned his Ph.D. in Sociology from the University of Colorado in 1987. He has authored more than fifty peer-reviewed publications on a variety of topics, including policing, probation and parole, and criminal justice theory. In addition, he has authored or edited eight books, including *Imagining Justice*, which received the Anderson Outstanding Book award from the Academy of Criminal Justice Sciences in 2004. His 2011 book, *Mission Based Policing* (with Rebecca Murray, Dawn Irlbeck, and Mark Sundermeier), explores how to reorganize policing around the mission of reducing serious crime. His 2014 book, *Crime, Violence, and Global Warming* (with Linda Jacoby), discusses the social impacts of climate change. Other current research examines the applications of Shotspotter technology to the police, reintegration of offenders, and gangs and violent crime.

David E. Duffee is Professor Emeritus of Criminal Justice, University at Albany, and former dean of the School of Criminal Justice, from which he received his Ph.D. in 1973. His research interests are in planned change in criminal justice agencies and communities and in criminal justice theory. His first work in criminal justice theory, *Explaining Criminal Justice*, received the Outstanding Book Award from the Academy of Criminal Justice Sciences. His two most recent projects were (1) as a member of the research team of Service Outcomes Action Research (SOAR), a continuing partnership between two child welfare agencies and the University at Albany, and (2) as study director for the Assessment Protocol in the Arizona State University sites of Criminal Justice Drug Abuse Treatment Studies II.

John Hagan is the John D. MacArthur Professor of Sociology and Law at Northwestern University. He serves as editor of the *Annual Review of Law and Social Science.* He is co-author with Wenona Rymond-Richmond of the book *Darfur and the Crime of Genocide* (Cambridge University Press, 2009). He developed an early interest in the social organization of subjective justice that is continued in his 2005 *American Sociological Review* article with Carla Shedd and Monique Payne on race, ethnicity, and perceptions of criminal injustice. His articles and book *Structural Criminology* present a power-control theory of crime and delinquency. Hagan's presidential address to the American Society of Criminology underlined the role of poverty in crime. This theme is central to his research with Bill McCarthy on homeless youth for their book *Mean Streets.* As a Guggenheim Fellow, Hagan studied the migration of American Vietnam war resisters to Canada that is described in the book *Northern Passage.* Hagan's recent work has focused on the international tribunal where Slobodan Milosevic was tried. His book *Justice in the Balkans* is a social history of this tribunal.

Paula M. Kautt is a lecturer of applied criminology at the University of Cambridge. She is currently engaged in a nationwide project funded by the Home Office to evaluate sentencing outcomes in England and Wales. She has a doctorate in criminal justice as well as extensive practitioner experience. Her research interests include criminal courts and sentencing, advanced quantitative methods, policing, and hate crime statute implementation and enforcement in addition to a wide variety of correctional topics. Her research has been published by *Justice Quarterly*, *Criminal Justice Review*, *The Federal Sentencing Reporter*, and the *National Institute of Justice.* She has also received research grants from the American Statistical Association and the National Institute of Justice.

Megan Kennedy is a Ph.D. student at the School of Criminal Justice at the University at Albany. She holds a J.D. from the Gonzaga University School of Law. Her research interests include the exercise of discretion and decision making by prosecutors, sexual assault and domestic violence, policy and legal reform, and qualitative research methods.

Eric G. Lambert is a faculty member in the Department of Legal Studies at the University of Mississippi. He received his Ph.D. from the School of Criminal Justice at the University at Albany. His research interests include organizational issues; job and organizational effects on the attitudes, intentions, and behaviors of criminal justice employees;

and international perceptions, attitudes, and views on criminal justice issues.

Edward R. Maguire is Professor of Justice, Law & Criminology in the School of Public Affairs at American University in Washington, DC. Professor Maguire received his Ph.D. in Criminal Justice from the University at Albany in 1997. He has held previous positions at George Mason University, the University of Nebraska, the U.S. Department of Justice, and the United Nations. From 2004–2010, he led a series of studies that examined gangs, guns, and violence in Trinidad and Tobago. From 2006–2010, he led a field study of sex trafficking in minors in the Philippines. He is currently leading impact evaluations and other studies related to policing, gangs, firearms, violence, and youth risk in El Salvador, Uruguay, the United States, and several Caribbean nations. He has written or edited three books and more than sixty journal articles and book chapters on a variety of topics in criminology and criminal justice.

Edmund F. McGarrell is director and professor in the School of Criminal Justice at Michigan State University. McGarrell's research focuses on communities and crime with a particular focus on violence prevention and control. Since 2002 he has led a team that has served as the national research partner for the U.S. Department of Justice's Project Safe Neighborhoods (PSN) program. His co-edited book *The New Criminal Justice* (with John Klofas and Natalie Hipple) presents the key findings from PSN and serves as a foundation for research-based, strategic problem solving for violence reduction. Recent articles have appeared in *Crime and Delinquency*, *Criminology and Public Policy*, and *Journal of Experimental Criminology*. His research has been funded by the Bureau of Justice Assistance, National Institute of Justice, Office of Juvenile Justice and Delinquency Prevention, state and local agencies, and foundations.

Brian C. Renauer is chair of the Criminology & Criminal Justice Division and director of the Criminal Justice Policy Research Institute at Portland State University. He received his Ph.D. in Criminal Justice in 2000 from the University at Albany. Dr. Renauer's expertise lies in the area of community- and problem-oriented policing, community crime prevention, public attitudes towards the police, and racial profiling/implicit bias in law enforcement. Dr. Renauer has been a principal investigator on numerous federal grants, including a Weed & Seed evaluation (BJA), Project Safe Neighborhoods (BJA), and Prohibit Racial Profiling (NHTSA). Since 2008 Dr. Renauer has helped to coordinate the training of over 2,000 Oregon police officers in partnership with Oregon's Department of Public Safety Standards and Training (DPSST) around issues of racial profiling and implicit bias.

Jeffrey B. Snipes is an associate professor of criminal justice at San Francisco State University. He holds a Ph.D. in Criminal Justice from the University at Albany and a J.D. from Stanford University. His areas of interest are policing, theories of crime, and criminal law. He has been involved in significant international projects in Trinidad and Tobago and the Philippines.

Cassia C. Spohn is a foundation professor and director of the School of Criminology and Criminal Justice at Arizona State University. She is the author or co-author of six books, including *Policing and Prosecuting Sexual Assault: Inside the Criminal Justice System*, which was published in 2013. Her research interests include prosecutorial and judicial decision making; the intersections of race, ethnicity, crime and justice; and sexual assault case processing decisions. In 2013 she received ASU's Award for Leading Edge Research in the Social Sciences and was selected as a Fellow of the American Society of Criminology.

Craig D. Uchida is the president and founder of Justice & Security Strategies, Inc. (JSS), a consulting firm that specializes in law enforcement, criminal justice, homeland security, children and youth violence, public health, and public policy. At JSS he oversees contracts and grants with cities, counties, criminal justice agencies, foundations, and foreign nations. Dr. Uchida is the author of numerous journal articles on policing and criminal justice, has co-edited two books, and co-authored a National Academy of Sciences book on the security of America's dams. Dr. Uchida received his Ph.D. in Criminal Justice from the University at Albany and holds two master's degrees, one in Criminal Justice and one in American History.

Alissa Pollitz Worden is an associate professor in the School of Criminal Justice at the University at Albany. She holds a Ph.D. in political science from the University of North Carolina at Chapel Hill. Much of her research examines criminal justice structures and policy, with a particular focus on decision processes and patterns in trial courts. Her recent work includes studies of misdemeanor court behavior and the intersection of policing and court practices and priorities, and the role of community politics in court practices and policy. Her current agenda includes both national and subnational investigations of the political and economic determinants and consequences of public defense policy.

Robert E. Worden is associate professor of Criminal Justice and Public Policy at the University at Albany, State University of New York, and the director of the John F. Finn Institute for Public Safety. He holds a Ph.D. in Political Science from the University of North Carolina at Chapel Hill, and previously served on the faculties of the University of Georgia and Michigan State University. His scholarship has appeared in a number of academic journals, and his research has been funded by the National Institute of Justice, the Bureau of Justice Assistance, the New York State Division of Criminal Justice Services, and other sponsors.

NAME INDEX

SUBJECT INDEX